CELEBRITY
DEATH
CERTIFICATES 2

CELEBRITY DEATH CERTIFICATES 2

by M. F. STEEN

McFarland & Company, Inc., Publishers
Jefferson, North Carolina, and London

To the people who love and support me every day:
Bill, Marian, Judi, Judi, Lee and Erika

Also to my Friday Letter Club:
Marge Van Meter, Doris Sexton, Elsie Horni,
Leo Beranek, Rev. M. Evely Kinser, Howard, Linda and
Roger Meierhenry, Paul Hall, PhD, Thom Hall, Marie and
Raymond Nelson, and Joyce Nore

Acknowledgments: The success of *Celebrity Death Certificates* and the encouragement to do *Celebrity Death Certificates 2* was not one person's effort. I would like to acknowledge the work, support and encouragement of the following: Judi Adams, Lee Adams, Yee Alchan, Kathy Conner, Erika Fabian, Steve Goldstein, Bernard Johnson, Sid Keating, Jim Lemmon, David Lotz, Karen McHale, Scott Michaels, R. Bart Mruz, Bill Schneid, Anna Stack, Jim Stepkowski, Kathy Steplowsek, Jim Tipton, Marge Van Meter

LIBRARY OF CONGRESS CATALOGUING-IN-PUBLICATION DATA

Steen, M. F.
Celebrity death certificates 2 / M. F. Steen.
p.   cm.

ISBN 0-7864-2346-3 (softcover : 50# alkaline paper) ∞

1. Actors—United States—Death.   2. Celebrities—United States—Death.
3. Death certificates—United States.
I. Title: Celebrity death certificates, two.
II. Steen, M. F. (Michael F.), 1946–
PN2285.C343   2005   791'.092'273—dc22   2005024720

British Library cataloguing data are available

On the cover: rose image © 2005 PhotoSpin; border © 2005 EclectiCollections Publishing Ltd.

Manufactured in the United States of America

*McFarland & Company, Inc., Publishers
Box 611, Jefferson, North Carolina 28640
www.mcfarlandpub.com*

Table of Contents

Preface

A death certificate is an intriguing document. On one page, a person's life is encapsulated. It's all there! Where the person was born and to whom, in the case of adoption by whom; amount of education and length of career; place of residence; whether the person was married at the time of death, and if so, to whom; what caused the death; and finally, what happened to the "remains."

A death certificate is a state-originated document. The information required on the certificate may vary from year to year and state to state.

Each state views a death certificate in a different way. California and Connecticut think of them as public documents, available to anyone. Other states, such as Texas and New York, do not. In those states, death certificates are officially available only to family members and others showing a direct need for a copy. Satisfying curiosity is not considered a need.

Florida will offer a death certificate to anyone, but the cause of death is not disclosed for 50 years.

This book contains death certificates of Hollywood's famous and infamous. You will find examples from the Silent Era; some from Hollywood's Golden Era; and some recent names. You will find people who worked behind the scenes, or who made their fame on the small screen in song or the written word.

Many famous people, whose certificates I would have liked to include, died in New York. The restrictions mentioned above prevented their inclusion.

The certificates are presented in alphabetical order by familiar name. Otherwise, people like Troy Donahue (whose certificate lists his name as Merle Johnson) and Susan Hayward (Edythe Marrener Chalkley) would be hard to find.

It was a challenge to decide which certificates to include. I sent my list of death certificates to family members and friends and asked them to select the ones they would be interested in. Whenever several friends suggested the same people, I knew that those certificates needed to be included. I took their suggestions and added some of my favorite certificates.

Collecting death certificates is surely an unusual hobby. If you are interested in starting a collection, you do not need to limit it to motion picture people. Sports figures, authors, or presidents of the United States are just a few other possibilities.

I started my collection in July of 1991.

I began my collection by ordering the death certificate of my 10 favorite celebrities. Marilyn Monroe was one of the first. I had worked at Pierce Brothers Westwood Memorial Park for 11 years. I had assisted her fans on a daily basis. I knew how important she was to them. Many of them were not even born when she died, so clearly her legacy continues.

Death certificates are available from the county health departments in the county where the death occurred. The fees usually range from $5.00 to $28.00, but they change from time to time, so it is necessary to check before ordering. Many states offer applications for death certificates on-line.

State health departments are another place to order death certificates. In most instances, getting them from the state takes a lot longer than ordering from the county health department.

The county or state often will not search for a certificate if the information provided is incorrect or incomplete. This can cause guessing games, particularly where women are concerned. Was the certificate filed under a birth name, professional name, or married name? Sometimes several attempts are necessary to get it right.

If you order certificates from the same place over a period of time, you may develop a relationship with the person filling your order. This can be quite beneficial if a problem or question should arise.

Following the 181 pages of actual certificates is a section containing biographical notes about each of the deceased, providing information to help identify the celebrity.

I had such positive responses from *Celebrity Death Certificates* that I was encouraged to offer *Celebrity Death Certificates 2*. This also permitted me to share a number of certificates from my collection and to add some of the celebrities who had died since *Celebrity Death Certificates* was published.

THE DEATH
CERTIFICATES

CERTIFICATE OF DEATH
STATE OF CALIFORNIA
USE BLACK INK ONLY/NO ERASURES, WHITEOUTS OR ALTERATIONS
VS-11 (REV. 7/93)

STATE FILE NUMBER		LOCAL REGISTRATION NUMBER

DECEDENT PERSONAL DATA

1. NAME OF DECEDENT—FIRST (GIVEN)	2. MIDDLE	3. LAST (FAMILY)
Claude	A.	Akins

4. DATE OF BIRTH MM/DD/CCYY	5. AGE YRS.	IF UNDER 1 YEAR MONTHS/DAYS	IF UNDER 24 HOURS HOURS/MINUTES	6. SEX	7. DATE OF DEATH MM/DD/CCYY	8. HOUR
05/25/1926	67			Male	01/27/1994	1425

9. STATE OF BIRTH	10. SOCIAL SECURITY NO.	11. MILITARY SERVICE	12. MARITAL STATUS	13. EDUCATION—YEARS COMPLETED
GA	308-22-8685	19__ To 19__ X NONE	Married	16

14. RACE	15. HISPANIC—SPECIFY	16. USUAL EMPLOYER
White	YES / X No	Self

17. OCCUPATION	18. KIND OF BUSINESS	19. YEARS IN OCCUPATION
Actor	Motion Picture & Television	40

USUAL RESIDENCE

20. RESIDENCE—STREET AND NUMBER OR LOCATION: 1927 North Midlothian

21. CITY	22. COUNTY	23. ZIP CODE	24. YRS IN COUNTY	25. STATE OR FOREIGN COUNTRY
Altadena	Los Angeles	91001	40	California

INFORMANT

26. NAME, RELATIONSHIP	27. MAILING ADDRESS
Therese Akins (Wife)	1927 North Midlothian Altadena CA 91001

SPOUSE AND PARENT INFORMATION

28. NAME OF SURVIVING SPOUSE—FIRST	29. MIDDLE	30. LAST (MAIDEN NAME)
Therese	–	Fairfield

31. NAME OF FATHER—FIRST	32. MIDDLE	33. LAST	34. BIRTH STATE
Ernest	–	Akins	GA

35. NAME OF MOTHER—FIRST	36. MIDDLE	37. LAST (MAIDEN)	38. BIRTH STATE
Anna	–	Howell	GA

DISPOSITION(S)

39. DATE MM/DD/CCYY	40. PLACE OF FINAL DISPOSITION
01/28/1994	1927 North Midlothian Altadena CA 91001

FUNERAL DIRECTOR AND LOCAL REGISTRAR

41. TYPE OF DISPOSITION(S)	42. SIGNATURE OF EMBALMER	43. LICENSE NO.
Cremation / Residence	▶ not embalmed	–

44. NAME OF FUNERAL DIRECTOR	45. LICENSE NO.	46. SIGNATURE OF LOCAL REGISTRAR	47. DATE MM/DD/CCYY
Cabot & Sons	FD 341	▶ Robert C. Natt	01/28/1994

PLACE OF DEATH

101. PLACE OF DEATH	102. IF HOSPITAL, SPECIFY ONE:	103. FACILITY OTHER THAN HOSPITAL:	104. COUNTY
Residence	IP / ER/OP / DOA	CONV. HOSP. / X RES. / OTHER	Los Angeles

105. STREET ADDRESS—STREET AND NUMBER OR LOCATION	106. CITY
1927 North Midlothian	Altadena

CAUSE OF DEATH

107. DEATH WAS CAUSED BY:	TIME INTERVAL BETWEEN ONSET AND DEATH	
IMMEDIATE CAUSE (A) Cardiopulmonary Arrest	Mins	108. DEATH REPORTED TO CORONER: YES / X NO
DUE TO (B) Congestive Heart Failure	days	109. BIOPSY PERFORMED: YES / X NO
DUE TO (C) Cancer of Stomach with Metastases	6 mos	110. AUTOPSY PERFORMED: YES / X NO
DUE TO (D)		111. USED IN DETERMINING CAUSE: YES / NO

112. OTHER SIGNIFICANT CONDITIONS CONTRIBUTING TO DEATH BUT NOT RELATED TO CAUSE GIVEN IN 107: None

113. WAS OPERATION PERFORMED FOR ANY CONDITION IN ITEM 107 OR 112? IF YES, LIST TYPE OF OPERATION AND DATE. Laporatomy 11/04/1993

PHYSICIAN'S CERTIFICATION

114. I CERTIFY ...	115. SIGNATURE AND TITLE OF CERTIFIER	116. LICENSE NO.	117. DATE MM/DD/CCYY
DECEDENT ATTENDED SINCE 08/19/1993 / DECEDENT LAST SEEN ALIVE 01/26/1994	▶ Banskota MD	AO 44429	01/27/1994

118. TYPE ATTENDING PHYSICIAN'S NAME, MAILING ADDRESS + ZIP: N.K. Banskota MD 301 W. Huntington Dr Arcadia CA 91107

CORONER'S USE ONLY

119. MANNER OF DEATH: NATURAL / SUICIDE / HOMICIDE / ACCIDENT / PENDING INVESTIGATION / COULD NOT BE DETERMINED

120. INJURY AT WORK: YES / No	121. INJURY DATE	122. HOUR	123. PLACE OF INJURY

124. DESCRIBE HOW INJURY OCCURRED

125. LOCATION

126. SIGNATURE OF CORONER OR DEPUTY CORONER	127. DATE MM/DD/CCYY	128. TYPED NAME, TITLE OF CORONER OR DEPUTY CORONER

STATE	A	B	C	D	E	F	G	H	FAX AUTH. #	CENSUS TRACT

CERTIFICATION OF VITAL RECORD

COUNTY OF LOS ANGELES • REGISTRAR-RECORDER/COUNTY CLERK

CERTIFICATE OF DEATH
STATE OF CALIFORNIA

0190-053506

STATE FILE NUMBER				LOCAL REGISTRATION DISTRICT AND CERTIFICATE NUMBER	
1A. NAME OF DECEDENT—FIRST: JACK	1B. MIDDLE	1C. LAST: ALBERTSON		2A. DATE OF DEATH (MONTH, DAY, YEAR): NOVEMBER 25, 1981	2B. HOUR: 1330

DECEDENT PERSONAL DATA

3. SEX: Male	4. RACE: Cauc.	5. ETHNICITY: American	6. DATE OF BIRTH: June 16, 1907	7. AGE: 74 YEARS	IF UNDER 1 YEAR MONTHS/DAYS	IF UNDER 24 HOURS HOURS/MINUTES

8. BIRTHPLACE OF DECEDENT (STATE OR FOREIGN COUNTRY): Massachusetts	9. NAME AND BIRTHPLACE OF FATHER: Leo Albertson - Poland	10. BIRTH NAME AND BIRTHPLACE OF MOTHER: Flora Craft - Russia

11. CITIZEN OF WHAT COUNTRY: U.S.A.	12. SOCIAL SECURITY NUMBER: 545-18-1254	13. MARITAL STATUS: Married	14. NAME OF SURVIVING SPOUSE (IF WIFE, ENTER BIRTH NAME): Wallace Thomson

15. PRIMARY OCCUPATION: Actor	16. NUMBER OF YEARS THIS OCCUPATION: 53	17. EMPLOYER (IF SELF-EMPLOYED, SO STATE): Self	18. KIND OF INDUSTRY OR BUSINESS: Motion Pictures, Television and Stage

USUAL RESIDENCE

19A. USUAL RESIDENCE—STREET ADDRESS (STREET AND NUMBER OR LOCATION): 1618 Sunset Plaza Drive	19B.	19C. CITY OR TOWN: Los Angeles

19D. COUNTY: Los Angeles	19E. STATE: California	20. NAME AND ADDRESS OF INFORMANT—RELATIONSHIP: Wallace Albertson (Wife) 1618 Sunset Plaza Drive Los Angeles, California 90069

PLACE OF DEATH

21A. PLACE OF DEATH: Residence	21B. COUNTY: Los Angeles	
21C. STREET ADDRESS (STREET AND NUMBER OR LOCATION): 1618 Sunset Plaza Drive	21D. CITY OR TOWN: Los Angeles	

CAUSE OF DEATH

22. DEATH WAS CAUSED BY: (ENTER ONLY ONE CAUSE PER LINE FOR A, B, AND C) IMMEDIATE CAUSE		
(A) Adenocarcinoma Colon	3 yrs	23. APPROXIMATE INTERVAL BETWEEN ONSET AND DEATH
CONDITIONS, IF ANY, WHICH GAVE RISE TO THE IMMEDIATE CAUSE, STATING THE UNDERLYING CAUSE LAST. (B) Metastases to liver		24. WAS DEATH REPORTED TO CORONER? Yes 81-15098
(C) Adenocarcinoma Colon		25. WAS AUTOPSY PERFORMED? Yes 26. WAS AUTOPSY PERFORMED? No

23. OTHER CONDITIONS CONTRIBUTING BUT NOT RELATED TO THE IMMEDIATE CAUSE OF DEATH	27. WAS OPERATION PERFORMED FOR ANY CONDITION IN ITEMS 22 OR 23? TYPE OPERATION: Resection of Colon	DATE: 1978

PHYSICIAN'S CERTIFICATION

28A. I CERTIFY THAT DEATH OCCURRED AT THE HOUR, DATE AND PLACE STATED FROM THE CAUSES STATED. I ATTENDED DECEDENT SINCE (ENTER MO. DA. YR.): 5-12-1971	I LAST SAW DECEDENT ALIVE (ENTER MO. DA. YR.): 10-21-1981	28B. PHYSICIAN—SIGNATURE AND DEGREE OR TITLE: Melvin Schlemenson MD	28C. DATE SIGNED: 11/27/81	28D. PHYSICIAN'S LICENSE NUMBER: C11881
		28E. TYPE PHYSICIAN'S NAME AND ADDRESS: MELVIN SCHLEMENSON, M.D. 465 N. Roxbury Drive Beverly Hills, California		

INJURY INFORMATION

29. SPECIFY ACCIDENT, SUICIDE, ETC.	30. PLACE OF INJURY	31. INJURY AT WORK	32A. DATE OF INJURY—MONTH, DAY, YEAR	32B. HOUR
33. LOCATION (STREET AND NUMBER OR LOCATION AND CITY OR TOWN)		34. DESCRIBE HOW INJURY OCCURRED (EVENTS WHICH RESULTED IN INJURY)		

CORONER'S USE ONLY

35A. I CERTIFY THAT DEATH OCCURRED AT THE HOUR, DATE AND PLACE STATED FROM THE CAUSES STATED. AS REQUIRED BY LAW I HAVE HELD AN (INQUEST-INVESTIGATION)	35B. CORONER—SIGNATURE AND DEGREE OR TITLE	35C. DATE SIGNED

36. DISPOSITION: Cremation	37. DATE—MONTH, DAY, YEAR: 11-30-1981	38. NAME AND ADDRESS OF CEMETERY: Rosedale Cem. 1831 W. Wash. Blvd. Los Angeles, Calif.	39. EMBALMER'S LICENSE NUMBER AND SIGNATURE: Not Embalmed

40. NAME OF FUNERAL DIRECTOR (OR PERSON ACTING AS SUCH): Cremation Society of California Inc.	41. LOCAL REGISTRAR	42. DATE ACCEPTED BY LOCAL REGISTRAR: NOV 30 1981

STATE REGISTRAR

A.	B.	C.	D.	E.	F.

01-8-1-7005

VS-11 (10-78)

This is to certify that this document is a true copy of the official record filed with the Registrar-Recorder/County Clerk.

Beatriz Valdez
BEATRIZ VALDEZ
Registrar-Recorder/County Clerk

AUG 16 1995
19-397056

This copy not valid unless prepared on engraved border displaying the Seal and Signature of the Registrar-Recorder/County Clerk.

American BankNote Company   ANY ALTERATION OR ERASURE VOIDS THIS CERTIFICATE

CERTIFICATE OF DEATH
STATE OF CALIFORNIA
USE BLACK INK ONLY/NO ERASURES, WHITEOUTS OR ALTERATIONS
VS-11 (REV. 7/93)

STATE FILE NUMBER   LOCAL REGISTRATION NUMBER

DECEDENT PERSONAL DATA

1. NAME OF DECEDENT—FIRST (GIVEN)	2. MIDDLE	3. LAST (FAMILY)
Morey	–	Amsterdam

4. DATE OF BIRTH MM/DD/CCYY	5. AGE YRS.	6. SEX	7. DATE OF DEATH MM/DD/CCYY	8. HOUR
12/14/1908	87	M	10/27/1996	2300

IF UNDER 1 YEAR: MONTHS / DAYS   IF UNDER 24 HOURS: HOURS / MINUTES

9. STATE OF BIRTH	10. SOCIAL SECURITY NO.	11. MILITARY SERVICE	12. MARITAL STATUS	13. EDUCATION—YEARS COMPLETED
ILLINOIS	319-14-6800	19 ___ To 19 ___ [X] NONE	MARRIED	13

14. RACE	15. HISPANIC—SPECIFY	16. USUAL EMPLOYER
CAUCASIAN	[ ] YES [X] NO	SELF EMPLOYED

17. OCCUPATION	18. KIND OF BUSINESS	19. YEARS IN OCCUPATION
ENTERTAINER	ENTERTAINMENT	74

USUAL RESIDENCE

20. RESIDENCE—STREET AND NUMBER OR LOCATION
1012 N. HILLCREST RD.

21. CITY	22. COUNTY	23. ZIP CODE	24. YRS IN COUNTY	25. STATE OR FOREIGN COUNTRY
BEVERLY HILLS	LOS ANGELES	90210	35	CA

INFORMANT

26. NAME, RELATIONSHIP	27. MAILING ADDRESS (STREET AND NUMBER OR RURAL ROUTE NUMBER, CITY OR TOWN, STATE, ZIP)
CATHERINE A. AMSTERDAM, WIFE	1012 N. HILLCREST RD., BEVERLY HILLS, CA. 90210

SPOUSE AND PARENT INFORMATION

28. NAME OF SURVIVING SPOUSE—FIRST	29. MIDDLE	30. LAST (MAIDEN NAME)
CATHERINE	A.	PATRICK

31. NAME OF FATHER—FIRST	32. MIDDLE	33. LAST	34. BIRTH STATE
MAX	–	AMSTERDAM	AUSTRIA

35. NAME OF MOTHER—FIRST	36. MIDDLE	37. LAST (MAIDEN)	38. BIRTH STATE
JENNY	–	FINDER	AUSTRIA

DISPOSITION(S)

39. DATE MM/DD/CCYY	40. PLACE OF FINAL DISPOSITION
11/04/1996	FOREST LAWN MEMORIAL PARK, LOS ANGELES, CA. 90068

FUNERAL DIRECTOR AND LOCAL REGISTRAR

41. TYPE OF DISPOSITION(S)	42. SIGNATURE OF EMBALMER	43. LICENSE NO.
ENTOMBMENT	▶ Christina Sorensen	7835

44. NAME OF FUNERAL DIRECTOR	45. LICENSE NO.	46. SIGNATURE OF LOCAL REGISTRAR	47. DATE MM/DD/CCYY
FOREST LAWN HOLLYWOOD HILLS	F 904	▶ Mark Finerman	11/04/1996

PLACE OF DEATH

101. PLACE OF DEATH	102. IF HOSPITAL, SPECIFY ONE:	103. FACILITY OTHER THAN HOSPITAL:	104. COUNTY
Cedars Sinai Med Ctr	[X] IP [ ] ER/OP [ ] DOA	[ ] CONV. HOSP. [ ] RES. [ ] OTHER	Los Angeles

105. STREET ADDRESS—STREET AND NUMBER OR LOCATION	106. CITY
8700 Beverly Blvd	Los Angeles

CAUSE OF DEATH

107. DEATH WAS CAUSED BY: (ENTER ONLY ONE CAUSE PER LINE FOR A, B, C, AND D)

		TIME INTERVAL BETWEEN ONSET AND DEATH	108. DEATH REPORTED TO CORONER
IMMEDIATE CAUSE	(A) Cardiopulmonary Arrest	1 hr	[X] YES [ ] NO
DUE TO	(B) Acute Myocardial Infarction	1 hr	REFERRAL NUMBER 96-57269
DUE TO	(C) Coronary Artery Disease	20 yrs	109. BIOPSY PERFORMED [ ] YES [X] NO
DUE TO	(D)		110. AUTOPSY PERFORMED [ ] YES [X] NO
			111. USED IN DETERMINING CAUSE [ ] YES [X] NO

112. OTHER SIGNIFICANT CONDITIONS CONTRIBUTING TO DEATH BUT NOT RELATED TO CAUSE GIVEN IN 107
None

113. WAS OPERATION PERFORMED FOR ANY CONDITION IN ITEM 107 OR 112? IF YES, LIST TYPE OF OPERATION AND DATE.
No

PHYSICIAN'S CERTIFICATION

114. I CERTIFY THAT TO THE BEST OF MY KNOWLEDGE DEATH OCCURRED AT THE HOUR, DATE AND PLACE STATED FROM THE CAUSES STATED.	115. SIGNATURE AND TITLE OF CERTIFIER	116. LICENSE NO.	117. DATE MM/DD/CCYY
	▶ A. M. Mondkar	A35142	10/29/1996

DECEDENT ATTENDED SINCE MM/DD/CCYY	DECEDENT LAST SEEN ALIVE MM/DD/CCYY	118. TYPE ATTENDING PHYSICIAN'S NAME, MAILING ADDRESS + ZIP
11/01/1984	10/04/1996	A. M. Mondkar, MD 8641 Wilshire Blvd #300, Beverly Hills, CA 90211

CORONER'S USE ONLY

12

I CERTIFY THAT IN MY OPINION DEATH OCCURRED AT THE HOUR, DATE AND PLACE STATED FROM THE CAUSES STATED.

119. MANNER OF DEATH	120. INJURY AT WORK	121. INJURY DATE MM/DD/CCYY	122. HOUR	123. PLACE OF INJURY
[ ] NATURAL [ ] SUICIDE [ ] HOMICIDE [ ] ACCIDENT [ ] PENDING INVESTIGATION [ ] COULD NOT BE DETERMINED	[ ] YES [ ] NO			

124. DESCRIBE HOW INJURY OCCURRED (EVENTS WHICH RESULTED IN INJURY)

410

125. LOCATION (STREET AND NUMBER OR LOCATION AND CITY AND ZIP CODE)

126. SIGNATURE OF CORONER OR DEPUTY CORONER	127. DATE MM/DD/CCYY	128. TYPED NAME, TITLE OF CORONER OR DEPUTY CORONER
▶		

CERTIFICATE OF DEATH
STATE OF CALIFORNIA
USE BLACK INK ONLY / NO ERASURES, WHITEOUTS OR ALTERATIONS
VS-11 (REV 1/03)

STATE FILE NUMBER		LOCAL REGISTRATION NUMBER

DECEDENT'S PERSONAL DATA

1. NAME OF DECEDENT --- FIRST (Given)	2. MIDDLE	3. LAST (Family)
ROYCE	DWAYNE	APPLEGATE

4. DATE OF BIRTH mm/dd/ccyy	5. AGE Yrs.	IF UNDER ONE YEAR Months / Days	IF UNDER 24 HOURS Hours / Minutes	6. SEX
AKA. ALSO KNOWN AS --- Include full AKA (FIRST, MIDDLE, LAST) —	12/25/1939	63			MALE

9. BIRTH STATE/FOREIGN COUNTRY	10. SOCIAL SECURITY NUMBER	11. EVER IN U.S. ARMED FORCES?	12. MARITAL STATUS (at Time of Death)	7. DATE OF DEATH mm/dd/ccyy	8. HOUR (24 Hours)
OKLAHOMA	448-36-4927	YES / [X] NO / UNK	DIVORCED	01/01/2003	0847

13. EDUCATION --- Highest Level/Degree (see worksheet on back)	14/15. WAS DECEDENT SPANISH/HISPANIC/LATINO? (If yes, see worksheet on back.)	16. DECEDENT'S RACE --- Up to 3 races may be listed (see worksheet on back)
BACHELOR'S	YES ___ [X] NO	WHITE

17. USUAL OCCUPATION --- Type of work for most of life. DO NOT USE RETIRED	18. KIND OF BUSINESS OR INDUSTRY (e.g., grocery store, road construction, employment agency, etc.)	19. YEARS IN OCCUPATION
ACTOR	ENTERTAINMENT	30

1OF 2

USUAL RESIDENCE

20. DECEDENT'S RESIDENCE (Street and number or location)
2616 HOLLYRIDGE DR.

21. CITY	22. COUNTY/PROVINCE	23. ZIP CODE	24. YEARS IN COUNTY	25. STATE/FOREIGN COUNTRY
LOS ANGELES	LOS ANGELES	90068	30	CALIFORNIA

INFORMANT

26. INFORMANT'S NAME, RELATIONSHIP	27. INFORMANT'S MAILING ADDRESS (Street and number or rural route number, city or town, state, ZIP)
SCOTT D. APPLEGATE -- SON	221 BELLHAVEN CIRCLE, CLOVER, SOUTH CAROLINA 29710

SPOUSE AND PARENT INFORMATION

28. NAME OF SURVIVING SPOUSE --- FIRST	29. MIDDLE	30. LAST (Maiden Name)
—	—	—

31. NAME OF FATHER --- FIRST	32. MIDDLE	33. LAST	34. BIRTH STATE
ROY	GILBERT	APPLEGATE	OKLAHOMA

35. NAME OF MOTHER --- FIRST	36. MIDDLE	37. LAST (Maiden)	38. BIRTH STATE
DOROTHY	OPAL	McGRAY	OKLAHOMA

FUNERAL DIRECTOR/ LOCAL REGISTRAR

39. DISPOSITION DATE mm/dd/ccyy	40. PLACE OF FINAL DISPOSITION
01/13/2003	WOODLAND MEM PARK, 1200 N. CLEVELAND, SAND SPRINGS, OKLAHOMA 74063

41. TYPE OF DISPOSITION(S)	42. SIGNATURE OF EMBALMER	43. LICENSE NUMBER
TR/BU	*Scott Fow*	8257

44. NAME OF FUNERAL ESTABLISHMENT	45. LICENSE NUMBER	46. SIGNATURE OF LOCAL REGISTRAR	47. DATE mm/dd/ccyy
FOREST LAWN MTY GLENDALE	FD 656	*Thomas W Gutherie*	01/07/2003

PLACE OF DEATH

101. PLACE OF DEATH	102. IF HOSPITAL, SPECIFY ONE	103. IF OTHER THAN HOSPITAL, SPECIFY ONE
RESIDENCE	IP / ER/OP / DOA	Hospice / Nursing Home/LTC / [X] Decedent's Home / Other

104. COUNTY	105. FACILITY ADDRESS OR LOCATION WHERE FOUND (Street and number or location)	106. CITY
LOS ANGELES	2616 HOLLYRIDGE DR.	LOS ANGELES

CAUSE OF DEATH

107. CAUSE OF DEATH	Enter the chain of events --- diseases, injuries, or complications --- that directly caused death. DO NOT enter terminal events such as cardiac arrest, respiratory arrest, or ventricular fibrillation without showing the etiology. DO NOT ABBREVIATE.	Time Interval Between Onset and Death	108. DEATH REPORTED TO CORONER?
IMMEDIATE CAUSE (A) (Final disease or condition resulting in death) →	DEFERRED	(AT)	[X] YES / NO REFERRAL NUMBER 2003-00007
Sequentially, list conditions, if any, leading to cause on Line A. Enter (B)		(BT)	109. BIOPSY PERFORMED? YES / NO
UNDERLYING CAUSE (disease or injury that (C)		(CT)	110. AUTOPSY PERFORMED? [X] YES / NO
initiated the events resulting in death) LAST (D)		(DT)	111. USED IN DETERMINING CAUSE? YES / NO

112. OTHER SIGNIFICANT CONDITIONS CONTRIBUTING TO DEATH BUT NOT RESULTING IN THE UNDERLYING CAUSE GIVEN IN 107

113. WAS OPERATION PERFORMED FOR ANY CONDITION IN ITEM 107 OR 112? (If yes, list type of operation and date.)	113A. IF FEMALE, PREGNANT IN LAST YEAR? YES / NO / UNK

PHYSICIAN'S CERTIFICATION

114. I CERTIFY THAT TO THE BEST OF MY KNOWLEDGE DEATH OCCURRED AT THE HOUR, DATE, AND PLACE STATED FROM THE CAUSES STATED.	115. SIGNATURE AND TITLE OF CERTIFIER	116. LICENSE NUMBER	117. DATE mm/dd/ccyy
Decedent Attended Since / Decedent Last Seen Alive (A) mm/dd/ccyy (B) mm/dd/ccyy	118. TYPE ATTENDING PHYSICIAN'S NAME, MAILING ADDRESS, ZIP CODE		

CORONER'S USE ONLY

119. I CERTIFY THAT IN MY OPINION DEATH OCCURRED AT THE HOUR, DATE, AND PLACE STATED FROM THE CAUSES STATED.	120. INJURED AT WORK?	121. INJURY DATE mm/dd/ccyy	122. HOUR (24 Hours)
MANNER OF DEATH: Natural / Accident / Homicide / Suicide / [X] Pending Investigation / Could not be determined	YES / NO / UNK		

123. PLACE OF INJURY (e.g., home, construction site, wooded area, etc.)

INFORMATIONAL, NOT A VALID DOCUMENT TO ESTABLISH IDENTITY

124. DESCRIBE HOW INJURY OCCURRED (Events which resulted in injury)

125. LOCATION OF INJURY (Street and number, or location, and city, and ZIP)

126. SIGNATURE OF CORONER / DEPUTY CORONER	127. DATE mm/dd/ccyy	128. TYPE NAME, TITLE OF CORONER / DEPUTY CORONER
Mary T. Macias	01/04/2003	MARY T. MACIAS　DEPUTY CORONER

STATE REGISTRAR	A	B	C	D	E	FAX AUTH. # 273/4401	CENSUS TRACT

This is a true certified copy of the record filed in the County of Los Angeles Department of Health Services if it bears the Registrar's signature in purple ink.

STATE OF CALIFORNIA
CERTIFICATION OF VITAL RECORD

COUNTY OF LOS ANGELES
DEPARTMENT OF HEALTH SERVICES

AMENDMENT OF MEDICAL AND HEALTH DATA—DEATH

INFORMATIONAL, NOT A VALID DOCUMENT TO ESTABLISH IDENTITY

STATE FILE NUMBER	USE BLACK INK ONLY—NO ERASURES, WHITEOUT, OR ALTERATIONS	LOCAL REGISTRATION DISTRICT AND CERTIFICATE NUMBER

STATE/LOCAL REGISTRAR USE ONLY   1   2   3

TYPE OR PRINT IN BLACK INK ONLY

PART I — INFORMATION TO LOCATE RECORD

1. NAME—FIRST (GIVEN)	2. MIDDLE	3. LAST (FAMILY)	4. SEX
ROYCE	DWAYNE	APPLEGATE	MALE

5. DATE OF EVENT—MM/DD/CCYY	6. CITY OF OCCURENCE	7. COUNTY OF OCCURRENCE	
01/01/2003	LOS ANGELES	LOS ANGELES	2OF2

PART II — INFORMATION AS IT APPEARS ON RECORD

107. DEATH WAS CAUSED BY ENTER ONLY ONE CAUSE PER LINE FOR A, B, C, AND D)

IMMEDIATE CAUSE (A)   DEFERRED

(B)

(C)

DUE TO (D)

TIME INTERVAL BETWEEN ONSET AND DEATH	108. DEATH REPORTED TO CORONER
	[X] YES [ ] NO
	REFERRAL NUMBER 2003-00007

109. BIOPSY PERFORMED [ ] YES [ ] NO
110. AUTOPSY PERFORMED [X] YES [ ] NO
111. USED IN DETERMINING CAUSE [ ] YES [ ] NO

112. OTHER SIGNIFICANT CONDITIONS CONTRIBUTING TO DEATH BUT NOT RELATED TO CAUSE GIVEN IN 107

113. WAS OPERATION PERFORMED FOR ANY CONDITION IN ITEM 107 or 112? IF YES, LIST TYPE OF OPERATION AND DATE.

119. MANNER OF DEATH
[ ] NATURAL [ ] SUICIDE [ ] HOMICIDE
[ ] ACCIDENT [X] PENDING INVESTIGATION [ ] COULD NOT BE DETERMINED

120. INJURY AT WORK [ ] YES [ ] NO
121. INJURY DATE—MM/DD/CCYY
122. HOUR
123. PLACE OF INJURY
124. DESCRIBE HOW INJURY OCCURED (EVENTS WHICH RESULTED IN INJURY)

125. LOCATION (STREET AND NUMBER OR LOCATION AND CITY AND ZIP CODE)

PART III — INFORMATION AS IT SHOULD APPEAR

107. DEATH WAS CAUSED BY ENTER ONLY ONE CAUSE PER LINE FOR A, B, C, AND D)

IMMEDIATE CAUSE (A)   SMOKE INHALATION

(B)

(C)

DUE TO (D)

TIME INTERVAL BETWEEN ONSET AND DEATH	108. DEATH REPORTED TO CORONER
RAPID	[X] YES [ ] NO
	REFERRAL NUMBER 2003-00007

109. BIOPSY PERFORMED [ ] YES [X] NO
110. AUTOPSY PERFORMED [X] YES [ ] NO
111. USED IN DETERMINING CAUSE [X] YES [ ] NO

112. OTHER SIGNIFICANT CONDITIONS CONTRIBUTING TO DEATH BUT NOT RELATED TO CAUSE GIVEN IN 107
CORONARY ATHEROSCLEROSIS

113. WAS OPERATION PERFORMED FOR ANY CONDITION IN ITEM 107 or 112? IF YES, LIST TYPE OF OPERATION AND DATE.
NO

119. MANNER OF DEATH
[ ] NATURAL [ ] SUICIDE [ ] HOMICIDE
[X] ACCIDENT [ ] PENDING INVESTIGATION [ ] COULD NOT BE DETERMINED

120. INJURY AT WORK [ ] YES [X] NO
121. INJURY DATE—MM/DD/CCYY 01/01/2003
122. HOUR 0802
123. PLACE OF INJURY OWN RESIDENCE
124. DESCRIBE HOW INJURY OCCURRED (EVENTS WHICH RESULTED IN INJURY)
RESIDENTIAL FIRE

125. LOCATION (STREET AND NUMBER OR LOCATION AND CITY AND ZIP CODE)
2616 HOLLYRIDGE DR.   LOS ANGELES   90068

DECLARATION OF CERTIFYING PHYSICIAN OR CORONER

I HEREBY DECLARE UNDER PENALTY OF PERJURY THAT THE ABOVE INFORMATION IS TRUE AND CORRECT TO THE BEST OF MY KNOWLEDGE.

8. SIGNATURE OF CERTIFYING PHYSICIAN OR CORONER	9. DATE SIGNED—MM/DD/CCYY	10. TYPED OR PRINTED NAME AND DEGREE/TITLE OF CERTIFIER
▶ *Stephen Scholtz*	01/22/2003	STEPHEN SCHOLTZ, M.D. DME

11. ADDRESS—STREET AND NUMBER	12. CITY	13. STATE	14. ZIP CODE
1104 N. MISSION ROAD	LOS ANGELES	CA	90033

STATE/LOCAL REGISTRAR USE ONLY

15. OFFICE OF STATE REGISTRAR OR SIGNATURE OF LOCAL REGISTRAR	16. DATE ACCEPTED FOR REGISTRATION—MM/DD/CCYY
▶ *Thomas J. Garthwaite*	01/27/2003

STATE OF CALIFORNIA, DEPARTMENT OF HEALTH SERVICES, OFFICE OF STATE REGISTRAR   VS-24 B (1/94)

090592882

CERTIFICATION OF VITAL RECORD

COUNTY OF LOS ANGELES • REGISTRAR-RECORDER/COUNTY CLERK

CERTIFICATE OF DEATH 38919032033
STATE OF CALIFORNIA
USE BLACK INK ONLY

STATE FILE NUMBER | LOCAL REGISTRATION DISTRICT AND CERTIFICATE NUMBER

DECEDENT PERSONAL DATA	1A. NAME OF DECEDENT—FIRST (GIVEN) James	1B. MIDDLE Gilmore	1C. LAST (FAMILY) Backus	2A. DATE OF DEATH—MONTH, DAY, YEAR July 3, 1989 / 2B. HOUR 0845 / 3. SEX Male
	4. RACE Caucasian	5. SPANISH/HISPANIC ☐ YES ☐ NO SPECIFY XX	6. DATE OF BIRTH—MONTH, DAY, YEAR February 25, 1913	7. AGE IN YEARS 76 / IF UNDER 1 YEAR MONTHS DAYS / IF UNDER 24 HOURS HOURS MINUTES
	8. STATE OF BIRTH Ohio	9. CITIZEN OF WHAT COUNTRY USA	10A. FULL NAME OF FATHER Russell Gould Backus / 10B. STATE OF BIRTH N.J.	11A. FULL MAIDEN NAME OF MOTHER Daisy Gilmore / 11B. STATE OF BIRTH Penn
	12. MILITARY SERVICE? 19___ To 19___ XX None	13. SOCIAL SECURITY NUMBER 112-10-9265	14. MARITAL STATUS Married	15. NAME OF SURVIVING SPOUSE (IF WIFE, ENTER MAIDEN NAME) Henny Kaye
	16A. USUAL OCCUPATION Actor	16B. USUAL KIND OF BUSINESS OR INDUSTRY Motion Picture	16C. USUAL EMPLOYER Various	16D. YEARS IN USUAL OCCUPATION 50+ / 17. NUMBER OF HIGHEST GRADE COMPLETED (1-12 OR COLLEGE 13-17+) 14
USUAL RESIDENCE	18A. RESIDENCE—STREET AND NUMBER OR LOCATION 10914 Bellagio Road		18B. CITY Los Angeles	18C. ZIP CODE 90077
	18D. COUNTY Los Angeles	18E. NUMBER OF YEARS IN THIS COUNTY 40+	18F. STATE OR FOREIGN COUNTRY California	20. NAME, RELATIONSHIP, MAILING ADDRESS AND ZIP CODE OF INFORMANT Charles Goldring- Trustee 9044 Melrose Avenue #101 Los Angeles, California 90069
PLACE OF DEATH	19A. PLACE OF DEATH St John's Hospital	19B. IF HOSPITAL, SPECIFY ONE: IP, ER/OP, DOA IP	19C. COUNTY Los Angeles	
	19D. STREET ADDRESS—STREET AND NUMBER OR LOCATION 1328 22nd Street		19E. CITY Santa Monica	TIME INTERVAL BETWEEN ONSET AND DEATH / 22. WAS DEATH REPORTED TO CORONER? ☐ Yes ☒ No / REFERRAL NUMBER
CAUSE OF DEATH	21. DEATH WAS CAUSED BY: (ENTER ONLY ONE CAUSE PER LINE FOR A, B, AND C) TYPE OR PRINT IMMEDIATE CAUSE (A) Pneumonia due to Klebsiella ▶ 10 days			23. WAS BIOPSY PERFORMED? ☐ Yes ☒ No
	DUE TO (B) ▶			24A. WAS AUTOPSY PERFORMED? ☐ Yes ☒ No
	DUE TO (C) ▶			24B. IF YES, WAS IT USED IN DETERMINING CAUSE OF DEATH? ☐ Yes ☐ No
	25. OTHER SIGNIFICANT CONDITIONS CONTRIBUTING TO DEATH BUT NOT RELATED TO CAUSE GIVEN IN 21 Parkinsons Disease		26. WAS OPERATION PERFORMED FOR ANY CONDITION IN ITEM 21 OR 25? No MONTH, DAY, YEAR / TYPE	
PHYSICIAN'S CERTIFICATION	I CERTIFY THAT DEATH OCCURRED AT THE HOUR, DATE, AND PLACE STATED FROM THE CAUSES STATED.	27B. SIGNATURE AND DEGREE OR TITLE OF PHYSICIAN Douglas L Forde MD ▶	27C. PHYSICIAN'S LICENSE NUMBER A10268	27D. DATE SIGNED 7/1/89
	27A. DECEDENT ATTENDED SINCE MONTH, DAY, YEAR 1954 / 27E. DECEDENT LAST SEEN ALIVE MONTH, DAY, YEAR July 2, 1989	27F. TYPE ATTENDING PHYSICIAN'S NAME AND ADDRESS Douglas L. Forde, MD 2001 Santa Monica Blvd Santa Monica, California 90404		
CORONER'S USE ONLY	I CERTIFY THAT DEATH OCCURRED AT THE HOUR, DATE AND PLACE STATED FROM THE CAUSES STATED. ▶	28A. SIGNATURE OF CORONER OR DEPUTY CORONER ▶		28B. DATE SIGNED
	29. MANNER OF DEATH—specify one: natural, accident, suicide, homicide, pending investigation or could not be determined	30A. PLACE OF INJURY	30B. INJURY AT WORK ☐ YES ☐ NO / 30C. DATE OF INJURY MONTH, DAY, YEAR	31. HOUR
	32. LOCATION (STREET AND NUMBER OR LOCATION AND CITY)	33. DESCRIBE HOW INJURY OCCURRED (EVENTS WHICH RESULTED IN INJURY)		
FUNERAL DIRECTOR AND LOCAL REGISTRAR	34A. DISPOSITION Burial	34B. PLACE OF FINAL DISPOSITION Westwood Memorial Park Los Angeles, California	34C. DATE OF DISPOSITION MONTH, DAY, YEAR July 8, 1989	35A. SIGNATURE OF EMBALMER / 35B. LICENSE NUMBER 5595
	36A. NAME OF FUNERAL DIRECTOR (OR PERSON ACTING AS SUCH) Pierce Bros Westwood Village	36B. LICENSE NO. F-951	37. SIGNATURE OF LOCAL REGISTRAR ▶	38. REGISTRATION DATE JUL 07 1989
STATE REGISTRAR	A.	B.	C.	D. E. F. / CENSUS TRACT
I-11 (REV. 1-89)	4820	MAKE NO ERASURES, WHITEOUTS, OR OTHER ALTERATIONS		0-9-1-0756

This is to certify that this document is a true copy of the official record filed with the Registrar-Recorder/County Clerk.

Beatriz Valdez
BEATRIZ VALDEZ
Registrar-Recorder/County Clerk

AUG 25 1995
19-399445

This copy not valid unless prepared on engraved border displaying the Seal and Signature of the Registrar-Recorder/County Clerk.

American Bank Note Company ANY ALTERATION OR ERASURE VOIDS THIS CERTIFICATE

STATE OF CALIFORNIA
CERTIFICATION OF VITAL RECORD

COUNTY OF LOS ANGELES • REGISTRAR-RECORDER/COUNTY CLERK

CERTIFICATE OF DEATH
STATE OF CALIFORNIA

0190-032471

STATE FILE NUMBER				LOCAL REGISTRATION DISTRICT AND CERTIFICATE NUMBER
1A. NAME OF DECEDENT—FIRST DONALD	1B. MIDDLE MICHAEL	1C. LAST BARRY	2A. DATE OF DEATH July 17, 1980	2B. HOUR 2152

DECEDENT PERSONAL DATA

3. SEX Male	4. RACE Caucasian	5. ETHNICITY	6. DATE OF BIRTH January 11,1911	7. AGE 69 YEARS	IF UNDER 1 YEAR	IF UNDER 24 HOURS

8. BIRTHPLACE OF DECEDENT Texas	9. NAME AND BIRTHPLACE OF FATHER Leonce DeAcosta. (Unknown)	10. NAME AND BIRTHPLACE OF MOTHER Emma Barry, Texas

11. CITIZEN OF WHAT COUNTRY United States	12. SOCIAL SECURITY NUMBER 563-18-4636	13. MARITAL STATUS Married	14. NAME OF SURVIVING SPOUSE Barbara E. Patin

15. PRIMARY OCCUPATION Actor	16. NUMBER OF YEARS THIS OCCUPATION 40	17. EMPLOYER Free Lance	18. KIND OF INDUSTRY OR BUSINESS Entertainment

USUAL RESIDENCE

19A. USUAL RESIDENCE—STREET ADDRESS 4729 Farmdale Avenue	19B.	19C. CITY OR TOWN North Hollywood

19D. COUNTY Los Angeles	19C. STATE California	20. NAME AND ADDRESS OF INFORMANT—RELATIONSHIP Mrs. Barbara Barry (wife)

PLACE OF DEATH

21A. PLACE OF DEATH Riverside Hospital	21B. COUNTY Los Angeles	11538 Riverside Drive ,Apt.A North Hollywood,
21C. STREET ADDRESS 12629 Riverside Dr	21D. CITY OR TOWN North Hollywood	California 91602

CAUSE OF DEATH

22. DEATH WAS CAUSED BY: (ENTER ONLY ONE CAUSE PER LINE FOR A. B. AND C) IMMEDIATE CAUSE		24. WAS DEATH REPORTED TO CORONER? 80-9178
(A) GUNSHOT WOUND PERFORATING HEAD AND NECK	APPROXIMATE INTERVAL BETWEEN ONSET AND DEATH	25. WAS BIOPSY PERFORMED? no
(B)		26. WAS AUTOPSY PERFORMED? no
(C)		

23. OTHER CONDITIONS CONTRIBUTING BUT NOT RELATED TO THE IMMEDIATE CAUSE OF DEATH	27. WAS OPERATION PERFORMED FOR ANY CONDITION IN ITEMS 22 OR 23? TYPE OF OPERATION DATE no

PHYSICIAN'S CERTIFICATION

28A. I CERTIFY THAT DEATH OCCURRED AT THE HOUR, DATE AND PLACE STATED FROM THE CAUSES STATED. I ATTENDED DECEDENT SINCE	I LAST SAW DECEDENT ALIVE	28B. PHYSICIAN—SIGNATURE AND DEGREE OR TITLE	28C. DATE SIGNED	28D. PHYSICIAN'S LICENSE NUMBER
		28E. TYPE PHYSICIAN'S NAME AND ADDRESS		

INJURY INFORMATION

29. SPECIFY ACCIDENT, SUICIDE, ETC. suicide	30. PLACE OF INJURY residence	31. INJURY AT WORK no	32A. DATE OF INJURY 7-17-80	32B. HOUR 2125

CORONER'S USE ONLY

33. LOCATION 4729 Farmdale, North Hollywood	34. DESCRIBE HOW INJURY OCCURRED as above
35A. I CERTIFY THAT DEATH OCCURRED AT THE HOUR, DATE AND PLACE STATED FROM THE CAUSES STATED. AS REQUIRED BY LAW I HAVE HELD AN INQUEST/INVESTIGATION. ANGELES. CALIF. 90053	35B. CORONER—SIGNATURE AND TITLE NOGUCHI M.D. CORONER DEPUTY	35C. DATE SIGNED 7-18-80

36. DISPOSITION Burial	37. DATE July 21,1980	38. NAME AND ADDRESS OF CEMETERY OR CREMATORY FOREST LAWN MEMORIAL PARK 6300 Forest Lawn Dr., Los Angeles, Ca.	39. EMBALMER—LICENSE NUMBER AND SIGNATURE 6707 Jaquine Morris

40. NAME OF FUNERAL DIRECTOR Forest Lawn Hollywood Hills Mty.	41. LOCAL REGISTRAR	DATE ACCEPTED BY LOCAL REGISTRAR JUL 21 1980

STATE REGISTRAR	A.	B.	C.	D.	E.	F.

VS-11 (5-78)

01-9-3-0654

This is to certify that this document is a true copy of the official record filed with the Registrar-Recorder/County Clerk.

Conny B. McCormack

CONNY B. McCORMACK
Registrar-Recorder/County Clerk

NOV 28 2000
19-116325

This copy not valid unless prepared on engraved border displaying the Seal and Signature of the Registrar-Recorder/County Clerk.

MIDWEST BANK NOTE COMPANY   ANY ALTERATION OR ERASURE VOIDS THIS CERTIFICATE

STATE OF CALIFORNIA
CERTIFICATION OF VITAL RECORD

COUNTY OF LOS ANGELES
DEPARTMENT OF HEALTH SERVICES

CERTIFICATE OF DEATH
STATE OF CALIFORNIA
USE BLACK INK ONLY/NO ERASURES, WHITEOUTS OR ALTERATIONS
VS-11 (REV. 1/00)

STATE FILE NUMBER   LOCAL REGISTRATION NUMBER

	1. NAME OF DECEDENT—FIRST (GIVEN)	2. MIDDLE	3. LAST (FAMILY)
	WILLIAM	JOHN	BARTY

	4. DATE OF BIRTH M M / D D / C C Y Y	5. AGE-YRS.	IF UNDER 1 YEAR MONTHS / DAYS	IF UNDER 24 HOURS HOURS / MINUTES	6. SEX	7. DATE OF DEATH M M / D D / C C Y Y	8. HOUR
DECEDENT PERSONAL DATA	10/25/1924	76			MALE	12/23/2000	0922

	9. STATE OF BIRTH	10. SOCIAL SECURITY NO.	11. MILITARY SERVICE	12. MARITAL STATUS	13. EDUCATION—YEARS COMPLETED
	PA	569-01-0590	YES ☐ NO ☐ UNK ☒	MARRIED	14

	14. RACE	15. HISPANIC—SPECIFY		16. USUAL EMPLOYER
	WHITE	YES ☐	NO ☒	SELF EMPLOYED

	17. OCCUPATION	18. KIND OF BUSINESS	19. YEARS IN OCCUPATION
	ACTOR	ENTERTAINMENT	73

	20. RESIDENCE—(STREET AND NUMBER OR LOCATION)
USUAL RESIDENCE	4502 FARMDALE AVE

	21. CITY	22. COUNTY	23. ZIP CODE	24. YRS IN COUNTY	25. STATE OR FOREIGN COUNTRY
	STUDIO CITY	LOS ANGELES	91602	73	CALIFORNIA

	26. NAME, RELATIONSHIP	27. MAILING ADDRESS (STREET AND NUMBER OR RURAL ROUTE NUMBER, CITY OR TOWN, STATE, ZIP)
INFORMANT	LORI NEILSON - DAUGHTER	11043 CANBY AVE, NORTHRIDGE CA 91326

	28. NAME OF SURVIVING SPOUSE—FIRST	29. MIDDLE	30. LAST (MAIDEN NAME)
	SHIRLEY	-	BOLINGBROKE

SPOUSE AND PARENT INFORMATION	31. NAME OF FATHER—FIRST	32. MIDDLE	33. LAST	34. BIRTH STATE
	ALBERT	-	BARTY	ITALY

	35. NAME OF MOTHER—FIRST	36. MIDDLE	37. LAST (MAIDEN)	38. BIRTH STATE
	ELLEN	-	CECELLIA	ITALY

	39. DATE M M / D D / C C Y Y	40. PLACE OF FINAL DISPOSITION
DISPOSITION(S)	12/27/2000	FOREST LAWN MEM. PARK 1712 S GLENDALE AVE, GLENDALE CA 91205

	41. TYPE OF DISPOSITION(S)	42. SIGNATURE OF EMBALMER	43. LICENSE NO.
FUNERAL DIRECTOR AND LOCAL REGISTRAR	CR/BU	▶ NOT EMBALMED	-
	44. NAME OF FUNERAL DIRECTOR	45. LICENSE NO.	46. SIGNATURE OF LOCAL REGISTRAR	47. DATE M M / D D / C C Y Y
	FOREST LAWN MTY GLENDALE	FD 656	▶ Mark Simmon	12/26/2000

	101. PLACE OF DEATH	102. IF HOSPITAL, SPECIFY ONE:	103. FACILITY OTHER THAN HOSPITAL	104. COUNTY
PLACE OF DEATH	GLENDALE MEMORIAL HOSPITAL	IP ☒ ER/OP ☐ DOA ☐	CONV. HOSP. ☐ RES. CARE ☐ OTHER ☐	LOS ANGELES
	105. STREET ADDRESS—(STREET AND NUMBER OR LOCATION)			106. CITY
	1420 S CENTRAL AVE			GLENDALE

	107. DEATH WAS CAUSED BY: (ENTER ONLY ONE CAUSE PER LINE FOR A, B, C, AND D)	TIME INTERVAL BETWEEN ONSET AND DEATH	108. DEATH REPORTED TO CORONER
IMMEDIATE CAUSE	(A) CARDIOPULMONARY ARREST	MINS	YES ☐ NO ☒
	DUE TO (B) ATHEROSCLEROTIC CARDIOVASCULAR DISEASE	YEARS	REFERRAL NUMBER
CAUSE OF DEATH	DUE TO (C)		109. BIOPSY PERFORMED YES ☐ NO ☒
			110. AUTOPSY PERFORMED YES ☐ NO ☒
	DUE TO (D)		111. USED IN DETERMINING CAUSE YES ☐ NO ☒

	112. OTHER SIGNIFICANT CONDITIONS CONTRIBUTING TO DEATH BUT NOT RELATED TO CAUSE GIVEN IN 107
	NONE

	113. WAS OPERATION PERFORMED FOR ANY CONDITION IN ITEM 107 OR 112? IF YES, LIST TYPE OF OPERATION AND DATE.
	NO

	114. I CERTIFY THAT TO THE BEST OF MY KNOWLEDGE DEATH OCCURRED AT THE HOUR, DATE AND PLACE STATED FROM THE CAUSES STATED.	115. SIGNATURE AND TITLE OF CERTIFIER	116. LICENSE NO.	117. DATE M M / D D / C C Y Y
PHYSICIAN'S CERTIFICATION	DECEDENT ATTENDED SINCE M M / D D / C C Y Y: 12/18/2000 DECEDENT LAST SEEN ALIVE M M / D D / C C Y Y: 12/22/2000	▶ Bruce B. Bagheri, MD	G70830	12/24/2000
		118. TYPE ATTENDING PHYSICIAN'S NAME, MAILING ADDRESS, ZIP. BRUCE BAGHERI, MD 1100 W. GLENOAKS BLVD, GLENDALE CA 91202		

	I CERTIFY THAT IN MY OPINION DEATH OCCURRED AT THE HOUR, DATE AND PLACE STATED FROM THE CAUSES STATED.	120. INJURY AT WORK YES ☐ NO ☐	121. INJURY DATE M M / D D / C C Y Y	122. HOUR	123. PLACE OF INJURY
CORONER'S USE ONLY	119. MANNER OF DEATH: NATURAL ☐ SUICIDE ☐ HOMICIDE ☐ ACCIDENT ☐ PENDING INVESTIGATION ☐ COULD NOT BE DETERMINED ☐	124. DESCRIBE HOW INJURY OCCURRED (EVENTS WHICH RESULTED IN INJURY)			
	125. LOCATION (STREET AND NUMBER OR LOCATION AND CITY, ZIP)				

	126. SIGNATURE OF CORONER OR DEPUTY CORONER	127. DATE M M / D D / C C Y Y	128. TYPED NAME, TITLE OF CORONER OR DEPUTY CORONER
	▶		090393843

STATE REGISTRAR	A	B	C	D	E	F	G	H	FAX AUTH. #	CENSUS TRACT
									273/7798	

This is a true certified copy of the record filed in the County of Los Angeles Department of Health Services if it bears the Registrar's signature in purple ink.

259
DATE ISSUED JAN 02 2001

Director of Health Services and Registrar

This copy not valid unless prepared on engraved border displaying seal and signature of Registrar.

ANY ALTERATION OR ERASURE VOIDS THIS CERTIFICATE

CERTIFICATE OF DEATH
STATE OF CALIFORNIA
USE BLACK INK ONLY

STATE FILE NUMBER		LOCAL REGISTRATION DISTRICT AND CERTIFICATE NUMBER

DECEDENT PERSONAL DATA

1A. NAME OF DECEDENT—First (Given)	1B. MIDDLE	1C. LAST (FAMILY)	2A. DATE OF DEATH—Mo, Day, Yr	2B. HOUR	3. SEX
RALPH	REXFORD	BELLAMY	November 29, 1991	0221	M

4. RACE	5. HISPANIC—SPECIFY	6. DATE OF BIRTH—Mo, Day, Yr	7. AGE IN YEARS	IF UNDER 1 YEAR MONTHS / DAYS	IF UNDER 24 HOURS HOURS / MINUTES
White	[ ] YES ____ [X] NO	June 17, 1904	87		

8. STATE OF BIRTH	9. CITIZEN OF WHAT COUNTRY	10A. FULL NAME OF FATHER	10B. STATE OF BIRTH	11A. FULL MAIDEN NAME OF MOTHER	11B. STATE OF BIRTH
IL	USA	Rexford Bellamy	Unk	Lilla Smith	Unk

12. MILITARY SERVICE?	13. SOCIAL SECURITY NO.	14. MARITAL STATUS	15. NAME OF SURVIVING SPOUSE (IF WIFE, ENTER MAIDEN NAME)
19__ TO 19__ [X] NONE	568-14-5982	Married	Alice Murphy

16A. USUAL OCCUPATION	16B. USUAL KIND OF BUSINESS OR INDUSTRY	16C. USUAL EMPLOYER	16D. YEARS IN OCCUPATION	17. EDUCATION—YEARS COMPLETED
Actor	Motion pictures	Self-employed	60	12

USUAL RESIDENCE

18A. RESIDENCE—STREET AND NUMBER OR LOCATION	18B. CITY	18C. ZIP CODE
8173 Mulholland Terrace	Los Angeles	90046

18D. COUNTY	18E. NUMBER OF YEARS IN THIS COUNTY	18F. STATE OR FOREIGN COUNTRY	20. NAME, RELATIONSHIP, MAILING ADDRESS AND ZIP CODE OF INFORMANT
Los Angeles	42	California	Alice Bellamy, wife 8173 Mulholland Terrace Los Angeles, CA 90046

PLACE OF DEATH

19A. PLACE OF DEATH	19B. IF HOSPITAL, SPECIFY ONE: IP, ER/OP, DOA	19C. COUNTY
ST. JOHN'S HOSPITAL	IP	LOS ANGELES

19D. STREET ADDRESS—STREET AND NUMBER OR LOCATION	19E. CITY
1328 22nd STREET	SANTA MONICA

TIME INTERVAL BETWEEN ONSET AND DEATH	22. WAS DEATH REPORTED TO CORONER? REFERRAL NUMBER
	[ ] YES [X] NO

CAUSE OF DEATH

21. DEATH WAS CAUSED BY: (ENTER ONLY ONE CAUSE PER LINE FOR A, B, AND C)		
IMMEDIATE CAUSE (A) *Cardiac Insufficiency*	▶ 3 days	23. WAS BIOPSY PERFORMED? [ ] YES [X] NO
DUE TO (B) *Chronic Obstructive Pulmonary Disease*	▶ 3 yrs	24A. WAS AUTOPSY PERFORMED? [ ] YES [X] NO
DUE TO (C)	▶	24B. WAS IT USED IN DETERMINING CAUSE OF DEATH? [ ] YES [X] NO

25. OTHER SIGNIFICANT CONDITIONS CONTRIBUTING TO DEATH BUT NOT RELATED TO CAUSE GIVEN IN 21	26. WAS OPERATION PERFORMED FOR ANY CONDITION IN ITEM 21 OR 25? IF YES, LIST TYPE OF OPERATION AND DATE.
none	no

PHYSICIAN'S CERTIFICATION

I CERTIFY THAT TO THE BEST OF MY KNOWLEDGE DEATH OCCURRED AT THE HOUR, DATE AND PLACE STATED FROM THE CAUSES STATED.	27B. SIGNATURE AND DEGREE OR TITLE OF CERTIFIER	27C. CERTIFIER'S LICENSE NUMBER	27D. DATE SIGNED
27A. DECEDENT ATTENDED SINCE MONTH, DAY, YEAR: 9/19/75 DECEDENT LAST SEEN ALIVE MONTH, DAY, YEAR: 11/28/91	▶ Wm W Smith MD	A08479	11/29/91 CA
	27E. TYPE ATTENDING PHYSICIAN'S NAME AND ADDRESS: William W. Smith, M.D., 9675 Brighton Way, Beverly Hills,		

CORONER'S USE ONLY

I CERTIFY THAT IN MY OPINION DEATH OCCURRED AT THE HOUR, DATE AND PLACE STATED FROM THE CAUSES STATED.	28A. SIGNATURE AND TITLE OF CORONER OR DEPUTY CORONER	28B. DATE SIGNED
	▶	

29. MANNER OF DEATH—specify one: natural, accident, suicide, homicide, pending investigation or could not be determined	30A. PLACE OF INJURY	30B. INJURY AT WORK [ ] YES [ ] NO	30C. DATE OF INJURY MONTH, DAY, YEAR	31. HOUR

32. LOCATION (STREET AND NUMBER OR LOCATION AND CITY)	33. DESCRIBE HOW INJURY OCCURRED (EVENTS WHICH RESULTED IN INJURY)

FUNERAL DIRECTOR AND LOCAL REGISTRAR

34A. DISPOSITION(S)	34B. PLACE OF FINAL DISPOSITION—NAME AND ADDRESS	34C. DATE MO, DAY, YEAR	35A. SIGNATURE OF EMBALMER	35B. LICENSE NUMBER
Burial	Forest Lawn Memorial Park Los Angeles, CA 90068	12-3-1991	Not embalmed	None

36A. NAME OF FUNERAL DIRECTOR (OR PERSON ACTING AS SUCH)	36B. LICENSE NO.	37. SIGNATURE OF LOCAL REGISTRAR	38. REGISTRATION DATE
Forest Lawn Hollywood Hills Mty.	F-904	▶ Robert C. Hate	DEC 02 1991

STATE REGISTRAR

A.	B.	C.	D.	E.	F.	CENSUS TRACT

VS-11 (REV. 3-91)   496   MAKE NO ERASURES, WHITEOUTS, OR OTHER ALTERATIONS   01-4-1-075

CERTIFICATION OF VITAL RECORD

COUNTY OF LOS ANGELES • REGISTRAR-RECORDER/COUNTY CLERK

CERTIFICATE OF DEATH
STATE OF CALIFORNIA—DEPARTMENT OF PUBLIC HEALTH

STATE FILE NUMBER

LOCAL REGISTRATION DISTRICT AND CERTIFICATE NUMBER 7053 25076

1a. NAME OF DECEASED—FIRST NAME / 1b. MIDDLE NAME	William
1c. LAST NAME	Bendix
2a. DATE OF DEATH—MONTH, DAY, YEAR / 2b. HOUR	December 14, 1964 4 PM
3. SEX	Male
4. COLOR OR RACE	Cauc.
5. BIRTHPLACE (STATE OR FOREIGN COUNTRY)	New York
6. DATE OF BIRTH	January 14, 1906
7. AGE (LAST BIRTHDAY)	58 YEARS
8. NAME AND BIRTHPLACE OF FATHER	Oscar Bendix Ohio
9. MAIDEN NAME AND BIRTHPLACE OF MOTHER	Hilda Carnell England
10. CITIZEN OF WHAT COUNTRY	U S A
11. SOCIAL SECURITY NUMBER	NONE
12. LAST OCCUPATION	Actor
13. NUMBER OF YEARS IN THIS OCCUPATION	26
14. NAME OF LAST EMPLOYING COMPANY OR FIRM	Self Employed
15. KIND OF INDUSTRY OR BUSINESS	Entertainment
16. IF DECEASED WAS EVER IN U.S. ARMED FORCES GIVE WAR OR DATES OF SERVICE	No
17. SPECIFY MARRIED NEVER MARRIED WIDOWED DIVORCED	Married
18a. NAME OF PRESENT SPOUSE	Teresa Bendix
18b. PRESENT OR LAST OCCUPATION OF SPOUSE	Housewife

DECEDENT PERSONAL DATA

Cleared for Dr. Chapman Coroner's Office

PLACE OF DEATH	
19a. PLACE OF DEATH—NAME OF HOSPITAL	Good Samaritan Hospital
19b. STREET ADDRESS	1212 Shatto St
19c. CITY OR TOWN	Los Angeles
19d. COUNTY	Los Angeles
19e. LENGTH OF STAY IN COUNTY OF DEATH	23 YEARS
19f. LENGTH OF STAY IN CALIFORNIA	23 YEARS

LAST USUAL RESIDENCE	
20a. LAST USUAL RESIDENCE—STREET ADDRESS	4848 Oak Park Ave 2433
20c. CITY OR TOWN	Los Angeles (Encino)
20b. COUNTY	Los Angeles
20c. STATE	Calif.
21a. NAME OF INFORMANT	

PHYSICIAN'S OR CORONER'S CERTIFICATION

22a. PHYSICIAN: I HEREBY CERTIFY THAT DEATH OCCURRED AT THE HOUR DATE AND PLACE STATED ABOVE, FROM THE CAUSES STATED BELOW AND THAT I ATTENDED THE DECEASED FROM 10-8-64 AND THAT I LAST SAW THE DECEASED ALIVE ON 12-14-64

22c. PHYSICIAN OR CORONER—SIGNATURE: J Howard Payne M.D.
ADDRESS 1930 Wilshire Blvd.
22a. DATE SIGNED 12-15-64

FUNERAL DIRECTOR AND LOCAL REGISTRAR

23. SPECIFY BURIAL ENTOMBMENT OR CREMATION	Burial
24. DATE	Dec. 17, 1964
25. NAME OF CEMETERY OR CREMATORY	San Fernando Mission
26. EMBALMER—SIGNATURE / LICENSE NUMBER	William P Beaty 7634
27. NAME OF FUNERAL DIRECTOR	Praiswater Funeral Home
28. DATE ACCEPTED FOR REGISTRATION BY LOCAL REGISTRAR	DEC 16 1964
29. LOCAL REGISTRAR—SIGNATURE	K.H. — M.D.

CAUSE OF DEATH

30. CAUSE OF DEATH
PART I. DEATH WAS CAUSED BY IMMEDIATE CAUSE (A) Pneumonia — APPROXIMATE INTERVAL BETWEEN ONSET AND DEATH 1 wk

CONDITIONS, IF ANY, WHICH GAVE RISE TO THE ABOVE CAUSE (A) STATING THE UNDERLYING CAUSE LAST DUE TO (B) DUE TO (C)

PART II. OTHER SIGNIFICANT CONDITIONS CONTRIBUTING TO DEATH BUT NOT RELATED TO THE TERMINAL DISEASE CONDITION GIVEN IN PART I (A): Malnutrition — Recurrent Carcinoma of Stomach

OPERATION AND AUTOPSY

31. OPERATION—CHECK ONE [X] NO OPERATION PERFORMED
32. DATE OF OPERATION
33. AUTOPSY—CHECK ONE [X] NO AUTOPSY PERFORMED

INJURY INFORMATION

35a. TIME OF INJURY HOUR MONTH DAY YEAR
35b. INJURY OCCURRED [ ] WHILE AT WORK [X] NOT WHILE AT WORK
35c. PLACE OF INJURY
35d. CITY, TOWN, OR LOCATION COUNTY STATE

MEDICAL AND HEALTH DATA

This is to certify that this document is a true copy of the official record on file with the Registrar-Recorder/County Clerk.

FILED JAN 15 1965

Beatriz Valdez
BEATRIZ VALDEZ
Registrar-Recorder/County Clerk

AUG 10 1995
19-389295

This copy not valid unless prepared on engraved border displaying the Seal and Signature of the Registrar-Recorder/County Clerk.

ANY ALTERATION OR ERASURE VOIDS THIS CERTIFICATE

STATE OF CALIFORNIA
CERTIFICATION OF VITAL RECORD

COUNTY OF LOS ANGELES • REGISTRAR-RECORDER/COUNTY CLERK

STATE OF CALIFORNIA   *1901*   DEPARTMENT OF PUBLIC HEALTH
VITAL STATISTICS

1. PLACE OF DEATH: DIST. NO._____   STANDARD CERTIFICATE OF DEATH

COUNTY OF Los Angeles   LOCAL REGISTERED NO. 10179

CITY, TOWN OR RURAL DISTRICT OF West Los Angeles   DO NOT WRITE IN THIS SPACE   STREET AND NO. 9820 Easton Drive

IF DEATH OCCURRED IN HOSPITAL OR INSTITUTION, GIVE ITS NAME

2. FULL NAME PAUL BERN

RESIDENCE: No. 9820 Easton Drive, W.L.A. ST.   IF NON RESIDENT, GIVE CITY OR TOWN, AND STATE

USUAL PLACE OF ABODE

3. SEX	4. COLOR OR RACE	5. SINGLE, MARRIED, WIDOWED OR DIVORCED? (WRITE THE WORD)
Male	White	Married

22. DATE OF DEATH September 5th 1932

5A. IF MARRIED, WIDOWED OR DIVORCED, NAME OF HUSBAND OR WIFE
Jean Harlow

6. DATE OF BIRTH December 3rd, 1889

7. AGE 42 YR. 9 MO. 2 DAYS. IF LESS THAN ONE DAY ___ HRS. ___ MIN.

8. TRADE, PROFESSION OR KIND OF WORK DONE AS SPINNER, SAWYER, BOOKKEEPER, ETC. Producer

9. INDUSTRY OR BUSINESS IN WHICH WORK WAS DONE, AS SILK MILL, SAW MILL, BANK, ETC. Producer M.G.M.

10. DATE DECEASED LAST WORKED AT THIS OCCUPATION (MONTH AND YEAR)

11. TOTAL YEARS SPENT IN THIS OCCUPATION

12. BIRTHPLACE (CITY OR TOWN) Wandersbeck
STATE OR COUNTRY Germany

13. NAME Levy Bern

14. BIRTHPLACE (CITY OR TOWN) Not Known
STATE OR COUNTRY Germany

15. MAIDEN NAME Henrietta Hersch

16. BIRTHPLACE (CITY OR TOWN) Not Known
STATE OR COUNTRY Germany

17. LENGTH OF RESIDENCE
A. CITY, TOWN OR RURAL DISTRICT OF DEATH 2 YRS. ___ MOS. ___ DAYS
B. IN CALIFORNIA 12 YRS. ___ MOS. ___ DAYS
C. IN U.S., IF OF FOREIGN BIRTH 25 YRS. ___ MOS. ___ DAYS

18. INFORMANT (SIGNATURE) M.E. Greenwood
ADDRESS 7902 Fairholm Drive

19. BURIAL, CREMATION OR REMOVAL Cremation
PLACE Inglewood   WRITE THE WORD   DATE

20. EMBALMER { LICENSE NO. 2135
SIGNATURE _____
FUNERAL DIRECTOR Price-Daniel Co., Inc.,
ADDRESS West Los Angeles, Calif

21. FILED SEP 12 1932 DATE _____ REGISTRAR _____ DEPUTY

23. MEDICAL CERTIFICATE OF DEATH
I HEREBY CERTIFY, THAT I ATTENDED DECEASED FROM _____ TO _____
THAT I LAST SAW H___ ALIVE ON _____ AND THAT DEATH OCCURRED ON THE ABOVE STATED DATE AT THE HOUR OF _____ M.

24. CORONER'S CERTIFICATE OF DEATH
I HEREBY CERTIFY, THAT I TOOK CHARGE OF THE REMAINS DESCRIBED ABOVE, HELD AN Autopsy INQUEST, AUTOPSY OR INQUIRY THEREON, AND FROM SUCH ACTION FIND THAT SAID DECEASED CAME TO H___ DEATH ON THE DATE STATED ABOVE.

THE PRINCIPAL CAUSE OF DEATH AND RELATED CAUSES OF IMPORTANCE, IN ORDER OF ONSET, WERE AS FOLLOWS: Gun shot wound of head. DATE OF ONSET

OTHER CONTRIBUTORY CAUSES OF IMPORTANCE:

IF OPERATION, DATE OF _____ WAS THERE AN AUTOPSY? yes
CONDITION FOR WHICH PERFORMED _____
NAME LABORATORY TEST CONFIRMING DIAGNOSIS _____

25. IF DEATH WAS DUE TO EXTERNAL CAUSES (VIOLENCE) FILL IN THE FOLLOWING:
ACCIDENT, SUICIDE OR HOMICIDE? Suicide DATE OF INJURY 9/5/32
INJURED CITY OR TOWN OF W. Los Angeles Cal
AT COUNTY AND STATE OF _____
DID INJURY OCCUR IN HOME, INDUSTRY, OR PUBLIC PLACE? Home
MANNER OF INJURY Gunshot wound
NATURE OF INJURY Gunshot through head.

26. IF DISEASE/INJURY RELATED TO OCCUPATION, SPECIFY _____

27. SIGNATURE Frank R Webb M.D. PHYSICIAN, AUTOPSY SURGEON M.D.
ADDRESS Coroners Office L.A.

28. WHEN REQUIRED BY LAW Frank A. Nance CORONER
COUNTY OF Los Angeles

This is to certify that this document is a true copy of the official record filed with the Registrar-Recorder/County Clerk.

Conny B. McCormack

CONNY B. McCORMACK
Registrar-Recorder/County Clerk

This copy not valid unless prepared on engraved border displaying the Seal and Signature of the Registrar-Recorder/County Clerk.

APR 28 2003

190916158

MIDWEST BANK NOTE COMPANY   ANY ALTERATION OR ERASURE VOIDS THIS CERTIFICATE

STATE OF CALIFORNIA
CERTIFICATION OF VITAL RECORD

COUNTY OF LOS ANGELES • REGISTRAR-RECORDER/COUNTY CLERK

CERTIFICATE OF DEATH
STATE OF CALIFORNIA
USE BLACK INK ONLY/NO ERASURES, WHITEOUTS OR ALTERATIONS
VS-11 (REV. 7/93)

39619041999

STATE FILE NUMBER		LOCAL REGISTRATION NUMBER

DECEDENT PERSONAL DATA

1. NAME OF DECEDENT — FIRST (GIVEN)	2. MIDDLE	3. LAST (FAMILY)	
HOWARD	WESTON	BESSELL, JR	

4. DATE OF BIRTH MM/DD/CCYY	5. AGE YRS	IF UNDER 1 YEAR (MONTHS / DAYS)	IF UNDER 24 HOURS (HOURS / MINUTES)	6. SEX	7. DATE OF DEATH MM/DD/CCYY	8. HOUR
03/20/1935	61			MALE	10/06/1996	0106

9. STATE OF BIRTH	10. SOCIAL SECURITY NO.	11. MILITARY SERVICE	12. MARITAL STATUS	13. EDUCATION — YEARS COMPLETED
NEW YORK	075-30-8880	19 __ TO 19 __ [X] NONE	MARRIED	16

14. RACE	15. HISPANIC — SPECIFY		16. USUAL EMPLOYER
CAUCASIAN	[ ] YES	[X] NO	BESSELL PRODUCTIONS

17. OCCUPATION	18. KIND OF BUSINESS	19. YEARS IN OCCUPATION
DIRECTOR/ACTOR	ENTERTAINMENT	14

USUAL RESIDENCE

20. RESIDENCE — STREET AND NUMBER OR LOCATION				
1454 STONE CANYON ROAD				

21. CITY	22. COUNTY	23. ZIP CODE	24. YRS. IN COUNTY	25. STATE OR FOREIGN COUNTRY
LOS ANGELES	LOS ANGELES	90077	30	CALIFORNIA

INFORMANT

26. NAME, RELATIONSHIP	27. MAILING ADDRESS (STREET AND NUMBER OR RURAL ROUTE NUMBER, CITY OR TOWN, STATE, ZIP)
LINNELL SUMIKO BESSELL — WIFE	1454 STONE CANYON ROAD

SPOUSE AND PARENT INFORMATION

28. NAME OF SURVIVING SPOUSE — FIRST	29. MIDDLE	30. LAST (MAIDEN NAME)	
LINNELL	SUMIKO	NOBORI	

31. NAME OF FATHER — FIRST	32. MIDDLE	33. LAST	34. BIRTH STATE
HOWARD	WESTON	BESSELL, SR.	NEW YORK

35. NAME OF MOTHER — FIRST	36. MIDDLE	37. LAST (MAIDEN)	38. BIRTH STATE
M.	JO	DAINESE	CONNECTICUT

FUNERAL DIRECTOR AND LOCAL REGISTRAR

39. DATE MM/DD/CCYY	40. PLACE OF FINAL DISPOSITION
10/14/1996	WOODLAWN CEMETERY, SANTA MONICA, CA

41. TYPE OF DISPOSITION(S)	42. SIGNATURE OF EMBALMER	43. LICENSE NO.
BU	▶ William L Abel	7981

44. NAME OF FUNERAL DIRECTOR	45. LICENSE NO.	46. SIGNATURE OF LOCAL REGISTRAR	47. DATE MM/DD/CCYY
GATES, KINGSLEY & GATES — S.M.	FD-451	▶ Mark _____	10/09/1996

PLACE OF DEATH

101. PLACE OF DEATH	102. IF HOSPITAL, SPECIFY ONE	103. FACILITY OTHER THAN HOSPITAL	104. COUNTY
UCLA MEDICAL CENTER	[ ] IP [X] ER/OP [ ] DOA	[ ] CONV. HOSP. [ ] RES. [ ] OTHER	Los Angeles

105. STREET ADDRESS — STREET AND NUMBER OR LOCATION	106. CITY
10833 LeConte Avenue	Los Angeles

CAUSE OF DEATH

107. DEATH WAS CAUSED BY: (ENTER ONLY ONE CAUSE PER LINE FOR A, B, C, AND D)	TIME INTERVAL BETWEEN ONSET AND DEATH	108. DEATH REPORTED TO CORONER
IMMEDIATE CAUSE (A) CARDIAC ARREST	10 mins	[ ] YES [X] NO
DUE TO (B) DISSECTING AORTIC ANEURYSM	48 hrs	109. BIOPSY PERFORMED [ ] YES [X] NO
DUE TO (C)		110. AUTOPSY PERFORMED [X] YES [ ] NO
DUE TO (D)		111. USED IN DETERMINING CAUSE [ ] YES [X] NO

112. OTHER SIGNIFICANT CONDITIONS CONTRIBUTING TO DEATH BUT NOT RELATED TO CAUSE GIVEN IN 107
None

113. WAS OPERATION PERFORMED FOR ANY CONDITION IN ITEM 107 OR 112? IF YES, LIST TYPE OF OPERATION AND DATE.
No

PHYSICIAN'S CERTIFICATION

114. I CERTIFY THAT TO THE BEST OF MY KNOWLEDGE DEATH OCCURRED AT THE HOUR, DATE AND PLACE STATED FROM THE CAUSES STATED. DECEDENT ATTENDED SINCE / DECEDENT LAST SEEN ALIVE MM/DD/CCYY	115. SIGNATURE AND TITLE OF CERTIFIER	116. LICENSE NO.	117. DATE MM/DD/CCYY
01/10/1990 10/06/1996	▶ David Kipper MD	G29776	10/06/1996

118. TYPE ATTENDING PHYSICIAN'S NAME, MAILING ADDRESS, ZIP
David Kipper, M.D., 153 S. Lasky Dr., Beverly Hills, CA 90210

CORONER'S USE ONLY

119. I CERTIFY THAT IN MY OPINION DEATH OCCURRED AT THE HOUR, DATE AND PLACE STATED FROM THE CAUSES STATED. MANNER OF DEATH	120. INJURY AT WORK	121. INJURY DATE MM/DD/CCYY	122. HOUR	123. PLACE OF INJURY
[ ] NATURAL [ ] SUICIDE [ ] HOMICIDE [ ] ACCIDENT [ ] PENDING INVESTIGATION [ ] COULD NOT BE DETERMINED	[ ] YES [ ] NO			

124. DESCRIBE HOW INJURY OCCURRED (EVENTS WHICH RESULTED IN INJURY)

125. LOCATION (STREET AND NUMBER OR LOCATION AND CITY AND ZIP CODE)

414

126. SIGNATURE OF CORONER OR DEPUTY CORONER	127. DATE MM/DD/CCYY	128. TYPED NAME, TITLE OF CORONER OR DEPUTY CORONER
▶		

STATE REGISTRAR

A	B	C	D	E	F	G	H	FAX AUTH. #	CENSUS TRACT

This is to certify that this document is a true copy of the official record filed with the Registrar-Recorder/County Clerk.

Conny B. McCormack

NOV 2 8 2000
19-116309

CERTIFICATION OF VITAL RECORD

COUNTY OF LOS ANGELES • REGISTRAR-RECORDER/COUNTY CLERK

CERTIFICATE OF DEATH
STATE OF CALIFORNIA

0190-002290

STATE FILE NUMBER				LOCAL REGISTRATION DISTRICT AND CERTIFICATE NUMBER

1A. NAME OF DECEDENT—FIRST	1B. MIDDLE	1C. LAST	2A. DATE OF DEATH (MONTH, DAY, YEAR)	2B. HOUR
Carl	Lawrence	Betz	Jan 18 1978	1420

3. SEX	4. RACE	5. ETHNICITY	6. DATE OF BIRTH	7. AGE	IF UNDER 1 YEAR MONTHS / DAYS	IF UNDER 24 HOURS HOURS / MINUTES
male	cauc		March 9 1921	56 YEARS		

DECEDENT PERSONAL DATA

8. BIRTHPLACE OF DECEDENT (STATE OR FOREIGN COUNTRY)	9. NAME AND BIRTHPLACE OF FATHER	10. BIRTH NAME AND BIRTHPLACE OF MOTHER
Pa.	Carl William Betz- Mo.	Leona Malenfant- Pa.

11. CITIZEN OF WHAT COUNTRY	12. SOCIAL SECURITY NUMBER	13. MARITAL STATUS	14. NAME OF SURVIVING SPOUSE (IF WIFE, ENTER BIRTH NAME)
U.S.A.	181 12 4956	married	Gloria Sokal

15. PRIMARY OCCUPATION	16. NUMBER OF YEARS THIS OCCUPATION	17. EMPLOYER (IF SELF-EMPLOYED, SO STATE)	18. KIND OF INDUSTRY OR BUSINESS
Actor	40	Free Lance	Acting

USUAL RESIDENCE

19A. USUAL RESIDENCE—STREET ADDRESS (STREET AND NUMBER OR LOCATION)	19B.	20. NAME AND ADDRESS OF INFORMANT—RELATIONSHIP
30810 Broad Beach Rd.		Gloria Betz wife

19C. CITY OR TOWN	19D. COUNTY	19E. STATE	
Malibu	Los Angeles	Calif	same address

PLACE OF DEATH

21A. PLACE OF DEATH	21B. STREET ADDRESS (STREET AND NUMBER OR LOCATION)
Cedars Sinai Hospital	8720 Beverly Blvd.

21C. CITY OR TOWN	21D. COUNTY
Los Angeles	Los Angeles

CAUSE OF DEATH

22. DEATH WAS CAUSED BY: (ENTER ONLY ONE CAUSE PER LINE FOR A, B, AND C) IMMEDIATE CAUSE		APPROXIMATE INTERVAL BETWEEN ONSET AND DEATH	24. WAS DEATH REPORTED TO CORONER? NO
(A)	Bronchogenic Carcinoma BMW		
CONDITIONS, IF ANY, WHICH GAVE RISE TO THE IMMEDIATE CAUSE, STATING THE UNDERLYING CAUSE LAST. (B) DUE TO, OR AS A CONSEQUENCE OF			25. WAS BIOPSY PERFORMED? yes
(C) DUE TO, OR AS A CONSEQUENCE OF			26. WAS AUTOPSY PERFORMED? NO

23. OTHER CONDITIONS CONTRIBUTING BUT NOT RELATED TO THE IMMEDIATE CAUSE OF DEATH	27. WAS OPERATION PERFORMED FOR ANY CONDITION IN ITEMS 22 OR 23? DATE
NONE	OPERATION NO

PHYSICIAN'S CERTIFICATION

28A. I CERTIFY THAT DEATH OCCURRED AT THE HOUR, DATE AND PLACE STATED FROM THE CAUSES STATED. I ATTENDED DECEDENT SINCE (ENTER MO. DA. YR.)	I LAST SAW DECEDENT ALIVE (ENTER MO. DA. YR.)	28B. PHYSICIAN—SIGNATURE AND DEGREE OR TITLE	28C. DATE SIGNED	28D. PHYSICIAN'S LICENSE NUMBER
7/77	1/18/78	Michael Engleberg M.D.	1/19/78	G19143

29E. TYPE PHYSICIAN'S NAME AND ADDRESS
Michael Engleberg M.D. 9735 Wilshire Blvd. Beverly Hills

INJURY INFORMATION

29. SPECIFY ACCIDENT, SUICIDE, ETC.	30. PLACE OF INJURY	31. INJURY AT WORK	32A. DATE OF INJURY—MONTH, DAY, YEAR	32B. HOUR

33. LOCATION (STREET AND NUMBER OR LOCATION AND CITY OR TOWN)	34. DESCRIBE HOW INJURY OCCURRED (EVENTS WHICH RESULTED IN INJURY)

CORONER'S USE ONLY

35A. I CERTIFY THAT DEATH OCCURRED AT THE HOUR, DATE AND PLACE STATED FROM THE CAUSES STATED. AS REQUIRED BY LAW I HAVE HELD AN (INQUEST-INVESTIGATION)	35B. CORONER—SIGNATURE AND DEGREE OR TITLE	35C. DATE SIGNED

FUNERAL DIRECTOR AND LOCAL REGISTRAR 15

36. DISPOSITION	37. DATE—MONTH, DAY, YEAR	38. NAME AND ADDRESS OF CEMETERY OR CREMATORY	39. EMBALMER'S LICENSE NUMBER
Cremation	1-20-78	Grandview Crem 1341 Glenwood Rd Glendale	not embalmed

40. NAME OF FUNERAL DIRECTOR (OR PERSON ACTING AS SUCH)	41. LOCAL REGISTRAR—SIGNATURE	42. DATE ACCEPTED BY LOCAL REGISTRAR
Westwood Village Mortuary	Morrison L. Chamberlin MD	JAN 19 1978

STATE REGISTRAR

A.	B.	C.	D.	E.	F.
					61-8-1-0355

VS-11 (1-75)

This is to certify that this document is a true copy of the official record filed with the Registrar-Recorder/County Clerk.

Beatriz Valdez
BEATRIZ VALDEZ
Registrar-Recorder/County Clerk

AUG 16 1995

19-397054

This copy not valid unless prepared on engraved border displaying the Seal and Signature of the Registrar-Recorder/County Clerk.

American Bank Note Company   ANY ALTERATION OR ERASURE VOIDS THIS CERTIFICATE

STATE OF CALIFORNIA
CERTIFICATION OF VITAL RECORD

COUNTY OF LOS ANGELES • REGISTRAR-RECORDER/COUNTY CLERK

CERTIFICATE OF DEATH — STATE OF CALIFORNIA—DEPARTMENT OF PUBLIC HEALTH

7069 281

STATE FILE NUMBER | LOCAL REGISTRATION DISTRICT AND CERTIFICATE NUMBER

1A. NAME OF DECEASED—FIRST NAME **MADGE**	1B. MIDDLE NAME **C.**	1C. LAST NAME **BLAKE**	2A. DATE OF DEATH—MONTH, DAY, YEAR **Feb. 19, 1969** 2B. HOUR **9A** M.

DECEDENT PERSONAL DATA

| 3. SEX **Female** | 4. COLOR OR RACE **White** | 5. BIRTHPLACE (STATE OR FOREIGN COUNTRY) **Kansas** | 6. DATE OF BIRTH **May 31, 1899** | 7. AGE (LAST BIRTHDAY) **69** YEARS | IF UNDER 1 YEAR | IF UNDER 24 HOURS |

8. NAME AND BIRTHPLACE OF FATHER **Albert W. Cummings, Unk.** | 9. MAIDEN NAME AND BIRTHPLACE OF MOTHER **Alice Stone; Unk.**

| 10. CITIZEN OF WHAT COUNTRY **USA** | 11. SOCIAL SECURITY NUMBER **549-22-1926** | 12. MARRIED, NEVER MARRIED, WIDOWED, DIVORCED (SPECIFY) **Divorced** | 13. NAME OF SURVIVING SPOUSE (IF WIFE, ENTER MAIDEN NAME) |

| 14. LAST OCCUPATION **Actress** | 15. NUMBER OF YEARS IN THIS OCCUPATION **24** | 16. NAME OF LAST EMPLOYING COMPANY OR FIRM (IF SELF EMPLOYED, SO STATE) **Self-Employed** | 17. KIND OF INDUSTRY OR BUSINESS **Motion Pictures & Stage** |

PLACE OF DEATH

| 18A. PLACE OF DEATH—NAME OF HOSPITAL OR OTHER IN-PATIENT FACILITY **Huntington Memorial Hospital** | 18B. STREET ADDRESS—(STREET AND NUMBER, OR LOCATION) **100 Congress St.** | 18C. INSIDE CITY CORPORATE LIMITS (SPECIFY YES OR NO) **Yes** |
| 18D. CITY OR TOWN **Pasadena** | 18E. COUNTY **Los Angeles** | 18F. LENGTH OF STAY IN COUNTY OF DEATH **57** YEARS | 18G. LENGTH OF STAY IN CALIFORNIA **57** YEARS |

USUAL RESIDENCE (IF DEATH OCCURRED IN INSTITUTION, ENTER RESIDENCE BEFORE ADMISSION)

| 19A. USUAL RESIDENCE—STREET ADDRESS (STREET AND NUMBER OR LOCATION) **729-B Park Ave.** | 19B. INSIDE CITY CORPORATE LIMITS (SPECIFY YES OR NO) **Yes** | 20. NAME AND MAILING ADDRESS OF INFORMANT **Edwin Raymond Blake** |
| 19C. CITY OR TOWN **South Pasadena** | 19D. COUNTY **Los Angeles** | 19E. STATE **Calif.** | **317 E. Adele St. Anaheim, Calif.** |

PHYSICIAN'S OR CORONER'S CERTIFICATION

| 21A. CORONER: I HEARBY CERTIFY THAT DEATH OCCURRED AT THE HOUR, DATE AND PLACE STATED ABOVE FROM THE CAUSES STATED BELOW AND THAT I HAVE HELD OR THE REMAINS OF DECEASED AS REQUIRED BY LAW **Investigation** (INVESTIGATION OR INQUEST) | 21B. PHYSICIAN: I HEREBY CERTIFY THAT DEATH OCCURRED AT THE HOUR, DATE, AND PLACE STATED BELOW AND THAT I ATTENDED THE DECEASED FROM ___ TO ___ ENTER MONTH, DAY, YEAR ___ | 21C. PHYSICIAN OR CORONER—SIGNATURE AND DEGREE OR TITLE _____ Deputy 21E. ADDRESS _____ **Hall of Justice, Los Angeles** | 21D. DATE SIGNED **2-20-65** 21F. PHYSICIAN'S CALIFORNIA LICENSE NUMBER |

FUNERAL DIRECTOR AND LOCAL REGISTRAR

| 22A. SPECIFY BURIAL, ENTOMBMENT OR CREMATION **Cremation** | 22B. DATE **2/24/69** | 23. NAME OF CEMETERY OR CREMATORY **Grand View Crematory** | 24. EMBALMER—SIGNATURE (IF BODY EMBALMED) LICENSE NUMBER **William B. Anderson 3978** |
| 25. NAME OF FUNERAL DIRECTOR (OR PERSON ACTING AS SUCH) **Glendale, Calif. Kiefer & Eyerick Mortuary** | 26. IF NOT CERTIFIED BY CORONER, WAS THIS DEATH REPORTED TO CORONER? (SPECIFY YES OR NO) | 27. LOCAL REGISTRAR—SIGNATURE | 28. DATE ACCEPTED FOR REGISTRATION BY **FEB 21 1969** |

MEDICAL AND HEALTH DATA

CAUSE OF DEATH

29. PART I. DEATH WAS CAUSED BY:	ENTER ONLY ONE CAUSE PER LINE FOR A, B, AND C		APPROXIMATE INTERVAL BETWEEN ONSET AND DEATH
IMMEDIATE CAUSE (A)	**Arteriosclerotic cardiovascular disease.**		
CONDITIONS, IF ANY, WHICH GAVE RISE TO THE IMMEDIATE CAUSE (A), STATING THE UNDERLYING CAUSE LAST.	DUE TO, OR AS A CONSEQUENCE OF (B) **Fracture of left ankle.**		
	DUE TO, OR AS A CONSEQUENCE OF (C)		

| 30. PART II. OTHER SIGNIFICANT CONDITIONS— CONTRIBUTING TO DEATH BUT NOT RELATED TO THE IMMEDIATE CAUSE GIVEN IN PART I. | 31. WAS OPERATION OR BIOPSY PERFORMED FOR ANY CONDITION IN ITEMS 29 OR 30? (SPECIFY OPERATION AND/OR BIOPSY) **no** | 32A. AUTOPSY (SPECIFY YES OR NO) **no** | 32B. IF YES, WERE FINDINGS CONSIDERED IN DETERMINING CAUSE OF DEATH? (SPECIFY YES OR NO) |

INJURY INFORMATION

33. SPECIFY ACCIDENT, SUICIDE OR HOMICIDE **ACCIDENT**	34. PLACE OF INJURY (SPECIFY HOME, FARM, FACTORY, OFFICE BUILDING, ETC.) **HOME**	35. INJURY AT WORK (SPECIFY YES OR NO) **NO**	36A. DATE OF INJURY—MONTH, DAY, YEAR **2-18-69**	36B. HOUR **unknown** M.
37A. PLACE OF INJURY (STREET AND NUMBER OR LOCATION AND CITY OR TOWN) **729 B. PARK AVE SO. PASADENA**	37B. DISTANCE FROM PLACE OF INJURY TO USUAL RESIDENCE, ITEM 19. **0** MILES	38. WERE LABORATORY TESTS DONE FOR DRUGS OR TOXIC CHEMICALS (SPECIFY YES OR NO) **no**	39. WERE LABORATORY TESTS DONE FOR ALCOHOL? (SPECIFY YES OR NO) **no**
40. DESCRIBE HOW INJURY OCCURRED (ENTER SEQUENCE OF EVENTS WHICH RESULTED IN INJURY, NATURE OF INJURY SHOULD BE ENTERED IN ITEM 29) **FELL ON FLOOR**			

STATE REGISTRAR

| A. | B. | C. | D. | E. | F. **4806** |

REV. 1-1-65 FORM VS-11

This is to certify that this document is a true copy of the official record filed with the Registrar-Recorder/County Clerk.

Conny B. McCormack

STATE OF CALIFORNIA
CERTIFICATION OF VITAL RECORD

COUNTY OF LOS ANGELES • REGISTRAR-RECORDER/COUNTY CLERK

CERTIFICATE OF DEATH
STATE OF CALIFORNIA
USE BLACK INK ONLY

38919033522

STATE FILE NUMBER			LOCAL REGISTRATION DISTRICT AND CERTIFICATE NUMBER

	1A. NAME OF DECEDENT—FIRST (GIVEN)	1B. MIDDLE	1C. LAST (FAMILY)	2A. DATE OF DEATH—MONTH, DAY, YEAR	2B. HOUR	3. SEX
DECEDENT PERSONAL DATA	Melvin	Jerome	Blanc	July 10, 1989	1430	Male

4. RACE	5. SPANISH/HISPANIC	6. DATE OF BIRTH—MONTH, DAY, YEAR	7. AGE IN YEARS	IF UNDER 1 YEAR MONTHS / DAYS	IF UNDER 24 HOURS HOURS / MINUTES
Cauc./Hebrew	☐ YES　XX NO SPECIFY	May 30, 1908	81	— / —	— / —

8. STATE OF BIRTH	9. CITIZEN OF WHAT COUNTRY	10A. FULL NAME OF FATHER	10B. STATE OF BIRTH	11A. FULL MAIDEN NAME OF MOTHER	11B. STATE OF BIRTH
CA	U S A	Frederick Blank	NY	Eva Katz	Unknown

12. MILITARY SERVICE?	13. SOCIAL SECURITY NUMBER	14. MARITAL STATUS	15. NAME OF SURVIVING SPOUSE (IF WIFE, ENTER MAIDEN NAME)
19__ TO 19__　XX NONE	562-14-5542	Married	Estelle Rosenbaum

16A. USUAL OCCUPATION	16B. USUAL KIND OF BUSINESS OR INDUSTRY	16C. USUAL EMPLOYER	16D. YEARS IN USUAL OCCUPATION	17. NUMBER OF HIGHEST GRADE COMPLETED (1–12 OR COLLEGE 13–17+)
Voice Specialist	Entertainment	Self	63	11

	18A. RESIDENCE—STREET AND NUMBER OR LOCATION	18B. CITY	18C. ZIP CODE
USUAL RESIDENCE	266 Toyopa Drive	Pacific Palisades	91272

18D. COUNTY	18E. NUMBER OF YEARS IN THIS COUNTY	18F. STATE OR FOREIGN COUNTRY	20. NAME, RELATIONSHIP, MAILING ADDRESS AND ZIP CODE OF INFORMANT
Los Angeles	56	California	Noel Blanc - SON

	19A. PLACE OF DEATH	19B. IF HOSPITAL, SPECIFY ONE: IP, ER/OP, DOA	19C. COUNTY	702 N. Rodeo Drive
PLACE OF DEATH	Cedars Sinai Medical Center	I P	Los Angeles	Beverly Hills, CA 90210

19D. STREET ADDRESS—STREET AND NUMBER OR LOCATION	19E. CITY	21. TIME INTERVAL BETWEEN ONSET AND DEATH	22. WAS DEATH REPORTED TO CORONER?
8700 Beverly Boulevard	Los Angeles		☐ YES　XX NO REFERRAL NUMBER

	21. DEATH WAS CAUSED BY: (ENTER ONLY ONE CAUSE PER LINE FOR A, B, AND C)—TYPE OR PRINT		
CAUSE OF DEATH	IMMEDIATE CAUSE (A) Cardiopulmonary Collapse	▶ 4 Mins.	23. WAS BIOPSY PERFORMED? ☐ YES　XX NO
	DUE TO (B) Coma	▶ 10 Days	24A. WAS AUTOPSY PERFORMED? ☐ YES　XX NO
	DUE TO (C) Stroke	▶ 3 Weeks	24B. IF YES, WAS IT USED IN DETERMINING CAUSE OF DEATH? ☐ YES ☐ NO

25. OTHER SIGNIFICANT CONDITIONS CONTRIBUTING TO DEATH BUT NOT RELATED TO CAUSE GIVEN IN 21	26. WAS OPERATION PERFORMED FOR ANY CONDITION IN ITEM 21 OR 25? MONTH, DAY, YEAR	TYPE
Aortic Stenosis	No	

	I CERTIFY THAT DEATH OCCURRED AT THE HOUR, DATE AND PLACE STATED FROM THE CAUSES STATED.	27B. SIGNATURE AND DEGREE OR TITLE OF PHYSICIAN	27C. PHYSICIAN'S LICENSE NUMBER	27D. DATE SIGNED
PHYSICIAN'S CERTIFICATION		▶ *[signature]*	G 31116	7-11-89

27A. DECEDENT ATTENDED SINCE MONTH, DAY, YEAR	DECEDENT LAST SEEN ALIVE MONTH, DAY, YEAR	27E. TYPE ATTENDING PHYSICIAN'S NAME AND ADDRESS
6-28-79	7-7-89	Stephen R. Corday, M.D., 8635 W. Third St., Los Angeles, CA

	I CERTIFY THAT DEATH OCCURRED AT THE HOUR, DATE AND PLACE STATED FROM THE CAUSES STATED.	28A. SIGNATURE OF CORONER OR DEPUTY CORONER	28B. DATE SIGNED
CORONER'S USE ONLY		▶	

29. MANNER OF DEATH—specify one: natural, accident, suicide, homicide, pending investigation or could not be determined	30A. PLACE OF INJURY	30B. INJURY AT WORK ☐ YES ☐ NO	30C. DATE OF INJURY MONTH, DAY, YEAR	31. HOUR

32. LOCATION (STREET AND NUMBER OR LOCATION AND CITY)	33. DESCRIBE HOW INJURY OCCURRED (EVENTS WHICH RESULTED IN INJURY)

	34A. DISPOSITION	34B. PLACE OF FINAL DISPOSITION	34C. DATE OF DISPOSITION MONTH, DAY, YEAR	35A. SIGNATURE OF EMBALMER	35B. LICENSE NUMBER
FUNERAL DIRECTOR AND LOCAL REGISTRAR	Burial	Beth Olam Cemetery Los Angeles, CA	July 13, 1989	Not Embalmed	---

36A. NAME OF FUNERAL DIRECTOR (OR PERSON ACTING AS SUCH)	36B. LICENSE NO.	37. SIGNATURE OF LOCAL REGISTRAR	38. REGISTRATION DATE
Groman Mortuary	696	▶ *Robt. A. Bate*	JUL 13 1989

STATE REGISTRAR	A.	B.	C.	D.	E.	F.	CENSUS TRACT

VS-11 (REV. 1-89)　　MAKE NO ERASURES, WHITEOUTS, OR OTHER ALTERATIONS

This is to certify that this document is a true copy of the official record filed with the Registrar-Recorder/County Clerk.

Conny B. McCormack

CONNY B. McCORMACK
Registrar-Recorder/County Clerk

This copy not valid unless prepared on engraved border displaying the Seal and Signature of the Registrar-Recorder/County Clerk.

OCT 04 2000
19-673795

ANY ALTERATION OR ERASURE VOIDS THIS CERTIFICATE

CERTIFICATION OF VITAL RECORD

COUNTY OF LOS ANGELES • REGISTRAR-RECORDER/COUNTY CLERK

CERTIFICATE OF DEATH 7097-021984

STATE OF CALIFORNIA—DEPARTMENT OF PUBLIC HEALTH

Text printed vertically in left margin: removal of gall bladder for gall stones. djs

STATE FILE NUMBER			LOCAL REGISTRATION DISTRICT AND CERTIFICATE NUMBER	

DECEDENT PERSONAL DATA

1A. NAME OF DECEASED—FIRST NAME: Dan
1B. MIDDLE NAME: Davis
1C. LAST NAME: Blocker
2A. DATE OF DEATH—MONTH, DAY, YEAR: May 13, 1972
2B. HOUR: 4:00 P

3. SEX: Male
4. COLOR OR RACE: Caucasian
5. BIRTHPLACE (STATE OR FOREIGN COUNTRY): Texas
6. DATE OF BIRTH: December 10, 1928
7. AGE (LAST BIRTHDAY): 43 YEARS
IF UNDER 1 YEAR / IF UNDER 24 HOURS

8. NAME AND BIRTHPLACE OF FATHER: Shack Blocker - Texas
9. MAIDEN NAME AND BIRTHPLACE OF MOTHER: Mary Davis - Texas

10. CITIZEN OF WHAT COUNTRY: United States
11. SOCIAL SECURITY NUMBER: 454-30-4824
12. MARRIED, NEVER MARRIED, WIDOWED, DIVORCED (SPECIFY): Married
13. NAME OF SURVIVING SPOUSE (IF WIFE, ENTER MAIDEN NAME): Dolphia Parker

14. LAST OCCUPATION: Actor
15. NUMBER OF YEARS IN THIS OCCUPATION: 17 years
16. NAME OF LAST EMPLOYING COMPANY OR FIRM: National Broadcasting Co.
17. KIND OF INDUSTRY OR BUSINESS: Television

PLACE OF DEATH

18A. PLACE OF DEATH—NAME OF HOSPITAL OR OTHER IN-PATIENT FACILITY: Daniel Freeman Memorial Hospital
18B. STREET ADDRESS: 333 North Prairie Avenue
18C. INSIDE CITY CORPORATE LIMITS (SPECIFY YES OR NO): Yes

18D. CITY OR TOWN: Inglewood
18E. COUNTY: Los Angeles
18F. LENGTH OF STAY IN COUNTY OF DEATH: 17 YEARS
18G. LENGTH OF STAY IN CALIFORNIA: 17 YEARS

USUAL RESIDENCE (IF DEATH OCCURRED IN INSTITUTION, ENTER RESIDENCE BEFORE ADMISSION)

19A. USUAL RESIDENCE—STREET ADDRESS: 555 South Muirfield Road
19B. INSIDE CITY CORPORATE LIMITS (SPECIFY YES OR NO): Yes
20. NAME AND MAILING ADDRESS OF INFORMANT: Jay J. Eller (Attorney) 3700 Wilshire Blvd. Los Angeles

19C. CITY OR TOWN: Los Angeles
19D. COUNTY: Los Angeles
19E. STATE: California

PHYSICIAN'S OR CORONER'S CERTIFICATION

21A. CORONER: I HEREBY CERTIFY THAT DEATH OCCURRED AT THE HOUR, DATE, AND PLACE STATED ABOVE FROM THE CAUSES STATED BELOW AND THAT I HELD ON THE REMAINS OF DECEASED AS REQUIRED BY LAW AN INVESTIGATION OR INQUEST.
21B. PHYSICIAN: I HEREBY CERTIFY THAT DEATH OCCURRED AT THE HOUR, DATE, AND PLACE STATED ABOVE FROM THE CAUSES STATED BELOW AND THAT I ATTENDED THE DECEASED FROM 12/24/62 TO 5/13/72 AND LAST SAW HIM 5/13/72
21C. PHYSICIAN OR CORONER—SIGNATURE AND DEGREE OR TITLE: Marvin Blumberg
21D. DATE SIGNED: 5/15/72
21E. ADDRESS: 4314 W Slauson LA
21F. PHYSICIAN CALIFORNIA LICENSE NUMBER: A10531

FUNERAL DIRECTOR AND LOCAL REGISTRAR

22A. SPECIFY BURIAL, ENTOMBMENT, OR CREMATION: Burial
22B. DATE: Shipped 5/16/72
23. NAME OF CEMETERY OR CREMATORY: Woodmen Cemetery De Kalb, Texas
24. EMBALMER—SIGNATURE (IF BODY EMBALMED) LICENSE NUMBER: George E. Oard 5643

25. NAME OF FUNERAL DIRECTOR (OR PERSON ACTING AS SUCH): McCormick Mortuary
26. IF NOT CERTIFIED BY CORONER WAS THIS DEATH REPORTED TO CORONER? (SPECIFY YES OR NO): No
27. LOCAL REGISTRAR—SIGNATURE: Edward Riedel MD
28. DATE ACCEPTED FOR REGISTRATION BY LOCAL REGISTRAR: MAY 1 5 1972

CAUSE OF DEATH

29. PART I. DEATH WAS CAUSED BY: (ENTER ONLY ONE CAUSE PER LINE FOR A, B, AND C)
(A) IMMEDIATE CAUSE: Pulmonary Embolism — 1 day
CONDITIONS IF ANY WHICH GAVE RISE TO THE IMMEDIATE CAUSE (A) STATING THE UNDERLYING CAUSE LAST
(B) DUE TO, OR AS A CONSEQUENCE OF: Phlebo Thrombosis — 14 d
(C) DUE TO, OR AS A CONSEQUENCE OF: Cholecystectomy — 14 d

APPROXIMATE INTERVAL BETWEEN ONSET AND DEATH

30. PART II. OTHER SIGNIFICANT CONDITIONS—CONTRIBUTING TO DEATH BUT NOT RELATED TO THE IMMEDIATE CAUSE GIVEN IN PART I.
31. WAS OPERATION OR BIOPSY PERFORMED FOR ANY CONDITION IN ITEMS 29 OR 30? SPECIFY OPERATION AND/OR BIOPSY: Operation
32A. AUTOPSY (SPECIFY YES OR NO): Yes
32B. IF YES, WERE FINDINGS CONSIDERED IN DETERMINING CAUSE OF DEATH? (SPECIFY YES OR NO): Yes

INJURY INFORMATION

33. SPECIFY ACCIDENT, SUICIDE OR HOMICIDE
34. PLACE OF INJURY (SPECIFY HOME, FARM, FACTORY, OFFICE BUILDING ETC.)
35. INJURY AT WORK (SPECIFY YES OR NO)
36A. DATE OF INJURY—MONTH DAY YEAR
36B. HOUR

37A. PLACE OF INJURY (STREET AND NUMBER OR LOCATION AND CITY OR TOWN)
37B. DISTANCE FROM PLACE OF INJURY TO USUAL RESIDENCE ITEM 19 ... MILES
38. WERE LABORATORY TESTS DONE FOR DRUGS OR TOXIC CHEMICALS (SPECIFY YES OR NO)
39. WERE LABORATORY TESTS DONE FOR ALCOHOL? (SPECIFY YES OR NO)

40. DESCRIBE HOW INJURY OCCURRED (ENTER SEQUENCE OF EVENTS WHICH RESULTED IN INJURY, NATURE OF INJURY SHOULD BE ENTERED IN ITEM 29)

STATE REGISTRAR

A.	B.	C.	D.	E.	F.
					2116

REV. 1-1-68 Form VS-11

This is to certify that this document is a true copy of the official record filed with the Registrar-Recorder/County Clerk.

Beatriz Valdez
BEATRIZ VALDEZ
Registrar-Recorder/County Clerk

19-397410

This copy not valid unless prepared on engraved border displaying the Seal and Signature of the Registrar-Recorder/County Clerk.

American Bank Note Company — ANY ALTERATION OR ERASURE VOIDS THIS CERTIFICATE

STATE OF CALIFORNIA
CERTIFICATION OF VITAL RECORD

COUNTY OF LOS ANGELES • REGISTRAR-RECORDER/COUNTY CLERK

STATE FILE NO

CERTIFICATE OF DEATH
STATE OF CALIFORNIA— DEPARTMENT OF PUBLIC HEALTH

REGISTRATION DISTRICT NO **7053** REGISTRAR'S NUMBER **825**

1A. NAME OF DECEASED—FIRST NAME **HUMPHREY**	1B. MIDDLE NAME **De Forest**	1C. LAST NAME **BOGART**	2A. DATE OF DEATH—MONTH, DAY, YEAR **JANUARY 14 1957** 2B. HOUR **2:25 A M**

| 3. SEX **Male** | 4. COLOR OR RACE **White** | 5. SPECIFY MARRIED, NEVER MARRIED, WIDOWED, DIVORCED **Married** | 6. DATE OF BIRTH **Dec 25, 1899** | 7. AGE (LAST BIRTHDAY) **57 YEARS**   IF UNDER 1 YEAR MONTHS DAYS   IF UNDER 24 HOURS HOURS MINUTES |

DECEDENT PERSONAL DATA (TYPE OR PRINT NAME)

| 8A. USUAL OCCUPATION (GIVE KIND OF WORK DONE DURING MOST OF WORKING LIFE, EVEN IF RETIRED) **Actor** | 8B. KIND OF BUSINESS OR INDUSTRY **Motion Pictures** | 9. BIRTHPLACE (STATE OR FOREIGN COUNTRY) **New York City** | 10. CITIZEN OF WHAT COUNTRY **United States** |

| 11. NAME AND BIRTHPLACE OF FATHER **Belmont De Forest Bogart New York** | 12. MAIDEN NAME AND BIRTHPLACE OF MOTHER **Maud Humphrey New York** | 13. NAME OF PRESENT SPOUSE (IF MARRIED) **Betty Bacall Bogart (aka Lauren Bacall Bogart)** |

| 14. WAS DECEASED EVER IN U.S. ARMED FORCES? SPECIFY YES, NO, UNKNOWN **Yes**   IF YES, GIVE WAR OR DATES OF SERVICE **World War I** | 15. SOCIAL SECURITY NUMBER **548 07 6990** | 16. INFORMANT **A. Morgan Maree III** |

PLACE OF DEATH

| 17A. COUNTY **Los Angeles** | 17B. CITY OR TOWN **Los Angeles** | OUTSIDE CORPO RATE LIMITS   INSIDE CORPO RATE LIMITS **X** | 17C. LENGTH OF STAY IN THIS CITY OR TOWN **22 to 23 years** |

17D. FULL NAME OF HOSPITAL OR INSTITUTION

17E. ADDRESS (IF NOT IN HOSPITAL OR INSTITUTION GIVE STREET AND NUMBER OR LOCATION. DO NOT USE P.O. BOX NUMBERS) **232 S. Mapleton Drive, Los Angeles, California**

LAST USUAL RESIDENCE (WHERE DECEASED LIVED. IF INSTITUTION, RESIDENCE BEFORE ADMISSION)

| 18A. STATE **California** | 18B. COUNTY **Los Angeles** | 18C. CITY OR TOWN **Los Angeles** | OUTSIDE CORPO RATE LIMITS   INSIDE CORPO RATE LIMITS **X** | 18D. STREET OR RURAL ADDRESS (DO NOT USE P.O. BOX NUMBERS) **232 S. Mapleton Drive** |

PHYSICIAN'S OR CORONER'S CERTIFICATION

19A. CORONER: I HEREBY CERTIFY THAT DEATH OCCURRED AT THE HOUR, DATE AND PLACE STATED ABOVE FROM THE CAUSES STATED BELOW AND THAT I HAVE HELD AN _____ INVESTIGATION, AUTOPSY, INQUEST ON THE REMAINS OF DECEASED AS REQUIRED BY LAW.

19B. PHYSICIAN: I HEREBY CERTIFY THAT DEATH OCCURRED AT THE HOUR, DATE AND PLACE STATED ABOVE, FROM THE CAUSES STATED BELOW, AND THAT I ATTENDED THE DECEASED FROM **12/27/55** TO **1/14/57** AND THAT I LAST SAW THE DECEASED ALIVE ON **1/13/57**

| 19C. SIGNATURE **M. Mondora** | DEGREE OR TITLE **M.D.** | 19D. **133 S. Lasky Dr, Bev. Hills** | 19E. DATE SIGNED **1/14/57** |

FUNERAL DIRECTOR AND REGISTRAR

| 20A. SPECIFY BURIAL, CREMATION OR REMOVAL **Cremation** | 20B. DATE **1/17/57** | 20C. CEMETERY OR CREMATORY **Forest Lawn Memorial-Park Crematory** | 21. SIGNATURE OF EMBALMER (IF BODY EMBALMED) **Richard B. Pichler**   LICENSE NUMBER **2899** |

| 22. FUNERAL DIRECTOR **Forest Lawn Memorial Park Ass'n., Glendale, California** | 23. DATE RECEIVED BY LOCAL REGISTRAR **JAN 16 1957** | 24. SIGNATURE OF LOCAL REGISTRAR **George M. Uhl, M.D.** |

MEDICAL AND HEALTH DATA

CAUSE OF DEATH (ENTER ONLY ONE CAUSE PER LINE FOR (A), (B) AND (C))

THIS DOES NOT MEAN THE MODE OF DYING SUCH AS HEART FAILURE, ASTHENIA, ETC. IT MEANS THE DISEASE, INJURY OR COMPLICATIONS WHICH CAUSED DEATH.

25. DISEASE OR CONDITION DIRECTLY LEADING TO DEATH (A) **Generalized Carcinomatosis**	**3 mos.**
ANTECEDENT CAUSES MORBID CONDITIONS, IF ANY, GIVING RISE TO THE ABOVE CAUSE (A) STATING THE UNDERLYING CAUSE LAST. DUE TO (B) **Carcinoma of esophagus**	**13 mo.**
DUE TO (C)	

APPROXIMATE INTERVAL BETWEEN ONSET AND DEATH

OTHER SIGNIFICANT CONDITIONS: 26. CONDITIONS CONTRIBUTING TO THE DEATH BUT NOT RELATED TO THE DISEASE OR CONDITION CAUSING DEATH.

OPERATIONS

| 27A. DATE OF OPERATION **1/1/56** | 27B. MAJOR FINDINGS OF OPERATION **Carcinoma of esophagus** | 28. AUTOPSY **YES** ☒   NO ☐ |

DEATH DUE TO EXTERNAL VIOLENCE

| 29A. SPECIFY ACCIDENT, SUICIDE OR HOMICIDE | 29B. PLACE OF INJURY (E.G. IN OR ABOUT HOME, FARM, FACTORY, STREET, OFFICE BUILDING) | 29C. LOCATION CITY OR TOWN COUNTY STATE |
| 29D. TIME MONTH DAY YEAR HOUR OF INJURY M | 29E. INJURY OCCURRED WHILE AT WORK ☐   NOT WHILE AT WORK ☐ | 29F. HOW DID INJURY OCCUR? |

REV. 1-1-52. FORM R&S-11

This is to certify that this document is a true copy of the official record filed with the Registrar-Recorder/County Clerk.

CONNY B. McCORMACK
Registrar-Recorder/County Clerk

This copy not valid unless prepared on engraved border displaying the Seal and Signature of the Registrar-Recorder/County Clerk.

JAN 3 1 2005

019147564

MIDWEST BANK NOTE COMPANY   ANY ALTERATION OR ERASURE VOIDS THIS CERTIFICATE

STATE OF CALIFORNIA
CERTIFICATION OF VITAL RECORD

COUNTY OF LOS ANGELES
DEPARTMENT OF HEALTH SERVICES

CERTIFICATE OF DEATH
STATE OF CALIFORNIA
USE BLACK INK ONLY-NO ERASURES, WHITEOUTS OR ALTERATIONS
VS-11 (REV. 1/00)

STATE FILE NUMBER		LOCAL REGISTRATION NUMBER

DECEDENT PERSONAL DATA

1. NAME OF DECEDENT—FIRST (GIVEN)	2. MIDDLE	3. LAST (FAMILY)
MARGARET	ELIZABETH	BOOTH

4. DATE OF BIRTH MM/DD/CCYY	5. AGE YRS.	IF UNDER 1 YEAR MONTHS / DAYS	IF UNDER 24 HOURS HOURS / MINUTES	6. SEX	7. DATE OF DEATH MM/DD/CCYY	8. HOUR
01/16/1898	104			F	10/28/2002	1432

9. STATE OF BIRTH	10. SOCIAL SECURITY NO.	11. MILITARY SERVICE	12. MARITAL STATUS	13. EDUCATION—YEARS COMPLETED
CA	569-18-8084	YES [X] No [ ] UNK	NEVER MARRIED	12

14. RACE	15. HISPANIC—SPECIFY	16. USUAL EMPLOYER
CAUCASIAN	YES [ ] [X] No	RAY STARK

17. OCCUPATION	18. KIND OF BUSINESS	19. YEARS IN OCCUPATION
FILM EDITOR	MOTION PICTURES	78

USUAL RESIDENCE

20. RESIDENCE—(STREET AND NUMBER OR LOCATION)
9920 DURANT DR.

21. CITY	22. COUNTY	23. ZIP CODE	24. YRS IN COUNTY	25. STATE OR FOREIGN COUNTRY
BEVERLY HILLS	LOS ANGELES	90212	104	CA

INFORMANT

26. NAME, RELATIONSHIP	27. MAILING ADDRESS (STREET AND NUMBER OR RURAL ROUTE NUMBER, CITY OR TOWN, STATE, ZIP)
MARIE CETNER - COUSIN	900 EUCLID ST. #209 SANTA MONICA, CA. 90403

SPOUSE AND PARENT INFORMATION

28. NAME OF SURVIVING SPOUSE—FIRST	29. MIDDLE	30. LAST (MAIDEN NAME)
-	-	-

31. NAME OF FATHER—FIRST	32. MIDDLE	33. LAST	34. BIRTH STATE
EDWARD	-	BOOTH	OH

35. NAME OF MOTHER—FIRST	36. MIDDLE	37. LAST (MAIDEN)	38. BIRTH STATE
MARGARET	-	BOLAND	NY

DISPOSITION(S)

39. DATE MM/DD/CCYY	40. PLACE OF FINAL DISPOSITION
10/31/2002	INGLEWOOD PARK CEMETERY 720 E.FLORENCE AVE. INGLEWOOD, CA. 90301

FUNERAL DIRECTOR AND LOCAL REGISTRAR

41. TYPE OF DISPOSITION(S)	42. SIGNATURE OF EMBALMER	43. LICENSE NO.
BURIAL	▶ Juleen Lade	8251

44. NAME OF FUNERAL DIRECTOR	45. LICENSE NO.	46. SIGNATURE OF LOCAL REGISTRAR	47. DATE MM/DD/CCYY
PIERCE BROS. WESTWOOD	FD-951	Thomas G [signature]	10/30/2002

PLACE OF DEATH

101. PLACE OF DEATH	102. IF HOSPITAL, SPECIFY ONE:	103. FACILITY OTHER THAN HOSPITAL:	104. COUNTY
CENTURY CITY HOSPITAL	[X] IP [ ] ER/OP [ ] DOA	[ ] CONV. HOSP. [ ] RES. CARE [ ] OTHER	LOS ANGELES

105. STREET ADDRESS—(STREET AND NUMBER OR LOCATION)	106. CITY
2070 CENTURY PARK EAST	CENTURY CITY

CAUSE OF DEATH

107. DEATH WAS CAUSED BY: (ENTER ONLY ONE CAUSE PER LINE FOR A, B, C, AND D)		TIME INTERVAL BETWEEN ONSET AND DEATH	108. DEATH REPORTED TO CORONER
IMMEDIATE CAUSE (A)	RESPIRATORY FAILURE	2hours	[ ] YES [X] No REFERRAL NUMBER
DUE TO (B)	PNEUMONIA	3days	109. BIOPSY PERFORMED [ ] YES [X] No
DUE TO (C)	CEREBROVASCULAR ACCIDENT	3days	110. AUTOPSY PERFORMED [ ] YES [X] No
DUE TO (D)			111. USED IN DETERMINING CAUSE [ ] YES [ ] NO

112. OTHER SIGNIFICANT CONDITIONS CONTRIBUTING TO DEATH BUT NOT RELATED TO CAUSE GIVEN IN 107
NONE

113. WAS OPERATION PERFORMED FOR ANY CONDITION IN ITEM 107 OR 112? IF YES, LIST TYPE OF OPERATION AND DATE.
NO

PHYSICIAN'S CERTIFICATION

114. I CERTIFY THAT TO THE BEST OF MY KNOWLEDGE DEATH OCCURRED AT THE HOUR, DATE, AND PLACE STATED FROM THE CAUSES STATED. DECEDENT ATTENDED SINCE MM/DD/CCYY / DECEDENT LAST SEEN ALIVE MM/DD/CCYY	115. SIGNATURE AND TITLE OF CERTIFIER	116. LICENSE NO.	117. DATE MM/DD/CCYY
10/21/2002 / 10/25/2002	▶ Rajwar [signature]	A68598	10/29/2002

118. TYPE ATTENDING PHYSICIAN'S NAME, MAILING ADDRESS, ZIP
RAJ PRASAD, M.D. 2080 CENTURY PARK EAST LOS ANGELES, CA 90067

CORONER'S USE ONLY

119. I CERTIFY THAT IN MY OPINION DEATH OCCURRED AT THE HOUR, DATE AND PLACE STATED FROM THE CAUSES STATED.	120. INJURY AT WORK [ ] YES [ ] NO	121. INJURY DATE MM/DD/CCYY	122. HOUR	123. PLACE OF INJURY
119. MANNER OF DEATH [ ] NATURAL [ ] SUICIDE [ ] HOMICIDE [ ] ACCIDENT [ ] PENDING INVESTIGATION [ ] COULD NOT BE DETERMINED	124. DESCRIBE HOW INJURY OCCURRED (EVENTS WHICH RESULTED IN INJURY)			

125. LOCATION (STREET AND NUMBER OR LOCATION AND CITY, ZIP)

126. SIGNATURE OF CORONER OR DEPUTY CORONER	127. DATE MM/DD/CCYY	128. TYPED NAME, TITLE OF CORONER OR DEPUTY CORONER
▶		

090583426

STATE REGISTRAR

A	B	C	D	E	F	G	H	FAX AUTH. #	CENSUS TRACT

INFORMATIONAL, NOT A VALID DOCUMENT TO ESTABLISH IDENTITY

This is a true certified copy of the record filed in the County of Los Angeles Department of Health Services if it bears the Registrar's signature in purple ink.

DATE ISSUED

Director of Health Services and Registrar

NOV 20 2002

This copy not valid unless prepared on engraved border displaying seal and signature of Registrar.

MIDWEST BANK NOTE COMPANY   ANY ALTERATION OR ERASURE VOIDS THIS CERTIFICATE

CERTIFICATION OF VITAL RECORD

COUNTY OF ORANGE
SANTA ANA, CALIFORNIA

CERTIFICATE OF DEATH
STATE OF CALIFORNIA—DEPARTMENT OF PUBLIC HEALTH

3000 06178

STATE FILE NUMBER				LOCAL REGISTRATION DISTRICT AND CERTIFICATE NUMBER

DECEDENT PERSONAL DATA

1A. NAME OF DECEASED—FIRST NAME	1B. MIDDLE NAME	1C. LAST NAME	2A. DATE OF DEATH—MONTH, DAY, YEAR	2B. HOUR
WILLIAM	LAWRENCE	BOYD	September 12, 1972	11:28 P.M.

3. SEX	4. COLOR OR RACE	5. BIRTHPLACE (STATE OR FOREIGN COUNTRY)	6. DATE OF BIRTH	7. AGE (LAST BIRTHDAY)	IF UNDER 1 YEAR MONTHS DAYS	IF UNDER 24 HOURS HOURS MINUTES
Male	Caucasian	Ohio	June 5, 1895	77 YEARS		

8. NAME AND BIRTHPLACE OF FATHER		9. MAIDEN NAME AND BIRTHPLACE OF MOTHER	
Charles W. Boyd	Unknown	Lyda Wilkins	Unknown

10. CITIZEN OF WHAT COUNTRY	11. SOCIAL SECURITY NUMBER	12. MARRIED, NEVER MARRIED, WIDOWED, DIVORCED (SPECIFY)	13. NAME OF SURVIVING SPOUSE (IF WIFE, ENTER MAIDEN NAME)
U.S.A.	568-03-4357	Married	Grace Bradley

14. LAST OCCUPATION	15. NUMBER OF YEARS THIS OCCUPATION	16. NAME OF LAST EMPLOYING COMPANY OR FIRM (IF SELF EMPLOYED SO STATE)	17. KIND OF INDUSTRY OR BUSINESS
Hop-A-Long Cassidy	53	William Boyd Enterprises	Movies, T.V. Radio & Etc.

PLACE OF DEATH

18A. PLACE OF DEATH—NAME OF HOSPITAL OR OTHER IN PATIENT FACILITY	18B. STREET ADDRESS—(STREET AND NUMBER OR LOCATION)	18C. INSIDE CITY CORPORATE LIMITS (SPECIFY YES OR NO)
South Coast Community Hospital	31872 Coast Highway	No

18D. CITY OR TOWN	18E. COUNTY	18F. LENGTH OF STAY IN COUNTY OF DEATH	18G. LENGTH OF STAY IN CALIFORNIA
South Laguna	Orange	12 YEARS	53 YEARS

USUAL RESIDENCE (IF DEATH OCCURRED IN INSTITUTION, ENTER RESIDENCE BEFORE ADMISSION)

19A. USUAL RESIDENCE—STREET ADDRESS (STREET AND NUMBER OR LOCATION)	19B. INSIDE CITY CORPORATE LIMITS (SPECIFY YES OR NO)	20. NAME AND MAILING ADDRESS OF INFORMANT
Dana Strand Club #17 34001 Dana Strand Road	No	Mrs. Marguerite Cherry-Pus. Mgr. 3447 Virginia Avenue

19C. CITY OR TOWN	19D. COUNTY	19E. STATE	
Dana Point	Orange	California	Santa Monica, California

PHYSICIAN'S OR CORONER'S CERTIFICATION

21A. CORONER	21B. PHYSICIAN	21C. PHYSICIAN OR CORONER SIGNATURE AND DEGREE OR TITLE	21D. DATE SIGNED
FROM 8-1-72 TO 9-12-72 AND 9-13-72		John H. Hagen M.D.	9-13-72
		21E. ADDRESS 31872 Coast Hwy, South Laguna	21F. PHYSICIAN'S CALIFORNIA LICENSE NUMBER A19129

FUNERAL DIRECTOR AND LOCAL REGISTRAR

22A. SPECIFY BURIAL, ENTOMBMENT OR CREMATION	22B. DATE	23. NAME OF CEMETERY OR CREMATORY	24. EMBALMER—SIGNATURE (IF BODY EMBALMED) LICENSE NUMBER
Entombment	9/15/72	FOREST LAWN MEMORIAL PARK ASS'N GLENDALE CALIFORNIA	Frederick B. Macdonald 3657

25. NAME OF FUNERAL DIRECTOR (OR PERSON ACTING AS SUCH)	26. IF NOT CERTIFIED BY CORONER HAS THIS DEATH BEEN REFERRED TO CORONER (SPECIFY YES OR NO)	27. LOCAL REGISTRAR—SIGNATURE	28. DATE ACCEPTED FOR REGISTRATION BY LOCAL REGISTRAR
FOREST LAWN MEMORIAL PARK ASS'N GLENDALE CALIFORNIA	No	John E. Philips, M.D.	SEP 15 1972

CAUSE OF DEATH

29. PART I. DEATH WAS CAUSED BY:	ENTER ONLY ONE CAUSE PER LINE FOR A, B AND C	APPROXIMATE INTERVAL BETWEEN ONSET AND DEATH
IMMEDIATE CAUSE (A)	Bronchopneumonia and congestive Heart failure	2 day
CONDITIONS IF ANY WHICH GAVE RISE TO THE IMMEDIATE CAUSE (A) STATING THE UNDERLYING CAUSE LAST. DUE TO, OR AS A CONSEQUENCE OF: (B)	Metastatic Squamous cell carcinoma Primary site unknown	3 years
DUE TO, OR AS A CONSEQUENCE OF: (C)	dis -- Quadriplegia 2° Probable Intracerebral metastases	2 months

30. PART II. OTHER SIGNIFICANT CONDITIONS—CONTRIBUTING TO DEATH BUT NOT RELATED TO THE IMMEDIATE CAUSE GIVEN IN PART I	31. WAS OPERATION OR BIOPSY PERFORMED FOR ANY CONDITION IN ITEMS 29 OR 30? SPECIFY OPERATION AND/OR BIOPSE	32A. AUTOPSY SPECIFY YES OR NO	32B. IF YES WERE FINDINGS CONSIDERED IN DETERMINING CAUSE OF DEATH SPECIFY YES OR NO
	Operation	No	

INJURY INFORMATION

33. SPECIFY ACCIDENT, SUICIDE OR HOMICIDE	34. PLACE OF INJURY (SPECIFY HOME, FARM, FACTORY, OFFICE BUILDING, ETC.)	35. INJURY AT WORK (SPECIFY YES OR NO)	36A. DATE OF INJURY—MONTH DAY YEAR	36B. HOUR M

37A. PLACE OF INJURY (STREET AND NUMBER OR LOCATION AND CITY OR TOWN)	37B. DISTANCE FR WORK-LT.? INJURY TO USUAL RESIDENCE-ITEM 19 MILES	38. WERE LABORATORY TESTS DONE FOR DRUGS OR TOXIC CHEMICALS (SPECIFY YES OR NO)	39. WERE LABORATORY TESTS DONE FOR ALCOHOL (SPECIFY YES OR NO)

40. DESCRIBE HOW INJURY OCCURRED (ENTER SEQUENCE OF EVENTS WHICH RESULTED IN INJURY, NATURE OF INJURY SHOULD BE ENTERED IN ITEM 29)

STATE REGISTRAR

A	B	C	D	E	F

213504

CERTIFIED COPY OF VITAL RECORDS

STATE OF CALIFORNIA
CERTIFICATION OF VITAL RECORD

COUNTY OF LOS ANGELES
DEPARTMENT OF HEALTH SERVICES

CERTIFICATE OF DEATH
STATE OF CALIFORNIA
USE BLACK INK ONLY / NO ERASURES, WHITEOUTS OR ALTERATIONS
VS-11 (REV 1/03)

INFORMATIONAL, NOT A VALID DOCUMENT TO ESTABLISH IDENTITY

STATE FILE NUMBER		LOCAL REGISTRATION NUMBER

DECEDENTS PERSONAL DATA

1. NAME OF DECEDENT — FIRST (Given)	2. MIDDLE	3. LAST (Family)
HARRY	WILLIAM	BOYETT

AKA, ALSO KNOWN AS — Include full AKA (FIRST, MIDDLE, LAST)	4. DATE OF BIRTH mm/dd/ccyy	5. AGE Yrs.	IF UNDER ONE YEAR Months/Days	IF UNDER 24 HOURS Hours/Minutes	6. SEX
H.W. BOYETT, WILLIAM BOYETT	01/03/1927	77			M

9. BIRTH STATE/FOREIGN COUNTRY	10. SOCIAL SECURITY NUMBER	11. EVER IN U.S. ARMED FORCES?	12. MARITAL STATUS (at Time of Death)	7. DATE OF DEATH mm/dd/ccyy	8. HOUR (24 Hours)
OHIO	571-24-2349	[X] YES [ ] NO [ ] UNK	MARRIED	12/29/2004	0250

13. EDUCATION — (Highest Level/Degree)	14/15. WAS DECEDENT SPANISH/HISPANIC/LATINO? (If yes, see worksheet on back.)	16. DECEDENT'S RACE — Up to 3 races may be listed (see worksheet on back)
SOME COLLEGE	[ ] YES [X] NO	CAUCASIAN

17. USUAL OCCUPATION — Type of work for most of life, DO NOT USE RETIRED	18. KIND OF BUSINESS OR INDUSTRY (e.g., grocery store, road construction, employment agency, etc.)	19. YEARS IN OCCUPATION
ACTOR	TELEVISION/RADIO	50

USUAL RESIDENCE

20. DECEDENT'S RESIDENCE (Street and number or location)
11595 DILLING STREET

21. CITY	22. COUNTY/PROVINCE	23. ZIP CODE	24. YEARS IN COUNTY	25. STATE/FOREIGN COUNTRY
STUDIO CITY	LOS ANGELES	91604	62	CALIFORNIA

INFORMANT

26. INFORMANT'S NAME, RELATIONSHIP	27. INFORMANT'S MAILING ADDRESS (Street and number or rural route number, city or town, state, ZIP)
JOAN A. BOYETT - SPOUSE	11595 DILLING ST., STUDIO CITY CA. 91604

SPOUSE AND PARENT INFORMATION

28. NAME OF SURVIVING SPOUSE — FIRST	29. MIDDLE	30. LAST (Maiden Name)
JOAN	A.	REYNOLDS

31. NAME OF FATHER — FIRST	32. MIDDLE	33. LAST	34. BIRTH STATE
HARRY	D.	BOYETT	UNK

35. NAME OF MOTHER — FIRST	36. MIDDLE	37. LAST (Maiden)	38. BIRTH STATE
MARGARET	-	MCCUBBIN	ENGLAND

FUNERAL DIRECTOR/LOCAL REGISTRAR

39. DISPOSITION DATE mm/dd/ccyy	40. PLACE OF FINAL DISPOSITION
01/05/2005	JOAN A. BOYETT RES: 11595 DILLING ST., STUDIO CITY CA. 91604

41. TYPE OF DISPOSITION(S)	42. SIGNATURE OF EMBALMER	43. LICENSE NUMBER
CREMATION/RESIDENCE	NOT EMBALMED	-

44. NAME OF FUNERAL ESTABLISHMENT	45. LICENSE NUMBER	46. SIGNATURE OF LOCAL REGISTRAR	47. DATE mm/dd/ccyy
SENSIBLE ALTERNATIVES FUNERAL SERVICES	FD 1732	Thomas W Garthwaite	01/05/2005

PLACE OF DEATH

101. PLACE OF DEATH	102. IF HOSPITAL, SPECIFY ONE	103. IF OTHER THAN HOSPITAL, SPECIFY ONE
PROVIDENCE HOLY CROSS MEDICAL CENTER	[X] IP [ ] ER/OP [ ] DOA	[ ] Hospice [ ] Nursing Home/LTC [ ] Decedent's Home [ ] Other

104. COUNTY	105. FACILITY ADDRESS OR LOCATION WHERE FOUND. (Street and number or location)	106. CITY
LOS ANGELES	15031 RINALDI ST.	MISSION HILLS

CAUSE OF DEATH

107. CAUSE OF DEATH	Enter the chain of events — diseases, injuries, or complications — that directly caused death. DO NOT enter terminal events such as cardiac arrest, respiratory arrest, or ventricular fibrillation without showing the etiology. DO NOT ABBREVIATE.	Time Interval Between Onset and Death	108. DEATH REPORTED TO CORONER?
IMMEDIATE CAUSE (Final disease or condition resulting in death) (A) →	BLUNT HEAD TRAUMA	DAYS	[X] YES [ ] NO Referral Number 2004-09910
Sequentially list conditions, if any, leading to cause on Line A. Enter UNDERLYING CAUSE (disease or injury that initiated the events resulting in death) LAST (B)			109. BIOPSY PERFORMED? [ ] YES [X] NO
(C)			110. AUTOPSY PERFORMED? [ ] YES [X] NO
			111. USED IN DETERMINING CAUSE? [ ] YES [ ] NO

112. OTHER SIGNIFICANT CONDITIONS CONTRIBUTING TO DEATH BUT NOT RESULTING IN THE UNDERLYING CAUSE GIVEN IN 107
CHRONIC RENAL FAILURE, ARTERIOSCLEROTIC CARDIOVASCULAR DISEASE

113. WAS OPERATION PERFORMED FOR ANY CONDITION IN ITEM 107 OR 112? (If yes, list type of operation and date.)	113A. IF FEMALE, PREGNANT IN LAST YEAR?
PACEMAKER PLACEMENT 09/--/2001, RELEASE SUBDURAL HEMATOMA 12/18/2004	[ ] YES [ ] NO [ ] UNK

PHYSICIAN'S CERTIFICATION

114. I CERTIFY THAT TO THE BEST OF MY KNOWLEDGE DEATH OCCURRED AT THE HOUR, DATE, AND PLACE STATED FROM THE CAUSES STATED.	115. SIGNATURE AND TITLE OF CERTIFIER	116. LICENSE NUMBER	117. DATE mm/dd/ccyy
Decedent Attended Since (A) mm/dd/ccyy / Decedent Last Seen Alive (B) mm/dd/ccyy			
	118. TYPE ATTENDING PHYSICIAN'S NAME, MAILING ADDRESS, ZIP CODE		

CORONER'S USE ONLY

119. I CERTIFY THAT IN MY OPINION DEATH OCCURRED AT THE HOUR, DATE, AND PLACE STATED FROM THE CAUSES STATED.	120. INJURED AT WORK?	121. INJURY DATE mm/dd/ccyy	122. HOUR (24 Hours)
MANNER OF DEATH [ ] Natural [X] Accident [ ] Homicide [ ] Suicide [ ] Pending Investigation [ ] Could not be determined	[ ] YES [X] NO [ ] UNK	12/17/2004	UNK

123. PLACE OF INJURY (e.g., home, construction site, wooded area, etc.)
RESIDENCE

124. DESCRIBE HOW INJURY OCCURRED (Events which resulted in injury)
FELL AT HOME

125. LOCATION OF INJURY (Street and number, or location, and city and, ZIP)
11595 DILLING ST., STUDIO CITY 91604

126. SIGNATURE OF CORONER / DEPUTY CORONER	127. DATE mm/dd/ccyy	128. TYPE NAME, TITLE OF CORONER / DEPUTY CORONER
Barbara A Nelson	01/05/2005	BARBARA L. NELSON DEP. CORONER

STATE REGISTRAR	A	B	C	D	E	FAX AUTH. #	*5B0056645*

This is a true certified copy of the record filed in the County of Los Angeles
Department of Health Services if it bears the Registrar's signature in purple ink.

DATE ISSUED

Director of Health Services and Registrar 312 FEB 0 1 2005

This copy not valid unless prepared on engraved border displaying seal and signature of Registrar.

MIDWEST BANK NOTE COMPANY · ANY ALTERATION OR ERASURE VOIDS THIS CERTIFICATE

CERTIFICATE OF DEATH
STATE OF CALIFORNIA
USE BLACK INK ONLY / NO ERASURES, WHITEOUTS OR ALTERATIONS
VS-11 (REV 1/03)

3 2004 19 028189
LOCAL REGISTRATION NUMBER

STATE FILE NUMBER

1 NAME OF DECEDENT — FIRST (Given)	2. MIDDLE	3. LAST (Family)
MARLON	–	BRANDO

AKA ALSO KNOWN AS — Include full AKA (FIRST, MIDDLE, LAST)	4. DATE OF BIRTH mm/dd/ccyy	5. AGE Yrs.	IF UNDER ONE YEAR Months Days	IF UNDER 24 HOURS Hours Minutes	6. SEX
–	04/03/1924	80			M

9. BIRTH STATE/FOREIGN COUNTRY	10 SOCIAL SECURITY NUMBER	11. EVER IN U.S. ARMED FORCES?	12. MARITAL STATUS (at Time of Death)	7. DATE OF DEATH mm/dd/ccyy	8. HOUR (24 Hours)
NE	337-12-6854	YES [X] NO UNK	DIVORCED	07/01/2004	1830

13 EDUCATION — Highest Level/Degree (see worksheet on back)	14/15 WAS DECEDENT SPANISH/HISPANIC/LATINO? (If yes, see worksheet on back)	16. DECEDENT'S RACE — Up to 3 races may be listed (see worksheet on back)
12	YES _____ [X] NO	WHITE

17. USUAL OCCUPATION — Type of work for most of life. DO NOT USE RETIRED	18. KIND OF BUSINESS OR INDUSTRY (e.g. grocery store, road construction, employment agency, etc.)	19. YEARS IN OCCUPATION
ACTOR	ENTERTAINMENT	60

20. DECEDENT'S RESIDENCE (Street and number or location)
12900 MULHOLLAND DRIVE

21. CITY	22. COUNTY/PROVINCE	23. ZIP CODE	24. YEARS IN COUNTY	25. STATE/FOREIGN COUNTRY
BEVERLY HILLS	LOS ANGELES	90210	50	CA

26. INFORMANT'S NAME, RELATIONSHIP	27. INFORMANT'S MAILING ADDRESS (Street and number or rural route number, city or town, state, ZIP)
MIKO C. BRANDO-SON	2766 MOTOR AVENUE LOS ANGELES CA 90064

28. NAME OF SURVIVING SPOUSE — FIRST	29. MIDDLE	30. LAST (Maiden Name)
–	–	–

31. NAME OF FATHER — FIRST	32. MIDDLE	33. LAST	34. BIRTH STATE
MARLON	–	BRANDO	NE

35. NAME OF MOTHER — FIRST	36. MIDDLE	37. LAST (Maiden)	38. BIRTH STATE
DOROTHY	–	PENNEBAKER	NE

39. DISPOSITION DATE mm/dd/ccyy	40. PLACE OF FINAL DISPOSITION
07/05/2004	RESIDENCE: MIKO C. BRANDO 2766 MOTOR AVENUE LOS ANGELES CA 90064

41. TYPE OF DISPOSITION(S)	42. SIGNATURE OF EMBALMER	43. LICENSE NUMBER
CR/RES	NOT EMBALMED	–

44. NAME OF FUNERAL ESTABLISHMENT	45. LICENSE NUMBER	46. SIGNATURE OF LOCAL REGISTRAR	47. DATE mm/dd/ccyy
GATES, KINGSLEY & GATES MOELLER MURPHY	FD451	Thomas H Arthmore PC	07/03/2004

101. PLACE OF DEATH	102. IF HOSPITAL, SPECIFY ONE	103. IF OTHER THAN HOSPITAL, SPECIFY ONE
UCLA MEDICAL CENTER	[X] IP ER/OP DOA	Hospice Nursing Home/LTC Decedent's Home Other

104. COUNTY	105. FACILITY ADDRESS OR LOCATION WHERE FOUND (Street and number or location)	106. CITY
Los Angeles	10833 LeConte Avenue	Los Angeles

107. CAUSE OF DEATH Enter the chain of events — diseases, injuries, or complications — that directly caused death. DO NOT enter terminal events such as cardiac arrest, respiratory arrest, or ventricular fibrillation without showing the etiology. DO NOT ABBREVIATE.	Time Interval Between Onset and Death	108. DEATH REPORTED TO CORONER?
IMMEDIATE CAUSE (A) (Final disease or condition resulting in death) → PULMONARY FIBROSIS IDIOPATHIC	(AT) 6 years	YES [X] NO REFERRAL NUMBER
Sequentially list conditions, if any leading to cause on Line A. Enter UNDERLYING CAUSE (disease or injury that initiated the events resulting in death) LAST (B)	(BT)	109. BIOPSY PERFORMED? YES [X] NO
(C)	(CT)	110. AUTOPSY PERFORMED? YES [X] NO
(D)	(DT)	111. USED IN DETERMINING CAUSE? YES [X] NO

112. OTHER SIGNIFICANT CONDITIONS CONTRIBUTING TO DEATH BUT NOT RESULTING IN THE UNDERLYING CAUSE GIVEN IN 107
None

113. WAS OPERATION PERFORMED FOR ANY CONDITION IN ITEM 107 OR 112? (If yes, list type of operation and date.)	113A. IF FEMALE, PREGNANT IN LAST YEAR?
No	YES NO UNK

114. I CERTIFY THAT TO THE BEST OF MY KNOWLEDGE DEATH OCCURRED AT THE HOUR, DATE, AND PLACE STATED FROM THE CAUSES STATED.	115. SIGNATURE AND TITLE OF CERTIFIER	116. LICENSE NUMBER	117. DATE mm/dd/ccyy
Decedent Attended Since / Decedent Last Seen Alive	John Belperio	A72669	07/01/2004

(A) mm/dd/ccyy	(B) mm/dd/ccyy	118. TYPE ATTENDING PHYSICIAN'S NAME, MAILING ADDRESS, ZIP CODE
06/30/2004	07/01/2004	John Belperio, M.D., 10833 LeConte Ave, L.A., CA 90095

119. I CERTIFY THAT IN MY OPINION DEATH OCCURRED AT THE HOUR, DATE, AND PLACE STATED FROM THE CAUSES STATED. MANNER OF DEATH	120. INJURED AT WORK?	121. INJURY DATE mm/dd/ccyy	122. HOUR (24 Hours)
Natural Accident Homicide Suicide Pending Investigation Could not be determined	YES NO UNK		

123. PLACE OF INJURY (e.g. home, construction site, wooded area, etc.)

124. DESCRIBE HOW INJURY OCCURRED (Events which resulted in injury)

125. LOCATION OF INJURY (Street and number, or location, and city, and ZIP)

126. SIGNATURE OF CORONER / DEPUTY CORONER	127. DATE mm/dd/ccyy	128. TYPE NAME, TITLE OF CORONER / DEPUTY CORONER

STATE REGISTRAR	A	B	C	D	E	FAX AUTH. #	CENSUS TRACT

CERTIFICATE OF DEATH
STATE OF CALIFORNIA
USE BLACK INK ONLY/NO ERASURES, WHITEOUTS OR ALTERATIONS
VS-11 (REV. 7/97)

STATE FILE NUMBER		LOCAL REGISTRATION NUMBER

DECEDENT PERSONAL DATA

1. NAME OF DECEDENT—FIRST (GIVEN)	2. MIDDLE	3. LAST (FAMILY)
LLOYD	VERNET	BRIDGES

4. DATE OF BIRTH MM/DD/CCYY	5. AGE YRS.	IF UNDER 1 YEAR MONTHS / DAYS	IF UNDER 24 HOURS HOURS / MINUTES	6. SEX	7. DATE OF DEATH MM/DD/CCYY	8. HOUR
01/15/1913	85			M	03/10/1998	1250

9. STATE OF BIRTH	10. SOCIAL SECURITY NO.	11. MILITARY SERVICE	12. MARITAL STATUS	13. EDUCATION—YEARS COMPLETED
CA	109-10-9154	☐ YES ☒ No ☐ UNK	MARRIED	16

14. RACE	15. HISPANIC—SPECIFY	16. USUAL EMPLOYER
WHITE	☐ YES ☒ No	SELF EMPLOYED

17. OCCUPATION	18. KIND OF BUSINESS	19. YEARS IN OCCUPATION
ACTOR	ENTERTAINMENT	65

USUAL RESIDENCE

20. RESIDENCE—(STREET AND NUMBER OR LOCATION)
225 LORING AVE.

21. CITY	22. COUNTY	23. ZIP CODE	24. YRS IN COUNTY	25. STATE OR FOREIGN COUNTRY
LOS ANGELES	LOS ANGELES	90024	65	CA

INFORMANT

26. NAME, RELATIONSHIP	27. MAILING ADDRESS (STREET AND NUMBER OR RURAL ROUTE NUMBER, CITY OR TOWN, STATE, ZIP)
DOROTHY L. BRIDGES - WIFE	225 LORING AVE. LOS ANGELES, CA 90024

SPOUSE AND PARENT INFORMATION

28. NAME OF SURVIVING SPOUSE—FIRST	29. MIDDLE	30. LAST (MAIDEN NAME)	
DOROTHY	LOUISE	SIMPSON	

31. NAME OF FATHER—FIRST	32. MIDDLE	33. LAST	34. BIRTH STATE
LLOYD	VERNET	BRIDGES	KS

35. NAME OF MOTHER—FIRST	36. MIDDLE	37. LAST (MAIDEN)	38. BIRTH STATE
HARRIET	-	BROWN	MO

DISPOSITION(S)

39. DATE MM/DD/CCYY	40. PLACE OF FINAL DISPOSITION
03/12/1998	PVT RES. DOROTHY L. BRIDGES, 225 LORING AVE. LOS ANGELES, CA 90024

FUNERAL DIRECTOR AND LOCAL REGISTRAR

41. TYPE OF DISPOSITION(S)	42. SIGNATURE OF EMBALMER	43. LICENSE NO.
CR/RES	▶ NOT EMBLAMED	-

44. NAME OF FUNERAL DIRECTOR	45. LICENSE NO.	46. SIGNATURE OF LOCAL REGISTRAR	47. DATE MM/DD/CCYY
FOREST LAWN MTY GLENDALE	FD 656	▶	03/11/1998

PLACE OF DEATH

101. PLACE OF DEATH	102. IF HOSPITAL, SPECIFY ONE:	103. FACILITY OTHER THAN HOSPITAL:	104. COUNTY
RESIDENCE	☐ IP ☐ ER/OP ☐ DOA	☐ CONV. HOSP. ☐ RES. CARE ☐ OTHER	LOS ANGELES

105. STREET ADDRESS—(STREET AND NUMBER OR LOCATION)	106. CITY
225 LORING AVENUE	LOS ANGELES

CAUSE OF DEATH

107. DEATH WAS CAUSED BY: (ENTER ONLY ONE CAUSE PER LINE FOR A, B, C, AND D)	TIME INTERVAL BETWEEN ONSET AND DEATH	108. DEATH REPORTED TO CORONER
IMMEDIATE CAUSE (A) CARDIOPULMONARY ARREST	MINS	☐ YES ☒ No / REFERRAL NUMBER
DUE TO (B) CONGESTIVE HEART FAILURE	YEARS	109. BIOPSY PERFORMED ☐ YES ☒ No
DUE TO (C)		110. AUTOPSY PERFORMED ☐ YES ☒ No
DUE TO (D)		111. USED IN DETERMINING CAUSE ☐ YES ☒ No

112. OTHER SIGNIFICANT CONDITIONS CONTRIBUTING TO DEATH BUT NOT RELATED TO CAUSE GIVEN IN 107
CORONARY ARTERY DISEASE

113. WAS OPERATION PERFORMED FOR ANY CONDITION IN ITEM 107 OR 112? IF YES, LIST TYPE OF OPERATION AND DATE.
NONE

PHYSICIAN'S CERTIFICATION

114. I CERTIFY THAT TO THE BEST OF MY KNOWLEDGE DEATH OCCURRED AT THE HOUR, DATE AND PLACE STATED FROM THE CAUSES STATED. DECEDENT ATTENDED SINCE MM/DD/CCYY / DECEDENT LAST SEEN ALIVE MM/DD/CCYY	115. SIGNATURE AND TITLE OF CERTIFIER	116. LICENSE NO.	117. DATE MM/DD/CCYY
--/--/1987 / 03/10/1998	▶ Richard A. Johnson, M.D.	G37531	03/11/1998

118. TYPE ATTENDING PHYSICIAN'S NAME, MAILING ADDRESS, ZIP
RICHARD JOHNSON, MD 200 UCLA MEDICAL PLAZA #220 LOS ANGELES CA 90024

CORONER'S USE ONLY

119. I CERTIFY THAT IN MY OPINION DEATH OCCURRED AT THE HOUR, DATE AND PLACE STATED FROM THE CAUSES STATED.	120. INJURY AT WORK	121. INJURY DATE MM/DD/CCYY	122. HOUR	123. PLACE OF INJURY
	☐ YES ☐ No			

119. MANNER OF DEATH	124. DESCRIBE HOW INJURY OCCURRED (EVENTS WHICH RESULTED IN INJURY)
☐ NATURAL ☐ SUICIDE ☐ HOMICIDE ☐ ACCIDENT ☐ PENDING INVESTIGATION ☐ COULD NOT BE DETERMINED	

125. LOCATION (STREET AND NUMBER OR LOCATION AND CITY, ZIP)

126. SIGNATURE OF CORONER OR DEPUTY CORONER	127. DATE MM/DD/CCYY	128. TYPED NAME, TITLE OF CORONER OR DEPUTY CORONER
▶		

STATE REGISTRAR

A	B	C	D	E	F	G	H	FAX AUTH. #	CENSUS TRACT
								273/19867	09007

CERTIFICATE OF DEATH
STATE OF CALIFORNIA
USE BLACK INK ONLY / NO ERASURES, WHITEOUTS OR ALTERATIONS
VS-11 (REV 1/03)

3 2003190 037424

STATE FILE NUMBER | LOCAL REGISTRATION NUMBER

DECEDENT'S PERSONAL DATA

1. NAME OF DECEDENT — FIRST (Given)	2. MIDDLE	3. LAST (Family)
CHARLES	DENNIS	BRONSON

AKA. ALSO KNOWN AS — include full AKA (FIRST, MIDDLE, LAST)	4. DATE OF BIRTH mm/dd/ccyy	5. AGE Yrs.	IF UNDER ONE YEAR: Months / Days	IF UNDER 24 HOURS: Hours / Minutes	6. SEX
-	11/03/1921	81			M

9. BIRTH STATE/FOREIGN COUNTRY	10. SOCIAL SECURITY NUMBER	11. EVER IN U.S. ARMED FORCES?	12. MARITAL STATUS (at Time of Death)	7. DATE OF DEATH mm/dd/ccyy	8. HOUR (24 Hours)
PA	176-16-1681	X YES ☐ NO ☐ UNK	MARRIED	08/30/2003	1235

13. EDUCATION — Highest Level/Degree	14/15. WAS DECEDENT SPANISH/HISPANIC/LATINO? (If yes, see worksheet on back)	16. DECEDENT'S RACE — Up to 3 races may be listed (see worksheet on back)
BACHELOR'S	☐ YES / X NO	CAUCASIAN

17. USUAL OCCUPATION — Type of work for most of life. DO NOT USE RETIRED	18. KIND OF BUSINESS OR INDUSTRY (e.g., grocery store, road construction, employment agency, etc.)	19. YEARS IN OCCUPATION
ACTOR	MOTION PICTURES	55

USUAL RESIDENCE

20. DECEDENT'S RESIDENCE (Street and number or location)
3210 RETREAT COURT

21. CITY	22. COUNTY/PROVINCE	23. ZIP CODE	24. YEARS IN COUNTY	25. STATE/FOREIGN COUNTRY
MALIBU	LOS ANGELES	90265	60	CALIFORNIA

INFORMANT

26. INFORMANT'S NAME, RELATIONSHIP	27. INFORMANT'S MAILING ADDRESS (Street and number or rural route number, city or town, state, ZIP)
KIM M. BRONSON - WIFE	P.O. BOX 2644 MALIBU, CA 90265

SPOUSE AND PARENT INFORMATION

28. NAME OF SURVIVING SPOUSE — FIRST	29. MIDDLE	30. LAST (Maiden Name)
KIM	M.	WEEKS

31. NAME OF FATHER — FIRST	32. MIDDLE	33. LAST	34. BIRTH STATE
WALTER	-	BUCHINSKY	LITHUANIA

35. NAME OF MOTHER — FIRST	36. MIDDLE	37. LAST (Maiden)	38. BIRTH STATE
MARY	-	VALINSKY	PA

FUNERAL DIRECTOR/ LOCAL REGISTRAR

39. DISPOSITION DATE mm/dd/ccyy	40. PLACE OF FINAL DISPOSITION
09/04/2003	BROWNSVILLE CEMETERY WEST WINDSOR, VERMONT

41. TYPE OF DISPOSITION(S)	42. SIGNATURE OF EMBALMER	43. LICENSE NUMBER
TR/BU	▶ Todd Weisweaver	8842

44. NAME OF FUNERAL ESTABLISHMENT	45. LICENSE NUMBER	46. SIGNATURE OF LOCAL REGISTRAR	47. DATE mm/dd/ccyy
PIERCE BROS. WESTWOOD	FD-951	▶ Thomas W. Harthwaite	09/03/2003

PLACE OF DEATH

101. PLACE OF DEATH	102. IF HOSPITAL, SPECIFY ONE	103. IF OTHER THAN HOSPITAL, SPECIFY ONE
CEDARS SINAI MEDICAL CENTER	X IP ☐ ER/OP ☐ DOA	☐ Hospice ☐ Nursing Home/LTC ☐ Decedent's Home ☐ Other

104. COUNTY	105. FACILITY ADDRESS OR LOCATION WHERE FOUND (Street and number or location)	106. CITY
LOS ANGELES	8700 BEVERLY BLVD.	LOS ANGELES

CAUSE OF DEATH

107. CAUSE OF DEATH	Enter the chain of events — diseases, injuries, or complications — that directly caused death. DO NOT enter terminal events such as cardiac arrest, respiratory arrest, or ventricular fibrillation without showing the etiology. DO NOT ABBREVIATE.	Time Interval Between Onset and Death	108. DEATH REPORTED TO CORONER?
IMMEDIATE CAUSE (Final disease or condition resulting in death) → (A)	RESPIRATORY FAILURE	(AT) 1month	☐ YES X NO REFERRAL NUMBER
(B)	METASTATIC LUNG CANCER	(BT) 1month	109. BIOPSY PERFORMED? X YES ☐ NO
Sequentially list conditions, if any, leading to cause on Line A. Enter UNDERLYING CAUSE (disease or injury that initiated the events resulting in death) LAST (C)		(CT)	110. AUTOPSY PERFORMED? ☐ YES X NO
(D)		(DT)	111. USED IN DETERMINING CAUSE? ☐ YES ☐ NO

112. OTHER SIGNIFICANT CONDITIONS CONTRIBUTING TO DEATH BUT NOT RESULTING IN THE UNDERLYING CAUSE GIVEN IN 107
CHRONIC OBSTRUCTIVE PULMONARY DISEASE, CONGESTIVE CARDIOMYOPATHY

113. WAS OPERATION PERFORMED FOR ANY CONDITION IN ITEM 107 OR 112? (If yes, list type of operation and date.)	113A. IF FEMALE, PREGNANT IN LAST YEAR?
GASTROSTOMY 07/23/2003, TRACHEOSTOMY 08/12/2003	☐ YES ☐ NO ☐ UNK

PHYSICIAN'S CERTIFICATION

114. I CERTIFY THAT TO THE BEST OF MY KNOWLEDGE DEATH OCCURRED AT THE HOUR, DATE, AND PLACE STATED FROM THE CAUSES STATED.	115. SIGNATURE AND TITLE OF CERTIFIER	116. LICENSE NUMBER	117. DATE mm/dd/ccyy
Decedent Attended Since / Decedent Last Seen Alive	▶ Arthur Waltuch	G34111	09/03/2003

(A) mm/dd/ccyy	(B) mm/dd/ccyy	118. TYPE ATTENDING PHYSICIAN'S NAME, MAILING ADDRESS, ZIP CODE
07/23/2003	08/30/2003	ARTHUR I. WALTUCH, M.D. 8635 W. 3RD. ST. LOS ANGELES, CA 90048

CORONER'S USE ONLY

119. I CERTIFY THAT IN MY OPINION DEATH OCCURRED AT THE HOUR, DATE, AND PLACE STATED FROM THE CAUSES STATED.	120. INJURED AT WORK?	121. INJURY DATE mm/dd/ccyy	122. HOUR (24 Hours)
MANNER OF DEATH ☐ Natural ☐ Accident ☐ Homicide ☐ Suicide ☐ Pending Investigation ☐ Could not be determined	☐ YES ☐ NO ☐ UNK		

123. PLACE OF INJURY (e.g., home, construction site, wooded area, etc.)

124. DESCRIBE HOW INJURY OCCURRED (Events which resulted in injury)
INFORMATIONAL, NOT A VALID DOCUMENT TO ESTABLISH IDENTITY

125. LOCATION OF INJURY (Street and number, or location, and city, and ZIP)

126. SIGNATURE OF CORONER / DEPUTY CORONER	127. DATE mm/dd/ccyy	128. TYPE NAME, TITLE OF CORONER / DEPUTY CORONER
▶		

STATE REGISTRAR	A	B	C	D	E		FAX AUTH. #	CENSUS TRACT

CERTIFICATE OF DEATH
STATE OF CALIFORNIA
USE BLACK INK ONLY/NO ERASURES, WHITEOUTS OR ALTERATIONS
VS-11 (REV. 1/OC)

STATE FILE NUMBER   LOCAL REGISTRATION NUMBER

1. NAME OF DECEDENT—FIRST (GIVEN) Foster	2. MIDDLE M.	3. LAST (FAMILY) Brooks

DECEDENT PERSONAL DATA

4. DATE OF BIRTH MM/DD/CCYY 05/11/1912	5. AGE YRS. 89	IF UNDER 1 YEAR MONTHS / DAYS	IF UNDER 24 HOURS HOURS / MINUTES	6. SEX M	7. DATE OF DEATH MM/DD/CCYY 12/20/2001	8. HOUR 1320

9. STATE OF BIRTH KY	10. SOCIAL SECURITY NO. 401-07-9362	11. MILITARY SERVICE YES [X] NO UNK	12. MARITAL STATUS Married	13. EDUCATION—YEARS COMPLETED 6

14. RACE White	15. HISPANIC—SPECIFY YES [X] No	16. USUAL EMPLOYER Self Employed

17. OCCUPATION Comedian/Actor	18. KIND OF BUSINESS Entertainment	19. YEARS IN OCCUPATION 77

USUAL RESIDENCE

20. RESIDENCE—(STREET AND NUMBER OR LOCATION) 18116 Chardon Circle				
21. CITY Encino	22. COUNTY Los Angeles	23. ZIP CODE 91316	24. YRS IN COUNTY 40	25. STATE OR FOREIGN COUNTRY CA

INFORMANT

26. NAME, RELATIONSHIP Teri Brooks Wife	27. MAILING ADDRESS (STREET AND NUMBER OR RURAL ROUTE NUMBER, CITY OR TOWN, STATE, ZIP) 18116 Chardon Circle, Encino, CA 91316

SPOUSE AND PARENT INFORMATION

28. NAME OF SURVIVING SPOUSE—FIRST Teri	29. MIDDLE G.	30. LAST (MAIDEN NAME) Gawron	
31. NAME OF FATHER—FIRST Pleasant	32. MIDDLE Malone	33. LAST Brooks	34. BIRTH STATE KY
35. NAME OF MOTHER—FIRST Edna	36. MIDDLE Foster	37. LAST (MAIDEN) Megowan	38. BIRTH STATE KY

DISPOSITION(S)

39. DATE MM/DD/CCYY 12/26/2001	40. PLACE OF FINAL DISPOSITION Res: Teri Brooks, 18116 Chardon Circle, encino, CA 91316

FUNERAL DIRECTOR AND LOCAL REGISTRAR

41. TYPE OF DISPOSITION(S) CRE/RES	42. SIGNATURE OF EMBALMER ▶ Not Embalmed	43. LICENSE NO. –
44. NAME OF FUNERAL DIRECTOR Crawford Mortuary	45. LICENSE NO. FD1228	46. SIGNATURE OF LOCAL REGISTRAR ▶ Fred Leaf	47. DATE MM/DD/CCYY 12/21/2001

PLACE OF DEATH

101. PLACE OF DEATH Residence	102. IF HOSPITAL, SPECIFY ONE: IP / ER/OP / DOA	103. FACILITY OTHER THAN HOSPITAL CONV. HOSP. / RES. CARE / [X] OTHER	104. COUNTY Los Angeles
105. STREET ADDRESS—(STREET AND NUMBER OR LOCATION) 18116 Chardon Circle			106. CITY Encino

CAUSE OF DEATH

107. DEATH WAS CAUSED BY: (ENTER ONLY ONE CAUSE PER LINE FOR A, B, C, AND D)	TIME INTERVAL BETWEEN ONSET AND DEATH	
IMMEDIATE CAUSE (A) Cardiorespiratory Arrest	mins	108. DEATH REPORTED TO CORONER [X] YES / [X] NO REFERRAL NUMBER 2001-58871
DUE TO (B) Arteriosclerotic Heart Disease	yrs	109. BIOPSY PERFORMED YES [X] NO
DUE TO (C)		110. AUTOPSY PERFORMED YES [X] NO
DUE TO (D)		111. USED IN DETERMINING CAUSE YES [X] NO

112. OTHER SIGNIFICANT CONDITIONS CONTRIBUTING TO DEATH BUT NOT RELATED TO CAUSE GIVEN IN 107   Cerebrovascular Accident

113. WAS OPERATION PERFORMED FOR ANY CONDITION IN ITEM 107 OR 112? IF YES, LIST TYPE OF OPERATION AND DATE.   No

PHYSICIAN'S CERTIFICATION

114. I CERTIFY THAT TO THE BEST OF MY KNOWLEDGE DEATH OCCURRED AT THE HOUR, DATE AND PLACE STATED FROM THE CAUSES STATED. DECEDENT ATTENDED SINCE MM/DD/CCYY 11/22/1999 / DECEDENT LAST SEEN ALIVE MM/DD/CCYY 11/10/2001	115. SIGNATURE AND TITLE OF CERTIFIER ▶ David Zarian	116. LICENSE NO. A 04350	117. DATE MM/DD/CCYY 12/21/2001
118. TYPE ATTENDING PHYSICIAN'S NAME, MAILING ADDRESS, ZIP David H. Zarian, MD. 16661 Ventura Blvd. Encino, CA 91436			

CORONER'S USE ONLY

I CERTIFY THAT IN MY OPINION DEATH OCCURRED AT THE HOUR, DATE AND PLACE STATED FROM THE CAUSES STATED.	120. INJURY AT WORK YES / NO	121. INJURY DATE MM/DD/CCYY	122. HOUR	123. PLACE OF INJURY
119. MANNER OF DEATH NATURAL / SUICIDE / HOMICIDE / ACCIDENT / PENDING INVESTIGATION / COULD NOT BE DETERMINED	124. DESCRIBE HOW INJURY OCCURRED (EVENTS WHICH RESULTED IN INJURY)			
125. LOCATION (STREET AND NUMBER OR LOCATION AND CITY, ZIP)				

126. SIGNATURE OF CORONER OR DEPUTY CORONER ▶	127. DATE MM/DD/CCYY	128. TYPED NAME, TITLE OF CORONER OR DEPUTY CORONER

STATE REGISTRAR

A	B	C	D	E	F	G	H	FAX AUTH. # 197/4932	CENSUS TRACT 090

COUNTY OF LOS ANGELES
DEPARTMENT OF HEALTH SERVICES

CERTIFICATE OF DEATH
STATE OF CALIFORNIA
USE BLACK INK ONLY/NO ERASURES, WHITEOUTS OR ALTERATIONS
VS-11 (REV. 7/97)

STATE FILE NUMBER		LOCAL REGISTRATION NUMBER

DECEDENT PERSONAL DATA

1. NAME OF DECEDENT—FIRST (GIVEN): RORY
2. MIDDLE: —
3. LAST (FAMILY): CALHOUN
4. DATE OF BIRTH: 08/08/1922
5. AGE YRS: 76
6. SEX: M
7. DATE OF DEATH: 04/28/1999
8. HOUR: 1855
9. STATE OF BIRTH: CALIFORNIA
10. SOCIAL SECURITY NO.: 562-30-8917
11. MILITARY SERVICE: [X] No
12. MARITAL STATUS: MARRIED
13. EDUCATION—YEARS COMPLETED: 12
14. RACE: CAUCASIAN
15. HISPANIC—SPECIFY: [X] No
16. USUAL EMPLOYER: SELF EMPLOYED
17. OCCUPATION: ACTOR
18. KIND OF BUSINESS: MOTION PICTURE & TELEVISION
19. YEARS IN OCCUPATION: 50

USUAL RESIDENCE

20. RESIDENCE: 8929 FOX TRAIL
21. CITY: MORONGO VALLEY
22. COUNTY: SAN BERNARDINO
23. ZIP CODE: 92256
24. YRS IN COUNTY: 5
25. STATE OR FOREIGN COUNTRY: CALIFORNIA

INFORMANT

26. NAME, RELATIONSHIP: SUSAN K. CALHOUN - WIFE
27. MAILING ADDRESS: P.O.BOX 689 - MORONGO VALLEY CA. 92256

SPOUSE AND PARENT INFORMATION

28. NAME OF SURVIVING SPOUSE—FIRST: SUSAN
29. MIDDLE: K.
30. LAST (MAIDEN NAME): RHODES
31. NAME OF FATHER—FIRST: UNKNOWN
32. MIDDLE: UNKNOWN
33. LAST: UNKNOWN
34. BIRTH STATE: UNKNOWN
35. NAME OF MOTHER—FIRST: ELIZABETH
36. MIDDLE: —
37. LAST (MAIDEN): CUTHBERT
38. BIRTH STATE: CALIFORNIA

DISPOSITION(S)

39. DATE: 05/05/1999
40. PLACE OF FINAL DISPOSITION: RES. SUSAN K. CALHOUN - 8929 FOX TRAIL, MORONGO VALLEY CA. 92256
41. TYPE OF DISPOSITION(S): CR/RES
42. SIGNATURE OF EMBALMER: ▶ NOT EMBALMED
43. LICENSE NO.
44. NAME OF FUNERAL DIRECTOR: NEPTUNE SOCIETY BURBANK
45. LICENSE NO.: FD1359
46. SIGNATURE OF LOCAL REGISTRAR: ▶ Mark [illegible]
47. DATE: 05/04/1999

PLACE OF DEATH

101. PLACE OF DEATH: PROVIDENCE ST JOSEPH MED/CTR
102. IF HOSPITAL, SPECIFY ONE: [X] IP
103. FACILITY OTHER THAN HOSPITAL
104. COUNTY: LOS ANGELES
105. STREET ADDRESS: 501 S. BUENA VISTA
106. CITY: BURBANK

CAUSE OF DEATH

107. DEATH WAS CAUSED BY:
- IMMEDIATE CAUSE (A) CARDIORESPIRATORY ARREST — MINUTES
- DUE TO (B) EMPHYSEMA — YEARS
- DUE TO (C)
- DUE TO (D)

108. DEATH REPORTED TO CORONER: [X] No
109. BIOPSY PERFORMED: [X] YES
110. AUTOPSY PERFORMED: [X] NO
111. USED IN DETERMINING CAUSE

112. OTHER SIGNIFICANT CONDITIONS: LIVER ABSCESS, SEPSIS
113. WAS OPERATION PERFORMED: LIVER ASPIRATION OF ABSCESS 04/02/1999

PHYSICIAN'S CERTIFICATION

114. DECEDENT ATTENDED SINCE 01/28/1994 / LAST SEEN ALIVE 04/28/1999
115. SIGNATURE AND TITLE OF CERTIFIER: ▶ [signature] M.D.
116. LICENSE NO.: G035739
117. DATE: 04/30/1999
118. TYPE ATTENDING PHYSICIAN'S NAME: STEVEN DRESS, M.D. 13220 RIVERSIDE DR. SHERMAN OAKS, CA 91423

CORONER'S USE ONLY

119. MANNER OF DEATH: NATURAL
120. INJURY AT WORK
121. INJURY DATE
122. HOUR
123. PLACE OF INJURY
124. DESCRIBE HOW INJURY OCCURRED
125. LOCATION
126. SIGNATURE OF CORONER OR DEPUTY CORONER
127. DATE
128. TYPED NAME, TITLE OF CORONER

STATE REGISTRAR

FAX AUTH. #: 195/10442
CENSUS TRACT: 090232590

This is a true certified copy of the record filed in the County of Los Angeles Department of Health Services if it bears the Registrar's signature in purple ink.

DATE ISSUED MAY 10 1999

Director of Health Service and Registrar

This copy not valid unless prepared on engraved border displaying seal and signature of Registrar.

ANY ALTERATION OR ERASURE VOIDS THIS CERTIFICATE

CERTIFICATE OF DEATH
STATE OF CALIFORNIA
USE BLACK INK ONLY/NO ERASURES, WHITEOUTS OR ALTERATIONS
VS-11 (REV. 7/93)

STATE FILE NUMBER		LOCAL REGISTRATION NUMBER

	1. NAME OF DECEDENT—FIRST (GIVEN)	2. MIDDLE	3. LAST (FAMILY)
	Edward	Macdonald	Carey

DECEDENT PERSONAL DATA

4. DATE OF BIRTH MM/DD/CCYY	5. AGE YRS.	IF UNDER 1 YEAR MONTHS / DAYS	IF UNDER 24 HOURS HOURS / MINUTES	6. SEX	7. DATE OF DEATH MM/DD/CCYY	8. HOUR
03/15/1913	81			M	03/21/1994	0230

9. STATE OF BIRTH	10. SOCIAL SECURITY NO.	11. MILITARY SERVICE	12. MARITAL STATUS	13. EDUCATION —YEARS COMPLETED
IA	346-01-5678	19 42 TO 1945 ☐ NONE	DIVORCED	17

14. RACE	15. HISPANIC—SPECIFY		16. USUAL EMPLOYER
CAUCASIAN	☐ YES _____	☒ No	NBC STUDIOS

17. OCCUPATION	18. KIND OF BUSINESS	19. YEARS IN OCCUPATION
ACTOR	ENTERTAINMENT	60

USUAL RESIDENCE

20. RESIDENCE—STREET AND NUMBER OR LOCATION
1543 BENEDICT CANYON

21. CITY	22. COUNTY	23. ZIP CODE	24. YRS IN COUNTY	25. STATE OR FOREIGN COUNTRY
BEVERLY HILLS	LOS ANGELES	90210	49	CA

INFORMANT

26. NAME, RELATIONSHIP	27. MAILING ADDRESS (STREET AND NUMBER OR RURAL ROUTE NUMBER, CITY OR TOWN, STATE, ZIP)
STEVEN CAREY, SON	9357 CRESTA DRIVE, LOS ANGELES, CA 90039

SPOUSE AND PARENT INFORMATION

28. NAME OF SURVIVING SPOUSE—FIRST	29. MIDDLE	30. LAST (MAIDEN NAME)
-	-	-

31. NAME OF FATHER—FIRST	32. MIDDLE	33. LAST	34. BIRTH STATE
CHARLES	SPILLANE	CAREY	UNK

35. NAME OF MOTHER—FIRST	36. MIDDLE	37. LAST (MAIDEN)	38. BIRTH STATE
ELIZABETH	-	MACDONALD	UNK

DISPOSITION(S)

39. DATE MM/DD/CCYY	40. PLACE OF FINAL DISPOSITION
03/26/1994	HOLY CROSS CEMETERY, 5835 W. SLAUSON AVE., CULVER CITY, CA 90230

FUNERAL DIRECTOR AND LOCAL REGISTRAR

41. TYPE OF DISPOSITION(S)	42. SIGNATURE OF EMBALMER	43. LICENSE NO.
BURIAL	▶ Kim Evans	7917

44. NAME OF FUNERAL DIRECTOR	45. LICENSE NO.	46. SIGNATURE OF LOCAL REGISTRAR	47. DATE MM/DD/CCYY
FOREST LAWN HOLLYWOOD HILLS	F-904	▶ Robert C. Nate	03/25/1994

PLACE OF DEATH

101. PLACE OF DEATH	102. IF HOSPITAL, SPECIFY ONE:	103. FACILITY OTHER THAN HOSPITAL:	104. COUNTY
Residence	☐ IP ☐ ER/OP ☐ DOA	☐ CONV. HOSP. ☒ RES. ☐ OTHER	Los Angeles

105. STREET ADDRESS—STREET AND NUMBER OR LOCATION	106. CITY
1543 BENEDICT CANYON	BEVERLY HILLS

CAUSE OF DEATH

107. DEATH WAS CAUSED BY: (ENTER ONLY ONE CAUSE PER LINE FOR A, B, C, AND D)		TIME INTERVAL BETWEEN ONSET AND DEATH	108. DEATH REPORTED TO CORONER
IMMEDIATE CAUSE (A)	CARDIOPULMONARY ARREST	MINS	☐ YES ☒ NO / REFERRAL NUMBER
DUE TO (B)	METASTATIC LUNG CANCER	3 MOS	109. BIOPSY PERFORMED ☒ YES ☐ NO
DUE TO (C)	PRIMARY ADENOCARCINOMA LUNG	2½ YRS	110. AUTOPSY PERFORMED ☐ YES ☒ NO
DUE TO (D)			111. USED IN DETERMINING CAUSE ☐ YES ☒ NO

112. OTHER SIGNIFICANT CONDITIONS CONTRIBUTING TO DEATH BUT NOT RELATED TO CAUSE GIVEN IN 107
METASTATIC PROSTATE CANCER

113. WAS OPERATION PERFORMED FOR ANY CONDITION IN ITEM 107 OR 112? IF YES, LIST TYPE OF OPERATION AND DATE.
LEFT UPPER LOBECTOMY 09/--/1991

PHYSICIAN'S CERTIFICATION

114. I CERTIFY THAT TO THE BEST OF MY KNOWLEDGE DEATH OCCURRED AT THE HOUR, DATE AND PLACE STATED FROM THE CAUSES STATED.	115. SIGNATURE AND TITLE OF CERTIFIER	116. LICENSE NO.	117. DATE MM/DD/CCYY
DECEDENT ATTENDED SINCE MM/DD/CCYY 04/15/1993 — DECEDENT LAST SEEN ALIVE MM/DD/CCYY 03/19/1994	▶ Sheldon P Herman MD	025603	3/21/94

118. TYPE ATTENDING PHYSICIAN'S NAME, MAILING ADDRESS + ZIP
SHELDON P.HERMAN,MD, 2428 SANTA MONICA BLVD, SANTA MONICA, CA 90404

CORONER'S USE ONLY

I CERTIFY THAT IN MY OPINION DEATH OCCURRED AT THE HOUR, DATE AND PLACE STATED FROM THE CAUSES STATED.	120. INJURY AT WORK ☐ YES ☐ NO	121. INJURY DATE MM/DD/CCYY	122. HOUR	123. PLACE OF INJURY
119. MANNER OF DEATH	124. DESCRIBE HOW INJURY OCCURRED (EVENTS WHICH RESULTED IN INJURY)			
☐ NATURAL ☐ SUICIDE ☐ HOMICIDE ☐ ACCIDENT ☐ PENDING INVESTIGATION ☐ COULD NOT BE DETERMINED				

125. LOCATION (STREET AND NUMBER OR LOCATION AND CITY AND ZIP CODE)

126. SIGNATURE OF CORONER OR DEPUTY CORONER	127. DATE MM/DD/CCYY	128. TYPED NAME, TITLE OF CORONER OR DEPUTY CORONER
▶		

STATE REGISTRAR

A	B	C	D	E	F	G	H	FAX AUTH. #	CENSUS TRACT

STATE OF CALIFORNIA
CERTIFICATION OF VITAL RECORD

COUNTY OF LOS ANGELES • REGISTRAR-RECORDER/COUNTY CLERK

CERTIFICATE OF DEATH
STATE OF CALIFORNIA
USE BLACK INK ONLY / NO ERASURES, WHITEOUTS OR ALTERATIONS
VS-11 (REV. 1/04)

3 2005 19 003593

LOCAL REGISTRATION NUMBER

DECEDENT'S PERSONAL DATA

1. NAME OF DECEDENT — FIRST (Given)	2. MIDDLE	3. LAST (Family)
JOHN	WILLIAM	CARSON

AKA, ALSO KNOWN AS — Include full AKA (FIRST, MIDDLE, LAST): —

4. DATE OF BIRTH mm/dd/ccyy	5. AGE Yrs.	IF UNDER ONE YEAR Months / Days	IF UNDER 24 HOURS Hours / Minutes	6. SEX
10/23/1925	79			M

9. BIRTH STATE/FOREIGN COUNTRY	10. SOCIAL SECURITY NUMBER	11. EVER IN U.S. ARMED FORCES?	12. MARITAL STATUS (at Time of Death)	7. DATE OF DEATH mm/dd/ccyy	8. HOUR (24 Hours)
IOWA	508-14-8695	X YES ☐ NO	MARRIED	01/23/2005	0650

13. EDUCATION — Highest Level/Degree	14/15. WAS DECEDENT HISPANIC/LATINO(A)/SPANISH?	16. DECEDENT'S RACE
BACHELOR'S	☐ YES　☒ NO	WHITE

17. USUAL OCCUPATION — Type of work for most of life. DO NOT USE RETIRED	18. KIND OF BUSINESS OR INDUSTRY	19. YEARS IN OCCUPATION
ENTERTAINER/TALK SHOW HOST	ENTERTAINMENT	40

USUAL RESIDENCE

20. DECEDENT'S RESIDENCE (Street and number or location)
6962 WILDLIFE RD.

21. CITY	22. COUNTY/PROVINCE	23. ZIP CODE	24. YEARS IN COUNTY	25. STATE/FOREIGN COUNTRY
MALIBU	LOS ANGELES	90265	30	CA

INFORMANT

26. INFORMANT'S NAME, RELATIONSHIP	27. INFORMANT'S MAILING ADDRESS
ALEXIS ANN CARSON, WIFE	6962 WILDLIFE RD., MALIBU, CA 90265

SPOUSE AND PARENT INFORMATION

28. NAME OF SURVIVING SPOUSE — FIRST	29. MIDDLE	30. LAST (Maiden Name)
ALEXIS	ANN	MASS

31. NAME OF FATHER — FIRST	32. MIDDLE	33. LAST	34. BIRTH STATE
HOMER	—	CARSON	IOWA

35. NAME OF MOTHER — FIRST	36. MIDDLE	37. LAST (Maiden)	38. BIRTH STATE
RUTH	—	HOOK	IOWA

FUNERAL DIRECTOR / LOCAL REGISTRAR

39. DISPOSITION DATE mm/dd/ccyy	40. PLACE OF FINAL DISPOSITION
01/27/2005	RES: ALEXIS ANN CARSON, 6962 WILDLIFE RD., MALIBU, CA 90265

41. TYPE OF DISPOSITION(S)	42. SIGNATURE OF EMBALMER	43. LICENSE NUMBER
CR/RES	NOT EMBALMED	—

44. NAME OF FUNERAL ESTABLISHMENT	45. LICENSE NUMBER	46. SIGNATURE OF LOCAL REGISTRAR	47. DATE mm/dd/ccyy
FOREST LAWN HOLLYWOOD HILLS	FD904	Thomas W. Wattworth　MCA	01/25/2005

PLACE OF DEATH

101. PLACE OF DEATH	102. IF HOSPITAL, SPECIFY ONE	103. IF OTHER THAN HOSPITAL, SPECIFY ONE
CEDARS SINAI MED CTR	☒ IP　☐ ER/OP　☐ DOA	☐ Hospice　☐ Nursing Home/LTC　☐ Decedent's Home　☐ Other

104. COUNTY	105. FACILITY ADDRESS OR LOCATION WHERE FOUND	106. CITY
LOS ANGELES	8700 BEVERLY BLVD	LOS ANGELES

CAUSE OF DEATH

107. CAUSE OF DEATH		Time Interval Between Onset and Death	108. DEATH REPORTED TO CORONER?
IMMEDIATE CAUSE (A)	RESPIRATORY ARREST	(AT) 10 MIN	☐ YES　☒ NO
(B)		(BT)	RETRIEVAL NUMBER
Sequentially list conditions (C)	EMPHYSEMA	(CT) 20 YRS	109. BIOPSY PERFORMED? ☐ YES ☒ NO
(D)		(DT)	110. AUTOPSY PERFORMED? ☐ YES ☒ NO
			111. USED IN DETERMINING CAUSE? ☐ YES ☒ NO

112. OTHER SIGNIFICANT CONDITIONS CONTRIBUTING TO DEATH BUT NOT RESULTING IN THE UNDERLYING CAUSE GIVEN IN 107
NONE

113. WAS OPERATION PERFORMED FOR ANY CONDITION IN ITEM 107 OR 112?	113A. IF FEMALE, PREGNANT IN LAST YEAR?
NO	☐ YES　☐ NO　☐ UNK

PHYSICIAN'S CERTIFICATION

114. I CERTIFY THAT TO THE BEST OF MY KNOWLEDGE DEATH OCCURRED AT THE HOUR, DATE, AND PLACE STATED FROM THE CAUSES STATED.	115. SIGNATURE AND TITLE OF CERTIFIER	116. LICENSE NUMBER	117. DATE mm/dd/ccyy
	Richard N Goldberg	G25597	01/24/2005

Decedent Attended Since (A) mm/dd/ccyy	Decedent Last Seen Alive (B) mm/dd/ccyy	118. TYPE ATTENDING PHYSICIAN'S NAME, MAILING ADDRESS, ZIP CODE
04/07/2003	01/22/2005	RICHARD N GOLD, MD 8631 W 3RD ST #815, LA, CA 90048

CORONER'S USE ONLY

119. I CERTIFY THAT IN MY OPINION DEATH OCCURRED AT THE HOUR, DATE, AND PLACE STATED FROM THE CAUSES STATED.	120. INJURED AT WORK?	121. INJURY DATE mm/dd/ccyy	122. HOUR (24 Hours)
MANNER OF DEATH: ☐ Natural ☐ Accident ☐ Homicide ☐ Suicide ☐ Pending Investigation ☐ Could not be determined	☐ YES ☐ NO ☐ UNK		

123. PLACE OF INJURY (e.g., home, construction site, wooded area, etc.)

124. DESCRIBE HOW INJURY OCCURRED (Events which resulted in injury)

125. LOCATION OF INJURY (Street and number, or location, and city, and ZIP)

126. SIGNATURE OF CORONER / DEPUTY CORONER	127. DATE mm/dd/ccyy	128. TYPE NAME, TITLE OF CORONER / DEPUTY CORONER

STATE REGISTRAR	A	B	C	D	E	FAX AUTH. #	CENSUS TRACT
						273/7256	

This is to certify that this document is a true copy of the official record filed with the Registrar-Recorder/County Clerk.

Conny B. McCormack

CONNY B. McCORMACK
Registrar-Recorder/County Clerk

JUN 13 2005

019406550

This copy not valid unless prepared on engraved border displaying the Seal and Signature of the Registrar-Recorder/County Clerk.

INFORMATIONAL, NOT A VALID DOCUMENT TO ESTABLISH IDENTITY

ANY ALTERATION OR ERASURE VOIDS THIS CERTIFICATE

STATE OF CALIFORNIA
CERTIFICATION OF VITAL RECORD

COUNTY OF LOS ANGELES
DEPARTMENT OF HEALTH SERVICES

CERTIFICATE OF DEATH
STATE OF CALIFORNIA
USE BLACK INK ONLY / NO ERASURES, WHITEOUTS OR ALTERATIONS
VS-11 (REV 1/02)

| STATE FILE NUMBER | | | | | LOCAL REGISTRATION NUMBER |

DECEDENT'S PERSONAL DATA

1. NAME OF DECEDENT --- FIRST (Given)	2. MIDDLE	3. LAST (Family)
Nell	Ruth	Carter

AKA, ALSO KNOWN AS --- include full AKA (FIRST, MIDDLE, LAST)	4. DATE OF BIRTH mm/dd/ccyy	5. AGE Yrs.	IF UNDER ONE YEAR Months / Days	IF UNDER 24 HOURS Hours / Minutes	6. SEX
	09/13/1948	54			F

9. BIRTH STATE/FOREIGN COUNTRY	10. SOCIAL SECURITY NUMBER	11. EVER IN U.S. ARMED FORCES?	12. MARITAL STATUS (at Time of Death)	7. DATE OF DEATH mm/dd/ccyy	8. HOUR (24 Hours)
AL	419-70-6591	☐ YES ☒ NO ☐ UNK	Divorced	01/23/2003	0653

13. EDUCATION --- Highest Level/Degree (see worksheet on back)	14/15. WAS DECEDENT SPANISH/HISPANIC/LATINO? (If yes, see worksheet on back.)	16. DECEDENT'S RACE --- Up to 3 races may be listed (see worksheet on back)
Some College	☐ YES ☒ NO	Black

17. USUAL OCCUPATION --- Type of work for most of life. DO NOT USE RETIRED	18. KIND OF BUSINESS OR INDUSTRY (e.g., grocery store, road construction, employment agency, etc.)	19. YEARS IN OCCUPATION
Actress & Singer	Entertainment 1OF2	38

USUAL RESIDENCE

20. DECEDENT'S RESIDENCE (Street and number or location)
420 South Spalding Drive #B

21. CITY	22. COUNTY/PROVINCE	23. ZIP CODE	24. YEARS IN COUNTY	25. STATE/FOREIGN COUNTRY
Beverly Hills	Los Angeles	90212	25	California

INFORMANT

26. INFORMANT'S NAME, RELATIONSHIP	27. INFORMANT'S MAILING ADDRESS (Street and number or rural route number, city or town, state, ZIP)
Ann Kaser, Domestic Partner	1001 Hammond Street, Los Angeles, CA 90069

SPOUSE AND PARENT INFORMATION

28. NAME OF SURVIVING SPOUSE --- FIRST	29. MIDDLE	30. LAST (Maiden Name)
-	-	-

31. NAME OF FATHER --- FIRST.	32. MIDDLE	33. LAST	34. BIRTH STATE
Horace	Lee	Hardy	Alabama

35. NAME OF MOTHER --- FIRST	36. MIDDLE	37. LAST (Maiden)	38. BIRTH STATE
Edna	Mae	Lee	Alabama

FUNERAL DIRECTOR / LOCAL REGISTRAR

39. DISPOSITION DATE mm/dd/ccyy	40. PLACE OF FINAL DISPOSITION
01/27/2003	Hillside Memorial Park 6001 Centinela Avenue, Los Angeles, CA 90045

41. TYPE OF DISPOSITION(S)	42. SIGNATURE OF EMBALMER	43. LICENSE NUMBER
BU	▶ Not Embalmed	

44. NAME OF FUNERAL ESTABLISHMENT	45. LICENSE NUMBER	46. SIGNATURE OF LOCAL REGISTRAR	47. DATE mm/dd/ccyy
Hillside Memorial Park Mortuary	FD 1358	▶ Thomas J. Garthwaite ✒	01/27/2003

PLACE OF DEATH

101. PLACE OF DEATH	102. IF HOSPITAL, SPECIFY ONE	103. IF OTHER THAN HOSPITAL, SPECIFY ONE
Residence	☐ IP ☐ ER/OP ☐ DOA	☐ Hospice ☐ Nursing Home/LTC ☒ Decedent's Home ☐ Other

104. COUNTY	105. FACILITY ADDRESS OR LOCATION WHERE FOUND (Street and number or location)	106. CITY
Los Angeles	420 S. Spalding Drive #B	Beverly Hills

CAUSE OF DEATH

107. CAUSE OF DEATH		Time Interval Between Onset and Death	108. DEATH REPORTED TO CORONER?
IMMEDIATE CAUSE (Final disease or condition resulting in death) → (A) Deferred		(AT)	☒ YES ☐ NO REFERRAL NUMBER 2003-00660
(B)		(BT)	109. BIOPSY PERFORMED? ☐ YES ☒ NO
Sequentially list conditions, if any, leading to cause on Line A. Enter UNDERLYING CAUSE (disease or injury that initiated the events resulting in death) LAST (C)		(CT)	110. AUTOPSY PERFORMED? ☐ YES ☒ NO
(D)		(DT)	111. USED IN DETERMINING CAUSE? ☐ YES ☐ NO

112. OTHER SIGNIFICANT CONDITIONS CONTRIBUTING TO DEATH BUT NOT RESULTING IN THE UNDERLYING CAUSE GIVEN IN 107

113. WAS OPERATION PERFORMED FOR ANY CONDITION IN ITEM 107 OR 112? (If yes, list type of operation and date.)	113A. IF FEMALE, PREGNANT IN LAST YEAR?
	☐ YES ☐ NO ☐ UNK

PHYSICIAN'S CERTIFICATION

114. I CERTIFY THAT TO THE BEST OF MY KNOWLEDGE DEATH OCCURRED AT THE HOUR, DATE, AND PLACE STATED FROM THE CAUSES STATED. Decedent Attended Since mm/dd/ccyy / Decedent Last Seen Alive mm/dd/ccyy	115. SIGNATURE AND TITLE OF CERTIFIER ▶	116. LICENSE NUMBER	117. DATE mm/dd/ccyy

118. TYPE ATTENDING PHYSICIAN'S NAME, MAILING ADDRESS, ZIP CODE

CORONER'S USE ONLY

119. I CERTIFY THAT IN MY OPINION DEATH OCCURRED AT THE HOUR, DATE, AND PLACE STATED FROM THE CAUSES STATED. MANNER OF DEATH ☐ Natural ☐ Accident ☐ Homicide ☐ Suicide ☒ Pending Investigation ☐ Could not be determined	120. INJURED AT WORK? ☐ YES ☐ NO ☐ UNK	121. INJURY DATE mm/dd/ccyy	122. HOUR (24 Hours)

123. PLACE OF INJURY (e.g., home, construction site, wooded area, etc.)

124. DESCRIBE HOW INJURY OCCURRED (Events which resulted in injury)

125. LOCATION OF INJURY (Street and number, or location, and city, and ZIP)

126. SIGNATURE OF CORONER / DEPUTY CORONER	127. DATE mm/dd/ccyy	128. TYPE NAME, TITLE OF CORONER / DEPUTY CORONER	
E143 ▶ Mary T. Macias	01/25/2003	Mary T. Macias Deputy Coroner	090603640

| STATE REGISTRAR | A | B | C | D | E | FAX AUTH. # | CENSUS TRACT |

This is a true certified copy of the record filed in the County of Los Angeles Department of Health Services if it bears the Registrar's signature in purple ink.

Thomas J. Garthwaite

DATE ISSUED MAR 18 2003

Director of Health Services and Registrar

This copy not valid unless prepared on engraved border displaying seal and signature of Registrar.

ANY ALTERATION OR ERASURE VOIDS THIS CERTIFICATE

STATE OF CALIFORNIA
CERTIFICATION OF VITAL RECORD

COUNTY OF LOS ANGELES
DEPARTMENT OF HEALTH SERVICES

CERTIFICATE OF DEATH
STATE OF CALIFORNIA
USE BLACK INK ONLY / NO ERASURES, WHITEOUTS OR ALTERATIONS
VS-11 (REV V03)

STATE FILE NUMBER		LOCAL REGISTRATION NUMBER

DECEDENT'S PERSONAL DATA

1. NAME OF DECEDENT — FIRST (Given)	2. MIDDLE	3. LAST (Family)		
Ray	Charles	Robinson, Sr.		

AKA, ALSO KNOWN AS — include full AKA (FIRST, MIDDLE, LAST)	4. DATE OF BIRTH mm/dd/ccyy	5. AGE Yrs.	IF UNDER ONE YEAR Months / Days	IF UNDER 24 HOURS Hours / Minutes	6. SEX
Ray Charles	09/23/1930	73			Male

9. BIRTH STATE/FOREIGN COUNTRY	10. SOCIAL SECURITY NUMBER	11. EVER IN U.S. ARMED FORCES?	12. MARITAL STATUS (at Time of Death)	7. DATE OF DEATH mm/dd/ccyy	8. HOUR (24 Hours)
GA	267-38-1715	YES ☒ NO	Divorced	06/10/2004	1135

13. EDUCATION — Highest Level/Degree	14/15. WAS DECEDENT SPANISH/HISPANIC/LATINO? (If yes, see worksheet on back.)	16. DECEDENT'S RACE — Up to 3 races may be listed (see worksheet on back)
12	YES ☒ NO	African American

17. USUAL OCCUPATION — Type of work for most of life. DO NOT USE RETIRED	18. KIND OF BUSINESS OR INDUSTRY (e.g., grocery store, road construction, employment agency, etc.)	19. YEARS IN OCCUPATION
Musician	Entertainment	65

USUAL RESIDENCE

20. DECEDENT'S RESIDENCE (Street and number or location)
2107 W. Washington Blvd.,

21. CITY	22. COUNTY/PROVINCE	23. ZIP CODE	24. YEARS IN COUNTY	25. STATE/FOREIGN COUNTRY
Los Angeles	Los Angeles	90008	56	California

INFORMANT

26. INFORMANT'S NAME, RELATIONSHIP	27. INFORMANT'S MAILING ADDRESS (Street and number or rural route number, city or town, state, ZIP)
Joseph E. Adams, Friend	2107 W. Washington Blvd. Los Angeles, Ca. 90008

SPOUSE AND PARENT INFORMATION

28. NAME OF SURVIVING SPOUSE — FIRST	29. MIDDLE	30. LAST (Maiden Name)	
—	—	—	

31. NAME OF FATHER — FIRST	32. MIDDLE	33. LAST	34. BIRTH STATE
Unknown	Unknown	Robinson	Unk

35. NAME OF MOTHER — FIRST	36. MIDDLE	37. LAST (Maiden)	38. BIRTH STATE
Reatha	Unknown	Unknown	Unk

FUNERAL DIRECTOR / LOCAL REGISTRAR

39. DISPOSITION DATE mm/dd/ccyy	40. PLACE OF FINAL DISPOSITION
06/18/2004	Inglewood Pk. Cem., 720 E. Florence Ave., Inglewood, Ca., 90301

41. TYPE OF DISPOSITION(S)	42. SIGNATURE OF EMBALMER	43. LICENSE NUMBER
Burial	▶ Joseph I. Davis	5894

44. NAME OF FUNERAL ESTABLISHMENT	45. LICENSE NUMBER	46. SIGNATURE OF LOCAL REGISTRAR	47. DATE mm/dd/ccyy
Angelus Funeral Home	FD 243	▶ Thomas L. Garthwaite	06/17/2004

PLACE OF DEATH

101. PLACE OF DEATH	102. IF HOSPITAL, SPECIFY ONE	103. IF OTHER THAN HOSPITAL, SPECIFY ONE
Residence	IP ☐ ER/OP ☐ DOA ☐	Hospice ☐ Nursing Home/LTC ☐ Decedent's Home ☐ Other ☒

104. COUNTY	105. FACILITY ADDRESS OR LOCATION WHERE FOUND (Street and number or location)	106. CITY
Los Angeles	349 S. Linden Dr.	Beverly Hills

CAUSE OF DEATH

107. CAUSE OF DEATH — Enter the chain of events — diseases, injuries, or complications — that directly caused death, DO NOT enter terminal events such as cardiac arrest, respiratory arrest, or ventricular fibrillation without showing the etiology. DO NOT ABBREVIATE.

		Time Interval Between Onset and Death	108. DEATH REPORTED TO CORONER?
IMMEDIATE CAUSE (A) (Final disease or condition resulting in death)	→ Hepatocellular Carcinoma	(AT) 11 Mons	YES ☐ NO ☒ REFERRAL NUMBER
(B)		(BT)	109. BIOPSY PERFORMED? YES ☐ NO ☒
Sequentially list conditions, if any, leading to cause on Line A. Enter UNDERLYING CAUSE (disease or injury that initiated the events resulting in death) LAST (C)		(CT)	110. AUTOPSY PERFORMED? YES ☐ NO ☒
(D)		(DT)	111. USED IN DETERMINING CAUSE? YES ☐ NO ☒

112. OTHER SIGNIFICANT CONDITIONS CONTRIBUTING TO DEATH BUT NOT RESULTING IN THE UNDERLYING CAUSE GIVEN IN 107
Non Alcoholic Cirrhosis

113. WAS OPERATION PERFORMED FOR ANY CONDITION IN ITEM 107 OR 112? (If yes, list type of operation and date.)	113A. IF FEMALE, PREGNANT IN LAST YEAR?
No	YES ☐ NO ☐ UNK ☐

PHYSICIAN'S CERTIFICATION

114. I CERTIFY THAT TO THE BEST OF MY KNOWLEDGE DEATH OCCURRED AT THE HOUR, DATE, AND PLACE STATED FROM THE CAUSES STATED.	115. SIGNATURE AND TITLE OF CERTIFIER	116. LICENSE NUMBER	117. DATE mm/dd/ccyy
Decedent Attended Since / Decedent Last Seen Alive	▶ Arthur L. Steinberg M.D.	G53431	6/16/2004
(A) mm/dd/ccyy 07/21/2003	(B) mm/dd/ccyy 06/05/2004	118. TYPE ATTENDING PHYSICIAN'S NAME, MAILING ADDRESS, ZIP CODE P.F. McAndrew, M.D., 9090 Wilshire Blvd., Beverly Hills, Ca. 90211	

CORONER'S USE ONLY

119. I CERTIFY THAT IN MY OPINION DEATH OCCURRED AT THE HOUR, DATE, AND PLACE STATED FROM THE CAUSES STATED.	120. INJURED AT WORK?	121. INJURY DATE mm/dd/ccyy	122. HOUR (24 Hours)
MANNER OF DEATH ☐ Natural ☐ Accident ☐ Homicide ☐ Suicide ☐ Pending Investigation ☐ Could not be determined	YES ☐ NO ☐ UNK ☐		

123. PLACE OF INJURY (e.g., home, construction site, wooded area, etc.)

124. DESCRIBE HOW INJURY OCCURRED (Events which resulted in injury)

125. LOCATION OF INJURY (Street and number, or location, and city, and ZIP)

126. SIGNATURE OF CORONER / DEPUTY CORONER	127. DATE mm/dd/ccyy	128. TYPE NAME, TITLE OF CORONER / DEPUTY CORONER
▶		

STATE REGISTRAR	A	B	C	D	E	FAX AUTH. #	CENSUS TRACT
							09071 7343

This is a true certified copy of the record filed in the County of Los Angeles Department of Health Services if it bears the Registrar's signature in purple ink.

Thomas L. Garthwaite
Director of Health Services and Registrar

219   DATE ISSUED   JUN 2 8 2004

This copy not valid unless prepared on engraved border displaying seal and signature of Registrar.

ANY ALTERATION OR ERASURE VOIDS THIS CERTIFICATE

CERTIFICATE OF DEATH
STATE OF CALIFORNIA
USE BLACK INK ONLY / NO ERASURES, WHITEOUTS OR ALTERATIONS
VS 11 (REV 1/03)

3 2003 9 0 1 2 5 1 2

STATE FILE NUMBER   LOCAL REGISTRATION NUMBER

DECEDENT'S PERSONAL DATA

1 NAME OF DECEDENT — FIRST (Given)	2 MIDDLE	3 LAST (Family)
Lana	Jean	Clarkson

AKA, ALSO KNOWN AS -- Include full AKA (FIRST, MIDDLE, LAST)

4 DATE OF BIRTH mm/dd/ccyy	5 AGE Yrs.	IF UNDER ONE YEAR Months / Days	IF UNDER 24 HOURS Hours / Minutes	6 SEX
04/05/1962	40			F

9 BIRTH STATE/FOREIGN COUNTRY	10 SOCIAL SECURITY NUMBER	11 EVER IN U S ARMED FORCES?	12 MARITAL STATUS (at Time of Death)	7 DATE OF DEATH mm/dd/ccyy	8 HOUR (24 Hours)
California	548-15-6434	YES / X NO / UNK	Never Married	02/03/2003	0625

13 EDUCATION - Highest Level/Degree	14/15 WAS DECEDENT SPANISH/HISPANIC/LATINO?	16 DECEDENT'S RACE
Some College	YES / X NO	White

17 USUAL OCCUPATION — Type of work for most of life DO NOT USE RETIRED	18 KIND OF BUSINESS OR INDUSTRY	19 YEARS IN OCCUPATION
Actress	Entertainment	24

USUAL RESIDENCE

20 DECEDENT'S RESIDENCE (Street and number or location)
3005 Grand Canal

21 CITY	22 COUNTY/PROVINCE	23 ZIP CODE	24 YEARS IN COUNTY	25 STATE/FOREIGN COUNTRY
Venice	Los Angeles	90291	25	California

INFORMANT

26 INFORMANT'S NAME, RELATIONSHIP	27 INFORMANT'S MAILING ADDRESS
Donna J.Clarkson Mother	P.O.Box 85648.Los Angeles,CA 90072

SPOUSE AND PARENT INFORMATION

28 NAME OF SURVIVING SPOUSE — FIRST	29 MIDDLE	30 LAST (Maiden Name)
-	-	-

31 NAME OF FATHER — FIRST	32 MIDDLE	33 LAST	34 BIRTH STATE
James	Michael	Clarkson	Illinois

35 NAME OF MOTHER — FIRST	36 MIDDLE	37 LAST (Maiden)	38 BIRTH STATE
Donna	Jean	Smith	Oklahoma

FUNERAL DIRECTOR/ LOCAL REGISTRAR

39 DISPOSITION DATE mm/dd/ccyy	40 PLACE OF FINAL DISPOSITION
02/12/2003	Res:Donna J.Clarkson,3005 Grand Canal,Venice,CA 90291

41 TYPE OF DISPOSITION(S)	42 SIGNATURE OF EMBALMER	43 LICENSE NUMBER
CR/RES	Not Embalmed	-

44 NAME OF FUNERAL ESTABLISHMENT	45 LICENSE NUMBER	46 SIGNATURE OF LOCAL REGISTRAR	47 DATE mm/dd/ccyy
Rose Hills Mortuary W.Hollywood	FD 727	thomas W. Cuthmore	02/11/2003

PLACE OF DEATH

101 PLACE OF DEATH	102 IF HOSPITAL, SPECIFY ONE	103 IF OTHER THAN HOSPITAL, SPECIFY ONE
Private Residence	IP / ER/OP / DOA	Hospice / Nursing Home/LTC / Decedent's Home / X Other

104 COUNTY	105 FACILITY ADDRESS OR LOCATION WHERE FOUND	106 CITY
Los Angeles	1700 Grandview Drive	Albambra

CAUSE OF DEATH

107 CAUSE OF DEATH — Enter the chain of events — diseases, injuries, or complications — that directly caused death DO NOT enter terminal events such as cardiac arrest, respiratory arrest, or ventricular fibrillation without showing the etiology. DO NOT ABBREVIATE

		Time Interval Between Onset and Death
IMMEDIATE CAUSE (A)	Deferred	(AT)
Sequentially list conditions, if any, leading to cause on Line A. (B)		(BT)
Enter UNDERLYING CAUSE (C)		(CT)
(disease or injury that initiated the events resulting in death) LAST (D)		(DT)

108 DEATH REPORTED TO CORONER?
X YES / NO
REFERRAL NUMBER 2003-00937
109 BIOPSY PERFORMED? YES / NO
110 AUTOPSY PERFORMED? X YES / NO
111 USED IN DETERMINING CAUSE? YES / NO

112 OTHER SIGNIFICANT CONDITIONS CONTRIBUTING TO DEATH BUT NOT RESULTING IN THE UNDERLYING CAUSE GIVEN IN 107

113 WAS OPERATION PERFORMED FOR ANY CONDITION IN ITEM 107 OR 112? (If yes, list type of operation and date)

113A IF FEMALE, PREGNANT IN LAST YEAR? YES / NO / UNK

PHYSICIAN'S CERTIFICATION

114 I CERTIFY THAT TO THE BEST OF MY KNOWLEDGE DEATH OCCURRED AT THE HOUR, DATE, AND PLACE STATED FROM THE CAUSES STATED	115 SIGNATURE AND TITLE OF CERTIFIER	116 LICENSE NUMBER	117 DATE mm/dd/ccyy
Decedent Attended Since / Decedent Last Seen Alive			
(A) mm/dd/ccyy (B) mm/dd/ccyy	118 TYPE ATTENDING PHYSICIAN'S NAME, MAILING ADDRESS, ZIP CODE		

CORONER'S USE ONLY

119 I CERTIFY THAT IN MY OPINION DEATH OCCURRED AT THE HOUR, DATE, AND PLACE STATED FROM THE CAUSES STATED	120 INJURED AT WORK?	121 INJURY DATE mm/dd/ccyy	122 HOUR (24 Hours)
MANNER OF DEATH: Natural / Accident / Homicide / Suicide / X Pending Investigation / Could not be determined	YES / NO / UNK		

123 PLACE OF INJURY (e g , home, construction site, wooded area, etc)

124 DESCRIBE HOW INJURY OCCURRED (Events which resulted in injury)

125 LOCATION OF INJURY (Street and number, or location, and city, and ZIP)

126 SIGNATURE OF CORONER / DEPUTY CORONER	127 DATE mm/dd/ccyy	128 TYPE NAME, TITLE OF CORONER / DEPUTY CORONER
Lavette Egans	02/10/2003	Lavette Egans Deputy Coroner

STATE REGISTRAR

A	B	C	D	E	FAX AUTH. #	CENSUS TRACT

AMENDMENT OF MEDICAL AND HEALTH DATA—DEATH

3 05 2003 068653

3200319012512

STATE FILE NUMBER	USE BLACK INK ONLY—NO ERASURES, WHITEOUT, OR ALTERATIONS	LOCAL REGISTRATION DISTRICT AND CERTIFICATE NUMBER

STATE/LOCAL REGISTRAR USE ONLY	1	2	3

TYPE OR PRINT IN BLACK INK ONLY

PART I
INFORMATION TO LOCATE RECORD

1. NAME—FIRST (GIVEN)	2. MIDDLE	3. LAST (FAMILY)	4. SEX
LANA	JEAN	CLARKSON	F

5. DATE OF EVENT—MM/DD/CCYY	6. CITY OF OCCURRENCE	7. COUNTY OF OCCURRENCE
02/03/2003	ALHAMBRA	LOS ANGELES

PART II
INFORMATION AS IT APPEARS ON RECORD

107. DEATH WAS CAUSED BY ENTER ONLY ONE CAUSE PER LINE FOR A, B, C, AND D)

IMMEDIATE CAUSE (A) DEFERRED

(B)

(C)

DUE TO (D)

2 of 2

TIME INTERVAL BETWEEN ONSET AND DEATH	108. DEATH REPORTED TO CORONER
	[X] YES [ ] NO
	REFERRAL NUMBER 2003-00937
	109. BIOPSY PERFORMED [ ] YES [ ] NO
	110. AUTOPSY PERFORMED [X] YES [ ] NO
	111. USED IN DETERMINING CAUSE [ ] YES [ ] NO

112. OTHER SIGNIFICANT CONDITIONS CONTRIBUTING TO DEATH BUT NOT RELATED TO CAUSE GIVEN IN 107

113. WAS OPERATION PERFORMED FOR ANY CONDITION IN ITEM 107 or 112? IF YES, LIST TYPE OF OPERATION AND DATE.

119. MANNER OF DEATH	120. INJURY AT WORK	121. INJURY DATE—MM/DD/CCYY	122. HOUR	123. PLACE OF INJURY
[ ] NATURAL [ ] SUICIDE [ ] HOMICIDE [ ] ACCIDENT [X] PENDING INVESTIGATION [ ] COULD NOT BE DETERMINED	[ ] YES [ ] NO			

124. DESCRIBE HOW INJURY OCCURED (EVENTS WHICH RESULTED IN INJURY)

125. LOCATION (STREET AND NUMBER OR LOCATION AND CITY AND ZIP CODE)

PART III
INFORMATION AS IT SHOULD APPEAR

107. DEATH WAS CAUSED BY ENTER ONLY ONE CAUSE PER LINE FOR A, B, C, AND D)

IMMEDIATE CAUSE (A) GUNSHOT WOUND OF HEAD AND NECK

(B)

(C)

DUE TO (D)

TIME INTERVAL BETWEEN ONSET AND DEATH	108. DEATH REPORTED TO CORONER
RAPID	[X] YES [ ] NO
	REFERRAL NUMBER 2003-00937
	109. BIOPSY PERFORMED [ ] YES [X] NO
	110. AUTOPSY PERFORMED [X] YES [ ] NO
	111. USED IN DETERMINING CAUSE [X] YES [ ] NO

112. OTHER SIGNIFICANT CONDITIONS CONTRIBUTING TO DEATH BUT NOT RELATED TO CAUSE GIVEN IN 107
NONE

113. WAS OPERATION PERFORMED FOR ANY CONDITION IN ITEM 107 or 112? IF YES, LIST TYPE OF OPERATION AND DATE.
NO

119. MANNER OF DEATH	120. INJURY AT WORK	121. INJURY DATE—MM/DD/CCYY	122. HOUR	123. PLACE OF INJURY
[ ] NATURAL [ ] SUICIDE [X] HOMICIDE [ ] ACCIDENT [ ] PENDING INVESTIGATION [ ] COULD NOT BE DETERMINED	[ ] YES [X] NO	02/03/2003	0530	PRIVATE RESIDENCE

124. DESCRIBE HOW INJURY OCCURRED (EVENTS WHICH RESULTED IN INJURY)
SHOT BY ANOTHER

125. LOCATION (STREET AND NUMBER OR LOCATION AND CITY AND ZIP CODE)
1700 GRANDVIEW DRIVE   ALHAMBRA   91803

DECLARATION OF CERTIFYING PHYSICIAN OR CORONER

I HEREBY DECLARE UNDER PENALTY OF PERJURY THAT THE ABOVE INFORMATION IS TRUE AND CORRECT TO THE BEST OF MY KNOWLEDGE.

8. SIGNATURE OF CERTIFYING PHYSICIAN OR CORONER	9. DATE SIGNED—MM/DD/CCYY	10. TYPED OR PRINTED NAME AND DEGREE/TITLE OF CERTIFIER
Louis A. Peña	09/19/2003	LOUIS A. PENA, M.D DME

11. ADDRESS—STREET AND NUMBER	12. CITY	13. STATE	14. ZIP CODE
1104 N. MISSION ROAD	LOS ANGELES	CA	90033

STATE/LOCAL REGISTRAR USE ONLY

15. OFFICE OF STATE REGISTRAR OR SIGNATURE OF LOCAL REGISTRAR	16. DATE ACCEPTED FOR REGISTRATION—MM/DD/CCYY
OFFICE OF THE STATE REGISTRAR OF VITAL STATISTICS	06/17/2004

STATE OF CALIFORNIA, DEPARTMENT OF HEALTH SERVICES, OFFICE OF STATE REGISTRAR

VS-24 B(1/94

STATE OF CALIFORNIA
CERTIFICATION OF VITAL RECORD

COUNTY OF LOS ANGELES
DEPARTMENT OF HEALTH SERVICES

CERTIFICATE OF DEATH
STATE OF CALIFORNIA
USE BLACK INK ONLY/NO ERASURES, WHITEOUTS OR ALTERATIONS
VS-11 (REV. 1/00)

STATE FILE NUMBER — LOCAL REGISTRATION NUMBER

DECEDENT PERSONAL DATA

1. NAME OF DECEDENT—FIRST (GIVEN)	Rosemary
2. MIDDLE	-
3. LAST (FAMILY)	Clooney
4. DATE OF BIRTH MM/DD/CCYY	05/23/1928
5. AGE YRS.	74
6. SEX	Female
7. DATE OF DEATH MM/DD/CCYY	06/29/2002
8. HOUR	1750
9. STATE OF BIRTH	KY
10. SOCIAL SECURITY NO.	273-26-2624
11. MILITARY SERVICE	X No
12. MARITAL STATUS	Married
13. EDUCATION—YEARS COMPLETED	12
14. RACE	White
15. HISPANIC—SPECIFY	X No
16. USUAL EMPLOYER	Self Employed
17. OCCUPATION	Singer
18. KIND OF BUSINESS	Entertainment
19. YEARS IN OCCUPATION	72
20. RESIDENCE—(STREET AND NUMBER OR LOCATION)	1019 North Roxbury Drive
21. CITY	Beverly Hills
22. COUNTY	Los Angeles
23. ZIP CODE	90210
24. YRS IN COUNTY	50
25. STATE OR FOREIGN COUNTRY	CA

INFORMANT

26. NAME, RELATIONSHIP	Maria Ferrer-Murdock, Daughter
27. MAILING ADDRESS (STREET AND NUMBER OR RURAL ROUTE NUMBER, CITY OR TOWN, STATE, ZIP)	1019 North Roxbury Drive Beverly Hills, Ca. 90210

SPOUSE AND PARENT INFORMATION

28. NAME OF SURVIVING SPOUSE—FIRST	Dante
29. MIDDLE	Cesare
30. LAST (MAIDEN NAME)	Dipaolo
31. NAME OF FATHER—FIRST	Andrew
32. MIDDLE	-
33. LAST	Clooney
34. BIRTH STATE	KY
35. NAME OF MOTHER—FIRST	Marie
36. MIDDLE	Frances
37. LAST (MAIDEN)	Guilfoyle
38. BIRTH STATE	KY

DISPOSITION(S)

39. DATE MM/DD/CCYY	07/02/2002
40. PLACE OF FINAL DISPOSITION	St. Patrick's Cemetery- Washington, Kentucky

FUNERAL DIRECTOR AND LOCAL REGISTRAR

41. TYPE OF DISPOSITION(S)	TR/BU
42. SIGNATURE OF EMBALMER	Not Embalmed
43. LICENSE NO.	
44. NAME OF FUNERAL DIRECTOR	Holy Cross Mortuary
45. LICENSE NO.	FD 1167
46. SIGNATURE OF LOCAL REGISTRAR	Thomas L. Garthwaite
47. DATE MM/DD/CCYY	07/01/2002

PLACE OF DEATH

101. PLACE OF DEATH	Residence
102. IF HOSPITAL, SPECIFY ONE:	
103. FACILITY OTHER THAN HOSPITAL:	
104. COUNTY	Los Angeles
105. STREET ADDRESS—(STREET AND NUMBER OR LOCATION)	1019 North Roxbury Drive
106. CITY	Beverly Hills

107. DEATH WAS CAUSED BY: (ENTER ONLY ONE CAUSE PER LINE FOR A, B, C, AND D)

CAUSE OF DEATH

		TIME INTERVAL BETWEEN ONSET AND DEATH
IMMEDIATE CAUSE (A)	Respiratory Arrest	immed.
DUE TO (B)	End Stage Lung Cancer	7 mons.
DUE TO (C)		
DUE TO (D)		

108. DEATH REPORTED TO CORONER: X No
109. BIOPSY PERFORMED: X No
110. AUTOPSY PERFORMED: X No
111. USED IN DETERMINING CAUSE:

112. OTHER SIGNIFICANT CONDITIONS CONTRIBUTING TO DEATH BUT NOT RELATED TO CAUSE GIVEN IN 107: None

113. WAS OPERATION PERFORMED FOR ANY CONDITION IN ITEM 107 OR 112? IF YES, LIST TYPE OF OPERATION AND DATE. — Lymph Node Dissection 01/11/2002

PHYSICIAN'S CERTIFICATION

114. I CERTIFY THAT TO THE BEST OF MY KNOWLEDGE DEATH OCCURRED AT THE HOUR, DATE AND PLACE STATED FROM THE CAUSES STATED.
DECEDENT ATTENDED SINCE MM/DD/CCYY: 06/03/2002
DECEDENT LAST SEEN ALIVE MM/DD/CCYY: 06/27/2002

115. SIGNATURE AND TITLE OF CERTIFIER — Peiman Berdjis
116. LICENSE NO. — A067173
117. DATE MM/DD/CCYY — 07/01/2002
118. TYPE ATTENDING PHYSICIAN'S NAME, MAILING ADDRESS, ZIP — Peiman Berdjis-MD 1125 S. Beverly Dr. Los Angeles, Ca. 90035

CORONER'S USE ONLY

119. I CERTIFY THAT IN MY OPINION DEATH OCCURRED AT THE HOUR, DATE AND PLACE STATED FROM THE CAUSES STATED.
119. MANNER OF DEATH: NATURAL / ACCIDENT / SUICIDE / PENDING INVESTIGATION / HOMICIDE / COULD NOT BE DETERMINED
120. INJURY AT WORK: YES / NO
121. INJURY DATE MM/DD/CCYY
122. HOUR
123. PLACE OF INJURY
124. DESCRIBE HOW INJURY OCCURRED (EVENTS WHICH RESULTED IN INJURY)
125. LOCATION (STREET AND NUMBER OR LOCATION AND CITY, ZIP)

126. SIGNATURE OF CORONER OR DEPUTY CORONER
127. DATE MM/DD/CCYY
128. TYPED NAME, TITLE OF CORONER OR DEPUTY CORONER

30

C349

STATE REGISTRAR — A B C D E F G H — FAX AUTH. # — CENSUS TRACT 090543012

STATE OF CALIFORNIA
CERTIFICATION OF VITAL RECORD

COUNTY OF LOS ANGELES
DEPARTMENT OF HEALTH SERVICES

CERTIFICATE OF DEATH
STATE OF CALIFORNIA
USE BLACK INK ONLY/NO ERASURES, WHITEOUTS OR ALTERATIONS
VS-11 (REV. 1/00)

STATE FILE NUMBER   3 2002 19 048624
LOCAL REGISTRATION NUMBER

	1. NAME OF DECEDENT—First (Given)	2. MIDDLE	3. LAST (FAMILY)
	JAMES	HARRISON	COBURN III

	4. DATE OF BIRTH MM/DD/CCYY	5. AGE YRS.	IF UNDER 1 YEAR / IF UNDER 24 HOURS	6. SEX	7. DATE OF DEATH MM/DD/CCYY	8. HOUR
	08/31/1928	74	MONTHS / DAYS / HOURS / MINUTES	M	11/18/2002	1732

DECEDENT PERSONAL DATA

9. STATE OF BIRTH	10. SOCIAL SECURITY NO.	11. MILITARY SERVICE	12. MARITAL STATUS	13. EDUCATION—YEARS COMPLETED
NEBRASKA	563-30-5489	[X] YES [ ] NO [ ] UNK	MARRIED	16

14. RACE	15. HISPANIC—SPECIFY		16. USUAL EMPLOYER
CAUCASIAN	[ ] YES	[X] NO	SELF EMPLOYED

17. OCCUPATION	18. KIND OF BUSINESS	19. YEARS IN OCCUPATION
ACTOR	ENTERTAINMENT	50

USUAL RESIDENCE

20. RESIDENCE—(STREET AND NUMBER OR LOCATION)
3550 WILSHIRE BLVD. #840

21. CITY	22. COUNTY	23. ZIP CODE	24. YRS IN COUNTY	25. STATE OR FOREIGN COUNTRY
LOS ANGELES	LOS ANGELES	90010	30	CA

INFORMANT

26. NAME, RELATIONSHIP	27. MAILING ADDRESS (STREET AND NUMBER OR RURAL ROUTE NUMBER, CITY OR TOWN, STATE, ZIP)
PAULA COBURN - WIFE	3550 WILSHIRE BLVD. #840 LOS ANGELES, CA. 90010

SPOUSE AND PARENT INFORMATION

28. NAME OF SURVIVING SPOUSE—FIRST	29. MIDDLE	30. LAST (MAIDEN NAME)
PAULA	JOSEPHINE	MURAD

31. NAME OF FATHER—FIRST	32. MIDDLE	33. LAST	34. BIRTH STATE
JAMES	HARRISON	COBURN II	NE

35. NAME OF MOTHER—FIRST	36. MIDDLE	37. LAST (MAIDEN)	38. BIRTH STATE
MYLET	–	JOHNSON	NE

DISPOSITION(S)

39. DATE MM/DD/CCYY	40. PLACE OF FINAL DISPOSITION
11/22/2002	RES:PAULA COBURN 3550 WILSHIRE BLVD. #840 LOS ANGELES, CA. 90010

FUNERAL DIRECTOR AND LOCAL REGISTRAR

41. TYPE OF DISPOSITION(S)	42. SIGNATURE OF EMBALMER	43. LICENSE NO.
CR/RES	▶ NOT EMBALMED	–

44. NAME OF FUNERAL DIRECTOR	45. LICENSE NO.	46. SIGNATURE OF LOCAL REGISTRAR	47. DATE MM/DD/CCYY
PIERCE BROS. WESTWOOD	FD-951	▶ *Thomas G. gutierrez*	11/21/2002

PLACE OF DEATH

101. PLACE OF DEATH	102. IF HOSPITAL, SPECIFY ONE:	103. FACILITY OTHER THAN HOSPITAL	104. COUNTY
CEDARS SINAI MEDICAL CENTER	[X] IP [ ] ER/OP [ ] DOA	[ ] CONV. HOSP. [ ] RES. CARE [ ] OTHER	LOS ANGELES

105. STREET ADDRESS—(STREET AND NUMBER OR LOCATION)	106. CITY
8700 BEVERLY BLVD.	LOS ANGELES

CAUSE OF DEATH

107. DEATH WAS CAUSED BY: (ENTER ONLY ONE CAUSE PER LINE FOR A, B, C, AND D)	TIME INTERVAL BETWEEN ONSET AND DEATH	108. DEATH REPORTED TO CORONER
IMMEDIATE CAUSE (A) CARDIAC ARREST	20mins.	[ ] YES [X] NO / REFERRAL NUMBER
DUE TO (B) CORONARY ARTERY DISEASE	years	109. BIOPSY PERFORMED [ ] YES [X] NO
DUE TO (C)		110. AUTOPSY PERFORMED [ ] YES [X] NO
DUE TO (D)		111. USED IN DETERMINING CAUSE [ ] YES [ ] NO

112. OTHER SIGNIFICANT CONDITIONS CONTRIBUTING TO DEATH BUT NOT RELATED TO CAUSE GIVEN IN 107
NONE

113. WAS OPERATION PERFORMED FOR ANY CONDITION IN ITEM 107 OR 112? IF YES, LIST TYPE OF OPERATION AND DATE.
NO

PHYSICIAN'S CERTIFICATION

114. I CERTIFY THAT TO THE BEST OF MY KNOWLEDGE DEATH OCCURRED AT THE HOUR, DATE AND PLACE STATED FROM THE CAUSES STATED. DECEDENT ATTENDED SINCE MM/DD/CCYY / DECEDENT LAST SEEN ALIVE MM/DD/CCYY	115. SIGNATURE AND TITLE OF CERTIFIER	116. LICENSE NO.	117. DATE MM/DD/CCYY
10/12/2001 / 11/18/2002	▶ *Richard N. Gold MD*	G25597	11/21/2002

118. TYPE ATTENDING PHYSICIAN'S NAME, MAILING ADDRESS, ZIP
RICHARD N.GOLD,M.D.8631 W.3RD ST. LOS ANGELES, CA. 90048

CORONER'S USE ONLY

I CERTIFY THAT IN MY OPINION DEATH OCCURRED AT THE HOUR, DATE AND PLACE STATED FROM THE CAUSES STATED.	120. INJURY AT WORK	121. INJURY DATE MM/DD/CCYY	122. HOUR	123. PLACE OF INJURY
119. MANNER OF DEATH	[ ] YES [ ] NO			

18+F

119. MANNER OF DEATH	124. DESCRIBE HOW INJURY OCCURRED (EVENTS WHICH RESULTED IN INJURY)
[ ] NATURAL [ ] SUICIDE [ ] HOMICIDE [ ] ACCIDENT [ ] PENDING INVESTIGATION [ ] COULD NOT BE DETERMINED	

I25?

125. LOCATION (STREET AND NUMBER OR LOCATION AND CITY, ZIP)

126. SIGNATURE OF CORONER OR DEPUTY CORONER	127. DATE MM/DD/CCYY	128. TYPED NAME, TITLE OF CORONER OR DEPUTY CORONER
▶		

STATE REGISTRAR

A	B	C	D	E	F	G	H	FAX AUTH. #	CENSUS TRACT
									090582778

This is a true certified copy of the record filed in the County of Los Angeles
Department of Health Services if it bears the Registrar's signature in purple ink.

Thomas L. Gutierrez   DATE ISSUED 234   DEC 3 0 2002

Director of Health Services and Registrar

This copy not valid unless prepared on engraved border displaying seal and signature of Registrar.

MIDWEST BANK NOTE COMPANY   ANY ALTERATION OR ERASURE VOIDS THIS CERTIFICATE

Imogene (handwritten overlay on name field)

VS-4 REV. 9/95
STATE OF CONNECTICUT
DEPARTMENT OF PUBLIC HEALTH

CERTIFICATE OF DEATH

I O 6 2001 19370

STATE FILE NUMBER

I certify that this is a true copy of the certificate received for record. — Fairfield Registrar of Vital Statistics

1 DECEASED NAME — FIRST: Imogene MIDDLE: Coca Donovan LAST: Coca			SEX: F	3 DATE OF DEATH (Month, Day, Year): 6/2/01	

| DATE OF BIRTH (Month, Day, Year): 4 November 18, 1908 | 5 AGE-Last Birthday: 92 | UNDER 1 YEAR Mos. / Days | UNDER 1 DAY Hours / Mins. | 6 RACE-White, Black, American Indian, Other (Specify): white | 7 OF HISPANIC ORIGIN? (If Yes, specify Cuban, Mexican, Puerto Rican, Other): ☐Y ☒N |

| 8 COUNTY OF DEATH: Fairfield | TOWN OF DEATH: Fairfield | 10 PLACE OF DEATH (Check one) Hospital: ☐ ER/outpatient ☐ DOA ☐ Inpatient | OTHER ☒ Nursing Home ☐ Residence ☐ Other: Carlton |

| 11 CITY & STATE OF BIRTH (Country if not U.S.): Philadelphia, PA. | 12 CITIZEN OF: U.S.A. | 13 ☐MARRIED ☐NEVER MARRIED ☒WIDOWED ☐DIVORCED ☐LEGALLY SEPARATED | 14 LAST SPOUSE (If wife, give maiden name): King Donovan |

| 15 SOCIAL SECURITY NUMBER: 439-14-4496 | 16 USUAL OCCUPATION (Give kind of work done during most working life, even if retired): Actress | 17 KIND OF BUSINESS OR INDUSTRY: self employed |

| 18 RESIDENCE STATE: Connecticut | 19 COUNTY: Fairfield | 20 TOWN: Weston | 21 NUMBER AND STREET: 54 Davis Hill Rd. |

| 22 WAS DECEASED A VETERAN IF YES GIVE WAR: ☐YES ☒NO | 23 BRANCH OF SERVICE: | 24 EDUCATION (Specify highest grade completed): Primary/Secondary: 8 College: — 0-12 / 1-4 / 5+ |

| 25 FATHER - NAME FIRST: Joseph MIDDLE: Coca LAST: | 26 MOTHER FIRST: Sadie MIDDLE: Brady MAIDEN: |

| 27 INFORMANT - NAME: Mark N. Basile | 28 MAILING ADDRESS: 54 Davis Hill Rd. Weston, Ct. 06883 | 29 RELATIONSHIP TO DECEASED: conservato |

PART 1. DEATH WAS CAUSED BY (ENTER ONLY ONE CAUSE PER LINE FOR (a), (b) AND (c))

APPROXIMATE INTERVAL BETWEEN ONSET AND DEATH

30 CONDITIONS, IF ANY WHICH GAVE RISE TO IMMEDIATE CAUSE (a) STATING THE UNDERLYING CAUSE LAST.

(a) IMMEDIATE CAUSE: Cerebrovascular Accident — hours.
DUE TO, OR AS A CONSEQUENCE OF:
(b) Alzheimer's Disease — years
DUE TO, OR AS A CONSEQUENCE OF:
(c)

31 PART II. OTHER SIGNIFICANT CONDITIONS: CONDITIONS CONTRIBUTING TO DEATH BUT NOT RELATED TO CAUSE

32 AUTOPSY ☐Y ☒N   33 IF YES, Were findings considered in determining cause of death.

| 34 NURSE PRONOUNCEMENT TYPE OR PRINT NAME: Catherine Tobyn RN AS | DEGREE | 35 SIGNATURE: Catherine Thomn | 36 DATE AND TIME PRONOUNCED MONTH: 6 DAY: 2 YEAR: 01 TIME: 7.05 ☒A.M. ☐P.M. |

| 37 CERTIFICATION - PHYSICIAN I attended the deceased from Mo. 2 Day 15 Year 01 TO Mo. 6 Day 2 Year 01 | 38 AND LAST SAW HIM/HER ALIVE ON Month 4 Day 5 Year 01 | 39 DEATH OCCURRED On the date, and to the best of my knowledge, due to the cause(s) stated. (Time) 6/2/01 |

| 40 WAS CASE REFERRED TO MEDICAL EXAMINER: ☐YES ☒NO | 41 SURGERY RELEVANT TO CONDITION REPORTED IN ITEM 30 (Name of Operation) | 42 (Date Performed) | 43 THE DECEDENT WAS PRONOUNCED DEAD: Month 6 Day 2 Year 01 Time 7.05 A.M. |

| 44 CERTIFIER - NAME (type or print): Peter Tortora, MD | 45 SIGNATURE: P Tortora, MD | DEGREE OR TITLE |

| 46 MAILING - CERTIFIER STREET OR R.F.D. NO.: 1300 Post Road, CITY OR TOWN: Fairfield STATE: CT ZIP: 06430 | DATE SIGNED (Month, Day, Year): 6/4/01 |

| 48 BURIAL, CREMATION, REMOVAL (Specify): Cremation | 49 CEMETERY OR CREMATORY - NAME: Lakeview | 50 LOCATION CITY OR TOWN: Bridgeport, Ct. STATE |

| 51 DATE (MONTH, DAY, YEAR): June 6, 2001 | 52 FUNERAL HOME - NAME AND ADDRESS: Daystar Cremation Service 39 So. Benson Rd. Fairfield, C |

| 53 FUNERAL DIRECTOR OR EMBALMER - SIGNATURE: | 54 NAME OF EMBALMER IF BODY WAS EMBALMED: N/A | 55 LICENSE NUMBER: 2006 |

| THIS CERTIFICATE RECEIVED FOR RECORD ON: JUN - 5 2001 | BY: Ann E Hradsky | REGISTRAR: asst |

THE SEAL OF THE STATE OF CONNECTICUT IS AFFIXED TO CERTIFY THAT THE ABOVE IS A TRUE COPY OF A RECORD FILED WITH THE STATE OF CONNECTICUT DEPARTMENT OF PUBLIC HEALTH PURSUANT TO THE PROVISIONS OF THE GENERAL STATUTES OF CONNECTICUT.

Suzanne Speers
Suzanne Speers, R.H.I.A., M.P.H.
Registrar of Vital Records

NOV 27 2001

Date of Issue

COUNTY OF LOS ANGELES

DEPARTMENT OF HEALTH SERVICES

CERTIFICATE OF DEATH

STATE OF CALIFORNIA
USE BLACK INK ONLY/NO ERASURES, WHITEOUTS OR ALTERATIONS
VS-11 (REV. 7/97)

STATE OF CALIFORNIA
CERTIFICATION OF VITAL RECORD

STATE FILE NUMBER		LOCAL REGISTRATION NUMBER

DECEDENT PERSONAL DATA

1. NAME OF DECEDENT—FIRST (GIVEN)	2. MIDDLE	3. LAST (FAMILY)
Oscar	Iron Eyes	Cody

4. DATE OF BIRTH MM/DD/CCYY	5. AGE YRS.	IF UNDER 1 YEAR MONTHS / DAYS	IF UNDER 24 HOURS HOURS / MINUTES	6. SEX	7. DATE OF DEATH MM/DD/CCYY	8. HOUR
04/03/1904	94			M	01/04/1999	1309

9. STATE OF BIRTH	10. SOCIAL SECURITY NO.	11. MILITARY SERVICE	12. MARITAL STATUS	13. EDUCATION—YEARS COMPLETED
Oklahoma	568-16-8865	☐ YES ☒ NO ☐ UNK	Widow	10

14. RACE	15. HISPANIC—SPECIFY		16. USUAL EMPLOYER
American Indian	☐ YES	☒ No	Disney

17. OCCUPATION	18. KIND OF BUSINESS	19. YEARS IN OCCUPATION
Actor	Entertainment	80

USUAL RESIDENCE

20. RESIDENCE—(STREET AND NUMBER OR LOCATION)
2013 N. Griffith Park Blvd.

21. CITY	22. COUNTY	23. ZIP CODE	24. YRS IN COUNTY	25. STATE OR FOREIGN COUNTRY
Los Angeles	Los Angeles	90039	80	CA

INFORMANT

26. NAME, RELATIONSHIP	27. MAILING ADDRESS (STREET AND NUMBER OR RURAL ROUTE NUMBER, CITY OR TOWN, STATE, ZIP)
Victor Buck - Trustee	1337 S. Oak Knoll Dr. Prescott, AZ 86303

SPOUSE AND PARENT INFORMATION

28. NAME OF SURVIVING SPOUSE—FIRST	29. MIDDLE	30. LAST (MAIDEN NAME)
-	-	-

31. NAME OF FATHER—FIRST	32. MIDDLE	33. LAST	34. BIRTH STATE
Thomas	-	Unk.	Unk.

35. NAME OF MOTHER—FIRST	36. MIDDLE	37. LAST (MAIDEN)	38. BIRTH STATE
Frances	-	Salpet	Unk.

DISPOSITION(S)

39. DATE MM/DD/CCYY	40. PLACE OF FINAL DISPOSITION
01/08/1999	Hollywood Forever Cemetery 6000 Santa Monica Bl. Los Angeles, CA 90038

FUNERAL DIRECTOR AND LOCAL REGISTRAR

41. TYPE OF DISPOSITION(S)	42. SIGNATURE OF EMBALMER	43. LICENSE NO.
BURIAL	▶ Not Embalmed	-

44. NAME OF FUNERAL DIRECTOR	45. LICENSE NO.	46. SIGNATURE OF LOCAL REGISTRAR	47. DATE MM/DD/CCYY
Hollywood Funeral Home	FD1651	▶ Mark _____	01/08/1999

PLACE OF DEATH

101. PLACE OF DEATH	102. IF HOSPITAL, SPECIFY ONE:	103. FACILITY OTHER THAN HOSPITAL:	104. COUNTY
Residence	☐ IP ☐ ER/OP ☐ DOA	☐ CONV. HOSP. ☐ RES. CARE ☐ OTHER	Los Angeles

105. STREET ADDRESS—(STREET AND NUMBER OR LOCATION)	106. CITY
2013 N. Griffith Park Blvd.	Los Angeles

CAUSE OF DEATH

107. DEATH WAS CAUSED BY: (ENTER ONLY ONE CAUSE PER LINE FOR A, B, C, AND D)	TIME INTERVAL BETWEEN ONSET AND DEATH	108. DEATH REPORTED TO CORONER
IMMEDIATE CAUSE (A) Cardio Respiratory Arrest	Mins.	☒ YES ☐ NO REFERRAL NUMBER 99-50121
DUE TO (B) Congestive Heart Failure	Yrs.	109. BIOPSY PERFORMED ☐ YES ☒ NO
DUE TO (C)		110. AUTOPSY PERFORMED ☐ YES ☒ NO
DUE TO (D)		111. USED IN DETERMINING CAUSE ☐ YES ☐ NO

112. OTHER SIGNIFICANT CONDITIONS CONTRIBUTING TO DEATH BUT NOT RELATED TO CAUSE GIVEN IN 107
Anemia

113. WAS OPERATION PERFORMED FOR ANY CONDITION IN ITEM 107 OR 112? IF YES, LIST TYPE OF OPERATION AND DATE.
No

PHYSICIAN'S CERTIFICATION

114. I CERTIFY THAT TO THE BEST OF MY KNOWLEDGE DEATH OCCURRED AT THE HOUR, DATE AND PLACE STATED FROM THE CAUSES STATED. DECEDENT ATTENDED SINCE MM/DD/CCYY / DECEDENT LAST SEEN ALIVE MM/DD/CCYY	115. SIGNATURE AND TITLE OF CERTIFIER	116. LICENSE NO.	117. DATE MM/DD/CCYY
09/30/1994 / 10/20/1998	▶ M. Frieberg M.D.	A42970	01/07/1999

118. TYPE ATTENDING PHYSICIAN'S NAME, MAILING ADDRESS, ZIP
Moshe Frieberg MD. 1510 S. Central Ave. Glendale, CA 91204

CORONER'S USE ONLY

119. I CERTIFY THAT IN MY OPINION DEATH OCCURRED AT THE HOUR, DATE AND PLACE STATED FROM THE CAUSES STATED. 119. MANNER OF DEATH	120. INJURY AT WORK	121. INJURY DATE MM/DD/CCYY	122. HOUR	123. PLACE OF INJURY
☐ NATURAL ☐ SUICIDE ☐ HOMICIDE ☐ ACCIDENT ☐ PENDING INVESTIGATION ☐ COULD NOT BE DETERMINED	☐ YES ☐ NO			

124. DESCRIBE HOW INJURY OCCURRED (EVENTS WHICH RESULTED IN INJURY)

125. LOCATION (STREET AND NUMBER OR LOCATION AND CITY, ZIP)

126. SIGNATURE OF CORONER OR DEPUTY CORONER	127. DATE MM/DD/CCYY	128. TYPED NAME, TITLE OF CORONER OR DEPUTY CORONER
▶		

STATE REGISTRAR

A	B	C	D	E	F	G	H	FAX AUTH. #	CENSUS TRACT
									090206701

This is a true certified copy of the record filed in the County of Los Angeles Department of Health Services if it bears the Registrar's signature in purple ink.

Mark _____   DATE ISSUED JAN 26 1999

Director of Health Service and Registrar

This copy not valid unless prepared on engraved border displaying seal and signature of Registrar.

CERTIFICATION OF VITAL RECORD

COUNTY OF LOS ANGELES • REGISTRAR-RECORDER/COUNTY CLERK

CERTIFICATE OF DEATH
STATE OF CALIFORNIA — DEPARTMENT OF PUBLIC HEALTH

LOCAL REGISTRATION DISTRICT AND CERTIFICATE NUMBER 26570

DECEDENT PERSONAL DATA

1. NAME OF DECEASED — FIRST NAME	Nathaniel
1b. MIDDLE NAME	Adams
1c. LAST NAME	Cole
2a. DATE OF DEATH	Feb. 15, 1965
3. SEX	Male
4. COLOR OR RACE	Negro
5. BIRTHPLACE	Alabama
6. DATE OF BIRTH	March 17, 1919
7. AGE	45 YEARS
8. NAME AND BIRTHPLACE OF FATHER	Edward J. Coles, unknown
9. MAIDEN NAME AND BIRTHPLACE OF MOTHER	Perlina Adams, unknown
10. CITIZEN OF WHAT COUNTRY	USA
11. SOCIAL SECURITY NUMBER	340-03-1210
12. LAST OCCUPATION	Entertainer
13. NUMBER OF YEARS	26
14. NAME OF LAST EMPLOYING COMPANY OR FIRM	Self Employed
15. KIND OF INDUSTRY OR BUSINESS	Entertainment
16. IF DECEASED WAS EVER IN U.S. ARMED FORCES	No
17. MARRIED / NEVER MARRIED / WIDOWED / DIVORCED	Married
18a. NAME OF PRESENT SPOUSE	Maria Cole
18b. PRESENT OR LAST OCCUPATION OF SPOUSE	Homemaker

PLACE OF DEATH

19a. PLACE OF DEATH — NAME OF HOSPITAL	St. John's Hospital
19b. STREET ADDRESS	1328 22nd St.
19c. CITY OR TOWN	Santa Monica
19d. COUNTY	Los Angeles
19f. LENGTH OF STAY IN COUNTY OF DEATH	28 YEARS
19g. LENGTH OF STAY IN CALIFORNIA	28 YEARS

LAST USUAL RESIDENCE

20a. LAST USUAL RESIDENCE — STREET ADDRESS	401 S. Muirfield Rd.
20c. CITY OR TOWN	Los Angeles
20d. COUNTY	Los Angeles
20e. STATE	California

PHYSICIAN'S OR CORONER'S CERTIFICATION

22a. PHYSICIAN — I HEREBY CERTIFY THAT DEATH OCCURRED AT THE HOUR DATE AND PLACE STATED ABOVE FROM THE CAUSES STATED BELOW AND THAT I ATTENDED THE DECEASED FROM 1/15/65 AND THAT I LAST SAW THE DECEASED ALIVE ON 2/14/65

22c. ADDRESS 9301 Sunset Blvd., Los Angeles 22d. DATE SIGNED 2/15/65

FUNERAL DIRECTOR AND LOCAL REGISTRAR

23. SPECIFY BURIAL / ENTOMBMENT OR CREMATION	Burial
24. DATE	2/18/65
25. NAME OF CEMETERY OR CREMATORY	Forest Lawn Cemetery
26. EMBALMER SIGNATURE — LICENSE NUMBER	5109
27. NAME OF FUNERAL DIRECTOR	Angelus Funeral Home
28. DATE RECEIVED FOR REGISTRATION	FEB 17 1965

CAUSE OF DEATH

	Cause	Approximate Interval Between Onset and Death
PART I — IMMEDIATE CAUSE (A)	Tumor Cerebrum	2 months
DUE TO (B)	Metastatic CA to all organs	1 month
DUE TO (C)	Primary Metastatic CA of Lung	3 months

PART II. OTHER SIGNIFICANT CONDITIONS CONTRIBUTING TO DEATH BUT NOT RELATED TO THE TERMINAL DISEASE CONDITION GIVEN IN PART I (A)

OPERATION AND AUTOPSY

31. OPERATION — CHECK ONE: OPERATION PERFORMED — FINDINGS USED IN DETERMINING ABOVE STATED CAUSES OF DEATH
32. DATE OF OPERATION 1-25-65
33. AUTOPSY — CHECK ONE: NO AUTOPSY PERFORMED

INJURY INFORMATION

34a. SPECIFY ACCIDENT, SUICIDE OR HOMICIDE
34b. DESCRIBE HOW INJURY OCCURRED
35a. TIME OF INJURY
35b. INJURY OCCURRED: WHILE AT WORK / NOT WHILE AT WORK
35c. PLACE OF INJURY
35d. CITY, TOWN OR LOCATION

This is to certify that this document is a true copy of the official record filed with the Registrar-Recorder/County Clerk.

CHARLES WEISSBURD
Registrar-Recorder/County Clerk

FEB 12 2002
19-314770

This copy not valid unless prepared on engraved border displaying the Seal and Signature of the Registrar-Recorder/County Clerk.

ANY ALTERATION OR ERASURE VOIDS THIS CERTIFICATE

CERTIFICATION OF VITAL RECORD

COUNTY OF LOS ANGELES • REGISTRAR-RECORDER/COUNTY CLERK

STATE FILE NUMBER	**CERTIFICATE OF DEATH** STATE OF CALIFORNIA—DEPARTMENT OF PUBLIC HEALTH	LOCAL REGISTRATION DISTRICT AND 7080 CERTIFICATE NUMBER 27921

DECEDENT PERSONAL DATA

1A. NAME OF DECEASED—FIRST NAME	1B. MIDDLE NAME	1C. LAST NAME	2A. DATE OF DEATH—MONTH, DAY, YEAR	2B. HOUR
RAY	BIDWELL	COLLINS	JULY 11, 1965	4:05 P.M.

3. SEX	4. COLOR OR RACE	5. BIRTHPLACE (STATE OR FOREIGN COUNTRY)	6. DATE OF BIRTH	7. AGE (LAST BIRTHDAY)	IF UNDER 1 YEAR	IF UNDER 24 HOURS
male	caucasian	California	December 10, 1889	75 YEARS		

8. NAME AND BIRTHPLACE OF FATHER	9. MAIDEN NAME AND BIRTHPLACE OF MOTHER	10. CITIZEN OF WHAT COUNTRY	11. SOCIAL SECURITY NUMBER
Wilkie B. Collins - California	Lillian Bidwell - Calif.	U.S.A.	124 01 2093

12. LAST OCCUPATION	13. NUMBER OF YEARS IN THIS OCCUPATION	14. NAME OF LAST EMPLOYING COMPANY OR FIRM	15. KIND OF INDUSTRY OR BUSINESS
Actor	58	Paisano Productions	T. V. Producers

16. IF DECEASED WAS EVER IN U. S. ARMED FORCES GIVE WAR OR DATES OF SERVICE	17. SPECIFY MARRIED, NEVER MARRIED, WIDOWED, DIVORCED	18A. NAME OF PRESENT SPOUSE	18B. PRESENT OR LAST OCCUPATION OF SPOUSE
none	Married	Mrs. Joan E. Collins	housewife

PLACE OF DEATH

19A. PLACE OF DEATH—NAME OF HOSPITAL	19B. STREET ADDRESS		
St. John's Hospital	1328 22nd Street	INSIDE CITY CORPORATE LIMITS	OUTSIDE CITY CORPORATE LIMITS

19C. CITY OR TOWN	19D. COUNTY	19E. LENGTH OF STAY IN COUNTY OF DEATH	19F. LENGTH OF STAY IN CALIFORNIA
Santa Monica	Los Angeles	31 YEARS	31 YEARS

LAST USUAL RESIDENCE (WHERE DID DECEASED LIVE—IF IN INSTITUTION ENTER RESIDENCE BEFORE ADMISSION)

20A. LAST USUAL RESIDENCE—STREET ADDRESS	20B. IF INSIDE CITY CORPORATE LIMITS	21A. NAME OF INFORMANT (IF OTHER THAN SPOUSE) (friend)
918 Third Street	INSIDE / ON A FARM / NOT ON A FARM	Mrs. Margaret A. MacGeorge

20C. CITY OR TOWN	20D. COUNTY	20E. STATE	21B. ADDRESS OF INFORMANT
Santa Monica	Los Angeles	Calif.	2130 Tondolea Lane La Canada, California

PHYSICIAN'S OR CORONER'S CERTIFICATION

22A. PHYSICIAN: I HEREBY CERTIFY THAT DEATH OCCURRED AT THE HOUR DATE AND PLACE STATED ABOVE, FROM THE CAUSES STATED BELOW AND THAT I ATTENDED THE DECEASED FROM 10-14-47 TO 7-11-65 AND THAT I LAST SAW THE DECEASED ALIVE ON 7-11-65	22C. PHYSICIAN OR CORONER — SIGNATURE	DEGREE OR TITLE
22B. CORONER: I HEREBY CERTIFY THAT DEATH OCCURRED AT THE HOUR DATE AND PLACE STATED ABOVE FROM THE CAUSES STATED BELOW AND THAT I HAVE HELD... ON THE REMAINS OF DECEASED AS REQUIRED BY LAW	John C. Sloane M.D. 22D. ADDRESS Beverly Hills 1335 Leaksy Dr B.H.	22E. DATE SIGNED 7-13-65

FUNERAL DIRECTOR AND LOCAL REGISTRAR

23. SPECIFY BURIAL, ENTOMBMENT OR CREMATION	24. DATE	25. NAME OF CEMETERY OR CREMATORY FOREST LAWN HOLLYWOOD HILLS 6300 FOREST LAWN DR - LOS ANGELES 28, CALIF.	26. EMBALMER—SIGNATURE (IF BODY EMBALMED) LICENSE NUMBER
Burial	July 14, 1965		Wayne A. Bowman 4365

27. NAME OF FUNERAL DIRECTOR (OR PERSON ACTING) FOREST LAWN HOLLYWOOD HILLS 6300 FOREST LAWN DR - LOS ANGELES 28, CALIF.	28. DATE ACCEPTED FOR REGISTRATION BY LOCAL REGISTRAR JUL 14 1965	29. LOCAL REGISTRAR—SIGNATURE R. V. Sutherland M.D.

CAUSE OF DEATH

30. CAUSE OF DEATH		APPROXIMATE INTERVAL BETWEEN ONSET AND DEATH
PART I. DEATH WAS CAUSED BY IMMEDIATE CAUSE (A)	Broncho pneumonia, terminal	1 wk
CONDITIONS, IF ANY, WHICH GAVE RISE TO THE ABOVE CAUSE (A) STATING THE UNDERLYING CAUSE LAST — DUE TO (B)	Pulmonary emphysema, severe	10 yrs
DUE TO (C)		

PART II. OTHER SIGNIFICANT CONDITIONS CONTRIBUTING TO DEATH BUT NOT RELATED TO THE TERMINAL DISEASE CONDITION GIVEN IN PART I (A)

Aneurysm - abdominal aorta - small

OPERATION AND AUTOPSY

31. OPERATION—CHECK ONE	32. DATE OF OPERATION	33. AUTOPSY—CHECK ONE
☒ NO OPERATION PERFORMED		☒ AUTOPSY PERFORMED

34A. SPECIFY ACCIDENT, SUICIDE OR HOMICIDE	34B. DESCRIBE HOW INJURY OCCURRED

INJURY INFORMATION

35A. TIME OF INJURY	HOUR	MONTH	DAY	YEAR	M.

35B. INJURY OCCURRED	35C. PLACE OF INJURY	35D. CITY, TOWN, OR LOCATION	COUNTY	STATE
☐ WHILE AT WORK ☒ NOT WHILE AT WORK				

Rev. 1 1 58 Form VS 11

This is to certify that this document is a true copy of the official record filed with the Registrar-Recorder/County Clerk.

OCT 02 1995

19 034108

This copy not valid unless prepared on engraved border displaying the Seal of the Registrar-Recorder/County Clerk.

ANY ALTERATION OR ERASURE VOIDS THIS CERTIFICATE

CERTIFICATE OF DEATH
STATE OF CALIFORNIA
USE BLACK INK ONLY/NO ERASURES, WHITEOUTS OR ALTERATIONS
VS-11 (REV. 7/93)

39619030463

STATE FILE NUMBER | LOCAL REGISTRATION NUMBER

DECEDENT PERSONAL DATA

1. NAME OF DECEDENT—FIRST (GIVEN)	2. MIDDLE	3. LAST (FAMILY)
RAYMOND	NEIL	COMBS JR.

4. DATE OF BIRTH MM/DD/CCYY	5. AGE YRS.	IF UNDER 1 YEAR MONTHS / DAYS	IF UNDER 24 HOURS HOURS / MINUTES	6. SEX	7. DATE OF DEATH MM/DD/CCYY	8. HOUR
04/03/1956	40			MALE	06/02/1996	0453

9. STATE OF BIRTH	10. SOCIAL SECURITY NO.	11. MILITARY SERVICE	12. MARITAL STATUS	13. EDUCATION —YEARS COMPLETED
OH	282-56-9477	19___ To 19___ [X] NONE	MARRIED	14

14. RACE	15. HISPANIC—SPECIFY	16. USUAL EMPLOYER	
CAUCASIAN	[ ] Yes ___ [X] No	SELF EMPLOYED	1OF?

17. OCCUPATION	18. KIND OF BUSINESS	19. YEARS IN OCCUPATION
ACTOR	ENTERTAINMENT	16

USUAL RESIDENCE

20. RESIDENCE—STREET AND NUMBER OR LOCATION
1318 SONORA AVENUE

21. CITY	22. COUNTY	23. ZIP CODE	24. YRS IN COUNTY	25. STATE OR FOREIGN COUNTRY
GLENDALE	LOS ANGELES	91201	14	CALIFORNIA

INFORMANT

26. NAME, RELATIONSHIP	27. MAILING ADDRESS (STREET AND NUMBER OR RURAL ROUTE NUMBER, CITY OR TOWN, STATE, ZIP)
DEBRA JO COMBS - WIFE	1318 SONORA AVENUE GLENDALE CA 91201

SPOUSE AND PARENT INFORMATION

28. NAME OF SURVIVING SPOUSE—FIRST	29. MIDDLE	30. LAST (MAIDEN NAME)	
DEBRA	JO	MINK	

31. NAME OF FATHER—FIRST	32. MIDDLE	33. LAST	34. BIRTH STATE
RAYMOND	NEIL	COMBS SR.	OH

35. NAME OF MOTHER—FIRST	36. MIDDLE	37. LAST (MAIDEN)	38. BIRTH STATE
ANITA	JEAN	WATERS	NC

DISPOSITION(S)

39. DATE MM/DD/CCYY	40. PLACE OF FINAL DISPOSITION
06/10/1996	GREENWOOD CEMETERY 1602 GREENWOOD HAMILTON OHIO 45011

FUNERAL DIRECTOR AND LOCAL REGISTRAR

41. TYPE OF DISPOSITION(S)	42. SIGNATURE OF EMBALMER	43. LICENSE NO.
TR/BURIAL	▶ B Tomey	8245

44. NAME OF FUNERAL DIRECTOR	45. LICENSE NO.	46. SIGNATURE OF LOCAL REGISTRAR	47. DATE MM/DD/CCYY
PRAISWATER MEYER MITCHELL MORTUARY	FD-549	▶ Mark Trumm HS	06/07/1996

PLACE OF DEATH

101. PLACE OF DEATH	102. IF HOSPITAL, SPECIFY ONE:	103. FACILITY OTHER THAN HOSPITAL:	104. COUNTY
Glendale Adventist Hospital	[X] IP [ ] ER/OP [ ] DOA	[ ] CONV. HOSP. [ ] RES. [ ] OTHER	Los Angeles

105. STREET ADDRESS—STREET AND NUMBER OR LOCATION	106. CITY
1509 East Wilson Terrace	Glendale

CAUSE OF DEATH

107. DEATH WAS CAUSED BY: (ENTER ONLY ONE CAUSE PER LINE FOR A, B, C, AND D)	TIME INTERVAL BETWEEN ONSET AND DEATH	
IMMEDIATE CAUSE (A) Deferred		108. DEATH REPORTED TO CORONER [ ] YES [ ] NO
		REFERRAL NUMBER 96-04224
DUE TO (B)		109. BIOPSY PERFORMED [ ] YES [ ] NO
DUE TO (C)		110. AUTOPSY PERFORMED [X] YES [ ] NO
DUE TO (D)		111. USED IN DETERMINING CAUSE [ ] YES [ ] NO

112. OTHER SIGNIFICANT CONDITIONS CONTRIBUTING TO DEATH BUT NOT RELATED TO CAUSE GIVEN IN 107

113. WAS OPERATION PERFORMED FOR ANY CONDITION IN ITEM 107 OR 112? IF YES, LIST TYPE OF OPERATION AND DATE.

PHYSICIAN'S CERTIFICATION

114. I CERTIFY THAT TO THE BEST OF MY KNOWLEDGE DEATH OCCURRED AT THE HOUR, DATE AND PLACE STATED FROM THE CAUSES STATED.	115. SIGNATURE AND TITLE OF CERTIFIER	116. LICENSE NO.	117. DATE MM/DD/CCYY
DECEDENT ATTENDED SINCE MM/DD/CCYY / DECEDENT LAST SEEN ALIVE MM/DD/CCYY	▶		
	118. TYPE ATTENDING PHYSICIAN'S NAME, MAILING ADDRESS + ZIP		

CORONER'S USE ONLY

I CERTIFY THAT IN MY OPINION DEATH OCCURRED AT THE HOUR, DATE AND PLACE STATED FROM THE CAUSES STATED.	120. INJURY AT WORK [ ] YES [ ] NO	121. INJURY DATE MM/DD/CCYY	122. HOUR	123. PLACE OF INJURY
119. MANNER OF DEATH	124. DESCRIBE HOW INJURY OCCURRED (EVENTS WHICH RESULTED IN INJURY)			
[ ] NATURAL [ ] SUICIDE [ ] HOMICIDE [ ] ACCIDENT [X] PENDING INVESTIGATION [ ] COULD NOT BE DETERMINED				

125. LOCATION (STREET AND NUMBER OR LOCATION AND CITY AND ZIP CODE)

126. SIGNATURE OF CORONER OR DEPUTY CORONER	127. DATE MM/DD/CCYY	128. TYPED NAME, TITLE OF CORONER OR DEPUTY CORONER
9530 ▶ Rachel Zaragoza	06/04/1996	Rachel Zaragoza Deputy Coroner

STATE REGISTRAR

A	B	C	D	E	F	G	H	FAX AUTH. #	CENSUS TRACT

AMENDMENT OF MEDICAL AND HEALTH DATA—DEATH

STATE FILE NUMBER	USE BLACK INK ONLY—NO ERASURES, WHITEOUT, OR ALTERATIONS	3961903046 5
		LOCAL REGISTRATION DISTRICT AND CERTIFICATE NUMBER

STATE/LOCAL REGISTRAR USE ONLY	1	2	3

TYPE OR PRINT IN BLACK INK ONLY

PART I — INFORMATION TO LOCATE RECORD

1. NAME—FIRST (GIVEN)	2. MIDDLE	3. LAST (FAMILY)	4. SEX
RAYMOND	NEIL	COMBS JR.	Male

5. DATE OF EVENT—MM/DD/CCYY	6. CITY OF OCCURENCE	7. COUNTY OF OCCURRENCE	
06/02/1996	Glendale	Los Angeles	1 OF 2

PART II — INFORMATION AS IT APPEARS ON RECORD

107. DEATH WAS CAUSED BY ENTER ONLY ONE CAUSE PER LINE FOR A, B, C, AND D)

			TIME INTERVAL BETWEEN ONSET AND DEATH	108. DEATH REPORTED TO CORONER
IMMEDIATE CAUSE	(A)	Deferred		[X] YES [ ] NO
				REFERRAL NUMBER 96-04224
	(B)			109. BIOPSY PERFORMED [ ] YES [ ] NO
	(C)			110. AUTOPSY PERFORMED [X] YES [ ] NO
DUE TO	(D)			111. USED IN DETERMINING CAUSE [ ] YES [ ] NO

112. OTHER SIGNIFICANT CONDITIONS CONTRIBUTING TO DEATH BUT NOT RELATED TO CAUSE GIVEN IN 107

113. WAS OPERATION PERFORMED FOR ANY CONDITION IN ITEM 107 or 112? IF YES, LIST TYPE OF OPERATION AND DATE.

119. MANNER OF DEATH	120. INJURY AT WORK	121. INJURY DATE—MM/DD/CCYY	122. HOUR	123. PLACE OF INJURY
[ ] NATURAL [ ] SUICIDE [ ] HOMICIDE	[ ] YES [ ] NO			
[ ] ACCIDENT [X] PENDING INVESTIGATION [ ] COULD NOT BE DETERMINED	124. DESCRIBE HOW INJURY OCCURED (EVENTS WHICH RESULTED IN INJURY)			

125. LOCATION (STREET AND NUMBER OR LOCATION AND CITY AND ZIP CODE)

PART III — INFORMATION AS IT SHOULD APPEAR

107. DEATH WAS CAUSED BY ENTER ONLY ONE CAUSE PER LINE FOR A, B, C, AND D)

			TIME INTERVAL BETWEEN ONSET AND DEATH	108. DEATH REPORTED TO CORONER
IMMEDIATE CAUSE	(A)	HANGING	Mins	[X] YES [ ] NO
				REFERRAL NUMBER 96-04224
	(B)			109. BIOPSY PERFORMED [ ] YES [X] NO
	(C)			110. AUTOPSY PERFORMED [X] YES [ ] NO
DUE TO	(D)			111. USED IN DETERMINING CAUSE [X] YES [ ] NO

112. OTHER SIGNIFICANT CONDITIONS CONTRIBUTING TO DEATH BUT NOT RELATED TO CAUSE GIVEN IN 107
None

113. WAS OPERATION PERFORMED FOR ANY CONDITION IN ITEM 107 or 112? IF YES, LIST TYPE OF OPERATION AND DATE.
No

119. MANNER OF DEATH	120. INJURY AT WORK	121. INJURY DATE—MM/DD/CCYY	122. HOUR	123. PLACE OF INJURY
[ ] NATURAL [X] SUICIDE [ ] HOMICIDE	[ ] YES [X] NO	06/02/1996	Unk.	Hospital Room
[ ] ACCIDENT [ ] PENDING INVESTIGATION [ ] COULD NOT BE DETERMINED	124. DESCRIBE HOW INJURY OCCURRED (EVENTS WHICH RESULTED IN INJURY) With sheet			

125. LOCATION (STREET AND NUMBER OR LOCATION AND CITY AND ZIP CODE)
1509 East Wilson Terrace, Glendale, CA 91206

DECLARATION OF CERTIFYING PHYSICIAN OR CORONER

I HEREBY DECLARE UNDER PENALTY OF PERJURY THAT THE ABOVE INFORMATION IS TRUE AND CORRECT TO THE BEST OF MY KNOWLEDGE.

8. SIGNATURE OF CERTIFYING PHYSICIAN OR CORONER	9. DATE SIGNED—MM/DD/CCYY	10. TYPED OR PRINTED NAME AND DEGREE/TITLE OF CERTIFIER
▶ Christopher Rogers	7-25-96	CHRISTOPHER B. ROGERS, M.D. DME

11. ADDRESS—STREET AND NUMBER	12. CITY	13. STATE	14. ZIP CODE
1104 North Mission Road	Los Angeles	CA	90033

STATE/LOCAL REGISTRAR USE ONLY

15. OFFICE OF STATE REGISTRAR OR SIGNATURE OF LOCAL REGISTRAR	16. DATE ACCEPTED FOR REGISTRATION—MM/DD/CCYY
▶	08/05/1996

STATE OF CALIFORNIA, DEPARTMENT OF HEALTH SERVICES, OFFICE OF STATE REGISTRAR

VS-24 B (1/94)
93 24457

STATE OF CALIFORNIA
CERTIFICATION OF VITAL RECORD

COUNTY OF LOS ANGELES • REGISTRAR-RECORDER/COUNTY CLERK

CERTIFICATE OF DEATH
STATE OF CALIFORNIA

0190-009987

STATE FILE NUMBER				LOCAL REGISTRATION DISTRICT AND CERTIFICATE NUMBER
1A. NAME OF DECEDENT—FIRST John aka: Jackie	1B. MIDDLE Leslie	1C. LAST Coogan Coogan	2A. DATE OF DEATH (MONTH, DAY, YEAR) March 1, 1984	2B. HOUR 1337

3. SEX Male	4. RACE/ETHNICITY White	5. SPANISH/HISPANIC NO	6. DATE OF BIRTH October 26, 1914	7. AGE 69 YEARS	IF UNDER 1 YEAR MONTHS DAYS	IF UNDER 24 HOURS HOURS MINUTES

DECEDENT PERSONAL DATA

8. BIRTHPLACE OF DECEDENT (STATE OR...) California	9. NAME AND BIRTHPLACE OF FATHER John H. Coogan, New York	10. BIRTH NAME AND BIRTHPLACE OF MOTHER Lillian Dolovier, California

11. CITIZEN OF WHAT COUNTRY United States	12. SOCIAL SECURITY NUMBER 547-12-5128	13. MARITAL STATUS Married	14. NAME OF SURVIVING SPOUSE (IF WIFE, ENTER...) Dorothea Hanson

15. PRIMARY OCCUPATION Actor	16. NUMBER OF YEARS THIS OCCUPATION 65 Yrs.	17. EMPLOYER (IF SELF-EMPLOYED, SO STATE) Self-Employed	18. KIND OF INDUSTRY OR BUSINESS Entertainment

USUAL RESIDENCE

19A. USUAL RESIDENCE—STREET ADDRESS (STR... AND NUMBER OR LOCATION) 1250 East Racquet Club Road	19B.	19C. CITY OR TOWN Palm Springs

19D. COUNTY Riverside	19E. STATE California	20. NAME AND ADDRESS OF INFORMANT—RELATIONSHIP Mrs. Dorothea Coogan = Wife 1050 E. Racquet Club Road Palm Springs, California 92262

PLACE OF DEATH

21A. PLACE OF DEATH Santa Monica Medical Center	21B. COUNTY Los Angeles	
21C. STREET ADDRESS (STREET AND NUMBER OR LOCATION) 1225 15th Street	21D. CITY OR TOWN Santa Monica	

CAUSE OF DEATH

22. DEATH WAS CAUSED BY: IMMEDIATE CAUSE (ENTER ONLY ONE CAUSE PER LINE FOR A, B, AND C)		APPROXIMATE INTERVAL BETWEEN ONSET AND DEATH	
CONDITIONS, IF ANY, WHICH GAVE RISE TO THE IMMEDIATE CAUSE, STATING THE UNDERLYING CAUSE LAST	(A) Cardiac arrest	3hn	24. WAS DEATH REPORTED TO CORONER? NO
	(B) Arteriosclerotic heart disease	20yr	25. WAS BIOPSY PERFORMED? NO
	(C) Hypertensive cardiovascular disease	25yr	26. WAS AUTOPSY PERFORMED? NO

23. OTHER CONDITIONS CONTRIBUTING BUT NOT RELATED TO THE IMMEDIATE CAUSE OF DEATH Chronic Renal failure	27. WAS OPERATION PERFORMED FOR ANY CONDITION IN ITEMS 22 OR 23? TYPE OF OPERATION arteriovenous fistule DATE May 1981

PHYSICIAN'S CERTIFICATION

28A. I CERTIFY THAT DEATH OCCURRED AT THE HOUR, DATE AND PLACE STATED FROM THE CAUSES STATED. I ATTENDED DECEDENT SINCE (ENTER MO. DA. YR.) July 7, 1977	I LAST SAW DECEDENT ALIVE (ENTER MO. DA. YR.) Mar 1, 1984	28B. PHYSICIAN—SIGNATURE AND DEGREE OR TITLE David L. Hartenbower MD	28C. DATE SIGNED Mar 2, 1984	28D. PHYSICIAN'S LICENSE NUMBER C30071
		28E. TYPE PHYSICIAN'S NAME AND ADDRESS David L. Hartenbower, M.D. 1260 15th St.; Santa Monica, Ca.		

INJURY INFORMATION

29. SPECIFY ACCIDENT, SUICIDE, ETC.	30. PLACE OF INJURY	31. INJURY AT WORK	32A. DATE OF INJURY—MONTH DAY YEAR	32B. HOUR
33. LOCATION (STREET AND NUMBER OR LOCATION AND CITY OR TOWN)		34. DESCRIBE HOW INJURY OCCURRED (EVENTS WHICH RESULTED IN INJURY)		

CORONER'S USE ONLY

35A. I CERTIFY THAT DEATH OCCURRED AT THE HOUR, DATE AND PLACE STATED FROM THE CAUSES STATED, AS REQUIRED BY LAW I HAVE HELD AN (INQUEST-INVESTIGATION) 10	35B. CORONER—SIGNATURE AND DEGREE OR TITLE	35C. DATE SIGNED

36. DISPOSITION Burial	37. DATE—MONTH, DAY, YEAR 3/5/84	38. NAME AND ADDRESS OF CEM 5835 W. Slauson Ave Holy Cross Cemetery Culver City, Calif.	39. EMBALMER'S LICENSE NUMBER AND SIGNATURE #949 David L. Meyer

40A. NAME OF FUNERAL DIRECTOR (OR PERSON ACTING AS SUCH) Cunningham & O'Connor – L.A.	40B. LICENSE NO. F-13	41. LOCAL REGISTRAR...	42... MAR 2 1984

STATE REGISTRAR

A.	B.	C.	D.	E.	F.

VS-11 (6-82)

This is to certify that this document is a true copy of the official record filed with the Registrar-Recorder/County Clerk.

CONNY B. McCORMACK
Registrar-Recorder/County Clerk

DEC 0 7 2000
19-149010

This copy not valid unless prepared on engraved border displaying the Seal and Signature of the Registrar-Recorder/County Clerk.

ANY ALTERATION OR ERASURE VOIDS THIS CERTIFICATE

STATE OF CALIFORNIA
CERTIFICATION OF VITAL RECORD

COUNTY OF LOS ANGELES

DEPARTMENT OF HEALTH SERVICES

CERTIFICATE OF DEATH

STATE OF CALIFORNIA
USE BLACK INK ONLY/NO ERASURES, WHITEOUTS OR ALTERATIONS
VS-11 (REV. 7/97)

STATE FILE NUMBER		LOCAL REGISTRATION NUMBER

	1. NAME OF DECEDENT—FIRST (GIVEN)	2. MIDDLE	3. LAST (FAMILY)
	ELLEN	–	CORBY

DECEDENT PERSONAL DATA

4. DATE OF BIRTH MM/DD/CCYY	5. AGE YRS.	IF UNDER 1 YEAR MONTHS / DAYS	IF UNDER 24 HOURS HOURS / MINUTES	6. SEX	7. DATE OF DEATH MM/DD/CCYY	8. HOUR
06/03/1911	87			Fem.	04/14/1999	2320

9. STATE OF BIRTH	10. SOCIAL SECURITY NO.	11. MILITARY SERVICE	12. MARITAL STATUS	13. EDUCATION—YEARS COMPLETED
WI	568-01-3291	Yes / X No / UNK	Married	Unknown

14. RACE	15. HISPANIC—SPECIFY		16. USUAL EMPLOYER
White	Yes /	X No	Self employed

17. OCCUPATION	18. KIND OF BUSINESS	19. YEARS IN OCCUPATION
Actress	Entertainment	Unknown

USUAL RESIDENCE

20. RESIDENCE—(STREET AND NUMBER OR LOCATION)
9026 Harrett St.

21. CITY	22. COUNTY	23. ZIP CODE	24. YRS IN COUNTY	25. STATE OR FOREIGN COUNTRY
Los Angeles	Los Angeles	90069	70	California

INFORMANT

26. NAME, RELATIONSHIP	27. MAILING ADDRESS (STREET AND NUMBER OR RURAL ROUTE NUMBER, CITY OR TOWN, STATE, ZIP)
Stella Lucheta - Friend	9026 Harrett Street, L.A., CA 90069

SPOUSE AND PARENT INFORMATION

28. NAME OF SURVIVING SPOUSE—FIRST	29. MIDDLE	30. LAST (MAIDEN NAME)
–		

31. NAME OF FATHER—FIRST	32. MIDDLE	33. LAST	34. BIRTH STATE
Fred	–	Hansen	Denmark

35. NAME OF MOTHER—FIRST	36. MIDDLE	37. LAST (MAIDEN)	38. BIRTH STATE
Dagmar	–	Nelleman	Denmark

FUNERAL DIRECTOR AND LOCAL REGISTRAR

39. DATE MM/DD/CCYY	40. PLACE OF FINAL DISPOSITION
04/23/1999	Forest Lawn Memorial Park, 1712 S. Glendale Ave.,Glendale, CA 91205

41. TYPE OF DISPOSITION(S)	42. SIGNATURE OF EMBALMER	43. LICENSE NO.
CR/BU	▶ Robert P Haggetty	5249

44. NAME OF FUNERAL DIRECTOR	45. LICENSE NO.	46. SIGNATURE OF LOCAL REGISTRAR	47. DATE MM/DD/CCYY
Forest Lawn Mortuary/Glendale	FD 656	▶ Mark Loman MS	04/21/1999

PLACE OF DEATH

101. PLACE OF DEATH	102. IF HOSPITAL, SPECIFY ONE:	103. FACILITY OTHER THAN HOSPITAL:	104. COUNTY
MOTION PICTURE HOSPITAL	X IP / ER/OP / DOA	CONV. HOSP. / RES. CARE / OTHER	LOS ANGELES

105. STREET ADDRESS—(STREET AND NUMBER OR LOCATION)	106. CITY
23388 MULHOLLAND DRIVE	WOODLAND HILLS

CAUSE OF DEATH

107. DEATH WAS CAUSED BY: (ENTER ONLY ONE CAUSE PER LINE FOR A, B, C, AND D)		TIME INTERVAL BETWEEN ONSET AND DEATH	
IMMEDIATE CAUSE	(A) CARDIOPULMONARY FAILURE	15 MINS	108. DEATH REPORTED TO CORONER Yes / X No — REFERRAL NUMBER
DUE TO	(B) ISCHEMIC ENTEROCOLITIS	12 HRS	109. BIOPSY PERFORMED Yes / X No
DUE TO	(C) ARTERIOSCLEROSIS	12 YRS	110. AUTOPSY PERFORMED Yes / X No
DUE TO	(D)		111. USED IN DETERMINING CAUSE Yes / No

112. OTHER SIGNIFICANT CONDITIONS CONTRIBUTING TO DEATH BUT NOT RELATED TO CAUSE GIVEN IN 107
CHRONIC STROKE, DIABETES MELLITUS

113. WAS OPERATION PERFORMED FOR ANY CONDITION IN ITEM 107 OR 112? IF YES, LIST TYPE OF OPERATION AND DATE.
NO

PHYSICIAN'S CERTIFICATION

114. I CERTIFY THAT TO THE BEST OF MY KNOWLEDGE DEATH OCCURRED AT THE HOUR, DATE AND PLACE STATED FROM THE CAUSES STATED. DECEDENT ATTENDED SINCE MM/DD/CCYY / DECEDENT LAST SEEN ALIVE MM/DD/CCYY	115. SIGNATURE AND TITLE OF CERTIFIER	116. LICENSE NO.	117. DATE MM/DD/CCYY
03/16/1999 / 04/14/1999	▶ Humayun MD	A39209	04/16/1999

118. TYPE ATTENDING PHYSICIAN'S NAME, MAILING ADDRESS, ZIP
SAEED HUMAYUN,MD 23388 MULHOLLAND DR.,WOODLAND HILLS,CA 91364

CORONER'S USE ONLY

119. I CERTIFY THAT IN MY OPINION DEATH OCCURRED AT THE HOUR, DATE AND PLACE STATED FROM THE CAUSES STATED. MANNER OF DEATH	120. INJURY AT WORK	121. INJURY DATE MM/DD/CCYY	122. HOUR	123. PLACE OF INJURY
NATURAL / SUICIDE / HOMICIDE / ACCIDENT / PENDING INVESTIGATION / COULD NOT BE DETERMINED	Yes / No			

124. DESCRIBE HOW INJURY OCCURRED (EVENTS WHICH RESULTED IN INJURY)

125. LOCATION (STREET AND NUMBER OR LOCATION AND CITY, ZIP)

126. SIGNATURE OF CORONER OR DEPUTY CORONER	127. DATE MM/DD/CCYY	128. TYPED NAME, TITLE OF CORONER OR DEPUTY CORONER
▶		

STATE REGISTRAR

A	B	C	D	E	F	G	H	FAX AUTH. #	CENSUS TRACT
								273/27102	090228273

This is a true certified copy of the record filed in the County of Los Angeles
Department of Health Services if it bears the Registrar's signature in purple ink.

Mark Loman   263   DATE ISSUED APR 27 1999

Director of Health Service and Registrar

This copy not valid unless prepared on engraved border displaying seal and signature of Registrar.

DE LA RUE   **ANY ALTERATION OR ERASURE VOIDS THIS CERTIFICATE**

CERTIFICATE OF DEATH
STATE OF CALIFORNIA
USE BLACK INK ONLY/NO ERASURES, WHITEOUTS OR ALTERATIONS
VS-11 (REV. 7/93)

STATE FILE NUMBER

LOCAL REGISTRATION NUMBER

DECEDENT PERSONAL DATA

1. NAME OF DECEDENT—FIRST (GIVEN)	2. MIDDLE	3. LAST (FAMILY)
Joseph	C	Cotten

4. DATE OF BIRTH MM/DD/CCYY	5. AGE YRS.	IF UNDER 1 YEAR MONTHS / DAYS	IF UNDER 24 HOURS HOURS / MINUTES	6. SEX	7. DATE OF DEATH MM/DD/CCYY	8. HOUR
05/15/1905	88			M	02/06/1994	0635

9. STATE OF BIRTH	10. SOCIAL SECURITY NO.	11. MILITARY SERVICE	12. MARITAL STATUS	13. EDUCATION —YEARS COMPLETED
VA	123-01-7286	19___ TO 19___ [X] NONE	MARRIED	16

14. RACE	15. HISPANIC— SPECIFY	16. USUAL EMPLOYER
WHITE	[ ] YES _____ [X] NO	SELF EMPLOYED

17. OCCUPATION	18. KIND OF BUSINESS	19. YEARS IN OCCUPATION
ACTOR	MOTION PICTURES	70

USUAL RESIDENCE

20. RESIDENCE—STREET AND NUMBER OR LOCATION
6363 WILSHIRE BLVD #600

21. CITY	22. COUNTY	23. ZIP CODE	24. YRS IN COUNTY	25. STATE OR FOREIGN COUNTRY
LOS ANGELES	LOS ANGELES	90048	2	CALIFORNIA

INFORMANT

26. NAME, RELATIONSHIP	27. MAILING ADDRESS (STREET AND NUMBER OR RURAL ROUTE NUMBER, CITY OR TOWN, STATE, ZIP)
PATRICIA M. COTTEN - WIFE	6363 WILSHIRE BLVD. #600

SPOUSE AND PARENT INFORMATION

28. NAME OF SURVIVING SPOUSE—FIRST	29. MIDDLE	30. LAST (MAIDEN NAME)
PATRICIA	-	MEDINA

31. NAME OF FATHER—FIRST	32. MIDDLE	33. LAST	34. BIRTH STATE
JOSEPH	C	COTTEN	NC

35. NAME OF MOTHER—FIRST	36. MIDDLE	37. LAST (MAIDEN)	38. BIRTH STATE
SALLY	-	WILLSON	VA

DISPOSITION(S)

39. DATE MM/DD/CCYY	40. PLACE OF FINAL DISPOSITION
02/11/1994	BLANDFORD CEMETERY - PETERSBURG, VA

FUNERAL DIRECTOR AND LOCAL REGISTRAR

41. TYPE OF DISPOSITION(S)	42. SIGNATURE OF EMBALMER	43. LICENSE NO.
CR/TR/BU	▶ NOT EMBALMED	NONE

44. NAME OF FUNERAL DIRECTOR	45. LICENSE NO.	46. SIGNATURE OF LOCAL REGISTRAR	47. DATE MM/DD/CCYY
Inglewood Cemetery Mortuary	FD 1101	▶ Robert C. ___	02/10/1994

PLACE OF DEATH

101. PLACE OF DEATH	102. IF HOSPITAL, SPECIFY ONE:	103. FACILITY OTHER THAN HOSPITAL:	104. COUNTY
Residence	[ ] IP [ ] ER/OP [ ] DOA	[ ] CONV. HOSP. [X] RES. [ ] OTHER	Los Angeles

105. STREET ADDRESS—STREET AND NUMBER OR LOCATION	106. CITY
10590 Wilshire Blvd. #1202	Los Angeles

CAUSE OF DEATH

107. DEATH WAS CAUSED BY: (ENTER ONLY ONE CAUSE PER LINE FOR A, B, C AND D)	TIME INTERVAL BETWEEN ONSET AND DEATH	108. DEATH REPORTED TO CORONER
IMMEDIATE CAUSE (A) PNEUMONIA	10DAYS	[ ] YES [X] NO — REFERRAL NUMBER
DUE TO (B) COPD	10YRS	109. BIOPSY PERFORMED [ ] YES [X] NO
DUE TO (C)		110. AUTOPSY PERFORMED [ ] YES [X] NO
DUE TO (D)		111. USED IN DETERMINING CAUSE [ ] YES [X] NO

112. OTHER SIGNIFICANT CONDITIONS CONTRIBUTING TO DEATH BUT NOT RELATED TO CAUSE GIVEN IN 107
CARCINOMA OF LARYNX, PROSTATE CANCER

113. WAS OPERATION PERFORMED FOR ANY CONDITION IN ITEM 107 OR 112? IF YES, LIST TYPE OF OPERATION AND DATE.
LARYNGECTOMY 1990

PHYSICIAN'S CERTIFICATION

114. I CERTIFY THAT TO THE BEST OF MY KNOWLEDGE DEATH OCCURRED AT THE HOUR, DATE AND PLACE STATED FROM THE CAUSES STATED.	115. SIGNATURE AND TITLE OF CERTIFIER	116. LICENSE NO.	117. DATE MM/DD/CCYY
DECEDENT ATTENDED SINCE MM/DD/CCYY: 1963 / DECEDENT LAST SEEN ALIVE MM/DD/CCYY: 02/05/1994	▶ Douglas L. Forde MD	A 10268	2-9-94

118. TYPE ATTENDING PHYSICIAN'S NAME, MAILING ADDRESS + ZIP
DOUGLAS L. FORDE MD. 2001 SANTA MONICA BLVD. S.M., CA 90404

CORONER'S USE ONLY

119. I CERTIFY THAT IN MY OPINION DEATH OCCURRED AT THE HOUR, DATE AND PLACE STATED FROM THE CAUSES STATED.	120. INJURY AT WORK [ ] YES [ ] NO	121. INJURY DATE MM/DD/CCYY	122. HOUR	123. PLACE OF INJURY

119. MANNER OF DEATH	124. DESCRIBE HOW INJURY OCCURRED (EVENTS WHICH RESULTED IN INJURY)
[ ] NATURAL [ ] SUICIDE [ ] HOMICIDE [ ] ACCIDENT [ ] PENDING INVESTIGATION [ ] COULD NOT BE DETERMINED	

125. LOCATION (STREET AND NUMBER OR LOCATION AND CITY AND ZIP CODE)

126. SIGNATURE OF CORONER OR DEPUTY CORONER	127. DATE MM/DD/CCYY	128. TYPED NAME, TITLE OF CORONER OR DEPUTY CORONER
▶		

13

STATE REGISTRAR

A	B	C	D	E	F	G	H	FAX AUTH. #	CENSUS TRACT

STATE OF CALIFORNIA
CERTIFICATION OF VITAL RECORD

COUNTY OF LOS ANGELES • REGISTRAR-RECORDER/COUNTY CLERK

CERTIFICATE OF DEATH

STATE OF CALIFORNIA—DEPARTMENT OF PUBLIC HEALTH

7097-008675

STATE FILE NUMBER   LOCAL REGISTRATION DISTRICT AND CERTIFICATE NUMBER

DECEDENT / PERSONAL DATA

1A. NAME OF DECEASED — FIRST NAME: Wallace	1B. MIDDLE NAME: Maynard	1C. LAST NAME: Cox
2A. DATE OF DEATH — MONTH, DAY, YEAR: February 15, 1973	2B. HOUR: 0800	HRS
3. SEX: Male	4. COLOR OR RACE: Caucasian	5. BIRTHPLACE (STATE OR FOREIGN COUNTRY): Michigan
6. DATE OF BIRTH: December 6, 1924	7. AGE (LAST BIRTHDAY): 48 YEARS	IF UNDER 1 YEAR / IF UNDER 24 HOURS
8. NAME AND BIRTHPLACE OF FATHER: Douglas Cox; Michigan	9. MAIDEN NAME AND BIRTHPLACE OF MOTHER: Eleanor Blake; Michigan	AMENDED
10. CITIZEN OF WHAT COUNTRY: United States	11. SOCIAL SECURITY NUMBER: No Record Available	12. MARRIED, NEVER MARRIED, WIDOWED DIVORCED (SPECIFY): married
13. NAME OF SURVIVING SPOUSE (IF WIFE, ENTER MAIDEN NAME): Patricia Tiernan		
14. LAST OCCUPATION: Actor	15. NUMBER OF YEARS IN THIS OCCUPATION: 20	16. NAME OF LAST EMPLOYING COMPANY OR FIRM (IF SELF EMPLOYED, SO STATE): National Broadcasting Co.
17. KIND OF INDUSTRY OR BUSINESS: Radio & Television		

PLACE OF DEATH

18A. PLACE OF DEATH — NAME OF HOSPITAL OR OTHER IN-PATIENT FACILITY	18B. STREET ADDRESS — (STREET AND NUMBER, OR LOCATION): 2928 Roscomare Road	18C. INSIDE CITY CORPORATE LIMITS (SPECIFY YES OR NO): Yes
18D. CITY OR TOWN: Los Angeles	18E. COUNTY: Los Angeles	18F. LENGTH OF STAY IN COUNTY OF DEATH: 10 YEARS / 18G. LENGTH OF STAY IN CALIFORNIA: 10 YEARS

USUAL RESIDENCE (IF DEATH OCCURRED IN INSTITUTION, ENTER RESIDENCE BEFORE ADMISSION)

19A. USUAL RESIDENCE — STREET ADDRESS (STREET AND NUMBER OR LOCATION): 2928 Roscomare Road	19B. INSIDE CITY CORPORATE LIMITS (SPECIFY YES OR NO): yes	20. NAME AND MAILING ADDRESS OF INFORMANT: Mrs. Wallace M. Cox, 2928 Roscomare Road, Los Angeles, Cal.
19C. CITY OR TOWN: Los Angeles	19D. COUNTY: Los Angeles	19E. STATE: California

PHYSICIAN'S OR CORONER'S CERTIFICATION

21A. CORONER: ... Investigation of Inquest	21B. PHYSICIAN: ... FROM / TO / AND	21C. PHYSICIAN OR CORONER — SIGNATURE AND DEGREE OR TITLE: Harold ... DEPUTY
21D. ADDRESS: ... RD. LOS ANGELES, CALIF. 90033	21E. DATE SIGNED: 2-15-73	21F. PHYSICIAN'S CALIFORNIA LICENSE NUMBER

FUNERAL DIRECTOR AND LOCAL REGISTRAR

22A. SPECIFY BURIAL, ENTOMBMENT OR CREMATION: Cremation	22B. DATE: Feb. 16, 1973	23. NAME OF CEMETERY OR CREMATORY: Odd Fellows Crematory
24. EMBALMER — SIGNATURE (IF BODY EMBALMED): LICENSE NUMBER 3166		
25. NAME OF FUNERAL DIRECTOR (OR PERSON ACTING AS SUCH): Cunningham & O'Connor, Hollywood	26. IF NOT CERTIFIED BY CORONER, WAS THIS DEATH REPORTED TO CORONER? (SPECIFY YES OR NO)	27. LOCAL REGISTRAR — SIGNATURE: ... MD
28. DATE ACCEPTED FOR REGISTRATION BY LOCAL REGISTRAR: FEB 16 1973		

MEDICAL AND HEALTH DATA

CAUSE OF DEATH

29. PART I. DEATH WAS CAUSED BY: IMMEDIATE CAUSE (A)	Deferred	APPROXIMATE INTERVAL BETWEEN ONSET AND DEATH
CONDITIONS, IF ANY, WHICH GAVE RISE TO THE IMMEDIATE CAUSE (A), STATING THE UNDERLYING CAUSE LAST — DUE TO, OR AS A CONSEQUENCE OF (B)		
DUE TO, OR AS A CONSEQUENCE OF (C)		
30. PART II. OTHER SIGNIFICANT CONDITIONS — CONTRIBUTING TO DEATH BUT NOT RELATED TO THE IMMEDIATE CAUSE GIVEN IN PART I.	31. WAS OPERATION OR BIOPSY PERFORMED FOR ANY CONDITION IN ITEMS 29 OR 30?	32A. AUTOPSY: Yes / 32B. IF YES, WERE FINDINGS CONSIDERED IN DETERMINING CAUSE OF DEATH?

INJURY INFORMATION

33. SPECIFY ACCIDENT, SUICIDE OR HOMICIDE	34. PLACE OF INJURY	35. INJURY AT WORK (SPECIFY YES OR NO)
36A. DATE OF INJURY — MONTH DAY YEAR	36B. HOUR	
37A. PLACE OF INJURY (STREET AND NUMBER OR LOCATION AND CITY OR TOWN)	37B. DISTANCE FROM PLACE OF INJURY TO USUAL RESIDENCE — ITEM 19: MILES	38. WERE LABORATORY TESTS DONE FOR DRUGS OR TOXIC CHEMICALS (SPECIFY YES OR NO) / 39. WERE LABORATORY TESTS DONE FOR ALCOHOL? (SPECIFY YES OR NO)
40. DESCRIBE HOW INJURY OCCURRED (ENTER SEQUENCE OF EVENTS WHICH RESULTED IN INJURY, NATURE OF INJURY SHOULD BE ENTERED IN ITEM 20)		

STATE REGISTRAR

A	B	C	D	E	F

REV 11-68 Form VS-11

This is to certify that this document is a true copy of the official record filed with the Registrar-Recorder/County Clerk.

Conny B. McCormack

CONNY B. McCORMACK
Registrar-Recorder/County Clerk

APR 07 2000

19-552330

This copy not valid unless prepared on engraved border displaying the Seal and Signature of the Registrar-Recorder/County Clerk.

MIDWEST BANK NOTE COMPANY — ANY ALTERATION OR ERASURE VOIDS THIS CERTIFICATE

STATE OF CALIFORNIA
CERTIFICATION OF VITAL RECORD

COUNTY OF LOS ANGELES
DEPARTMENT OF HEALTH SERVICES

CERTIFICATE OF DEATH
STATE OF CALIFORNIA
USE BLACK INK ONLY / NO ERASURES, WHITEOUTS OR ALTERATIONS
VS-11 (REV 1/03)

STATE FILE NUMBER		LOCAL REGISTRATION NUMBER

DECEDENT'S PERSONAL DATA

1. NAME OF DECEDENT --- FIRST (Given)	2. MIDDLE	3. LAST (Family)
RICHARD	DONALD	CRENNA

AKA, ALSO KNOWN AS --- Include full AKA (FIRST, MIDDLE, LAST)	4. DATE OF BIRTH mm/dd/ccyy	5. AGE Yrs.	IF UNDER ONE YEAR Months / Days	IF UNDER 24 HOURS Hours / Minutes	6. SEX
---	11/30/1926	76			M

9. BIRTH STATE/FOREIGN COUNTRY	10. SOCIAL SECURITY NUMBER	11. EVER IN U.S. ARMED FORCES?	12. MARITAL STATUS (at Time of Death)	7. DATE OF DEATH mm/dd/ccyy	8. HOUR (24 Hours)
CA	567-20-8482	[X] YES [ ] NO [ ] UNK	MARRIED	01/17/2003	1756

13. EDUCATION --- Highest Level/Degree (see worksheet on back)	14/15. WAS DECEDENT SPANISH/HISPANIC/LATINO? (If yes, see worksheet on back)	16. DECEDENT'S RACE --- Up to 3 races may be listed (see worksheet on back)
BACHELOR'S	[ ] YES [X] NO	WHITE

17. USUAL OCCUPATION --- Type of work for most of life. DO NOT USE RETIRED	18. KIND OF BUSINESS OR INDUSTRY (e.g., grocery store, road construction, employment agency, etc.)	19. YEARS IN OCCUPATION
ACTOR/DIRECTOR	ENTERTAINMENT	65

USUAL RESIDENCE

20. DECEDENT'S RESIDENCE (Street and number or location)
3951 VALLEY MEADOW RD

21. CITY	22. COUNTY/PROVINCE	23. ZIP CODE	24. YEARS IN COUNTY	25. STATE/FOREIGN COUNTRY
ENCINO	LOS ANGELES	91436	76	CA

INFORMANT

26. INFORMANT'S NAME, RELATIONSHIP	27. INFORMANT'S MAILING ADDRESS (Street and number or rural route number, city or town, state, ZIP)
PENNI CRENNA, WIFE	3951 VALLEY MEADOW RD ENCINO CA 91436

SPOUSE AND PARENT INFORMATION

28. NAME OF SURVIVING SPOUSE --- FIRST	29. MIDDLE	30. LAST (Maiden Name)
PENNI	---	SMITH

31. NAME OF FATHER --- FIRST	32. MIDDLE	33. LAST	34. BIRTH STATE
DOMENICK	ANTHONY	CRENNA	CA

35. NAME OF MOTHER --- FIRST	36. MIDDLE	37. LAST (Maiden)	38. BIRTH STATE
EDITH	JOSEPHINE	POLETTE	UT

FUNERAL DIRECTOR / LOCAL REGISTRAR

39. DISPOSITION DATE mm/dd/ccyy	40. PLACE OF FINAL DISPOSITION
01/24/2003	AT SEA OFF THE COAST OF LOS ANGELES

41. TYPE OF DISPOSITION(S)	42. SIGNATURE OF EMBALMER	43. LICENSE NUMBER
CR/SEA	NOT EMBALMED	---

44. NAME OF FUNERAL ESTABLISHMENT	45. LICENSE NUMBER	46. SIGNATURE OF LOCAL REGISTRAR	47. DATE mm/dd/ccyy
FOREST LAWN HOLLYWOOD HILLS	FD 904	Thomas L Garwhwate MCA	01/23/2003

PLACE OF DEATH

101. PLACE OF DEATH	102. IF HOSPITAL, SPECIFY ONE	103. IF OTHER THAN HOSPITAL, SPECIFY ONE
CEDARS SINAI MED CTR	[X] IP [ ] ER/OP [ ] DOA	[ ] Hospice [ ] Nursing Home/LTC [ ] Decedent's Home [ ] Other

104. COUNTY	105. FACILITY ADDRESS OR LOCATION WHERE FOUND (Street and number or location)	106. CITY
LOS ANGELES	8700 BEVERLY BLVD	LOS ANGELES

CAUSE OF DEATH

107. CAUSE OF DEATH	Enter the chain of events --- diseases, injuries, or complications --- that directly caused death. DO NOT enter terminal events such as cardiac arrest, respiratory arrest, or ventricular fibrillation without showing the etiology. DO NOT ABBREVIATE.	Time Interval Between Onset and Death	108. DEATH REPORTED TO CORONER?
IMMEDIATE CAUSE (Final disease or condition resulting in death) → (A)	CARCINOMA OF PANCREAS	(A↑) 2 MOS	[ ] YES [X] NO REFERRAL NUMBER
(B)		(B↑)	109. BIOPSY PERFORMED? [X] YES [ ] NO
Sequentially, list conditions, if any, leading to cause on Line A. Enter UNDERLYING CAUSE (disease or injury that initiated the events resulting in death) LAST. (C)		(C↑)	110. AUTOPSY PERFORMED? [ ] YES [X] NO
(D)		(D↑)	111. USED IN DETERMINING CAUSE? [ ] YES [X] NO

112. OTHER SIGNIFICANT CONDITIONS CONTRIBUTING TO DEATH BUT NOT RESULTING IN THE UNDERLYING CAUSE GIVEN IN 107
NONE

113. WAS OPERATION PERFORMED FOR ANY CONDITION IN ITEM 107 OR 112? (If yes, list type of operation and date.)	113A. IF FEMALE, PREGNANT IN LAST YEAR?
NO	[ ] YES [ ] NO [ ] UNK

PHYSICIAN'S CERTIFICATION

114. I CERTIFY THAT TO THE BEST OF MY KNOWLEDGE DEATH OCCURRED AT THE HOUR, DATE, AND PLACE STATED FROM THE CAUSES STATED.	115. SIGNATURE AND TITLE OF CERTIFIER	116. LICENSE NUMBER	117. DATE mm/dd/ccyy
Decedent Attended Since (A) 01/25/1983 / Decedent Last Seen Alive (B) 01/07/2003	Richard M Gold MD	G25597	01/21/2003

118. TYPE ATTENDING PHYSICIAN'S NAME, MAILING ADDRESS, ZIP CODE
RICHARD GOLD, MD 8631 W 3RD ST #815, LA, CA 90048

CORONER'S USE ONLY

119. I CERTIFY THAT IN MY OPINION DEATH OCCURRED AT THE HOUR, DATE, AND PLACE STATED FROM THE CAUSES STATED.		
MANNER OF DEATH [ ] Natural [ ] Accident [ ] Homicide [ ] Suicide [ ] Pending Investigation [ ] Could not be determined	120. INJURED AT WORK? [ ] YES [ ] NO [ ] UNK	121. INJURY DATE mm/dd/ccyy	122. HOUR (24 Hours)

123. PLACE OF INJURY (e.g. home, construction site, wooded area, etc.)

124. DESCRIBE HOW INJURY OCCURRED (Events which resulted in injury)

125. LOCATION OF INJURY (Street and number, or location, and city, and ZIP)

126. SIGNATURE OF CORONER / DEPUTY CORONER	127. DATE mm/dd/ccyy	128. TYPE NAME, TITLE OF CORONER / DEPUTY CORONER
		090591988

STATE REGISTRAR	A	B	C	D	E	FAX AUTH. #	CENSUS TRACT
						273/9529	

This is a true certified copy of the record filed in the County of Los Angeles
Department of Health Services if it bears the Registrar's signature in purple ink.

Thomas L Garwhwate
Director of Health Services and Registrar

DATE ISSUED 234 JAN 30 2003

This copy not valid unless prepared on engraved border displaying seal and signature of Registrar.

ANY ALTERATION OR ERASURE VOIDS THIS CERTIFICATE

STATE OF CONNECTICUT
DEPARTMENT OF PUBLIC HEALTH

CERTIFICATE OF DEATH

#10 corrected 15-SEP-03

STATE FILE NUMBER: 2003-07-013893

	FIRST	MIDDLE	LAST	SEX	DATE OF DEATH (Month, Day, Year)
1 DECEDENT'S LEGAL NAME	Hume		CRONYN	2 M	3 6/15/2003

COUNTY OF DEATH	TOWN OF DEATH	PLACE OF DEATH (Check One) Hospital:	OTHER ☐ Nursing Home ☒ Residence
4 Fairfield	5 Fairfield	6 ☐ ER/Outpatient ☐ DOA ☐ Inpatient	7 3100 Bronson Rd. ☐ Other

DATE OF BIRTH (Month, Day, Year)	AGE-Last Birthday	UNDER 1 YEAR Mos. Days	UNDER 1 DAY Hours Mins.	CITY & STATE OF BIRTH (Country if not U.S)	CITIZEN OF (Country)
8 7/18/1911	9 91	a.	b.	10 London, Ontario Canada	11 U.S.A.

☒ MARRIED ☐ NEVER MARRIED ☐ WIDOWED	LAST SPOUSE (If wife, give maiden name)	WAS DECEASED A VETERAN IF YES GIVE WAR	BRANCH OF SERVICE
12 ☐ DIVORCED ☐ LEGALLY SEPARATED	13 Susan Cooper Cronyn	14 ☐ YES ☒ NO	15

RESIDENCE STATE	COUNTY	TOWN	NUMBER AND STREET
16 Connecticut	17 Fairfield	18 Fairfield	19 3100 Bronson Rd.

FATHER – NAME FIRST	MIDDLE	LAST	MOTHER – NAME FIRST	MIDDLE	MAIDEN
20 Hume	Blake	Cronyn	21 Frances		Labatt

INFORMANT – NAME	MAILING ADDRESS	RELATIONSHIP TO DECEASED
22 Susan Cooper Cronyn	23 3100 Bronson Rd. Ffld.,CT	24 Wife

PART I. DEATH WAS CAUSED BY (ENTER ONLY ONE CAUSE PER LINE FOR (a), (b), AND (c))	APPROXIMATE INTERVAL BETWEEN ONSET AND DEATH
25 CONDITIONS, IF ANY WHICH GAVE RISE TO IMMEDIATE CAUSE (a) STATING THE UNDERLYING CAUSE LAST. IMMEDIATE CAUSE (a) Hemoptysis	3 weeks
DUE TO, OR AS A CONSEQUENCE OF: (b) Thrombocytopenia	weeks
DUE TO, OR AS A CONSEQUENCE OF: (c) metastatic prostate carcinoma	months.

PART II. OTHER SIGNIFICANT CONDITIONS: CONDITIONS CONTRIBUTING TO DEATH BUT NOT RELATED TO CAUSE	AUTOPSY	IF YES, were findings considered in determining cause of death:
26 — old age, Bronchiectasis	27 ☐ Y ☒ N	28

NURSE PRONOUNCEMENT TYPE OR PRINT NAME	DEGREE	SIGNATURE	DATE AND TIME PRONOUNCED
29 Stefanie Ehnot, A.S.N., RN		30 Stefanie J Ehnot RN	31 MONTH 06 DAY 15 YEAR 2003 TIME 808 ☒ A.M. ☐ P.M.

CERTIFICATION – PHYSICIAN	Mo. Day Year	Mo. Day Year	AND LAST SAW HIM/HER ALIVE ON	ACTUAL OR PRESUMED DATE AND TIME OF DEATH
32 I attended the deceased from	5-1-1998	TO 6-15-2003	33 Month 6-11-2003 Day Year	34 M.

WAS CASE REFERRED TO MEDICAL EXAMINER	SURGERY RELEVANT TO CONDITION REPORTED IN ITEM 25	THE DECEDENT WAS PRONOUNCED DEAD:
35 ☐ YES ☒ NO	36 (Name of Operation) 37 (Date Performed)	38 Month Day Year Time 6-15-03 808 ☒ A.M. ☐ P.M.

CERTIFIER – NAME (type or print) To the best of my knowledge, death occurred on the date and time and due to the causes stated	SIGNATURE	DEGREE OR TITLE
39 Warren Heller MD	40 Warren Heller MD	MD

MAILING – CERTIFIER (STREET)	(CITY OR TOWN)	(STATE) (ZIP)	DATE SIGNED (Month, Day, Year)
41 Warren Heller MD 4644 Main St Bpt, CT 06666			42 6/16/03

BURIAL, CREMATION, REMOVAL (Specify)	CEMETERY OR CREMATORY – NAME	LOCATION (CITY OR TOWN) (STATE)
43 Cremation	44 Mt. Grove Crematory	45 Bridgeport, CT

DATE (MONTH, DAY, YEAR)	FUNERAL HOME – NAME AND ADDRESS (STREET, CITY OR TOWN, STATE, ZIP)
46 6/17/03	47 Larson Funeral Home, 2496 North Ave. Bpt., CT

FUNERAL DIRECTOR OR EMBALMER – SIGNATURE	WAS BODY EMBALMED? ☐ YES ☒ NO	LICENSE NUMBER
48 Robert J. Carroll	49 IF YES, NAME OF EMBALMER:	50 2244

THIS CERTIFICATE RECEIVED FOR RECORD ON **JUN 1 7 2003** BY Elizabeth P Greene Asst. REGISTRAR

***************************** ADMINISTRATIVE USE ONLY *****************************

THE SEAL OF THE STATE OF CONNECTICUT IS AFFIXED TO CERTIFY THAT THE ABOVE IS A TRUE COPY OF A RECORD FILED WITH THE STATE OF CONNECTICUT DEPARTMENT OF PUBLIC HEALTH PURSUANT TO THE PROVISIONS OF THE GENERAL STATUTES OF CONNECTICUT.

Suzanne Speers, R.H.I.A., M.P.H.
Registrar of Vital Records
OCT 0 8 2003
Date of Issue

QUI TRANSTULIT SUSTINET

CERTIFICATION OF VITAL RECORD

COUNTY OF LOS ANGELES • REGISTRAR-RECORDER/COUNTY CLERK

CERTIFICATE OF DEATH
STATE OF CALIFORNIA
USE BLACK INK ONLY

39019053185

STATE FILE NUMBER			LOCAL REGISTRATION DISTRICT AND CERTIFICATE NUMBER

1A. NAME OF DECEDENT—FIRST (GIVEN): ROBERT	1B. MIDDLE: O.	1C. LAST (FAMILY): CUMMINGS	2A. DATE OF DEATH—MO, DAY, YR: December 2, 1990	2B. HOUR: 2027	3. SEX: M

DECEDENT PERSONAL DATA

4 RACE: WHITE	5. HISPANIC—SPECIFY: ☐ YES ____ [XX] NO	6. DATE OF BIRTH—MO, DAY, YR: JUNE 9, 1910	7. AGE IN YEARS: 80	IF UNDER 1 YEAR MONTHS DAYS	IF UNDER 24 HOURS HOURS MINUTES

8. STATE OF BIRTH: MO	9. CITIZEN OF WHAT COUNTRY: USA	10A. FULL NAME OF FATHER: CHARLES C. CUMMINGS	10B. STATE OF BIRTH: IN	11A. FULL MAIDEN NAME OF MOTHER: RUTH A. KRAFT	11B. STATE OF BIRTH: IN

12. MILITARY SERVICE? 19__ To 19__ [X] NONE	13. SOCIAL SECURITY NO.: 563-14-0218	14. MARITAL STATUS: MARRIED	15. NAME OF SURVIVING SPOUSE (IF WIFE, ENTER MAIDEN NAME): MARTHA JANE BURZYNSKI

16A. USUAL OCCUPATION: ACTOR	16B. USUAL KIND OF BUSINESS OR INDUSTRY: ENTERTAINMENT	16C. USUAL EMPLOYER: SELF EMPLOYED	16D. YEARS IN OCCUPATION: 68	17. EDUCATION YEARS COMPLETED: 15

USUAL RESIDENCE

18A. RESIDENCE—STREET AND NUMBER OR LOCATION: 14155 MAGNOLIA BLVD, APT 124	18B. CITY: SHERMAN OAKS	18C. ZIP CODE: 91423

18D. COUNTY: LOS ANGELES	18E. NUMBER OF YEARS IN THIS COUNTY: 50	18F. STATE OR FOREIGN COUNTRY: CALIFORNIA	20. NAME, RELATIONSHIP, MAILING ADDRESS AND ZIP CODE OF INFORMANT: MARTHA JANE CUMMINGS – WIFE 14155 MAGNOLIA BLVD. APT 124 SHERMAN OAKS, CA. 91423

PLACE OF DEATH

19A. PLACE OF DEATH: Motion Picture/TV Hosp.	19B. IF HOSPITAL, SPECIFY ONE: IP, ER/OP, DOA: IP	19C. COUNTY: Los Angeles

19D. STREET ADDRESS—STREET AND NUMBER OR LOCATION: 23388 Mulholland Drive	19E. CITY: Woodland Hills

TIME INTERVAL BETWEEN ONSET AND DEATH	22. WAS DEATH REPORTED TO CORONER? REFERRAL NUMBER: ☐ YES [X] NO

CAUSE OF DEATH

21. DEATH WAS CAUSED BY: (ENTER ONLY ONE CAUSE PER LINE FOR A, B, AND C)		
IMMEDIATE CAUSE (A) Cardiac Arrest	► 6 min.	23. WAS BIOPSY PERFORMED? [X] YES ☐ NO
DUE TO (B) Hypotension	► 10 hrs.	24A. WAS AUTOPSY PERFORMED? [X] YES ☐ NO
DUE TO (C) Thrombotic Thrombocytopenic Purpura	► 15 days	24B. WAS IT USED IN DETERMINING CAUSE OF DEATH?

25. OTHER SIGNIFICANT CONDITIONS CONTRIBUTING TO DEATH BUT NOT RELATED TO CAUSE GIVEN IN 21: Acute Interstitial Pneumonitis, Hepatitis, Renal Failure, Gangrene, GI Bleeding, Arterial Occlusion	26. WAS OPERATION PERFORMED FOR ANY CONDITION IN ITEM 21 OR 25? IF YES, LIST TYPE OF OPERATION AND DATE: Open Lung Biopsy 11/21/90

PHYSICIAN'S CERTIFICATION

I CERTIFY THAT TO THE BEST OF MY KNOWLEDGE DEATH OCCURRED AT THE HOUR, DATE AND PLACE STATED FROM THE CAUSES STATED.	27B. SIGNATURE AND DEGREE OR TITLE OF CERTIFIER: ► L. Brostoff M.D.	27C. CERTIFIER'S LICENSE NUMBER: G061694	27D. DATE SIGNED: 12/05/90

27A. DECEDENT ATTENDED SINCE MONTH, DAY, YEAR: 11/18/90	DECEDENT LAST SEEN ALIVE MONTH, DAY, YEAR: 12/02/90	27E. TYPE ATTENDING PHYSICIAN'S NAME AND ADDRESS: L. Brostoff, M.D. 23388 Mulholland Drive, Woodland Hills, CA 91364

CORONER'S USE ONLY

I CERTIFY THAT IN MY OPINION DEATH OCCURRED AT THE HOUR, DATE AND PLACE STATED FROM THE CAUSES STATED.	28A. SIGNATURE AND TITLE OF CORONER OR DEPUTY CORONER: ►	28B. DATE SIGNED

29. MANNER OF DEATH—specify one: natural, accident, suicide, homicide, pending investigation or could not be determined	30A. PLACE OF INJURY	30B. INJURY AT WORK: ☐ YES ☐ NO	30C. DATE OF INJURY MONTH, DAY, YEAR	31. HOUR

32. LOCATION (STREET AND NUMBER OR LOCATION AND CITY)	33. DESCRIBE HOW INJURY OCCURRED (EVENTS WHICH RESULTED IN INJURY)

FUNERAL DIRECTOR AND LOCAL REGISTRAR

34A. DISPOSITION(S): CR/BU	34B. PLACE OF FINAL DISPOSITION—NAME AND ADDRESS: FOREST LAWN MEMORIAL PARK 1712 S. GLENDALE AVE., GLENDALE, CA.	34C. DATE MO, DAY, YEAR: 12-6-1990	35A. SIGNATURE OF EMBALMER: Kay Morris	35B. LICENSE NUMBER: 7079

36A. NAME OF FUNERAL DIRECTOR (OR PERSON ACTING AS SUCH): FOREST LAWN GLENDALE	36B. LICENSE NO.: 656	37. SIGNATURE OF LOCAL REGISTRAR: ► Robert ...	38. REGISTRATION DATE: DEC 05 1990

STATE REGISTRAR

A.	B.	C.	D.	E.	F.	CENSUS TRACT

VS-11 (REV. 1-90)   MAKE NO ERASURES, WHITEOUTS, OR OTHER ALTERATIONS

01-9-2-055

STATE OF CALIFORNIA
CERTIFICATION OF VITAL RECORD

COUNTY OF LOS ANGELES
DEPARTMENT OF HEALTH SERVICES

CERTIFICATE OF DEATH
STATE OF CALIFORNIA
USE BLACK INK ONLY / NO ERASURES, WHITEOUTS OR ALTERATIONS
VS-11 (REV 1/03)

3 2004 9 04 512

STATE FILE NUMBER						LOCAL REGISTRATION NUMBER

DECEDENT'S PERSONAL DATA

1. NAME OF DECEDENT — FIRST (Given)	2. MIDDLE	3. LAST (Family)
RODNEY	–	DANGERFIELD

AKA, ALSO KNOWN AS — Include full AKA (FIRST, MIDDLE, LAST)	4. DATE OF BIRTH mm/dd/ccyy	5. AGE Yrs.	IF UNDER ONE YEAR (Months / Days)	IF UNDER 24 HOURS (Hours / Minutes)	6. SEX
JACK – ROY	11/22/1921	82			MALE

9. BIRTH STATE/FOREIGN COUNTRY	10. SOCIAL SECURITY NUMBER	11. EVER IN U.S. ARMED FORCES?	12. MARITAL STATUS (at Time of Death)	7. DATE OF DEATH mm/dd/ccyy	8. HOUR (24 Hours)
NEW YORK	105-16-7569	YES [X] NO UNK	MARRIED	10/05/2004	1320

13. EDUCATION — Highest Level/Degree	14/15. WAS DECEDENT SPANISH/HISPANIC/LATINO? (If yes, see worksheet on back)	16. DECEDENT'S RACE — Up to 3 races may be listed (see worksheet on back)
UNKNOWN	YES / [X] NO	CAUCASIAN

17. USUAL OCCUPATION — Type of work for most of life. DO NOT USE RETIRED	18. KIND OF BUSINESS OR INDUSTRY (e.g., grocery store, road construction, employment agency, etc.)		19. YEARS IN OCCUPATION
ENTERTAINER	ENTERTAINMENT	1 OF 2	40

USUAL RESIDENCE

20. DECEDENT'S RESIDENCE (Street and number or location)
10580 WILSHIRE BLVD.

21. CITY	22. COUNTY/PROVINCE	23. ZIP CODE	24. YEARS IN COUNTY	25. STATE/FOREIGN COUNTRY
LOS ANGELES	LOS ANGELES	90024	15	CA

INFORMANT

26. INFORMANT'S NAME, RELATIONSHIP	27. INFORMANT'S MAILING ADDRESS (Street and number or rural route number, city or town, state, ZIP)
DAVID PERMUT – FRIEND	9150 WILSHIRE BLVD. #401 LOS ANGELES, CA. 90024

SPOUSE AND PARENT INFORMATION

28. NAME OF SURVIVING SPOUSE — FIRST	29. MIDDLE	30. LAST (Maiden Name)
JOAN	SANDRA	CHILD

31. NAME OF FATHER — FIRST	32. MIDDLE	33. LAST	34. BIRTH STATE
PHILIP	–	COHEN	NY

35. NAME OF MOTHER — FIRST	36. MIDDLE	37. LAST (Maiden)	38. BIRTH STATE
DOROTHY	–	NITELBAUM	NY

FUNERAL DIRECTOR/LOCAL REGISTRAR

39. DISPOSITION DATE mm/dd/ccyy	40. PLACE OF FINAL DISPOSITION
10/10/2004	WESTWOOD VILLAGE MEMORIAL PARK 1218 GLENDON AVE. LOS ANGELES, CA. 90024

41. TYPE OF DISPOSITION(S)	42. SIGNATURE OF EMBALMER	43. LICENSE NUMBER
BURIAL	Randyn M. Ziegler	7516

44. NAME OF FUNERAL ESTABLISHMENT	45. LICENSE NUMBER	46. SIGNATURE OF LOCAL REGISTRAR	47. DATE mm/dd/ccyy
PIERCE BROS. WESTWOOD	FD-951	Thomas M Garthwaite	10/07/2004

PLACE OF DEATH

101. PLACE OF DEATH	102. IF HOSPITAL, SPECIFY ONE	103. IF OTHER THAN HOSPITAL, SPECIFY ONE
UCLA MEDICAL CENTER	[X] IP / ER/OP / DOA	Hospice / Nursing Home/LTC / Decedent's Home / Other

104. COUNTY	105. FACILITY ADDRESS OR LOCATION WHERE FOUND (Street and number or location)	106. CITY
Los Angeles	10833 LeConte Avenue	Los Angeles

CAUSE OF DEATH

107. CAUSE OF DEATH	Enter the chain of events — diseases, injuries, or complications — that directly caused death. DO NOT enter terminal events such as cardiac arrest, respiratory arrest, or ventricular fibrillation without showing the etiology. DO NOT ABBREVIATE.	Time Interval Between Onset and Death	108. DEATH REPORTED TO CORONER?
IMMEDIATE CAUSE (A) (Final disease or condition resulting in death) → SEPSIS		(A) 3 days	YES [X] NO
Sequentially, list conditions, if any, leading to cause on Line A. Enter UNDERLYING CAUSE (disease or injury that initiated the events resulting in death) LAST (B) ISCHEMIC COLITIS		(B) 3 days	REFERRAL NUMBER — 109. BIOPSY PERFORMED? YES [X] NO
(C) ATHEROSCLEROTIC VASCULAR HEART DISEASE		(C) years	110. AUTOPSY PERFORMED? YES [X] NO
(D)		(D)	111. USED IN DETERMINING CAUSE? YES [X] NO

112. OTHER SIGNIFICANT CONDITIONS CONTRIBUTING TO DEATH BUT NOT RESULTING IN THE UNDERLYING CAUSE GIVEN IN 107
Aortic Stenosis, Ischemic Cardiomyopathy, Cerebrovascular Accident

113. WAS OPERATION PERFORMED FOR ANY CONDITION IN ITEM 107 OR 112? (If yes, list type of operation and date.)	113A. IF FEMALE, PREGNANT IN LAST YEAR?
Ventricle to Aortic Conduit 06/21/2004, Exploratory Laparotomy 10/03/2004	YES / NO / UNK

PHYSICIAN'S CERTIFICATION

114. I CERTIFY THAT TO THE BEST OF MY KNOWLEDGE DEATH OCCURRED AT THE HOUR, DATE, AND PLACE STATED FROM THE CAUSES STATED.	115. SIGNATURE AND TITLE OF CERTIFIER	116. LICENSE NUMBER	117. DATE mm/dd/ccyy
Decedent Attended Since (A) 03/17/2003 / Decedent Last Seen Alive (B) 10/05/2004	Jaime Moriguchi	G48967	10/05/2004

118. TYPE ATTENDING PHYSICIAN'S NAME, MAILING ADDRESS, ZIP CODE
Jaime Moriguchi, M.D., 100 UCLA Medical Plaza, Ste 630, LA CA 90095

CORONER'S USE ONLY

119. I CERTIFY THAT IN MY OPINION DEATH OCCURRED AT THE HOUR, DATE, AND PLACE STATED FROM THE CAUSES STATED.	120. INJURED AT WORK?	121. INJURY DATE mm/dd/ccyy	122. HOUR (24 Hours)
MANNER OF DEATH: Natural / Accident / Homicide / Suicide / Pending investigation / Could not be determined	YES / NO / UNK		

123. PLACE OF INJURY (e.g., home, construction site, wooded area, etc.)

124. DESCRIBE HOW INJURY OCCURRED (Events which resulted in injury)

125. LOCATION OF INJURY (Street and number; or location, and city, and ZIP)

126. SIGNATURE OF CORONER / DEPUTY CORONER	127. DATE mm/dd/ccyy	128. TYPE NAME, TITLE OF CORONER / DEPUTY CORONER
		090772321

STATE REGISTRAR	A	B	C	D	E	FAX AUTH. #	CENSUS TRACT

This is a true certified copy of the record filed in the County of Los Angeles
Department of Health Services if it bears the Registrar's signature in purple ink.

DATE ISSUED

CERTIFICATION OF VITAL RECORD

COUNTY OF LOS ANGELES • REGISTRAR-RECORDER/COUNTY CLERK

CERTIFICATE OF DEATH   3051923215
STATE OF CALIFORNIA

STATE FILE NUMBER				LOCAL REGISTRATION DISTRICT AND CERTIFICATE NUMBER

1A. NAME OF DECEDENT—FIRST	1B. MIDDLE	1C. LAST	2A. DATE OF DEATH (MONTH, DAY, YEAR)	2B. HOUR
Selma		Diamond	May 13, 1985	0324

DECEDENT PERSONAL DATA

3. SEX	4. RACE/ETHNICITY	5. SPANISH/HISPANIC	6. DATE OF BIRTH	7. AGE	IF UNDER 1 YEAR MONTHS DAYS	IF UNDER 24 HOURS HOURS MINUTES
Female	White/Jewish	No	August 5, 1920	64 YEARS		

8. BIRTHPLACE OF DECEDENT (STATE OR FOREIGN COUNTRY)	9. NAME AND BIRTHPLACE OF FATHER	10. BIRTH NAME AND BIRTHPLACE OF MOTHER
Canada	Samuel Diamond (Unknown)	Edith Farfel (Unknown)

11A. CITIZEN OF WHAT COUNTRY	11B. IF DECEASED WAS EVER IN MILITARY GIVE DATES OF SERVICE	12. SOCIAL SECURITY NUMBER	13. MARITAL STATUS	14. NAME OF SURVIVING SPOUSE (IF WIFE, ENTER BIRTH NAME)
USA	19__ TO 19__	055-16-2305	Never Married	

15. PRIMARY OCCUPATION	16. NUMBER OF YEARS THIS OCCUPATION	17. EMPLOYER (IF SELF-EMPLOYED, SO STATE)	18. KIND OF INDUSTRY OR BUSINESS
Actress-Writer	30	Warner Bros. Television	Entertainment

USUAL RESIDENCE

19A. USUAL RESIDENCE—STREET ADDRESS (STREET AND NUMBER OR LOCATION)	19B.	19C. CITY OR TOWN
886 N. Hillgard Ave.		Los Angeles

19D. COUNTY	19E. STATE	20. NAME AND ADDRESS OF INFORMANT—RELATIONSHIP
Los Angeles	California	Harvey Medlinsky Friend

PLACE OF DEATH

21A. PLACE OF DEATH	21B. COUNTY	9555 W. Olympic Blvd.
Cedars Sinai Medical Center	Los Angeles	Beverly Hills, California 90212

21C. STREET ADDRESS (STREET AND NUMBER OR LOCATION)	21D. CITY OR TOWN
8700 Beverly Blvd.	Los Angeles

CAUSE OF DEATH

22. DEATH WAS CAUSED BY: (ENTER ONLY ONE CAUSE PER LINE FOR A, B, AND C) IMMEDIATE CAUSE			24. WAS DEATH REPORTED TO CORONER?
(A) Bronchogenic Carcinoma 2 mos		APPROXIMATE INTERVAL BETWEEN ONSET AND DEATH	NO
CONDITIONS, IF ANY, WHICH GAVE RISE TO THE IMMEDIATE CAUSE, STATING THE UNDERLYING CAUSE LAST. DUE TO, OR AS A CONSEQUENCE OF (B)			25. WAS BIOPSY PERFORMED? Yes
DUE TO, OR AS A CONSEQUENCE OF (C)			26. WAS AUTOPSY PERFORMED? NO

23. OTHER SIGNIFICANT CONDITIONS—CONTRIBUTING TO DEATH BUT NOT RELATED TO CAUSE GIVEN IN 22A	27. WAS OPERATION PERFORMED FOR ANY CONDITION IN ITEMS 22 OR 23? TYPE OF OPERATION None	DATE

PHYSICIAN'S CERTIFICATION

28A. I CERTIFY THAT DEATH OCCURRED AT THE HOUR, DATE AND PLACE STATED FROM THE CAUSES STATED. I ATTENDED DECEDENT SINCE (ENTER MO. DA. YR.)	I LAST SAW DECEDENT ALIVE (ENTER MO. DA. YR.)	28B. PHYSICIAN—SIGNATURE AND DEGREE OR TITLE	28C. DATE SIGNED	28D. PHYSICIAN'S LICENSE NUMBER
4/8/85	5/13/85	Clarence Engelberg M.D.	5/14/85	GC9143
		28E. TYPE PHYSICIAN'S NAME AND ADDRESS Clarence Engelberg, M.D. 9735 Wilshire Blvd. Beverly Hills		

INJURY INFORMATION

29. SPECIFY ACCIDENT, SUICIDE, ETC.	30. PLACE OF INJURY	31. INJURY AT WORK	32A. DATE OF INJURY—MONTH, DAY, YEAR	32B. HOUR
33. LOCATION (STREET AND NUMBER OF LOCATION AND CITY OR TOWN)	34. DESCRIBE HOW INJURY OCCURRED (EVENTS WHICH RESULTED IN INJURY)			

CORONER'S USE ONLY

35A. I CERTIFY THAT DEATH OCCURRED AT THE HOUR, DATE AND PLACE STATED FROM THE CAUSES STATED. AS REQUIRED BY LAW I HAVE HELD AN (INQUEST-INVESTIGATION)	35B. CORONER—SIGNATURE AND DEGREE OR TITLE	35C. DATE SIGNED

36. DISPOSITION	37. DATE—MONTH, DAY, YEAR	38. NAME AND ADDRESS OF CEMETERY OR CREMATORY	39. EMBALMER'S LICENSE NUMBER AND SIGNATURE
Entomb.	5/15/85	Hillside Memorial Park 6001 Centinela Ave. L.A.	NOT EMBALMED

40A. NAME OF FUNERAL DIRECTOR (OR PERSON ACTING AS SUCH)	40B. LICENSE NO.	41. LOCAL REGISTRAR—SIGNATURE	42. DATE ACCEPTED BY LOCAL REGISTRAR
Hillside Mem. Pk. Mort. bb	1358	Robert Matz KS	MAY 15 1985

STATE REGISTRAR	A.	B.	C.	D.	E.	F.

VS-11 (1-85)   1639

This is to certify that this document is a true copy of the official record filed with the Registrar-Recorder/County Clerk.

Beatriz Valdez
BEATRIZ VALDEZ
Registrar-Recorder/County Clerk

AUG 10 1995

19-389405

This copy not valid unless prepared on engraved border displaying the Seal and Signature of the Registrar-Recorder/County Clerk.

ANY ALTERATION OR ERASURE VOIDS THIS CERTIFICATE

STATE OF CALIFORNIA
CERTIFICATION OF VITAL RECORD

COUNTY OF LOS ANGELES
DEPARTMENT OF HEALTH SERVICES

CERTIFICATE OF DEATH
STATE OF CALIFORNIA
USE BLACK INK ONLY/NO ERASURES, WHITEOUTS OR ALTERATIONS
VS-11 (REV. 1/00)

STATE FILE NUMBER		LOCAL REGISTRATION NUMBER

DECEDENT PERSONAL DATA

1. NAME OF DECEDENT—FIRST (GIVEN)	2. MIDDLE	3. LAST (FAMILY)
MERLE	–	JOHNSON

4. DATE OF BIRTH MM/DD/CCYY	5. AGE YRS.	IF UNDER 1 YEAR MONTHS / DAYS	IF UNDER 24 HOURS HOURS / MINUTES	6. SEX	7. DATE OF DEATH MM/DD/CCYY	8. HOUR
01/27/1936	65			M	09/02/2001	0615

9. STATE OF BIRTH	10. SOCIAL SECURITY NO.	11. MILITARY SERVICE	12. MARITAL STATUS	13. EDUCATION—YEARS COMPLETED
NY	089-30-9609	☐ YES ☒ NO ☐ UNK	DIVORCED	13

14. RACE	15. HISPANIC—SPECIFY		16. USUAL EMPLOYER
CAUC	☐ YES	☒ NO	SELF EMPLOYED

17. OCCUPATION	18. KIND OF BUSINESS	19. YEARS IN OCCUPATION
ACTOR	TELEVISION/MOVIES	45

I OF 2

USUAL RESIDENCE

20. RESIDENCE—(STREET AND NUMBER OR LOCATION)
1022 EUCLID ST. #2

21. CITY	22. COUNTY	23. ZIP CODE	24. YRS IN COUNTY	25. STATE OR FOREIGN COUNTRY
SANTA MONICA	LOS ANGELES	90403	30	CA

INFORMANT

26. NAME, RELATIONSHIP	27. MAILING ADDRESS (STREET AND NUMBER OR RURAL ROUTE NUMBER, CITY OR TOWN, STATE, ZIP)
JANE NUNEZ – FRIEND	7985 SANTA MONICA BLVD. #109-29 W.HOLLYWOOD, CA. 90046

SPOUSE AND PARENT INFORMATION

28. NAME OF SURVIVING SPOUSE—FIRST	29. MIDDLE	30. LAST (MAIDEN NAME)
–	–	–

31. NAME OF FATHER—FIRST	32. MIDDLE	33. LAST	34. BIRTH STATE
MERLE	–	JOHNSON	IL

35. NAME OF MOTHER—FIRST	36. MIDDLE	37. LAST (MAIDEN)	38. BIRTH STATE
EDITH	DOROTHY	FREDRICKSON	NY

DISPOSITION(S)

39. DATE MM/DD/CCYY	40. PLACE OF FINAL DISPOSITION
09/14/2001	RES:JANE NUNEZ 1022 EUCLID ST. #2 SANTA MONICA, CA. 90403

FUNERAL DIRECTOR AND LOCAL REGISTRAR

41. TYPE OF DISPOSITION(S)	42. SIGNATURE OF EMBALMER	43. LICENSE NO.
CR/RES	▶ NOT EMBALMED	–

44. NAME OF FUNERAL DIRECTOR	45. LICENSE NO.	46. SIGNATURE OF LOCAL REGISTRAR	47. DATE MM/DD/CCYY
GATES KINGSLEY GATES MOELLER MURPHY	FD451	▶ Jonathan E Fielding ms	09/12/2001

PLACE OF DEATH

101. PLACE OF DEATH	102. IF HOSPITAL, SPECIFY ONE:	103. FACILITY OTHER THAN HOSPITAL:	104. COUNTY
ST. JOHN'S HEALTH CENTER	☒ IP ☐ ER/OP ☐ DOA	☐ CONV. HOSP. ☐ RES. CARE ☐ OTHER	LOS ANGELES

105. STREET ADDRESS—(STREET AND NUMBER OR LOCATION)	106. CITY
1328 22ND. STREET	SANTA MONICA

CAUSE OF DEATH

107. DEATH WAS CAUSED BY: (ENTER ONLY ONE CAUSE PER LINE FOR A, B, C, AND D)

		TIME INTERVAL BETWEEN ONSET AND DEATH	108. DEATH REPORTED TO CORONER
IMMEDIATE CAUSE (A)	CARDIAC ARREST	mins	☐ YES ☒ NO REFERRAL NUMBER
DUE TO (B)	CARDIOGENIC SHOCK	3days	109. BIOPSY PERFORMED ☐ YES ☒ NO
DUE TO (C)	MYOCARDIAL INFARCTION	3days	110. AUTOPSY PERFORMED ☐ YES ☒ NO
DUE TO (D)			111. USED IN DETERMINING CAUSE ☐ YES ☐ NO

112. OTHER SIGNIFICANT CONDITIONS CONTRIBUTING TO DEATH BUT NOT RELATED TO CAUSE GIVEN IN 107
NONE

113. WAS OPERATION PERFORMED FOR ANY CONDITION IN ITEM 107 OR 112? IF YES, LIST TYPE OF OPERATION AND DATE.
CORONARY ARTERY BYPASS GRAFT X6 AND INTRA-AORTIC BALLON PLACEMENT, LEFT LEG 08/30/2001

PHYSICIAN'S CERTIFICATION

114. I CERTIFY THAT TO THE BEST OF MY KNOWLEDGE DEATH OCCURRED AT THE HOUR, DATE AND PLACE STATED FROM THE CAUSES STATED. DECEDENT ATTENDED SINCE MM/DD/CCYY	DECEDENT LAST SEEN ALIVE MM/DD/CCYY	115. SIGNATURE AND TITLE OF CERTIFIER	116. LICENSE NO.	117. DATE MM/DD/CCYY
08/30/2001	09/02/2001	▶ [signature]	A26596	09/10/2001

118. TYPE ATTENDING PHYSICIAN'S NAME, MAILING ADDRESS, ZIP
AURELIO CHAUX, MD. 1328 22ND. ST. SANTA MONICA, CA. 90404

CORONER'S USE ONLY

119. I CERTIFY THAT IN MY OPINION DEATH OCCURRED AT THE HOUR, DATE AND PLACE STATED FROM THE CAUSES STATED. 119. MANNER OF DEATH	120. INJURY AT WORK	121. INJURY DATE MM/DD/CCYY	122. HOUR	123. PLACE OF INJURY
☐ NATURAL ☐ SUICIDE ☐ HOMICIDE ☐ ACCIDENT ☐ PENDING INVESTIGATION ☐ COULD NOT BE DETERMINED	☐ YES ☐ NO			

124. DESCRIBE HOW INJURY OCCURRED (EVENTS WHICH RESULTED IN INJURY)

125. LOCATION (STREET AND NUMBER OR LOCATION AND CITY, ZIP)

126. SIGNATURE OF CORONER OR DEPUTY CORONER	127. DATE MM/DD/CCYY	128. TYPED NAME, TITLE OF CORONER OR DEPUTY CORONER
▶		

STATE REGISTRAR

A	B	C	D	E	F	G	H	FAX AUTH. #	CENSUS TRACT

090466792

This is a true certified copy of the record filed in the County of Los Angeles Department of Health Services if it bears the Registrar's signature in purple ink.

Jonathan E Fielding ms
Director of Health Services and Registrar

DATE ISSUED
033
OCT 03 2001

This copy not valid unless prepared on engraved border displaying seal and signature of Registrar.

ANY ALTERATION OR ERASURE VOIDS THIS CERTIFICATE

STATE OF CALIFORNIA
CERTIFICATION OF VITAL RECORD

COUNTY OF LOS ANGELES
DEPARTMENT OF HEALTH SERVICES
AFFIDAVIT TO AMEND A RECORD

STATE FILE NUMBER	DEATHS AFTER 1-1994 NO ERASURES, WHITEOUTS, OR ALTERATIONS	LOCAL REGISTRATION DISTRICT AND CERTIFICATE NUMBER

STATE/LOCAL REGISTRAR USE ONLY	1.	2.	3.

PART I   INFORMATION TO LOCATE RECORD—TYPE OR PRINT IN BLACK INK ONLY

NAME AS IT APPEARS ON RECORD	1. NAME—FIRST (GIVEN) MERLE	2. MIDDLE –	3. LAST (FAMILY) JOHNSON

ADDITIONAL INFORMATION TO LOCATE RECORD	4. SEX M	5. DATE OF EVENT—MM/DD/CCYY 09/02/2001	6. CITY OF OCCURRENCE SANTA MONICA	7. COUNTY OF OCCURRENCE LOS ANGELES
	8. FATHER'S NAME AS STATED ON ORIGINAL MERLE – JOHNSON		9. MOTHER'S NAME AS STATED ON ORIGINAL EDITH DOROTHY FREDRICKSON	

PART II   STATEMENT OF CORRECTIONS—NO ERASURES, WHITEOUTS, OR ALTERATIONS   2 OF 2

	10. CERTIFICATE ITEM NUMBER	11. INFORMATION AS IT APPEARS ON ORIGINAL RECORD	12. INFORMATION AS IT SHOULD APPEAR
LIST ONE ITEM PER LINE	1,2,3	MERLE – JOHNSON	MERLE – JOHNSON AKA TROY – DONAHUE

REASON FOR CORRECTION	13. TO SHOW MULTIPLE NAMES

AFFIDAVITS AND SIGNATURES	We, the undersigned, hereby certify under penalty of perjury that we have personal knowledge of the above facts and that the information given above is true and correct.		
TWO PERSONS MUST SIGN THIS FORM	14. SIGNATURE OF FIRST PERSON *Laura Cox*	15. TITLE/RELATIONSHIP TO PERSON IN PART I FUNERAL DIRECTOR	16. DATE SIGNED—MM/DD/CCYY 09/10/2001
	17. AGE ADULT	18. ADDRESS (STREET, CITY, STATE, ZIP) 1925 ARIZONA AVE. SANTA MONICA, CA. 90404	
USE BLACK INK ONLY	19. SIGNATURE OF SECOND PERSON *Wm Wms*	20. TITLE/RELATIONSHIP TO PERSON IN PART I FUNERAL DIRECTOR	21. DATE SIGNED—MM/DD/CCYY 09/10/2001
	22. AGE ADULT	23. ADDRESS (STREET, CITY, STATE, ZIP) 1925 ARIZONA AVE. SANTA MONICA, CA. 90404	
STATE/LOCAL REGISTRAR USE ONLY	24. SIGNATURE OF STATE OR LOCAL REGISTRAR *Jonathan E Fielding ms JK*		25. DATE ACCEPTED FOR REGISTRATION—MM/DD/CCYY 09/12/2001

STATE OF CALIFORNIA, DEPARTMENT OF HEALTH SERVICES, OFFICE OF STATE REGISTRAR   VS 24(L) (Rev. 1/95)

090466793

This is a true certified copy of the record filed in the County of Los Angeles
Department of Health Services if it bears the Registrar's signature in purple ink.

Jonathan E Fielding ms   DATE ISSUED
                                033
Director of Health Services and Registrar   OCT 0 3 2001

This copy not valid unless prepared on engraved border displaying seal and signature of Registrar.

ANY ALTERATION OR ERASURE VOIDS THIS CERTIFICATE

STATE OF CALIFORNIA
CERTIFICATION OF VITAL RECORD

COUNTY OF LOS ANGELES • REGISTRAR-RECORDER/COUNTY CLERK

CERTIFICATE OF DEATH
STATE OF CALIFORNIA
USE BLACK INK ONLY/NO ERASURES, WHITEOUTS OR ALTERATIONS
VS-11 (REV. 11/96)

3 1997 19 009770
LOCAL REGISTRATION NUMBER
STATE FILE NUMBER

1. NAME OF DECEDENT—FIRST GIVEN	2. MIDDLE	3. LAST (FAMILY)
DAVID	FITZGERALD	DOYLE

DECEDENT PERSONAL DATA

4. DATE OF BIRTH MM/DD/CCYY	5. AGE YRS	IF UNDER 1 YEAR MONTHS/DAYS	IF UNDER 24 HOURS HOURS/MINUTES	6. SEX	7. DATE OF DEATH MM/DD/CCYY	8. HOUR
12/01/1929	67			M	02/26/1997	1765

9. STATE OF BIRTH	10. SOCIAL SECURITY NO.	11. MILITARY SERVICE	12. MARITAL STATUS	13. EDUCATION—YEARS COMPLETED
NEBRASKA	506-24-3835	[X] YES ☐ NO	MARRIED	15

14. RACE	15. HISPANIC—SPECIFY	16. USUAL EMPLOYER
CAUCASIAN	☐ YES [X] NO	SELF-EMPLOYED

17. OCCUPATION	18. KIND OF BUSINESS	19. YEARS IN OCCUPATION
ACTOR/DIRECTOR	ENTERTAINMENT	47

1 OF 2

USUAL RESIDENCE

20. RESIDENCE—STREET AND NUMBER OR LOCATION
4731 NOLELINE AVE.

21. CITY	22. COUNTY	23. ZIP CODE	24. YRS IN COUNTY	25. STATE OR FOREIGN COUNTRY
ENCINO	LOS ANGELES	91347	25	CALIFORNIA

INFORMANT

26. NAME, RELATIONSHIP	27. MAILING ADDRESS (STREET AND NUMBER OR RURAL ROUTE NUMBER, CITY OR TOWN, STATE, ZIP)
ANITA DOYLE – WIFE	4731 NOLELINE AVE. ENCINO CA 91437

SPOUSE AND PARENT INFORMATION

28. NAME OF SURVIVING SPOUSE—FIRST	29. MIDDLE	30. LAST (MAIDEN NAME)
ANITA	C.	SUSSMAN

31. NAME OF FATHER—FIRST	32. MIDDLE	33. LAST	34. BIRTH STATE
LOUIS	R.	DOYLE	NB

35. NAME OF MOTHER—FIRST	36. MIDDLE	37. LAST (MAIDEN)	38. BIRTH STATE
RUTH		FITZGERALD	NB

DISPOSITION(S)

39. DATE MM/DD/CCYY	40. PLACE OF FINAL DISPOSITION
03/05/1997	RES ANITA DOYLE 4731 NOLELINE AVE. ENCINO CA 91347

FUNERAL DIRECTOR AND LOCAL REGISTRAR

41. TYPE OF DISPOSITION(S)	42. SIGNATURE OF EMBALMER	43. LICENSE NO.
CR/RES	NOT EMBALMED	-

44. NAME OF FUNERAL DIRECTOR	45. LICENSE NO.	46. SIGNATURE OF LOCAL REGISTRAR	47. DATE MM/DD/CCYY
PRAISWATER MEYER MITCHELL	FD-549	Mark _____ ns	03/04/1997

PLACE OF DEATH

101. PLACE OF DEATH	102. IF HOSPITAL, SPECIFY ONE:	103. FACILITY OTHER THAN HOSPITAL	104. COUNTY
ENCINO HOSPITAL	[X] IP ☐ ER/OP ☐ DOA	☐ CONV. HOSP. ☐ RES. CARE ☐ OTHER	LOS ANGELES

105. STREET ADDRESS—STREET AND NUMBER OR LOCATION	106. CITY
16237 VENTURA BLVD.	ENCINO

CAUSE OF DEATH

107. DEATH WAS CAUSED BY (ENTER ONLY ONE CAUSE PER LINE FOR A, B, C, AND D)

		TIME INTERVAL BETWEEN ONSET AND DEATH	
IMMEDIATE CAUSE (A)	ACUTE PULMONARY EDEMA	HOURS	108. DEATH REPORTED TO CORONER ☐ YES [X] NO — REFERRAL NUMBER
DUE TO (B)	ACUTE MYOCARDIAL INFARCTION	HOURS	109. BIOPSY PERFORMED ☐ YES [X] NO
DUE TO (C)	ARTERIOSCLEROTIC HEART DISEASE	YEARS	110. AUTOPSY PERFORMED ☐ YES [X] NO
DUE TO (D)			111. USED IN DETERMINING CAUSE ☐ YES [X] NO

112. OTHER SIGNIFICANT CONDITIONS CONTRIBUTING TO DEATH BUT NOT RELATED TO CAUSE GIVEN IN 107
CANCER OF THE LUNG METASTATIC TO LIVER

113. WAS OPERATION PERFORMED FOR ANY CONDITION IN ITEM 107 OR 112? IF YES, LIST TYPE OF OPERATION AND DATE.
LIVER BIOPSY 02/22/1997

PHYSICIAN'S CERTIFICATION

114. I CERTIFY THAT TO THE BEST OF MY KNOWLEDGE DEATH OCCURRED AT THE HOUR, DATE AND PLACE STATED FROM THE CAUSES STATED. DECEDENT ATTENDED SINCE / DECEDENT LAST SEEN ALIVE MM/DD/CCYY

08/15/1989	02/26/1997	115. SIGNATURE AND TITLE OF CERTIFIER	116. LICENSE NO.	117. DATE MM/DD/CCYY
		_____	A17238	02/28/1997

118. TYPE ATTENDING PHYSICIAN'S NAME, MAILING ADDRESS, ZIP
KENNETH BLIEFER, M.D. 15211 VANOWEN ST. #300 VAN NUYS CA 91405

CORONER'S USE ONLY

119. I CERTIFY THAT IN MY OPINION DEATH OCCURRED AT THE HOUR, DATE AND PLACE STATED FROM THE CAUSES STATED.

119. MANNER OF DEATH
☐ NATURAL ☐ SUICIDE ☐ HOMICIDE ☐ ACCIDENT ☐ PENDING INVESTIGATION ☐ COULD NOT BE DETERMINED

120. INJURY AT WORK ☐ YES ☐ NO	121. INJURY DATE MM/DD/CCYY	122. HOUR	123. PLACE OF INJURY

124. DESCRIBE HOW INJURY OCCURRED (EVENTS WHICH RESULTED IN INJURY)

125. LOCATION, STREET AND NUMBER OR LOCATION AND CITY, ZIP.

126. SIGNATURE OF CORONER OR DEPUTY CORONER	127. DATE MM/DD/CCYY	128. TYPED NAME, TITLE OF CORONER OR DEPUTY CORONER

STATE REGISTRAR

A	B	C	D	E	F	G	H	FAX AUTH. #	CENSUS TRACT

This is to certify that this document is a true copy of the official record filed with the Registrar-Recorder/County Clerk.

Conny B. McCormack

CONNY B. McCORMACK
Registrar-Recorder/County Clerk

OCT 04 200_
19-673790

This copy not valid unless prepared on engraved border displaying the Seal and Signature of the Registrar-Recorder/County Clerk.

ANY ALTERATION OR ERASURE VOIDS THIS CERTIFICATE

STATE OF CALIFORNIA
CERTIFICATION OF VITAL RECORD

SANTA BARBARA COUNTY
SANTA BARBARA, CALIFORNIA

STATE OF CALIFORNIA
DEPARTMENT OF PUBLIC HEALTH
VITAL STATISTICS

STANDARD CERTIFICATE OF DEATH

110

1. PLACE OF DEATH: DIST. No. 4256

COUNTY OF Santa Barbara

LOCAL REGISTERED No. 104

CITY, TOWN OR RURAL DISTRICT OF Montecito

STREET AND NO.
IF DEATH OCCURRED IN A HOSPITAL OR INSTITUTION, GIVE ITS NAME INSTEAD OF STREET AND NO.

2. FULL NAME MARIE DRESSLER

RESIDENCE: No. 801 North Alpine Drive
IF NON-RESIDENT, GIVE
ST. CITY OR TOWN, AND STATE Beverly Hills, Calif

USUAL PLACE OF ABODE

3. SEX	4. COLOR OR RACE	5. SINGLE, MARRIED, WIDOWED OR DIVORCED? (WRITE THE WORD)
Female	White	Single

22. DATE OF DEATH July 28 1934
MONTH   DAY   YEAR

5A. IF MARRIED, WIDOWED OR DIVORCED, NAME OF HUSBAND OR WIFE

23. MEDICAL CERTIFICATE OF DEATH

24. CORONER'S CERTIFICATE OF DEATH

6. DATE OF BIRTH November 9 1871
MONTH   DAY   YEAR

I HEREBY CERTIFY, THAT I ATTENDED DECEASED FROM Feb.10-34
TO July 28-34

I HEREBY CERTIFY, THAT I TOOK CHARGE OF THE REMAINS DESCRIBED ABOVE, HELD

7. AGE 62 YR. 8 MO.19 DAYS. IF LESS THAN ONE DAY ___ HRS. ___ MIN.

THAT I LAST SAW HER ALIVE ON 7-28-34
AND THAT DEATH OCCURRED ON THE ABOVE STATED DATE AT THE HOUR OF 3:30 P M.

AN ___ INQUEST, AUTOPSY OR INQUIRY THEREON, AND FROM SUCH ACTION FIND THAT SAID DECEASED CAME TO H ___ DEATH ON THE DATE STATED ABOVE.

8. TRADE, PROFESSION OR KIND OF WORK DONE AS SPINNER, SAWYER, BOOKKEEPER, ETC. Star Actress

9. INDUSTRY OR BUSINESS IN WHICH WORK WAS DONE, AS SILKMILL, SAWMILL, BANK, ETC. Motion Picture

10. DATE DECEASED LAST WORKED AT THIS OCCUPATION (MO. AND YR.)

11. TOTAL YEARS SPENT IN THIS OCCUPATION

THE PRINCIPAL CAUSE OF DEATH AND RELATED CAUSES OF IMPORTANCE, IN ORDER OF ONSET, WERE AS FOLLOWS:

DATE OF ONSET

12. BIRTHPLACE (CITY OR TOWN) Cobourg
STATE OR COUNTRY Canada

Congestive heart failure

13. NAME Alexander Rudolph Koerber
14. BIRTHPLACE (CITY OR TOWN) Unknown
STATE OR COUNTRY Canada

OTHER CONTRIBUTORY CAUSES OF IMPORTANCE:
Uremia

15. MAIDEN NAME Unknown
16. BIRTHPLACE (CITY OR TOWN) Unknown
STATE OR COUNTRY Unknown

Recurrent carcinoma 7-1-31

IF OPERATION, DATE OF Sept.1932
CONDITION FOR WHICH PERFORMED Tumor of vulva
NAME LABORATORY TEST CONFIRMING DIAGNOSIS

WAS THERE AN AUTOPSY?

A. CITY, TOWN OR RURAL DISTRICT OF DEATH ___ YRS. 2 MOS. 15 DAYS
B. IN CALIFORNIA 7 YRS. ___ MOS. ___ DAYS
C. IN U.S., IF OF FOREIGN BIRTH 60 YRS. ___ MOS. ___ DAYS

25. IF DEATH WAS DUE TO EXTERNAL CAUSES (VIOLENCE) FILL IN THE FOLLOWING:
ACCIDENT, SUICIDE OR HOMICIDE?   DATE OF INJURY

INJURED CITY OR TOWN OF
AT   COUNTY AND STATE OF
DID INJURY OCCUR IN HOME, INDUSTRY, OR PUBLIC PLACE?
MANNER OF INJURY
NATURE OF INJURY

18. INFORMANT (SIGNATURE) Allen Breed Walker
ADDRESS Beverly Hills, Calif

19. BURIAL, CREMATION OR REMOVAL? Burial
PLACE Forest Lawn Memorial Park WRITE THE WORD DATE 7-31-34

26. IF DISEASE/INJURY RELATED TO OCCUPATION, SPECIFY

20. EMBALMER { LICENSE No. 378
SIGNATURE Charles T.Holland }

FUNERAL DIRECTOR Charles T.Holland
ADDRESS Santa Barbara, California

27. SIGNATURE F.R.Nuzum M.D.
PHYSICIAN, AUTOPSY SURGEON
ADDRESS Santa Barbara, Calif

21. FILED July 29,1934
DATE
R.C.MAIN, M.D
LOCAL REGISTRAR

28. WHEN REQUIRED BY LAW ___ CORONER
COUNTY OF

STATE OF CALIFORNIA
CERTIFICATION OF VITAL RECORD

COUNTY OF LOS ANGELES • REGISTRAR-RECORDER/COUNTY CLERK

CERTIFICATE OF DEATH
STATE OF CALIFORNIA
USE BLACK INK ONLY

39019039496

LOCAL REGISTRATION DISTRICT AND CERTIFICATE NUMBER

STATE FILE NUMBER				
1A. NAME OF DECEDENT—FIRST (GIVEN) **IRENE**	1B. MIDDLE **DUNNE**	1C. LAST (FAMILY) **GRIFFIN**	2A. DATE OF DEATH—MO. DAY, YR. **SEPT. 4, 1990** 2B. HOUR **1820**	3. SEX **FEMALE**

DECEDENT PERSONAL DATA

4. RACE **Caucasian**	5. HISPANIC—SPECIFY ☐ YES ☒ No	6. DATE OF BIRTH—MO. DAY, YR. **Dec. 20, 1901**	7. AGE IN YEARS **88**	IF UNDER 1 YEAR MONTHS DAYS	IF UNDER 24 HOURS HOURS MINUTES

8. STATE OF BIRTH **Ky**	9. CITIZEN OF WHAT COUNTRY **USA**	10A. FULL NAME OF FATHER **Joseph Dunne**	10B. STATE OF BIRTH **Ky**	11A. FULL MAIDEN NAME OF MOTHER **Adelaide Henry**	11B. STATE OF BIRTH **Ky**

12. MILITARY SERVICE? 19___ TO 19___ ☒ NONE	13. SOCIAL SECURITY NO. **563-10-1113**	14. MARITAL STATUS **Widowed**	15. NAME OF SURVIVING SPOUSE (IF WIFE, ENTER MAIDEN NAME) ----

16A. USUAL OCCUPATION **Actress**	16B. USUAL KIND OF BUSINESS OR INDUSTRY **Motion Picture**	16C. USUAL EMPLOYER **Self-Employed**	16D. YEARS IN OCCUPATION **30**	17 EDUCATION—YEARS COMPLETED **16**

USUAL RESIDENCE

18A. RESIDENCE—STREET AND NUMBER OR LOCATION **461 Faring Road**	18B. CITY **Los Angeles**	18C. ZIP CODE **90077**

18D. COUNTY **Los Angeles**	18E. NUMBER OF YEARS IN THIS COUNTY **60**	18F. STATE OR FOREIGN COUNTRY **California**	20. NAME, RELATIONSHIP, MAILING ADDRESS AND ZIP CODE OF INFORMANT **Allen Dunne – Nephew 1101 Charmacres Pl. Pacific Palisades, Ca. 90272**

PLACE OF DEATH

19A. PLACE OF DEATH **RESIDENCE**	19B. IF HOSPITAL, SPECIFY ONE: IP, ER/OP, DOA ----	19C. COUNTY **LOS ANGELES**	
19D. STREET ADDRESS—STREET AND NUMBER OR LOCATION **461 FARING ROAD**		19E. CITY **LOS ANGELES**	TIME INTERVAL BETWEEN ONSET AND DEATH	22. WAS DEATH REPORTED TO CORONER? REFERRAL NUMBER ☐ YES ☒ NO

CAUSE OF DEATH

21. DEATH WAS CAUSED BY: (ENTER ONLY ONE CAUSE PER LINE FOR A, B, AND C)		
IMMEDIATE CAUSE (A) **Myocardial Insufficiency**	▶ 10 hrs	23. WAS BIOPSY PERFORMED? ☐ YES ☒ NO
DUE TO (B) **Arteriosclerosis, general**	▶ 10 yrs	24A. WAS AUTOPSY PERFORMED? ☐ YES ☒ NO
DUE TO (C)	▶	24B. WAS IT USED IN DETERMINING CAUSE OF DEATH? ☐ YES ☐ NO

25. OTHER SIGNIFICANT CONDITIONS CONTRIBUTING TO DEATH BUT NOT RELATED TO CAUSE GIVEN IN 21 **None**	26. WAS OPERATION PERFORMED FOR ANY CONDITION IN ITEM 21 OR 25? IF YES, LIST TYPE OF OPERATION AND DATE. **No**

PHYSICIAN'S CERTIFICATION

I CERTIFY THAT TO THE BEST OF MY KNOWLEDGE DEATH OCCURRED AT THE HOUR, DATE AND PLACE STATED FROM THE CAUSES STATED.	27B. SIGNATURE AND DEGREE OR TITLE OF CERTIFIER *William West Smith M.D.*	27C. CERTIFIER'S LICENSE NUMBER **A08479**	27D. DATE SIGNED **09/05/90**
27A. DECEDENT ATTENDED SINCE MONTH, DAY, YEAR **07/18/81**	DECEDENT LAST SEEN ALIVE MONTH, DAY, YEAR **09/04/90**	27E. TYPE ATTENDING PHYSICIAN'S NAME AND ADDRESS **William W. Smith M.D. 9675 Brighton Wy. Bev. Hills, Ca.**	

CORONER'S USE ONLY

I CERTIFY THAT IN MY OPINION DEATH OCCURRED AT THE HOUR, DATE AND PLACE STATED FROM THE CAUSES STATED.	28A. SIGNATURE AND TITLE OF CORONER OR DEPUTY CORONER ▶	28B. DATE SIGNED
29. MANNER OF DEATH—specify one. natural, accident, suicide, homicide, pending investigation or could not be determined	30A. PLACE OF INJURY	30B. INJURY AT WORK ☐ YES ☐ NO	30C. DATE OF INJURY MONTH, DAY, YEAR	31. HOUR
32. LOCATION (STREET AND NUMBER OR LOCATION AND CITY)	33. DESCRIBE HOW INJURY OCCURRED (EVENTS WHICH RESULTED IN INJURY)			

FUNERAL DIRECTOR AND LOCAL REGISTRAR

34A. DISPOSITION(S) **Burial**	34B. PLACE OF FINAL DISPOSITION—NAME AND ADDRESS **Calvary Maus. Cem. E. L.A. Ca.**	34C. DATE MO. DAY, YEAR **Sept. 8, 1990**	35A. SIGNATURE OF EMBALMER *Jim Austin*	35B. LICENSE NUMBER **4350**
36A. NAME OF FUNERAL DIRECTOR (OR PERSON ACTING AS SUCH) **PIERCE BROTHERS, CUNNINGHAM AND O'CONNOR, UTTER McKINLEY**	36B. LICENSE NO. **F-168**	37. SIGNATURE OF LOCAL REGISTRAR ▶ *Robert C. Bart*	38. REGISTRATION DATE **SEP 7 1990**

STATE REGISTRAR

A.	B.	C.	D.	E.	F.	CENSUS TRACT

VS-11 (REV. 1-90)   MAKE NO ERASURES, WHITEOUTS, OR OTHER ALTERATIONS

INFORMATIONAL, NOT A VALID DOCUMENT TO ESTABLISH IDENTITY

This is to certify that this document is a true copy of the official record on file with the Registrar-Recorder/County Clerk.

JAN 24 2005

Conny B. McCormack

CONNY B. McCORMACK
Registrar-Recorder/County Clerk

This copy not valid unless prepared on engraved border displaying the Seal and Signature of the Registrar-Recorder/County Clerk.

019133229

MIDWEST BANK NOTE COMPANY   ANY ALTERATION OR ERASURE VOIDS THIS CERTIFICATE

CERTIFICATE OF DEATH
STATE OF CALIFORNIA
USE BLACK INK ONLY / NO ERASURES, WHITEOUTS OR ALTERATIONS
VS 11 (REV V03)

3 2003 19 029381

STATE FILE NUMBER			LOCAL REGISTRATION NUMBER

DECEDENT'S PERSONAL DATA

1 NAME OF DECEDENT -- FIRST (Given)	2 MIDDLE	3 LAST (Family)
CHRISTIAN	L.	EBSEN, JR.

AKA ALSO KNOWN AS - Include full AKA (FIRST, MIDDLE, LAST)	4 DATE OF BIRTH mm/dd/ccyy	5 AGE Yrs	IF UNDER ONE YEAR Months / Days	IF UNDER 24 HOURS Hours / Minutes	6 SEX
BUDDY EBSEN	04/02/1908	95			MALE

9 BIRTH STATE/FOREIGN COUNTRY	10 SOCIAL SECURITY NUMBER	11 EVER IN U S ARMED FORCES?	12 MARITAL STATUS (at Time of Death)	7 DATE OF DEATH mm/dd/ccyy	8 HOUR (24 Hours)
IL	562-01-3097	X YES	MARRIED	07/06/2003	0930

13 EDUCATION Highest Level/Degree	14/15 WAS DECEDENT SPANISH/HISPANIC/LATINO?	16 DECEDENT'S RACE
BACHELOR'S	X NO	WHITE

17 USUAL OCCUPATION - Type of work for most of life DO NOT USE RETIRED	18 KIND OF BUSINESS OR INDUSTRY	19 YEARS IN OCCUPATION
ENTERTAINER/ACTOR	ENTERTAINMENT	75

USUAL RESIDENCE

20 DECEDENT'S RESIDENCE (Street and number or location)
605 VIA HORQUILLA

21 CITY	22 COUNTY/PROVINCE	23 ZIP CODE	24 YEARS IN COUNTY	25 STATE/FOREIGN COUNTRY
PALOS VERDES ESTATES	LOS ANGELES	90274	75	CA

26 INFORMANT'S NAME, RELATIONSHIP	27 INFORMANT'S MAILING ADDRESS
DOROTHY EBSEN-WIFE	P.O. BOX 2069 PALOS VERDES, CA 90274

SPOUSE AND PARENT INFORMATION

28 NAME OF SURVIVING SPOUSE – FIRST	29 MIDDLE	30 LAST (Maiden Name)
DOROTHY		HINUBER

31 NAME OF FATHER – FIRST	32 MIDDLE	33 LAST	34 BIRTH STATE
CHRISTIAN	L.	EBSEN, SR.	GERMANY

35 NAME OF MOTHER – FIRST	36 MIDDLE	37 LAST (Maiden)	38 BIRTH STATE
FRANCES	-	WENDT	LATVIA

FUNERAL DIRECTOR/ LOCAL REGISTRAR

39 DISPOSITION DATE mm/dd/ccyy	40 PLACE OF FINAL DISPOSITION
07/09/2003	RES. DOROTHY EBSEN, 605 VIA HORQUILLA, PALOS VERDES ESTATES, CA 90274

41 TYPE OF DISPOSITION(S)	42 SIGNATURE OF EMBALMER	43 LICENSE NUMBER
CR/RES	NOT EMBALMED	-

44 NAME OF FUNERAL ESTABLISHMENT	45 LICENSE NUMBER	46 SIGNATURE OF LOCAL REGISTRAR	47 DATE mm/dd/ccyy
GREEN HILLS MORTUARY	FD 1175	Thomas G. Whitmore	07/08/2003

PLACE OF DEATH

101 PLACE OF DEATH	102 IF HOSPITAL, SPECIFY ONE	103 IF OTHER THAN HOSPITAL, SPECIFY ONE
TORRANCE MEM'L HOSPITAL	X IP ER/OP DOA	Hospice Nursing Home/LTC Decedent's Home Other

104 COUNTY	105 FACILITY ADDRESS OR LOCATION WHERE FOUND	106 CITY
LOS ANGELES	3330 W. LOMITA BLVD.	TORRANCE

CAUSE OF DEATH

107 CAUSE OF DEATH		Time Interval Between Onset and Death	108 DEATH REPORTED TO CORONER?
IMMEDIATE CAUSE (A)	VENTRICULAR ASYSTOLE	MINS	YES X NO
(B)	RESPIRATORY FAILURE	DAYS	109 BIOPSY PERFORMED? YES X NO
(C) UNDERLYING CAUSE	PNEUMONITIS	WEEKS	110 AUTOPSY PERFORMED? YES X NO
(D)			111 USED IN DETERMINING CAUSE? YES NO

112 OTHER SIGNIFICANT CONDITIONS CONTRIBUTING TO DEATH BUT NOT RESULTING IN THE UNDERLYING CAUSE GIVEN IN 107
CEREBROVASCULAR ACCIDENT

113 WAS OPERATION PERFORMED FOR ANY CONDITION IN ITEM 107 OR 112?	113A IF FEMALE PREGNANT IN LAST YEAR?
NO	YES NO UNK

PHYSICIAN'S CERTIFICATION

114 I CERTIFY THAT TO THE BEST OF MY KNOWLEDGE DEATH OCCURRED AT THE HOUR DATE AND PLACE STATED FROM THE CAUSES STATED	115 SIGNATURE AND TITLE OF CERTIFIER	116 LICENSE NUMBER	117 DATE mm/dd/ccyy
Decedent Attended Since / Decedent Last Seen Alive	Mark Lurie MD	G28221	07/07/2003

(A) mm/dd/ccyy	(B) mm/dd/ccyy	118 TYPE ATTENDING PHYSICIAN'S NAME, MAILING ADDRESS, ZIP CODE
12/28/1991	07/06/2003	MARK LURIE, MD 3475 TORRANCE BLVD. TORRANCE, CA 90503

CORONER'S USE ONLY

119 I CERTIFY THAT IN MY OPINION DEATH OCCURRED AT THE HOUR, DATE AND PLACE STATED FROM THE CAUSES STATED	120 INJURED AT WORK?	121 INJURY DATE mm/dd/ccyy	122 HOUR (24 Hours)
MANNER OF DEATH: Natural Accident Homicide Suicide Pending Investigation Could not be determined	YES NO UNK		

123 PLACE OF INJURY (e.g., home, construction site, wooded area, etc)

124 DESCRIBE HOW INJURY OCCURRED (Events which resulted in injury)

125 LOCATION OF INJURY (Street and number, or location and city, and ZIP)

126 SIGNATURE OF CORONER / DEPUTY CORONER	127 DATE mm/dd/ccyy	128 TYPE NAME, TITLE OF CORONER / DEPUTY CORONER

STATE REGISTRAR	A	B	C	D	E		FAX AUTH #	CENSUS TRACT
							312-939	

CERTIFICATION OF VITAL RECORD

COUNTY OF LOS ANGELES • REGISTRAR-RECORDER/COUNTY CLERK

STATE FILE NUMBER		**CERTIFICATE OF DEATH** STATE OF CALIFORNIA—DEPARTMENT OF PUBLIC HEALTH		LOCAL REGISTRATION DISTRICT AND CERTIFICATE NUMBER	7055 8841

DECEDENT PERSONAL DATA

1A. NAME OF DECEASED—FIRST NAME	1B. MIDDLE NAME	1C. LAST NAME	2A. DATE OF DEATH—MONTH, DAY, YEAR	2B. HOUR
Hope		Emerson	Apr 24, 1960	10:15 P.M.

3. SEX	4. COLOR OR RACE	5. BIRTHPLACE	6. DATE OF BIRTH	7. AGE	IF UNDER 1 YEAR	IF UNDER 24 HOURS
Female	Cauc	Iowa	Oct 30, 1897	62 YEARS		

8. NAME AND BIRTHPLACE OF FATHER	9. MAIDEN NAME AND BIRTHPLACE OF MOTHER	10. CITIZEN OF WHAT COUNTRY	11. SOCIAL SECURITY NUMBER
John A. Emerson - Iowa	Josie Washburn - Unknown	USA	060-10-6781

12. LAST OCCUPATION	13. NUMBER OF YEARS IN THIS OCCUPATION	14. NAME OF LAST EMPLOYING COMPANY OR FIRM	15. KIND OF INDUSTRY OR BUSINESS
Actress	57	Cypress Productions	Television

16. IF DECEASED WAS EVER IN U.S. ARMED FORCES GIVE WAR OR DATES OF SERVICE	17. SPECIFY MARRIED NEVER MARRIED WIDOWED DIVORCED	18A. NAME OF PRESENT SPOUSE	18B. PRESENT OR LAST OCCUPATION OF SPOUSE
No	Never Married		

PLACE OF DEATH

19A. PLACE OF DEATH—NAME OF HOSPITAL	19B. STREET ADDRESS		
Hollywood Presbyterian Hospital	1322 N. Vermont Ave.	INSIDE CITY CORPORATE LIMITS	OUTSIDE CITY CORPORATE LIMITS

19C. CITY OR TOWN	19D. COUNTY	19E. LENGTH OF STAY IN COUNTY OF DEATH	19F. LENGTH OF STAY IN CALIFORNIA
Los Angeles	Los Angeles	10 YEARS	10 YEARS

LAST USUAL RESIDENCE (WHERE DID DECEASED LIVE—IF IN INSTITUTION ENTER RESIDENCE BEFORE ADMISSION)

20A. LAST USUAL RESIDENCE—STREET ADDRESS	20B. INSIDE CITY CORPORATE LIMITS	IF OUTSIDE CITY CORPORATE LIMITS CHECK ONE	21A. NAME OF INFORMANT (IF OTHER THAN SPOUSE)
1036 S. Wooster	☒ CHECK HERE	ON A FARM / NOT ON A FARM	Ila Rutten

20C. CITY OR TOWN	20D. COUNTY	20E. STATE	21B. ADDRESS OF INFORMANT
Los Angeles 151-A	Los Angeles	Calif	2116 N. Frederic St. Burbank, Calif

PHYSICIAN'S OR CORONER'S CERTIFICATION

22A. PHYSICIAN: I HEREBY CERTIFY THAT DEATH OCCURRED AT THE HOUR DATE AND PLACE STATED ABOVE, FROM THE CAUSES STATED BELOW AND THAT I ATTENDED THE DECEASED FROM 4-9-60 AND THAT I LAST SAW THE DECEASED ALIVE ON 4-24-60	22B. PHYSICIAN OR CORONER—SIGNATURE	DEGREE OR TITLE
4-24-60	Paul Ribers	M.D.

22B. CORONER: I HEREBY CERTIFY THAT DEATH OCCURRED AT THE HOUR DATE AND PLACE STATED ABOVE FROM THE CAUSES STATED BELOW AND THAT I HAVE HELD AN INVESTIGATION AUTOPSY INQUEST ON THE REMAINS OF DECEASED AS REQUIRED BY LAW	22D. ADDRESS	22E. DATE SIGNED
	1400 No. Vermont.	4-25-60

FUNERAL DIRECTOR AND LOCAL REGISTRAR

23. SPECIFY BURIAL ENTOMBMENT OR CREMATION	24. DATE	25. NAME OF CEMETERY OR CREMATORY	26. EMBALMER—SIGNATURE (IF BODY EMBALMED) LICENSE NUMBER
Cremation	Apr 27, 1960	Chapel of the Pines	Not Embalmed

27. NAME OF FUNERAL DIRECTOR (OR PERSON ACTING AS SUCH)	28. DATE ACCEPTED FOR REGISTRATION BY LOCAL REGISTRAR	29. LOCAL REGISTRAR—SIGNATURE
Pierce Bros. Hollywood	APR 25 1960	Grace M. Wol, M.D.

MEDICAL AND HEALTH DATA

CAUSE OF DEATH

30. CAUSE OF DEATH ENTER ONLY ONE CAUSE PER LINE FOR (A), (B) AND (C)		APPROXIMATE INTERVAL BETWEEN ONSET AND DEATH
PART I. DEATH WAS CAUSED BY: IMMEDIATE CAUSE (A)	Carcinoma of colon with metastases	36 months
CONDITIONS, IF ANY, WHICH GAVE RISE TO THE ABOVE CAUSE (A) STATING THE UNDERLYING CAUSE LAST DUE TO (B)	to liver & lung	
DUE TO (C)		
PART II. OTHER SIGNIFICANT CONDITIONS CONTRIBUTING TO DEATH BUT NOT RELATED TO THE TERMINAL DISEASE CONDITION GIVEN IN PART I (A)		

OPERATION AND AUTOPSY

31. OPERATION—CHECK ONE	32. DATE OF OPERATION	33. AUTOPSY—CHECK ONE
☒ NO OPERATION PERFORMED ☒ OPERATION PERFORMED—FINDINGS USED IN DETERMINING ABOVE STATED CAUSES OF DEATH OPERATION PERFORMED—FINDINGS NOT USED IN DETERMINING ABOVE STATES CAUSES OF DEATH	1957	☒ NO AUTOPSY PERFORMED AUTOPSY PERFORMED—GROSS FINDINGS USED IN DETERMINING ABOVE CAUSES OF DEATH AUTOPSY PERFORMED—GROSS FINDINGS NOT USED IN DETERMINING ABOVE STATED CAUSES OF DEATH

INJURY INFORMATION

34A. SPECIFY ACCIDENT, SUICIDE OR HOMICIDE	34B. DESCRIBE HOW INJURY OCCURRED

35A. TIME OF INJURY	HOUR	MONTH	DAY	YEAR
	M.			

35B. INJURY OCCURRED	35C. PLACE OF INJURY	35D. CITY, TOWN, OR LOCATION	COUNTY	STATE
WHILE AT WORK / NOT WHILE AT WORK				

This is to certify that this document is a true copy of the official record filed with the Registrar-Recorder/County Clerk.

OCT 02 1995

19-033994

This copy not valid unless prepared on engraved border displaying the Seal of the Registrar-Recorder/County Clerk.

STATE OF CALIFORNIA
CERTIFICATION OF VITAL RECORD

COUNTY OF LOS ANGELES
DEPARTMENT OF HEALTH SERVICES

CERTIFICATE OF DEATH
STATE OF CALIFORNIA
USE BLACK INK ONLY/NO ERASURES, WHITEOUTS OR ALTERATIONS
VS-11 (REV. 7/97)

3 199819051634

STATE FILE NUMBER — LOCAL REGISTRATION NUMBER

DECEDENT PERSONAL DATA			
1. NAME OF DECEDENT—FIRST (GIVEN) NORMAN	2. MIDDLE NOAH	3. LAST (FAMILY) FELL	
4. DATE OF BIRTH MM/DD/CCYY 03/24/1924	5. AGE YRS. 74	6. SEX MALE	7. DATE OF DEATH MM/DD/CCYY 12/14/1998 8. HOUR 1443
9. STATE OF BIRTH PENNSYLVANIA	10. SOCIAL SECURITY NO. 194-18-4341	11. MILITARY SERVICE [X] YES [ ] NO [ ] UNK 12. MARITAL STATUS DIVORCED	13. EDUCATION—YEARS COMPLETED 16
14. RACE WHITE	15. HISPANIC—SPECIFY [ ] YES [X] NO	16. USUAL EMPLOYER SELF EMPLOYED	
17. OCCUPATION ACTOR	18. KIND OF BUSINESS ENTERTAINMENT	19. YEARS IN OCCUPATION 50	

USUAL RESIDENCE			
20. RESIDENCE—(STREET AND NUMBER OR LOCATION) 4240 PROMENADE WAY			
21. CITY MARINA DEL REY	22. COUNTY LOS ANGELES	23. ZIP CODE 90292	24. YRS IN COUNTY 40 25. STATE OR FOREIGN COUNTRY CALIFORNIA

INFORMANT		
26. NAME, RELATIONSHIP TRACY KLORMAN - DAUGHTER	27. MAILING ADDRESS (STREET AND NUMBER OR RURAL ROUTE NUMBER, CITY OR TOWN, STATE, ZIP) 10224 GOTHIC AVENUE, NORTH HILLS, CALIFORNIA 91343	

SPOUSE AND PARENT INFORMATION			
28. NAME OF SURVIVING SPOUSE—FIRST -	29. MIDDLE	30. LAST (MAIDEN NAME)	
31. NAME OF FATHER—FIRST SAMUEL	32. MIDDLE -	33. LAST FELL	34. BIRTH STATE AUSTRIA
35. NAME OF MOTHER—FIRST EDNA	36. MIDDLE -	37. LAST (MAIDEN) ROSENFELD	38. BIRTH STATE PA

DISPOSITION(S)		
39. DATE MM/DD/CCYY 12/17/1998	40. PLACE OF FINAL DISPOSITION MOUNT SINAI MEMORIAL PARK, 5950 FOREST LAWN DRIVE, LOS ANGELES, CALIFORNIA 90068	43. LICENSE NO.

FUNERAL DIRECTOR AND LOCAL REGISTRAR		
41. TYPE OF DISPOSITION(S) CREMATION/ENTOMBMENT	42. SIGNATURE OF EMBALMER ▶ NOT EMBALMED	47. DATE MM/DD/CCYY 12/17/1998
44. NAME OF FUNERAL DIRECTOR MOUNT SINAI MORTUARY	45. LICENSE NO. FD-1010 46. SIGNATURE OF LOCAL REGISTRAR ▶	

PLACE OF DEATH		
101. PLACE OF DEATH MOTION PICTURE AND TELEVISION FUND	102. IF HOSPITAL, SPECIFY ONE: [X] IP [ ] ER/OP [ ] DOA 103. FACILITY OTHER THAN HOSPITAL [ ] CONV. HOSP. [ ] RES. CARE [ ] OTHER	104. COUNTY LOS ANGELES
105. STREET ADDRESS—(STREET AND NUMBER OR LOCATION) 23388 MULHOLLAND DRIVE		106. CITY WOODLAND HILLS

CAUSE OF DEATH	107. DEATH WAS CAUSED BY: (ENTER ONLY ONE CAUSE PER LINE FOR A, B, C, AND D)	TIME INTERVAL BETWEEN ONSET AND DEATH	
	IMMEDIATE CAUSE (A) CARDIOPULMONARY FAILURE	15 MINS	108. DEATH REPORTED TO CORONER [ ] YES [X] NO REFERRAL NUMBER
	DUE TO (B) PNEUMONIA	1 DAY	109. BIOPSY PERFORMED [X] YES [ ] NO
	DUE TO (C) MULTIPLE MYELOMA	WEEKS	110. AUTOPSY PERFORMED [ ] YES [X] NO
	DUE TO (D)		111. USED IN DETERMINING CAUSE [ ] YES [ ] NO
	112. OTHER SIGNIFICANT CONDITIONS CONTRIBUTING TO DEATH BUT NOT RELATED TO CAUSE GIVEN IN 107 DEMENTIA OF ALZHEIMER'S TYPE		
	113. WAS OPERATION PERFORMED FOR ANY CONDITION IN ITEM 107 OR 112? IF YES, LIST TYPE OF OPERATION AND DATE. BONE MARROW BIOPSY 11/29/1998		

PHYSICIAN'S CERTIFICATION			
114. I CERTIFY THAT TO THE BEST OF MY KNOWLEDGE DEATH OCCURRED AT THE HOUR, DATE AND PLACE STATED FROM THE CAUSES STATED. DECEDENT ATTENDED SINCE MM/DD/CCYY 07/15/1998 DECEDENT LAST SEEN ALIVE MM/DD/CCYY 12/14/1998	115. SIGNATURE AND TITLE OF CERTIFIER ▶	116. LICENSE NO. A39209	117. DATE MM/DD/CCYY 12/15/1998
	118. TYPE ATTENDING PHYSICIAN'S NAME, MAILING ADDRESS, ZIP SAEED HUMAYUN, M.D., 23388 MULHOLLAND DRIVE, WOODLAND HILLS, CALIFORNIA 91364		

CORONER'S USE ONLY			
I CERTIFY THAT IN MY OPINION DEATH OCCURRED AT THE HOUR, DATE AND PLACE STATED FROM THE CAUSES STATED.	120. INJURY AT WORK [ ] YES [ ] NO	121. INJURY DATE MM/DD/CCYY	122. HOUR 123. PLACE OF INJURY
119. MANNER OF DEATH [ ] NATURAL [ ] SUICIDE [ ] HOMICIDE [ ] ACCIDENT [ ] PENDING INVESTIGATION [ ] COULD NOT BE DETERMINED	124. DESCRIBE HOW INJURY OCCURRED (EVENTS WHICH RESULTED IN INJURY)		
	125. LOCATION (STREET AND NUMBER OR LOCATION AND CITY, ZIP)		
126. SIGNATURE OF CORONER OR DEPUTY CORONER ▶	127. DATE MM/DD/CCYY	128. TYPED NAME, TITLE OF CORONER OR DEPUTY CORONER	

STATE REGISTRAR	A	B	C	D	E	F	G	H	FAX AUTH. #	CENSUS TRACT 090206692
▶										

This is a true certified copy of the record filed in the County of Los Angeles
Department of Health Services if it bears the Registrar's signature in purple ink.

DATE ISSUED   JAN 26 1999

Director of Health Service and Registrar

This copy not valid unless prepared on engraved border displaying seal and signature of Registrar.

ANY ALTERATION OR ERASURE VOIDS THIS CERTIFICATE

CERTIFICATION OF VITAL RECORD

COUNTY OF LOS ANGELES • REGISTRAR-RECORDER/COUNTY CLERK

CERTIFICATE OF DEATH
STATE OF CALIFORNIA—DEPARTMENT OF PUBLIC HEALTH

STATE FILE NUMBER

LOCAL REGISTRATION DISTRICT AND CERTIFICATE NUMBER   7097-052429

DECEDENT PERSONAL DATA

1A. NAME OF DECEASED—FIRST NAME: VERNA	1B. MIDDLE NAME: FELTON	1C. LAST NAME: MILLAR
2A. DATE OF DEATH—MONTH, DAY, YEAR: Dec 14 1966		2B. HOUR: 5:20 p M
3. SEX: Female	4. COLOR OR RACE: White	5. BIRTHPLACE (STATE OR FOREIGN COUNTRY): Calif
6. DATE OF BIRTH: July 20 1890	7. AGE (LAST BIRTHDAY): 76 YEARS	IF UNDER 1 YEAR / IF UNDER 24 HOURS
8. NAME AND BIRTHPLACE OF FATHER: Horace W Felton, Calif	9. MAIDEN NAME AND BIRTHPLACE OF MOTHER: Clara Lawrence, Calif	10. CITIZEN OF WHAT COUNTRY: USA / 11. SOCIAL SECURITY NUMBER: 561 03 1931
12. LAST OCCUPATION: Actress	13. NUMBER OF YEARS IN THIS OCCUPATION: 68	14. NAME OF LAST EMPLOYING COMPANY OR FIRM: Walt Disney Studio / 15. KIND OF INDUSTRY OR BUSINESS: Motion Picture and TV
16. IF DECEASED WAS EVER IN U.S. ARMED FORCES, GIVE WAR OR DATES OF SERVICE: none	17. SPECIFY MARRIED, NEVER MARRIED, WIDOWED, DIVORCED: Widowed	18A. NAME OF PRESENT SPOUSE: -- / 18B. PRESENT OR LAST OCCUPATION OF SPOUSE: --

PLACE OF DEATH

19A. PLACE OF DEATH—NAME OF HOSPITAL: 4147 Bakman Ave (home)	19B. STREET ADDRESS: 4147 Bakman Ave	INSIDE CITY CORPORATE LIMITS
19C. CITY OR TOWN: North Hollywood	19D. COUNTY: Los Angeles	19E. LENGTH OF STAY IN COUNTY OF DEATH: 28 YEARS / 19F. LENGTH OF STAY IN CALIFORNIA: life YEARS

LAST USUAL RESIDENCE (WHERE DID DECEASED LIVE—IF IN INSTITUTION ENTER RESIDENCE BEFORE ADMISSION)

20A. LAST USUAL RESIDENCE—STREET ADDRESS: 4147 Bakman Ave	20B. IF INSIDE CITY CORPORATE LIMITS CHECK HERE [X]	21A. NAME OF INFORMANT (IF OTHER THAN SPOUSE): Lee C. Millar (Son)
20C. CITY OR TOWN: North Hollywood	20D. COUNTY: Los Angeles / 20E. STATE: Calif	21B. ADDRESS OF INFORMANT: Same

PHYSICIAN'S OR CORONER'S CERTIFICATION

22A. PHYSICIAN: I HEREBY CERTIFY THAT DEATH OCCURRED AT THE HOUR, DATE AND PLACE STATED ABOVE, FROM THE CAUSES STATED BELOW AND THAT I ATTENDED THE DECEASED FROM 1940 TO 12-14-66 AND THAT I LAST SAW THE DECEASED ALIVE ON 12-14-66	22B. PHYSICIAN OR CORONER—SIGNATURE: Carlos Lund / DEGREE OR TITLE: MD
22B. CORONER: I HEREBY CERTIFY THAT DEATH OCCURRED AT THE HOUR, DATE AND PLACE STATED ABOVE FROM THE CAUSES STATED BELOW AND THAT I HAVE HELD	22D. ADDRESS: 10745 Riverside Dr NH / 22E. DATE SIGNED: 12/15/66

FUNERAL DIRECTOR AND LOCAL REGISTRAR

23. SPECIFY BURIAL, ENTOMBMENT OR CREMATION: Cremation	24. DATE: 12/17/66	25. NAME OF CEMETERY OR CREMATORY: Grand View crematory / 26. EMBALMER—SIGNATURE: Vernon D Steen / LICENSE NUMBER: 1861
27. NAME OF FUNERAL DIRECTOR: Steen Lorentzen Chapel	28. DATE ACCEPTED FOR REGISTRATION BY LOCAL REGISTRAR: DEC 16 1966	29. LOCAL REGISTRAR SIGNATURE: Alfred Leder MD

CAUSE OF DEATH (MEDICAL AND HEALTH DATA)

30. CAUSE OF DEATH — PART I. DEATH WAS CAUSED BY	APPROXIMATE INTERVAL BETWEEN ONSET AND DEATH
IMMEDIATE CAUSE (A): Cardiac Failure	24 hrs
CONDITIONS IF ANY WHICH GIVE RISE TO THE ABOVE CAUSE (A) STATING THE UNDERLYING CAUSE LAST — DUE TO (B): C.V.A.	48 hrs
DUE TO (C): Arteriosclerotic Heart Disease	10 yrs

PART II. OTHER SIGNIFICANT CONDITIONS CONTRIBUTING TO DEATH BUT NOT RELATED TO THE TERMINAL DISEASE CONDITION GIVEN IN PART I (A):

OPERATION AND AUTOPSY

31. OPERATION—CHECK ONE: [X] NO OPERATION PERFORMED	32. DATE OF OPERATION	33. AUTOPSY—CHECK ONE: [X] NO AUTOPSY PERFORMED

INJURY INFORMATION

34A. SPECIFY ACCIDENT, SUICIDE OR HOMICIDE	34B. DESCRIBE HOW INJURY OCCURRED
35A. TIME OF INJURY	
35B. INJURY OCCURRED [ ] WHILE AT WORK [ ] NOT WHILE AT WORK	35C. PLACE OF INJURY / 35D. CITY, TOWN, OR LOCATION / COUNTY / STATE

Rev 1-1-59 Form VS-11

This is to certify that this document is a true copy of the official record filed with the Registrar-Recorder/County Clerk.

OCT 6 1995
19-029349

This copy not valid unless prepared on engraved border displaying the Seal of the Registrar-Recorder/County Clerk.

ANY ALTERATION OR ERASURE VOIDS THIS CERTIFICATE

STATE OF CALIFORNIA
CERTIFICATION OF VITAL RECORD

COUNTY OF LOS ANGELES • REGISTRAR-RECORDER/COUNTY CLERK

CERTIFICATE OF DEATH
STATE OF CALIFORNIA
USE BLACK INK ONLY NO ERASURES, WHITEOUTS OR ALTERATIONS
VS 11 (REV 7-93)

39619026130

STATE FILE NUMBER / LOCAL REGISTRATION NUMBER

DECEDENT PERSONAL DATA

1. NAME OF DECEDENT FIRST (GIVEN): Ella
2. MIDDLE: Jane
3. LAST (FAMILY): Fitzgerald
4. DATE OF BIRTH MM/DD/CCYY: 04/25/1918
5. AGE YRS: 78
6. SEX: FE
7. DATE OF DEATH MM/DD/CCYY: 06/15/1996
8. HOUR: 0256
9. STATE OF BIRTH: VA
10. SOCIAL SECURITY NO: 059-12-2595
11. MILITARY SERVICE: 19 TO 19 — NONE
12. MARITAL STATUS: Divorced
13. EDUCATION - YEARS COMPLETED: 11
14. RACE: Black
15. HISPANIC: SPECIFY — YES / [X] NO
16. USUAL EMPLOYER: Self-Employed
17. OCCUPATION: Singer
18. KIND OF BUSINESS: Entertainment
19. YEARS IN OCCUPATION: 55

USUAL RESIDENCE

20. RESIDENCE — STREET AND NUMBER OR LOCATION: 908 Whittier Drive
21. CITY: Beverly Hills
22. COUNTY: Los Angeles
23. ZIP CODE: 90210
24. YRS IN COUNTY: 38
25. STATE OR FOREIGN COUNTRY: California

INFORMANT

26. NAME, RELATIONSHIP: Raymond M. Brown Jr-Son
27. MAILING ADDRESS: 908 Whittier Drive Beverly Hills, Ca. 90210

SPOUSE AND PARENT INFORMATION

28. NAME OF SURVIVING SPOUSE—FIRST: —
29. MIDDLE: —
30. LAST (MAIDEN NAME): —
31. NAME OF FATHER—FIRST: William
32. MIDDLE: —
33. LAST: Fitzgerald
34. BIRTH STATE: VA
35. NAME OF MOTHER—FIRST: Temple
36. MIDDLE: —
37. LAST (MAIDEN): Williams
38. BIRTH STATE: NC

DISPOSITION(S)

39. DATE MM/DD/CCYY: 06/20/1996
40. PLACE OF FINAL DISPOSITION: Inglewood Park Cemetery 720 E. Florence Avenue Inglewood, Calif.

FUNERAL DIRECTOR AND LOCAL REGISTRAR

41. TYPE OF DISPOSITION(S): Burial
42. SIGNATURE OF EMBALMER: Eleanor Richardson
43. LICENSE NO.: 7668
44. NAME OF FUNERAL DIRECTOR: HARRISON ROSS MORTUARY
45. LICENSE NO.: FD 551
46. SIGNATURE OF LOCAL REGISTRAR: Mark Simmons
47. DATE MM/DD/CCYY: 06/18/1996

PLACE OF DEATH

101. PLACE OF DEATH: RESIDENCE
102. IF HOSPITAL, SPECIFY ONE: IP / ER/OP / DOA
103. FACILITY OTHER THAN HOSPITAL: CONV HOSP / [X] RES / OTHER
104. COUNTY: LOS ANGELES
105. STREET ADDRESS: 908 WHITTIER DRIVE
106. CITY: BEVERLY HILLS

CAUSE OF DEATH

107. DEATH WAS CAUSED BY:
IMMEDIATE CAUSE (A) CEREBRAL VASCULAR ACCIDENT — TIME INTERVAL: 12 DAYS
DUE TO (B) DIABETES MELLITUS — 30 YRS
DUE TO (C)
DUE TO (D)
108. DEATH REPORTED TO CORONER: YES / [X] NO — REFERRAL NUMBER
109. BIOPSY PERFORMED: YES / [X] NO
110. AUTOPSY PERFORMED: YES / [X] NO
111. USED IN DETERMINING CAUSE: YES / [X] NO
112. OTHER SIGNIFICANT CONDITIONS CONTRIBUTING TO DEATH BUT NOT RELATED TO CAUSE GIVEN IN 107: CHRONIC RENAL FAILURE
113. WAS OPERATION PERFORMED FOR ANY CONDITION IN ITEM 107 OR 112? IF YES, LIST TYPE OF OPERATION AND DATE: NO

PHYSICIANS CERTIFICATION

114. I CERTIFY THAT TO THE BEST OF MY KNOWLEDGE DEATH OCCURRED AT THE HOUR, DATE AND PLACE STATED FROM THE CAUSES STATED.
DECEDENT ATTENDED SINCE: 07/01/1970
DECEDENT LAST SEEN ALIVE: 06/14/1996
115. SIGNATURE AND TITLE OF CERTIFIER
116. LICENSE NO.: C29672
117. DATE MM/DD/CCYY: 06/17/1996
118. TYPE ATTENDING PHYSICIAN'S NAME, MAILING ADDRESS - ZIP: Norman S. Bobes MD 9763 W. Pico Blvd. Los Angeles, Calif. 90035

CORONER'S USE ONLY

119. MANNER OF DEATH: NATURAL / SUICIDE / HOMICIDE / ACCIDENT / PENDING INVESTIGATION / COULD NOT BE DETERMINED
120. INJURY AT WORK: YES / NO
121. INJURY DATE MM/DD/CCYY
122. HOUR
123. PLACE OF INJURY
124. DESCRIBE HOW INJURY OCCURRED (EVENTS WHICH RESULTED IN INJURY)
125. LOCATION (STREET AND NUMBER OR LOCATION AND CITY AND ZIP CODE)
126. SIGNATURE OF CORONER OR DEPUTY CORONER
127. DATE MM/DD/CCYY
128. TYPED NAME, TITLE OF CORONER OR DEPUTY CORONER

STATE REGISTRAR
A / B / C / D / E / F / G / H / FAX AUTH. # / CENSUS TRACT

This is to certify that this document is a true copy of the official record filed with the Registrar-Recorder/County Clerk.

Conny B. McCormack

CONNY B. McCORMACK
Registrar-Recorder/County Clerk

This copy not valid unless prepared on engraved border displaying the Seal and Signature of the Registrar-Recorder/County Clerk.

APR 0 7 2000
19-555656

MIDWEST BANK NOTE COMPANY — ANY ALTERATION OR ERASURE VOIDS THIS CERTIFICATE

STATE OF CALIFORNIA
CERTIFICATION OF VITAL RECORD

COUNTY OF LOS ANGELES • REGISTRAR-RECORDER/COUNTY CLERK

FILED JAN 17 1941 MAME B. BEATTY, Registrar of Vital Statistics   12635

DISTRICT No. **1953**   REGISTRAR'S No. **171**

1. FULL NAME **F. Scott Fitzgerald**

2. PLACE OF DEATH: (A) COUNTY **Los Angeles**
   (B) CITY OR TOWN **West Hollywood Rural**   1-53
   IF OUTSIDE CITY OR TOWN LIMITS, WRITE RURAL
   (C) NAME OF HOSPITAL OR INSTITUTION **1443 No. Hayworth**
   IF NOT IN HOSPITAL OR INSTITUTION, GIVE STREET NUMBER OR LOCATION
   (D) LENGTH OF STAY: (SPECIFY WHETHER YEARS, MONTHS OR DAYS)
   IN HOSPITAL OR INSTITUTION
   IN THIS COMMUNITY **3 yrs.** IN CALIFORNIA **3 yrs.**
   (E) IF FOREIGN BORN, HOW LONG IN THE U.S.A. ____ YEARS

3. USUAL RESIDENCE OF DECEASED:
   (A) STATE **California**
   (B) COUNTY **Los Angeles**
   (C) CITY OR TOWN **West Hollywood Rural**   1-53
   IF OUTSIDE CITY OR TOWN LIMITS, WRITE RURAL
   (D) STREET No. **1403 N. Laurel**

20. DATE OF DEATH: MONTH **Dec.** DAY **21** YEAR **1940** HOUR **5** MINUTE **15 pm**

3. (A) IF VETERAN, NAME OF WAR **None**
3. (B) SOCIAL SECURITY NO. **None**

4. SEX **Male**
5. COLOR OR RACE **Cauc.**
6. (A) SINGLE, MARRIED, WIDOWED OR DIVORCED **Married**

6. (D) NAME OF HUSBAND OR WIFE **Zelda Fitzgerald**
6. (C) AGE OF HUSBAND OR WIFE, IF ALIVE **Unk.** YEARS

21. MEDICAL CERTIFICATE
I HEREBY CERTIFY, THAT I ATTENDED THE DECEASED
FROM **Nov 15** 1940
TO **Dec 21** 1940
THAT I LAST SAW HIM **1m** ALIVE ON **Dec 14** 1940
AND THAT DEATH OCCURRED ON THE DATE AND HOUR STATED ABOVE.

22. CORONER'S CERTIFICATE
I HEREBY CERTIFY, THAT I HELD AN AUTOPSY, INQUEST OR INVESTIGATION ON THE REMAINS OF THE DECEASED AND FIND FROM SUCH ACTION THAT DECEASED CAME TO DEATH ON THE DATE AND HOUR STATED ABOVE.

7. BIRTHDATE OF DECEASED **Sept.** MONTH **24** DAY **1896** YEAR

IMMEDIATE CAUSE OF DEATH **Coronary occlusion** | DURATION **6 wks.**

8. AGE **44** YRS. **2** MOS. **27** DAYS ____ IF LESS THAN ONE DAY OLD HRS. ____ MIN. ____

DUE TO **Arteriosclerotic Heart Disease**   ?

9. BIRTHPLACE **St Paul, Minn.**
10. USUAL OCCUPATION **Writer**
11. INDUSTRY OR BUSINESS **Books**

DUE TO ____   93d   44a

FATHER
12. NAME **Unk.**
13. BIRTHPLACE **Unk.**

OTHER CONDITIONS (INCLUDE PREGNANCY WITHIN THREE MONTHS OF DEATH)

MOTHER
14. MAIDEN NAME **Unk.**
15. BIRTHPLACE **Unk.**

MAJOR FINDINGS: OF OPERATIONS ____ DATE OF OPERATION ____

(2)

PHYSICIAN UNDERLINE THE CAUSE TO WHICH DEATH SHOULD BE CHARGED STATISTICALLY

16. (A) INFORMANT **Frances Kroll**
    (B) ADDRESS **921 S. Shenandoah**

OF AUTOPSY **none**

17. (A) **Removal** BURIAL, CREMATION OR REMOVAL (B) DATE **12-23-40**
    (C) PLACE **Baltimore, Maryland**
18. (A) EMBALMER SIGNATURE **Thomas J. Clougherty** LICENSE No. **2556**
    (B) FUNERAL DIRECTOR **Pierce Brothers**
    ADDRESS **720 W. Washington Los Angeles**
    BY **C. H. Hess**

23. IF DEATH WAS DUE TO EXTERNAL CAUSES, FILL IN THE FOLLOWING:
    (A) ACCIDENT, SUICIDE OR HOMICIDE? ____
    (B) DATE OF INJURY ____
    (C) WHERE DID INJURY OCCUR? ____ CITY OR TOWN ____ COUNTY ____ STATE ____
    (D) DID INJURY OCCUR IN OR ABOUT HOME, ON FARM, IN INDUSTRIAL PLACE, OR IN PUBLIC PLACE? ____ SPECIFY TYPE OF PLACE ____ WHILE AT WORK? ____
    (E) MEANS OF INJURY ____

J L Pomeroy MD

19. (A) **Dec 23 1940** DATE FILED **Effa M. Brannies** REGISTRAR'S SIGNATURE

24. CORONER OR PHYSICIAN'S SIGNATURE **Clarence H Nelson M.D.** (SPECIFY WHICH)
    ADDRESS **3130 W 6th St. Los Angeles, Dec 21/40**

STATE OF CALIFORNIA
DEPARTMENT OF PUBLIC HEALTH

CERTIFICATE OF DEATH

U. S. DEPT. OF COMMERCE
BUREAU OF THE CENSUS

STATE OF CALIFORNIA
CERTIFICATION OF VITAL RECORD

COUNTY OF RIVERSIDE
RIVERSIDE, CALIFORNIA

CERTIFICATE OF DEATH
STATE OF CALIFORNIA
USE BLACK INK ONLY/NO ERASURES, WHITEOUTS OR ALTERATIONS
VS-11 (REV. 1/00)

3 2002 33012021

STATE FILE NUMBER | LOCAL REGISTRATION NUMBER

DECEDENT PERSONAL DATA

1. NAME OF DECEDENT—FIRST (GIVEN)	2. MIDDLE	3. LAST (FAMILY)
SUSAN	ALVA	FLEMING- MARX

4. DATE OF BIRTH MM/DD/CCYY	5. AGE YRS.	IF UNDER 1 YEAR MONTHS/DAYS	IF UNDER 24 HOURS HOURS/MINUTES	6. SEX	7. DATE OF DEATH MM/DD/CCYY	8. HOUR
02/19/1908	94			F	12/22/2002	2330

9. STATE OF BIRTH	10. SOCIAL SECURITY NO.	11. MILITARY SERVICE	12. MARITAL STATUS	13. EDUCATION—YEARS COMPLETED
NEW YORK	559-70-2180	YES [X] NO [ ] UNK	WIDOWED	14

14. RACE	15. HISPANIC—SPECIFY	16. USUAL EMPLOYER
WHITE	Yes [ ] [X] No	SELF EMPLOYED

17. OCCUPATION	18. KIND OF BUSINESS	19. YEARS IN OCCUPATION
ACTRESS	MOTION PICTURES	12

USUAL RESIDENCE

20. RESIDENCE—STREET AND NUMBER OR LOCATION: 44600 MONTEREY AVENUE B107

21. CITY	22. COUNTY	23. ZIP CODE	24. YRS IN COUNTY	25. STATE OR FOREIGN COUNTRY
PALM DESERT	RIVERSIDE	92260	55	CALIFORNIA

INFORMANT

26. NAME, RELATIONSHIP	27. MAILING ADDRESS (STREET AND NUMBER OR RURAL ROUTE NUMBER, CITY OR TOWN, STATE, ZIP)
WILLIAM W MARX - SON	7 BUCKINGHAM WAY, RANCHO MIRAGE, CA 92270

SPOUSE AND PARENT INFORMATION

28. NAME OF SURVIVING SPOUSE—FIRST	29. MIDDLE	30. LAST (MAIDEN NAME)
-	-	-

31. NAME OF FATHER—FIRST	32. MIDDLE	33. LAST	34. BIRTH STATE
WILLIAM	-	FLEMING	UNKNOWN

35. NAME OF MOTHER—FIRST	36. MIDDLE	37. LAST (MAIDEN)	38. BIRTH STATE
GUNHILD	-	VON PHILP	UNKNOWN

DISPOSITION(S)

39. DATE MM/DD/CCYY	40. PLACE OF FINAL DISPOSITION
12/27/2002	RES: WILLIAM W MARX, 7 BUCKINGHAM WAY, RANCHO MIRAGE, CA 92270

FUNERAL DIRECTOR AND LOCAL REGISTRAR

41. TYPE OF DISPOSITION(S)	42. SIGNATURE OF EMBALMER	43. LICENSE NO.
CR/RES	▶ NOT EMBALMED	

44. NAME OF FUNERAL DIRECTOR	45. LICENSE NO.	46. SIGNATURE OF LOCAL REGISTRAR	47. DATE MM/DD/CCYY
PALM SPRINGS MORTUARY, CATHEDRAL CITY	FD 1513	▶ Gary Feldman MD	12/27/2002

PLACE OF DEATH

101. PLACE OF DEATH	102. IF HOSPITAL, SPECIFY ONE:	103. FACILITY OTHER THAN HOSPITAL:	104. COUNTY
EISENHOWER MEMORIAL HOSPITAL	[X] IP [ ] ER/OP [ ] DOA	[ ] CONV. HOSP. [ ] RES. CARE [ ] OTHER	RIVERSIDE

105. STREET ADDRESS—STREET AND NUMBER OR LOCATION	106. CITY
39000 BOB HOPE DRIVE	RANCHO MIRAGE

CAUSE OF DEATH

107. DEATH WAS CAUSED BY: (ENTER ONLY ONE CAUSE PER LINE FOR A, B, C, AND D)

			TIME INTERVAL BETWEEN ONSET AND DEATH	108. DEATH REPORTED TO CORONER
IMMEDIATE CAUSE	(A)	CARDIOPULMONARY FAILURE	DAYS	YES [ ] [X] NO — REFERRAL NUMBER
DUE TO	(B)	CARDIOMYOPATHY	DAYS	109. BIOPSY PERFORMED YES [ ] [X] NO
DUE TO	(C)	MYOCARDIAL INFARCTION	DAYS	110. AUTOPSY PERFORMED YES [ ] [X] NO
DUE TO	(D)	PROBABLE CORONARY ARTERY DISEASE	YEARS	111. USED IN DETERMINING CAUSE YES [ ] NO [ ]

112. OTHER SIGNIFICANT CONDITIONS CONTRIBUTING TO DEATH BUT NOT RELATED TO CAUSE GIVEN IN 107
LEUKOCYTOSIS, D J D, C H F, PERIPHERAL VASCULAR DISEASE, POSSIBLE TRANSIENT ISCHEMIC ATTACK

113. WAS OPERATION PERFORMED FOR ANY CONDITION IN ITEM 107 OR 112? IF YES, LIST TYPE OF OPERATION AND DATE.
NO

PHYSICIAN'S CERTIFICATION

114. I CERTIFY THAT TO THE BEST OF MY KNOWLEDGE DEATH OCCURRED AT THE HOUR, DATE AND PLACE STATED FROM THE CAUSES STATED.		115. SIGNATURE AND TITLE OF CERTIFIER	116. LICENSE NO.	117. DATE MM/DD/CCYY
DECEDENT ATTENDED SINCE MM/DD/CCYY 12/15/2002	DECEDENT LAST SEEN ALIVE MM/DD/CCYY 12/22/2002	▶ Arnd Liffler	20 A 5819	12/23/2002

118. TYPE ATTENDING PHYSICIAN'S NAME, MAILING ADDRESS, ZIP
MASSOUD G DEZFULI, DO 39000 BOB HOPE DRIVE, RANCHO MIRAGE, CA 92270

CORONER'S USE ONLY

119. I CERTIFY THAT IN MY OPINION DEATH OCCURRED AT THE HOUR, DATE AND PLACE FROM THE CAUSES STATED.	120. INJURY AT WORK	121. INJURY DATE MM/DD/CCYY	122. HOUR	123. PLACE OF INJURY
119. MANNER OF DEATH	YES [ ] NO [ ]			

124. DESCRIBE HOW INJURY OCCURRED (EVENTS WHICH RESULTED IN INJURY)

[ ] NATURAL	[ ] SUICIDE	[ ] HOMICIDE
[ ] ACCIDENT	[ ] PENDING INVESTIGATION	[ ] COULD NOT BE DETERMINED

125. LOCATION (STREET AND NUMBER OR LOCATION AND CITY, ZIP)

126. SIGNATURE OF CORONER OR DEPUTY CORONER	127. DATE MM/DD/CCYY	128. TYPED NAME, TITLE OF CORONER OR DEPUTY CORONER
▶		

STATE REGISTRAR

A	B	C	D	E	F	G	H	FAX AUTH. #	CENSUS TRACT
								452306	

33372531

CERTIFIED COPY OF VITAL RECORDS
STATE OF CALIFORNIA, COUNTY OF RIVERSIDE

This is a true and exact reproduction of the document officially registered and placed on file in the office of the County of Riverside, County Clerk-Recorder.

DATE ISSUED   JAN 1 4 2003

Gary L. Orso

GARY L. ORSO
COUNTY CLERK-RECORDER
RIVERSIDE COUNTY, CALIFORNIA

This copy is not valid unless prepared on engraved border displaying date, seal and signature of the County Clerk-Recorder.

ANY ALTERATION OR ERASURE VOIDS THIS CERTIFICATE

COUNTY OF LOS ANGELES • REGISTRAR-RECORDER/ COUNTY CLERK

CERTIFICATE OF DEATH
STATE OF CALIFORNIA
USE BLACK INK ONLY

39119043131

LOCAL REGISTRATION DISTRICT AND CERTIFICATE NUMBER

1A. NAME OF DECEDENT—FIRST (Given)	1B. MIDDLE	1C. LAST (Family)	2A. DATE OF DEATH—MO. DAY. YR.	2B. HOUR	3. SEX
REDD		FOXX	OCTOBER 11, 1991	7:45	MALE

4. RACE	5. HISPANIC—SPECIFY	6. DATE OF BIRTH—MO. DAY. YR	7. AGE IN YEARS	IF UNDER 1 YEAR MONTHS / DAYS	IF UNDER 24 HOURS HOURS / MINUTES
BLACK	☐ YES ☒ NO	DECEMBER 9, 1922	68		

DECEDENT PERSONAL DATA

8. STATE OF BIRTH	9. CITIZEN OF WHAT COUNTRY	10A. FULL NAME OF FATHER	10B. STATE OF BIRTH	11A. FULL MAIDEN NAME OF MOTHER	11B. STATE OF BIRTH
MO	USA	UNKNOWN SANFORD	UNK.	MARY HUGHES	MS

12. MILITARY SERVICE? 19___ TO 19___ ☒ NONE	13. SOCIAL SECURITY NO. 101-18-7943	14. MARITAL STATUS MARRIED	15. NAME OF SURVIVING SPOUSE (IF WIFE, ENTER MAIDEN NAME) KAHO CHO

16A. USUAL OCCUPATION	16B. USUAL KIND OF BUSINESS OR INDUSTRY	16C. USUAL EMPLOYER	16D. YEARS IN OCCUPATION	17. EDUCATION - YEARS COMPLETED
ACTOR-COMEDIAN	ENTERTAINMENT	SELF EMPLOYED	55	12

USUAL RESIDENCE

18A. RESIDENCE—STREET AND NUMBER OR LOCATION	18B. CITY	18C. ZIP CODE
5460 S. EASTERN AVE.	LAS VEGAS	89119

18D. COUNTY	18E. NUMBER OF YEARS IN THIS COUNTY	18F. STATE OR FOREIGN COUNTRY	20. NAME, RELATIONSHIP, MAILING ADDRESS AND ZIP CODE OF INFORMANT
CLARK	22	NEVADA	KAHO CHO FOXX - WIFE 5460 S. EASTERN AVE. LAS VEGAS, NEVADA 89119

PLACE OF DEATH

19A. PLACE OF DEATH	19B. IF HOSPITAL SPECIFY ONE: IP, ER/OP, DOA	19C. COUNTY
QUEEN OF ANGELS/HOLLYWOOD PRESBYTERIAN MED. CTR.	IP	LOS ANGELES

19D. STREET ADDRESS—STREET AND NUMBER OR LOCATION	19E. CITY
1300 N. VERMONT AVENUE	LOS ANGELES

TIME INTERVAL BETWEEN ONSET AND DEATH	22. WAS DEATH REPORTED TO CORONER? REFERRAL NUMBER ☐ YES ☒ NO

CAUSE OF DEATH

21. DEATH WAS CAUSED BY (ENTER ONLY ONE CAUSE PER LINE FOR A, B, AND C)		23. WAS BIOPSY PERFORMED?
IMMEDIATE CAUSE (A) Cardiorespiratory arrest	▶ 45 min	☐ YES ☒ NO
DUE TO (B) Cardiogenic Shock	▶ 1½ hr	24A. WAS AUTOPSY PERFORMED? ☐ YES ☒ NO
DUE TO (C) Acute myocardial infarction	▶ 2½ hr	24B. WAS IT USED IN DETERMINING CAUSE OF DEATH? ☐ YES ☒ NO

25. OTHER SIGNIFICANT CONDITIONS CONTRIBUTING TO DEATH BUT NOT RELATED TO CAUSE GIVEN IN 21 None	26. WAS OPERATION PERFORMED FOR ANY CONDITION IN ITEM 21 OR 25? IF YES, LIST TYPE OF OPERATION AND DATE None

PHYSICIAN'S CERTIFICATION

27A. DECEDENT ATTENDED SINCE MONTH, DAY, YEAR / DECEDENT LAST SEEN ALIVE MONTH, DAY, YEAR	27B. SIGNATURE AND DEGREE OR TITLE OF CERTIFIER ▶ M. A. Latif, MD	27C. CERTIFIER'S LICENSE NUMBER A29695	27D. DATE SIGNED 10/12/91
I CERTIFY THAT TO THE BEST OF MY KNOWLEDGE DEATH OCCURRED AT THE HOUR, DATE AND PLACE STATED FROM THE CAUSES STATED. 10/11/91 10/11/91	27E. TYPE ATTENDING PHYSICIAN'S NAME AND ADDRESS Mohamad Latif, MD 1300 N. Vermont, LA, CA 90027		

CORONER'S USE ONLY

I CERTIFY THAT IN MY OPINION DEATH OCCURRED AT THE HOUR, DATE AND PLACE STATED FROM THE CAUSES STATED.	28A. SIGNATURE AND TITLE OF CORONER OR DEPUTY CORONER ▶	28B. DATE SIGNED

29. MANNER OF DEATH	30A. PLACE OF INJURY	30B. INJURY AT WORK? ☐ YES ☐ NO	30C. DATE OF INJURY MONTH DAY, YEAR	31. HOUR

32. LOCATION (STREET AND NUMBER OR LOCATION AND CITY)	33. DESCRIBE HOW INJURY OCCURRED (EVENTS WHICH RESULTED IN INJURY)

FUNERAL DIRECTOR AND LOCAL REGISTRAR

34A. DISPOSITION(S) TR/BU	34B. PLACE OF FINAL DISPOSITION—NAME AND ADDRESS PALM VALLEY VIEW MEMORIAL PARK LAS VEGAS, NEVADA	34C. DATE MO. DAY, YEAR 10-12-1991	35A. SIGNATURE OF EMBALMER Ray Morris	35B. LICENSE NUMBER 7079
36A. NAME OF FUNERAL DIRECTOR (OR PERSON ACTING AS SUCH) FOREST LAWN MTY GLENDALE	36B. LICENSE NO. 656	37. SIGNATURE OF LOCAL REGISTRAR ▶ Robert C. Britt	38. REGISTRATION DATE OCT 12 1991

STATE REGISTRAR	A	B	C	D	E	F	CENSUS TRACT

VS-11 (REV. 1-90)   410   MAKE NO ERASURES, WHITEOUTS, OR OTHER ALTERATIONS   04-9-1-0382

CERTIFICATION OF VITAL RECORD

COUNTY OF LOS ANGELES • REGISTRAR-RECORDER/COUNTY CLERK

CERTIFICATE OF DEATH
STATE OF CALIFORNIA
USE BLACK INK ONLY

39119029782

STATE FILE NUMBER		LOCAL REGISTRATION DISTRICT AND CERTIFICATE NUMBER

DECEDENT PERSONAL DATA

1A. NAME OF DECEDENT—FIRST (GIVEN): James
1B. MIDDLE: G.
1C. LAST (FAMILY): Franciscus
2A. DATE OF DEATH—MO, DAY, YR: July 8, 1991
2B. HOUR: 1300
3. SEX: M

4. RACE: Caucasian
5. HISPANIC—SPECIFY: [X] NO
6. DATE OF BIRTH—MO, DAY, YR: January 31, 1934
7. AGE IN YEARS: 57
IF UNDER 1 YEAR MONTHS / DAYS
IF UNDER 24 HOURS HOURS / MINUTES

8. STATE OF BIRTH: MO
9. CITIZEN OF WHAT COUNTRY: USA
10A. FULL NAME OF FATHER: JOHN ALLEN FRANCISCUS
10B. STATE OF BIRTH: MO
11A. FULL MAIDEN NAME OF MOTHER: LORAINE GROVER
11B. STATE OF BIRTH: MO

12. MILITARY SERVICE? 19 ___ TO 19 ___ [X] NONE
13. SOCIAL SECURITY NO.: 049-28-6904
14. MARITAL STATUS: Married
15. NAME OF SURVIVING SPOUSE (IF WIFE, ENTER MAIDEN NAME): Carla Ankney

16A. USUAL OCCUPATION: Actor
16B. USUAL KIND OF BUSINESS OR INDUSTRY: Entertainment
16C. USUAL EMPLOYER: Self
16D. YEARS IN OCCUPATION: 30
17. EDUCATION—YEARS COMPLETED: 17

USUAL RESIDENCE

18A. RESIDENCE—STREET AND NUMBER OR LOCATION: 12549 Addison Street
18B. CITY: North Hollywood
18C. ZIP CODE: 91607

18D. COUNTY: Los Angeles
18E. NUMBER OF YEARS IN THIS COUNTY: 30
18F. STATE OR FOREIGN COUNTRY: California

20. NAME, RELATIONSHIP, MAILING ADDRESS AND ZIP CODE OF INFORMANT:
Carla Franciscus —Wife
12549 Addison Street
North Hollywood, Ca. 91607

PLACE OF DEATH

19A. PLACE OF DEATH: Medical Center of North Hollywood
19B. IF HOSPITAL, SPECIFY ONE: IP, ER/OP, DOA: IP
19C. COUNTY: Los Angeles

19D. STREET ADDRESS—STREET AND NUMBER OR LOCATION: 12629 Riverside Dr.
19E. CITY: North Hollywood

TIME INTERVAL BETWEEN ONSET AND DEATH

22. WAS DEATH REPORTED TO CORONER? [X] YES REFERRAL NUMBER 91-53131 [X] NO

CAUSE OF DEATH

21. DEATH WAS CAUSED BY: (ENTER ONLY ONE CAUSE PER LINE FOR A, B, AND C)

IMMEDIATE CAUSE (A): Respiratory arrest ▶ 5 HRS
23. WAS BIOPSY PERFORMED? [ ] YES [X] NO

DUE TO (B): Aspiration pneumonia ▶ 2 DAYS
24A. WAS AUTOPSY PERFORMED? [ ] YES [X] NO

DUE TO (C): Anoxic Encephalopathy d/t Cardiomyopathy ▶ YRS
24B. WAS IT USED IN DETERMINING CAUSE OF DEATH? [ ] YES [X] NO

25. OTHER SIGNIFICANT CONDITIONS CONTRIBUTING TO DEATH BUT NOT RELATED TO CAUSE GIVEN IN 21: Emphysema
26. WAS OPERATION PERFORMED FOR ANY CONDITION IN ITEM 21 OR 25? IF YES, LIST TYPE OF OPERATION AND DATE: No

PHYSICIAN'S CERTIFICATION

I CERTIFY THAT TO THE BEST OF MY KNOWLEDGE DEATH OCCURRED AT THE HOUR, DATE AND PLACE STATED FROM THE CAUSES STATED.

27A. DECEDENT ATTENDED SINCE MONTH, DAY, YEAR: 7-1-1991
DECEDENT LAST SEEN ALIVE MONTH, DAY, YEAR: 7-8-1991

27B. SIGNATURE AND DEGREE OR TITLE OF CERTIFIER: ▶ [signature] M
27C. CERTIFIER'S LICENSE NUMBER: 653079
27D. DATE SIGNED: 7/10/91

27E. TYPE ATTENDING PHYSICIAN'S NAME AND ADDRESS: J. Nathan Rubin, MD 4929 Van Nuys Blvd., Sherman Oaks, Ca

CORONER'S USE ONLY

I CERTIFY THAT IN MY OPINION DEATH OCCURRED AT THE HOUR, DATE AND PLACE STATED FROM THE CAUSES STATED. ▶
28A. SIGNATURE AND TITLE OF CORONER OR DEPUTY CORONER
28B. DATE SIGNED

29. MANNER OF DEATH—specify one natural, accident, suicide, homicide, pending investigation or could not be determined
30A. PLACE OF INJURY
30B. INJURY AT WORK [ ] YES [ ] NO
30C. DATE OF INJURY MONTH, DAY, YEAR
31. HOUR

32. LOCATION (STREET AND NUMBER OR LOCATION AND CITY)
33. DESCRIBE HOW INJURY OCCURRED (EVENTS WHICH RESULTED IN INJURY)

FUNERAL DIRECTOR AND LOCAL REGISTRAR

34A. DISPOSITION(S): Cr/Res
34B. PLACE OF FINAL DISPOSITION—NAME AND ADDRESS: Res: 12549 Addison Street North Hollywood, Ca.
34C. DATE MO, DAY, YEAR: 7-22-91
35A. SIGNATURE OF EMBALMER: Not Embalmed
35B. LICENSE NUMBER: None

36A. NAME OF FUNERAL DIRECTOR (OR PERSON ACTING AS SUCH): Aftercare Ca. crem & Bu Society
36B. LICENSE NO.: F 1166
37. SIGNATURE OF LOCAL REGISTRAR: ▶ [signature] Robert C. Nata Jr.
38. REGISTRATION DATE: JUL 18 1991

STATE REGISTRAR
A. B. C. D. E. F. CENSUS TRACT

VS-11 (REV. 1-90)

MAKE NO ERASURES, WHITEOUTS, OR OTHER ALTERATIONS

This is to certify that this document is a true copy of the official record filed with the Registrar-Recorder/County Clerk.

[signature] Beatriz Valdez
BEATRIZ VALDEZ
Registrar-Recorder/County Clerk

AUG 16 1995
19-397090

This copy not valid unless prepared on engraved border displaying the Seal and Signature of the Registrar-Recorder/County Clerk.

American Bank Note Company   ANY ALTERATION OR ERASURE VOIDS THIS CERTIFICATE

CERTIFICATE OF DEATH
STATE OF CALIFORNIA
USE BLACK INK ONLY/NO ERASURES, WHITEOUTS OR ALTERATIONS
VS-11 (REV. 1/00)

3 2002 19 029366

STATE FILE NUMBER		LOCAL REGISTRATION NUMBER

DECEDENT PERSONAL DATA

1. NAME OF DECEDENT—FIRST (GIVEN)	2. MIDDLE	3. LAST (FAMILY)
John	Michael	Frankenheimer

4. DATE OF BIRTH MM/DD/CCYY	5. AGE YRS.	IF UNDER 1 YEAR MONTHS / DAYS	IF UNDER 24 HOURS HOURS / MINUTES	6. SEX	7. DATE OF DEATH MM/DD/CCYY	8. HOUR
02/19/1930	72			M	07/06/2002	0800

9. STATE OF BIRTH	10. SOCIAL SECURITY NO.	11. MILITARY SERVICE	12. MARITAL STATUS	13. EDUCATION—YEARS COMPLETED
NY	110-24-6438	[X] YES [ ] NO [ ] UNK	Married	16

14. RACE	15. HISPANIC—SPECIFY	16. USUAL EMPLOYER
Caucasian	[ ] YES [X] No	Self Employed

17. OCCUPATION	18. KIND OF BUSINESS	19. YEARS IN OCCUPATION
Film Director	Motion Picture	48

USUAL RESIDENCE

20. RESIDENCE—(STREET AND NUMBER OR LOCATION)
3114 Abington Dr.

21. CITY	22. COUNTY	23. ZIP CODE	24. YRS IN COUNTY	25. STATE OR FOREIGN COUNTRY
Beverly Hills	Los Angeles	90210	41	CA

INFORMANT

26. NAME, RELATIONSHIP	27. MAILING ADDRESS (STREET AND NUMBER OR RURAL ROUTE NUMBER, CITY OR TOWN, STATE, ZIP)
Evans Frankenheimer-Wife	3114 Abington Dr. Beverly Hills, CA 90210

SPOUSE AND PARENT INFORMATION

28. NAME OF SURVIVING SPOUSE—FIRST	29. MIDDLE	30. LAST (MAIDEN NAME)
Evans	-	Evans

31. NAME OF FATHER—FIRST	32. MIDDLE	33. LAST	34. BIRTH STATE
Walter	-	Frankenheimer	NY

35. NAME OF MOTHER—FIRST	36. MIDDLE	37. LAST (MAIDEN)	38. BIRTH STATE
Helen	-	Sheedy	unk

DISPOSITION(S)

39. DATE MM/DD/CCYY	40. PLACE OF FINAL DISPOSITION
07/09/2002	Res:Evans Frankenheimer:3114 Abington Dr.,Beverly Hills, CA 90210

FUNERAL DIRECTOR AND LOCAL REGISTRAR

41. TYPE OF DISPOSITION(S)	42. SIGNATURE OF EMBALMER	43. LICENSE NO.
Cr/Res	▶ not embalmed	-

44. NAME OF FUNERAL DIRECTOR	45. LICENSE NO.	46. SIGNATURE OF LOCAL REGISTRAR	47. DATE MM/DD/CCYY
Callanan Mortuary	FD-86	▶ *Thomas W. Gutheroth* AN	07/08/2002

PLACE OF DEATH

101. PLACE OF DEATH	102. IF HOSPITAL, SPECIFY ONE!	103. FACILITY OTHER THAN HOSPITAL	104. COUNTY
Cedars Sinai Med. Ctr.	[X] IP [ ] ER/OP [ ] DOA	[ ] CONV. HOSP. [ ] RES. CARE [ ] OTHER	Los Angeles

105. STREET ADDRESS—(STREET AND NUMBER OR LOCATION)	106. CITY
8700 Beverly Blvd.	Los Angeles

CAUSE OF DEATH

107. DEATH WAS CAUSED BY: (ENTER ONLY ONE CAUSE PER LINE FOR A, B, C, AND D)	TIME INTERVAL BETWEEN ONSET AND DEATH	108. DEATH REPORTED TO CORONER
IMMEDIATE CAUSE (A) Bilateral Cerebral Infarct	Days	[ ] YES [X] No — REFERRAL NUMBER
DUE TO (B) Pulmonary Embolus	Wks.	109. BIOPSY PERFORMED — [X] YES [ ] No
DUE TO (C) Metastatic Lung Cancer	Yrs.	110. AUTOPSY PERFORMED — [ ] YES [X] No
DUE TO (D) Thoracic Spinal Metastasis	Yrs.	111. USED IN DETERMINING CAUSE — [ ] YES [X] No

112. OTHER SIGNIFICANT CONDITIONS CONTRIBUTING TO DEATH BUT NOT RELATED TO CAUSE GIVEN IN 107
Bilateral DVT, Atrial Fibrillation

113. WAS OPERATION PERFORMED FOR ANY CONDITION IN ITEM 107 OR 112? IF YES, LIST TYPE OF OPERATION AND DATE.
T6 Exploration for Metastatic Module/Cord compression 06/22/2002
T4-5 Disc&Vertebral Reconstruction for pathological fracture/cord compression 05/01/2002

PHYSICIAN'S CERTIFICATION

114. I CERTIFY THAT TO THE BEST OF MY KNOWLEDGE DEATH OCCURRED AT THE HOUR, DATE AND PLACE STATED FROM THE CAUSES STATED. DECEDENT ATTENDED SINCE MM/DD/CCYY / DECEDENT LAST SEEN ALIVE MM/DD/CCYY	115. SIGNATURE AND TITLE OF CERTIFIER	116. LICENSE NO.	117. DATE MM/DD/CCYY
06/01/1985 / 07/05/2002	▶ *R. Huizenga* LMD	G-40228	7/6/02

118. TYPE ATTENDING PHYSICIAN'S NAME, MAILING ADDRESS, ZIP
Robert Huizenga M.D. 150 N. Robertson Blvd.Beverly Hills, CA 90211

CORONER'S USE ONLY

30

I CERTIFY THAT IN MY OPINION DEATH OCCURRED AT THE HOUR, DATE AND PLACE STATED FROM THE CAUSES STATED.	120. INJURY AT WORK [ ] YES [ ] No	121. INJURY DATE MM/DD/CCYY	122. HOUR	123. PLACE OF INJURY

119. MANNER OF DEATH	124. DESCRIBE HOW INJURY OCCURRED (EVENTS WHICH RESULTED IN INJURY)
[ ] NATURAL [ ] SUICIDE [ ] HOMICIDE [ ] ACCIDENT [ ] PENDING INVESTIGATION [ ] COULD NOT BE DETERMINED	INFORMATIONAL, NOT A VALID DOCUMENT TO ESTABLISH IDENTITY

125. LOCATION (STREET AND NUMBER OR LOCATION AND CITY, ZIP)

126. SIGNATURE OF CORONER OR DEPUTY CORONER	127. DATE MM/DD/CCYY	128. TYPED NAME, TITLE OF CORONER OR DEPUTY CORONER
▶		

STATE REGISTRAR

A	B	C	D	E	F	G	H	FAX AUTH. #	CENSUS TRACT
								344-4343	

CERTIFICATE OF DEATH
STATE OF CALIFORNIA
USE BLACK INK ONLY/NO ERASURES, WHITEOUTS OR ALTERATIONS
VS-11 (REV. 7/97)

3199927   001562

STATE FILE NUMBER · LOCAL REGISTRATION NUMBER

	1. NAME OF DECEDENT—FIRST (GIVEN)	2. MIDDLE	3. LAST (FAMILY)
	Allen	Albert	FUNT

DECEDENT PERSONAL DATA

4. DATE OF BIRTH MM/DD/CCYY	5. AGE YRS.	IF UNDER 1 YEAR MONTHS / DAYS	IF UNDER 24 HOURS HOURS / MINUTES	6. SEX	7. DATE OF DEATH MM/DD/CCYY	8. HOUR
09/16/1914	84			Male	09/05/1999	1628

9. STATE OF BIRTH	10. SOCIAL SECURITY NO.	11. MILITARY SERVICE	12. MARITAL STATUS	13. EDUCATION—YEARS COMPLETED
NY	113-07-6293	X YES ☐ NO ☐ UNK	Divorced	16

14. RACE	15. HISPANIC—SPECIFY	16. USUAL EMPLOYER
White	☐ YES _____ X NO	Self-employed

17. OCCUPATION	18. KIND OF BUSINESS	19. YEARS IN OCCUPATION
Television Producer	Television	47

USUAL RESIDENCE

20. RESIDENCE—(STREET AND NUMBER OR LOCATION)
3132 Spruance Road

21. CITY	22. COUNTY	23. ZIP CODE	24. YRS IN COUNTY	25. STATE OR FOREIGN COUNTRY
Pebble Beach	Monterey	93953	21	California

INFORMANT

26. NAME, RELATIONSHIP	27. MAILING ADDRESS (STREET AND NUMBER OR RURAL ROUTE NUMBER, CITY OR TOWN, STATE, ZIP)
Peter Funt, Son	1270 Lisbon Lane, Pebble Beach, CA 93953

SPOUSE AND PARENT INFORMATION

28. NAME OF SURVIVING SPOUSE—FIRST	29. MIDDLE	30. LAST (MAIDEN NAME)	
-	-	-	

31. NAME OF FATHER—FIRST	32. MIDDLE	33. LAST	34. BIRTH STATE
Isidor	Peter	Funt	Russia

35. NAME OF MOTHER—FIRST	36. MIDDLE	37. LAST (MAIDEN)	38. BIRTH STATE
Pauline	-	Schaferstein	Russia

DISPOSITION(S)

39. DATE MM/DD/CCYY	40. PLACE OF FINAL DISPOSITION
09/06/1999	Res/Peter Funt,3132 Spruance Rd.,Pebble Beach, CA

FUNERAL DIRECTOR AND LOCAL REGISTRAR

41. TYPE OF DISPOSITION(S)	42. SIGNATURE OF EMBALMER	43. LICENSE NO.
CR/Res	▶Not Embalmed	-

44. NAME OF FUNERAL DIRECTOR	45. LICENSE NO.	46. SIGNATURE OF LOCAL REGISTRAR	47. DATE MM/DD/CCYY
The Paul Mortuary	FD-280	▶Robert Imeltumo	09/06/1999 MD

PLACE OF DEATH

101. PLACE OF DEATH	102. IF HOSPITAL, SPECIFY ONE:	103. FACILITY OTHER THAN HOSPITAL:	104. COUNTY
Residence	☐ IP ☐ ER/OP ☐ DOA	☐ CONV. HOSP. ☐ RES. CARE ☐ OTHER	Monterey

105. STREET ADDRESS—(STREET AND NUMBER OR LOCATION)	106. CITY
3132 Spruance Road	Pebble Beach

CAUSE OF DEATH

107. DEATH WAS CAUSED BY: (ENTER ONLY ONE CAUSE PER LINE FOR A, B, C, AND D)	TIME INTERVAL BETWEEN ONSET AND DEATH	108. DEATH REPORTED TO CORONER
IMMEDIATE CAUSE (A) Congestive Heart Failure	1 Year	☐ YES X NO REFERRAL NUMBER
DUE TO (B) Cardiomyopathy	2 Years	109. BIOPSY PERFORMED ☐ YES X NO
DUE TO (C)		110. AUTOPSY PERFORMED ☐ YES X NO
DUE TO (D)		111. USED IN DETERMINING CAUSE ☐ YES ☐ NO

112. OTHER SIGNIFICANT CONDITIONS CONTRIBUTING TO DEATH BUT NOT RELATED TO CAUSE GIVEN IN 107
Renal Insufficiancy

113. WAS OPERATION PERFORMED FOR ANY CONDITION IN ITEM 107 OR 112? IF YES, LIST TYPE OF OPERATION AND DATE.
None

PHYSICIAN'S CERTIFICATION

114. I CERTIFY THAT TO THE BEST OF MY KNOWLEDGE DEATH OCCURRED AT THE HOUR, DATE AND PLACE STATED FROM THE CAUSES STATED.	115. SIGNATURE AND TITLE OF CERTIFIER	116. LICENSE NO.	117. DATE MM/DD/CCYY
DECEDENT ATTENDED SINCE MM/DD/CCYY 09/--/1998 — DECEDENT LAST SEEN ALIVE MM/DD/CCYY 09/05/1999	▶ Stephen Brabeck MD	G-083279	09/06/1999

118. TYPE ATTENDING PHYSICIAN'S NAME, MAILING ADDRESS, ZIP
Stephen Brabeck,MD, 23845 Holman Highway,Monterey,CA93940

CORONER'S USE ONLY

I CERTIFY THAT IN MY OPINION DEATH OCCURRED AT THE HOUR, DATE AND PLACE STATED FROM THE CAUSES STATED.	120. INJURY AT WORK	121. INJURY DATE MM/DD/CCYY	122. HOUR	123. PLACE OF INJURY
	☐ YES ☐ NO			

119. MANNER OF DEATH	124. DESCRIBE HOW INJURY OCCURRED (EVENTS WHICH RESULTED IN INJURY)
☐ NATURAL ☐ SUICIDE ☐ HOMICIDE ☐ ACCIDENT ☐ PENDING INVESTIGATION ☐ COULD NOT BE DETERMINED	

125. LOCATION (STREET AND NUMBER OR LOCATION AND CITY, ZIP)

CERTIFICATE OF DEATH
STATE OF CALIFORNIA
USE BLACK INK ONLY/NO ERASURES, WHITEOUTS OR ALTERATIONS
VS 11 (REV 7/99)

39519028690

STATE FILE NUMBER	LOCAL REGISTRATION NUMBER

DECEDENT PERSONAL DATA

1 NAME OF DECEDENT — FIRST (GIVEN)	2 MIDDLE	3 LAST (FAMILY)
EVA	-	GABOR

4 DATE OF BIRTH MM/DD/CCYY	5 AGE YRS	IF UNDER 1 YEAR — MONTHS	DAYS	IF UNDER 24 HOURS — HOURS	MINUTES	6 SEX	7 DATE OF DEATH MM/DD/CCYY	8 HOUR
02/11/1919	76					F	07/04/1995	1005

9 STATE OF BIRTH	10 SOCIAL SECURITY NO.	11 MILITARY SERVICE	12 MARITAL STATUS	13 EDUCATION YEARS COMPLETED
HUNGARY	556-22-8699	19 __ TO 19 __ ☐ NONE	DIVORCED	16

14 RACE	15 HISPANIC — SPECIFY	16 USUAL EMPLOYER
CAUCASIAN	☐ YES _____ ☒ NO	SELF EMPLOYED

17 OCCUPATION	18 KIND OF BUSINESS	19 YEARS IN OCCUPATION
ACTRESS	ENTERTAINMENT	55

USUAL RESIDENCE

20 RESIDENCE — STREET AND NUMBER OR LOCATION
100 DELFERN DR.

21 CITY	22 COUNTY	23 ZIP CODE	24 YRS IN COUNTY	25 STATE OR FOREIGN COUNTRY
LOS ANGELES	LOS ANGELES	90077	56	CA

INFORMANT

26 NAME, RELATIONSHIP	27 MAILING ADDRESS (STREET AND NUMBER OR RURAL ROUTE NUMBER, CITY OR TOWN, STATE, ZIP)
RAYMOND KATZ — CO EXECUTOR	335 N. MAPLE DR., BEVERLY HILLS, CA 90210

SPOUSE AND PARENT INFORMATION

28 NAME OF SURVIVING SPOUSE — FIRST	29 MIDDLE	30 LAST (MAIDEN NAME)
-	-	-

31 NAME OF FATHER — FIRST	32 MIDDLE	33 LAST	34 BIRTH STATE
WILLIAM	-	GABOR	HUNGARY

35 NAME OF MOTHER — FIRST	36 MIDDLE	37 LAST (MAIDEN)	38 BIRTH STATE
JOLIE	-	KENDE	HUNGARY

DISPOSITION(S)

39 DATE MM/DD/CCYY	40 PLACE OF FINAL DISPOSITION
07/14/1995	WESTWOOD MEMORIAL PARK, LOS ANGELES, CA

FUNERAL DIRECTOR AND LOCAL REGISTRAR

41 TYPE OF DISPOSITION(S)	42 SIGNATURE OF EMBALMER	43 LICENSE NO.
CR/BU	▶ Henri Petrocchi	4281

44 NAME OF FUNERAL DIRECTOR	45 LICENSE NO.	46 SIGNATURE OF LOCAL REGISTRAR	47 DATE MM/DD/CCYY
PIERCE BROTHERS CUNNINGHAM & O'CONNOR	FD-168	▶ Robert C. Statz	07/13/1995

PLACE OF DEATH

101 PLACE OF DEATH	102 IF HOSPITAL, SPECIFY ONE:	103 FACILITY OTHER THAN HOSPITAL	104 COUNTY
CEDARS-SINAI MEDICAL CENTER	☒ IP ☐ ER/OP ☐ DOA	☐ CONV HOSP ☐ RES ☐ OTHER	LOS ANGELES

105 STREET ADDRESS — STREET AND NUMBER OR LOCATION	106 CITY
8700 W. BEVERLY BLVD.	LOS ANGELES

CAUSE OF DEATH

107 DEATH WAS CAUSED BY: (ENTER ONLY ONE CAUSE PER LINE FOR A, B, C, AND D)		TIME INTERVAL BETWEEN ONSET AND DEATH	108 DEATH REPORTED TO CORONER
IMMEDIATE CAUSE	(A) RESPIRATORY FAILURE	1 DAY	☐ YES ☒ NO REFERRAL NUMBER
DUE TO	(B) ADULT RESPIRATORY DISTRESS SYNDROME	12 DAYS	109 BIOPSY PERFORMED ☐ YES ☒ NO
DUE TO	(C) PNEUMOCCAL PNEUMONIA, BILATERAL	13 DAYS	110 AUTOPSY PERFORMED ☐ YES ☒ NO
DUE TO	(D)		111 USED IN DETERMINING CAUSE ☐ YES ☐ NO

112 OTHER SIGNIFICANT CONDITIONS CONTRIBUTING TO DEATH BUT NOT RELATED TO CAUSE GIVEN IN 107
NONE

113 WAS OPERATION PERFORMED FOR ANY CONDITION IN ITEM 107 OR 112? IF YES, LIST TYPE OF OPERATION AND DATE
NO

PHYSICIAN'S CERTIFICATION

114 I CERTIFY THAT TO THE BEST OF MY KNOWLEDGE DEATH OCCURRED AT THE HOUR, DATE AND PLACE STATED FROM THE CAUSES STATED	115 SIGNATURE AND TITLE OF CERTIFIER	116 LICENSE NO.	117 DATE MM/DD/CCYY
DECEDENT ATTENDED SINCE MM/DD/CCYY: 01/14/1993 — DECEDENT LAST SEEN ALIVE MM/DD/CCYY: 07/04/1995	▶ Kobl	97117	07-05-95

118 TYPE ATTENDING PHYSICIAN'S NAME, MAILING ADDRESS · ZIP
ROBERT KOBLIN, MD 150 N. ROBERTSON BLVD. #205, BEVERLY HILLS, CA 90211

CORONER'S USE ONLY

119 I CERTIFY THAT IN MY OPINION DEATH OCCURRED AT THE HOUR, DATE AND PLACE STATED FROM THE CAUSES STATED.	120 INJURY AT WORK ☐ YES ☐ NO	121 INJURY DATE MM/DD/CCYY	122 HOUR	123 PLACE OF INJURY
119 MANNER OF DEATH ☐ NATURAL ☐ SUICIDE ☐ HOMICIDE ☐ ACCIDENT ☐ PENDING INVESTIGATION ☐ COULD NOT BE DETERMINED	124 DESCRIBE HOW INJURY OCCURRED			

INFORMATIONAL, NOT A VALID DOCUMENT TO ESTABLISH IDENTITY

125 LOCATION (STREET AND NUMBER OR LOCATION AND CITY AND ZIP CODE)

126 SIGNATURE OF CORONER OR DEPUTY CORONER	127 DATE MM/DD/CCYY	128 TYPED NAME, TITLE OF CORONER OR DEPUTY CORONER

STATE REGISTRAR

A	B	C	D	E	F	G	H	FAX AUTH #	CENSUS TRACT

CERTIFICATE OF DEATH
STATE OF CALIFORNIA
USE BLACK INK ONLY/NO ERASURES, WHITEOUTS OR ALTERATIONS
VS-11 (REV. 11/96)

STATE FILE NUMBER

3 1997 33004859

LOCAL REGISTRATION NUMBER

1. NAME OF DECEDENT—FIRST (GIVEN) Magda	2. MIDDLE -	3. LAST (FAMILY) Gabor

DECEDENT PERSONAL DATA

| 4. DATE OF BIRTH MM/DD/CCYY 06/11/1918 | 5. AGE YRS. 78 | IF UNDER 1 YEAR MONTHS | DAYS | IF UNDER 24 HOURS HOURS | MINUTES | 6. SEX F | 7. DATE OF DEATH MM/DD/CCYY 06/06/1997 | 8. HOUR 0750 |

| 9. STATE OF BIRTH HUNG | 10. SOCIAL SECURITY NO. 131-24-3874 | 11. MILITARY SERVICE ☐ YES ☒ NO | 12. MARITAL STATUS Widowed | 13. EDUCATION—YEARS COMPLETED 12 |

| 14. RACE White | 15. HISPANIC—SPECIFY ☐ YES ____ ☒ NO | 16. USUAL EMPLOYER Self-Employed |

| 17. OCCUPATION Owner | 18. KIND OF BUSINESS Retail Jewelry | 19. YEARS IN OCCUPATION 40 |

USUAL RESIDENCE

| 20. RESIDENCE—STREET AND NUMBER OR LOCATION 1090 Cielo Drive | | | | |
| 21. CITY Palm Springs | 22. COUNTY Riverside | 23. ZIP CODE 92262 | 24. YRS IN COUNTY 28 | 25. STATE OR FOREIGN COUNTRY CA |

INFORMANT

| 26. NAME, RELATIONSHIP Zsa Zsa Gabor - Sister | 27. MAILING ADDRESS (STREET AND NUMBER OR RURAL ROUTE NUMBER, CITY OR TOWN, STATE, ZIP) 1001 Bel Air Road, Los Angeles, CA 90077 |

SPOUSE AND PARENT INFORMATION

28. NAME OF SURVIVING SPOUSE—FIRST -	29. MIDDLE	30. LAST (MAIDEN NAME)
31. NAME OF FATHER—FIRST Vilmos	32. MIDDLE -	33. LAST Gabor	34. BIRTH STATE HUNG
35. NAME OF MOTHER—FIRST Jolie	36. MIDDLE -	37. LAST (MAIDEN) Kende	38. BIRTH STATE HUNG

DISPOSITION(S)

| 39. DATE MM/DD/CCYY 06/10/1997 | 40. PLACE OF FINAL DISPOSITION Desert Memorial Park, 69920 E. Ramon Rd., Cathedral City, CA 92234 |

FUNERAL DIRECTOR AND LOCAL REGISTRAR

| 41. TYPE OF DISPOSITION(S) Burial | 42. SIGNATURE OF EMBALMER ▶ Not embalmed | 43. LICENSE NO. - |
| 44. NAME OF FUNERAL DIRECTOR Wiefels & Son, Palm Springs | 45. LICENSE NO. FD 836 | 46. SIGNATURE OF LOCAL REGISTRAR P.C. Eggan MD | 47. DATE MM/DD/CCYY 06/09/1997 |

PLACE OF DEATH

| 101. PLACE OF DEATH Eisenhower Medical Center | 102. IF HOSPITAL, SPECIFY ONE: ☒ IP ☐ ER/OP ☐ DOA | 103. FACILITY OTHER THAN HOSPITAL: ☐ CONV. HOSP. ☐ RES. CARE ☐ OTHER | 104. COUNTY Riverside |
| 105. STREET ADDRESS—STREET AND NUMBER OR LOCATION 39000 Bob Hope Drive | | | 106. CITY Rancho Mirage |

CAUSE OF DEATH

107. DEATH WAS CAUSED BY: (ENTER ONLY ONE CAUSE PER LINE FOR A, B, C, AND D)	TIME INTERVAL BETWEEN ONSET AND DEATH	108. DEATH REPORTED TO CORONER
IMMEDIATE CAUSE (A) Sepsis	Weeks	☐ YES ☒ NO REFERRAL NUMBER
DUE TO (B) Acute Renal Failure	Weeks	109. BIOPSY PERFORMED ☐ YES ☒ NO
DUE TO (C) Pyonephritis	Weeks	110. AUTOPSY PERFORMED ☐ YES ☒ NO
DUE TO (D) Urinary Tract Infection	Weeks	111. USED IN DETERMINING CAUSE ☐ YES ☐ NO

| 112. OTHER SIGNIFICANT CONDITIONS CONTRIBUTING TO DEATH BUT NOT RELATED TO CAUSE GIVEN IN 107 Chronic Obstructive Lung Disease |
| 113. WAS OPERATION PERFORMED FOR ANY CONDITION IN ITEM 107 OR 112? IF YES, LIST TYPE OF OPERATION AND DATE. No |

PHYSICIAN'S CERTIFICATION

| 114. I CERTIFY THAT TO THE BEST OF MY KNOWLEDGE DEATH OCCURRED AT THE HOUR, DATE AND PLACE STATED FROM THE CAUSES STATED. DECEDENT ATTENDED SINCE MM/DD/CCYY --/--/1987 DECEDENT LAST SEEN ALIVE MM/DD/CCYY 06/06/1997 | 115. SIGNATURE AND TITLE OF CERTIFIER ▶ | 116. LICENSE NO. G40006 | 117. DATE MM/DD/CCYY 06/06/1997 |
| | 118. TYPE ATTENDING PHYSICIAN'S NAME, MAILING ADDRESS, ZIP Joel M. Hirschberg, M.D., 39000 Bob Hope Drive, P-102 Rancho Mirage, CA 92270 | | |

CORONER'S USE ONLY

| 119. MANNER OF DEATH ☐ NATURAL ☐ SUICIDE ☐ HOMICIDE ☐ ACCIDENT ☐ PENDING INVESTIGATION ☐ COULD NOT BE DETERMINED | 120. INJURY AT WORK ☐ YES ☐ NO | 121. INJURY DATE MM/DD/CCYY | 122. HOUR | 123. PLACE OF INJURY |
| 124. DESCRIBE HOW INJURY OCCURRED (EVENTS WHICH RESULTED IN INJURY) | | | | |

| 125. LOCATION (STREET AND NUMBER OR LOCATION AND CITY, ZIP) |
| 126. SIGNATURE OF CORONER OR DEPUTY CORONER ▶ | 127. DATE MM/DD/CCYY | 128. TYPED NAME, TITLE OF CORONER OR DEPUTY CORONER |

STATE REGISTRAR

| A | B | C | D | E | F | G | H | FAX AUTH. # 096169 | CENSUS TRACT 44803 |

STATE OF CALIFORNIA
CERTIFICATION OF VITAL RECORD

COUNTY OF LOS ANGELES • REGISTRAR-RECORDER/COUNTY CLERK

CERTIFICATE OF DEATH
STATE OF CALIFORNIA

0190-053169

LOCAL REGISTRATION DISTRICT AND CERTIFICATE NUMBER

STATE FILE NUMBER					
1A. NAME OF DECEDENT—FIRST	1B. MIDDLE	1C. LAST	2A. DATE OF DEATH (MONTH, DAY, YEAR)		2B. HOUR
Christopher	John	George	Nov 29 1983		0314
3. SEX	4. RACE/ETHNICITY	5. SPANISH/HISPANIC NO xx	6. DATE OF BIRTH	7. AGE	IF UNDER 1 YEAR / IF UNDER 24 HOURS
male	cauc		Feb 24 1931	52 YEARS	MONTHS DAYS / HOURS MINUTES

DECEDENT PERSONAL DATA

8. BIRTHPLACE OF DECEDENT (STATE OR FOREIGN COUNTRY)	9. NAME AND BIRTHPLACE OF FATHER		10. BIRTH NAME AND BIRTHPLACE OF MOTHER
Michigan	John George-Greece		Vaseleke Nicholas-Greece
11. CITIZEN OF WHAT COUNTRY	12. SOCIAL SECURITY NUMBER	13. MARITAL STATUS	14. NAME OF SURVIVING SPOUSE (IF WIFE, ENTER BIRTH NAME)
U.S.A.	265 40 0107	married	Lynda Day
15. PRIMARY OCCUPATION	16. NUMBER OF YEARS THIS OCCUPATION	17. EMPLOYER (IF SELF-EMPLOYED, SO STATE)	18. KIND OF INDUSTRY OR BUSINESS
Actor	Adult life	Freelance	Entertainment

USUAL RESIDENCE

19A. USUAL RESIDENCE—STREET ADDRESS (STREET AND NUMBER OR LOCATION)	19B.	19C. CITY OR TOWN
602 S Hudson		Los Angeles
19D. COUNTY	19E. STATE	20. NAME AND ADDRESS OF INFORMANT—RELATIONSHIP
Los Angeles	Calif	Lynda Day George (Wife)

PLACE OF DEATH

21A. PLACE OF DEATH	21B. COUNTY	
Westside Hospital	Los Angeles	same address
21C. STREET ADDRESS (STREET AND NUMBER OR LOCATION)	21D. CITY OR TOWN	
910 S Fairfax	Los Angeles	

CAUSE OF DEATH

22. DEATH WAS CAUSED BY: IMMEDIATE CAUSE (ENTER ONLY ONE CAUSE PER LINE FOR A, B, AND C)			24. WAS DEATH REPORTED TO CORONER?
(A) VENTRICULAR FIBRILLATION	1 Hr	APPROXIMATE INTERVAL BETWEEN ONSET AND DEATH	No
CONDITIONS, IF ANY, WHICH GAVE RISE TO THE IMMEDIATE CAUSE, STATING THE UNDERLYING CAUSE LAST DUE TO, OR AS A CONSEQUENCE OF (B) CORONARY INSUFFICIENCY	12 Yrs		25. WAS BIOPSY PERFORMED? No
DUE TO, OR AS A CONSEQUENCE OF (C) ARTERIOSCLEROTIC HEART DISEASE	12 yrs		26. WAS AUTOPSY PERFORMED? No

23. OTHER CONDITIONS CONTRIBUTING BUT NOT RELATED TO THE IMMEDIATE CAUSE OF DEATH	27. WAS OPERATION PERFORMED FOR ANY CONDITION IN ITEMS 22 OR 23? TYPE OF OPERATION / DATE
	By Pass Surgery 1973

PHYSICIAN'S CERTIFICATION

28A. I CERTIFY THAT DEATH OCCURRED AT THE HOUR, DATE AND PLACE STATED FROM THE CAUSES STATED. I ATTENDED DECEDENT SINCE / I LAST SAW DECEDENT ALIVE (ENTER MO. DA. YR.)	28B. PHYSICIAN—SIGNATURE AND DEGREE OR TITLE	28C. DATE SIGNED	28D. PHYSICIAN'S LICENSE NUMBER
6-15-83 / 11-19-83	Wiel R Broom, M.D.	11-29-83	G 3430
	28E. TYPE PHYSICIAN'S NAME AND ADDRESS F Pearl McBroom M.D. 12732 W Washington Blvd. Los Angeles Ca.		

INJURY INFORMATION

29. SPECIFY ACCIDENT SUICIDE, ETC.	30. PLACE OF INJURY	31. INJURY AT WORK	32A. DATE OF INJURY—MONTH DAY YEAR	32B. HOUR
33. LOCATION (STREET AND NUMBER OR LOCATION AND CITY OR TOWN)		34. DESCRIBE HOW INJURY OCCURRED (EVENTS WHICH RESULTED IN INJURY)		

CORONER'S USE ONLY

35A. I CERTIFY THAT DEATH OCCURRED AT THE HOUR, DATE AND PLACE STATED FROM THE CAUSES STATED, AS REQUIRED BY LAW. I HAVE HELD AN (INQUEST) INVESTIGATION	35B. CORONER—SIGNATURE AND DEGREE OR TITLE	35C. DATE SIGNED

36. DISPOSITION	37. DATE—MONTH DAY YEAR	38. NAME AND ADDRESS OF CEMETERY OR CREMATORY	39. EMBALMER'S LICENSE NUMBER AND SIGNATURE
Entombment	12-2-83	Westwood Memorial Park Los Angeles Calif	5595 William R. Pierce
40A. NAME OF FUNERAL DIRECTOR (OR PERSON ACTING AS SUCH)	40B. LICENSE NO.	41. LOCAL REGISTRAR—SIGNATURE	42. DATE ACCEPTED BY LOCAL REGISTRAR
Westwood Village Mortuary		Robert White	DEC 1 1983

STATE REGISTRAR | A. | B. | C. | D. | E. | F.

This is to certify that this document is a true copy of the official record filed with the Registrar-Recorder/County Clerk.

Conny B. McCormack

CONNY B. McCORMACK
Registrar-Recorder/County Clerk

This copy not valid unless prepared on engraved border displaying the Seal and Signature of the Registrar-Recorder/County Clerk.

MAY 14 2002
19-254954

ANY ALTERATION OR ERASURE VOIDS THIS CERTIFICATE

CERTIFICATE OF DEATH
STATE OF CALIFORNIA
USE BLACK INK ONLY · NO ERASURES, WHITEOUTS OR ALTERATIONS
VS 11 (REV 1-03)

3 2003 19 025592

STATE FILE NUMBER		LOCAL REGISTRATION NUMBER

DECEDENT'S PERSONAL DATA

1 NAME OF DECEDENT -- FIRST (Given)	2 MIDDLE	3 LAST (Family)
Trevor	John	Goddard

AKA ALSO KNOWN AS · Include full AKA (FIRST MIDDLE, LAST): –

4 DATE OF BIRTH mm/dd/ccyy	5 AGE Yrs	IF UNDER ONE YEAR — Months / Days	IF UNDER 24 HOURS — Hours / Minutes	6 SEX
10/14/1962	40			Male

9 BIRTH STATE/FOREIGN COUNTRY	10 SOCIAL SECURITY NUMBER	11 EVER IN U.S ARMED FORCES?	12 MARITAL STATUS (at Time of Death)	7 DATE OF DEATH mm/dd/ccyy	8 HOUR (24 Hours)
United Kingdom	551-91-9984	YES / X NO / UNK	Married	06/08/2003	1215

EDUCATION highest Level/Degree	14/15 WAS DECEDENT SPANISH/HISPANIC/LATINO?	16 DECEDENT'S RACE
Unknown	YES / X NO	Caucasian

17 USUAL OCCUPATION -- Type of work for most of life DO NOT USE RETIRED	18 KIND OF BUSINESS OR INDUSTRY	19 YEARS IN OCCUPATION
Actor	Entertainment 1OF2	12

USUAL RESIDENCE

20 DECEDENT'S RESIDENCE (Street and number or location)
6261 Ben Avenue

21 CITY	22 COUNTY/PROVINCE	23 ZIP CODE	24 YEARS IN COUNTY	25 STATE/FOREIGN COUNTRY
North Hollywood	Los Angeles	91606	17	CA

INFORMANT

26 INFORMANT'S NAME RELATIONSHIP	27 INFORMANT'S MAILING ADDRESS
Ruthann Goddard, Wife	6378 Ivarene Avenue Hollywood CA 90068

SPOUSE AND PARENT INFORMATION

28 NAME OF SURVIVING SPOUSE -- FIRST	29 MIDDLE	30 LAST (Maiden Name)
Ruthann	–	McCarthy

31 NAME OF FATHER -- FIRST	32 MIDDLE	33 LAST	34 BIRTH STATE
Eric	James William	Goddard	U.K.

35 NAME OF MOTHER -- FIRST	36 MIDDLE	37 LAST (Maiden)	38 BIRTH STATE
Adelaide	Clara	Hayes	Ireland

FUNERAL DIRECTOR / LOCAL REGISTRAR

39 DISPOSITION DATE mm/dd/ccyy	40 PLACE OF FINAL DISPOSITION
06/16/2003	Res Ruthann Goddard 6378 Ivarene Avenue Hollywood CA 90068

41 TYPE OF DISPOSITION(S)	42 SIGNATURE OF EMBALMER	43 LICENSE NUMBER
CR/RES	Not Embalmed	–

44 NAME OF FUNERAL ESTABLISHMENT	45 LICENSE NUMBER	46 SIGNATURE OF LOCAL REGISTRAR	47 DATE mm/dd/ccyy
Neptune Society Sherman Oaks	FD 1359	Thomas W...ville MO	06/13/2003

PLACE OF DEATH

101 PLACE OF DEATH	102 IF HOSPITAL, SPECIFY ONE	103 IF OTHER THAN HOSPITAL, SPECIFY ONE
RESIDENCE	IP / ER/OP / DOA	Hospice / Nursing Home/LTC / X Decedent's Home / Other

104 COUNTY	105 FACILITY ADDRESS OR LOCATION WHERE FOUND	106 CITY
LOS ANGELES	6261 BEN AVE.	NORTH HOLLYWOOD

CAUSE OF DEATH

107 CAUSE OF DEATH		Time Interval Between Onset and Death	108 DEATH REPORTED TO CORONER?
IMMEDIATE CAUSE (A)	DEFERRED	(AT)	X YES / NO — REFERRAL NUMBER 2003-04329
(B)		(BT)	109 BIOPSY PERFORMED? YES / NO
(C)		(CT)	110 AUTOPSY PERFORMED? X YES / NO
(D)		(DT)	111 USED IN DETERMINING CAUSE? YES / NO

112 OTHER SIGNIFICANT CONDITIONS CONTRIBUTING TO DEATH BUT NOT RESULTING IN THE UNDERLYING CAUSE GIVEN IN 107

113 WAS OPERATION PERFORMED FOR ANY CONDITION IN ITEM 107 OR 112?	113A IF FEMALE, PREGNANT IN LAST YEAR?
	YES / NO / UNK

PHYSICIAN'S CERTIFICATION

114 I CERTIFY THAT TO THE BEST OF MY KNOWLEDGE DEATH OCCURRED AT THE HOUR, DATE AND PLACE STATED FROM THE CAUSES STATED	115 SIGNATURE AND TITLE OF CERTIFIER	116 LICENSE NUMBER	117 DATE mm/dd/ccyy
Decedent Attended Since (A) mm/dd/ccyy — Decedent Last Seen Alive (B) mm/dd/ccyy			

118 TYPE ATTENDING PHYSICIAN'S NAME, MAILING ADDRESS, ZIP CODE

CORONER'S USE ONLY

119 I CERTIFY THAT IN MY OPINION DEATH OCCURRED AT THE HOUR, DATE, AND PLACE STATED FROM THE CAUSES STATED — MANNER OF DEATH	120 INJURED AT WORK?	121 INJURY DATE mm/dd/ccyy	122 HOUR (24 Hours)
Natural / Accident / Homicide / Suicide / X Pending Investigation / Could not be determined	YES / NO / UNK		

123 PLACE OF INJURY (e.g. home, construction site, wooded area, etc.)

124 DESCRIBE HOW INJURY OCCURRED (Events which resulted in injury)

125 LOCATION OF INJURY (Street and number, or location, and city, and ZIP)

126 SIGNATURE OF CORONER / DEPUTY CORONER	127 DATE mm/dd/ccyy	128 TYPE NAME, TITLE OF CORONER / DEPUTY CORONER
[signature]	06/12/2003	REGINA AUGUSTINE DEPUTY CORONER

STATE REGISTRAR	A	B	C	D	E	FAX AUTH #	CENSUS TRACT
						195/5727	

AMENDMENT OF MEDICAL AND HEALTH DATA—DEATH 3 2003 9 025592

USE BLACK INK ONLY—NO ERASURES, WHITEOUT, OR ALTERATIONS

	STATE FILE NUMBER			LOCAL REGISTRATION DISTRICT AND CERTIFICATE NUMBER
STATE/LOCAL REGISTRAR USE ONLY	1	2	3	

TYPE OR PRINT IN BLACK INK ONLY

PART I
INFORMATION TO LOCATE RECORD

1. NAME -FIRST (GIVEN)	2. MIDDLE	3. LAST (FAMILY)	4. SEX
TREVOR	JOHN	GODDARD	MALE

5. DATE OF EVENT MM/DD/CCYY	6. CITY OF OCCURRENCE	7. COUNTY OF OCCURRENCE	
06/08/2003	NORTH HOLLYWOOD	LOS ANGELES	2OF2

PART II
INFORMATION AS IT APPEARS ON RECORD

107. DEATH WAS CAUSED BY ENTER ONLY ONE CAUSE PER LINE FOR A, B, C AND D

		TIME INTERVAL BETWEEN ONSET AND DEATH
IMMEDIATE CAUSE (A)	DEFERRED	
(B)		
(C)		
DUE TO (D)		

108. DEATH REPORTED TO CORONER [X] YES [ ] NO
REFERRAL NUMBER 2003-04329
109. BIOPSY PERFORMED [ ] YES [ ] NO
110. AUTOPSY PERFORMED [X] YES [ ] NO
111. USED IN DETERMINING CAUSE [ ] YES [ ] NO

112. OTHER SIGNIFICANT CONDITIONS CONTRIBUTING TO DEATH BUT NOT RELATED TO CAUSE GIVEN IN 107

113. WAS OPERATION PERFORMED FOR ANY CONDITION IN ITEM 107 or 112? IF YES, LIST TYPE OF OPERATION AND DATE.

119. MANNER OF DEATH	120. INJURY AT WORK	121. INJURY DATE—MM/DD/CCYY	122. HOUR	123. PLACE OF INJURY
[ ] NATURAL [ ] SUICIDE [ ] HOMICIDE [ ] ACCIDENT [X] PENDING INVESTIGATION [ ] COULD NOT BE DETERMINED	[ ] YES [ ] NO			

124. DESCRIBE HOW INJURY OCCURED (EVENTS WHICH RESULTED IN INJURY)

125. LOCATION (STREET AND NUMBER OR LOCATION AND CITY AND ZIP CODE)

PART III
INFORMATION AS IT SHOULD APPEAR

107. DEATH WAS CAUSED BY ENTER ONLY ONE CAUSE PER LINE FOR A, B, C AND D

		TIME INTERVAL BETWEEN ONSET AND DEATH
IMMEDIATE CAUSE (A)	MULTIPLE DRUG INTOXICATION	UNK
(B)		
(C)		
DUE TO (D)		

108. DEATH REPORTED TO CORONER [X] YES [ ] NO
REFERRAL NUMBER 2003-04329
109. BIOPSY PERFORMED [ ] YES [X] NO
110. AUTOPSY PERFORMED [X] YES [ ] NO
111. USED IN DETERMINING CAUSE [X] YES [ ] NO

112. OTHER SIGNIFICANT CONDITIONS CONTRIBUTING TO DEATH BUT NOT RELATED TO CAUSE GIVEN IN 107
NONE

113. WAS OPERATION PERFORMED FOR ANY CONDITION IN ITEM 107 or 112? IF YES, LIST TYPE OF OPERATION AND DATE.
NO

119. MANNER OF DEATH	120. INJURY AT WORK	121. INJURY DATE—MM/DD/CCYY	122. HOUR	123. PLACE OF INJURY
[ ] NATURAL [ ] SUICIDE [ ] HOMICIDE [X] ACCIDENT [ ] PENDING INVESTIGATION [ ] COULD NOT BE DETERMINED	[ ] YES [X] NO	UNKNOWN	UNK	RESIDENCE

124. DESCRIBE HOW INJURY OCCURRED (EVENTS WHICH RESULTED IN INJURY)
HEROIN, COCAINE, AND PRESCRIPTION DRUGS USE

125. LOCATION (STREET AND NUMBER OR LOCATION AND CITY AND ZIP CODE)
6261 BEN AVE.   NORTH HOLLYWOOD   91605

DECLARATION OF CERTIFYING PHYSICIAN OR CORONER

I HEREBY DECLARE UNDER PENALTY OF PERJURY THAT THE ABOVE INFORMATION IS TRUE AND CORRECT TO THE BEST OF MY KNOWLEDGE.

8. SIGNATURE OF CERTIFYING PHYSICIAN OR CORONER	9. DATE SIGNED—MM/DD/CCYY	10. TYPED OR PRINTED NAME AND DEGREE/TITLE OF CERTIFIER
Raffi Djal	08/05/2003	RAFFI SARKIS DJABOURIAN, M.D. DME

11. ADDRESS—STREET AND NUMBER	12. CITY	13. STATE	14. ZIP CODE
1104 N. MISSION ROAD	LOS ANGELES	CA	90033

STATE/LOCAL REGISTRAR USE ONLY

15. OFFICE OF STATE REGISTRAR OR SIGNATURE OF LOCAL REGISTRAR	16. DATE ACCEPTED FOR REGISTRATION—MM/DD/CCYY
Thomas W. Gutmacile rb	08/08/2003

STATE OF CALIFORNIA, DEPARTMENT OF HEALTH SERVICES, OFFICE OF STATE REGISTRAR

VS-24 B (1/94)

CERTIFICATE OF DEATH
STATE OF CALIFORNIA
USE BLACK INK ONLY/NO ERASURES, WHITEOUTS OR ALTERATIONS
VS-11 (REV. 7/93)

395!9021402

STATE FILE NUMBER		LOCAL REGISTRATION NUMBER

	1. NAME OF DECEDENT — FIRST (GIVEN)	2. MIDDLE	3. LAST (FAMILY)
	ALEXANDER	BORIS	GODUNOV

	4. DATE OF BIRTH MM/DD/CCYY	5. AGE YRS	IF UNDER 1 YEAR — MONTHS/DAYS	IF UNDER 24 HOURS — HOURS/MINUTES	6. SEX	7. DATE OF DEATH MM/DD/CCYY	8. HOUR
DECEDENT PERSONAL DATA	11/28/1949	45			M	FOUND 05/18/1995	1000

	9. STATE OF BIRTH	10. SOCIAL SECURITY NO	11. MILITARY SERVICE	12. MARITAL STATUS	13. EDUCATION — YEARS COMPLETED
	USSR	220-90-0493	19___ TO 19___ ☐ NONE	DIVORCED	19

	14. RACE	15. HISPANIC — SPECIFY		16. USUAL EMPLOYER
	CAUCASIAN	☐ YES	[X] NO	SELF EMPLOYED

	17. OCCUPATION	18. KIND OF BUSINESS	AMENDED	19. YEARS IN OCCUPATION
	ACTOR/BALLET ARTIST	ENTERTAINMENT	1 OF 2	35

	20. RESIDENCE — STREET AND NUMBER OR LOCATION
USUAL RESIDENCE	8787 SHOREHAM DRIVE #1001

	21. CITY	22. COUNTY	23. ZIP CODE	24. YRS IN COUNTY	25. STATE OR FOREIGN COUNTRY
	WEST HOLLYWOOD	LOS ANGELES	90069	14	CA

	26. NAME, RELATIONSHIP	27. MAILING ADDRESS (STREET AND NUMBER OR RURAL ROUTE NUMBER, CITY OR TOWN, STATE, ZIP)
INFORMANT	ARLYNE MEDANN-EXECUTRIX	1640 5TH STREET SUITE 106 SANTA MONICA CA 90401

	28. NAME OF SURVIVING SPOUSE — FIRST	29. MIDDLE	30. LAST MAIDEN NAME
SPOUSE AND PARENT INFORMATION	–	–	–

	31. NAME OF FATHER — FIRST	32. MIDDLE	33. LAST	34. BIRTH STATE
	BORIS	–	GODUNOV	USSR

	35. NAME OF MOTHER — FIRST	36. MIDDLE	37. LAST MAIDEN	38. BIRTH STATE
	LIDIA	NICHOLAEVNA	STUDENTOVA	USSR

	39. DATE MM/DD/CCYY	40. PLACE OF FINAL DISPOSITION
DISPOSITION(S)	05/24/1995	PRIVATE RESIDENCE ARLYNE MEDANN 1640 5TH ST. STE 106 SANTA MONICA CA

	41. TYPE OF DISPOSITION(S)	42. SIGNATURE OF EMBALMER	43. LICENSE NO.
FUNERAL DIRECTOR AND LOCAL REGISTRAR	CR/RES	▶ NOT EMBALMED	–

	44. NAME OF FUNERAL DIRECTOR	45. LICENSE NO.	46. SIGNATURE OF LOCAL REGISTRAR	47. DATE MM/DD/CCYY
	GATES, KINGSLEY & GATES SM	F451	▶ Robert C. Gates	4 05/23/1995

	101. PLACE OF DEATH	102. IF HOSPITAL, SPECIFY ONE	103. FACILITY OTHER THAN HOSPITAL	104. COUNTY
PLACE OF DEATH	RESIDENCE	☐ IP ☐ ER/OP ☐ DOA	☐ CONV. HOSP. [X] RES. ☐ OTHER	LOS ANGELES

	105. STREET ADDRESS — STREET AND NUMBER OR LOCATION	106. CITY
	8787 SHOREHAM DRIVE #1001	WEST HOLLYWOOD

	107. DEATH WAS CAUSED BY: (ENTER ONLY ONE CAUSE PER LINE FOR A, B, C, AND D)	TIME INTERVAL BETWEEN ONSET AND DEATH	108. DEATH REPORTED TO CORONER
	IMMEDIATE CAUSE (A) CHRONIC ALCOHOLISM	YEARS	☐ YES [X] NO — REFERRAL NUMBER
	DUE TO (B)		109. BIOPSY PERFORMED ☐ YES [X] NO
CAUSE OF DEATH	DUE TO (C)		110. AUTOPSY PERFORMED ☐ YES [X] NO
	DUE TO (D)		111. USED IN DETERMINING CAUSE ☐ YES ☐ NO

	112. OTHER SIGNIFICANT CONDITIONS CONTRIBUTING TO DEATH BUT NOT RELATED TO CAUSE GIVEN IN 107
	HEPATITIS

	113. WAS OPERATION PERFORMED FOR ANY CONDITION IN ITEM 107 OR 112? IF YES, LIST TYPE OF OPERATION AND DATE.
	NO

	114. I CERTIFY THAT TO THE BEST OF MY KNOWLEDGE DEATH OCCURRED AT THE HOUR, DATE AND PLACE STATED FROM THE CAUSES STATED.	115. SIGNATURE AND TITLE OF CERTIFIER	116. LICENSE NO.	117. DATE MM/DD/CCYY
PHYSICIAN'S CERTIFICATION	DECEDENT ATTENDED SINCE MM/DD/CCYY 07/25/1990 — DECEDENT LAST SEEN ALIVE MM/DD/CCYY 05/08/1995	▶ Maurice LEVY MD	A41579	05/19/1995
		118. TYPE ATTENDING PHYSICIAN'S NAME, MAILING ADDRESS, ZIP — MAURICE LEVY MD 8641 WILSHIRE BLVD BEVERLY HILLS CA 90211		

	I CERTIFY THAT IN MY OPINION DEATH OCCURRED AT THE HOUR, DATE AND PLACE STATED FROM THE CAUSES STATED.	120. INJURY AT WORK	121. INJURY DATE MM/DD/CCYY	122. HOUR	123. PLACE OF INJURY
	119. MANNER OF DEATH	☐ YES ☐ NO			
CORONER'S USE ONLY	☐ NATURAL ☐ SUICIDE ☐ HOMICIDE ☐ ACCIDENT ☐ PENDING INVESTIGATION ☐ COULD NOT BE DETERMINED	124. DESCRIBE HOW INJURY OCCURRED (EVENTS WHICH RESULTED IN INJURY)			
	125. LOCATION (STREET AND NUMBER OR LOCATION AND CITY AND ZIP CODE)				

	126. SIGNATURE OF CORONER OR DEPUTY CORONER	127. DATE MM/DD/CCYY	128. TYPED NAME, TITLE OF CORONER OR DEPUTY CORONER
	▶		

	A	B	C	D	E	F	G	H	FAX AUTH #	CENSUS TRACT
STATE REGISTRAR										

STATE OF CALIFORNIA
CERTIFICATION OF VITAL RECORD

COUNTY OF LOS ANGELES • REGISTRAR-RECORDER/COUNTY CLERK

CERTIFICATE OF DEATH
STATE OF CALIFORNIA
USE BLACK INK ONLY

393 5035062

STATE FILE NUMBER			LOCAL REGISTRATION DISTRICT AND CERTIFICATE NUMBER

DECEDENT PERSONAL DATA

1A. NAME OF DECEDENT—FIRST (GIVEN)	1B. MIDDLE	1C. LAST (FAMILY)	2A. DATE OF DEATH—MO, DAY, YR	2B. HOUR	3. SEX
JAMES	STEWART	GRANGER	August 16, 1993	1555	Male

4. RACE	5. HISPANIC—SPECIFY	6. DATE OF BIRTH—MO, DAY, YR	7. AGE IN YEARS	IF UNDER 1 YEAR MONTHS / DAYS	IF UNDER 24 HOURS HOURS / MINUTES
Caucasian	☐ YES ____ ☒ NO	May 6, 1913	80		

8. STATE OF BIRTH	9. CITIZEN OF WHAT COUNTRY	10A. FULL NAME OF FATHER	10B. STATE OF BIRTH	11A. FULL MAIDEN NAME OF MOTHER	11B. STATE OF BIRTH
England	England	James Stewart	England	Frederica LaBlache	England

12. MILITARY SERVICE?	13. SOCIAL SECURITY NO.	14. MARITAL STATUS	15. NAME OF SURVIVING SPOUSE (IF WIFE, ENTER MAIDEN NAME)
19__ TO 19__ ☒ NONE	557-42-5469	Divorced	----

16A. USUAL OCCUPATION	16B. USUAL KIND OF BUSINESS OR INDUSTRY	16C. USUAL EMPLOYER	16D. YEARS IN OCCUPATION	17. EDUCATION—YEARS COMPLETED
Actor	Entertainment	MGM Studios	60	12

USUAL RESIDENCE

18A. RESIDENCE—STREET AND NUMBER OR LOCATION	18B. CITY	18C. ZIP CODE
17331 Tramonto Drive #1	Pacific Palisades	90272

18D. COUNTY	18E. NUMBER OF YEARS IN THIS COUNTY	18F. STATE OR FOREIGN COUNTRY	20. NAME, RELATIONSHIP, MAILING ADDRESS AND ZIP CODE OF INFORMANT
Los Angeles	12	CA	Marilyn L. Ball - Companion 27200 Pacific Coast Highway Malibu, CA 90265

PLACE OF DEATH

19A. PLACE OF DEATH	19B. IF HOSPITAL, SPECIFY ONE: IP, ER/OP, DOA	19C. COUNTY
St. John's Hospital	IP	Los Angeles

19D. STREET ADDRESS—STREET AND NUMBER OR LOCATION	19E. CITY
1328 22nd Street	Santa Monica

TIME INTERVAL BETWEEN ONSET AND DEATH	22. WAS DEATH REPORTED TO CORONER? REFERRAL NUMBER
	☐ YES ☒ NO

CAUSE OF DEATH

21. DEATH WAS CAUSED BY: (ENTER ONLY ONE CAUSE PER LINE FOR A, B, AND C)

IMMEDIATE CAUSE	(A)	CHRONIC RESPIRATORY FAILURE ►	Hours
DUE TO	(B)	METASTIC PROSTATE CANCER ►	Years
DUE TO	(C)	►	

23. WAS BIOPSY PERFORMED?	☐ YES ☒ NO
24A. WAS AUTOPSY PERFORMED?	☐ YES ☒ NO
24B. WAS IT USED IN DETERMINING CAUSE OF DEATH?	☐ YES ☐ NO

25. OTHER SIGNIFICANT CONDITIONS CONTRIBUTING TO DEATH BUT NOT RELATED TO CAUSE GIVEN IN 21	26. WAS OPERATION PERFORMED FOR ANY CONDITION IN ITEM 21 OR 25? IF YES, LIST TYPE OF OPERATION AND DATE.
LOBECTOMY AND CHRONIC OBSTRUCTIVE LUNG DISEASE	Lobectomy-1950 TURP-1990

PHYSICIAN'S CERTIFICATION

I CERTIFY THAT TO THE BEST OF MY KNOWLEDGE DEATH OCCURRED AT THE HOUR, DATE AND PLACE STATED FROM THE CAUSES STATED.

27A. DECEDENT ATTENDED SINCE MONTH, DAY, YEAR	DECEDENT LAST SEEN ALIVE MONTH, DAY, YEAR	27B. SIGNATURE AND DEGREE OR TITLE OF CERTIFIER	27C. CERTIFIER'S LICENSE NUMBER	27D. DATE SIGNED
2/3/1992	8/16/1993	► Susan Sprau MD	G44652	8/18/1993

27E. TYPE ATTENDING PHYSICIAN'S NAME AND ADDRESS: Susan Sprau M.D. 2021 Santa Monica Bl. Suite 525 E, Santa Monica, CA

CORONER'S USE ONLY

I CERTIFY THAT IN MY OPINION DEATH OCCURRED AT THE HOUR, DATE AND PLACE STATED FROM THE CAUSES STATED.

28A. SIGNATURE AND TITLE OF CORONER OR DEPUTY CORONER	28B. DATE SIGNED
►	

29. MANNER OF DEATH—specify one: natural, accident, suicide, homicide, pending investigation or could not be determined	30A. PLACE OF INJURY	30B. INJURY AT WORK ☐ YES ☐ NO	30C. DATE OF INJURY MONTH, DAY, YEAR	31. HOUR

32. LOCATION (STREET AND NUMBER OR LOCATION AND CITY)	33. DESCRIBE HOW INJURY OCCURRED (EVENTS WHICH RESULTED IN INJURY)

FUNERAL DIRECTOR AND LOCAL REGISTRAR

34A. DISPOSITION(S)	34B. PLACE OF FINAL DISPOSITION—NAME AND ADDRESS	34C. DATE MO, DAY, YEAR	35A. SIGNATURE OF EMBALMER	35B. LICENSE NUMBER
CR/RES	27200 Pacific Coast Hwy, Malibu, CA	8/20/1993	No Embalming	----

36A. NAME OF FUNERAL DIRECTOR (OR PERSON ACTING AS SUCH)	36B. LICENSE NO.	37. SIGNATURE OF LOCAL REGISTRAR	38. REGISTRATION DATE
Gates, Kingsley & Gates - S.M.	FD 451	► Robert C. Nate	AUG 18 1993

STATE REGISTRAR

A.	B.	C.	D.	E.	F.	CENSUS TRACT

VS-11 (REV. 3-91)   185   MAKE NO ERASURES, WHITEOUTS, OR OTHER ALTERATIONS   01-9-1-0756

CERTIFICATE OF DEATH
STATE OF CALIFORNIA
USE BLACK INK ONLY/NO ERASURES, WHITEOUTS OR ALTERATIONS
VS-11 (REV. 1/00)

STATE FILE NUMBER		LOCAL REGISTRATION NUMBER

DECEDENT PERSONAL DATA

1. NAME OF DECEDENT—FIRST (GIVEN)	2. MIDDLE	3. LAST (FAMILY)
Teresa	–	Graves

4. DATE OF BIRTH MM/DD/CCYY	5. AGE YRS.	IF UNDER 1 YEAR MONTHS / DAYS	IF UNDER 24 HOURS HOURS / MINUTES	6. SEX	7. DATE OF DEATH MM/DD/CCYY	8. HOUR
01/10/1948	54			F	10/10/2002	0104

9. STATE OF BIRTH	10. SOCIAL SECURITY NO.	11. MILITARY SERVICE	12. MARITAL STATUS	13. EDUCATION—YEARS COMPLETED
TX	547-70-9349	☐ YES ☒ NO ☐ UNK	Divorced	14

14. RACE	15. HISPANIC—SPECIFY		16. USUAL EMPLOYER
Black	☐ YES_____	☒ NO	Aaron Spelling Productions

17. OCCUPATION	18. KIND OF BUSINESS	19. YEARS IN OCCUPATION
Actress	Production Co.	10　　1 OF 2

USUAL RESIDENCE

20. RESIDENCE—(STREET AND NUMBER OR LOCATION)
3437 W. 78th Pl.

21. CITY	22. COUNTY	23. ZIP CODE	24. YRS IN COUNTY	25. STATE OR FOREIGN COUNTRY
Los Angeles	Los Angeles	90043	48	CA

INFORMANT

26. NAME, RELATIONSHIP	27. MAILING ADDRESS (STREET AND NUMBER OR RURAL ROUTE NUMBER, CITY OR TOWN, STATE, ZIP)
Marise Graves Regalado, sister	3622 W. 105th St. Apt. 4, Inglewood, CA 90303

SPOUSE AND PARENT INFORMATION

28. NAME OF SURVIVING SPOUSE—FIRST	29. MIDDLE	30. LAST (MAIDEN NAME)
–	–	–

31. NAME OF FATHER—FIRST	32. MIDDLE	33. LAST	34. BIRTH STATE
Mannie	–	Graves	TX

35. NAME OF MOTHER—FIRST	36. MIDDLE	37. LAST (MAIDEN)	38. BIRTH STATE
Willie	–	Patterson	TX

DISPOSITION(S)

39. DATE MM/DD/CCYY	40. PLACE OF FINAL DISPOSITION
10/25/2002	At Sea off the Coast of Los Angeles County

FUNERAL DIRECTOR AND LOCAL REGISTRAR

41. TYPE OF DISPOSITION(S)	42. SIGNATURE OF EMBALMER	43. LICENSE NO.
CR/SEA	► Jeri McWilliams	8163

44. NAME OF FUNERAL DIRECTOR	45. LICENSE NO.	46. SIGNATURE OF LOCAL REGISTRAR	47. DATE MM/DD/CCYY
Ashley-Grigsby Mort., Inc.	FD 586	► Thomas Whitworth Jr.	10/24/2002

PLACE OF DEATH

101. PLACE OF DEATH	102. IF HOSPITAL, SPECIFY ONE:	103. FACILITY OTHER THAN HOSPITAL:	104. COUNTY
Daniel Freeman Memorial	☐ IP ☒ ER/OP ☐ DOA	☐ CONV. HOSP. ☐ RES. CARE ☐ OTHER	Los Angeles

105. STREET ADDRESS—(STREET AND NUMBER OR LOCATION)	106. CITY
333 North Prairie Avenue	Inglewood

CAUSE OF DEATH

107. DEATH WAS CAUSED BY: (ENTER ONLY ONE CAUSE PER LINE FOR A, B, C, AND D)	TIME INTERVAL BETWEEN ONSET AND DEATH	108. DEATH REPORTED TO CORONER
IMMEDIATE CAUSE (A) Deferred		☒ YES ☐ NO
		REFERRAL NUMBER 2002-07612
DUE TO (B)		109. BIOPSY PERFORMED ☐ YES ☐ NO
DUE TO (C)		110. AUTOPSY PERFORMED ☒ YES ☐ NO
DUE TO (D)		111. USED IN DETERMINING CAUSE ☐ YES ☐ NO

112. OTHER SIGNIFICANT CONDITIONS CONTRIBUTING TO DEATH BUT NOT RELATED TO CAUSE GIVEN IN 107

113. WAS OPERATION PERFORMED FOR ANY CONDITION IN ITEM 107 OR 112? IF YES, LIST TYPE OF OPERATION AND DATE.

PHYSICIAN'S CERTIFICATION

114. I CERTIFY THAT TO THE BEST OF MY KNOWLEDGE DEATH OCCURRED AT THE HOUR, DATE AND PLACE STATED FROM THE CAUSES STATED. DECEDENT ATTENDED SINCE MM/DD/CCYY / DECEDENT LAST SEEN ALIVE MM/DD/CCYY	115. SIGNATURE AND TITLE OF CERTIFIER ►	116. LICENSE NO.	117. DATE MM/DD/CCYY
	118. TYPE ATTENDING PHYSICIAN'S NAME, MAILING ADDRESS, ZIP		

CORONER'S USE ONLY

I CERTIFY THAT IN MY OPINION DEATH OCCURRED AT THE HOUR, DATE AND PLACE STATED FROM THE CAUSES STATED.	120. INJURY AT WORK ☐ YES ☐ NO	121. INJURY DATE MM/DD/CCYY	122. HOUR	123. PLACE OF INJURY
119. MANNER OF DEATH ☐ NATURAL ☐ SUICIDE ☐ HOMICIDE ☐ ACCIDENT ☐ PENDING INVESTIGATION ☐ COULD NOT BE DETERMINED	124. DESCRIBE HOW INJURY OCCURRED (EVENTS WHICH RESULTED IN INJURY)			

INFORMATIONAL NOT A VALID DOCUMENT TO ESTABLISH IDENTITY

125. LOCATION (STREET AND NUMBER OR LOCATION AND CITY, ZIP)

X00

126. SIGNATURE OF CORONER OR DEPUTY CORONER	127. DATE MM/DD/CCYY	128. TYPED NAME, TITLE OF CORONER OR DEPUTY CORONER
► Pamela K. Euher	10/23/2002	Pamela K. Euher, Deputy Coroner

STATE REGISTRAR

A	B	C	D	E	F	G	H	FAX AUTH. #	CENSUS TRACT

This is a true certified copy of the record filed in the County of Los Angeles Department of Health Services if it bears the Registrar's signature in purple ink

AMENDMENT OF MEDICAL AND HEALTH DATA—DEATH

STATE FILE NUMBER	USE BLACK INK ONLY—NO ERASURES, WHITEOUT, OR ALTERATIONS	LOCAL REGISTRATION DISTRICT AND CERTIFICATE NUMBER

STATE/LOCAL REGISTRAR USE ONLY	1	2	3

TYPE OR PRINT IN BLACK INK ONLY

PART I
INFORMATION TO LOCATE RECORD

1. NAME—FIRST (GIVEN) TERESA	2. MIDDLE –	3. LAST (FAMILY) GRAVES	4. SEX F
5. DATE OF EVENT—MM/DD/CCYY 10/10/2002	6. CITY OF OCCURENCE Inglewood	7. COUNTY OF OCCURRENCE Los Angeles	2 OF 2

PART II
INFORMATION AS IT APPEARS ON RECORD

107. DEATH WAS CAUSED BY ENTER ONLY ONE CAUSE PER LINE FOR A, B, C, AND D)

IMMEDIATE CAUSE (A) Deferred

(B)

(C)

DUE TO (D)

TIME INTERVAL BETWEEN ONSET AND DEATH	108. DEATH REPORTED TO CORONER [X] YES [ ] NO REFERRAL NUMBER 2002-07612
	109. BIOPSY PERFORMED [ ] YES [ ] NO
	110. AUTOPSY PERFORMED [X] YES [ ] NO
	111. USED IN DETERMINING CAUSE [ ] YES [ ] NO

112. OTHER SIGNIFICANT CONDITIONS CONTRIBUTING TO DEATH BUT NOT RELATED TO CAUSE GIVEN IN 107

113. WAS OPERATION PERFORMED FOR ANY CONDITION IN ITEM 107 or 112? IF YES, LIST TYPE OF OPERATION AND DATE.

119. MANNER OF DEATH [ ] NATURAL [ ] SUICIDE [ ] HOMICIDE [ ] ACCIDENT [X] PENDING INVESTIGATION [ ] COULD NOT BE DETERMINED	120. INJURY AT WORK [ ] YES [ ] NO	121. INJURY DATE—MM/DD/CCYY	122. HOUR	123. PLACE OF INJURY
	124. DESCRIBE HOW INJURY OCCURED (EVENTS WHICH RESULTED IN INJURY)			

125. LOCATION (STREET AND NUMBER OR LOCATION AND CITY AND ZIP CODE)

INFORMATION AS IT SHOULD APPEAR

107. DEATH WAS CAUSED BY ENTER ONLY ONE CAUSE PER LINE FOR A, B, C, AND D)

IMMEDIATE CAUSE (A) THERMAL INJURIES WITH INHALATION OF PRODUCTS

(B) OF COMBUSTION

(C)

DUE TO (D)

TIME INTERVAL BETWEEN ONSET AND DEATH	108. DEATH REPORTED TO CORONER [X] YES [ ] NO REFERRAL NUMBER 2002-07612
	109. BIOPSY PERFORMED [ ] YES [X] NO
Mins	110. AUTOPSY PERFORMED [X] YES [ ] NO
	111. USED IN DETERMINING CAUSE [X] YES [ ] NO

112. OTHER SIGNIFICANT CONDITIONS CONTRIBUTING TO DEATH BUT NOT RELATED TO CAUSE GIVEN IN 107
None

113. WAS OPERATION PERFORMED FOR ANY CONDITION IN ITEM 107 or 112? IF YES, LIST TYPE OF OPERATION AND DATE.
No

119. MANNER OF DEATH [ ] NATURAL [ ] SUICIDE [ ] HOMICIDE [X] ACCIDENT [ ] PENDING INVESTIGATION [ ] COULD NOT BE DETERMINED	120. INJURY AT WORK [ ] YES [X] NO	121. INJURY DATE—MM/DD/CCYY 10/10/2002	122. HOUR 0030	123. PLACE OF INJURY Residence
	124. DESCRIBE HOW INJURY OCCURRED (EVENTS WHICH RESULTED IN INJURY) Fire At Residence			

125. LOCATION (STREET AND NUMBER OR LOCATION AND CITY AND ZIP CODE)
3437 W. 78th Pl., Los Angeles, CA 90043

DECLARATION OF CERTIFYING PHYSICIAN OR CORONER

I HEREBY DECLARE UNDER PENALTY OF PERJURY THAT THE ABOVE INFORMATION IS TRUE AND CORRECT TO THE BEST OF MY KNOWLEDGE.

8. SIGNATURE OF CERTIFYING PHYSICIAN OR CORONER *Louis A. Peña*	9. DATE SIGNED—MM/DD/CCYY 11/21/2002	10. TYPED OR PRINTED NAME AND DEGREE/TITLE OF CERTIFIER LOUIS A. PENA, M.D. DME
11. ADDRESS—STREET AND NUMBER 1104 North Mission Road	12. CITY Los Angeles	13. STATE CA	14. ZIP CODE 90033

STATE/LOCAL REGISTRAR USE ONLY

15. OFFICE OF STATE REGISTRAR OR SIGNATURE OF LOCAL REGISTRAR *Thomas Garthwaite*	16. DATE ACCEPTED FOR REGISTRATION—MM/DD/CCYY 12/04/2002

STATE OF CALIFORNIA, DEPARTMENT OF HEALTH SERVICES, OFFICE OF STATE REGISTRAR

VS-24 B (1/94)

This is a true certified copy of the record filed in the County of Los Angeles Department of Health Services if it bears the Registrar's signature in purple ink.

STATE OF CALIFORNIA
CERTIFICATION OF VITAL RECORD

COUNTY OF LOS ANGELES • REGISTRAR-RECORDER/ COUNTY CLERK

CERTIFICATE OF DEATH
STATE OF CALIFORNIA

387 9040054

STATE FILE NUMBER			LOCAL REGISTRATION DISTRICT AND CERTIFICATE NUMBER

1A. NAME OF DECEDENT—FIRST	1B. MIDDLE	1C. LAST	2A. DATE OF DEATH (MONTH, DAY, YEAR)	2B. HOUR
Lorne	Hyman	Greene	September 11, 1987	1214

DECEDENT PERSONAL DATA

3. SEX	4. RACE/ETHNICITY	5. SPANISH/HISPANIC NO	6. DATE OF BIRTH	7. AGE	IF UNDER 1 YEAR MONTHS/DAYS	IF UNDER 24 HOURS HOURS/MINUTES
Male	White/Jewish		February 12, 1915	72 YEARS		

8. BIRTHPLACE OF DECEDENT (STATE OR FOREIGN COUNTRY)	9. NAME AND BIRTHPLACE OF FATHER	10. BIRTH NAME AND BIRTHPLACE OF MOTHER
Canada	Daniel Green, Russia	Dora Slavin, Russia

11A. CITIZEN OF WHAT COUNTRY	11B. IF DECEASED WAS EVER IN MILITARY GIVE DATES OF SERVICE	12. SOCIAL SECURITY NUMBER	13. MARITAL STATUS	14. NAME OF SURVIVING SPOUSE (IF WIFE, ENTER BIRTH NAME)
Canada	19__ TO 19__	055-30-0061	Married	Nancy Ann Deale

15. PRIMARY OCCUPATION	16. NUMBER OF YEARS THIS OCCUPATION	17. EMPLOYER (IF SELF-EMPLOYED SO STATE)	18. KIND OF INDUSTRY OR BUSINESS
Actor	48	Self Employed	Entertainment

USUAL RESIDENCE

19A. USUAL RESIDENCE—STREET ADDRESS (STREET AND NUMBER OR LOCATION)	19B.	19C. CITY OR TOWN
10351 Santa Monica Bl. Ste 402		Los Angeles

19D. COUNTY	19E. STATE	20. NAME AND ADDRESS OF INFORMANT—RELATIONSHIP
Los Angeles	California	Nancy Ann Greene Wife 10351 Santa Monica Bl. Ste 402 Los Angeles, Ca. 90025

PLACE OF DEATH

21A. PLACE OF DEATH	21B. COUNTY
St. John's Medical Center	Los Angeles

21C. STREET ADDRESS (STREET AND NUMBER OR LOCATION)	21D. CITY OR TOWN
1328 22nd St.	Santa Monica

CAUSE OF DEATH

22. DEATH WAS CAUSED BY: (ENTER ONLY ONE CAUSE PER LINE FOR A, B, AND C) IMMEDIATE CAUSE		APPROXIMATE INTERVAL BETWEEN ONSET AND DEATH	24. WAS DEATH REPORTED TO CORONER? No
(A) Cardiovascular Collapse		minutes	
CONDITIONS, IF ANY, WHICH GAVE RISE TO THE IMMEDIATE CAUSE (B) Adult Respiratory Distress Syndrome		3 days	25. WAS BIOPSY PERFORMED? No
STATING THE UNDERLYING CAUSE LAST. (C) Metastatic Prostate Cancer		yrs	26. WAS AUTOPSY PERFORMED? No

23. OTHER SIGNIFICANT CONDITIONS—CONTRIBUTING TO DEATH BUT NOT RELATED TO CAUSE GIVEN IN 22A Pleural Effusion , Perforated Stomach	27. WAS OPERATION PERFORMED FOR ANY CONDITION IN ITEMS 22 OR 23? TYPE OF OPERATION Repair of the Stomach wall	DATE 8/19/87

PHYSICIAN'S CERTIFICATION

28A. I CERTIFY THAT DEATH OCCURRED AT THE HOUR, DATE AND PLACE STATED FROM THE CAUSES STATED. ATTENDED DECEDENT SINCE (ENTER MO. DA. YR.) 10-21-82	LAST SAW DECEDENT ALIVE (ENTER MO. DA. YR.) 9-11-87	28B. PHYSICIAN—SIGNATURE AND DEGREE OR TITLE David S David MD	28C. DATE SIGNED 9-14-87	28D. PHYSICIAN'S LICENSE NUMBER G035123
		28E. TYPE PHYSICIAN'S NAME AND ADDRESS David S.David MD 2001 Santa Monica Bl.Santa Monica,Ca.		

INJURY INFORMATION

29. SPECIFY ACCIDENT, SUICIDE, ETC.	30. PLACE OF INJURY	31. INJURY AT WORK	32A. DATE OF INJURY—MONTH, DAY, YEAR	32B. HOUR

33. LOCATION (STREET AND NUMBER OR LOCATION AND CITY OR TOWN)	34. DESCRIBE HOW INJURY OCCURRED (EVENTS WHICH RESULTED IN INJURY)

CORONER'S USE ONLY

35A. I CERTIFY THAT DEATH OCCURRED AT THE HOUR, DATE AND PLACE STATED FROM THE CAUSES STATED, AS REQUIRED BY LAW I HAVE HELD AN (INQUEST-INVESTIGATION)	35B. CORONER—SIGNATURE AND DEGREE OR TITLE	35C. DATE SIGNED

36. DISPOSITION	37. DATE—MONTH, DAY, YEAR	38. NAME AND ADDRESS OF CEMETERY OR CREMATORY	39. EMBALMER'S LICENSE NUMBER AND SIGNATURE
Entomb.	9-14-87	Hillside Mem.Pk.6001 Centinela Ave.LA,CA.	7516 Randy M. [signature]

40A. NAME OF FUNERAL DIRECTOR (OR PERSON ACTING AS SUCH)	40B. LICENSE NO.	41. LOCAL REGISTRAR—SIGNATURE	42. DATE ACCEPTED BY LOCAL REGISTRAR
Hillside Mem.Pk.Mort. cb	1358	[signature]	SEP 14 1987

STATE REGISTRAR	A.	B.	C.	D.	E.	F.
VS-11 (11-85)	185					5

This is to certify that this document is a true copy of the official record filed with the Registrar-Recorder/County Clerk.

Conny B. McCormack

CONNY B. McCORMACK
Registrar-Recorder/County Clerk

This copy not valid unless prepared on engraved border displaying the Seal and Signature of the Registrar-Recorder/County Clerk.

NOV 0 6 1998
19-602413

DE LA RUE | ANY ALTERATION OR ERASURE VOIDS THIS CERTIFICATE

STATE OF CALIFORNIA

CERTIFICATION OF VITAL RECORD

COUNTY OF LOS ANGELES
DEPARTMENT OF HEALTH SERVICES

CERTIFICATE OF DEATH
STATE OF CALIFORNIA
USE BLACK INK ONLY / NO ERASURES, WHITEOUTS OR ALTERATIONS
VS-11 (REV 1/03)

STATE FILE NUMBER   LOCAL REGISTRATION NUMBER

1. NAME OF DECEDENT — FIRST (Given)	2. MIDDLE	3. LAST (Family)
MARGUERITE	–	GILFORD

AKA, ALSO KNOWN AS — Include full AKA (FIRST, MIDDLE, LAST)	4. DATE OF BIRTH mm/dd/ccyy	5. AGE Yrs.	IF UNDER ONE YEAR Months / Days	IF UNDER 24 HOURS Hours / Minutes	6. SEX
ANNE GWYNNE	12/10/1918	84			F.

9. BIRTH STATE/FOREIGN COUNTRY	10. SOCIAL SECURITY NUMBER	11. EVER IN U.S. ARMED FORCES?	12. MARITAL STATUS (at Time of Death)	7. DATE OF DEATH mm/dd/ccyy	8. HOUR (24 Hours)
TEXAS	548-28-8919	YES [X] NO UNK	WIDOWED	03/31/2003	0345

13. EDUCATION — Highest Level/Degree (see worksheet on back)	14/15. WAS DECEDENT SPANISH/HISPANIC/LATINO? (If yes, see worksheet on back.)	16. DECEDENT'S RACE — Up to 3 races may be listed (see worksheet on back)
16	YES [X] NO	CAUCASIAN

17. USUAL OCCUPATION — Type of work for most of life. DO NOT USE RETIRED	18. KIND OF BUSINESS OR INDUSTRY (e.g., grocery store, road construction, employment agency, etc.)	19. YEARS IN OCCUPATION
ACTRESS	MOTION PICTURE	30

20. DECEDENT'S RESIDENCE (Street and number or location)
23388 MULHOLLAND DR.

21. CITY	22. COUNTY/PROVINCE	23. ZIP CODE	24. YEARS IN COUNTY	25. STATE/FOREIGN COUNTRY
WOODLAND HILLS	LOS ANGELES	91364	64	CA.

26. INFORMANT'S NAME, RELATIONSHIP	27. INFORMANT'S MAILING ADDRESS (Street and number or rural route number, city or town, state, ZIP)
GWYNNE GILFORD PINE – DAUGHTER	11923 ADDISON ST. VALLEY VILLAGE, CA. 91607

28. NAME OF SURVIVING SPOUSE — FIRST	29. MIDDLE	30. LAST (Maiden Name)
–	–	

31. NAME OF FATHER — FIRST	32. MIDDLE	33. LAST	34. BIRTH STATE
JEFFERSON	BENJAMIN	TRICE	TEXAS

35. NAME OF MOTHER — FIRST	36. MIDDLE	37. LAST (Maiden)	38. BIRTH STATE
PEARL	–	GUINN	TEXAS

39. DISPOSITION DATE mm/dd/ccyy	40. PLACE OF FINAL DISPOSITION
04/04/2003	AT SEA OFF THE COAST OF LOS ANGELES COUNTY

41. TYPE OF DISPOSITION(S)	42. SIGNATURE OF EMBALMER	43. LICENSE NUMBER
CR/SEA	NOT EMBALMED	–

44. NAME OF FUNERAL ESTABLISHMENT	45. LICENSE NUMBER	46. SIGNATURE OF LOCAL REGISTRAR	47. DATE mm/dd/ccyy
ARMSTRONG FAMILY MALLOY-MITTEN	FD-380	Thomas L. Garthwaite RC	04/03/2003

101. PLACE OF DEATH	102. IF HOSPITAL, SPECIFY ONE	103. IF OTHER THAN HOSPITAL, SPECIFY ONE
MOTION PICTURE HOSPITAL	IP [X] ER/OP DOA	Hospice / Nursing Home/LTC / Decedent's Home / Other

104. COUNTY	105. FACILITY ADDRESS OR LOCATION WHERE FOUND (Street and number or location)	106. CITY
LOS ANGELES	23388 MULHOLLAND DR.	WOODLAND HILLS

107. CAUSE OF DEATH — Enter the chain of events — diseases, injuries, or complications — that directly caused death. DO NOT enter terminal events such as cardiac arrest, respiratory arrest, or ventricular fibrillation without showing the etiology. DO NOT ABBREVIATE.

		Time Interval Between Onset and Death	108. DEATH REPORTED TO CORONER?
IMMEDIATE CAUSE (A) (Final disease or condition resulting in death)	ACUTE CEREBRAL INFARCTION	72 HRS	YES [X] NO REFERRAL NUMBER
Sequentially, list conditions, if any, leading to cause on Line A. Enter UNDERLYING CAUSE (disease or injury that initiated the events resulting in death) LAST (C)	ATHEROSCLEROSIS	6 YRS	109. BIOPSY PERFORMED? YES [X] NO
(D)			110. AUTOPSY PERFORMED? YES [X] NO
			111. USED IN DETERMINING CAUSE? YES [X] NO

112. OTHER SIGNIFICANT CONDITIONS CONTRIBUTING TO DEATH BUT NOT RESULTING IN THE UNDERLYING CAUSE GIVEN IN 107
CHRONIC ATRIAL FIBRILLATION, DIABETES MELLITUS

113. WAS OPERATION PERFORMED FOR ANY CONDITION IN ITEM 107 OR 112? (If yes, list type of operation and date.)	113A. IF FEMALE, PREGNANT IN LAST YEAR?
NO	YES [X] NO UNK

114. I CERTIFY THAT TO THE BEST OF MY KNOWLEDGE DEATH OCCURRED AT THE HOUR, DATE, AND PLACE STATED FROM THE CAUSES STATED.	115. SIGNATURE AND TITLE OF CERTIFIER	116. LICENSE NUMBER	117. DATE mm/dd/ccyy
Decedent Attended Since / Decedent Last Seen Alive	M. Humyan MD	A39209	03/31/2003

(A) mm/dd/ccyy	mm/dd/ccyy	118. TYPE ATTENDING PHYSICIAN'S NAME, MAILING ADDRESS, ZIP CODE
09/01/1997	03/28/2003	S HUMUYAN MD 23388 MULHOLLAND DR WOODLAND HILLS CA 91364

CORONER'S USE ONLY

119. I CERTIFY THAT IN MY OPINION DEATH OCCURRED AT THE HOUR, DATE, AND PLACE STATED FROM THE CAUSES STATED.			
MANNER OF DEATH: Natural / Accident / Homicide / Suicide / Pending Investigation / Could not be determined	120. INJURED AT WORK? YES NO UNK	121. INJURY DATE mm/dd/ccyy	122. HOUR (24 Hours)

123. PLACE OF INJURY (e.g., home, construction site, wooded area, etc.)

124. DESCRIBE HOW INJURY OCCURRED (Events which resulted in injury)

125. LOCATION OF INJURY (Street and number, or location, city, and ZIP)

126. SIGNATURE OF CORONER / DEPUTY CORONER	127. DATE mm/dd/ccyy	128. TYPE NAME, TITLE OF CORONER / DEPUTY CORONER

STATE REGISTRAR	A	B	C	D	E	FAX AUTH. #	CENSUS TRACT

090615394

This is a true certified copy of the record filed in the County of Los Angeles Department of Health Services if it bears the Registrar's signature in purple ink.

Thomas L. Garthwaite DATE ISSUED   APR 29 2003

Director of Health Services and Registrar

This copy not valid unless prepared on engraved border displaying seal and signature of Registrar.

ANY ALTERATION OR ERASURE VOIDS THIS CERTIFICATE

CERTIFICATE OF DEATH
STATE OF CALIFORNIA
USE BLACK INK ONLY / NO ERASURES WHITEOUTS OR ALTERATIONS

3 2003 19 028308

1 NAME OF DECEDENT—FIRST (Given) Buddy	2 MIDDLE -	3 LAST (Family) Hackett

4 DATE OF BIRTH 08/31/1924 5 AGE 78 6 SEX M

9 BIRTH STATE/FOREIGN COUNTRY New York 10 SOCIAL SECURITY NUMBER 089-16-8630 11 EVER IN U.S ARMED FORCES? X YES 12 MARITAL STATUS Married 7 DATE OF DEATH 06/30/2003 8 HOUR 1130

Professional 15 WAS DECEDENT SPANISH/HISPANIC/LATINO? X NO 16 RACE White

17 USUAL OCCUPATION Entertainer 18 KIND OF BUSINESS Show Business 19 YEARS IN OCCUPATION 60

USUAL RESIDENCE: 800 North Whittier Drive Beverly Hills 22 COUNTY Los Angeles 23 ZIP 90210 24 YEARS IN COUNTY 35 25 STATE California

INFORMANT: Sherry Hackett, Wife 27 INFORMANT'S MAILING ADDRESS 800 North Whittier Drive, Beverly Hills, CA 90210

28 NAME OF SURVIVING SPOUSE—FIRST Sherry 29 MIDDLE - 30 LAST (Maiden Name) Cohen

31 NAME OF FATHER—FIRST Phillip 32 MIDDLE - 33 LAST Hacker 34 BIRTH STATE Italy

35 NAME OF MOTHER—FIRST Anna 36 MIDDLE 37 LAST (Maiden) Hacker 38 BIRTH STATE New York

39 DISPOSITION DATE 07/02/2003 40 PLACE OF FINAL DISPOSITION Residence Of Sherry Hackett 800 North Whittier Drive, Beverly Hills, CA 90210

41 TYPE OF DISPOSITION CR/RES 42 SIGNATURE OF EMBALMER Not Embalmed 43 LICENSE NUMBER

44 NAME OF FUNERAL ESTABLISHMENT Hillside Memorial Park Mortuary 45 LICENSE NUMBER FD 1358 46 SIGNATURE OF LOCAL REGISTRAR Thomas W... 47 DATE 07/01/2003

PLACE OF DEATH: Residence Los Angeles 104 32232 Pacific Coast Highway 106 CITY Malibu 103 X Decedent's Home

CAUSE OF DEATH:
- IMMEDIATE CAUSE (A) Acute Myocardial Infarction — 1 Hour
- (B) Arteriosclerotic Heart Disease — 5 Years
- (C) Diabetes Mellitus — 10 Years

108 DEATH REPORTED TO CORONER? X NO 109 BIOPSY PERFORMED? X NO 110 AUTOPSY PERFORMED? X NO

112 OTHER SIGNIFICANT CONDITIONS: Hyperlipidemia

113 WAS OPERATION PERFORMED: No

114/115 SIGNATURE AND TITLE OF CERTIFIER [signature] 116 LICENSE NUMBER G 7677 117 DATE 07/01/2003

01/01/1993 06/28/2003 118 Robert Karns, M.D., 8920 Wilshire Boulevard, Beverly Hills, CA 90211

STATE OF CALIFORNIA
CERTIFICATION OF VITAL RECORD

COUNTY OF LOS ANGELES • REGISTRAR-RECORDER/COUNTY CLERK

CERTIFICATE OF DEATH
STATE OF CALIFORNIA

0190-045597

STATE FILE NUMBER			LOCAL REGISTRATION DISTRICT AND CERTIFICATE NUMBER
1A. NAME OF DECEDENT—FIRST	1B. MIDDLE	1C. LAST	2A. DATE OF DEATH (MONTH, DAY, YEAR) 2B. HOUR
Joan		Hackett	October 8, 1983 ⎪ 2115

DECEDENT PERSONAL DATA

3. SEX	4. RACE	5. ETHNICITY	6. DATE OF BIRTH	7. AGE	IF UNDER 1 YEAR MONTHS / DAYS	IF UNDER 24 HOURS HOURS / MINUTES
F	White		March 1, 1934	49 YEARS		

8. BIRTHPLACE OF DECEDENT (STATE OR FOREIGN COUNTRY)	9. NAME AND BIRTHPLACE OF FATHER	10. BIRTH NAME AND BIRTHPLACE OF MOTHER
New York	John Hackett-New York	Mary Esposito-Italy

11. CITIZEN OF WHAT COUNTRY	12. SOCIAL SECURITY NUMBER	13. MARITAL STATUS	14. NAME OF SURVIVING SPOUSE (IF WIFE, ENTER BIRTH NAME)
U.S.A.	082-26-0193	Divorced	None

15. PRIMARY OCCUPATION	16. NUMBER OF YEARS THIS OCCUPATION	17. EMPLOYER (IF SELF-EMPLOYED, SO STATE)	18. KIND OF INDUSTRY OR BUSINESS
Actress	30 years	Self-Employed	Entertainment

USUAL RESIDENCE

19A. USUAL RESIDENCE—STREET ADDRESS (STREET AND NUMBER OR LOCATION)	19B.	19C. CITY OR TOWN
1364 Angelo Dr.		Beverly Hills

19D. COUNTY	19E. STATE	20. NAME AND ADDRESS OF INFORMANT—RELATIONSHIP
Los Angeles	California	Richard M. Smyser-Bus. Manager

PLACE OF DEATH

21A. PLACE OF DEATH	21B. COUNTY	2331 Allview Dr.
Encino Hospital	Los Angeles	

21C. STREET ADDRESS (STREET AND NUMBER OR LOCATION)	21D. CITY OR TOWN	Los Angeles, CA 90068
16237 Ventura Blvd.	Encino	

CAUSE OF DEATH

22. DEATH WAS CAUSED BY: (ENTER ONLY ONE CAUSE PER LINE FOR A, B, AND C) IMMEDIATE CAUSE		24. WAS DEATH REPORTED TO CORONER?
(A) Abdominal metastases	5 mo	No
CONDITIONS, IF ANY, WHICH GAVE RISE TO THE IMMEDIATE CAUSE, STATING THE UNDERLYING CAUSE LAST. (B) Clear cell carcinoma of the kidney	22 mo	25. WAS BIOPSY PERFORMED? yes
(C)		26. WAS AUTOPSY PERFORMED? No

APPROXIMATE INTERVAL BETWEEN ONSET AND DEATH

23. OTHER CONDITIONS CONTRIBUTING BUT NOT RELATED TO THE IMMEDIATE CAUSE OF DEATH	27. WAS OPERATION PERFORMED FOR ANY CONDITION IN ITEMS 22 OR 23? TYPE OF OPERATION / DATE
Pulmonary metastases	1/20/82 - hysterectomy + oophorectomy 1-20-82

PHYSICIAN'S CERTIFICATION

28A. I CERTIFY THAT DEATH OCCURRED AT THE HOUR, DATE AND PLACE STATED FROM THE CAUSES STATED. I ATTENDED DECEDENT SINCE (ENTER MO. DA. YR.) / I LAST SAW DECEDENT ALIVE (ENTER MO. DA. YR.)	28B. PHYSICIAN—SIGNATURE AND DEGREE OR TITLE	28C. DATE SIGNED	28D. PHYSICIAN'S LICENSE NUMBER
1-10-83 / 10-7-83	Avrum Bluming, M.D.	10-10-83	G15859
28E. TYPE PHYSICIAN'S NAME AND ADDRESS	A. Bluming 16311 Ventura Blvd, Encino. Calif		

INJURY INFORMATION

29. SPECIFY ACCIDENT, SUICIDE, ETC.	30. PLACE OF INJURY	31. INJURY AT WORK	32A. DATE OF INJURY—MONTH, DAY, YEAR	32B. HOUR

33. LOCATION (STREET AND NUMBER OR LOCATION AND CITY OR TOWN)	34. DESCRIBE HOW INJURY OCCURRED (EVENTS WHICH RESULTED IN INJURY)

CORONER'S USE ONLY

35A. I CERTIFY THAT DEATH OCCURRED AT THE HOUR, DATE AND PLACE STATED FROM THE CAUSES STATED, AS REQUIRED BY LAW I HAVE HELD AN (INQUEST-INVESTIGATION)	35B. CORONER—SIGNATURE AND DEGREE OR TITLE	35C. DATE SIGNED

36. DISPOSITION	37. DATE—MONTH, DAY, YEAR	38. NAME AND ADDRESS OF CEMETERY OR CREMATORY	39. EMBALMER'S LICENSE NUMBER AND SIGNATURE
Burial	10-12-1983	Hollywood Cemetery 6000 Santa Monica Blvd.	3296 Ed Kell

40. NAME OF FUNERAL DIRECTOR (OR PERSON ACTING AS SUCH)	41. LOCAL REGISTRAR—SIGNATURE	42. DATE ACCEPTED BY LOCAL REGISTRAR
Gold Cross Mortuary F-1303	Robert Wolstein	OCT 11 1983

STATE REGISTRAR

A.	B.	C.	D.	E.	F.

VS-11 (10-78) 1800

This is to certify that this document is a true copy of the official record filed with the Registrar-Recorder/County Clerk.

Conny B. McCormack

CONNY B. McCORMACK
Registrar-Recorder/County Clerk

This copy not valid unless prepared on engraved border displaying the Seal and Signature of the Registrar-Recorder/County Clerk.

OCT 04 2001
19-673800

ANY ALTERATION OR ERASURE VOIDS THIS CERTIFICATE

STATE OF CALIFORNIA
CERTIFICATION OF VITAL RECORD

COUNTY OF LOS ANGELES • REGISTRAR-RECORDER/COUNTY CLERK

CERTIFICATE OF DEATH
STATE OF CALIFORNIA

STATE FILE NUMBER

0190-026669

LOCAL REGISTRATION DISTRICT AND CERTIFICATE NUMBER

DECEDENT PERSONAL DATA				
1A. NAME OF DECEDENT—FIRST aka Jack JOHN	1B. MIDDLE JOSEPH	1C. LAST HALEY Haley	2A. DATE OF DEATH (MONTH, DAY, YEAR) June 6, 1979	2B. HOUR 1304
3. SEX Male	4. RACE White	5. ETHNICITY	6. DATE OF BIRTH August 10, 1898	7. AGE 80 YEARS
8. BIRTHPLACE OF DECEDENT (STATE OR FOREIGN COUNTRY) Massachusetts	9. NAME AND BIRTHPLACE OF FATHER John J. Haley - Nova Scotia, Canada		10. BIRTH NAME AND BIRTHPLACE OF MOTHER Ellen F. Curley-Nova Scotia, Canada	
11. CITIZEN OF WHAT COUNTRY United States	12. SOCIAL SECURITY NUMBER 555 09 3034	13. MARITAL STATUS Married	14. NAME OF SURVIVING SPOUSE (IF WIFE, ENTER BIRTH NAME) Florence Mc Fadden	
15. PRIMARY OCCUPATION Actor	16. NUMBER OF YEARS THIS OCCUPATION 62	17. EMPLOYER (IF SELF-EMPLOYED, SO STATE) Self-employed	18. KIND OF INDUSTRY OR BUSINESS Entertainment	

USUAL RESIDENCE			
19A. USUAL RESIDENCE—STREET ADDRESS (STREET AND NUMBER OR LOCATION) 1001 No. Beverly Drive	19B.		19C. CITY OR TOWN Beverly Hills
19D. COUNTY Los Angeles	19E. STATE California	20. NAME AND ADDRESS OF INFORMANT—RELATIONSHIP Mrs. Florence Haley (wife) 1001 No. Beverly Drive Beverly Hills, CA. 90210	

PLACE OF DEATH		
21A. PLACE OF DEATH UCLA Hospital	21B. COUNTY Los Angeles	
21C. STREET ADDRESS (STREET AND NUMBER OR LOCATION) 10833 Le Conte Avenue	21D. CITY OR TOWN Los Angeles	

CAUSE OF DEATH

22. DEATH WAS CAUSED BY: (ENTER ONLY ONE CAUSE PER LINE FOR A, B, AND C)
IMMEDIATE CAUSE

(A) CARDIOPULMONARY ARREST — 1 HR.
CONDITIONS, IF ANY, WHICH GAVE RISE TO THE IMMEDIATE CAUSE, STATING THE UNDERLYING CAUSE LAST
(B) CARDIOGENIC SHOCK — 12 HRS.
DUE TO, OR AS A CONSEQUENCE OF
(C) MYOCARDIAL INFARCTION — 6 DAYS

APPROXIMATE INTERVAL BETWEEN ONSET AND DEATH

24. WAS DEATH REPORTED TO CORONER? NO
25. WAS BIOPSY PERFORMED? NO
26. WAS AUTOPSY PERFORMED? YES

23. OTHER CONDITIONS CONTRIBUTING BUT NOT RELATED TO THE IMMEDIATE CAUSE OF DEATH No
27. WAS OPERATION PERFORMED FOR ANY CONDITION IN ITEMS 22 OR 23? TYPE OF OPERATION NO DATE

PHYSICIAN'S CERTIFICATION

28A. I CERTIFY THAT DEATH OCCURRED AT THE HOUR, DATE AND PLACE STATED FROM THE CAUSES STATED
I ATTENDED DECEDENT SINCE (ENTER MO. DA. YR.) 6-1-79
I LAST SAW DECEDENT ALIVE (ENTER MO. DA. YR.) 6-6-79
28B. PHYSICIAN—SIGNATURE AND DEGREE OR TITLE David M. Berman MD
28C. DATE SIGNED 6-6-79
28D. PHYSICIAN'S LICENSE NUMBER 637827
28E. TYPE PHYSICIAN'S NAME AND ADDRESS David M. Berman, MD, 10833 Le Conte, Los Angeles, Calif.

INJURY INFORMATION

29. SPECIFY ACCIDENT, SUICIDE, ETC.
30. PLACE OF INJURY
31. INJURY AT WORK
32A. DATE OF INJURY—MONTH DAY YEAR
32B. HOUR

33. LOCATION (STREET AND NUMBER OR LOCATION AND CITY OR TOWN)
34. DESCRIBE HOW INJURY OCCURRED (EVENTS WHICH RESULTED IN INJURY)

CORONER'S USE ONLY

35A. I CERTIFY THAT DEATH OCCURRED AT THE HOUR, DATE AND PLACE STATED FROM THE CAUSES STATED, AS REQUIRED BY LAW I HAVE HELD AN (INQUEST/INVESTIGATION)
35B. CORONER—SIGNATURE AND DEGREE OR TITLE
35C. DATE SIGNED

36. DISPOSITION Burial	37. DATE—MONTH, DAY, YEAR 6-11-79	38. NAME AND ADDRESS OF CEMETERY OR CREMATORY Holy Cross 5835 W. Slauson Av, Los Angeles	39. EMBALMER'S LICENSE NUMBER AND SIGNATURE 6829
40. NAME OF FUNERAL DIRECTOR (OR PERSON ACTING AS SUCH) Cunningham & O'Connor Hwd.	41. LOCAL REGISTRAR—SIGNATURE		42. DATE ACCEPTED BY LOCAL REGISTRAR JUN 8 1979

12 STATE REGISTRAR | A. | B. | C. | D. | E. | F.

VS-11 (10-78)

This is to certify that this document is a true copy of the official record filed with the Registrar-Recorder/County Clerk.

Conny B. McCormack

CONNY B. McCORMACK
Registrar-Recorder/County Clerk

This copy not valid unless prepared on engraved border displaying the Seal and Signature of the Registrar-Recorder/County Clerk.

SEP 3 0 2002
19-540655

ANY ALTERATION OR ERASURE VOIDS THIS CERTIFICATE

CERTIFICATION OF VITAL RECORD

COUNTY OF LOS ANGELES • REGISTRAR-RECORDER/COUNTY CLERK

CERTIFICATE OF DEATH

STATE OF CALIFORNIA—DEPARTMENT OF PUBLIC HEALTH

LOCAL REGISTRATION DISTRICT AND CERTIFICATE NUMBER
7097-006556

DECEDENT PERSONAL DATA	1A. NAME OF DECEASED—FIRST NAME: GEORGE / 1B. MIDDLE NAME: FRANCIS / 1C. LAST NAME: HAYES	2A. DATE OF DEATH: February 9, 1969 / 2B. HOUR: 9:40 A.M.
	3. SEX: Male / 4. COLOR OR RACE: Caucasian / 5. BIRTHPLACE: New York / 6. DATE OF BIRTH: May 7, 1885	7. AGE (LAST BIRTHDAY): 83 YEARS
	8. NAME AND BIRTHPLACE OF FATHER: Clark R. Hayes – New York	9. MAIDEN NAME AND BIRTHPLACE OF MOTHER: Unknown – Morrison – New York
	10. CITIZEN OF WHAT COUNTRY: U.S.A. / 11. SOCIAL SECURITY NUMBER: 560-12-0306 / 12. MARRIED, NEVER MARRIED, WIDOWED, DIVORCED (SPECIFY): Widowed	13. NAME OF SURVIVING SPOUSE (IF WIFE, ENTER MAIDEN NAME): - - - - - - -
	14. LAST OCCUPATION: Actor / 15. NUMBER OF YEARS IN THIS OCCUPATION: 60 / 16. NAME OF LAST EMPLOYING COMPANY OR FIRM: R.K.O.	17. KIND OF INDUSTRY OR BUSINESS: Motion Pictures
PLACE OF DEATH	18A. PLACE OF DEATH—NAME OF HOSPITAL OR OTHER IN-PATIENT FACILITY: St. Joseph's Hospital / 18B. STREET ADDRESS: 501 South Buena Vista Street	18C. INSIDE CITY CORPORATE LIMITS: Yes
	18D. CITY OR TOWN: Burbank / 18E. CITY OR TOWN: Los Angeles / 18F. LENGTH OF STAY IN COUNTY OF DEATH: 40 YEARS	18G. LENGTH OF STAY IN CALIFORNIA: 40 YEARS
USUAL RESIDENCE	19A. USUAL RESIDENCE—STREET ADDRESS: 5011 Cahuenga Boulevard / 19B. INSIDE CITY CORPORATE LIMITS: Yes	20. NAME AND MAILING ADDRESS OF INFORMANT: Clark W. Hayes – Nephew, 4831 Biloxi Avenue, North Hollywood, California
	19C. CITY OR TOWN: North Hollywood / 19D. COUNTY: Los Angeles / 19E. STATE: California	
PHYSICIAN'S OR CORONER'S CERTIFICATION	21A. CORONER / 21B. PHYSICIAN: FROM Feb 3, 69 TO Feb 9, 69 AND LAST SAW HIM Feb 9, 69 / 21C. PHYSICIAN OR CORONER SIGNATURE: Raymond C. Perkins M.D. / 21D. DATE SIGNED: 10 Feb 69	21E. ADDRESS: 13320 Riverside Dr. / 21F. PHYSICIAN'S CALIFORNIA LICENSE NUMBER: G1114
FUNERAL DIRECTOR AND LOCAL REGISTRAR	22A. SPECIFY BURIAL, ENTOMBMENT OR CREMATION: Cremation / 22B. DATE: Feb 12, 1969 / 23. NAME OF CEMETERY OR CREMATORY: FOREST LAWN MEMORIAL PARK	24. EMBALMER—SIGNATURE: Fred A. Prevost 5166
	25. NAME OF FUNERAL DIRECTOR: Forest Lawn Hollywood Hills Mortuary / 26. IF NOT CERTIFIED BY CORONER, WAS THIS DEATH REPORTED TO CORONER: No / 27. LOCAL REGISTRAR—SIGNATURE: Alfred Becker MD	28. DATE ACCEPTED FOR REGISTRATION BY LOCAL REGISTRAR: FEB 11 1969

CAUSE OF DEATH	29. PART I. DEATH WAS CAUSED BY: ENTER ONLY ONE CAUSE PER LINE FOR A, B AND C		APPROXIMATE INTERVAL BETWEEN ONSET AND DEATH
	IMMEDIATE CAUSE (A): Acute Myocardial Infarction		7 day
	CONDITIONS, IF ANY, WHICH GAVE RISE TO THE IMMEDIATE CAUSE (A), STATING THE UNDERLYING CAUSE LAST. DUE TO, OR AS A CONSEQUENCE OF (B): Coronary Thrombosis		7 day
	DUE TO, OR AS A CONSEQUENCE OF (C): Arteriosclerotic Heart Disease		30 yrs
	30. PART II. OTHER SIGNIFICANT CONDITIONS	31. WAS OPERATION OR BIOPSY PERFORMED: no / 32A. AUTOPSY: no	32B. IF YES, WERE FINDINGS CONSIDERED IN DETERMINING CAUSE OF DEATH
INJURY INFORMATION	33. SPECIFY ACCIDENT, SUICIDE OR HOMICIDE / 34. PLACE OF INJURY / 35. INJURY AT WORK / 36A. DATE OF INJURY		36B. HOUR
	37A. PLACE OF INJURY / 37B. DISTANCE FROM PLACE OF INJURY TO USUAL RESIDENCE / 38. WERE LABORATORY TESTS DONE FOR DRUGS	39. WERE LABORATORY TESTS DONE FOR ALCOHOL	
	40. DESCRIBE HOW INJURY OCCURRED		
STATE REGISTRAR	A. / B. / C. / D. / E.		F. 1255

REV. 1-1-66 Form VS-11

This is to certify that this document is a true copy of the official record filed with the Registrar-Recorder/County Clerk.

Beatriz Valdez
BEATRIZ VALDEZ
Registrar-Recorder/County Clerk

AUG 10 1995
19-389291

This copy not valid unless prepared on engraved border displaying the Seal and Signature of the Registrar-Recorder/County Clerk.

American Bank Note Company   ANY ALTERATION OR ERASURE VOIDS THIS CERTIFICATE

CERTIFICATION OF VITAL RECORD

COUNTY OF LOS ANGELES · REGISTRAR-RECORDER/COUNTY CLERK

CERTIFICATE OF DEATH
STATE OF CALIFORNIA—DEPARTMENT OF HEALTH
OFFICE OF THE STATE REGISTRAR OF VITAL STATISTICS

0190-011922

STATE FILE NUMBER	LOCAL REGISTRATION DISTRICT AND CERTIFICATE NUMBER	

1A. NAME OF DECEASED—FIRST NAME	1B. MIDDLE NAME	1C. LAST NAME	2A. DATE OF DEATH—MONTH, DAY, YEAR	2B. HOUR
Edythe	Marrener	Chalkley	March 14, 1975	2:25 P.M.

3. SEX	4. COLOR OR RACE	5. BIRTHPLACE (STATE OR FOREIGN COUNTRY)	6. DATE OF BIRTH	7. AGE (LAST BIRTHDAY)	IF UNDER 1 YEAR	IF UNDER 24 HOURS
Female	Cauc.	New York	June 30, 1917	57 YEARS		

DECEDENT PERSONAL DATA

8. NAME AND BIRTHPLACE OF FATHER	9. MAIDEN NAME AND BIRTHPLACE OF MOTHER
Walter Marrener - New York	Ellen Pearson - New York

10. CITIZEN OF WHAT COUNTRY	11. SOCIAL SECURITY NUMBER	12. MARRIED, NEVER MARRIED, WIDOWED, DIVORCED (SPECIFY)	13. NAME OF SURVIVING SPOUSE (IF WIFE, ENTER MAIDEN NAME)
U.S.A.	577-28-3004	Divorced	

14. LAST OCCUPATION	15. NUMBER OF YEARS IN THIS OCCUPATION	16. NAME OF LAST EMPLOYING COMPANY OR FIRM (IF SELF EMPLOYED, SO STATE)	17. KIND OF INDUSTRY OR BUSINESS
Actress	36	American Broadcasting Co.	Motion Picture

PLACE OF DEATH

18A. PLACE OF DEATH—NAME OF HOSPITAL OR OTHER IN-PATIENT FACILITY	18B. STREET ADDRESS (STREET AND NUMBER OR LOCATION)	18C. INSIDE CITY CORPORATE LIMITS (SPECIFY YES OR NO)
Century City Hospital	2070 Century Park East	Yes

18D. CITY OR TOWN	18E. COUNTY	18F. LENGTH OF STAY IN COUNTY OF DEATH	18G. LENGTH OF STAY IN CALIFORNIA
Los Angeles	Los Angeles	3 YEARS	3 YEARS

USUAL RESIDENCE (IF DEATH OCCURRED IN INSTITUTION ENTER RESIDENCE BEFORE ADMISSION)

19A. USUAL RESIDENCE—STREET ADDRESS (STREET AND NUMBER OR LOCATION)	19B. INSIDE CITY CORPORATE LIMITS (SPECIFY YES OR NO)	20. NAME AND MAILING ADDRESS OF INFORMANT
1460 Laurel Way	Yes	Timothy Barker

19C. CITY OR TOWN	19D. COUNTY	19E. STATE	1451 No. Kings Road
Los Angeles	Los Angeles	California	Los Angeles, Calif. 90069

PHYSICIAN'S OR CORONER'S CERTIFICATION

21A. CORONER	21B. PHYSICIAN FROM ... TO ...	21C. PHYSICIAN OR CORONER SIGNATURE	21D. DATE SIGNED
	1-7-72 to 3-14-75 / 3-13-75	Carl Riegel M.D.	3-14-75
	21E. ADDRESS	9441 Wilshire Blvd.	21F. PHYSICIAN'S CALIFORNIA LICENSE NO. A04875

FUNERAL DIRECTOR AND LOCAL REGISTRAR

22A. SPECIFY BURIAL, ENTOMBMENT OR CREMATION	22B. DATE	23. NAME OF CEMETERY OR CREMATORY	24. EMBALMER SIGNATURE IF BODY EMBALMED / LICENSE NUMBER
Burial	3-17-75	Our Lady of Perpetual Health Carrollton Georgia	

25. NAME OF FUNERAL DIRECTOR (OR PERSON ACTING AS SUCH)	26. IF NOT CERTIFIED BY CORONER, WAS THIS DEATH REPORTED TO CORONER? (SPECIFY YES OR NO)	27. LOCAL REGISTRAR—SIGNATURE	28. DATE RECEIVED FOR REGISTRATION BY LOCAL REGISTRAR
Armstrong Family	No		MAR 14 1975

CAUSE OF DEATH

29. PART I. DEATH WAS CAUSED BY: IMMEDIATE CAUSE (A) *Cerebral seizure & bronchial pneumonia 1 week*

CONDITIONS, IF ANY, WHICH GAVE RISE TO THE IMMEDIATE CAUSE (A), STATING THE UNDERLYING CAUSE LAST. DUE TO, OR AS A CONSEQUENCE OF (B) *Ca of Brain with spreading metastasis 2½ yrs*

DUE TO, OR AS A CONSEQUENCE OF (C)

APPROXIMATE INTERVAL BETWEEN ONSET AND DEATH

30. PART II. OTHER SIGNIFICANT CONDITIONS	31. WAS OPERATION OR BIOPSY PERFORMED?	32A. AUTOPSY	32B. IF YES, WERE FINDINGS CONSIDERED IN DETERMINING CAUSE OF DEATH?
	Biopsy Brain	Yes	Yes

INJURY INFORMATION

33. SPECIFY ACCIDENT, SUICIDE OR HOMICIDE	34. PLACE OF INJURY	35. INJURY AT WORK (SPECIFY YES OR NO)	36A. DATE OF INJURY	36B. HOUR

37A. PLACE OF INJURY (STREET AND NUMBER OR LOCATION AND CITY OR TOWN)	37B. DISTANCE FROM PLACE OF INJURY TO USUAL RESIDENCE	38. WERE LABORATORY TESTS DONE (OF DRUGS OR TOXIC CHEMICALS)?	39. WERE LABORATORY TESTS DONE FOR ALCOHOL?

40. DESCRIBE HOW INJURY OCCURRED

STATE REGISTRAR	A.	B.	C.	D.	E.	F. 8-1-9

VS-4 REV. 9/95
STATE OF CONNECTICUT
DEPARTMENT OF PUBLIC HEALTH

CERTIFICATE OF DEATH

106 2001 0 2 8 5 4 4

STATE FILE NUMBER

1 DECEASED NAME — FIRST	MIDDLE	LAST	SEX 2 F	DATE OF DEATH (Month, Day, Year) 3 12-31-2001
Eileen		Yankee		

4 DATE OF BIRTH (Month, Day, Year) 03-29-1919	5 AGE-Last Birthday 82	UNDER 1 YEAR a. Mos. / Days	UNDER 1 DAY b. Hours / Mins.	6 RACE-White, Black, American Indian, Other (Specify) White	7 OF HISPANIC ORIGIN? (If Yes, specify Cuban, Mexican, Puerto Rican, Other) ☐Y ☒N

8 COUNTY OF DEATH Fairfield	9 TOWN OF DEATH Norwalk	10 PLACE OF DEATH (Check one) Hospital: ☐ER/outpatient ☐DOA ☐Inpatient	OTHER ☐ Nursing Home ☒Residence 1223 Foxboro Drive ☐ Other

11 CITY & STATE OF BIRTH (Country if not U.S.) Columbus, Ohio	12 CITIZEN OF USA	13 ☐MARRIED ☐NEVER MARRIED ☒WIDOWED ☐DIVORCED ☐LEGALLY SEPARATED	14 LAST SPOUSE (If wife, give maiden name) Jack Yankee

15 SOCIAL SECURITY NUMBER	16 USUAL OCCUPATION (Give kind of work done during most working life, even if retired) Actress	17 KIND OF BUSINESS OR INDUSTRY Broadway / Movies

18 RESIDENCE STATE CT	19 COUNTY Fairfield	20 TOWN Norwalk	21 NUMBER AND STREET 1223 Foxboro Drive

22 WAS DECEASED A VETERAN IF YES GIVE WAR ☐YES ☒NO	23 BRANCH OF SERVICE	24 EDUCATION (Specify highest grade completed): Primary/Secondary: _____ College: 4 0-12 1-4 5+

25 FATHER - NAME FIRST Leo	MIDDLE Herbert	LAST	26 MOTHER - FIRST Esther	MIDDLE Stark	MAIDEN

27 INFORMANT - NAME Mark Yankee	28 MAILING ADDRESS 28 Ellen Street, Norwalk, Conn.	29 RELATIONSHIP TO DECEASED Son

PART 1. DEATH WAS CAUSED BY (ENTER ONLY ONE CAUSE PER LINE FOR (a), (b) AND (c))

30 CONDITIONS, IF ANY WHICH GAVE RISE TO IMMEDIATE CAUSE (a) STATING THE UNDERLYING CAUSE LAST.	IMMEDIATE CAUSE (a) Lung Cancer	APPROXIMATE INTERVAL BETWEEN ONSET AND DEATH 2 mos.
	DUE TO, OR AS A CONSEQUENCE OF: (b)	
	DUE TO, OR AS A CONSEQUENCE OF: (c)	

31 PART II. OTHER SIGNIFICANT CONDITIONS: CONDITIONS CONTRIBUTING TO DEATH BUT NOT RELATED TO CAUSE Chronic Obstructive Pulmonary Disease	32 AUTOPSY ☐Y ☒N	33 IF YES, Were findings considered in determining cause of death.

34 NURSE PRONOUNCEMENT TYPE OR PRINT NAME Marie Spaight	DEGREE RN	35 SIGNATURE Marie Spaight	35 DATE AND TIME PRONOUNCED MONTH 12 / DAY 31 / YEAR 01 / TIME 10:00 ☐A.M. ☒P.M.

37 CERTIFICATION - PHYSICIAN I attended the deceased from Mo. 8 Day 20 Yr 99 T o Mo. 12 Day 30 Year 01	38 AND LAST SAW HIM/HER ALIVE ON Month 12 Day 30 Year 01	39 DEATH OCCURRED On the date, and to the best of my knowledge, due to the cause(s) stated. (Time) 10:00 A.M.

40 WAS CASE REFERRED TO MEDICAL EXAMINER ☐YES ☒NO	41 SURGERY RELEVANT TO CONDITION REPORTED IN ITEM 30 (Name of Operation)	42 (Date Performed)	43 THE DECEDENT WAS PRONOUNCED DEAD: Month / Day / Year / Time M.

44 CERTIFIER - NAME (type or print) D.J. Leone MD.	45 SIGNATURE Leone	DEGREE OR TITLE Attending

46 MAILING - CERTIFIER STREET OR R.F.D. NO. 40 Cross Street	CITY OR TOWN Norwalk	STATE CT	ZIP 0685?	47 DATE SIGNED (Month, Day, Year) 12-31-01

48 BURIAL, CREMATION, REMOVAL (Specify) Cremation	49 CEMETERY OR CREMATORY - NAME Stamford Crematory	50 LOCATION CITY OR TOWN Stamford, Conn.	STATE

51 DATE (MONTH, DAY, YEAR) January 3, 2002	52 FUNERAL HOME - NAME AND ADDRESS (STREET OR R.F.D. NO., CITY OR TOWN, STATE, ZIP) Gallagher Telophase 2900 Summer St. Stamford, Ct.

53 FUNERAL DIRECTOR OR EMBALMER - SIGNATURE Brien McMahon / Brien J. McMahon	54 NAME OF EMBALMER IF BODY WAS EMBALMED Not Embalmed	55 LICENSE NUMBER 2384

THIS CERTIFICATE RECEIVED FOR RECORD ON January 2, 2002	BY	REGISTRAR Jane M. Seymour, Asst.

(left margin, vertical) I certify that this is a true copy of the certificate received for record.   Attest: _____   Registrar.

THE SEAL OF THE STATE OF CONNECTICUT IS AFFIXED TO CERTIFY THAT THE ABOVE IS A TRUE COPY OF A RECORD FILED WITH THE STATE OF CONNECTICUT DEPARTMENT OF PUBLIC HEALTH PURSUANT TO THE PROVISIONS OF THE GENERAL STATUTES OF CONNECTICUT.

Suzanne Speers, R.H.I.A., M.P.H.
Registrar of Vital Records

JAN 3 0 2002

Date of Issue

CERTIFICATION OF VITAL RECORD

COUNTY OF LOS ANGELES • REGISTRAR-RECORDER/COUNTY CLERK

CERTIFICATE OF DEATH
STATE OF CALIFORNIA
USE BLACK INK ONLY

39219014884

LOCAL REGISTRATION DISTRICT AND CERTIFICATE NUMBER

1A. NAME OF DECEDENT—FIRST (GIVEN) PAUL	**1B. MIDDLE**	**1C. LAST (FAMILY)** HENREID	**2A. DATE OF DEATH—MO. DAY. YR.** MARCH 29, 1992 **2B. HOUR** 2020 **3. SEX** MALE

DECEDENT PERSONAL DATA

| 4. RACE CAUCASIAN | 5. HISPANIC—SPECIFY ☐ YES ☒ NO | 6. DATE OF BIRTH—MO. DAY. YR JANUARY 10, 1908 | 7. AGE IN YEARS 84 | IF UNDER 1 YEAR MONTHS DAYS | IF UNDER 24 HOURS HOURS MINUTES |

| 8. STATE OF BIRTH ITALY | 9. CITIZEN OF WHAT COUNTRY USA | 10A. FULL NAME OF FATHER CARL A. VON HERNRIED | 10B. STATE OF BIRTH AUSTRIA | 11A. FULL MAIDEN NAME OF MOTHER MARIA LOUISE LENDECKE | 11B. STATE OF BIRTH AUSTRIA |

| 12. MILITARY SERVICE? 19___ TO 19___ ☒ NONE | 13. SOCIAL SECURITY NO. 103-12-4215 | 14. MARITAL STATUS MARRIED | 15. NAME OF SURVIVING SPOUSE OF WIFE, ENTER MAIDEN NAME) LISL GLUCK |

| 16A. USUAL OCCUPATION ACTOR | 16B. USUAL KIND OF BUSINESS OR INDUSTRY ENTERTAINMENT | 16C. USUAL EMPLOYER SELF | 16D. YEARS IN OCCUPATION 60 | 17. EDUCATION—YEARS COMPLETED 15 |

USUAL RESIDENCE

| 18A. RESIDENCE—STREET AND NUMBER OR LOCATION 18068 BLUE SAIL DRIVE | 18B. CITY PACIFIC PALISADES | 18C. ZIP CODE 90272 |

| 18D. COUNTY LOS ANGELES | 18E. NUMBER OF YEARS IN THIS COUNTY 50 | 18F. STATE OR FOREIGN COUNTRY CALIFORNIA | 20. NAME, RELATIONSHIP, MAILING ADDRESS AND ZIP CODE OF INFORMANT MIMI HENREID DUNCAN - DAUGHTER 517 POMONA AVENUE CORONADO, CALIFORNIA 92118 |

PLACE OF DEATH

| 19A. PLACE OF DEATH SANTA MONICA HOSPITAL | 19B. IF HOSPITAL SPECIFY ONE: IP, ER/OP, DOA IP | 19C. COUNTY LOS ANGELES | |

| 19D. STREET ADDRESS—STREET AND NUMBER OR LOCATION 1250 16TH ST. | 19E. CITY SANTA MONICA | TIME INTERVAL BETWEEN ONSET AND DEATH | 22. WAS DEATH REPORTED TO CORONER? REFERRAL NUMBER ☐ YES ☒ NO |

CAUSE OF DEATH

21. DEATH WAS CAUSED BY: (ENTER ONLY ONE CAUSE PER LINE FOR A, B AND C)

IMMEDIATE CAUSE (A) Cardiorespiratory Arrest	▶ 5 Mins	23. WAS BIOPSY PERFORMED? ☐ YES ☒ NO
DUE TO (B) Progressive Respiratory Failure	▶ 3 Mos.	24A. WAS AUTOPSY PERFORMED? ☐ YES ☒ NO
DUE TO (C) Parkinsonism	▶ Years	24B. WAS IT USED IN DETERMINING CAUSE OF DEATH? ☐ YES ☐ NO

| 25. OTHER SIGNIFICANT CONDITIONS CONTRIBUTING TO DEATH BUT NOT RELATED TO CAUSE GIVEN IN 21 Dysphagia | 26. WAS OPERATION PERFORMED FOR ANY CONDITION IN ITEM 21 OR 25? IF YES, LIST TYPE OF OPERATION AND DATE. No |

PHYSICIAN'S CERTIFICATION

| I CERTIFY THAT TO THE ... OF MY KNOWLEDGE DEATH ...ATE AND PLACE STATED FROM THE CAUSES STATED. | 27B. SIGNATURE AND DEGREE OR TITLE OF CERTIFIER Karen Mercola M.D. | 27C. CERTIFIER'S LICENSE NUMBER G30394 | 27D. DATE SIGNED 3/30/92 |
| 27A. DECEDENT ATTENDED SINCE MONTH, DAY, YEAR 1/18/92 | DECEDENT LAST SEEN ALIVE MONTH, DAY, YEAR 3/29/92 | 27E. TYPE ATTENDING PHYSICIAN'S NAME AND ADDRESS KAREN MERCOLA, M.D. 9735 WILSHIRE BLVD., SUITE 400, BEVERLY HILLS, CA |

CORONER'S USE ONLY

| I CERTIFY THAT IN MY OPINION DEATH OCCURRED AT THE HOUR, DATE AND PLACE STATED FROM THE CAUSES STATED. ▶ | 28A. SIGNATURE AND TITLE OF CORONER OR DEPUTY CORONER | 28B. DATE SIGNED |

| 29. MANNER OF DEATH—specify one: natural, accident, suicide, homicide, pending investigation or could not be determined | 30A. PLACE OF INJURY | 30B. INJURY AT WORK ☐ YES ☐ NO | 30C. DATE OF INJURY MONTH, DAY, YEAR | 31. HOUR |

| 32. LOCATION (STREET AND NUMBER OR LOCATION AND CITY) | 33. DESCRIBE HOW INJURY OCCURRED (EVENTS WHICH RESULTED IN INJURY) |

FUNERAL DIRECTOR AND LOCAL REGISTRAR

| 34A. DISPOSITION(S) BURIAL | 34B. PLACE OF FINAL DISPOSITION—NAME AND ADDRESS WOODLAWN CEMETERY—1847 14th ST. SANTA MONICA, CALIFORNIA 90404 | 34C. DATE MO. DAY, YEAR 04/01/92 | 35A. SIGNATURE OF EMBALMER Lope Martinez | 35B. LICENSE NUMBER 7517 |
| 36A. NAME OF FUNERAL DIRECTOR (OR PERSON ACTING AS SUCH) PIERCE BROS. MOELLER-MURPHY | 36B. LICENSE NO. FD-695 | 37. SIGNATURE OF LOCAL REGISTRAR ▶ Robert C. Watt | 38. REGISTRATION DATE APR 01 1992 |

STATE REGISTRAR

| A. | B. | C. | D. | E. | F. | CENSUS TRACT |

VS-11 (REV. 3-91)   MAKE NO ERASURES, WHITEOUTS, OR OTHER ALTERATIONS

COPY REV. 7/02
OF CONNECTICUT
DEPARTMENT OF PUBLIC HEALTH   CERTIFICATE OF DEATH   STATE FILE NUMBER 2003 07 014314

DECEDENT'S LEGAL NAME	FIRST	MIDDLE	LAST	SEX	DATE OF DEATH (Month, Day, Year)
1 Katharine	H.		Hepburn	2 F	3 June 29, 2003

COUNTY OF DEATH	TOWN OF DEATH	PLACE OF DEATH (Check One)	OTHER ☐ Nursing Home XX Residence
4 Middlesex	5 Old Saybrook	Hospital 6 ☐ ER/Outpatient ☐ DOA ☐ Inpatient 7 ☐ Other	10 Mohegan Ave.

DATE OF BIRTH (Month, Day, Year)	Age-Last Birthday	UNDER 1 YEAR	UNDER 1 DAY	CITY & STATE OF BIRTH (Country if not U.S)	CITIZEN OF (Country)
8 May 12, 1907	9 96	Mos. a. / Days	Hours b. / Mins.	10 Hartford, CT	11 USA

☐ MARRIED ☐ NEVER MARRIED ☐ WIDOWED 12 X DIVORCED ☐ LEGALLY SEPARATED	LAST SPOUSE (If wife, give maiden name) 13 Ogden Ludlow Smith	WAS DECEASED A VETERAN IF YES GIVE WAR 14 ☐ YES XX NO	BRANCH OF SERVICE 15

RESIDENCE STATE	COUNTY	TOWN	NUMBER AND STREET
16 Connecticut	17 Middlesex	18 Old Saybrook	19 10 Mohegan Ave.

FATHER – NAME FIRST MIDDLE LAST	MOTHER – NAME FIRST MIDDLE MAIDEN
20 Thomas N. Hepburn, M.D.	21 Katharine Houghton

INFORMANT – NAME	MAILING ADDRESS	RELATIONSHIP TO DECEASED
22 Cynthia McFadden	23 150 Columbus Av. New York, NY 10023	24 Executrix

PART I. DEATH WAS CAUSED BY (ENTER ONLY ONE CAUSE PER LINE FOR (a), (b), AND (c))	APPROXIMATE INTERVAL BETWEEN ONSET AND DEATH
25 IMMEDIATE CAUSE (a) CARDIAC ARREST	
CONDITIONS, IF ANY WHICH GAVE RISE TO IMMEDIATE CAUSE (a) STATING THE UNDERLYING CAUSE LAST. DUE TO, OR AS A CONSEQUENCE OF: (b)	
DUE TO, OR AS A CONSEQUENCE OF: (c)	

PART II. OTHER SIGNIFICANT CONDITIONS: CONDITIONS CONTRIBUTING TO DEATH BUT NOT RELATED TO CAUSE 26 Ø	AUTOPSY 27 ☐ Y ☑ N	IF YES, were findings considered in determining cause of death: 28

NURSE PRONOUNCEMENT TYPE OR PRINT NAME 29 CHARLOTTE QUIGLEY RN	DEGREE	SIGNATURE 30 Charlotte Quigley	DATE AND TIME PRONOUNCED 31 MONTH 06 DAY 29 YEAR 2003 TIME 250 ☐ A.M. ☑ P.M.

CERTIFICATION – PHYSICIAN I attended the deceased from 32 Mo. Day Year 1993	Mo. Day Year 2003	AND LAST SAW HIM/HER ALIVE ON 33 Month 5 Day 7 Year 03	ACTUAL OR PRESUMED DATE AND TIME OF DEATH 34 6/29/03 2:50 PM M.

WAS CASE REFERRED TO MEDICAL EXAMINER 35 ☐ YES X NO	SURGERY RELEVANT TO CONDITION REPORTED IN ITEM 25 36 (Name of Operation) Ø (Date Performed) 37	THE DECEDENT WAS PRONOUNCED DEAD: 38 Month 6 Day 29 Year 03 Time 2:50 ☐ A.M. X P.M.

CERTIFIER – NAME (type or print) To the best of my knowledge, death occurred on the date and time and due to the causes stated 39 AMSHA R PAREKH	SIGNATURE 40 AParekh	DEGREE OR TITLE M.D

MAILING - CERTIFIER 41 8 VISTA DR	(STREET) OLD LYME CT 06371	(CITY OR TOWN)	(STATE) CT	(ZIP) 06371	DATE SIGNED (Month, Day, Year) 42 6/30/03

BURIAL, CREMATION, REMOVAL (Specify) 43 Cremation	CEMETERY OR CREMATORY – NAME 44 Cedar Hill Cemetery	LOCATION (CITY OR TOWN) 45 Hartford, CT	(STATE)

DATE (MONTH, DAY, YEAR) 46 July 1, 2003	FUNERAL HOME – NAME AND ADDRESS (STREET, CITY OR TOWN, STATE, ZIP) 47 James T. Pratt Co.,277 Folly Brook Blvd.Wethersfield,CT

FUNERAL DIRECTOR OR EMBALMER – SIGNATURE 48	WAS BODY EMBALMED? ☐ YES XX NO 49 IF YES NAME OF EMBALMER:	LICENSE NUMBER 50 2069

THIS CERTIFICATE RECEIVED FOR RECORD ON JUN 30, 2003	BY Sandra C. Swanson	REGISTRAR

OF HISPANIC ORIGIN? If yes, specify (e.g., Puerto Rican)	RACE – White, Black, American Indian, Asian, Other race	SOCIAL SECURITY NUMBER

THE SEAL OF THE STATE OF CONNECTICUT IS AFFIXED TO CERTIFY THAT THE ABOVE IS A TRUE COPY OF A RECORD FILED WITH THE STATE OF CONNECTICUT DEPARTMENT OF PUBLIC HEALTH PURSUANT TO THE PROVISIONS OF THE GENERAL STATUTES OF CONNECTICUT.

Suzanne Speers, R.H.I.A., M.P.H.
Registrar of Vital Records
AUG 12 2003
Date of Issue

QUI TRANSTULIT SUSTINET

CERTIFICATE OF DEATH
STATE OF CALIFORNIA
USE BLACK INK ONLY / NO ERASURES WHITEOUTS OR ALTERATIONS
VS 11 (REV 1-93)

3 2003 9 032342

LOCAL REGISTRATION NUMBER

STATE FILE NUMBER	

DECEDENT'S PERSONAL DATA

1 NAME OF DECEDENT - FIRST (Given)	2 MIDDLE	3 LAST (Family)
Leslie	Towns	Hope

AKA ALSO KNOWN AS - Include full AKA (FIRST MIDDLE LAST)	4 DATE OF BIRTH mm/dd/ccyy	5 AGE Yrs	IF UNDER ONE YEAR Months / Days	IF UNDER 24 HOURS Hours / Minutes	6 SEX
Bob Hope	05/29/1903	100			M

9 BIRTH STATE/FOREIGN COUNTRY	10 SOCIAL SECURITY NUMBER	11 EVER IN U S ARMED FORCES?	12 MARITAL STATUS (at Time of Death)	7 DATE OF DEATH mm/dd/ccyy	8 HOUR (24 Hours)
England	112-09-8770	X YES / NO / UNK	Married	07/27/2003	2128

13 EDUCATION - Highest Level/Degree (see worksheet on back)	14/15 WAS DECEDENT SPANISH/HISPANIC/LATINO? (If yes, see worksheet on back)	16 DECEDENT'S RACE -- Up to 3 races may be listed (see worksheet on back)
12	YES / X NO	Caucasian

17 USUAL OCCUPATION - Type of work for most of life DO NOT USE RETIRED	18 KIND OF BUSINESS OR INDUSTRY (e g , grocery store, road construction, employment agency, etc)	19 YEARS IN OCCUPATION
Entertainer	Entertainment	1 OF 2	80

USUAL RESIDENCE

20 DECEDENT'S RESIDENCE (Street and number or location)
10346 Moorpark Street

	22 COUNTY/PROVINCE	23 ZIP CODE	24 YEARS IN COUNTY	25 STATE/FOREIGN COUNTRY
North Hollywood	Los Angeles	91602	62	CA

INFORMANT

26 INFORMANT'S NAME RELATIONSHIP	27 INFORMANT'S MAILING ADDRESS (Street and number or rural route number, city or town, state, ZIP)
Dolores Hope - Wife	10346 Moorpark Street, North Hollywood, CA 91602

SPOUSE AND PARENT INFORMATION

28 NAME OF SURVIVING SPOUSE - FIRST	29 MIDDLE	30 LAST (Maiden Name)
Dolores	-	DeFina

31 NAME OF FATHER - FIRST	32 MIDDLE	33 LAST	34 BIRTH STATE
William	Henry	Hope	England

35 NAME OF MOTHER - FIRST	36 MIDDLE	37 LAST (Maiden)	38 BIRTH STATE
Avis	-	Towns	Wales

FUNERAL DIRECTOR/LOCAL REGISTRAR

39 DISPOSITION DATE mm/dd/ccyy	40 PLACE OF FINAL DISPOSITION
07/30/2003	San Fernando Mission Cemetery, 11160 Stranwood Ave., Mission Hills, CA 91345

41 TYPE OF DISPOSITION(S)	42 SIGNATURE OF EMBALMER	43 LICENSE NUMBER
BU	Claudia Kintzing	6984

44 NAME OF FUNERAL ESTABLISHMENT	45 LICENSE NUMBER	46 SIGNATURE OF LOCAL REGISTRAR	47 DATE mm/dd/ccyy
Holy Cross Mortuary	FD-1711	Thomas G. ...	07/29/2003

PLACE OF DEATH

101 PLACE OF DEATH	102 IF HOSPITAL SPECIFY ONE	103 IF OTHER THAN HOSPITAL SPECIFY ONE
Residence	IP / ER/OP / DOA	Hospice / Nursing Home/LTC / X Decedent's Home / Other

104 COUNTY	105 FACILITY ADDRESS OR LOCATION WHERE FOUND (Street and number or location)	106 CITY
Los Angeles	10346 Moorpark Street	North Hollywood

CAUSE OF DEATH

107 CAUSE OF DEATH Enter the chain of events -- diseases, injuries or complications -- that directly caused death DO NOT enter terminal events such as cardiac arrest, respiratory arrest, or ventricular fibrillation without showing the etiology DO NOT ABBREVIATE

		Time Interval Between Onset and Death	108 DEATH REPORTED TO CORONER?
IMMEDIATE CAUSE (Final disease or condition resulting in death) → A	Pneumonia	(A) 3 Weeks	YES / X NO REFERRAL NUMBER
Sequentially list conditions if any leading to cause on Line A Enter UNDERLYING CAUSE (disease or injury that initiated the events resulting in death) LAST → B		(B)	109 BIOPSY PERFORMED? YES / X NO
C		(C)	110 AUTOPSY PERFORMED? YES / X NO
D		(D)	111 USED IN DETERMINING CAUSE? YES / X NO

112 OTHER SIGNIFICANT CONDITIONS CONTRIBUTING TO DEATH BUT NOT RESULTING IN THE UNDERLYING CAUSE GIVEN IN 107
Aortic Stenosis, Atrial Fibrillation

113 WAS OPERATION PERFORMED FOR ANY CONDITION IN ITEM 107 OR 112? (If yes, list type of operation and date)	113A IF FEMALE PREGNANT IN LAST YEAR?
No	YES / NO / UNK

PHYSICIAN'S CERTIFICATION

114 I CERTIFY THAT TO THE BEST OF MY KNOWLEDGE DEATH OCCURRED AT THE HOUR DATE AND PLACE STATED FROM THE CAUSES STATED	115 SIGNATURE AND TITLE OF CERTIFIER	116 LICENSE NUMBER	117 DATE mm/dd/ccyy
Decedent Attended Since / Decedent Last Seen Alive	H. Lee Kagan MD	G33026	07/27/2003

07/20/1997	07/27/2003	118 TYPE ATTENDING PHYSICIAN'S NAME MAILING ADDRESS ZIP CODE
		H. Lee Kagan, MD, 13320 Riverside Dr #100, Sherman Oaks, CA 91423

CORONER'S USE ONLY

119 I CERTIFY THAT IN MY OPINION DEATH OCCURRED AT THE HOUR, DATE, AND PLACE STATED FROM THE CAUSES STATED	120 INJURED AT WORK?	121 INJURY DATE mm/dd/ccyy	122 HOUR (24 Hours)
MANNER OF DEATH: Natural / Accident / Homicide / Suicide / Pending Investigation / Could not be determined	YES / NO / UNK		

123 PLACE OF INJURY (e g home construction site wooded area etc)

124 DESCRIBE HOW INJURY OCCURRED (Events which resulted in injury)

125 LOCATION OF INJURY (Street and number or location, and city, and ZIP)

126 SIGNATURE OF CORONER - DEPUTY CORONER	127 DATE mm/dd/ccyy	128 TYPE NAME TITLE OF CORONER / DEPUTY CORONER

STATE REGISTRAR

A	B	C	D	E		FAX AUTH #	CENSUS TRACT

AFFIDAVIT TO AMEND A RECORD

3 200319 032342

DEATHS AFTER 1-1994

NO ERASURES, WHITEOUTS, OR ALTERATIONS

STATE FILE NUMBER		LOCAL REGISTRATION DISTRICT AND CERTIFICATE NUMBER
		03-010091

STATE/LOCAL REGISTRAR USE ONLY	1	2	3

PART I — INFORMATION TO LOCATE RECORD—TYPE OR PRINT IN BLACK INK ONLY

NAME AS IT APPEARS ON RECORD	1. NAME—FIRST (GIVEN) Leslie	2. MIDDLE Towns	3. LAST (FAMILY) Hope	2 OF 2

ADDITIONAL INFORMATION TO LOCATE RECORD	4. SEX M	5. DATE OF EVENT—MM/DD/CCYY 07/27/2003	6. CITY OF OCCURRENCE North Hollywood	7. COUNTY OF OCCURRENCE Los Angeles
	8. FATHER'S NAME AS STATED ON ORIGINAL William Henry Hope		9. MOTHER'S NAME AS STATED ON ORIGINAL Avis - Towns	

PART II — STATEMENT OF CORRECTIONS—NO ERASURES, WHITEOUTS, OR ALTERATIONS

	10. CERTIFICATE ITEM NUMBER	11. INFORMATION AS IT APPEARS ON ORIGINAL RECORD	12. INFORMATION AS IT SHOULD APPEAR
LIST ONE ITEM PER LINE	AKA	Bob Hope	Lester Townes Hope

REASON FOR CORRECTION	13. To Show AKA'S

We, the undersigned, hereby certify under penalty of perjury that we have personal knowledge of the above facts and that the information given above is true and correct.

AFFIDAVITS AND SIGNATURES	14. SIGNATURE OF FIRST PERSON	15. TITLE/RELATIONSHIP TO PERSON IN PART I Admin. Assist.	16. DATE SIGNED—MM/DD/CCYY 07/30/2003
TWO PERSONS MUST SIGN THIS FORM	17. AGE Legal	18. ADDRESS (STREET, CITY, STATE, ZIP) 4201 Whittier Blvd, Los Angeles, CA 90023	
	19. SIGNATURE OF SECOND PERSON	20. TITLE/RELATIONSHIP TO PERSON IN PART I Admin. Assist.	21. DATE SIGNED—MM/DD/CCYY 07/30/2003
USE BLACK INK ONLY	22. AGE Legal	23. ADDRESS (STREET, CITY, STATE, ZIP) 4201 Whittier Blvd, Los Angeles, CA 90023	
STATE/LOCAL REGISTRAR USE ONLY	24. SIGNATURE OF STATE OR LOCAL REGISTRAR		25. DATE ACCEPTED FOR REGISTRATION—MM/DD CCYY 08/08/2003

STATE OF CALIFORNIA, DEPARTMENT OF HEALTH SERVICES, OFFICE OF STATE REGISTRAR

VS 24(L) (Rev. 1/95)

STATE OF CALIFORNIA
CERTIFICATION OF VITAL RECORD

COUNTY OF LOS ANGELES
DEPARTMENT OF HEALTH SERVICES

CERTIFICATE OF DEATH
STATE OF CALIFORNIA
USE BLACK INK ONLY / NO ERASURES, WHITEOUTS OR ALTERATIONS
VS-11 (REV 1/03)

1. NAME OF DECEDENT --- FIRST (Given)	2. MIDDLE	3. LAST (Family)
GRAHAM	POWLEY	JARVIS

AKA, ALSO KNOWN AS --- Include full AKA (FIRST, MIDDLE, LAST)	4. DATE OF BIRTH mm/dd/ccyy	5. AGE Yrs.	IF UNDER ONE YEAR Months Days	IF UNDER 24 HOURS Hours Minutes	6. SEX
-	08/25/1930	72			M

9. BIRTH STATE/FOREIGN COUNTRY	10. SOCIAL SECURITY NUMBER	11. EVER IN U.S. ARMED FORCES?	12. MARITAL STATUS (at Time of Death)	7. DATE OF DEATH mm/dd/ccyy	8. HOUR (24 Hours)
CANADA	046-24-6081	YES [X] NO UNK	MARRIED	04/16/2003	0812

13. EDUCATION --- Highest Level/Degree	14/15. WAS DECEDENT SPANISH/HISPANIC/LATINO? (If yes, see worksheet on back)	16. DECEDENT'S RACE --- Up to 3 races may be listed (see worksheet on back)
SOME COLLEGE	YES [X] NO	CAUCASIAN

17. USUAL OCCUPATION --- Type of work for most of life. DO NOT USE RETIRED	18. KIND OF BUSINESS OR INDUSTRY (e.g. grocery store, road construction, employment agency, etc.)	19. YEARS IN OCCUPATION
ACTOR	MOTION PICTURES	52

20. DECEDENT'S RESIDENCE (Street and number or location)
15351 VIA DE LAS OLAS

21. CITY	22. COUNTY/PROVINCE	23. ZIP CODE	24. YEARS IN COUNTY	25. STATE/FOREIGN COUNTRY
PACIFIC PALISADES	LOS ANGELES	90272	29	CA

26. INFORMANT'S NAME, RELATIONSHIP	27. INFORMANT'S MAILING ADDRESS (Street and number or rural route number, city or town, state, ZIP)
JOANNA JARVIS - WIFE	15351 VIA DE LAS OLAS, PACIFIC PALISADES, CA 90272

28. NAME OF SURVIVING SPOUSE --- FIRST	29. MIDDLE	30. LAST (Maiden Name)
JOANNA	-	RADER

31. NAME OF FATHER --- FIRST	32. MIDDLE	33. LAST	34. BIRTH STATE
WILLIAM	HENRY REGINALD	JARVIS	CANADA

35. NAME OF MOTHER --- FIRST	36. MIDDLE	37. LAST (Maiden)	38. BIRTH STATE
MARGARET	BIDDAULPH	SCATCHERD	CANADA

39. DISPOSITION DATE mm/dd/ccyy	40. PLACE OF FINAL DISPOSITION
04/19/2003	VALLEY OAKS MEMORIAL PARK 5600 LINDERO CANYON RD. WESTLAKE VILLAGE, CA. 91361

41. TYPE OF DISPOSITION(S)	42. SIGNATURE OF EMBALMER	43. LICENSE NUMBER
BURIAL	▶ Denver Mason	8699

44. NAME OF FUNERAL ESTABLISHMENT	45. LICENSE NUMBER	46. SIGNATURE OF LOCAL REGISTRAR	47. DATE mm/dd/ccyy
GATES KINGSLEY GATES MOELLER MURPHY	FD-451	▶ Thomas W authorite	04/18/2003

101. PLACE OF DEATH	102. IF HOSPITAL, SPECIFY ONE	103. IF OTHER THAN HOSPITAL, SPECIFY ONE
OWN RESIDENCE	IP ER/OP DOA	Hospice Nursing Home/LTC [X] Decedent's Home Other

104. COUNTY	105. FACILITY ADDRESS OR LOCATION WHERE FOUND (Street and number or location)	106. CITY
LOS ANGELES	15351 VIA DE LAS OLAS	PACIFIC PALISADES

107. CAUSE OF DEATH Enter the chain of events --- diseases, injuries, or complications --- that directly caused death. DO NOT enter terminal events such as cardiac arrest, respiratory arrest, or ventricular fibrillation without showing the etiology. DO NOT ABBREVIATE.

		Time Interval Between Onset and Death	108. DEATH REPORTED TO CORONER?
IMMEDIATE CAUSE (A) (Final disease or condition resulting in death) →	MULTIPLE MYELOMA	(A) 3 yrs	[X] YES [X] NO REFERRAL NUMBER 2003-52922
Sequentially list conditions, if any, leading to cause on Line A. Enter UNDERLYING CAUSE (disease or injury that initiated the events resulting in death LAST	(B)	(B1)	109. BIOPSY PERFORMED? [X] YES NO
	(C)	(C1)	110. AUTOPSY PERFORMED? YES [X] NO
	(D)	(D1)	111. USED IN DETERMINING CAUSE? YES NO

112. OTHER SIGNIFICANT CONDITIONS CONTRIBUTING TO DEATH BUT NOT RESULTING IN THE UNDERLYING CAUSE GIVEN IN 107
NONE

113. WAS OPERATION PERFORMED FOR ANY CONDITION IN ITEM 107 OR 112? (If yes, list type of operation and date.)	113A. IF FEMALE, PREGNANT IN LAST YEAR?
NO	YES NO UNK

114. I CERTIFY THAT TO THE BEST OF MY KNOWLEDGE DEATH OCCURRED AT THE HOUR, DATE, AND PLACE STATED FROM THE CAUSES STATED.	115. SIGNATURE AND TITLE OF CERTIFIER	116. LICENSE NUMBER	117. DATE mm/dd/ccyy
Decedent Attended Since / Decedent Last Seen Alive	▶ Michael R. Block M.D.	G24174	04/17/2003
(A) mm/dd/ccyy 08/10/1984	(B) mm/dd/ccyy 03/26/2003	118. TYPE ATTENDING PHYSICIAN'S NAME, MAILING ADDRESS, ZIP CODE MICHAEL R.BLOCK, MD. 970 MONUMENT ST. PACIFIC PALISADES, CA. 90272	

119. I CERTIFY THAT IN MY OPINION DEATH OCCURRED AT THE HOUR, DATE, AND PLACE STATED FROM THE CAUSES STATED.	120. INJURED AT WORK?	121. INJURY DATE mm/dd/ccyy	122. HOUR (24 Hours)
MANNER OF DEATH Natural Accident Homicide Suicide Pending Investigation Could not be determined	YES NO UNK		

123. PLACE OF INJURY (e.g., home, construction site, wooded area, etc.)

124. DESCRIBE HOW INJURY OCCURRED (Events which resulted in injury)

125. LOCATION OF INJURY (Street and number, or location, and city, and ZIP)

126. SIGNATURE OF CORONER / DEPUTY CORONER	127. DATE mm/dd/ccyy	128. TYPE NAME, TITLE OF CORONER / DEPUTY CORONER
▶		

STATE REGISTRAR	A	B	C	D	E	FAX AUTH. #	CENSUS TRACT

090615395

This is a true certified copy of the record filed in the County of Los Angeles Department of Health Services if it bears the Registrar's signature in purple ink.

DATE ISSUED APR 29 2003

Director of Health Services and Registrar

This copy not valid unless prepared on engraved border displaying seal and signature of Registrar.

ANY ALTERATION OR ERASURE VOIDS THIS CERTIFICATE

STATE OF CALIFORNIA
CERTIFICATION OF VITAL RECORD

COUNTY OF LOS ANGELES • REGISTRAR-RECORDER/COUNTY CLERK

CERTIFICATE OF DEATH
STATE OF CALIFORNIA

0190-034858

STATE FILE NUMBER				LOCAL REGISTRATION DISTRICT AND CERTIFICATE NUMBER	

1A. NAME OF DECEDENT—FIRST	1B. MIDDLE	1C. LAST	2A. DATE OF DEATH (MONTH, DAY, YEAR)	2B. HOUR
Carolyn	Sue	Jones	August 3, 1983	1245

3. SEX	4. RACE	5. ETHNICITY	6. DATE OF BIRTH	7. AGE	IF UNDER 1 YEAR MONTHS / DAYS	IF UNDER 24 HOURS HOURS / MINUTES
Fem	Cauc		April 28, 1930	53 YEARS		

DECEDENT PERSONAL DATA

8. BIRTHPLACE OF DECEDENT (STATE OR FOREIGN COUNTRY)	9. NAME AND BIRTHPLACE OF FATHER		10. BIRTH NAME AND BIRTHPLACE OF MOTHER
Texas	Jones - Unk	Unk	Unknown

11. CITIZEN OF WHAT COUNTRY	12. SOCIAL SECURITY NUMBER	13. MARITAL STATUS	14. NAME OF SURVIVING SPOUSE (IF WIFE, ENTER BIRTH NAME)
U.S.A.	455-44-7353	Married	Peter Bailey-Britton

15. PRIMARY OCCUPATION	16. NUMBER OF YEARS THIS OCCUPATION	17. EMPLOYER (IF SELF-EMPLOYED, SO STATE)	18. KIND OF INDUSTRY OR BUSINESS
Actress	30	self-employed	Entertainment

USUAL RESIDENCE

19A. USUAL RESIDENCE—STREET ADDRESS (STREET AND NUMBER OR LOCATION)	19B.	19C. CITY OR TOWN
8967 Norma Place		Los Angeles

19D. COUNTY	19E. STATE	20. NAME AND ADDRESS OF INFORMANT—RELATIONSHIP
Los Angeles	California	Peter Bailey-Britton (husb) 8967 Norma Place Los Angeles, CA 90069

PLACE OF DEATH

21A. PLACE OF DEATH	21B. COUNTY	
Residence	Los Angeles	

21C. STREET ADDRESS (STREET AND NUMBER OR LOCATION)	21D. CITY OR TOWN
8967 Norma Place	Los Angeles

CAUSE OF DEATH

22. DEATH WAS CAUSED BY: (ENTER ONLY ONE CAUSE PER LINE FOR A, B, AND C) IMMEDIATE CAUSE		APPROXIMATE INTERVAL BETWEEN ONSET AND DEATH	24. WAS DEATH REPORTED TO CORONER?
CONDITIONS, IF ANY, WHICH GAVE RISE TO THE IMMEDIATE CAUSE, STATING THE UNDERLYING CAUSE LAST.	(A) Metastatic Carcinoma	2 yrs	NO
	DUE TO, OR AS A CONSEQUENCE OF		25. WAS BIOPSY PERFORMED?
	(B) Carcinoma of Colon	2 yrs	Yes
	DUE TO, OR AS A CONSEQUENCE OF		26. WAS AUTOPSY PERFORMED?
	(C)		NO

23. OTHER CONDITIONS CONTRIBUTING BUT NOT RELATED TO THE IMMEDIATE CAUSE OF DEATH	27. WAS OPERATION PERFORMED FOR ANY CONDITION IN ITEMS 22 OR 23? TYPE OF OPERATION	DATE
Bronchial asthma	laparotomy	6/23/81

PHYSICIAN'S CERTIFICATION

25A. I CERTIFY THAT DEATH OCCURRED AT THE HOUR, DATE AND PLACE STATED FROM THE CAUSES STATED. I ATTENDED DECEDENT SINCE (ENTER MO. DA. YR.)	I LAST SAW DECEDENT ALIVE (ENTER MO. DA. YR.)	28B. PHYSICIAN—SIGNATURE AND DEGREE OR TITLE	28C. DATE SIGNED	28D. PHYSICIAN'S LICENSE NUMBER
6/05/81	7/28/83	Michael Engelberg, M.D. 9,35 Wilshire Bl. Beverly Hills	8/3/83	G 19143

INJURY INFORMATION

29. SPECIFY ACCIDENT, SUICIDE, ETC.	30. PLACE OF INJURY	31. INJURY AT WORK	32A. DATE OF INJURY—MONTH, DAY, YEAR	32B. HOUR

33. LOCATION (STREET AND NUMBER OR LOCATION AND CITY OR TOWN)	34. DESCRIBE HOW INJURY OCCURRED (EVENTS WHICH RESULTED IN INJURY)

CORONER'S USE ONLY

35A. I CERTIFY THAT DEATH OCCURRED AT THE HOUR, DATE AND PLACE STATED FROM THE CAUSES STATED. AS REQUIRED BY LAW I HAVE HELD AN (INQUEST/INVESTIGATION)	35B. CORONER—SIGNATURE AND DEGREE OR TITLE	35C. DATE SIGNED

36. DISPOSITION	37. DATE—MONTH, DAY, YEAR	38. NAME AND ADDRESS OF CEMETERY OR CREMATORY	39. EMBALMER'S LICENSE NUMBER AND SIGNATURE
Cremation	8/4/83	Pasadena-2400 N. Fair Oaks, Altadena	Not Embalmed

40. NAME OF FUNERAL DIRECTOR (OR PERSON ACTING AS SUCH)	41. LOCAL REGISTRAR—SIGNATURE	42. DATE ACCEPTED BY LOCAL REGISTRAR
Glasband-Willen Mort. (F727)		AUG 4 1983

STATE REGISTRAR

A.	B.		E.	F.

This is to certify that this document is a true copy of the official record filed with the Registrar-Recorder/County Clerk.

Conny B. McCormack

CONNY B. McCORMACK
Registrar-Recorder/County Clerk

This copy not valid unless prepared on engraved border displaying the Seal and Signature of the Registrar-Recorder/County Clerk.

MAY 1 3 2003

190940719

STATE OF CALIFORNIA
CERTIFICATION OF VITAL RECORD

COUNTY OF LOS ANGELES • REGISTRAR-RECORDER/COUNTY CLERK

CERTIFICATE OF DEATH
STATE OF CALIFORNIA

38719010429

STATE FILE NUMBER		LOCAL REGISTRATION DISTRICT AND CERTIFICATE NUMBER

DECEDENT PERSONAL DATA

1A. NAME OF DECEDENT—FIRST	1B. MIDDLE	1C. LAST	2A. DATE OF DEATH (MONTH, DAY, YEAR)	2B. HOUR
DANNY		KAYE	MARCH 3 1987	0358

3. SEX	4. RACE/ETHNICITY	5. SPANISH/HISPANIC	6. DATE OF BIRTH	7. AGE	IF UNDER 1 YEAR MONTHS DAYS	IF UNDER 24 HOURS HOURS MINUTES
Male	White/Jewish	no x	January 18, 1913	74 YEARS		

8. BIRTHPLACE OF DECEDENT (STATE OR FOREIGN COUNTRY)	9. NAME AND BIRTHPLACE OF FATHER	10. BIRTH NAME AND BIRTHPLACE OF MOTHER
New York	Jacob Kaminsky, Russia	Clara Nemerozsky, Russia

11A. CITIZEN OF WHAT COUNTRY	11B. IF DECEASED WAS EVER IN MILITARY GIVE DATES OF SERVICE	12. SOCIAL SECURITY NUMBER	13. MARITAL STATUS	14. NAME OF SURVIVING SPOUSE (IF WIFE, ENTER BIRTH NAME)
USA	19__ TO 19__	129-12-6938	Married	Sylvia Fine

15. PRIMARY OCCUPATION	16. NUMBER OF YEARS THIS OCCUPATION	17. EMPLOYER (IF SELF-EMPLOYED, SO STATE)	18. KIND OF INDUSTRY OR BUSINESS
Entertainer	60	Self Employed	Entertainment

USUAL RESIDENCE

19A. USUAL RESIDENCE—STREET ADDRESS (STREET AND NUMBER OR LOCATION)	19B.	19C. CITY OR TOWN
1103 San Yisidro Dr.		Beverly Hills

19D. COUNTY	19E. STATE	20. NAME AND ADDRESS OF INFORMANT — RELATIONSHIP
Los Angeles	California	Sylvia Fine wife 1103 San Yisidro Dr. Beverly Hills, California 90210

PLACE OF DEATH

21A. PLACE OF DEATH	21B. COUNTY
CEDARS SINAI MEDICAL CENTER	LOS ANGELES

21C. STREET ADDRESS (STREET AND NUMBER OR LOCATION)	21D. CITY OR TOWN
8700 BEVERLY BLVD	LOS ANGELES

CAUSE OF DEATH

22. DEATH WAS CAUSED BY: (ENTER ONLY ONE CAUSE PER LINE FOR A, B, AND C)
IMMEDIATE CAUSE

		APPROXIMATE INTERVAL BETWEEN ONSET AND DEATH	24. WAS DEATH REPORTED TO CORONER?
(A) Gastrointestinal hem - Rage	◄	36 Hrs	No
(B) esophageal varices	◄	6 mo	25. WAS BIOPSY PERFORMED? No
(C) Non-A Non-B Post Hepatitic cirr	◄	2 yrs	26. WAS AUTOPSY PERFORMED? No

23. OTHER SIGNIFICANT CONDITIONS — CONTRIBUTING TO DEATH BUT NOT RELATED TO CAUSE GIVEN IN 22A
Myelo dysplastic syndrome - thrombocytopenia

27. WAS OPERATION PERFORMED FOR ANY CONDITION IN ITEMS 22 OR 23?	27. TYPE OF OPERATION	DATE
No		

PHYSICIAN'S CERTIFICATION

28A. I CERTIFY THAT DEATH OCCURRED AT THE HOUR, DATE AND PLACE STATED FROM THE CAUSES STATED.

I ATTENDED DECEDENT SINCE (ENTER MO. DA. YR.)	I LAST SAW DECEDENT ALIVE (ENTER MO. DA. YR.)	28B. PHYSICIAN — SIGNATURE AND DEGREE OR TITLE	28C. DATE SIGNED	28D. PHYSICIAN'S LICENSE NUMBER
2-1-83	3-2-87	Chas. Kivowitz	3-3-87	G16910

28E. TYPE PHYSICIAN'S NAME AND ADDRESS
Charles Kivowitz, M.D. 435 N. Roxbury Dr. Beverly Hills, Ca

INJURY INFORMATION

29. SPECIFY ACCIDENT, SUICIDE, ETC.	30. PLACE OF INJURY	31. INJURY AT WORK	32A. DATE OF INJURY—MONTH, DAY, YEAR	32B. HOUR

33. LOCATION (STREET AND NUMBER OR LOCATION AND CITY OR TOWN)	34. DESCRIBE HOW INJURY OCCURRED (EVENTS WHICH RESULTED IN INJURY)

CORONER'S USE ONLY

35A. I CERTIFY THAT DEATH OCCURRED AT THE HOUR, DATE AND PLACE STATED FROM THE CAUSES STATED. AS REQUIRED BY LAW I HAVE HELD AN (INQUEST-INVESTIGATION)	35B. CORONER — SIGNATURE AND DEGREE OR TITLE	35C. DATE SIGNED

36. DISPOSITION	37. DATE—MONTH, DAY, YEAR	38. NAME AND ADDRESS OF CEMETERY OR CREMATORY	39. EMBALMER'S LICENSE NUMBER AND SIGNATURE
Cremation	3/4/87	Rosedale Cemetery Crematory 1831 W. Washington Blvd. Los Angeles	NOT EMBALMED

40A. NAME OF FUNERAL DIRECTOR (OR PERSON ACTING AS SUCH)	40B. LICENSE NO.	41. LOCAL REGISTRAR—SIGNATURE	42. DATE ACCEPTED BY LOCAL REGISTRAR
Hillside Mem. Pk. Mort. bb	1358	Robert Marts R.R.	MAR 03 1987

STATE REGISTRAR

A.	B.	C.	D.	E.	F.
5715					01-91-053

VS-11 (1-85)

This is to certify that this document is a true copy of the official record filed with the Registrar-Recorder/County Clerk.

Conny B. McCormack
CONNY B. McCORMACK
Registrar-Recorder/County Clerk

This copy not valid unless prepared on engraved border displaying the Seal and Signature of the Registrar-Recorder/County Clerk.

NOV 28 2000
19-116317

ANY ALTERATION OR ERASURE VOIDS THIS CERTIFICATE

CERTIFICATE OF DEATH
STATE OF CALIFORNIA
USE BLACK INK ONLY/NO ERASURES, WHITEOUTS OR ALTERATIONS
VS-11 (REV. 7/93)

STATE FILE NUMBER		LOCAL REGISTRATION NUMBER

DECEDENT PERSONAL DATA

1. NAME OF DECEDENT—FIRST (GIVEN)	2. MIDDLE	3. LAST (FAMILY)
Eugene	Curran	Kelly

4. DATE OF BIRTH MM/DD/CCYY	5. AGE YRS.	IF UNDER 1 YEAR — MONTHS / DAYS	IF UNDER 24 HOURS — HOURS / MINUTES	6. SEX	7. DATE OF DEATH MM/DD/CCYY	8. HOUR
08/23/1912	83			M	02/02/1996	0817

9. STATE OF BIRTH	10. SOCIAL SECURITY NO.	11. MILITARY SERVICE	12. MARITAL STATUS	13. EDUCATION—YEARS COMPLETED
PA	210-10-7435	19 44 TO 19 46 □ None	Married	16

14. RACE	15. HISPANIC—SPECIFY		16. USUAL EMPLOYER
Caucasian	□ YES _____	X No	Self Employed

17. OCCUPATION	18. KIND OF BUSINESS	19. YEARS IN OCCUPATION
Director	Motion Picture Industry	50

USUAL RESIDENCE

20. RESIDENCE—STREET AND NUMBER OR LOCATION
725 No. Rodeo Drive

21. CITY	22. COUNTY	23. ZIP CODE	24. YRS IN COUNTY	25. STATE OR FOREIGN COUNTRY
Beverly Hills	Los Angeles	90210	54	California

INFORMANT

26. NAME, RELATIONSHIP	27. MAILING ADDRESS (STREET AND NUMBER OR RURAL ROUTE NUMBER, CITY OR TOWN, STATE, ZIP)
Patricia Ward Kelly – Wife	725 No. Rodeo Drive, Beverly Hills, CA 90210

SPOUSE AND PARENT INFORMATION

28. NAME OF SURVIVING SPOUSE—FIRST	29. MIDDLE	30. LAST (MAIDEN NAME)
Patricia	–	Ward

31. NAME OF FATHER—FIRST	32. MIDDLE	33. LAST	34. BIRTH STATE
James	Joseph Parick	Kelly	Canada

35. NAME OF MOTHER—FIRST	36. MIDDLE	37. LAST (MAIDEN)	38. BIRTH STATE
Harriet	–	Curran	Penn.

FUNERAL DIRECTOR AND LOCAL REGISTRAR

39. DATE MM/DD/CCYY	40. PLACE OF FINAL DISPOSITION
02/02/1996	Patricia Ward Kelly for Res: 725 No.Rodeo Drive, Beverly Hills,CA 9021

41. TYPE OF DISPOSITION(S)	42. SIGNATURE OF EMBALMER	43. LICENSE NO.
Cr/Res	▶ Not Embalmed	–

44. NAME OF FUNERAL DIRECTOR	45. LICENSE NO.	46. SIGNATURE OF LOCAL REGISTRAR	47. DATE MM/DD/CCYY
Pierce Bros.Westwood Village	f-951	▶	

PLACE OF DEATH

101. PLACE OF DEATH	102. IF HOSPITAL, SPECIFY ONE:	103. FACILITY OTHER THAN HOSPITAL:	104. COUNTY
Residence	□ IP □ ER/OP □ DOA	□ CONV. HOSP. X RES. □ OTHER	Los Angeles

105. STREET ADDRESS—STREET AND NUMBER OR LOCATION	106. CITY
725 No. Rodeo Drive	Beverly Hills

CAUSE OF DEATH

107. DEATH WAS CAUSED BY: (ENTER ONLY ONE CAUSE PER LINE FOR A, B, C, AND D)	TIME INTERVAL BETWEEN ONSET AND DEATH	
IMMEDIATE CAUSE (A) Sepsis	Days	108. DEATH REPORTED TO CORONER □ YES X No REFERRAL NUMBER
DUE TO (B) Renal Failure Acute	Days	109. BIOPSY PERFORMED □ YES X No
DUE TO (C) Cerebrovacular Accident	1 Year	110. AUTOPSY PERFORMED □ YES X No
DUE TO (D) Diabetes Mellitus	Years	111. USED IN DETERMINING CAUSE □ YES X No

112. OTHER SIGNIFICANT CONDITIONS CONTRIBUTING TO DEATH BUT NOT RELATED TO CAUSE GIVEN IN 107
Coronary Disease, Prostate Cancer

113. WAS OPERATION PERFORMED FOR ANY CONDITION IN ITEM 107 OR 112? IF YES, LIST TYPE OF OPERATION AND DATE.
No

PHYSICIAN'S CERTIFICATION

114. I CERTIFY THAT TO THE BEST OF MY KNOWLEDGE DEATH OCCURRED AT THE HOUR, DATE AND PLACE STATED FROM THE CAUSES STATED.	115. SIGNATURE AND TITLE OF CERTIFIER	116. LICENSE NO.	117. DATE MM/DD/CCYY
DECEDENT ATTENDED SINCE 06/20/1994 — DECEDENT LAST BEEN ALIVE 01/18/1996	▶ _____ M.D.	G 44264	02/02/1996

118. TYPE ATTENDING PHYSICIAN'S NAME, MAILING ADDRESS + ZIP
S.Saleh,MD 100 UCLA Med Plaza#690,Los Angeles, CA 90024

CORONER'S USE ONLY

I CERTIFY THAT IN MY OPINION DEATH OCCURRED AT THE HOUR, DATE AND PLACE STATED FROM THE CAUSES STATED.	120. INJURY AT WORK □ YES □ NO	121. INJURY DATE MM/DD/CCYY	122. HOUR	123. PLACE OF INJURY
119. MANNER OF DEATH □ NATURAL □ SUICIDE □ HOMICIDE □ ACCIDENT □ PENDING INVESTIGATION □ COULD NOT BE DETERMINED	124. DESCRIBE HOW INJURY OCCURRED (EVENTS WHICH RESULTED IN INJURY)			

125. LOCATION (STREET AND NUMBER OR LOCATION AND CITY AND ZIP CODE)

126. SIGNATURE OF CORONER OR DEPUTY CORONER	127. DATE MM/DD/CCYY	128. TYPED NAME, TITLE OF CORONER OR DEPUTY CORONER
▶		

STATE

A	B	C	D	E	F	G	H	FAX AUTH. #	CENSUS TRACT

CERTIFICATE OF DEATH   3 19931 9 045945
STATE OF CALIFORNIA
USE BLACK INK ONLY/NO ERASURES, WHITEOUTS OR ALTERATIONS
VS-11 (REV 7/97)

STATE FILE NUMBER   LOCAL REGISTRATION NUMBER

1. NAME OF DECEDENT—FIRST (GIVEN)	2. MIDDLE	3. LAST (FAMILY)
Mabel	W.	King

4. DATE OF BIRTH MM DD CCYY	5. AGE YRS	IF UNDER 1 YEAR — MONTHS / DAYS	IF UNDER 24 HOURS — HOURS / MINUTES	6. SEX	7. DATE OF DEATH MM/DD/CCYY	8. HOUR
12/25/1932	66			F	11/09/1999	0355

DECEDENT PERSONAL DATA

9. STATE OF BIRTH	10. SOCIAL SECURITY NO.	11. MILITARY SERVICE	12. MARITAL STATUS	13. EDUCATION—YEARS COMPLETED
SC	105-22-3965	YES / X NO / UNK	Divorced	12

14. RACE	15. HISPANIC—SPECIFY	16. USUAL EMPLOYER
Black	YES / X NO	Sony Pictures

17. OCCUPATION	18. KIND OF BUSINESS	19. YEARS IN OCCUPATION
Actress	Motion Pictures	30

USUAL RESIDENCE

20. RESIDENCE—STREET AND NUMBER OR LOCATION
20812 Exhibit Court

21. CITY	22. COUNTY	23. ZIP CODE	24. YRS IN COUNTY	25. STATE OR FOREIGN COUNTRY
Woodland Hills	Los Angeles	91367	20	CA

INFORMANT

26. NAME, RELATIONSHIP	27. MAILING ADDRESS (STREET AND NUMBER OR RURAL ROUTE NUMBER, CITY OR TOWN, STATE, ZIP)
Vickie L. Chamberlain - Power of Att.	20812 Exhibit Court, Woodland Hills, CA 91367

SPOUSE AND PARENT INFORMATION

28. NAME OF SURVIVING SPOUSE—FIRST	29. MIDDLE	30. LAST (MAIDEN NAME)
–	–	–

31. NAME OF FATHER—FIRST	32. MIDDLE	33. LAST	34. BIRTH STATE
Edward	–	Washington	SC

35. NAME OF MOTHER—FIRST	36. MIDDLE	37. LAST (MAIDEN)	38. BIRTH STATE
Rosalie	–	Fields	SC

DISPOSITION(S)

39. DATE MM/DD/CCYY	40. PLACE OF FINAL DISPOSITION
11/12/1999	Res: Vickie L. Chamberlain, 20812 Exhibit Court, Woodland Hills, CA91367

FUNERAL DIRECTOR AND LOCAL REGISTRAR

41. TYPE OF DISPOSITION(S)	42. SIGNATURE OF EMBALMER	43. LICENSE NO.
CR/RES	Not Embalmed	–

44. NAME OF FUNERAL DIRECTOR	45. LICENSE NO.	46. SIGNATURE OF LOCAL REGISTRAR	47. DATE MM/DD/CCYY
Crawford Mortuary	FD1228	Mark Shuman	11/12/19999

PLACE OF DEATH

101. PLACE OF DEATH	102. IF HOSPITAL, SPECIFY ONE:	103. FACILITY OTHER THAN HOSPITAL:	104. COUNTY
Kaiser Foundation Hospital	X IP / ER/OP / DOA	CONV. HOSP. / RES. CARE / OTHER	Los Angeles

105. STREET ADDRESS—(STREET AND NUMBER OR LOCATION)	106. CITY
5601 DeSoto Ave.	Woodland Hills

CAUSE OF DEATH

107. DEATH WAS CAUSED BY: (ENTER ONLY ONE CAUSE PER LINE FOR A, B, C, AND D)	TIME INTERVAL BETWEEN ONSET AND DEATH	108. DEATH REPORTED TO CORONER
IMMEDIATE CAUSE (A) End Stage Renal Failure	1 year	YES / X NO REFERRAL NUMBER
DUE TO (B)		109. BIOPSY PERFORMED YES / X NO
DUE TO (C)		110. AUTOPSY PERFORMED YES / X NO
DUE TO (D)		111. USED IN DETERMINING CAUSE YES / X NO

112. OTHER SIGNIFICANT CONDITIONS CONTRIBUTING TO DEATH BUT NOT RELATED TO CAUSE GIVEN IN 107
None

113. WAS OPERATION PERFORMED FOR ANY CONDITION IN ITEM 107 OR 112? IF YES, LIST TYPE OF OPERATION AND DATE.
No

PHYSICIAN'S CERTIFICATION

114. I CERTIFY THAT TO THE BEST OF MY KNOWLEDGE DEATH OCCURRED AT THE HOUR, DATE AND PLACE STATED FROM THE CAUSES STATED.	115. SIGNATURE AND TITLE OF CERTIFIER	116. LICENSE NO.	117. DATE MM/DD/CCYY
DECEDENT ATTENDED SINCE MM/DD/CCYY 10/01/1999 — DECEDENT LAST SEEN ALIVE MM/DD/CCYY 11/08/1999	Robert Lein MD	G063911	11/11/1999

118. TYPE ATTENDING PHYSICIAN'S NAME, MAILING ADDRESS, ZIP
Robert Lein, MD. 16030 Ventura Blvd, Encino, CA 91436

CORONER'S USE ONLY

119. I CERTIFY THAT IN MY OPINION DEATH OCCURRED AT THE HOUR, DATE AND PLACE STATED FROM THE CAUSES STATED. MANNER OF DEATH	120. INJURY AT WORK	121. INJURY DATE MM/DD/CCYY	122. HOUR	123. PLACE OF INJURY
NATURAL / SUICIDE / HOMICIDE / ACCIDENT / PENDING INVESTIGATION / COULD NOT BE DETERMINED	YES / NO			

124. DESCRIBE HOW INJURY OCCURRED (EVENTS WHICH RESULTED IN INJURY)

125. LOCATION (STREET AND NUMBER OR LOCATION AND CITY, ZIP)

126. SIGNATURE OF CORONER OR DEPUTY CORONER	127. DATE MM/DD/CCYY	128. TYPED NAME, TITLE OF CORONER OR DEPUTY CORONER

STATE REGISTRAR

A	B	C	D	E	F	G	H	FAX AUTH. #	CENSUS TRACT
								197/5935	

CERTIFICATION OF VITAL RECORD

COUNTY OF LOS ANGELES • REGISTRAR-RECORDER/COUNTY CLERK

STATE FILE NUMBER	CERTIFICATE OF DEATH	LOCAL REGISTRATION DISTRICT AND CERTIFICATE NUMBER	7053	1029

STATE OF CALIFORNIA—DEPARTMENT OF PUBLIC HEALTH

DECEDENT PERSONAL DATA

1A. NAME OF DECEASED—FIRST NAME	1B. MIDDLE NAME	1C. LAST NAME	2. DATE OF DEATH—MONTH, DAY, YEAR	2A. HOUR
ERNEST	E.	KOVACS	January 13, 1962	130 A.

3. SEX	4. COLOR OR RACE	5. BIRTHPLACE (STATE OR FOREIGN COUNTRY)	6. DATE OF BIRTH	7. AGE (LAST BIRTHDAY)	IF UNDER 1 YEAR	IF UNDER 24 HOURS
Male	Cauc.	New Jersey	January 23, 1919	42 YEARS		

8. NAME AND BIRTHPLACE OF FATHER	9. MAIDEN NAME AND BIRTHPLACE OF MOTHER	10. CITIZEN OF WHAT COUNTRY	11. SOCIAL SECURITY NUMBER
Andrew Kovacs, Hungary	Mary Chebonick, Hungary	U.S.A.	153-18-4764

12. LAST OCCUPATION	13. NUMBER OF YEARS IN THIS OCCUPATION	14. NAME OF LAST EMPLOYING COMPANY OR FIRM IF SELF EMPLOYED	15. KIND OF INDUSTRY OR BUSINESS
Actor	22 yrs.	Screen Gems	Stage and Screen

16. IF DECEASED WAS EVER IN U S ARMED FORCES, GIVE WAR OR DATES OF SERVICE	17. SPECIFY MARRIED NEVER MARRIED WIDOWED DIVORCED	18A. NAME OF PRESENT SPOUSE	18B. PRESENT OR LAST OCCUPATION OF SPOUSE
No	Married	Edith Adams Kovacs	Actress

PLACE OF DEATH

19A. PLACE OF DEATH—NAME OF HOSPITAL	19B. STREET ADDRESS—GIVE STREET OR RURAL ADDRESS OR LOCATION. DO NOT USE P. O. BOX NUMBERS
	10,000 Santa Monica Boulevard

19C. CITY OR TOWN	19D. COUNTY	19E. LENGTH OF STAY IN COUNTY OF DEATH	19F. LENGTH OF STAY IN CALIFORNIA
Los Angeles	Los Angeles	4 years	4 years

LAST USUAL RESIDENCE (WHERE DID DECEASED LIVE—IF IN INSTITUTION ENTER RESIDENCE BEFORE ADMISSION)

20A. LAST USUAL RESIDENCE—STREET ADDRESS (GIVE STREET AND RURAL ADDRESS OR LOCATION. DO NOT USE P. O. BOX NUMBERS)	20B. IF INSIDE CITY CORPORATE LIMITS	21A. NAME OF INFORMANT (IF OTHER THAN SPOUSE)
2301 Bowmont Drive 2611		

20C. CITY OR TOWN	20D. COUNTY	20E. STATE	21B. ADDRESS OF INFORMANT
Los Angeles	Los Angeles	California	

PHYSICIAN'S OR CORONER'S CERTIFICATION

22A. PHYSICIAN: I HEREBY CERTIFY THAT DEATH OCCURRED AT THE HOUR, DATE AND PLACE STATED ABOVE, FROM THE CAUSES STATED BELOW AND THAT I ATTENDED THE DECEASED FROM ____ AND THAT I LAST SAW THE DECEASED ALIVE ON ____	22C. PHYSICIAN OR CORONER—SIGNATURE ▶ By Theo. J. Curphey, M.D., Coroner	DEGREE OR TITLE
22B. CORONER: I HEREBY CERTIFY THAT DEATH OCCURRED AT THE HOUR, DATE AND PLACE STATED BELOW AND THAT I HAVE HELD ____ ON THE REMAINS OF DECEASED AS REQUIRED BY LAW. Autopsy	22D. ADDRESS HALL OF JUSTICE, LOS ANGELES	22E. DATE SIGNED 1-17-62

FUNERAL DIRECTOR AND LOCAL REGISTRAR

23. SPECIFY BURIAL ENTOMBMENT OR CREMATION	24. DATE	25. NAME OF CEMETERY OR CREMATORY	26. EMBALMER—SIGNATURE (IF BODY EMBALMED) LICENSE NUMBER
Burial	1-15-62	Forest Lawn Hollywood Hills	3458

27. NAME OF FUNERAL DIRECTOR (OR PERSON ACTING AS SUCH)	28. DATE ACCEPTED FOR REGISTRATION BY LOCAL REGISTRAR	29. LOCAL REGISTRAR—SIGNATURE
6240 Hollywood Boulevard UTTER-McKINLEY MORTUARIES	1-19-62	George M. Ukl, M.D.

CAUSE OF DEATH

30. CAUSE OF DEATH ENTER ONLY ONE CAUSE PER LINE FOR (A), (B), AND (C)	APPROXIMATE INTERVAL BETWEEN ONSET AND DEATH
PART I. DEATH WAS CAUSED BY: IMMEDIATE CAUSE (A) FRACTURED SKULL AND RIBS WITH RUPTURED AORTA	
CONDITIONS, IF ANY, WHICH GAVE RISE TO THE ABOVE CAUSE (A) STATING THE UNDERLYING CAUSE LAST. DUE TO (B) AND OTHER INJURIES.	
DUE TO (C)	
PART II. OTHER SIGNIFICANT CONDITIONS CONTRIBUTING TO DEATH BUT NOT RELATED TO THE TERMINAL DISEASE CONDITION GIVEN IN PART I (A)	

OPERATION AND AUTOPSY

31. OPERATION—CHECK ONE: ☒ NO OPERATION PERFORMED ☐ OPERATION PERFORMED—FINDINGS USED IN DETERMINING CAUSES OF DEATH ☐ OPERATION PERFORMED—FINDINGS NOT USED IN DETERMINING CAUSES OF DEATH	32. DATE OF OPERATION	33. AUTOPSY—CHECK ONE: ☐ NO AUTOPSY PERFORMED ☒ AUTOPSY PERFORMED—GROSS FINDINGS USED IN DETERMINING CAUSES OF DEATH

INJURY INFORMATION

34A. SPECIFY ACCIDENT, SUICIDE OR HOMICIDE Accident	34B. DESCRIBE HOW INJURY OCCURRED Auto struck Pole (driver)

35A. TIME OF INJURY HOUR 130 A. MONTH 1 DAY 13 YEAR 62	35B. INJURY OCCURRED ☐ WHILE AT WORK ☒ NOT WHILE AT WORK	35C. PLACE OF INJURY street	35D. CITY, TOWN, OR LOCATION Los Angeles, L.A., Calif.

Rev 1-1-58 Form VS-11

This is to certify that this document is a true copy of the official record filed with the Registrar-Recorder/County Clerk.

Beatriz Valdez
BEATRIZ VALDEZ
Registrar-Recorder/County Clerk

This copy not valid unless prepared on engraved border displaying the Seal and Signature of the Registrar-Recorder/County Clerk.

AUG 23 1995

THE GREAT SEAL OF THE STATE OF CALIFORNIA

REGISTRAR-RECORDER/COUNTY CLERK • LOS ANGELES, CALIFORNIA

BANKNOTE CORPORATION OF AMERICA

ANY ALTERATION OR ERASURE VOIDS THIS CERTIFICATE

CERTIFICATE OF DEATH
STATE OF CALIFORNIA
USE BLACK INK ONLY/NO ERASURES, WHITEOUTS OR ALTERATIONS
VS-11 (REV. 7/93)

STATE FILE NUMBER | LOCAL REGISTRATION NUMBER

DECEDENT PERSONAL DATA

1. NAME OF DECEDENT—FIRST (GIVEN)	2. MIDDLE	3. LAST (FAMILY)
WALTER	–	LANTZ

4. DATE OF BIRTH MM/DD/CCYY	5. AGE YRS.	IF UNDER 1 YEAR MONTHS / DAYS	IF UNDER 24 HOURS HOURS / MINUTES	6. SEX	7. DATE OF DEATH MM/DD/CCYY	8. HOUR
04/27/1899	94			M	03/22/1994	1015

9. STATE OF BIRTH	10. SOCIAL SECURITY NO.	11. MILITARY SERVICE	12. MARITAL STATUS	13. EDUCATION—YEARS COMPLETED
NY	557-40-2887	19___ TO 19___ [X] NONE	WIDOWED	6

14. RACE	15. HISPANIC—SPECIFY	16. USUAL EMPLOYER
CAUCASIAN	[ ] YES _____ [X] NO	SELF EMPLOYED

17. OCCUPATION	18. KIND OF BUSINESS	19. YEARS IN OCCUPATION
ANIMATOR	ENTERTAINMENT	80

USUAL RESIDENCE

20. RESIDENCE—STREET AND NUMBER OR LOCATION
1715 CARLA RIDGE

21. CITY	22. COUNTY	23. ZIP CODE	24. YRS IN COUNTY	25. STATE OR FOREIGN COUNTRY
BEVERLY HILLS	LOS ANGELES	90210	70	CALIFORNIA

INFORMANT

26. NAME, RELATIONSHIP	27. MAILING ADDRESS (STREET AND NUMBER OR RURAL ROUTE NUMBER, CITY OR TOWN, STATE, ZIP)
PEGGY JACKSON, FRIEND	4444 LAKESIDE DR. #310, BURBANK, CA. 91505

SPOUSE AND PARENT INFORMATION

28. NAME OF SURVIVING SPOUSE—FIRST	29. MIDDLE	30. LAST (MAIDEN NAME)
–	–	–

31. NAME OF FATHER—FIRST	32. MIDDLE	33. LAST	34. BIRTH STATE
FRANK	–	LANTZ	ITALY

35. NAME OF MOTHER—FIRST	36. MIDDLE	37. LAST (MAIDEN)	38. BIRTH STATE
MARY	–	JARVIS	ITALY

DISPOSITION(S)

39. DATE MM/DD/CCYY	40. PLACE OF FINAL DISPOSITION
04/05/1994	FOREST LAWN MEMORIAL PARK, LOS ANGELES, CA. 90068

FUNERAL DIRECTOR AND LOCAL REGISTRAR

41. TYPE OF DISPOSITION(S)	42. SIGNATURE OF EMBALMER	43. LICENSE NO.
CREMATION/BURIAL	▶ NOT EMBALMED	–

44. NAME OF FUNERAL DIRECTOR	45. LICENSE NO.	46. SIGNATURE OF LOCAL REGISTRAR	47. DATE MM/DD/CCYY
FOREST LAWN HOLLYWOOD HILLS	F 904	▶ Robert C. Mata AU	03/29/1994

PLACE OF DEATH

101. PLACE OF DEATH	102. IF HOSPITAL, SPECIFY ONE:	103. FACILITY OTHER THAN HOSPITAL:	104. COUNTY
ST. JOSEPH MED. CTR.	[X] IP [ ] ER/OP [ ] DOA	[ ] CONV. HOSP. [ ] RES. [ ] OTHER	LOS ANGELES

105. STREET ADDRESS—STREET AND NUMBER OR LOCATION	106. CITY
501 S. BUENA VISTA	BURBANK

CAUSE OF DEATH

107. DEATH WAS CAUSED BY: (ENTER ONLY ONE CAUSE PER LINE FOR A, B, C, AND D)	TIME INTERVAL BETWEEN ONSET AND DEATH	108. DEATH REPORTED TO CORONER
IMMEDIATE CAUSE (A) CARDIOPULMONARY ARREST	1 MIN	[ ] YES [X] NO — REFERRAL NUMBER
DUE TO (B) CONGESTIVE HEART FAILURE	7 DAYS	109. BIOPSY PERFORMED [ ] YES [X] NO
DUE TO (C) MITRAL REGURGITATION	10 YRS	110. AUTOPSY PERFORMED [ ] YES [X] NO
DUE TO (D)		111. USED IN DETERMINING CAUSE [ ] YES [ ] NO

112. OTHER SIGNIFICANT CONDITIONS CONTRIBUTING TO DEATH BUT NOT RELATED TO CAUSE GIVEN IN 107
PROSTATE CARCINOMA, CVA

113. WAS OPERATION PERFORMED FOR ANY CONDITION IN ITEM 107 OR 112? IF YES, LIST TYPE OF OPERATION AND DATE.
NO

PHYSICIAN'S CERTIFICATION

114. I CERTIFY THAT TO THE BEST OF MY KNOWLEDGE DEATH OCCURRED AT THE HOUR, DATE AND PLACE STATED FROM THE CAUSES STATED.	115. SIGNATURE AND TITLE OF CERTIFIER	116. LICENSE NO.	117. DATE MM/DD/CCYY
DECEDENT ATTENDED SINCE MM/DD/CCYY 01/19/1990 / DECEDENT LAST SEEN ALIVE MM/DD/CCYY 03/22/1994	▶ R.L. Anderson M.D.	G037464	03/23/1994

118. TYPE ATTENDING PHYSICIAN'S NAME, MAILING ADDRESS + ZIP
RICHARD L. ANDERSON, MD, 2701 W. ALAMEDA AVE., BURBANK, CA. 91505

CORONER'S USE ONLY

I CERTIFY THAT IN MY OPINION DEATH OCCURRED AT THE HOUR, DATE AND PLACE STATED FROM THE CAUSES STATED.	120. INJURY AT WORK	121. INJURY DATE MM/DD/CCYY	122. HOUR	123. PLACE OF INJURY
119. MANNER OF DEATH	[ ] YES [ ] NO			

119. MANNER OF DEATH: [ ] NATURAL [ ] SUICIDE [ ] HOMICIDE [ ] ACCIDENT [ ] PENDING INVESTIGATION [ ] COULD NOT BE DETERMINED	124. DESCRIBE HOW INJURY OCCURRED (EVENTS WHICH RESULTED IN INJURY)

125. LOCATION (STREET AND NUMBER OR LOCATION AND CITY AND ZIP CODE)

126. SIGNATURE OF CORONER OR DEPUTY CORONER	127. DATE MM/DD/CCYY	128. TYPED NAME, TITLE OF CORONER OR DEPUTY CORONER
▶		

CERTIFICATION OF VITAL RECORD

COUNTY OF LOS ANGELES • REGISTRAR-RECORDER/COUNTY CLERK

CERTIFICATE OF DEATH
STATE OF CALIFORNIA

90-041829

				LOCAL REGISTRATION DISTRICT AND CERTIFICATE NUMBER	
STATE FILE NUMBER					
1A. NAME OF DECEDENT—FIRST	1B. MIDDLE		1C. LAST	2A. DATE OF DEATH (MONTH, DAY, YEAR)	2B. HOUR
Wesley	Albert		Lau	August 30, 1984	1922
3. SEX	4. RACE/ETHNICITY	5. SPANISH/HISPANIC NO ☒	6. DATE OF BIRTH	7. AGE 63 YEARS	IF UNDER 1 YEAR MONTHS DAYS / IF UNDER 24 HOURS HOURS MINUTES
Male	White		June 18, 1921		

DECEDENT PERSONAL DATA

8. BIRTHPLACE OF DECEDENT (STATE OR FOREIGN COUNTRY)	9. NAME AND BIRTHPLACE OF FATHER	10. BIRTH NAME AND BIRTHPLACE OF MOTHER
Wisconsin	Albert Lau - Michigan	Agnes Feldner - Wisconsin
11. CITIZEN OF WHAT COUNTRY	12. SOCIAL SECURITY NUMBER	13. MARITAL STATUS	14. NAME OF SURVIVING SPOUSE (IF WIFE, ENTER BIRTH NAME)
U.S.A.	326-18-4591	Married	Mary L. Metcalf
15. PRIMARY OCCUPATION	16. NUMBER OF YEARS THIS OCCUPATION	17. EMPLOYER (IF SELF-EMPLOYED, SO STATE)	18. KIND OF INDUSTRY OR BUSINESS
Actor and Screenwriter	40	Self	Motion Picture & Television

USUAL RESIDENCE

19A. USUAL RESIDENCE—STREET ADDRESS (STREET AND NUMBER OR LOCATION)	19B.	19C. CITY OR TOWN
840 N. Kenter Ave.		Los Angeles
19D. COUNTY	19E. STATE	20. NAME AND ADDRESS OF INFORMANT—RELATIONSHIP
Los Angeles	California	Mary Louise Lau - Wife same as 19a

PLACE OF DEATH

21A. PLACE OF DEATH	21B. COUNTY
St. Johns Medical Center	Los Angeles
21C. STREET ADDRESS (STREET AND NUMBER OR LOCATION)	21D. CITY OR TOWN
1328 22nd St.	Santa Monica

CAUSE OF DEATH

22. DEATH WAS CAUSED BY: (ENTER ONLY ONE CAUSE PER LINE FOR A, B, AND C)		APPROXIMATE INTERVAL BETWEEN ONSET AND DEATH	
IMMEDIATE CAUSE (A)	Cardiac arrest	1 Hour	24. WAS DEATH REPORTED TO CORONER? Yes 84-10933
CONDITIONS, IF ANY, WHICH GAVE RISE TO THE IMMEDIATE CAUSE, STATING THE UNDERLYING CAUSE LAST. DUE TO, OR AS A CONSEQUENCE OF (B)	Acute Myocardial Infarct	1 Day	25. WAS BIOPSY PERFORMED? No
DUE TO, OR AS A CONSEQUENCE OF (C)	arteriosclerosis	years	26. WAS AUTOPSY PERFORMED? No
23. OTHER SIGNIFICANT CONDITIONS—CONTRIBUTING TO DEATH BUT NOT RELATED TO CAUSE GIVEN IN 22A		27. WAS OPERATION PERFORMED FOR ANY CONDITION IN ITEMS 22 OR 23? TYPE OF OPERATION No	DATE

PHYSICIAN'S CERTIFICATION

28A. I CERTIFY THAT DEATH OCCURRED AT THE HOUR, DATE AND PLACE STATED FROM THE CAUSES STATED. I ATTENDED DECEDENT SINCE (ENTER MO. DA. YR.) Jan 13 1972 / I LAST SAW DECEDENT ALIVE (ENTER MO. DA. YR.) July 28 1984	28B. PHYSICIAN—SIGNATURE AND DEGREE OR TITLE *Gilbert Gallis M.D.*	28C. DATE SIGNED 8/31/84	28D. PHYSICIAN'S LICENSE NUMBER C24147
	28E. TYPE PHYSICIAN'S NAME AND ADDRESS Gilbert P. Gallis, M.D. 8631 West Third St. Suite 715-E		

INJURY INFORMATION

29. SPECIFY ACCIDENT, SUICIDE, ETC.	30. PLACE OF INJURY	31. INJURY AT WORK	32A. DATE OF INJURY—MONTH, DAY, YEAR	32B. HOUR
33. LOCATION (STREET AND NUMBER OR LOCATION AND CITY OR TOWN)	34. DESCRIBE HOW INJURY OCCURRED (EVENTS WHICH RESULTED IN INJURY)			

CORONER'S USE ONLY

35A. I CERTIFY THAT DEATH OCCURRED AT THE HOUR, DATE AND PLACE STATED FROM THE CAUSES STATED. AS REQUIRED BY LAW I HAVE HELD AN (INQUEST-INVESTIGATION)	35B. CORONER—SIGNATURE AND DEGREE OR TITLE	35C. DATE SIGNED

36. DISPOSITION	37. DATE—MONTH, DAY, YEAR	38. NAME AND ADDRESS OF CEMETERY OR CREMATORY		39. EMBALMER'S LICENSE NUMBER AND SIGNATURE
Burial	Sept. 4, 1984	Forest Lawn Hollywood Hills Los Angeles, CA		Juan L. Werner 6449
40A. NAME OF FUNERAL DIRECTOR (OR PERSON ACTING AS SUCH)	40B. LICENSE NO.	41. LOCAL REGISTRAR		42. DATE ACCEPTED BY LOCAL REGISTRAR
Westwood Village Mortuary	951			SEP 4 1984

STATE REGISTRAR	A.	B.	C.	D.	E.	F.

VS-11 (7-83)

87504-449 9-83 400M DUP ① OSP

This is to certify that this document is a true copy of the official record filed with the Registrar-Recorder/County Clerk.

OCT 02 1995

19-033393

This copy not valid unless prepared on engraved border displaying the Seal of the Registrar-Recorder/County Clerk.

STATE OF CALIFORNIA
CERTIFICATION OF VITAL RECORD

COUNTY OF LOS ANGELES
DEPARTMENT OF HEALTH SERVICES

CERTIFICATE OF DEATH
STATE OF CALIFORNIA
USE BLACK INK ONLY/NO ERASURES, WHITEOUTS OR ALTERATIONS
VS-11 (REV. 7/00)

STATE FILE NUMBER | LOCAL REGISTRATION NUMBER

DECEDENT PERSONAL DATA

1. NAME OF DECEDENT—FIRST (GIVEN): PEGGY	2. MIDDLE: -	3. LAST (FAMILY): LEE

| 4. DATE OF BIRTH MM/DD/CCYY: 05/26/1920 | 5. AGE YRS: 81 | 6. SEX: F | 7. DATE OF DEATH MM/DD/CCYY: 01/21/2002 | 8. HOUR: 2025 |

| 9. STATE OF BIRTH: ND | 10. SOCIAL SECURITY NO: 502-09-3702 | 11. MILITARY SERVICE: YES / X NO / UNK | 12. MARITAL STATUS: DIVORCED | 13. EDUCATION—YEARS COMPLETED: 12 |

| 14. RACE: CAUCASIAN | 15. HISPANIC—SPECIFY: YES / X NO | 16. USUAL EMPLOYER: SELF EMPLOYED |

| 17. OCCUPATION: SINGER/ACTRESS | 18. KIND OF BUSINESS: ENTERTAINMENT | 19. YEARS IN OCCUPATION: 60 |

USUAL RESIDENCE

| 20. RESIDENCE—STREET AND NUMBER OR LOCATION: 11404 BELLAGIO RD. |

| 21. CITY: LOS ANGELES | 22. COUNTY: LOS ANGELES | 23. ZIP CODE: 90049 | 24. YRS IN COUNTY: 50 | 25. STATE OR FOREIGN COUNTRY: CA |

INFORMANT

| 26. NAME, RELATIONSHIP: NICKI FOSTER - DAUGHTER | 27. MAILING ADDRESS (STREET AND NUMBER OR RURAL ROUTE NUMBER, CITY OR TOWN, STATE, ZIP): P.O.BOX 815 SUN VALLEY, IDAHO 83353 |

SPOUSE AND PARENT INFORMATION

| 28. NAME OF SURVIVING SPOUSE—FIRST: - | 29. MIDDLE: - | 30. LAST (MAIDEN NAME): - |

| 31. NAME OF FATHER—FIRST: MARVIN | 32. MIDDLE: - | 33. LAST: EGSTROM | 34. BIRTH STATE: ND |

| 35. NAME OF MOTHER—FIRST: SELMA | 36. MIDDLE: - | 37. LAST (MAIDEN): ANDERSON | 38. BIRTH STATE: ND |

DISPOSITION(S)

| 39. DATE MM/DD/CCYY: 01/22/2002 | 40. PLACE OF FINAL DISPOSITION: WESTWOOD VILLAGE MEMORIAL PARK 1218 GLENDON AVE. LOS ANGELES,CA.90024 |

FUNERAL DIRECTOR AND LOCAL REGISTRAR

| 41. TYPE OF DISPOSITION(S): CR/BU | 42. SIGNATURE OF EMBALMER: ► NOT EMBALMED | 43. LICENSE NO. |

| 44. NAME OF FUNERAL DIRECTOR: PIERCE BROS. WESTWOOD | 45. LICENSE NO.: FD-951 | 46. SIGNATURE OF LOCAL REGISTRAR: Fred Leaf | 47. DATE MM/DD/CCYY: 01/22/2002 |

PLACE OF DEATH

| 101. PLACE OF DEATH: RESIDENCE | 102. IF HOSPITAL, SPECIFY ONE: IP / ER/OP / DOA | 103. FACILITY OTHER THAN HOSPITAL: CONV.HOSP. / RES.CARE / OTHER | 104. COUNTY: LOS ANGELES |

| 105. STREET ADDRESS—STREET AND NUMBER OR LOCATION: 11404 BELLAGIO RD. | 106. CITY: LOS ANGELES |

CAUSE OF DEATH

107. DEATH WAS CAUSED BY: (ENTER ONLY ONE CAUSE PER LINE FOR A, B, C, AND D)	TIME INTERVAL BETWEEN ONSET AND DEATH	108. DEATH REPORTED TO CORONER: YES / X NO REFERRAL NUMBER
IMMEDIATE CAUSE (A): CARDIORESPIRATORY ARREST	1min.	
DUE TO (B): MYOCARDIAL INFARCTION	mins.	109. BIOPSY PERFORMED: YES / X NO
DUE TO (C): ATHEROSCLEROTIC CARDIOVASCULAR DISEASE	years	110. AUTOPSY PERFORMED: YES / X NO
DUE TO (D):		111. USED IN DETERMINING CAUSE: YES / NO

| 112. OTHER SIGNIFICANT CONDITIONS CONTRIBUTING TO DEATH BUT NOT RELATED TO CAUSE GIVEN IN 107: CEREBROVASCULAR INFARCTION |

| 113. WAS OPERATION PERFORMED FOR ANY CONDITION IN ITEM 107 OR 112? IF YES, LIST TYPE OF OPERATION AND DATE: NO |

PHYSICIAN'S CERTIFICATION

| 114. I CERTIFY THAT TO THE BEST OF MY KNOWLEDGE DEATH OCCURRED AT THE HOUR, DATE AND PLACE STATED FROM THE CAUSES STATED. | 115. SIGNATURE AND TITLE OF CERTIFIER: ► Morris T. Grabie | 116. LICENSE NO: G34196 | 117. DATE MM/DD/CCYY: 01/22/2002 |

| DECEDENT ATTENDED SINCE MM/DD/CCYY: 12/10/1999 | DECEDENT LAST SEEN ALIVE MM/DD/CCYY: 01/20/2002 | 118. TYPE ATTENDING PHYSICIAN'S NAME, MAILING ADDRESS, ZIP: MORRIS T.GRABIE, MD. 1301 20TH ST. SANTA MONICA, CA. 90404 |

CORONER'S USE ONLY

| 119. I CERTIFY THAT IN MY OPINION DEATH OCCURRED AT THE HOUR, DATE AND PLACE STATED FROM THE CAUSES STATED. | 120. INJURY AT WORK: YES / NO | 121. INJURY DATE MM/DD/CCYY | 122. HOUR | 123. PLACE OF INJURY |

| 119. MANNER OF DEATH: NATURAL / SUICIDE / HOMICIDE / ACCIDENT / PENDING INVESTIGATION / COULD NOT BE DETERMINED | 124. DESCRIBE HOW INJURY OCCURRED (EVENTS WHICH RESULTED IN INJURY): |

| 125. LOCATION (STREET AND NUMBER OR LOCATION AND CITY, ZIP): |

| 126. SIGNATURE OF CORONER OR DEPUTY CORONER: ► | 127. DATE MM/DD/CCYY | 128. TYPED NAME, TITLE OF CORONER OR DEPUTY CORONER |

STATE REGISTRAR

| A | B | C | D | E | F | G | H | FAX AUTH. # | CENSUS TRACT |

090498251

This is a true certified copy of the record filed in the County of Los Angeles Department of Health Services if it bears the Registrar's signature in purple ink.

Fred Leaf

Director of Health Services and Registrar

140 DATE ISSUED JAN 28 2002

This copy not valid unless prepared on engraved border displaying seal and signature of Registrar.

CERTIFICATE OF DEATH
STATE OF CALIFORNIA
USE BLACK INK ONLY / NO ERASURES, WHITEOUTS OR ALTERATIONS
VS-11 (REV 1/04)

3 200419041246

STATE FILE NUMBER | LOCAL REGISTRATION NUMBER

DECEDENT'S PERSONAL DATA

1. NAME OF DECEDENT --- FIRST (Given)	2. MIDDLE	3. LAST (Family)
JANET	LEIGH	BRANDT

AKA, ALSO KNOWN AS — Include full AKA (FIRST, MIDDLE, LAST)	4. DATE OF BIRTH mm/dd/ccyy	5. AGE Yrs.	IF UNDER ONE YEAR Months / Days	IF UNDER 24 HOURS Hours / Minutes	6. SEX
--	07/06/1927	77			FEMALE

9. BIRTH STATE/FOREIGN COUNTRY	10. SOCIAL SECURITY NUMBER	11. EVER IN U.S. ARMED FORCES?	12. MARITAL STATUS (at Time of Death)	7. DATE OF DEATH mm/dd/ccyy	8. HOUR (24 Hours)
CALIFORNIA	573-26-9823	YES / X NO / UNK	MARRIED	10/03/2004	1847

13. EDUCATION — Highest Level/Degree	14/15. WAS DECEDENT HISPANIC/LATINO(A)/SPANISH? (If yes, see worksheet on back.)	16. DECEDENT'S RACE — Up to 3 races may be listed (see worksheet on back)
DOCTORATE	YES / X NO	CAUCASIAN

17. USUAL OCCUPATION --- Type of work for most of life. DO NOT USE RETIRED	18. KIND OF BUSINESS OR INDUSTRY (e.g., grocery store, road construction, employment agency, etc.)	19. YEARS IN OCCUPATION
ACTRESS	ENTERTAINMENT	57

USUAL RESIDENCE

20. DECEDENT'S RESIDENCE (Street and number or location)
1625 SUMMITRIDGE DRIVE

21. CITY	22. COUNTY/PROVINCE	23. ZIP CODE	24. YEARS IN COUNTY	25. STATE/FOREIGN COUNTRY
BEVERLY HILLS	LOS ANGELES	90210	53	CALIFORNIA

INFORMANT

26. INFORMANT'S NAME, RELATIONSHIP	27. INFORMANT'S MAILING ADDRESS (Street and number or rural route number, city or town, state, ZIP)
KELLY CURTIS, DAUGHTER	1625 SUMMITRIDGE DRIVE, BEVERLY HILLS, CA 90210

SPOUSE AND PARENT INFORMATION

28. NAME OF SURVIVING SPOUSE --- FIRST	29. MIDDLE	30. LAST (Maiden Name)
ROBERT	--	BRANDT

31. NAME OF FATHER --- FIRST	32. MIDDLE	33. LAST	34. BIRTH STATE
FRED	--	MORRISON	CALIFORNIA

35. NAME OF MOTHER --- FIRST	36. MIDDLE	37. LAST (Maiden)	38. BIRTH STATE
HELEN	--	WESTERGARD	CALIFORNIA

FUNERAL DIRECTOR/ LOCAL REGISTRAR

39. DISPOSITION DATE mm/dd/ccyy	40. PLACE OF FINAL DISPOSITION
10/05/2004	RES, KELLY CURTIS 1625 SUMMITRIDGE DRIVE, BEVERLY HILLS, CA 90210

41. TYPE OF DISPOSITION(S)	42. SIGNATURE OF EMBALMER	43. LICENSE NUMBER
CR/RES	NOT EMBALMED	--

44. NAME OF FUNERAL ESTABLISHMENT	45. LICENSE NUMBER	46. SIGNATURE OF LOCAL REGISTRAR	47. DATE mm/dd/ccyy
NEPTUNE SOCIETY	S.O. FD-1359	*Thomas W Whitworth* MS	10/04/2004 CeD

PLACE OF DEATH

101. PLACE OF DEATH	102. IF HOSPITAL, SPECIFY ONE	103. IF OTHER THAN HOSPITAL, SPECIFY ONE
RESIDENCE	IP / ER/OP / DOA	Hospice / Nursing Home/LTC / X Decedent's Home / Other

104. COUNTY	105. FACILITY ADDRESS OR LOCATION WHERE FOUND (Street and number or location)	106. CITY
LOS ANGELES	1625 SUMMITRIDGE DRIVE	BEVERLY HILLS

CAUSE OF DEATH

107. CAUSE OF DEATH — Enter the chain of events --- diseases, injuries, or complications --- that directly caused death. DO NOT enter terminal events such as cardiac arrest, respiratory arrest, or ventricular fibrillation without showing the etiology. DO NOT ABBREVIATE.

		Time Interval Between Onset and Death	108. DEATH REPORTED TO CORONER?
IMMEDIATE CAUSE (Final disease or condition resulting in death) (A)	CARDIOPULMONARY ARREST	(AT) MINUTES	X YES / NO REFERRAL NUMBER 2004-57250
Sequentially list conditions, if any, leading to cause on Line A. Enter UNDERLYING CAUSE (disease or injury that initiated the events resulting in death) LAST (B)	DILATED CARDIOMYOPATHY	(BT) MONTHS	109. BIOPSY PERFORMED? YES / X NO
(C)		(CT)	110. AUTOPSY PERFORMED? YES / X NO
(D)		(DT)	111. USED IN DETERMINING CAUSE? YES / X NO

112. OTHER SIGNIFICANT CONDITIONS CONTRIBUTING TO DEATH BUT NOT RESULTING IN THE UNDERLYING CAUSE GIVEN IN 107
VASCULITIS, PERIPHERAL NEUROPATHY, GANGRENE RIGHT HAND

113. WAS OPERATION PERFORMED FOR ANY CONDITION IN ITEM 107 OR 112? (If yes, list type of operation and date.)	113A. IF FEMALE, PREGNANT IN LAST YEAR?
GASTROSTOMY TUBE 12/02/2003	YES / X NO / UNK

PHYSICIAN'S CERTIFICATION

114. I CERTIFY THAT TO THE BEST OF MY KNOWLEDGE DEATH OCCURRED AT THE HOUR, DATE, AND PLACE STATED FROM THE CAUSES STATED.	115. SIGNATURE AND TITLE OF CERTIFIER	116. LICENSE NUMBER	117. DATE mm/dd/ccyy
Decedent Attended Since / Decedent Last Seen Alive	*John Gordon Harold MD*	G046536	10/04/2004

(A) mm/dd/ccyy	(B) mm/dd/ccyy	118. TYPE ATTENDING PHYSICIAN'S NAME, MAILING ADDRESS, ZIP CODE
08/18/2004	09/10/2004	JOHN GORDON HAROLD, MD 8635 W. THIRD STREET, LOS ANGELES, CA 90048

CORONER'S USE ONLY

T42g /5

119. I CERTIFY THAT IN MY OPINION DEATH OCCURRED AT THE HOUR, DATE, AND PLACE STATED FROM THE CAUSES STATED. MANNER OF DEATH	Natural / Accident / Homicide / Suicide / Pending Investigation / Could not be determined	120. INJURED AT WORK? YES / NO / UNK	121. INJURY DATE mm/dd/ccyy	122. HOUR (24 Hours)

123. PLACE OF INJURY (e.g., home, construction site, wooded area, etc.)

124. DESCRIBE HOW INJURY OCCURRED (Events which resulted in injury)

125. LOCATION OF INJURY (Street and number, or location, and city, and ZIP)

126. SIGNATURE OF CORONER / DEPUTY CORONER	127. DATE mm/dd/ccyy	128. TYPE NAME, TITLE OF CORONER / DEPUTY CORONER
		*0907

STATE REGISTRAR	A	B	C	D	E		FAX AUTH. # 195/842	CENSUS TRACT

STATE OF CALIFORNIA
CERTIFICATION OF VITAL RECORD

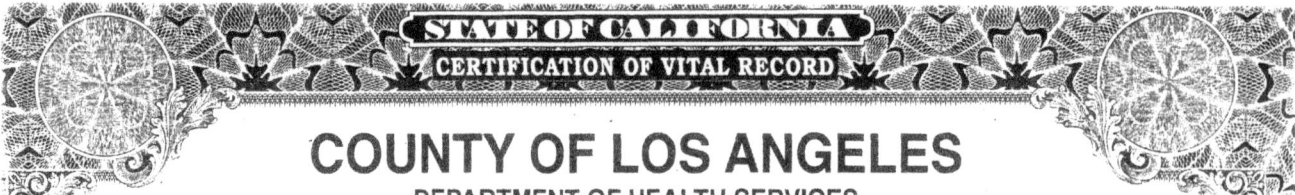

COUNTY OF LOS ANGELES
DEPARTMENT OF HEALTH SERVICES

CERTIFICATE OF DEATH
STATE OF CALIFORNIA
USE BLACK INK ONLY/NO ERASURES, WHITEOUTS OR ALTERATIONS
VS-11 (REV. 1/00)

STATE FILE NUMBER		LOCAL REGISTRATION NUMBER

DECEDENT PERSONAL DATA

1. NAME OF DECEDENT—FIRST (GIVEN)	2. MIDDLE	3. LAST (FAMILY)	
John	Uhler	Lemmon III	

4. DATE OF BIRTH MM/DD/CCYY	5. AGE YRS	IF UNDER 1 YEAR MONTHS / DAYS	IF UNDER 24 HOURS HOURS / MINUTES	6. SEX	7. DATE OF DEATH MM/DD/CCYY	8. HOUR
02/08/1925	76			M	06/27/2001	2111

9. STATE OF BIRTH	10. SOCIAL SECURITY NO.	11. MILITARY SERVICE	12. MARITAL STATUS	13. EDUCATION—YEARS COMPLETED
MA	030-20-3253	X YES NO UNK	MARRIED	16

14. RACE	15. HISPANIC—SPECIFY		16. USUAL EMPLOYER
CAUC	YES	X No	SELF EMPLOYED

17. OCCUPATION	18. KIND OF BUSINESS	19. YEARS IN OCCUPATION
ACTOR	ENTERTAINMENT	56

USUAL RESIDENCE

20. RESIDENCE—(STREET AND NUMBER OR LOCATION)
173 S. EL CAMINO #210

21. CITY	22. COUNTY	23. ZIP CODE	24. YRS IN COUNTY	25. STATE OR FOREIGN COUNTRY
BEVERLY HILLS	LOS ANGELES	90210	50	CA

INFORMANT

26. NAME, RELATIONSHIP	27. MAILING ADDRESS (STREET AND NUMBER OR RURAL ROUTE NUMBER, CITY OR TOWN, STATE, ZIP)
FELICIA FARR LEMMON - WIFE	173 S. EL CAMINO #210 BEVERLY HILLS, CA. 90210

SPOUSE AND PARENT INFORMATION

28. NAME OF SURVIVING SPOUSE—FIRST	29. MIDDLE	30. LAST (MAIDEN NAME)	
FELICIA	-	FARR	

31. NAME OF FATHER—FIRST	32. MIDDLE	33. LAST	34. BIRTH STATE
JOHN	UHLER	LEMMON II	MA

35. NAME OF MOTHER—FIRST	36. MIDDLE	37. LAST (MAIDEN)	38. BIRTH STATE
MILDRED	-	NOEL	MD

DISPOSITION(S)

39. DATE MM/DD/CCYY	40. PLACE OF FINAL DISPOSITION
07/01/2001	WESTWOOD VILLAGE MEMORIAL PARK 1218 GLENDON AVE. LOS ANGELES,CA.90024

FUNERAL DIRECTOR AND LOCAL REGISTRAR

41. TYPE OF DISPOSITION(S)	42. SIGNATURE OF EMBALMER	43. LICENSE NO.
BURIAL	▶ NOT EMBALMED	-

44. NAME OF FUNERAL DIRECTOR	45. LICENSE NO.	46. SIGNATURE OF LOCAL REGISTRAR	47. DATE MM/DD/CCYY
PIERCE BROS. WESTWOOD	FD951	▶ Mark Simmons	06/29/2001

PLACE OF DEATH

101. PLACE OF DEATH	102. IF HOSPITAL, SPECIFY ONE:	103. FACILITY OTHER THAN HOSPITAL:	104. COUNTY
USC/KENNETH NORRIS JR. COMP. CANCER CENTER AND HOSPITAL	X IP ER/OP DOA	CONV. HOSP. RES. CARE OTHER	LOS ANGELES

105. STREET ADDRESS—(STREET AND NUMBER OR LOCATION)	106. CITY
1441 EASTLAKE AVE.	LOS ANGELES

CAUSE OF DEATH

107. DEATH WAS CAUSED BY: (ENTER ONLY ONE CAUSE PER LINE FOR A, B, C, AND D)	TIME INTERVAL BETWEEN ONSET AND DEATH	108. DEATH REPORTED TO CORONER
IMMEDIATE CAUSE (A) CARCINOMATOSIS	2months	YES X NO — REFERRAL NUMBER
DUE TO (B) METASTATIC CANCER OF BLADDER TO COLON	2years	109. BIOPSY PERFORMED YES X NO
DUE TO (C)		110. AUTOPSY PERFORMED YES X NO
DUE TO (D)		111. USED IN DETERMINING CAUSE YES NO

112. OTHER SIGNIFICANT CONDITIONS CONTRIBUTING TO DEATH BUT NOT RELATED TO CAUSE GIVEN IN 107
NONE

113. WAS OPERATION PERFORMED FOR ANY CONDITION IN ITEM 107 OR 112? IF YES, LIST TYPE OF OPERATION AND DATE
RADICAL CYSTECTOMY 12/14/1999 EXPLORATORY LAPAROTOMY WITH SIGMOIDOSTOMY 12/19/2000

C679

PHYSICIAN'S CERTIFICATION

114. I CERTIFY THAT TO THE BEST OF MY KNOWLEDGE DEATH OCCURRED AT THE HOUR, DATE AND PLACE STATED FROM THE CAUSES STATED.		115. SIGNATURE AND TITLE OF CERTIFIER	116. LICENSE NO.	117. DATE MM/DD/CCYY
DECEDENT ATTENDED SINCE MM/DD/CCYY	DECEDENT LAST SEEN ALIVE MM/DD/CCYY	▶ Donald J. Skinner	G017316	06/28/2001
11/24/1999	06/27/2001	118. TYPE ATTENDING PHYSICIAN'S NAME, MAILING ADDRESS, ZIP DONALD SKINNER,MD. 1441 EASTLAKE AVE. LOS ANGELES,CA.90033		

CORONER'S USE ONLY

4+F

1889

C

I CERTIFY THAT IN MY OPINION DEATH OCCURRED AT THE HOUR, DATE AND PLACE STATED FROM THE CAUSES STATED.	120. INJURY AT WORK	121. INJURY DATE MM/DD/CCYY	122. HOUR	123. PLACE OF INJURY
119. MANNER OF DEATH	YES NO			
NATURAL SUICIDE HOMICIDE ACCIDENT PENDING INVESTIGATION COULD NOT BE DETERMINED	124. DESCRIBE HOW INJURY OCCURRED (EVENTS WHICH RESULTED IN INJURY)			

125. LOCATION (STREET AND NUMBER OR LOCATION AND CITY, ZIP)

126. SIGNATURE OF CORONER OR DEPUTY CORONER	127. DATE MM/DD/CCYY	128. TYPED NAME, TITLE OF CORONER OR DEPUTY CORONER
▶		

STATE REGISTRAR

A	B	C	D	E	F	G	H	FAX AUTH. #	CENSUS TRACT

090453628

This is a true certified copy of the record filed in the County of Los Angeles
Department of Health Services if it bears the Registrar's signature in purple ink.

DATE ISSUED

Director of Health Services and Registrar

This copy not valid unless prepared on engraved border displaying seal and signature of Registrar.

ANY ALTERATION OR ERASURE VOIDS THIS CERTIFICATE

STATE OF CALIFORNIA
CERTIFICATION OF VITAL RECORD

COUNTY OF LOS ANGELES • REGISTRAR-RECORDER/COUNTY CLERK

CERTIFICATE OF DEATH
STATE OF CALIFORNIA
USE BLACK INK ONLY

STATE FILE NUMBER — 39219045821

LOCAL REGISTRATION DISTRICT AND CERTIFICATE NUMBER

DECEDENT PERSONAL DATA

1A. NAME OF DECEDENT—FIRST (GIVEN)	1B. MIDDLE	1C. LAST (FAMILY)	2A. DATE OF DEATH—MO. DAY. YR. 2B. HOUR	3. SEX
Cleavon	Jake	Little	October 22, 1992 0745	M

4. RACE	5. HISPANIC—SPECIFY	6. DATE OF BIRTH—MO. DAY. YR	7. AGE IN YEARS	IF UNDER 1 YEAR MONTHS / DAYS	IF UNDER 24 HOURS HOURS / MINUTES
African American	YES X NO	June 1, 1939	53		

8. STATE OF BIRTH	9. CITIZEN OF WHAT COUNTRY	10A. FULL NAME OF FATHER	10B. STATE OF BIRTH	11A. FULL MAIDEN NAME OF MOTHER	11B. STATE OF BIRTH
OK	USA	Malchi Little	MS	De Etta Bowens	TX

12. MILITARY SERVICE	13. SOCIAL SECURITY NO.	14. MARITAL STATUS	15. NAME OF SURVIVING SPOUSE (IF WIFE, ENTER MAIDEN NAME)
19___ TO 19___ X NONE	571-54-5976	Divorced	None

16A. USUAL OCCUPATION	16B. USUAL KIND OF BUSINESS INDUSTRY	16C. USUAL EMPLOYER	16D. YEARS IN OCCUPATION	17. EDUCATION—YEARS COMPLETED
Actor	Film/Television	Self	30	16

USUAL RESIDENCE

18A. RESIDENCE—STREET AND NUMBER OR LOCATION	18B. CITY	18C. ZIP CODE
4374 Ventura Cyn Ave., #4	Sherman Oaks	91423

18D. COUNTY	18E. NUMBER OF YEARS IN THIS COUNTY	18F. STATE OR FOREIGN COUNTRY	20. NAME, RELATIONSHIP, MAILING ADDRESS AND ZIP CODE OF INFORMANT
Los Angeles	27	California	Diane Lewis-Guardian of Minor Child 2210 N. Kinnelea Cyn Rd. Pasadena, CA 91107

PLACE OF DEATH

19A. PLACE OF DEATH	19B. IF HOSPITAL SPECIFY ONE: IP. ER/OP. DOA	19C. COUNTY
Residence	—	Los Angeles

19D. STREET ADDRESS—STREET AND NUMBER OR LOCATION	19E. CITY
4374 Ventura Cyn. Avenue	Sherman Oaks

	TIME INTERVAL BETWEEN ONSET AND DEATH	22. WAS DEATH REPORTED TO CORONER REFERRAL NUMBER
		YES X NO

CAUSE OF DEATH

21. DEATH WAS CAUSED BY: (ENTER ONLY ONE CAUSE PER LINE FOR A, B, AND C)

IMMEDIATE CAUSE (A)	Obstructive Uropathy & GI Tract	▶ Months	23. WAS BIOPSY PERFORMED X YES ☐ NO
DUE TO (B)	Metastatic adenocarcinoma of the colon	▶ 1 year	24A. WAS AUTOPSY PERFORMED ☐ YES X NO
DUE TO (C)		▶	24B. WAS IT USED IN DETERMINING CAUSE OF DEATH ☐ YES X NO

25. OTHER SIGNIFICANT CONDITIONS CONTRIBUTING TO DEATH BUT NOT RELATED TO CAUSE GIVEN IN 21	26. WAS OPERATION PERFORMED FOR ANY CONDITION IN ITEM 21 OR 25, LIST TYPE OF OPERATION AND DATE
Sepsis due to abscess	Ex B/P of GI Trac, Gastrostomy 9/5/92 5/8/92,

PHYSICIAN'S CERTIFICATION

I CERTIFY THAT TO THE BEST OF MY KNOWLEDGE DEATH OCCURRED AT THE HOUR, DATE AND PLACE STATED FROM THE CAUSES STATED. 27B. SIGNATURE AND DEGREE OR TITLE OF CERTIFIER	27C. CERTIFIER'S LICENSE NUMBER	27D. DATE SIGNED
▶ Paul Rosoff, MD	G31898	10-23-92

27A. DECEDENT ATTENDED SINCE MONTH, DAY, YEAR	DECEDENT LAST SEEN ALIVE MONTH, DAY, YEAR	27E. TYPE ATTENDING PHYSICIAN'S NAME AND ADDRESS
11-12-1991	10-20-1992	Saul Rosoff, M.D. 2080 Century Pk. East, Ste.1209, L.A., CA., 90067

CORONER'S USE ONLY

I CERTIFY THAT IN MY OPINION DEATH OCCURRED AT THE HOUR, DATE AND PLACE STATED FROM THE CAUSES STATED.

28A. SIGNATURE AND TITLE OF CORONER OR DEPUTY CORONER	28B. DATE SIGNED

29. MANNER OF DEATH	30A. PLACE OF INJURY	30B. INJURY AT WORK YES ☐ NO ☐	30C. DATE OF INJURY MONTH, DAY, YEAR	31. HOUR

32. LOCATION (STREET AND NUMBER OR LOCATION AND CITY)

33. DESCRIBE HOW INJURY OCCURRED (EVENTS WHICH RESULTED IN INJURY)

FUNERAL DIRECTOR AND LOCAL REGISTRAR

34A. DISPOSITION(S)	34B. PLACE OF FINAL DISPOSITION—NAME AND ADDRESS	34C. DATE MO. DAY. YR.	35A. SIGNATURE OF EMBALMER	35B. LICENSE NO.
CR/TR/SEA	sea scattering in New York Harbor, New York	10-28-1992	Not Embalmed	None

36A. NAME OF FUNERAL DIRECTOR (OR PERSON ACTING AS SUCH)	36B. LICENSE NO.	37. SIGNATURE OF LOCAL REGISTRAR	38. REGISTRATION DATE
Aftercare CA Crem & BU Society	F-1166	▶ Robert ? Gate	OCT 27 1992

STATE REGISTRAR A.	B.	C.	D.	E.	F.	CENSUS TRACT

VS-11 (REV. 7-22)   1539   MAKE NO ERASURES, WHITEOUTS, OR OTHER ALTERATIONS

This is to certify that this document is a true copy of the official record filed with the Registrar-Recorder/County Clerk.

Conny B. McCormack

CONNY B. McCORMACK
Registrar-Recorder/County Clerk

This copy not valid unless prepared on engraved border displaying the Seal and Signature of the Registrar-Recorder/County Clerk.

NOV 2 8 2000
19-116315

ANY ALTERATION OR ERASURE VOIDS THIS CERTIFICATE

CERTIFICATE OF DEATH
STATE OF CALIFORNIA
USE BLACK INK ONLY/NO ERASURES, WHITEOUTS OR ALTERATIONS
VS-11 (REV. 1/00)

STATE FILE NUMBER

3 2000 19 043784

LOCAL REGISTRATION NUMBER

1. NAME OF DECEDENT—FIRST (Given) JULIE	2. MIDDLE LONDON	3. LAST (FAMILY) TROUP

DECEDENT PERSONAL DATA

4. DATE OF BIRTH MM/DD/CCYY 09/26/1926	5. AGE YRS. 74	IF UNDER 1 YEAR MONTHS / DAYS	IF UNDER 24 HOURS HOURS / MINUTES	6. SEX F	7. DATE OF DEATH MM/DD/CCYY 10/18/2000	8. HOUR 0530

9. STATE OF BIRTH CA	10. SOCIAL SECURITY NO. 573-20-9888	11. MILITARY SERVICE YES [X] NO UNK	12. MARITAL STATUS WIDOWED	13. EDUCATION—YEARS COMPLETED 12

14. RACE CAUCASIAN	15. HISPANIC—SPECIFY YES___ [X] NO	16. USUAL EMPLOYER UNIVERSAL STUDIOS

17. OCCUPATION ACTRESS/SINGER	18. KIND OF BUSINESS ENTERTAINMENT	19. YEARS IN OCCUPATION 57

USUAL RESIDENCE

20. RESIDENCE—STREET AND NUMBER OR LOCATION 16074 ROYAL OAK RD				
21. CITY ENCINO	22. COUNTY LOS ANGELES	23. ZIP CODE 91436	24. YRS IN COUNTY 60	25. STATE OR FOREIGN COUNTRY CA

INFORMANT

26. NAME, RELATIONSHIP JODY TROUP, SON	27. MAILING ADDRESS (STREET AND NUMBER OR RURAL ROUTE NUMBER, CITY OR TOWN, STATE, ZIP) 5120 KESTER AVE SHERMAN OAKS CA 91403

SPOUSE AND PARENT INFORMATION

28. NAME OF SURVIVING SPOUSE—FIRST –	29. MIDDLE –	30. LAST (MAIDEN NAME) –
31. NAME OF FATHER—FIRST JACK	32. MIDDLE –	33. LAST PECK	34. BIRTH STATE UNK
35. NAME OF MOTHER—FIRST JOSEPHINE	36. MIDDLE –	37. LAST (MAIDEN) TAYLOR	38. BIRTH STATE OK

DISPOSITION(S)

39. DATE MM/DD/CCYY 10/26/2000	40. PLACE OF FINAL DISPOSITION FOREST LAWN MEMORIAL PARK - 6800 FOREST LAWN DR LOS ANGELES CA 90068

FUNERAL DIRECTOR AND LOCAL REGISTRAR

41. TYPE OF DISPOSITION(S) CR/BU	42. SIGNATURE OF EMBALMER ▶ NOT EMBALMED	43. LICENSE NO.
44. NAME OF FUNERAL DIRECTOR FOREST LAWN HOLLYWOOD HILLS	45. LICENSE NO. FD 904	46. SIGNATURE OF LOCAL REGISTRAR Mark Summons	47. DATE MM/DD/CCYY 10/23/2000

PLACE OF DEATH

101. PLACE OF DEATH ENCINO TARZANA REG MED CTR	102. IF HOSPITAL, SPECIFY ONE: [X] IP ER/OP DOA	103. FACILITY OTHER THAN HOSPITAL CONV. HOSP. RES. CARE OTHER	104. COUNTY LOS ANGELES
105. STREET ADDRESS—STREET AND NUMBER OR LOCATION 16237 VENTURA BLVD			106. CITY ENCINO

CAUSE OF DEATH

107. DEATH WAS CAUSED BY: (ENTER ONLY ONE CAUSE PER LINE FOR A, B, C, AND D)		TIME INTERVAL BETWEEN ONSET AND DEATH	108. DEATH REPORTED TO CORONER
IMMEDIATE CAUSE (A)	Respiratory Arrest	mins	YES [X] NO REFERRAL NUMBER
DUE TO (B)	Chronic Obstructive Pulmonary Disease	yrs	109. BIOPSY PERFORMED [X] YES NO
DUE TO (C)			110. AUTOPSY PERFORMED YES [X] NO
DUE TO (D)			111. USED IN DETERMINING CAUSE YES [X] NO

112. OTHER SIGNIFICANT CONDITIONS CONTRIBUTING TO DEATH BUT NOT RELATED TO CAUSE GIVEN IN 107 Lung Carcinoma, Atherosclerotic Heart Disease

113. WAS OPERATION PERFORMED FOR ANY CONDITION IN ITEM 107 OR 112? IF YES, LIST TYPE OF OPERATION AND DATE. No

PHYSICIAN'S CERTIFICATION

114. I CERTIFY THAT TO THE BEST OF MY KNOWLEDGE DEATH OCCURRED AT THE HOUR, DATE AND PLACE STATED FROM THE CAUSES STATED. DECEDENT ATTENDED SINCE 09/15/2000 / DECEDENT LAST SEEN ALIVE 10/17/2000	115. SIGNATURE AND TITLE OF CERTIFIER ▶ Al Skinno	116. LICENSE NO. A49741	117. DATE MM/DD/CCYY 10/19/2000
	118. TYPE ATTENDING PHYSICIAN'S NAME, MAILING ADDRESS, ZIP L ROSEN, MD 200 MEDICAL PLAZA #120 LOS ANGELES CA 90095		

CORONER'S USE ONLY

I CERTIFY THAT IN MY OPINION DEATH OCCURRED AT THE HOUR, DATE AND PLACE STATED FROM THE CAUSES STATED. 119. MANNER OF DEATH NATURAL SUICIDE HOMICIDE ACCIDENT PENDING INVESTIGATION COULD NOT BE DETERMINED	120. INJURY AT WORK YES NO	121. INJURY DATE MM/DD/CCYY	122. HOUR	123. PLACE OF INJURY
	124. DESCRIBE HOW INJURY OCCURRED (EVENTS WHICH RESULTED IN INJURY)			
125. LOCATION (STREET AND NUMBER OR LOCATION AND CITY, ZIP)				

126. SIGNATURE OF CORONER OR DEPUTY CORONER ▶	127. DATE MM/DD/CCYY	128. TYPED NAME, TITLE OF CORONER OR DEPUTY CORONER

STATE REGISTRAR

A	B	C	D	E	F	G	H	FAX AUTH. # 273/2264	CENSUS TRACT

CERTIFICATION OF VITAL RECORD

COUNTY OF LOS ANGELES · REGISTRAR-RECORDER/COUNTY CLERK

CERTIFICATE OF DEATH

STATE OF CALIFORNIA—DEPARTMENT OF PUBLIC HEALTH

0190-056771

LOCAL REGISTRATION DISTRICT AND CERTIFICATE NUMBER

STATE FILE NUMBER		

DECEDENT PERSONAL DATA

1a. NAME OF DECEASED—FIRST NAME	1b. MIDDLE NAME	1c. LAST NAME	2a. DATE OF DEATH—MONTH, DAY, YEAR	2b. HOUR
Richard	McCord	Long	December 21, 1974	1:50 A.M.

3. SEX	4. COLOR OR RACE	5. BIRTHPLACE (STATE OR FOREIGN COUNTRY)	6. DATE OF BIRTH	7. AGE (LAST BIRTHDAY)	IF UNDER 1 YEAR	IF UNDER 24 HOURS
Male	Cauc	Illinois	December 17, 1927	47 YEARS		

8. NAME AND BIRTHPLACE OF FATHER	9. MAIDEN NAME AND BIRTHPLACE OF MOTHER
Sherman Long; Missouri	Dale McCord; Iowa

10. CITIZEN OF WHAT COUNTRY	11. SOCIAL SECURITY NUMBER	12. MARRIED, NEVER MARRIED, WIDOWED, DIVORCED (SPECIFY)	13. NAME OF SURVIVING SPOUSE (IF WIFE, ENTER MAIDEN NAME)
U.S.A.	351-14-3570	Married	Marilyn Watts

14. LAST OCCUPATION	15. NUMBER OF YEARS IN THIS OCCUPATION	16. NAME OF LAST EMPLOYING COMPANY OR FIRM (IF SELF EMPLOYED, SO STATE)	17. KIND OF INDUSTRY OR BUSINESS
Actor	30	Universal Studios	Motion Pictures & Television

PLACE OF DEATH

18a. PLACE OF DEATH—NAME OF HOSPITAL OR OTHER IN-PATIENT FACILITY	18a. STREET ADDRESS—(STREET AND NUMBER OR LOCATION)	18c. INSIDE CITY CORPORATE LIMITS (SPECIFY YES OR NO)
Medical Center of Tarzana	18321 Clark Street	Yes

18b. CITY OR TOWN	18c. COUNTY	18f. LENGTH OF STAY IN COUNTY OF DEATH	18s. LENGTH OF STAY IN CALIFORNIA
Tarzana	Los Angeles	31 YEARS	31 YEAR

USUAL RESIDENCE (IF DEATH OCCURRED IN INSTITUTION, ENTER RESIDENCE BEFORE ADMISSION)

19a. USUAL RESIDENCE—STREET ADDRESS (STREET AND NUMBER OR LOCATION)	19b. INSIDE CITY CORPORATE LIMITS (SPECIFY YES OR NO)	20. NAME AND MAILING ADDRESS OF INFORMANT
18105 Chardon Circle	Yes	Marilyn Long, 18105 Chardon Circle, Encino, California

19c. CITY OR TOWN	19d. COUNTY	19e. STATE
Encino	Los Angeles	California

PHYSICIAN'S OR CORONER'S CERTIFICATION

21. CORONER: I HEREBY CERTIFY THAT DEATH OCCURRED AT THE HOUR, DATE AND PLACE STATED ABOVE FROM THE CAUSES STATED BELOW AND THAT I HAVE HELD ON THE REMAINS OF DECEASED AS REQUIRED BY LAW	21a. PHYSICIAN: I HEREBY CERTIFY THAT DEATH OCCURRED AT THE HOUR, DATE AND PLACE STATED ABOVE FROM THE CAUSES STATED BELOW AND THAT I ATTENDED THE DECEASED	21c. PHYSICIAN OR CORONER—SIGNATURE AND DEGREE OR TITLE	21o. DATE SIGNED
(INVESTIGATION OR INQUEST)	FROM 4/25/61 TO 12/20/74 AND LAST SAW HIM ALIVE 12/20/74	Harold Long, M.D.	12/21/74
		21e. ADDRESS 6550 Ventura Blvd	21f. PHYSICIAN'S CALIFORNIA LICENSE NUMBER C-12537

FUNERAL DIRECTOR AND LOCAL REGISTRAR

22a. SPECIFY BURIAL, ENTOMBMENT OR CREMATION	22b. DATE	23. NAME OF CEMETERY OR CREMATORY	24. EMBALMER—SIGNATURE (IF BODY EMBALMED) LICENSE NUMBER
Cremation	12/23/74	Grand View Crematory	6159

25. NAME OF FUNERAL DIRECTOR (OR PERSON ACTING AS SUCH)	26. IF NOT CERTIFIED BY CORONER, WAS THIS DEATH REPORTED TO CORONER? (SPECIFY YES OR NO)	27. LOCAL REGISTRAR—SIGNATURE	28. DATE ACCEPTED FOR REGISTRATION BY LOCAL REGISTRAR
Utter-McKinley Van Nuys	No		DEC 23 1974

MEDICAL AND HEALTH DATA

CAUSE OF DEATH

29. PART I. DEATH WAS CAUSED BY: IMMEDIATE CAUSE	ENTER ONLY ONE CAUSE PER LINE FOR A, B AND C	APPROXIMATE INTERVAL BETWEEN ONSET AND DEATH
(A)	Cardiac Arrest	SEC.
CONDITIONS, IF ANY, WHICH GAVE RISE TO THE IMMEDIATE CAUSE (A), STATING THE UNDERLYING CAUSE LAST. DUE TO, OR AS A CONSEQUENCE OF (B)	Multiple Myocardial Infarctions	YRS.
DUE TO, OR AS A CONSEQUENCE OF (C)	Coronary Atherosclerosis	YRS

30. PART II. OTHER SIGNIFICANT CONDITIONS—CONTRIBUTING TO DEATH BUT NOT RELATED TO THE IMMEDIATE CAUSE GIVEN IN PART I	31. WAS OPERATION OR BIOPSY PERFORMED FOR ANY CONDITION IN ITEMS 29 OR 30? (SPECIFY OPERATION AND/OR BIOPSY)	32A. AUTOPSY (SPECIFY YES OR NO)	32B. IF YES, WERE FINDINGS CONSIDERED IN DETERMINING CAUSE OF DEATH? (SPECIFY YES OR NO)
	No	No	

INJURY INFORMATION

33. SPECIFY ACCIDENT, SUICIDE OR HOMICIDE	34. PLACE OF INJURY (SPECIFY HOME, FARM, FACTORY, OFFICE BUILDING, ETC.)	35. INJURY AT WORK (SPECIFY YES OR NO)	36A. DATE OF INJURY—MONTH, DAY, YEAR	36B. HOUR

37A. PLACE OF INJURY (STREET AND NUMBER OR LOCATION AND CITY OR TOWN)	37B. DISTANCE FROM PLACE OF INJURY TO USUAL RESIDENCE, ITEM 19 MILES	38. WERE LABORATORY TESTS DONE FOR DRUGS OR TOXIC CHEMICALS? (SPECIFY YES OR NO)	39. WERE LABORATORY TESTS DONE FOR ALCOHOL? (SPECIFY YES OR NO)

40. DESCRIBE HOW INJURY OCCURRED (ENTER SEQUENCE OF EVENTS WHICH RESULTED IN INJURY, NATURE OF INJURY SHOULD BE ENTERED IN ITEM 29)

STATE REGISTRAR

A.	B.	C.	D.	E.	F.

This is to certify that this document is a true copy of the official record filed with the Registrar-Recorder/County Clerk.

Conny B. McCormack

CONNY B. McCORMACK
Registrar-Recorder/County Clerk

OCT 3 1996

19-386514

This copy not valid unless prepared on engraved border displaying the Seal and Signature of the Registrar-Recorder/County Clerk.

ANY ALTERATION OR ERASURE VOIDS THIS CERTIFICATE

STATE OF CALIFORNIA
CERTIFICATION OF VITAL RECORD

COUNTY OF LOS ANGELES • REGISTRAR-RECORDER/COUNTY CLERK

CERTIFICATE OF DEATH
STATE OF CALIFORNIA
USE BLACK INK ONLY/NO ERASURES, WHITEOUTS OR ALTERATIONS
VS-11 (REV. 7/93)

39619003746

STATE FILE NUMBER   LOCAL REGISTRATION NUMBER

DECEDENT PERSONAL DATA

1. NAME OF DECEDENT—FIRST (GIVEN) **RITA**	2. MIDDLE **-**	3. LAST (FAMILY) **LYNN**

4. DATE OF BIRTH MM/DD/CCYY **12/02/1921**	5. AGE YRS. **74**	IF UNDER 1 YEAR / IF UNDER 24 HOURS — MONTHS / DAYS / HOURS / MINUTES	6. SEX **FEMALE**	7. DATE OF DEATH MM/DD/CCYY **01/21/1996**	8. HOUR **2300**

9. STATE OF BIRTH **LA**	10. SOCIAL SECURITY NO. **109-14-2947**	11. MILITARY SERVICE 19 __ To 19 __ [X] NONE	12. MARITAL STATUS **MARRIED**	13. EDUCATION—YEARS COMPLETED **14**

14. RACE **CAUCASIAN**	15. HISPANIC—SPECIFY [ ] YES [X] NO	16. USUAL EMPLOYER **FREE LANCE**

17. OCCUPATION **ACTRESS**	18. KIND OF BUSINESS **ENTERTAINMENT**	19. YEARS IN OCCUPATION **55**

USUAL RESIDENCE

20. RESIDENCE—STREET AND NUMBER OR LOCATION **446 SAN VICENTE BLVD. #301**				
21. CITY **SANTA MONICA**	22. COUNTY **LOS ANGELES**	23. ZIP CODE **90402**	24. YRS IN COUNTY **45**	25. STATE OR FOREIGN COUNTRY **CALIFORNIA**

INFORMANT

26. NAME, RELATIONSHIP **FRANK MAXWELL - HUSBAND**	27. MAILING ADDRESS (STREET AND NUMBER OR RURAL ROUTE NUMBER, CITY OR TOWN, STATE, ZIP) **446 SAN VICENTE BLVD. #301, SANTA MONICA, CA. 90402**

SPOUSE AND PARENT INFORMATION

28. NAME OF SURVIVING SPOUSE—FIRST **FRANK**	29. MIDDLE	30. LAST (MAIDEN NAME) **MAXWELL**	
31. NAME OF FATHER—FIRST **BENJAMIN**	32. MIDDLE **-**	33. LAST **PIAZZA**	34. BIRTH STATE **MS**
35. NAME OF MOTHER—FIRST **FRANCES**	36. MIDDLE **-**	37. LAST (MAIDEN) **CAPPELLANO**	38. BIRTH STATE **NY**

DISPOSITION(S)

39. DATE MM/DD/CCYY **01/26/1996**	40. PLACE OF FINAL DISPOSITION **HOLY CROSS CEMETERY, 5835 W. SLAUSON AVE., CULVER CITY, CA. 90230**

FUNERAL DIRECTOR AND LOCAL REGISTRAR

41. TYPE OF DISPOSITION(S) **BURIAL**	42. SIGNATURE OF EMBALMER ▸ *Kristen Dean*	43. LICENSE NO. **8265**
44. NAME OF FUNERAL DIRECTOR **PIERCE BROS. WESTWOOD VILLAGE**	45. LICENSE NO. **F-951**	46. SIGNATURE OF LOCAL REGISTRAR ▸ *Robert A. Getz*	47. DATE MM/DD/CCYY **01/25/1996**

PLACE OF DEATH

101. PLACE OF DEATH **RESIDENCE**	102. IF HOSPITAL, SPECIFY ONE: [ ] IP [ ] ER/OP [ ] DOA	103. FACILITY OTHER THAN HOSPITAL: [ ] CONV. HOSP [X] RES [ ] OTHER	104. COUNTY **LOS ANGELES**
105. STREET ADDRESS—STREET AND NUMBER OR LOCATION **446 SAN VICENTE BLVD. #301**			106. CITY **SANTA MONICA**

CAUSE OF DEATH

107. DEATH WAS CAUSED BY: (ENTER ONLY ONE CAUSE PER LINE FOR A, B, C, AND D)		TIME INTERVAL BETWEEN ONSET AND DEATH	108. DEATH REPORTED TO CORONER
IMMEDIATE CAUSE (A) **METASTATIC OVARIAN CANCER**		**2 yrs**	[ ] YES [X] NO — REFERRAL NUMBER
DUE TO (B)			109. BIOPSY PERFORMED [X] YES [ ] NO
DUE TO (C)			110. AUTOPSY PERFORMED [ ] YES [X] NO
DUE TO (D)			111. USED IN DETERMINING CAUSE [ ] YES [ ] NO

112. OTHER SIGNIFICANT CONDITIONS CONTRIBUTING TO DEATH BUT NOT RELATED TO CAUSE GIVEN IN 107 **NONE**

113. WAS OPERATION PERFORMED FOR ANY CONDITION IN ITEM 107 OR 112? IF YES, LIST TYPE OF OPERATION AND DATE. **02/02/1995 INSERTION OF PERITONEAL PORTACATH**

PHYSICIAN'S CERTIFICATION

114. I CERTIFY THAT TO THE BEST OF MY KNOWLEDGE DEATH OCCURRED AT THE HOUR, DATE AND PLACE STATED FROM THE CAUSES STATED.	115. SIGNATURE AND TITLE OF CERTIFIER ▸ *illegible*	116. LICENSE NO. **G20643**	117. DATE MM/DD/CCYY **1-23-96**
DECEDENT ATTENDED SINCE MM/DD/CCYY **03/02/1995** / DECEDENT LAST SEEN ALIVE MM/DD/CCYY **01/18/1996**	118. TYPE ATTENDING PHYSICIAN'S NAME, MAILING ADDRESS + ZIP **PETER BOASBERG, MD. 1301 20th ST. SANTA MONICA, CA. 90403**		

CORONER'S USE ONLY

119. I CERTIFY THAT IN MY OPINION DEATH OCCURRED AT THE HOUR, DATE AND PLACE STATED FROM THE CAUSES STATED. 119. MANNER OF DEATH [ ] NATURAL [ ] SUICIDE [ ] HOMICIDE [ ] ACCIDENT [ ] PENDING INVESTIGATION [ ] COULD NOT BE DETERMINED	120. INJURY AT WORK [ ] YES [ ] NO	121. INJURY DATE MM/DD/CCYY	122. HOUR	123. PLACE OF INJURY
	124. DESCRIBE HOW INJURY OCCURRED (EVENTS WHICH RESULTED IN INJURY)			

125. LOCATION (STREET AND NUMBER OR LOCATION AND CITY AND ZIP CODE)

126. SIGNATURE OF CORONER OR DEPUTY CORONER	127. DATE MM/DD/CCYY	128. TYPED NAME, TITLE OF CORONER OR DEPUTY CORONER

STATE REGISTRAR

A	B	C	D	E	F	G	H	FAX AUTH. #	CENSUS TRACT

This is to certify that this document is a true copy of the official record filed with the Registrar-Recorder/County Clerk.

Conny B. McCormack

CONNY B. McCORMACK
Registrar-Recorder/County Clerk

JUN 23 1999
19-123724

This copy not valid unless prepared on engraved border displaying the Seal and Signature of the Registrar-Recorder/County Clerk.

MIDWEST BANK NOTE COMPANY   ANY ALTERATION OR ERASURE VOIDS THIS CERTIFICATE

STATE OF CALIFORNIA
CERTIFICATION OF VITAL RECORD

COUNTY OF LOS ANGELES
DEPARTMENT OF HEALTH SERVICES

CERTIFICATE OF DEATH
STATE OF CALIFORNIA
USE BLACK INK ONLY/NO ERASURES, WHITEOUTS OR ALTERATIONS
VS-11 (REV. 1/00)

3 2000 19 029924

STATE FILE NUMBER		LOCAL REGISTRATION NUMBER

DECEDENT PERSONAL DATA

1. NAME OF DECEDENT—FIRST (GIVEN)	2. MIDDLE	3. LAST (FAMILY)
MEREDITH	MACRAE	NEAL

4. DATE OF BIRTH MM/DD/CCYY	5. AGE YRS.	IF UNDER 1 YEAR — MONTHS / DAYS	IF UNDER 24 HOURS — HOURS / MINUTES	6. SEX	7. DATE OF DEATH MM/DD/CCYY	8. HOUR
05/30/1944	56			F	07/14/2000	1142

9. STATE OF BIRTH	10. SOCIAL SECURITY NO.	11. MILITARY SERVICE	12. MARITAL STATUS	13. EDUCATION—YEARS COMPLETED
TX	567-46-1236	YES [X] NO [ ] UNK	MARRIED	16

14. RACE	15. HISPANIC—SPECIFY	16. USUAL EMPLOYER
CAUCASIAN	YES [ ] [X] NO	SELF EMPLOYED

17. OCCUPATION	18. KIND OF BUSINESS	19. YEARS IN OCCUPATION
ACTRESS	ENTERTAINMENT	30

USUAL RESIDENCE

20. RESIDENCE—(STREET AND NUMBER OR LOCATION)
518 PACIFIC AVENUE

21. CITY	22. COUNTY	23. ZIP CODE	24. YRS IN COUNTY	25. STATE OR FOREIGN COUNTRY
MANHATTAN BEACH	LOS ANGELES	90266	56	CA

INFORMANT

26. NAME, RELATIONSHIP	27. MAILING ADDRESS (STREET AND NUMBER OR RURAL ROUTE NUMBER, CITY OR TOWN, STATE, ZIP)
PHILIP MARK NEAL-HUSBAND	518 PACIFIC AVENUE MANHATTAN BEACH, CA 90266

SPOUSE AND PARENT INFORMATION

28. NAME OF SURVIVING SPOUSE—FIRST	29. MIDDLE	30. LAST (MAIDEN NAME)
PHILIP	MARK	NEAL

31. NAME OF FATHER—FIRST	32. MIDDLE	33. LAST	34. BIRTH STATE
GORDON	–	MACREA	NJ

35. NAME OF MOTHER—FIRST	36. MIDDLE	37. LAST (MAIDEN)	38. BIRTH STATE
SHEILA	–	STEPHENS	ENGLAND

DISPOSITION(S)

39. DATE MM/DD/CCYY	40. PLACE OF FINAL DISPOSITION
07/18/2000	AT SEA OFF THE COAST OF LOS ANGELES COUNTY

FUNERAL DIRECTOR AND LOCAL REGISTRAR

41. TYPE OF DISPOSITION(S)	42. SIGNATURE OF EMBALMER	43. LICENSE NO.
CR/SEA	▶ NOT EMBALMED	–

44. NAME OF FUNERAL DIRECTOR	45. LICENSE NO.	46. SIGNATURE OF LOCAL REGISTRAR	47. DATE MM/DD/CCYY
NEPTUNE SOCIETY-BURBANK	FD-1359	▶	07/17/2000

PLACE OF DEATH

101. PLACE OF DEATH	102. IF HOSPITAL, SPECIFY ONE:	103. FACILITY OTHER THAN HOSPITAL:	104. COUNTY
RESIDENCE	IP [ ] ER/OP [ ] DOA [ ]	CONV. HOSP. [ ] RES. CARE [ ] OTHER [ ]	LOS ANGELES

105. STREET ADDRESS—(STREET AND NUMBER OR LOCATION)	106. CITY
518 PACIFIC AVENUE	MANHATTAN BEACH

CAUSE OF DEATH

107. DEATH WAS CAUSED BY: (ENTER ONLY ONE CAUSE PER LINE FOR A, B, C, AND D)	TIME INTERVAL BETWEEN ONSET AND DEATH	108. DEATH REPORTED TO CORONER
IMMEDIATE CAUSE (A) GLIOBLASTOMA	19 MOS	YES [ ] [X] NO
DUE TO (B)		109. BIOPSY PERFORMED [X] YES [ ] NO
DUE TO (C)		110. AUTOPSY PERFORMED [ ] YES [X] NO
DUE TO (D)		111. USED IN DETERMINING CAUSE [ ] YES [X] NO

112. OTHER SIGNIFICANT CONDITIONS CONTRIBUTING TO DEATH BUT NOT RELATED TO CAUSE GIVEN IN 107
NONE

113. WAS OPERATION PERFORMED FOR ANY CONDITION IN ITEM 107 OR 112? IF YES, LIST TYPE OF OPERATION AND DATE.
YES CRANIOTOMY 01/29/1999

PHYSICIAN'S CERTIFICATION

114. I CERTIFY THAT TO THE BEST OF MY KNOWLEDGE DEATH OCCURRED AT THE HOUR, DATE AND PLACE STATED FROM THE CAUSES STATED. DECEDENT ATTENDED SINCE / DECEDENT LAST SEEN ALIVE MM/DD/CCYY	115. SIGNATURE AND TITLE OF CERTIFIER	116. LICENSE NO.	117. DATE MM/DD/CCYY
10/27/1999 / 06/30/2000	▶ Philomena F. McAndrew MD	G47403	07/17/2000

118. TYPE ATTENDING PHYSICIAN'S NAME, MAILING ADDRESS, ZIP
PHILOMENA F. MCANDREW MD 8635 W. THIRD ST. #665 W LOS ANGELES, CA 90048

CORONER'S USE ONLY

119. I CERTIFY THAT IN MY OPINION DEATH OCCURRED AT THE HOUR, DATE AND PLACE STATED FROM THE CAUSES STATED. 119. MANNER OF DEATH	120. INJURY AT WORK	121. INJURY DATE MM/DD/CCYY	122. HOUR	123. PLACE OF INJURY
NATURAL [ ] SUICIDE [ ] HOMICIDE [ ] ACCIDENT [ ] PENDING INVESTIGATION [ ] COULD NOT BE DETERMINED [ ]	YES [ ] NO [ ]			

124. DESCRIBE HOW INJURY OCCURRED (EVENTS WHICH RESULTED IN INJURY)

125. LOCATION (STREET AND NUMBER OR LOCATION AND CITY, ZIP)

126. SIGNATURE OF CORONER OR DEPUTY CORONER	127. DATE MM/DD/CCYY	128. TYPED NAME, TITLE OF CORONER OR DEPUTY CORONER
▶		

STATE REGISTRAR

A	B	C	D	E	F	G	H	FAX AUTH. #	CENSUS TRACT
								273/24415	090362188

This is a true certified copy of the record filed in the County of Los Angeles Department of Health Services if it bears the Registrar's signature in purple ink.

DATE ISSUED

Director of Health Services and Registrar

This copy not valid unless prepared on engraved border displaying seal and signature of Registrar.

ANY ALTERATION OR ERASURE VOIDS THIS CERTIFICATE

STATE OF CALIFORNIA
CERTIFICATION OF VITAL RECORD

COUNTY OF LOS ANGELES
DEPARTMENT OF HEALTH SERVICES

AFFIDAVIT TO AMEND A RECORD   3 200019029924

STATE FILE NUMBER

DEATHS AFTER 1-1994
NO ERASURES, WHITEOUTS, OR ALTERATIONS

LOCAL REGISTRATION DISTRICT AND CERTIFICATE NUMBER

STATE/LOCAL REGISTRAR USE ONLY	1.	2.	3.

PART I   INFORMATION TO LOCATE RECORD—TYPE OR PRINT IN BLACK INK ONLY

NAME AS IT APPEARS ON RECORD	1. NAME—FIRST (GIVEN) MEREDITH	2. MIDDLE MACRAE	3. LAST (FAMILY) NEAL

ADDITIONAL INFORMATION TO LOCATE RECORD	4. SEX F	5. DATE OF EVENT—MM/DD/CCYY 07/14/2000	6. CITY OF OCCURRENCE MANHATTAN BEACH	7. COUNTY OF OCCURRENCE LOS ANGELES

8. FATHER'S NAME AS STATED ON ORIGINAL GORDON - MACREA	9. MOTHER'S NAME AS STATED ON ORIGINAL SHEILA - STEPHENS 2OF2

PART II   STATEMENT OF CORRECTIONS—NO ERASURES, WHITEOUTS, OR ALTERATIONS

LIST ONE ITEM PER LINE	10. CERTIFICATE ITEM NUMBER	11. INFORMATION AS IT APPEARS ON ORIGINAL RECORD	12. INFORMATION AS IT SHOULD APPEAR
	33	MACREA	MACRAE

REASON FOR CORRECTION	13. TO CORRECT TYPING ERROR OF SPELLING

AFFIDAVITS AND SIGNATURES

We, the undersigned, hereby certify under penalty of perjury that we have personal knowledge of the above facts and that the information given above is true and correct.

TWO PERSONS MUST SIGN THIS FORM

USE BLACK INK ONLY

14. SIGNATURE OF FIRST PERSON *John A. Haughlin*	15. TITLE/RELATIONSHIP TO PERSON IN PART I FUNERAL DIRECTOR	16. DATE SIGNED—MM/DD/CCYY 07/19/2000
17. AGE ADULT	18. ADDRESS (STREET, CITY, STATE, ZIP) 1721 W MAGNOLIA BLVD. BURBANK, CA 91506	
19. SIGNATURE OF SECOND PERSON *Kim Ferreira*	20. TITLE/RELATIONSHIP TO PERSON IN PART I MORTUARY COUNSELOR	21. DATE SIGNED—MM/DD/CCYY 07/19/2000
22. AGE ADULT	23. ADDRESS (STREET, CITY, STATE, ZIP) 1721 W MAGNOLIA BLVD. BURBANK, CA 91506	

STATE/LOCAL REGISTRAR USE ONLY	24. SIGNATURE OF STATE OR LOCAL REGISTRAR *Mark Sum*	25. DATE ACCEPTED FOR REGISTRATION—MM/DD CCYY 07/27/2000

STATE OF CALIFORNIA DEPARTMENT OF HEALTH SERVICES, OFFICE OF STATE REGISTRAR   VS 24(I) (Rev. 1/95)

nqn362189

This is a true certified copy of the record filed in the County of Los Angeles Department of Health Services if it bears the Registrar's signature in purple ink.

DATE ISSUED

Director of Health Services and Registrar

This copy not valid unless prepared on engraved border displaying seal and signature of Registrar.

ANY ALTERATION OR ERASURE VOIDS THIS CERTIFICATE

VS-4 REV. 9/95
STATE OF CONNECTICUT
DEPARTMENT OF PUBLIC HEALTH

CERTIFICATE OF DEATH

106 2000013188

DECEASED NAME FIRST NANCY M. MIDDLE SPARER LAST
1 AKA NANCY MARCHAND 2 SEX F | STATE FILE NUMBER | DATE OF DEATH (Month, Day, Year) 06-18-00

DATE OF BIRTH (Month, Day, Year) 4 JUNE 19, 1928 | AGE-Last Birthday 5 71 | UNDER 1 YEAR Mos. Days a. | UNDER 1 DAY Hours Mins. b. | RACE-White, Black, American Indian, Other (Specify) 6 WHITE | OF HISPANIC ORIGIN? (If Yes, specify Cuban, Mexican, Puerto Rican, Other) 7 ☐ Y ☒ N

COUNTY OF DEATH 8 FAIRFIELD | TOWN OF DEATH 9 STRATFORD | PLACE OF DEATH (Check one) ☐ ER/outpatient Hospital: 10 ☐ DOA ☐ Inpatient | OTHER ☐ Nursing Home ☒ Residence 1 Pauline St ☐ Other

CITY & STATE OF BIRTH (Country if not U.S.) 11 BUFFALO, N.Y. | CITIZEN OF 12 U.S.A. | 13 ☐ MARRIED ☐ NEVER MARRIED ☒ WIDOWED ☐ DIVORCED ☐ LEGALLY SEPARATED | LAST SPOUSE (If wife, give maiden name) PAUL I. SPARER

SOCIAL SECURITY NUMBER 15 | USUAL OCCUPATION (Give kind of work done during most working life, even if retired) 16 ACTRESS | KIND OF BUSINESS OR INDUSTRY 17

RESIDENCE STATE 18 CONNECTICUT | COUNTY 19 FAIRFIELD | TOWN 20 STRATFORD | NUMBER AND STREET 21 1 PAULINE ST

WAS DECEASED A VETERAN IF YES GIVE WAR 22 ☐ YES ☒ NO | BRANCH OF SERVICE 23 | EDUCATION (Specify highest grade completed): Primary/Secondary: 24 12 College: 0-12 1-4 5+

FATHER - NAME FIRST RAYMOND MIDDLE LOUIS LAST MARCHAND 25 | MOTHER FIRST MARJORIE 26 MIDDLE FREEMAN MAIDEN

INFORMANT - NAME 27 KATHRYN BOWE | MAILING ADDRESS 28 31 PINE ST. STRATFORD CT 06615 | RELATIONSHIP TO DECEASED 29 DAUGHTER

PART 1. DEATH WAS CAUSED BY (ENTER ONLY ONE CAUSE PER LINE FOR (a), (b) AND (c))

30 IMMEDIATE CAUSE | APPROXIMATE INTERVAL BETWEEN ONSET AND DEATH

CONDITIONS, IF ANY WHICH GAVE RISE TO IMMEDIATE CAUSE (a) STATING THE UNDERLYING CAUSE LAST. (a) LUNG CANCER | years
DUE TO, OR AS A CONSEQUENCE OF: (b)
DUE TO, OR AS A CONSEQUENCE OF: (c)

PART II. OTHER SIGNIFICANT CONDITIONS: CONDITIONS CONTRIBUTING TO DEATH BUT NOT RELATED TO CAUSE 31 | AUTOPSY 32 ☐ Y ☒ N | IF YES, Were findings considered in determining cause of death. 33

NURSE PRONOUNCEMENT TYPE OR PRINT NAME 34 Helen M. Seferi RN | DEGREE | SIGNATURE Helen M Seferi | DATE AND TIME PRONOUNCED MONTH DAY YEAR 35 6 18 00 TIME 11:50 ☐ A.M. ☒ P.M.

CERTIFICATION - PHYSICIAN I attended the deceased from 37 06-17-00 | To 06-18-00 | AND LAST SAW HIM/HER ALIVE ON 38 06-17-00 | DEATH OCCURRED On the date, and to the best of my knowledge, due to the cause(s) stated. (Time) 39 11:50p M.

WAS CASE REFERRED TO MEDICAL EXAMINER 40 ☒ YES | SURGERY RELEVANT TO CONDITION REPORTED IN ITEM 30 (Name of Operation) 41 | (Date Performed) 42 | THE DECEDENT WAS PRONOUNCED DEAD: 43 Month 6 Day 18 Year 00 Time 11:50 P.M.

CERTIFIER - NAME (type or print) 44 Dr. Jerry Malefatto | SIGNATURE 45 Jerry P. Malefatto | DEGREE OR TITLE MD

MAILING - CERTIFIER 46 STREET OR R.F.D. NO. 15 Corporate Drive | CITY OR TOWN Trumbull, Ct | STATE ZIP 06611 | DATE SIGNED (Month, Day, Year) 47 6-19-00

BURIAL, CREMATION, REMOVAL (Specify) 48 CREMATION | CEMETERY OR CREMATORY - NAME 49 LAKEVIEW | LOCATION CITY OR TOWN 50 BRIDGEPORT CT | STATE

DATE (MONTH, DAY, YEAR) 51 JUNE 21, 2000 | FUNERAL HOME - NAME AND ADDRESS (STREET OR R.F.D. NO., CITY OR TOWN, STATE, ZIP) 52 W.B. McDONALD 2591 MAIN ST STRATFORD, CT 06615

FUNERAL DIRECTOR OR EMBALMER SIGNATURE Bernard E. Koitsch | NAME OF EMBALMER IF BODY WAS EMBALMED | LICENSE NUMBER 55 1876

THIS CERTIFICATE RECEIVED FOR RECORD ON 6-19-2000 BY | REGISTRAR Anne De Folkenville

(left margin, rotated) RECEIVED FOR RECORD. ATTEST: Patricia P. Wimpel REGISTRAR, TOWN OF USUAL RESIDENCE WHERE DECEASED LIVED. IF DEATH OCCURRED IN INSTITUTION, GIVE RESIDENCE BEFORE ADMISSION.

(left margin) NT INSTRUCTIONS CAREFULLY
LEGIBLY with a Black Record Ink.
COMPLETED, this uld be sent to the vital statistics in the death occurred.
AREA: to be com-hysician.
DED AREA: to be by Funeral Director.

THE SEAL OF THE STATE OF CONNECTICUT IS AFFIXED TO CERTIFY THAT THE ABOVE IS A TRUE COPY OF A RECORD FILED WITH THE STATE OF CONNECTICUT DEPARTMENT OF PUBLIC HEALTH PURSUANT TO THE PROVISIONS OF THE GENERAL STATUTES OF CONNECTICUT.

Suzanne Speers

Suzanne Speers, R.H.I.A., M.P.H.
Registrar of Vital Records

JAN 30 2002
Date of Issue

STATE OF CALIFORNIA
CERTIFICATION OF VITAL RECORD

COUNTY OF MONTEREY
Salinas, California
CERTIFIED COPY OF VITAL RECORDS

CERTIFICATE OF DEATH
STATE OF CALIFORNIA
USE BLACK INK ONLY — NO ERASURES WHITEOUTS OR ALTERATIONS
VS-11 (REV. 1/00)

3200027 000621

STATE FILE NUMBER	LOCAL REGISTRATION NUMBER

1. NAME OF DECEDENT—FIRST (GIVEN)	2. MIDDLE	3. LAST (FAMILY)
Helen	Dorothy	Martin

4. DATE OF BIRTH MM/DD/CCYY	5. AGE YRS	IF UNDER 1 YEAR MONTHS DAYS	IF UNDER 24 HOURS HOURS MINUTES	6. SEX	7. DATE OF DEATH MM/DD/CCYY	8. HOUR
07/28/1911	88			F	03/25/2000	0332

9. STATE OF BIRTH	10. SOCIAL SECURITY NO.	11. MILITARY SERVICE	12. MARITAL STATUS	13. EDUCATION—YEARS COMPLETED
MO	318-10-7937	YES [X] NO UNK	Widowed	14

14. RACE	15. HISPANIC—SPECIFY	16. USUAL EMPLOYER
Black	YES___ [X] NO	Self

17. OCCUPATION	18. KIND OF BUSINESS	19. YEARS IN OCCUPATION
Actress	Entertainment	64

DECEDENT PERSONAL DATA

20. RESIDENCE—(STREET AND NUMBER OR LOCATION): 7510 Sunset Boulevard #514

USUAL RESIDENCE

21. CITY	22. COUNTY	23. ZIP CODE	24. YRS IN COUNTY	25. STATE OR FOREIGN COUNTRY
Hollywood	Los Angeles	90068	30	CA

INFORMANT

26. NAME, RELATIONSHIP	27. MAILING ADDRESS (STREET AND NUMBER OR RURAL ROUTE NUMBER, CITY OR TOWN, STATE, ZIP)
Calvin Smith (Nephew)	7510 Sunset Blvd. #514 Hollywood, CA 90068

SPOUSE AND PARENT INFORMATION

28. NAME OF SURVIVING SPOUSE—FIRST	29. MIDDLE	30. LAST (MAIDEN NAME)
-	-	-

31. NAME OF FATHER—FIRST	32. MIDDLE	33. LAST	34. BIRTH STATE
William	-	Martin	USA--Unk

35. NAME OF MOTHER—FIRST	36. MIDDLE	37. LAST (MAIDEN)	38. BIRTH STATE
Amanda	Frank	Fox	USA--Unk

DISPOSITION(S):

39. DATE MM/DD/CCYY	40. PLACE OF FINAL DISPOSITION
04/03/2000	Res: Calvin Smith 7510 Sunset Blvd. #514 Hollywood, CA

FUNERAL DIRECTOR AND LOCAL REGISTRAR

41. TYPE OF DISPOSITION(S)	42. SIGNATURE OF EMBALMER	43. LICENSE NO.
CR/Res	▶ Not Embalmed	-

44. NAME OF FUNERAL DIRECTOR	45. LICENSE NO.	46. SIGNATURE OF LOCAL REGISTRAR	47. DATE MM/DD/CCYY
Neptune Society of Central CA	FD 1322	▶ Robert J Melton MD	03/30/2000 1w

PLACE OF DEATH

101. PLACE OF DEATH	102. IF HOSPITAL, SPECIFY ONE:	103. FACILITY OTHER THAN HOSPITAL	104. COUNTY
Community Hospital Monterey Peninsula	IP [X] ER/OP DOA	CONV. HOSP. RES. CARE OTHER	Monterey

105. STREET ADDRESS—(STREET AND NUMBER OR LOCATION):	106. CITY
23625 W. R. Holman Highway	Monterey

CAUSE OF DEATH

107. DEATH WAS CAUSED BY: (ENTER ONLY ONE CAUSE PER LINE FOR A, B, C, AND D)

		TIME INTERVAL BETWEEN ONSET AND DEATH
IMMEDIATE CAUSE (A)	Cardiopulmonary Arrest	1 hour
DUE TO (B)	Atherosclerotic Cardiovascular Disease	years
DUE TO (C)		
DUE TO (D)		

108. DEATH REPORTED TO CORONER: YES [X] NO — REFERRAL NUMBER

109. BIOPSY PERFORMED: YES [X] NO

110. AUTOPSY PERFORMED: YES [X] NO

111. USED IN DETERMINING CAUSE: YES NO

112. OTHER SIGNIFICANT CONDITIONS CONTRIBUTING TO DEATH BUT NOT RELATED TO CAUSE GIVEN IN 107

113. WAS OPERATION PERFORMED FOR ANY CONDITION IN ITEM 107 OR 112? IF YES, LIST TYPE OF OPERATION AND DATE.

PHYSICIAN'S CERTIFICATION

114. I CERTIFY THAT TO THE BEST OF MY KNOWLEDGE DEATH OCCURRED AT THE HOUR, DATE AND PLACE STATED FROM THE CAUSES STATED

DECEDENT ATTENDED SINCE MM/DD/CCYY	DECEDENT LAST SEEN ALIVE MM/DD/CCYY
3/15/00	3/15/00

115. SIGNATURE AND TITLE OF CERTIFIER	116. LICENSE NO.	117. DATE MM/DD/CCYY
▶ Stephen Brabeck MD	G83279	3/28/00

118. TYPE ATTENDING PHYSICIAN'S NAME, MAILING ADDRESS, ZIP
Stephen Brabeck MD 23845 Holman Hwy. Monterey, CA 93940

CORONER'S USE ONLY

I CERTIFY THAT IN MY OPINION DEATH OCCURRED AT THE HOUR, DATE AND PLACE STATED FROM THE CAUSES STATED.

120. INJURY AT WORK	121. INJURY DATE MM/DD/CCYY	122. HOUR	123. PLACE OF INJURY
YES NO			

119. MANNER OF DEATH	124. DESCRIBE HOW INJURY OCCURRED (EVENTS WHICH RESULTED IN INJURY)
NATURAL SUICIDE HOMICIDE ACCIDENT PENDING INVESTIGATION COULD NOT BE DETERMINED	

125. LOCATION (STREET AND NUMBER OR LOCATION AND CITY ZIP)

126. SIGNATURE OF CORONER OR DEPUTY CORONER	127. DATE MM/DD/CCYY	128. TYPED NAME, TITLE OF CORONER OR DEPUTY CORONER
▶		

STATE REGISTRAR

A	B	C	D	E	F	G	H	FAX AUTH. #	CENSUS TRACT
								0454	

APR 2 0 2000

MONTEREY CO. DEPT. OF HEALTH
STATE OF CALIFORNIA
COUNTY OF MONTEREY   DATE ISSUED

By Robert J Melton

73105

This is a true and exact reproduction of the document officially registered and placed on file in the Office of the Monterey County Vital Records.

This copy is not valid unless prepared on engraved border displaying seal and signature of local Registrar.

ANY ALTERATION OR ERASURE VOIDS THIS CERTIFICATE

STATE OF CALIFORNIA
CERTIFICATION OF VITAL RECORD

COUNTY OF RIVERSIDE
RIVERSIDE, CALIFORNIA

CERTIFICATE OF DEATH
STATE OF CALIFORNIA
USE BLACK INK ONLY

LOCAL REGISTRATION DISTRICT AND CERTIFICATE NUMBER: 39033007413

STATE FILE NUMBER	1A NAME OF DECEDENT- FIRST (Given): Mary	1B MIDDLE: Virginia	1C. LAST (FAMILY): Martin Halliday

2A. DATE OF DEATH—MO. DAY, YR: November 3, 1990 2B. HOUR: 1510 3. SEX: F

4 RACE: White 5. HISPANIC—SPECIFY: YES ☐ NO ☒ 6. DATE OF BIRTH—MO. DAY, YR: Dec. 1, 1913 7. AGE IN YEARS: 77 IF UNDER 1 YEAR MONTHS DAYS IF UNDER 24 HOURS HOURS MINUTES

DECEDENT PERSONAL DATA

8 STATE OF BIRTH: TX 9. CITIZEN OF WHAT COUNTRY: U.S.A. 10A. FULL NAME OF FATHER: Preston Martin 10B. STATE OF BIRTH: TX 11A. FULL MAIDEN NAME OF MOTHER: Juanita Presley 11B. STATE OF BIRTH: TX

12 MILITARY SERVICE?: 19___ TO 19___ NONE ☒ 13. SOCIAL SECURITY NO.: 568-10-3142 14. MARITAL STATUS: Widowed 15. NAME OF SURVIVING SPOUSE (IF WIFE, ENTER MAIDEN NAME): None

16A. USUAL OCCUPATION: Actress 16B. USUAL KIND OF BUSINESS OR INDUSTRY: Motion Picture 16C. USUAL EMPLOYER: Self-Employed 16D. YEARS IN OCCUPATION: 50 17. EDUCATION—YEARS COMPLETED: 12

USUAL RESIDENCE

18A RESIDENCE—STREET AND NUMBER OR LOCATION: 82 Princeton Way 18B. CITY: Rancho Mirage 18C. ZIP CODE: 92270

18D. COUNTY: Riverside 18E. NUMBER OF YEARS IN THIS COUNTY: 10 18F. STATE OR FOREIGN COUNTRY: CA 20. NAME, RELATIONSHIP, MAILING ADDRESS AND ZIP CODE OF INFORMANT: Larry M. Hagman - Son, 23730 Malibu Colony, Malibu, CA 90265

PLACE OF DEATH

19A. PLACE OF DEATH: Residence 19B. IF HOSPITAL, SPECIFY ONE: IP, ER/OP, DOA: – 19C. COUNTY: Riverside

19D. STREET ADDRESS—STREET AND NUMBER OR LOCATION: 82 Princeton Way 19E. CITY: Rancho Mirage

TIME INTERVAL BETWEEN ONSET AND DEATH 22. WAS DEATH REPORTED TO CORONER? REFERRAL NUMBER: ☒ YES 90M1915 ☐ NO

CAUSE OF DEATH

21. DEATH WAS CAUSED BY: (ENTER ONLY ONE CAUSE PER LINE FOR A, B, AND C)

IMMEDIATE CAUSE (A) Metastatic Colon Cancer ▶ 1 Yr

23. WAS BIOPSY PERFORMED? ☐ YES ☒ NO

DUE TO (B) Adenocarcinoma of Colon ▶ 18 Mos

24A. WAS AUTOPSY PERFORMED? ☐ YES ☒ NO

DUE TO (C) ▶

24B. WAS IT USED IN DETERMINING CAUSE OF DEATH? ☐ YES ☐ NO

25 OTHER SIGNIFICANT CONDITIONS CONTRIBUTING TO DEATH BUT NOT RELATED TO CAUSE GIVEN IN 21: Pneumonia 26. WAS OPERATION PERFORMED FOR ANY CONDITION IN ITEM 21 OR 25? IF YES, LIST TYPE OF OPERATION AND DATE.: Hemicolectomy - 1989

PHYSICIAN'S CERTIFICATION

I CERTIFY THAT TO THE BEST OF MY KNOWLEDGE DEATH OCCURRED AT THE HOUR, DATE AND PLACE STATED FROM THE CAUSES STATED.

27A. DECEDENT ATTENDED SINCE MONTH, DAY, YEAR: 2/15/90 DECEDENT LAST SEEN ALIVE MONTH, DAY, YEAR: 10/31/90

27B. SIGNATURE AND DEGREE OR TITLE OF CERTIFIER: Lawrence Cone, MD 27C. CERTIFIER'S LICENSE NUMBER: A24592 27D. DATE SIGNED: 11/5/90

27E. TYPE ATTENDING PHYSICIAN'S NAME AND ADDRESS: Lawrence A. Cone, M.D., 39000 Bob Hope Drive, P-308, Rancho Mirage, CA 92270

CORONER'S USE ONLY

I CERTIFY THAT IN MY OPINION DEATH OCCURRED AT THE HOUR, DATE AND PLACE STATED FROM THE CAUSES STATED.

28A. SIGNATURE AND TITLE OF CORONER OR DEPUTY CORONER 28B. DATE SIGNED

29. MANNER OF DEATH—specify one: natural, accident, suicide, homicide, pending investigation or could not be determined 30A. PLACE OF INJURY 30B. INJURY AT WORK ☐ YES ☐ NO 30C. DATE OF INJURY MONTH, DAY, YEAR 31. HOUR

32. LOCATION (STREET AND NUMBER OR LOCATION AND CITY) 33. DESCRIBE HOW INJURY OCCURRED (EVENTS WHICH RESULTED IN INJURY)

FUNERAL DIRECTOR AND LOCAL REGISTRAR

34A DISPOSITION(S): Cr/Res 34B. PLACE OF FINAL DISPOSITION—NAME AND ADDRESS: Residence, 23730 Malibu Colony, Malibu, CA 34C. DATE MO. DAY, YEAR: 11/7/90 35A. SIGNATURE OF EMBALMER: Not embalmed 35B. LICENSE NUMBER: –

36A. NAME OF FUNERAL DIRECTOR (OR PERSON ACTING AS SUCH): Wiefels & Son, Palm Springs 36B. LICENSE NO.: 836 37. SIGNATURE OF LOCAL REGISTRAR 38. REGISTRATION DATE: NOV 07 1990

STATE REGISTRAR A. B. C. D. E. CENSUS TRACT: 44902

VS-11 (REV 1-90) MAKE NO ERASURES, WHITEOUTS, OR OTHER ALTERATIONS

CERTIFICATION OF VITAL RECORD

COUNTY OF LOS ANGELES • REGISTRAR-RECORDER/COUNTY CLERK

STATE FILE NUMBER

CERTIFICATE OF DEATH
STATE OF CALIFORNIA—DEPARTMENT OF PUBLIC HEALTH

LOCAL REGISTRATION
DISTRICT AND 7013 — CERTIFICATE NUMBER — **17968**

1A. NAME OF DECEASED—FIRST NAME: LEO	1B. MIDDLE NAME: CHICO	1C. LAST NAME: MARX
2A. DATE OF DEATH—MONTH, DAY, YEAR: OCTOBER 11, 1961	2B. HOUR: 10:05 A M	

DECEDENT PERSONAL DATA

3. SEX: Male — 4. COLOR OR RACE: Caucasian — 5. BIRTHPLACE (STATE OR FOREIGN COUNTRY): New York — 6. DATE OF BIRTH: March 22, 1887 — 7. AGE (LAST BIRTHDAY): 74 YEARS

8. NAME AND BIRTHPLACE OF FATHER: Samuel Marx - Germany — 9. MAIDEN NAME AND BIRTHPLACE OF MOTHER: Minnie Shoemberg - Germany — 10. CITIZEN OF WHAT COUNTRY: U.S.A. — 11. SOCIAL SECURITY NUMBER: 564-18-0722

12. LAST OCCUPATION: Actor — 13. NUMBER OF YEARS IN THIS OCCUPATION: 60 — 14. NAME OF LAST EMPLOYING COMPANY OR FIRM: Self Employed — 15. KIND OF INDUSTRY OR BUSINESS: Entertainment

16. IF DECEASED WAS EVER IN U.S. ARMED FORCES, GIVE WAR OR DATES OF SERVICE: none — 17. SPECIFY MARRIED, NEVER MARRIED, WIDOWED, DIVORCED: Married — 18A. NAME OF PRESENT SPOUSE: Mary D. Marx — 18B. PRESENT OR LAST OCCUPATION OF SPOUSE: Housewife

PLACE OF DEATH

19A. PLACE OF DEATH—NAME OF HOSPITAL: (none) — 19B. STREET ADDRESS: 123 North Elm Drive — [X] INSIDE CITY CORPORATE LIMITS

19C. CITY OR TOWN: Beverly Hills — 19D. COUNTY: Los Angeles — 19E. LENGTH OF STAY IN COUNTY OF DEATH: 30 YEARS — 19F. LENGTH OF STAY IN CALIFORNIA: 30 YEARS

LAST USUAL RESIDENCE (WHERE DID DECEASED LIVE—IF IN INSTITUTION ENTER RESIDENCE BEFORE ADMISSION)

20A. LAST USUAL RESIDENCE—STREET ADDRESS: 123 N. Elm Dr. — 20B. IF INSIDE CITY CORPORATE LIMITS — 21A. NAME OF INFORMANT (IF OTHER THAN SPOUSE): - - - -

20C. CITY OR TOWN: Beverly Hills — 20D. COUNTY: Los Angeles — 20E. STATE: California — 21B. ADDRESS OF INFORMANT: - - - -

PHYSICIAN'S OR CORONER'S CERTIFICATION

22A. PHYSICIAN: I HEREBY CERTIFY THAT DEATH OCCURRED AT THE HOUR DATE AND PLACE STATED ABOVE, FROM THE CAUSES STATED BELOW AND THAT I ATTENDED THE DECEASED FROM 10/11/61 AND THAT I LAST SAW THE DECEASED ALIVE ON 10/11/61

22B. CORONER: I HEREBY CERTIFY THAT DEATH OCCURRED AT THE HOUR DATE AND PLACE STATED ABOVE FROM THE CAUSES STATED BELOW AND THAT I HAVE HELD

22C. PHYSICIAN OR CORONER—SIGNATURE: Frederick W Pobirs, MD — DEGREE OR TITLE

22D. ADDRESS: 240 So La Cienega Blvd Los Angeles — 22E. DATE SIGNED: 10/12/61

FUNERAL DIRECTOR AND LOCAL REGISTRAR

23. SPECIFY BURIAL, ENTOMBMENT OR CREMATION: Entombment — 24. DATE: 10-13-61 — 25. NAME OF CEMETERY OR CREMATORY: Forest Lawn Memorial-Park Mausoleum — 26. EMBALMER—SIGNATURE (IF BODY EMBALMED) LICENSE NUMBER: Joseph Jo B King 2375

27. NAME OF FUNERAL DIRECTOR (OR PERSON ACTING AS SUCH): FOREST LAWN MEMORIAL PARK ASS'N GLENDALE — 28. DATE ACCEPTED FOR REGISTRATION BY LOCAL REGISTRAR: OCT 17 — 29. LOCAL REGISTRAR—SIGNATURE: R.L... Virginia Mattley

CAUSE OF DEATH

30. CAUSE OF DEATH		APPROXIMATE INTERVAL BETWEEN ONSET AND DEATH
PART I DEATH WAS CAUSED BY IMMEDIATE CAUSE (A): Arteriosclerotic Heart Disease		10 yrs
CONDITIONS IF ANY WHICH GAVE RISE TO THE ABOVE CAUSE (A) STATING THE UNDERLYING CAUSE LAST DUE TO (B): with intractable Congestive failure		3 mos
DUE TO (C): and Nephro sclerosis & Uremia		3 mos

PART II OTHER SIGNIFICANT CONDITIONS CONTRIBUTING TO DEATH BUT NOT RELATED TO THE TERMINAL DISEASE CONDITION GIVEN IN PART I (A)

OPERATION AND AUTOPSY

31. OPERATION—CHECK ONE: [X] NO OPERATION PERFORMED — 32. DATE OF OPERATION — 33. AUTOPSY—CHECK ONE: [X] NO AUTOPSY PERFORMED

INJURY INFORMATION

34A. SPECIFY ACCIDENT, SUICIDE OR HOMICIDE — 34B. DESCRIBE HOW INJURY OCCURRED

35A. TIME OF INJURY: HOUR MONTH DAY YEAR M. — 35B. INJURY OCCURRED [ ] WHILE AT WORK [ ] NOT WHILE AT WORK — 35C. PLACE OF INJURY — 35D. CITY, TOWN, OR LOCATION — COUNTY — STATE

Rev 1 1-58 Form VS-11

Filed NOV 10 1961 RAY E. LEE, COUNTY RECORDER

This is to certify that this document is a true copy of the official record filed with the Registrar-Recorder/County Clerk.

Beatriz Valdez
BEATRIZ VALDEZ
Registrar-Recorder/County Clerk

AUG 0 1 1995
19-389814

This copy not valid unless prepared on engraved border displaying the Seal and Signature of the Registrar-Recorder/County Clerk.

ANY ALTERATION OR ERASURE VOIDS THIS CERTIFICATE

CERTIFICATION OF VITAL RECORD

COUNTY OF LOS ANGELES • REGISTRAR-RECORDER/COUNTY CLERK

CERTIFICATE OF DEATH

STATE OF CALIFORNIA—DEPARTMENT OF HEALTH
OFFICE OF THE STATE REGISTRAR OF VITAL STATISTICS

0190-036229

STATE FILE NUMBER			LOCAL REGISTRATION DISTRICT AND CERTIFICATE NUMBER

1A. NAME OF DECEASED—FIRST NAME **JULIUS**	1B. MIDDLE NAME **H.**	1C. LAST NAME **MARX**	2A. DATE OF DEATH—MONTH, DAY, YEAR **August 19, 1977** · 2B. HOUR **7:15 P.M.**

3. SEX **Male**	4. COLOR OR RACE **Cauc.**	5. BIRTHPLACE (STATE OR FOREIGN COUNTRY) **New York**	6. DATE OF BIRTH **Oct. 2, 1890**	7. AGE (LAST BIRTHDAY) **86** YEARS	IF UNDER 1 YEAR	IF UNDER 24 HOURS

DECEDENT PERSONAL DATA

8. NAME AND BIRTHPLACE OF FATHER **Samuel Marx, Alsace-Lorraine**	9. MAIDEN NAME AND BIRTHPLACE OF MOTHER **Minnie Schoenberg, Germany**

10. CITIZEN OF WHAT COUNTRY **USA**	11. SOCIAL SECURITY NUMBER **Unknown**	12. MARRIED, NEVER MARRIED, WIDOWED, DIVORCED (SPECIFY) **Divorced**	13. NAME OF SURVIVING SPOUSE (IF WIFE, ENTER MAIDEN NAME)

14. LAST OCCUPATION **Entertainer**	15. NUMBER OF YEARS THIS OCCUPATION **70**	16. NAME OF LAST EMPLOYING COMPANY OR FIRM (IF SELF EMPLOYED, SO STATE) **Self Employed**	17. KIND OF INDUSTRY OR BUSINESS **Entertainment**

PLACE OF DEATH

18A. PLACE OF DEATH—NAME OF HOSPITAL OR OTHER IN-PATIENT FACILITY **Cedars-Sinai Medical Center**	18B. STREET ADDRESS—(STREET AND NUMBER, OR LOCATION) **8720 Beverly Blvd.**	18C. INSIDE CITY CORPORATE LIMITS (SPECIFY YES OR NO) **yes**
18D. CITY OR TOWN **Los Angeles**	18E. COUNTY **Los Angeles**	18F. LENGTH OF STAY IN COUNTY OF DEATH **47** YEARS · 18G. LENGTH OF STAY IN CALIFORNIA **47** YEARS

USUAL RESIDENCE (IF DEATH OCCURRED IN INSTITUTION, ENTER RESIDENCE BEFORE ADMISSION)

19A. USUAL RESIDENCE—STREET ADDRESS (STREET AND NUMBER OR LOCATION) **1083 N. Hillcrest Rd.**	19B. INSIDE CITY CORPORATE LIMITS (SPECIFY YES OR NO) **yes**	20. NAME AND MAILING ADDRESS OF INFORMANT **Arthur J. Marx**
19C. CITY OR TOWN **Beverly Hills** · 19D. COUNTY **Los Angeles** · 19E. STATE **California**		**1244 Bel Air Rd.** **Los Angeles, California**

PHYSICIAN'S OR CORONER'S CERTIFICATION

20A. CORONER ...	21A. PHYSICIAN ... **8-19-77** FROM · **8-19-77** TO	21B. PHYSICIAN OR CORONER—SIGNATURE AND DEGREE OR TITLE *Richard Holtz* **8-19-77** · 21C. ADDRESS **8700 W. Beverly Bl., LA**	21D. DATE SIGNED **8-19-77** · 21E. PHYSICIAN'S CALIFORNIA LICENSE NUMBER **625597**

FUNERAL DIRECTOR AND LOCAL REGISTRAR

22A. SPECIFY BURIAL, ENTOMBMENT OR CREMATION **Cremation**	22B. DATE **8/22/77**	23. NAME OF CEMETERY OR CREMATORY **L.A. Oddfellows Crematory**	24. EMBALMER—SIGNATURE (IF BODY EMBALMED) / LICENSE NUMBER *Walter C. Dodder, Jr.* **45535**
25. NAME OF FUNERAL DIRECTOR (OR PERSON ACTING AS SUCH) **Groman Mortuary bb**	26. IF NOT CERTIFIED BY CORONER WAS THIS DEATH REPORTED TO CORONER (SPECIFY YES OR NO) **No**	27. LOCAL REGISTRAR—SIGNATURE *Morrison E Chamberlin*	28. DATE RECEIVED FOR REGISTRATION BY LOCAL REGISTRAR **AUG 22 1977**

CAUSE OF DEATH

29. PART I. DEATH WAS CAUSED BY:		ENTER ONLY ONE CAUSE PER LINE FOR A, B, AND C	APPROXIMATE INTERVAL BETWEEN ONSET AND DEATH
	IMMEDIATE CAUSE (A)	*Aspiration Pneumonia*	*1 hour*
CONDITIONS, IF ANY, WHICH GAVE RISE TO THE IMMEDIATE CAUSE (A), STATING THE UNDERLYING CAUSE LAST.	DUE TO, OR AS A CONSEQUENCE OF (B)	*Pseudobulbar Paralysis*	*2 wks*
	DUE TO, OR AS A CONSEQUENCE OF (C)	*Cerebrovascular Accident*	*several years*

30. PART II. OTHER SIGNIFICANT CONDITIONS—CONTRIBUTING TO DEATH BUT NOT RELATED TO THE IMMEDIATE CAUSE GIVEN IN PART I. *Congestive Heart Failure.*	31. WAS OPERATION OR BIOPSY PERFORMED FOR ANY CONDITION IN ITEMS 29 OR 30? (SPECIFY) OPERATION AND/OR BIOPSY **NO**	32A. AUTOPSY (SPECIFY YES OR NO) **NO**	32B. IF YES, WERE FINDINGS CONSIDERED IN DETERMINING CAUSE OF DEATH? (SPECIFY YES OR NO)

INJURY INFORMATION

33. SPECIFY ACCIDENT, SUICIDE OR HOMICIDE	34. PLACE OF INJURY (SPECIFY HOME, FARM, FACTORY, OFFICE BUILDING, ETC.)	35. INJURY AT WORK (SPECIFY YES OR NO)	36A. DATE OF INJURY—MONTH DAY YEAR	36B. HOUR M.
37A. PLACE OF INJURY (STREET AND NUMBER OR LOCATION AND CITY OR TOWN)		37B. DISTANCE FROM PLACE OF INJURY TO USUAL RESIDENCE IN MILES	38. WERE LABORATORY TESTS DONE FOR DRUGS OR TOXIC CHEMICALS (SPECIFY YES OR NO)	39. WERE LABORATORY TESTS DONE FOR ALCOHOL (SPECIFY YES OR NO)
40. DESCRIBE HOW INJURY OCCURRED (ENTER SEQUENCE OF EVENTS WHICH RESULTED IN INJURY. NATURE OF INJURY SHOULD BE ENTERED IN ITEM 29)				

STATE REGISTRAR — 15

A.	B.	C.	D.	E.	F. **01-9-1- 0555**

VS 11 (8-73)

This is to certify that this document is a true copy of the official record filed with the Registrar-Recorder/County Clerk.

Beatriz Valdez
BEATRIZ VALDEZ
Registrar-Recorder/County Clerk

AUG 18 1995

19-389401

CERTIFICATION OF VITAL RECORD

COUNTY OF LOS ANGELES • REGISTRAR-RECORDER/COUNTY CLERK

CERTIFICATE OF DEATH
STATE OF CALIFORNIA—DEPARTMENT OF PUBLIC HEALTH

STATE FILE NUMBER

LOCAL REGISTRATION DISTRICT AND CERTIFICATE NUMBER 7053 19411

1a. NAME OF DECEASED, FIRST NAME ARTHUR	1b MIDDLE NAME HARPO	1c. LAST NAME Marx

2a. DATE OF DEATH 9/28/64　2b. HOUR 8:35 P.M.

3. SEX MALE	4. COLOR OR RACE CAUC.	5. BIRTHPLACE NEW YORK	6. DATE OF BIRTH Nov. 23, 1888	7. AGE 75 YEARS

DECEDENT PERSONAL DATA

8. NAME AND BIRTHPLACE OF FATHER SAMUEL MARX, FRANCE	9. MAIDEN NAME AND BIRTHPLACE OF MOTHER MINNIE SCHOENBERG, GERMANY
10. CITIZEN OF WHAT COUNTRY USA	11 SOCIAL SECURITY NUMBER 564-18-0721

12. LAST OCCUPATION ENTERTAINER	13. NUMBER OF YEARS IN THIS OCCUPATION 50	14. NAME OF LAST EMPLOYING COMPANY OR FIRM SELF EMPLOYED	15. KIND OF INDUSTRY OR BUSINESS ACTOR

16. IF DECEASED WAS EVER IN U.S. ARMED FORCES No	17. SPECIFY MARRIED MARRIED	18a. NAME OF PRESENT SPOUSE SUSAN MARX	18b. PRESENT OR LAST OCCUPATION OF SPOUSE HOUSEWIFE

PLACE OF DEATH

19a. PLACE OF DEATH—NAME OF HOSPITAL MT. SINAI HOSPITAL	19b. STREET ADDRESS 8720 BEVERLY BLVD. INSIDE CITY CORPORATE LIMITS XX

19c. CITY OR TOWN LOS ANGELES	19d. COUNTY LOS ANGELES	19e. LENGTH OF STAY IN COUNTY OF DEATH 2 DAYS	19f. LENGTH OF STAY IN CALIFORNIA 23 YEARS

LAST USUAL RESIDENCE (WHERE DID DECEASED LIVE—IF IN INSTITUTION ENTER RESIDENCE BEFORE ADMISSION)

20a. LAST USUAL RESIDENCE—STREET ADDRESS 71-111 LA PAZ RD.	20b IF INSIDE CITY CORPORATE LIMITS	21a. NAME OF INFORMANT

20c. CITY OR TOWN CATHEDRAL CITY 3300	20d. COUNTY RIVERSIDE	20e. STATE CALIFORNIA	21b. ADDRESS OF INFORMANT

PHYSICIAN'S OR CORONER'S CERTIFICATION

22a. PHYSICIAN I HEREBY CERTIFY THAT DEATH OCCURRED AT THE HOUR DATE AND PLACE STATED ABOVE FROM THE CAUSES STATED BELOW AND THAT I ATTENDED THE DECEASED FROM 9/28/64 AND THAT I LAST SAW THE DECEASED ALIVE ON 9/28/64

22b. CORONER

22c. PHYSICIAN OR CORONER—SIGNATURE Lester W. Farr MD

22d. ADDRESS 9735 Wilshire Blvd.

22e. DATE SIGNED 9/28/64

FUNERAL DIRECTOR AND LOCAL REGISTRAR

23. SPECIFY BURIAL CREMATION	24. DATE SEPT. 30, 1964	25. NAME OF CEMETERY OR CREMATORY HOLLYWOOD CREMATORY

26. EMBALMER—SIGNATURE Meredith H. Secord 4619

27. NAME OF FUNERAL DIRECTOR GROMAN MORTUARY BB	28. DATE ACCEPTED FOR REGISTRATION BY LOCAL REGISTRAR SEP 30 1964

29. LOCAL REGISTRAR—SIGNATURE K. H. Sutherland M.D.

CAUSE OF DEATH

30. CAUSE OF DEATH

PART I DEATH WAS CAUSED BY

		APPROXIMATE INTERVAL BETWEEN ONSET AND DEATH
IMMEDIATE CAUSE (A)	Circulatory arrest (Ventricular asystole)	2 hrs.
CONDITIONS DUE TO (B)	Acute myocardial Infarction	2 hrs.
CAUSE LAST DUE TO (C)	Art. Sclerotic Heart Disease	15 yrs.

PART II OTHER SIGNIFICANT CONDITIONS CONTRIBUTING TO DEATH Status post resection of abdominal aortic aneurysm — 7 hrs.

OPERATION AND AUTOPSY

31. OPERATION—CHECK ONE	32. DATE OF OPERATION 9/28/64	33. AUTOPSY—CHECK ONE AUTOPSY PERFORMED GROSS FINDINGS NOT USED X

INJURY INFORMATION

34a. SPECIFY ACCIDENT, SUICIDE OR HOMICIDE

34b. DESCRIBE HOW INJURY OCCURRED

35a. TIME OF INJURY	35b. INJURY OCCURRED WHILE AT WORK / NOT WHILE AT WORK
35c. PLACE OF INJURY	35d. CITY, TOWN, OR LOCATION

Filed OCT 30 1964　RAY E. LEE, COUNTY RECORDER

This is to certify that this document is a true copy of the official record filed with the Registrar-Recorder/County Clerk.

Beatriz Valdez
BEATRIZ VALDEZ
Registrar-Recorder/County Clerk

AUG 1 0 1995

19-389282

This copy not valid unless prepared on engraved border displaying the Seal and Signature of the Registrar-Recorder/County Clerk.

CERTIFICATE OF DEATH
STATE OF CALIFORNIA

3397   **4876**

	STATE FILE NUMBER					LOCAL REGISTRATION DISTRICT AND CERTIFICATE NUMBER	

DECEDENT PERSONAL DATA

1A. NAME OF DECEDENT—FIRST	1B. MIDDLE	1C. LAST	2A. DATE OF DEATH (MONTH, DAY, YEAR)	2B. HOUR
HERBERT (AKA ZEPPO)	Z.	MARX	November 30, 1979	0010

3. SEX	4. RACE	5. ETHNICITY	6. DATE OF BIRTH	7. AGE	IF UNDER 1 YEAR MONTHS / DAYS	IF UNDER 24 HOURS HOURS / MINUTES
Male	White		February 25, 1901	78 YEARS		

8. BIRTHPLACE OF DECEDENT (STATE OR FOREIGN COUNTRY)	9. NAME AND BIRTHPLACE OF FATHER	10. BIRTH NAME AND BIRTHPLACE OF MOTHER
New York	Sam Marx – Unknown	Minnie Shoenberg – Unknown

11. CITIZEN OF WHAT COUNTRY	12. SOCIAL SECURITY NUMBER	13. MARITAL STATUS	14. NAME OF SURVIVING SPOUSE (IF WIFE, ENTER BIRTH NAME)
U.S.A.	559 12 5905 A	Divorced	None

15. PRIMARY OCCUPATION	16. NUMBER OF YEARS THIS OCCUPATION	17. EMPLOYER (IF SELF-EMPLOYED, SO STATE)	18. KIND OF INDUSTRY OR BUSINESS
Comedian	50	Self Employed	Entertainment

USUAL RESIDENCE

19A. USUAL RESIDENCE—STREET ADDRESS (STREET AND NUMBER OR LOCATION)	19B.	19C. CITY OR TOWN
38 899 Frank Sinatra Drive	45101	Rancho Mirage

19D. COUNTY	19E. STATE	20. NAME AND ADDRESS OF INFORMANT—RELATIONSHIP
Riverside	California	Pat Welch – Friend 36 928 Pinto Palm Rancho Mirage, California

PLACE OF DEATH

21A. PLACE OF DEATH	21B. COUNTY
Eisenhower Medical Center	Riverside

21C. STREET ADDRESS (STREET AND NUMBER OR LOCATION)	21D. CITY OR TOWN
39 000 Bob Hope Drive	Rancho Mirage

CAUSE OF DEATH

22. DEATH WAS CAUSED BY: IMMEDIATE CAUSE		APPROXIMATE INTERVAL BETWEEN ONSET AND DEATH	24. WAS DEATH REPORTED TO CORONER?
(A)	Cardiopulmonary Arrest	5 min	No
CONDITIONS, IF ANY, WHICH GAVE RISE TO THE IMMEDIATE CAUSE, STATING THE UNDERLYING CAUSE LAST. (B)	Pleural Effusion	1 month	25. WAS BIOPSY PERFORMED? No
(C)	Adenocarcinoma of lung	3 months	26. WAS AUTOPSY PERFORMED? No

23. OTHER CONDITIONS CONTRIBUTING BUT NOT RELATED TO THE IMMEDIATE CAUSE OF DEATH	27. WAS OPERATION PERFORMED FOR ANY CONDITION IN ITEMS 22 OR 23? TYPE OF OPERATION / DATE
	No

PHYSICIAN'S CERTIFICATION

28A. I CERTIFY THAT DEATH OCCURRED AT THE HOUR, DATE AND PLACE STATED FROM THE CAUSES STATED.		28B. PHYSICIAN—SIGNATURE AND DEGREE OR TITLE	28C. DATE SIGNED	28D. PHYSICIAN'S LICENSE NUMBER
I ATTENDED DECEDENT SINCE (ENTER MO. DA. YR.)	I LAST SAW DECEDENT ALIVE (ENTER MO. DA. YR.)	Philip B. Dreisbach MD	11/30/79	G 19293
11/12/79	11/29/79	TYPE PHYSICIAN'S NAME AND ADDRESS: Philip B. Dreisbach M.D. 39000 Bob Hope Dr., Rancho Mirage		

INJURY INFORMATION

29. SPECIFY ACCIDENT, SUICIDE, ETC.	30. PLACE OF INJURY	31. INJURY AT WORK	32A. DATE OF INJURY—MONTH, DAY, YEAR	32B. HOUR

33. LOCATION (STREET AND NUMBER OR LOCATION AND CITY OR TOWN)	34. DESCRIBE HOW INJURY OCCURRED (EVENTS WHICH RESULTED IN INJURY)

CORONER'S USE ONLY

35A. I CERTIFY THAT DEATH OCCURRED AT THE HOUR, DATE AND PLACE STATED FROM THE CAUSES STATED. AS REQUIRED BY LAW I HAVE HELD AN (INQUEST-INVESTIGATION)	35B. CORONER—SIGNATURE AND DEGREE OR TITLE	35C. DATE SIGNED

36. DISPOSITION	37. DATE—MONTH, DAY, YEAR	38. NAME AND ADDRESS OF CEMETERY OR CREMATORY	39. EMBALMER'S LICENSE NUMBER AND SIGNATURE
Cremation	November 30, 1979	Montecito Memorial Park, San Bernardino, Ca.	NOT EMBALMED

40. NAME OF FUNERAL DIRECTOR (OR PERSON ACTING AS SUCH)	41. LOCAL REGISTRAR—SIGNATURE	42. DATE ACCEPTED BY LOCAL REGISTRAR
Wiefels & Son – Palm Springs	[signature] M.D.	DEC 3 1979

STATE REGISTRAR	A.	B.	C.	D.	E.	F.

CERTIFICATE OF DEATH
STATE OF CALIFORNIA
USE BLACK INK ONLY/NO ERASURES, WHITEOUTS OR ALTERATIONS
VS-11 (REV. 7/93)

39519005762

STATE FILE NUMBER			LOCAL REGISTRATION NUMBER

	1. NAME OF DECEDENT—FIRST (GIVEN)	2. MIDDLE	3. LAST (FAMILY)	
DECEDENT PERSONAL DATA	DOUGLAS	OSBORNE	MC CLURE	

	4. DATE OF BIRTH MM/DD/CCYY	5. AGE YRS.	IF UNDER 1 YEAR MONTHS / DAYS	IF UNDER 24 HOURS HOURS / MINUTES	6. SEX	7. DATE OF DEATH MM/DD/CCYY	8. HOUR
	05/11/1935	59			MALE	02/05/1995	1924

9. STATE OF BIRTH	10. SOCIAL SECURITY NO.	11. MILITARY SERVICE	12. MARITAL STATUS	13. EDUCATION — YEARS COMPLETED
CA	566-42-6529	19 UNK TO 19 UNK ☐ NONE	MARRIED	16

14. RACE	15. HISPANIC—SPECIFY		16. USUAL EMPLOYER
WHITE	☐ YES	X NO	SELF-EMPLOYED

17. OCCUPATION	18. KIND OF BUSINESS	19. YEARS IN OCCUPATION
ACTOR	ENTERTAINMENT	39

USUAL RESIDENCE

20. RESIDENCE—STREET AND NUMBER OR LOCATION
14936 STONESBORO PL.

21. CITY	22. COUNTY	23. ZIP CODE	24. YRS IN COUNTY	25. STATE OR FOREIGN COUNTRY
SHERMAN OAKS	LOS ANGELES	91403	59	CALIFORNIA

INFORMANT

26. NAME, RELATIONSHIP	27. MAILING ADDRESS (STREET AND NUMBER OR RURAL ROUTE NUMBER, CITY OR TOWN, STATE, ZIP)
DIANE MC CLURE - WIFE	14936 STONESBORO PL. SHERMAN OAKS, CA 91403

SPOUSE AND PARENT INFORMATION

28. NAME OF SURVIVING SPOUSE—FIRST	29. MIDDLE	30. LAST (MAIDEN NAME)	
DIANE	-	FURNBERG	

31. NAME OF FATHER—FIRST	32. MIDDLE	33. LAST	34. BIRTH STATE
DONALD	REED	MC CLURE	PA

35. NAME OF MOTHER—FIRST	36. MIDDLE	37. LAST (MAIDEN)	38. BIRTH STATE
CLARA	ELSIE	BARKER	ENGLAND

DISPOSITION(S)

39. DATE MM/DD/CCYY	40. PLACE OF FINAL DISPOSITION
02/08/1995	WOODLAWN CEMETERY 1847 14TH ST. SANTA MONICA, CA

FUNERAL DIRECTOR AND LOCAL REGISTRAR

41. TYPE OF DISPOSITION(S)	42. SIGNATURE OF EMBALMER	43. LICENSE NO.
BURIAL	▶ NOT EMBALMED	

44. NAME OF FUNERAL DIRECTOR	45. LICENSE NO.	46. SIGNATURE OF LOCAL REGISTRAR	47. DATE MM/DD/CCYY
GATES, KINGSLEY & GATES - SM	F-451	▶ Robert C. Gates	02/08/1995

PLACE OF DEATH

101. PLACE OF DEATH	102. IF HOSPITAL, SPECIFY ONE	103. FACILITY OTHER THAN HOSPITAL	104. COUNTY
RESIDENCE	☐ IP ☐ ER/OP ☐ DOA	☐ CONV. HOSP. X RES. ☐ OTHER	LOS ANGELES

105. STREET ADDRESS—STREET AND NUMBER OR LOCATION	106. CITY
14936 STONESBORO PL.	SHERMAN OAKS

CAUSE OF DEATH

107. DEATH WAS CAUSED BY: (ENTER ONLY ONE CAUSE PER LINE FOR A, B, C, AND D)		TIME INTERVAL BETWEEN ONSET AND DEATH	108. DEATH REPORTED TO CORONER
IMMEDIATE CAUSE (A)	CARDIORESPIRATORY ARREST	5 MIN	☐ YES X NO
DUE TO (B)	METASTATIC LUNG CANCER	6 MOS	REFERRAL NUMBER
DUE TO (C)			109. BIOPSY PERFORMED X YES ☐ NO
DUE TO (D)			110. AUTOPSY PERFORMED ☐ YES X NO
			111. USED IN DETERMINING CAUSE ☐ YES X NO

112. OTHER SIGNIFICANT CONDITIONS CONTRIBUTING TO DEATH BUT NOT RELATED TO CAUSE GIVEN IN 107
THROMBOTIC CEREBRAL INFARCTION

113. WAS OPERATION PERFORMED FOR ANY CONDITION IN ITEM 107 OR 112? IF YES, LIST TYPE OF OPERATION AND DATE.
BRONCHOSCOPY 08/02/1994

23

PHYSICIAN'S CERTIFICATION

114. I CERTIFY THAT TO THE BEST OF MY KNOWLEDGE DEATH OCCURRED AT THE HOUR, DATE AND PLACE STATED FROM THE CAUSES STATED.	115. SIGNATURE AND TITLE OF CERTIFIER	116. LICENSE NO.	117. DATE MM/DD/CCYY
DECEDENT ATTENDED SINCE MM/DD/CCYY: 01/18/1990 DECEDENT LAST SEEN ALIVE MM/DD/CCYY: 02/05/1995	▶ H. Lee Kagan MD	G33026	02/06/1995
	118. TYPE ATTENDING PHYSICIAN'S NAME, MAILING ADDRESS + ZIP: H. LEE KAGAN, MD. 13320 RIVERSIDE DR. SHERMAN OAKS, CA 91423		

CORONER'S USE ONLY

I CERTIFY THAT IN MY OPINION DEATH OCCURRED AT THE HOUR, DATE AND PLACE STATED FROM THE CAUSES STATED.	120. INJURY AT WORK ☐ YES ☐ NO	121. INJURY DATE MM/DD/CCYY	122. HOUR	123. PLACE OF INJURY
119. MANNER OF DEATH: ☐ NATURAL ☐ SUICIDE ☐ HOMICIDE ☐ ACCIDENT ☐ PENDING INVESTIGATION ☐ COULD NOT BE DETERMINED	124. DESCRIBE HOW INJURY OCCURRED (EVENTS WHICH RESULTED IN INJURY)			

125. LOCATION (STREET AND NUMBER OR LOCATION AND CITY AND ZIP CODE)

126. SIGNATURE OF CORONER OR DEPUTY CORONER	127. DATE MM/DD/CCYY	128. TYPED NAME, TITLE OF CORONER OR DEPUTY CORONER
▶		

STATE REGISTRAR

A	B	C	D	E	F	G	H	FAX AUTH. #	CENSUS TRACT

1629

01-9-1-7005

CERTIFICATE OF DEATH
STATE OF CALIFORNIA
USE BLACK INK ONLY/NO ERASURES, WHITEOUTS OR ALTERATIONS
VS-11 (REV. 11/96)

3 H9719037900

STATE FILE NUMBER | LOCAL REGISTRATION NUMBER

DECEDENT PERSONAL DATA

1. NAME OF DECEDENT—FIRST (GIVEN)	2. MIDDLE	3. LAST (FAMILY)
Oliver	Burgess	Meredith

4. DATE OF BIRTH MM-DD-CCYY	5. AGE YRS	IF UNDER 1 YEAR MONTHS/DAYS	IF UNDER 24 HOURS HOURS/MINUTES	6. SEX	7. DATE OF DEATH MM/DD/CCYY	8. HOUR
11/16/1907	89			M	09/09/1997	0520

9. STATE OF BIRTH	10. SOCIAL SECURITY NO	11. MILITARY SERVICE	12. MARITAL STATUS	13. EDUCATION—YEARS COMPLETED
Ohio	113-10-2478	YES / [X] NO	Married	15

14. RACE	15. HISPANIC—SPECIFY	16. USUAL EMPLOYER
Caucasian	YES___ [X] NO	Self

17. OCCUPATION	18. KIND OF BUSINESS	19. YEARS IN OCCUPATION
Actor	Entertainment	73

USUAL RESIDENCE

20. RESIDENCE—STREET AND NUMBER OR LOCATION
23736 Malibu Road

21. CITY	22. COUNTY	23. ZIP CODE	24. YRS IN COUNTY	25. STATE OR FOREIGN COUNTRY
Malibu	Los Angeles	90265	26	California

INFORMANT

26. NAME, RELATIONSHIP	27. MAILING ADDRESS (STREET AND NUMBER OR RURAL ROUTE NUMBER, CITY OR TOWN, STATE, ZIP)
Jonathan Meredith SON	23736 Malibu Road., Malibu, Ca. 90265

SPOUSE AND PARENT INFORMATION

28. NAME OF SURVIVING SPOUSE—FIRST	29. MIDDLE	30. LAST (MAIDEN NAME)
Kaja	Karlyn	Sundsten

31. NAME OF FATHER—FIRST	32. MIDDLE	33. LAST	34. BIRTH STATE
William	George	Meredith	Canada

35. NAME OF MOTHER—FIRST	36. MIDDLE	37. LAST (MAIDEN)	38. BIRTH STATE
Ida	B.	Burgess	Ohio

DISPOSITION(S)

39. DATE MM/DD/CCYY	40. PLACE OF FINAL DISPOSITION
09/15/1997	RES-Jonathan Meredith: 23736 Malibu Rd., Malibu, Ca. 90265

FUNERAL DIRECTOR AND LOCAL REGISTRAR

41. TYPE OF DISPOSITION(S)	42. SIGNATURE OF EMBALMER	43. LICENSE NO.
CR / RES	▶ Not Embalmed	-

44. NAME OF FUNERAL DIRECTOR	45. LICENSE NO.	46. SIGNATURE OF LOCAL REGISTRAR	47. DATE MM/DD/CCYY
PB Valley Oaks Mortuary	FD-1344	▶ Mark Simmon	09/12/1997 AN

PLACE OF DEATH

101. PLACE OF DEATH	102. IF HOSPITAL, SPECIFY ONE:	103. FACILITY OTHER THAN HOSPITAL	104. COUNTY
Residence	IP / ER/OP / DOA	CONV. HOSP. / RES. CARE / [X] OTHER	Los Angeles

105. STREET ADDRESS—STREET AND NUMBER OR LOCATION	106. CITY
23736 Malibu Road	Malibu

CAUSE OF DEATH

107. DEATH WAS CAUSED BY (ENTER ONLY ONE CAUSE PER LINE FOR A, B, C, AND D)	TIME INTERVAL BETWEEN ONSET AND DEATH	108. DEATH REPORTED TO CORONER
IMMEDIATE CAUSE (A) Pneumonia	3 Days	YES / [X] NO REFERRAL NUMBER
DUE TO (B) Alzheimer's Disease	2 Yrs.	109. BIOPSY PERFORMED [X] YES / NO
DUE TO (C)		110. AUTOPSY PERFORMED YES / [X] NO
DUE TO (D)		111. USED IN DETERMINING CAUSE YES / [X] NO

112. OTHER SIGNIFICANT CONDITIONS CONTRIBUTING TO DEATH BUT NOT RELATED TO CAUSE GIVEN IN 107
Malignant Melanoma, Prostate Cancer

113. WAS OPERATION PERFORMED FOR ANY CONDITION IN ITEM 107 OR 112? IF YES, LIST TYPE OF OPERATION AND DATE.
Melanoma excision & Lymphnode biopsy --/--/1993., Anterior prostectomy --/--/1992

PHYSICIAN'S CERTIFICATION

114. I CERTIFY THAT TO THE BEST OF MY KNOWLEDGE DEATH OCCURRED AT THE HOUR, DATE AND PLACE STATED FROM THE CAUSES STATED. DECEDENT ATTENDED SINCE MM/DD/CCYY / DECEDENT LAST SEEN ALIVE MM/DD/CCYY	115. SIGNATURE AND TITLE OF CERTIFIER	116. LICENSE NO.	117. DATE MM/DD/CCYY
05/13/1997 / 08/22/1997	▶ _(signature)_ MD	G45287	09/09/1997

118. TYPE ATTENDING PHYSICIAN'S NAME, MAILING ADDRESS, ZIP
Lewis Kanengiser MD., 1301 20th St., Santa Monica, Ca. 90411

CORONER'S USE ONLY

I CERTIFY THAT IN MY OPINION DEATH OCCURRED AT THE HOUR, DATE AND PLACE STATED FROM THE CAUSES STATED	120. INJURY AT WORK	121. INJURY DATE MM/DD/CCYY	122. HOUR	123. PLACE OF INJURY
119. MANNER OF DEATH	YES / NO			

119. MANNER OF DEATH: NATURAL / SUICIDE / HOMICIDE / ACCIDENT / PENDING INVESTIGATION / COULD NOT BE DETERMINED	124. DESCRIBE HOW INJURY OCCURRED (EVENTS WHICH RESULTED IN INJURY)

125. LOCATION (STREET AND NUMBER OR LOCATION AND CITY, ZIP)

126. SIGNATURE OF CORONER OR DEPUTY CORONER	127. DATE MM/DD/CCYY	128. TYPED NAME, TITLE OF CORONER OR DEPUTY CORONER
▶		

STATE REGISTRAR

A	B	C	D	E	F	G	H	FAX AUTH. #	CENSUS TRACT
								197/6097	

CERTIFICATE OF DEATH
STATE OF CALIFORNIA
USE BLACK INK ONLY | NO ERASURES, WHITEOUTS OR ALTERATIONS
VS-11 (REV 1/00)

3 200419003640

STATE FILE NUMBER   LOCAL REGISTRATION NUMBER

1 NAME OF DECEDENT — FIRST (Given)	2 MIDDLE	3 LAST (Family)
Ann	-	Miller

AKA. ALSO KNOWN AS — Include full AKA (FIRST, MIDDLE, LAST): -

4 DATE OF BIRTH mm/dd/ccyy	5 AGE Yrs	IF UNDER ONE YEAR (Months / Days)	IF UNDER 24 HOURS (Hours / Minutes)	6 SEX
04/12/1923	80			F

9 BIRTH STATE/FOREIGN COUNTRY	10 SOCIAL SECURITY NUMBER	11 EVER IN US ARMED FORCES?	12 MARITAL STATUS (at Time of Death)	7 DATE OF DEATH mm/dd/ccyy	8 HOUR (24 Hours)
TX	562-09-6351	YES / [X] NO / UNK	Divorced	01/22/2004	0050

13 EDUCATION — Highest Level/Degree (see worksheet on back)	14/15 WAS DECEDENT SPANISH/HISPANIC/LATINO? (If yes, see worksheet on back)	16 DECEDENT'S RACE — Up to 3 races may be listed (see worksheet on back)
11	YES / [X] NO	White

17 USUAL OCCUPATION — Type of work for most of life DO NOT USE RETIRED	18 KIND OF BUSINESS OR INDUSTRY (e.g., grocery store, road construction, employment agency, etc.)	19 YEARS IN OCCUPATION
Dancer/Actress	Entertainment	70

USUAL RESIDENCE

20 DECEDENT'S RESIDENCE (Street and number or location)
618 N. Alta Dr

21 CITY	22 COUNTY/PROVINCE	23 ZIP CODE	24 YEARS IN COUNTY	25 STATE/FOREIGN COUNTRY
Beverly Hills	Los Angeles	90210	60	CA

INFORMANT

26 INFORMANT'S NAME, RELATIONSHIP	27 INFORMANT'S MAILING ADDRESS (Street and number or rural route number, city or town, state, ZIP)
Ronald C Pearson - Trustee	10100 Santa Monica Blvd #2200, Los Angeles, CA 90007

SPOUSE AND PARENT INFORMATION

28 NAME OF SURVIVING SPOUSE — FIRST	29 MIDDLE	30 LAST (Maiden Name)
-		

31 NAME OF FATHER — FIRST	32 MIDDLE	33 LAST	34 BIRTH STATE
John		Collier	TX

35 NAME OF MOTHER — FIRST	36 MIDDLE	37 LAST (Maiden)	38 BIRTH STATE
Clara	-	Birdwell	TX

FUNERAL DIRECTOR/ LOCAL REGISTRAR

39 DISPOSITION DATE mm/dd/ccyy	40 PLACE OF FINAL DISPOSITION
01/28/2004	Holy Cross Cemetery, 5835 W Slauson Ave, Culver City, CA 90230

41 TYPE OF DISPOSITION(S)	42 SIGNATURE OF EMBALMER	43 LICENSE NUMBER
BU	D.S Sada	8563

44 NAME OF FUNERAL ESTABLISHMENT	45 LICENSE NUMBER	46 SIGNATURE OF LOCAL REGISTRAR	47 DATE mm/dd/ccyy
Holy Cross Mortuary	FD-1711	Thomas W Gutherie	01/23/2004

PLACE OF DEATH

101 PLACE OF DEATH	102 IF HOSPITAL, SPECIFY ONE	103 IF OTHER THAN HOSPITAL, SPECIFY ONE
Cedars Sinai Medical Center	[X] IP / ER/OP / DOA	Hospice / Nursing Home/LTC / Decedent's Home / Other

104 COUNTY	105 FACILITY ADDRESS OR LOCATION WHERE FOUND (Street and number or location)	106 CITY
Los Angeles	8700 Beverly Blvd	Los Angeles

CAUSE OF DEATH

107 CAUSE OF DEATH	Time Interval Between Onset and Death	108 DEATH REPORTED TO CORONER?
IMMEDIATE CAUSE (A) (Final disease or condition resulting in death) → Arteriosclerotic Cardiovascular Disease	(AT) Yrs	[X] YES / NO — REFERRAL NUMBER 2004-00636
Sequentially, list conditions, if any, leading to cause on Line A. Enter UNDERLYING CAUSE (disease or injury that initiated the events resulting in death) LAST (B)	(BT)	109 BIOPSY PERFORMED? YES / [X] NO
(C)	(CT)	110 AUTOPSY PERFORMED? YES / [X] NO
(D)	(DT)	111 USED IN DETERMINING CAUSE? YES / [X] NO

112 OTHER SIGNIFICANT CONDITIONS CONTRIBUTING TO DEATH BUT NOT RESULTING IN THE UNDERLYING CAUSE GIVEN IN 107
Osteoporosis, Left Femoral Fracture, Chronic Obstructive Pulmonary Disease, History of Colon Cancer

113 WAS OPERATION PERFORMED FOR ANY CONDITION IN ITEM 107 OR 112? (If yes, list type of operation and date.)	113A. IF FEMALE, PREGNANT IN LAST YEAR?
No	YES / [X] NO / UNK

PHYSICIAN'S CERTIFICATION

114 I CERTIFY THAT TO THE BEST OF MY KNOWLEDGE DEATH OCCURRED AT THE HOUR, DATE, AND PLACE STATED FROM THE CAUSES STATED	115 SIGNATURE AND TITLE OF CERTIFIER	116 LICENSE NUMBER	117 DATE mm/dd/ccyy
Decedent Attended Since (A) mm/dd/ccyy — Decedent Last Seen Alive (B) mm/dd/ccyy			
118 TYPE ATTENDING PHYSICIAN'S NAME, MAILING ADDRESS, ZIP CODE			

CORONER'S USE ONLY

119 I CERTIFY THAT IN MY OPINION DEATH OCCURRED AT THE HOUR, DATE, AND PLACE STATED FROM THE CAUSES STATED. MANNER OF DEATH	120 INJURED AT WORK?	121 INJURY DATE mm/dd/ccyy	122 HOUR (24 Hours)
Natural / [X] Accident / Homicide / Suicide / Pending Investigation / Could not be determined	YES / [X] NO / UNK	01/17/2003	1451

123 PLACE OF INJURY (e.g., home, construction site, wooded area, etc.)
Residence

124 DESCRIBE HOW INJURY OCCURRED (Events which resulted in injury)
Fell in Bathroom

125 LOCATION OF INJURY (Street and number, or location, and city, and ZIP)
618 N. Alta Dr, Beverly Hills, CA 90210

126 SIGNATURE OF CORONER / DEPUTY CORONER	127 DATE mm/dd/ccyy	128 TYPE NAME, TITLE OF CORONER / DEPUTY CORONER
Denise Bertone	01/23/2004	Denise Bertone, Deputy Coroner

STATE REGISTRAR	A	B	C	D	E	FAX AUTH. #	CENSUS TRACT

STATE OF CALIFORNIA
CERTIFICATION OF VITAL RECORD

COUNTY OF LOS ANGELES • REGISTRAR-RECORDER/COUNTY CLERK

CERTIFICATE OF DEATH
STATE OF CALIFORNIA—DEPARTMENT OF PUBLIC HEALTH

STATE FILE No

REGISTRATION DISTRICT No 7013   REGISTRAR'S NUMBER **10983**

DECEDENT PERSONAL DATA (TYPE OR PRINT NAME)	1A NAME OF DECEASED—FIRST NAME: Maria Do Carmo also known as Carmen	1B MIDDLE NAME: Miranda Da Cunha	1C LAST NAME: Sebastian Miranda	2A DATE OF DEATH—MONTH, DAY, YEAR: August 5, 1955	2B HOUR: 4:00 A

3. SEX: Female	4. COLOR OR RACE: White	5 SPECIFY MARRIED, NEVER MARRIED, WIDOWED, DIVORCED: Married	6 DATE OF BIRTH: February 9, 1915

7 AGE (LAST BIRTHDAY): 40 YEARS   IF UNDER 1 YEAR MONTHS DAYS   IF UNDER 24 HOURS HOURS MINUTES

8A USUAL OCCUPATION: Actress   8B KIND OF BUSINESS OR INDUSTRY: Movie & Television   9 BIRTHPLACE STATE OR FOREIGN COUNTRY: Portugal   10 CITIZEN OF WHAT COUNTRY: Brazil

11 NAME AND BIRTHPLACE OF FATHER: Jose Pinto Da Cunha, Portugal   12 MAIDEN NAME AND BIRTHPLACE OF MOTHER: Emilia Miranda, Portugal   13 NAME OF PRESENT SPOUSE (IF MARRIED): David A. Sebastian

14. WAS DECEASED EVER IN U.S. ARMED FORCES? SPECIFY YES, NO, UNKNOWN: No   15. SOCIAL SECURITY NUMBER: None   16 INFORMANT: David A. Sebastian

PLACE OF DEATH
17A COUNTY: Los Angeles   17B CITY OR TOWN: Beverly Hills   1-11-13   17C LENGTH OF STAY IN THIS CITY OR TOWN: 11 years

17D FULL NAME OF HOSPITAL OR INSTITUTION: (none)   17E ADDRESS: 616 North Bedford Drive

LAST USUAL RESIDENCE
18A STATE: California   18B COUNTY: Los Angeles   18C CITY OR TOWN: Beverly Hills   11-13   18D STREET OR RURAL ADDRESS: 616 North Bedford Drive

PHYSICIAN'S OR CORONER'S CERTIFICATION
19A CORONER: ...   19B PHYSICIAN: ... FROM 1440 to date to 8-5-55 ... 8-5-55 (W.L.Marxer, M.D.)

19C SIGNATURE: M.D.   19D DEGREE OR TITLE   19D ADDRESS: 133 So. Lasky Drive, Beverly Hills   19E DATE SIGNED: 8-6-55

FUNERAL DIRECTOR AND REGISTRAR
20A SPECIFY BURIAL CREMATION OR REMOVAL: Removal   20B DATE: 8-10-55   20C CEMETERY OR CREMATORY: Sao Joao Baptista, Rio de Janeiro, Brazil   21 SIGNATURE OF EMBALMER: Ronald E. Patterson   LICENSE NUMBER: 4235

22 FUNERAL DIRECTOR: Cunningham & O'Connor Hollywood   23 DATE RECEIVED BY LOCAL REGISTRAR: AUG 8 1955   24 SIGNATURE OF LOCAL REGISTRAR: Roy O. Gilbert / Mae Morris

CAUSE OF DEATH (ENTER ONLY ONE CAUSE PER LINE FOR (A), (B) AND (C))
25. DISEASE OR CONDITION DIRECTLY LEADING TO DEATH (A): Coronary Occlusion
ANTECEDENT CAUSES — DUE TO (B):
DUE TO (C):

APPROXIMATE INTERVAL BETWEEN ONSET AND DEATH

OTHER SIGNIFICANT CONDITIONS
26. CONDITIONS CONTRIBUTING TO THE DEATH BUT NOT RELATED TO THE DISEASE OR CONDITION CAUSING DEATH

27A DATE OF OPERATION   27B MAJOR FINDINGS OF OPERATION   28 AUTOPSY: [ ] YES [X] NO

DEATH DUE TO EXTERNAL VIOLENCE
29A SPECIFY ACCIDENT, SUICIDE OR HOMICIDE   29B PLACE OF INJURY   29C LOCATION CITY OR TOWN COUNTY STATE
29D TIME MONTH DAY YEAR HOUR OF INJURY   29E INJURY OCCURRED [ ] WHILE AT WORK [ ] NOT WHILE AT WORK   29F HOW DID INJURY OCCUR?

REV. 1-1-52. FORM R&S-11

12881

This is to certify that this document is a true copy of the official record filed with the Registrar-Recorder/County Clerk.

JAN 2 4 2005

Conny B. McCormack

CONNY B. McCORMACK
Registrar-Recorder/County Clerk

This copy not valid unless prepared on engraved border displaying the Seal and Signature of the Registrar-Recorder/County Clerk.

019132796

MIDWEST BANK NOTE COMPANY   ANY ALTERATION OR ERASURE VOIDS THIS CERTIFICATE

CERTIFICATE OF DEATH
STATE OF CALIFORNIA
USE BLACK INK ONLY/NO ERASURES, WHITEOUTS OR ALTERATIONS
VS-11 (REV. 11/96)

STATE FILE NUMBER | LOCAL REGISTRATION NUMBER

	1. NAME OF DECEDENT—FIRST (GIVEN)	2. MIDDLE	3. LAST (FAMILY)	
	OWEN	HARLAN	MICKEL	

4. DATE OF BIRTH MM/DD/CCYY	5. AGE YRS.	IF UNDER 1 YEAR — MONTHS / DAYS	IF UNDER 24 HOURS — HOURS / MINUTES	6. SEX	7. DATE OF DEATH MM/DD/CCYY	8. HOUR
06/21/1910	87			M	05/20/1998	1330

DECEDENT PERSONAL DATA

9. STATE OF BIRTH	10. SOCIAL SECURITY NO.	11. MILITARY SERVICE	12. MARITAL STATUS	13. EDUCATION—YEARS COMPLETED
ND	568-09-9364	☐ YES ☒ No	MARRIED	UNKNOWN

14. RACE	15. HISPANIC—SPECIFY		16. USUAL EMPLOYER
CAUCASIAN	☐ YES ___	☒ No	SELF-EMPLOYED

17. OCCUPATION	18. KIND OF BUSINESS	19. YEARS IN OCCUPATION
ACTOR	ENTERTAINMENT	72

1 OF 2

USUAL RESIDENCE

20. RESIDENCE—STREET AND NUMBER OR LOCATION
10326 MONTANA LANE

21. CITY	22. COUNTY	23. ZIP CODE	24. YRS IN COUNTY	25. STATE OR FOREIGN COUNTRY
AGUA DULCE	LOS ANGELES	91350	69	CALIFORNIA

INFORMANT

26. NAME, RELATIONSHIP	27. MAILING ADDRESS (STREET AND NUMBER OR RURAL ROUTE NUMBER, CITY OR TOWN, STATE, ZIP)
MONTIE MONTANA JR. - SON	P.O. BOX 1060 SPRINGVILLE, CA 93265

SPOUSE AND PARENT INFORMATION

28. NAME OF SURVIVING SPOUSE—FIRST	29. MIDDLE	30. LAST (MAIDEN NAME)	
MARILEE	ELIZABETH	CROCKER	

31. NAME OF FATHER—FIRST	32. MIDDLE	33. LAST	34. BIRTH STATE
EDGAR	OWEN	MICKEL	NEW YORK

35. NAME OF MOTHER—FIRST	36. MIDDLE	37. LAST (MAIDEN)	38. BIRTH STATE
MARY	EDNA	HARLAN	IOWA

DISPOSITION(S)

39. DATE MM/DD/CCYY	40. PLACE OF FINAL DISPOSITION
05/26/1998	OAKWOOD MEMORIAL PARK CHATSWORTH, CA 91311

FUNERAL DIRECTOR AND LOCAL REGISTRAR

41. TYPE OF DISPOSITION(S)	42. SIGNATURE OF EMBALMER	43. LICENSE NO.
BURIAL	▶ LL Teeters	5940

44. NAME OF FUNERAL DIRECTOR	45. LICENSE NO.	46. SIGNATURE OF LOCAL REGISTRAR	47. DATE MM/DD/CCYY
SANTA CLARITA MORTUARY	FD-1560	▶ Mark Louma	05/22/1998

PLACE OF DEATH

101. PLACE OF DEATH	102. IF HOSPITAL, SPECIFY ONE:	103. FACILITY OTHER THAN HOSPITAL:	104. COUNTY
HENRY MAYO HOSPITAL	☒ IP ☐ ER/OP ☐ DOA	☐ CONV. HOSP. ☐ RES. CARE ☐ OTHER	LOS ANGELES

105. STREET ADDRESS—STREET AND NUMBER OR LOCATION	106. CITY
23845 MC BEAN PRKY	VALENCIA

CAUSE OF DEATH

107. DEATH WAS CAUSED BY: (ENTER ONLY ONE CAUSE PER LINE FOR A, B, C, AND D)	TIME INTERVAL BETWEEN ONSET AND DEATH	
IMMEDIATE CAUSE (A) RIGHT CEREBRAL INFARCTION	12 DAYS	108. DEATH REPORTED TO CORONER ☐ YES ☒ No / REFERRAL NUMBER
DUE TO (B) CEREBRAL ARTERIOSCLEROSIS	YEARS	109. BIOPSY PERFORMED ☐ YES ☒ No
DUE TO (C)		110. AUTOPSY PERFORMED ☐ YES ☒ No
DUE TO (D)		111. USED IN DETERMINING CAUSE ☐ YES ☐ No

112. OTHER SIGNIFICANT CONDITIONS CONTRIBUTING TO DEATH BUT NOT RELATED TO CAUSE GIVEN IN 107
NONE

113. WAS OPERATION PERFORMED FOR ANY CONDITION IN ITEM 107 OR 112? IF YES, LIST TYPE OF OPERATION AND DATE.
NO

PHYSICIAN'S CERTIFICATION

114. I CERTIFY THAT TO THE BEST OF MY KNOWLEDGE DEATH OCCURRED AT THE HOUR, DATE AND PLACE STATED FROM THE CAUSES STATED.	115. SIGNATURE AND TITLE OF CERTIFIER	116. LICENSE NO.	117. DATE MM/DD/CCYY
DECEDENT ATTENDED SINCE MM/DD/CCYY: 05/20/1997 — DECEDENT LAST SEEN ALIVE MM/DD/CCYY: 05/20/1998	▶ Mysko MD	614939	05/21/1998
	118. TYPE ATTENDING PHYSICIAN'S NAME, MAILING ADDRESS, ZIP: DAVID MYSKO MD 23928 LYONS AVE. #201 NEWHALL, CA 91321		

CORONER'S USE ONLY

I CERTIFY THAT IN MY OPINION DEATH OCCURRED AT THE HOUR, DATE AND PLACE STATED FROM THE CAUSES STATED.	120. INJURY AT WORK ☐ YES ☐ No	121. INJURY DATE MM/DD/CCYY	122. HOUR	123. PLACE OF INJURY
119. MANNER OF DEATH: ☐ NATURAL ☐ SUICIDE ☐ HOMICIDE ☐ ACCIDENT ☐ PENDING INVESTIGATION ☐ COULD NOT BE DETERMINED	124. DESCRIBE HOW INJURY OCCURRED (EVENTS WHICH RESULTED IN INJURY)			

125. LOCATION (STREET AND NUMBER OR LOCATION AND CITY, ZIP)

126. SIGNATURE OF CORONER OR DEPUTY CORONER	127. DATE MM/DD/CCYY	128. TYPED NAME, TITLE OF CORONER OR DEPUTY CORONER
▶		

STATE REGISTRAR

A	B	C	D	E	F	G	H	FAX AUTH. #	CENSUS TRACT

STATE OF CALIFORNIA
CERTIFICATION OF VITAL RECORD

COUNTY OF LOS ANGELES • REGISTRAR-RECORDER/COUNTY CLERK

CERTIFICATE OF DEATH
STATE OF CALIFORNIA
USE BLACK INK ONLY/NO ERASURES, WHITEOUTS OR ALTERATIONS
VS-11 (REV. 11/06)

3 1997 19 022822
LOCAL REGISTRATION NUMBER

STATE FILE NUMBER

DECEDENT PERSONAL DATA

1. NAME OF DECEDENT—FIRST (GIVEN)	2. MIDDLE	3. LAST (FAMILY)
EDWARD	–	MULHARE

4. DATE OF BIRTH MM/DD/CCYY	5. AGE YRS.	IF UNDER 1 YEAR MONTHS DAYS	IF UNDER 24 HOURS HOURS MINUTES	6. SEX	7. DATE OF DEATH MM/DD/CCYY	8. HOUR
04/08/1923	74			M	05/24/1997	0825

9. STATE OF BIRTH	10. SOCIAL SECURITY NO.	11. MILITARY SERVICE	12. MARITAL STATUS	13. EDUCATION—YEARS COMPLETED
IRELAND	074-32-9428	☐ YES [X] NO	NEVER MARRIED	12

14. RACE	15. HISPANIC—SPECIFY	16. USUAL EMPLOYER
CAUCASIAN	☐ YES [X] NO	INDEPENDENT PRODUCTION

17. OCCUPATION	18. KIND OF BUSINESS	19. YEARS IN OCCUPATION
ACTOR	FILM	55

USUAL RESIDENCE

20. RESIDENCE—STREET AND NUMBER OR LOCATION
6045 SUNNYSLOPE AVENUE

21. CITY	22. COUNTY	23. ZIP CODE	24. YRS IN COUNTY	25. STATE OR FOREIGN COUNTRY
VAN NUYS	LOS ANGELES	91401	20	CALIFORNIA

INFORMANT

26. NAME, RELATIONSHIP	27. MAILING ADDRESS (STREET AND NUMBER OR RURAL ROUTE NUMBER, CITY OR TOWN, STATE, ZIP)
PETER THOMPSON - FRIEND	4539 FULTON AVENUE SHERMAN OAKS, CA., 91423

SPOUSE AND PARENT INFORMATION

28. NAME OF SURVIVING SPOUSE—FIRST	29. MIDDLE	30. LAST (MAIDEN NAME)
	–	

31. NAME OF FATHER—FIRST	32. MIDDLE	33. LAST	34. BIRTH STATE
JOHN	–	MULHARE	IRELAND

35. NAME OF MOTHER—FIRST	36. MIDDLE	37. LAST (MAIDEN)	38. BIRTH STATE
CATHERINE	–	KEANE	IRELAND

DISPOSITION(S)

39. DATE MM/DD/CCYY	40. PLACE OF FINAL DISPOSITION
05/28/1997	SAINT JOSEPH CEMETERY CORK, IRELAND

FUNERAL DIRECTOR AND LOCAL REGISTRAR

41. TYPE OF DISPOSITION(S)	42. SIGNATURE OF EMBALMER	43. LICENSE NO.
CR/TR/BU	▶	6095

44. NAME OF FUNERAL DIRECTOR	45. LICENSE NO.	46. SIGNATURE OF LOCAL REGISTRAR	47. DATE MM/DD/CCYY
PRAISWATER MEYER MITCHELL	FD-549	▶	05/27/1997

PLACE OF DEATH

101. PLACE OF DEATH	102. IF HOSPITAL, SPECIFY ONE	103. FACILITY OTHER THAN HOSPITAL	104. COUNTY
RESIDENCE	☐ IP ☐ ER/OP ☐ DOA	☐ CONV. HOSP. ☐ RES. CARE ☐ OTHER	LOS ANGELES

105. STREET ADDRESS—STREET AND NUMBER OR LOCATION	106. CITY
6045 SUNNYSLOPE AVENUE	VAN NUYS

CAUSE OF DEATH

107. DEATH WAS CAUSED BY: (ENTER ONLY ONE CAUSE PER LINE FOR A, B, C, AND D)	TIME INTERVAL BETWEEN ONSET AND DEATH	108. DEATH REPORTED TO CORONER
IMMEDIATE CAUSE (A) METASTATIC LUNG CANCER	4 MOS.	[X] YES ☐ NO REFERRAL NUMBER 97-053585
DUE TO (B)		109. BIOPSY PERFORMED [X] YES ☐ NO
DUE TO (C)		110. AUTOPSY PERFORMED ☐ YES [X] NO
DUE TO (D)		111. USED IN DETERMINING CAUSE ☐ YES [X] NO

112. OTHER SIGNIFICANT CONDITIONS CONTRIBUTING TO DEATH BUT NOT RELATED TO CAUSE GIVEN IN 107
NONE

113. WAS OPERATION PERFORMED FOR ANY CONDITION IN ITEM 107 OR 112? IF YES, LIST TYPE OF OPERATION AND DATE.
NO

PHYSICIAN'S CERTIFICATION

114. I CERTIFY THAT TO THE BEST OF MY KNOWLEDGE DEATH OCCURRED AT THE HOUR, DATE AND PLACE STATED FROM THE CAUSES STATED. DECEDENT ATTENDED SINCE MM/DD/CCYY	DECEDENT LAST SEEN ALIVE MM/DD/CCYY 04/22/1997	115. SIGNATURE AND TITLE OF CERTIFIER ▶ MD	116. LICENSE NO. G072790	117. DATE MM/DD/CCYY 05/27/1997

118. TYPE ATTENDING PHYSICIAN'S NAME, MAILING ADDRESS, ZIP
STEVEN H. APPLEBAUM, M.D. 2601 W. ALAMEDA ST. BURBANK, CA., 91505

CORONER'S USE ONLY

119. I CERTIFY THAT IN MY OPINION DEATH OCCURRED AT THE HOUR, DATE AND PLACE STATED FROM THE CAUSES STATED.	120. INJURY AT WORK ☐ YES ☐ NO	121. INJURY DATE MM/DD/CCYY	122. HOUR	123. PLACE OF INJURY
119. MANNER OF DEATH ☐ NATURAL ☐ SUICIDE ☐ HOMICIDE ☐ ACCIDENT ☐ PENDING INVESTIGATION ☐ COULD NOT BE DETERMINED	124. DESCRIBE HOW INJURY OCCURRED (EVENTS WHICH RESULTED IN INJURY)			

125. LOCATION (STREET AND NUMBER OR LOCATION AND CITY, ZIP)

126. SIGNATURE OF CORONER OR DEPUTY CORONER ▶	127. DATE MM/DD/CCYY	128. TYPED NAME, TITLE OF CORONER OR DEPUTY CORONER

STATE REGISTRAR

A	B	C	D	E	F	G	H	FAX AUTH. #	CENSUS TRACT

This is to certify that this document is a true copy of the official record filed with the Registrar-Recorder/County Clerk.

Conny B. McCormack

CONNY B. McCORMACK
Registrar-Recorder/County Clerk

OCT 3 0 1997

19-064101

This copy not valid unless prepared on engraved border displaying the Seal and Signature of the Registrar-Recorder/County Clerk.

American Bank Note Company — ANY ALTERATION OR ERASURE VOIDS THIS CERTIFICATE

CERTIFICATE OF DEATH
STATE OF CALIFORNIA
USE BLACK INK ONLY/NO ERASURES, WHITEOUTS OR ALTERATIONS
VS-11 (REV. 1/00)

STATE FILE NUMBER   LOCAL REGISTRATION NUMBER

1. NAME OF DECEDENT—FIRST (GIVEN) GEORGE	2. MIDDLE GARFIELD	3. LAST (FAMILY) NADER JR

4. DATE OF BIRTH MM/DD/CCYY 10/19/1921	5. AGE YRS. 80	IF UNDER 1 YEAR MONTHS / DAYS	IF UNDER 24 HOURS HOURS / MINUTES	6. SEX M	7. DATE OF DEATH MM/DD/CCYY 02/04/2002	8. HOUR 0710

DECEDENT PERSONAL DATA

9. STATE OF BIRTH CA	10. SOCIAL SECURITY NO. 569-16-8378	11. MILITARY SERVICE [X] YES [ ] NO [ ] UNK	12. MARITAL STATUS NEVER MARRIED	13. EDUCATION—YEARS COMPLETED 20

14. RACE WHITE	15. HISPANIC—SPECIFY [ ] YES _____ [X] NO	16. USUAL EMPLOYER UNIVERSAL STUDIOS

17. OCCUPATION ACTOR/WRITER	18. KIND OF BUSINESS FILM	19. YEARS IN OCCUPATION 52

USUAL RESIDENCE

20. RESIDENCE—(STREET AND NUMBER OR LOCATION) 893 CAMINO SUR

21. CITY PALM SPRINGS	22. COUNTY RIVERSIDE	23. ZIP CODE 92262	24. YRS IN COUNTY 37	25. STATE OR FOREIGN COUNTRY CA

INFORMANT

26. NAME, RELATIONSHIP WALLACE SHEFT - EXECUTOR	27. MAILING ADDRESS (STREET AND NUMBER OR RURAL ROUTE NUMBER, CITY OR TOWN, STATE, ZIP) 125 JERICHO TURNPIKE, JERICHO, NY 11753

SPOUSE AND PARENT INFORMATION

28. NAME OF SURVIVING SPOUSE—FIRST -	29. MIDDLE -	30. LAST (MAIDEN NAME) -

31. NAME OF FATHER—FIRST GEORGE	32. MIDDLE GARFIELD	33. LAST NADER SR	34. BIRTH STATE IL

35. NAME OF MOTHER—FIRST ALICE	36. MIDDLE COGAR	37. LAST (MAIDEN) SCOTT	38. BIRTH STATE KS

DISPOSITION(S)

39. DATE MM/DD/CCYY 02/07/2002	40. PLACE OF FINAL DISPOSITION AT SEA OFF THE COAST OF ORANGE COUNTY

FUNERAL DIRECTOR AND LOCAL REGISTRAR

41. TYPE OF DISPOSITION(S) CR/SEA	42. SIGNATURE OF EMBALMER ▶ NOT EMBALMED	43. LICENSE NO. -

44. NAME OF FUNERAL DIRECTOR PALM SPRINGS MORTUARY, CATHEDRAL CITY	45. LICENSE NO. FD 1513	46. SIGNATURE OF LOCAL REGISTRAR ▶ *Fred Leaf*	47. DATE MM/DD/CCYY 02/07/2002

PLACE OF DEATH

101. PLACE OF DEATH MOTION PICTURE & TV FUND HOSPITAL	102. IF HOSPITAL, SPECIFY ONE: [X] IP [ ] ER/OP [ ] DOA	103. FACILITY OTHER THAN HOSPITAL [ ] CONV. HOSP. [ ] RES. CARE [ ] OTHER	104. COUNTY LOS ANGELES

105. STREET ADDRESS—(STREET AND NUMBER OR LOCATION) 23388 MULHOLLAND DRIVE	106. CITY WOODLAND HILLS

CAUSE OF DEATH

107. DEATH WAS CAUSED BY: (ENTER ONLY ONE CAUSE PER LINE FOR A, B, C, AND D)	TIME INTERVAL BETWEEN ONSET AND DEATH	108. DEATH REPORTED TO CORONER
IMMEDIATE CAUSE (A) CARDIOPULMONARY FAILURE	10 MINUTES	[X] YES [-X-] NO REFERRAL NUMBER 2002-51136
DUE TO (B) ASPIRATION PNEUMONIA	8 HOURS	109. BIOPSY PERFORMED [ ] YES [X] NO
DUE TO (C) MULTIPLE CEREBRAL INFARCTIONS	5 YEARS	110. AUTOPSY PERFORMED [ ] YES [X] NO
DUE TO (D) ATHEROSCLEROSIS	10 YEARS	111. USED IN DETERMINING CAUSE [ ] YES [ ] NO

112. OTHER SIGNIFICANT CONDITIONS CONTRIBUTING TO DEATH BUT NOT RELATED TO CAUSE GIVEN IN 107
CHRONIC ATRIAL FIBRILLATION

113. WAS OPERATION PERFORMED FOR ANY CONDITION IN ITEM 107 OR 112? IF YES, LIST TYPE OF OPERATION AND DATE.
NO

PHYSICIAN'S CERTIFICATION

114. I CERTIFY THAT TO THE BEST OF MY KNOWLEDGE DEATH OCCURRED AT THE HOUR, DATE AND PLACE STATED FROM THE CAUSES STATED. DECEDENT ATTENDED SINCE MM/DD/CCYY 10/15/2001	DECEDENT LAST SEEN ALIVE MM/DD/CCYY 02/01/2002	115. SIGNATURE AND TITLE OF CERTIFIER ▶	116. LICENSE NO. A 39209	117. DATE MM/DD/CCYY 02/04/2002

118. TYPE ATTENDING PHYSICIAN'S NAME, MAILING ADDRESS, ZIP
SAEED HUMAYAN, MD 23388 MULHOLLAND DRIVE, WOODLAND HILLS, CA 91364

CORONER'S USE ONLY

I CERTIFY THAT IN MY OPINION DEATH OCCURRED AT THE HOUR, DATE AND PLACE STATED FROM THE CAUSES STATED.	120. INJURY AT WORK [ ] YES [ ] NO	121. INJURY DATE MM/DD/CCYY	122. HOUR	123. PLACE OF INJURY

119. MANNER OF DEATH [ ] NATURAL [ ] SUICIDE [ ] HOMICIDE [ ] ACCIDENT [ ] PENDING INVESTIGATION [ ] COULD NOT BE DETERMINED	124. DESCRIBE HOW INJURY OCCURRED (EVENTS WHICH RESULTED IN INJURY)

125. LOCATION (STREET AND NUMBER OR LOCATION AND CITY, ZIP)

126. SIGNATURE OF CORONER OR DEPUTY CORONER ▶	127. DATE MM/DD/CCYY	128. TYPED NAME, TITLE OF CORONER OR DEPUTY CORONER

STATE REGISTRAR

A	B	C	D	E	F	G	H	FAX AUTH. # 545-966	CENSUS TRACT

STATE OF CALIFORNIA
CERTIFICATION OF VITAL RECORD

COUNTY OF LOS ANGELES • REGISTRAR-RECORDER/COUNTY CLERK

CERTIFICATE OF DEATH
STATE OF CALIFORNIA

3 8 8 1 9 0 3 5 9 5 0

STATE FILE NUMBER		LOCAL REGISTRATION DISTRICT AND CERTIFICATE NUMBER

1A. NAME OF DECEDENT—FIRST	1B. MIDDLE	1C. LAST	2A. DATE OF DEATH (MONTH, DAY, YEAR)	2B. HOUR
ALAN		NAPIER	August 8, 1988	0020

DECEDENT PERSONAL DATA

3. SEX	4. RACE/ETHNICITY	5. SPANISH/HISPANIC	6. DATE OF BIRTH	7. AGE	IF UNDER 1 YEAR MONTHS / DAYS	IF UNDER 24 HOURS HOURS / MINUTES
Male	Caucasian	NO ☒	January 7, 1903	85 YEARS		

8. BIRTHPLACE OF DECEDENT (STATE OR FOREIGN COUNTRY)	9. NAME AND BIRTHPLACE OF FATHER	10. BIRTH NAME AND BIRTHPLACE OF MOTHER
England	Claude Napier-England	Millicent Kenrick-England

11A. CITIZEN OF WHAT COUNTRY	11B. IF DECEASED WAS EVER IN MILITARY GIVE DATES OF SERVICE	12. SOCIAL SECURITY NUMBER	13. MARITAL STATUS	14. NAME OF SURVIVING SPOUSE (IF WIFE, ENTER BIRTH NAME)
U.S.A.	19 n/a TO 19 n/a	549-20-2229	Widowed	

15. PRIMARY OCCUPATION	16. NUMBER OF YEARS THIS OCCUPATION	17. EMPLOYER (IF SELF-EMPLOYED, SO STATE)	18. KIND OF INDUSTRY OR BUSINESS
Actor	60	Various Studios	Motion Picture

USUAL RESIDENCE

19A. USUAL RESIDENCE—STREET ADDRESS (STREET AND NUMBER OR LOCATION)	19B.	19C. CITY OR TOWN
17919 Porto Marina Way		Pacific Palisades

19D. COUNTY	19E. STATE	20. NAME AND ADDRESS OF INFORMANT—RELATIONSHIP
Los Angeles	California	Jennifer Nichols-Daughter Millington Green East Haddan, Connecticut 06423

PLACE OF DEATH

21A. PLACE OF DEATH	21B. COUNTY	
Berkeley East Convalescent Hosp.	Los Angeles	
21C. STREET ADDRESS (STREET AND NUMBER OR LOCATION)	21D. CITY OR TOWN	
2021 Arizona Avenue	Santa Monica	

CAUSE OF DEATH

22. DEATH WAS CAUSED BY: (ENTER ONLY ONE CAUSE PER LINE FOR A, B, AND C)		24. WAS DEATH REPORTED TO CORONER?
IMMEDIATE CAUSE (A) Respiratory Failure	◀ Sudden	APPROXIMATE INTERVAL BETWEEN ONSET AND DEATH — No
CONDITIONS, IF ANY, WHICH GAVE RISE TO THE IMMEDIATE CAUSE, STATING THE UNDERLYING CAUSE LAST. DUE TO, OR AS A CONSEQUENCE OF (B) Pneumonia	◀ 1 Week	25. WAS BIOPSY PERFORMED? No
DUE TO, OR AS A CONSEQUENCE OF (C) Pulmonary Emboli due to Deep Vein Thrombosis	◀ Several Weeks	26. WAS AUTOPSY PERFORMED? No

23. OTHER SIGNIFICANT CONDITIONS—CONTRIBUTING TO DEATH BUT NOT RELATED TO CAUSE GIVEN IN 22A Cerebral Vascular Accident	27. WAS OPERATION PERFORMED FOR ANY CONDITION IN ITEMS 22 OR 23? No	23. TYPE OF OPERATION	DATE

PHYSICIAN'S CERTIFICATION

28A. I CERTIFY THAT DEATH OCCURRED AT THE HOUR, DATE AND PLACE STATED FROM THE CAUSES STATED.	28B. PHYSICIAN—SIGNATURE AND DEGREE OR TITLE	28C. DATE SIGNED	28D. PHYSICIAN'S LICENSE NUMBER
I ATTENDED DECEDENT SINCE (ENTER MO. DA. YR.) 8-23-72 / LAST SAW DECEDENT ALIVE (ENTER MO. DA. YR.) 8-7-88	*Carleton K. Little*	8-8-88	G03307
	28E. TYPE PHYSICIAN'S NAME AND ADDRESS Carleton K. Little, M.D.	984 Monument St. #101 Pacific Palisades, Calif.	

INJURY INFORMATION

29. SPECIFY ACCIDENT, SUICIDE, ETC.	30. PLACE OF INJURY	31. INJURY AT WORK	32A. DATE OF INJURY—MONTH, DAY, YEAR	32B. HOUR

33. LOCATION (STREET AND NUMBER OR LOCATION AND CITY OR TOWN)	34. DESCRIBE HOW INJURY OCCURRED (EVENTS WHICH RESULTED IN INJURY)

CORONER'S USE ONLY

35A. I CERTIFY THAT DEATH OCCURRED AT THE HOUR, DATE AND PLACE STATED FROM THE CAUSES STATED. AS REQUIRED BY LAW I HAVE HELD AN (INQUEST-INVESTIGATION)	35B. CORONER—SIGNATURE AND DEGREE OR TITLE	35C. DATE SIGNED

36. DISPOSITION	37. DATE—MONTH, DAY, YEAR	38. NAME AND ADDRESS OF CEMETERY OR CREMATORY	39. EMBALMER'S LICENSE NUMBER AND SIGNATURE
Cremation	Aug. 10, 1988	Chapel of the Pines, Los Angeles, Calif.	Not Embalmed

40A. NAME OF FUNERAL DIRECTOR (OR PERSON ACTING AS SUCH)	40B. LICENSE NO.	41. LOCAL REGISTRAR—SIGNATURE	42. DATE ACCEPTED BY LOCAL REGISTRAR
Pierce Brothers Westwood Village	F-951	*Robert Hall R.R.*	AUG 0 9 1988

STATE REGISTRAR

A.	B.	C.	D.	E.	F.

This is to certify that this document is a true copy of the official record filed with the Registrar-Recorder/County Clerk.

Conny B. McCormack

CONNY B. McCORMACK
Registrar-Recorder/County Clerk

MAY 1 3 2003

190940715

This copy not valid unless prepared on engraved border displaying the Seal and Signature of the Registrar-Recorder/County Clerk.

ANY ALTERATION OR ERASURE VOIDS THIS CERTIFICATE

CERTIFICATE OF DEATH
STATE OF CALIFORNIA
USE BLACK INK ONLY/NO ERASURES, WHITEOUTS OR ALTERATIONS
VS-11 (REV. 7/97)

STATE FILE NUMBER		LOCAL REGISTRATION NUMBER

DECEDENT PERSONAL DATA

1. NAME OF DECEDENT—FIRST (GIVEN)	2. MIDDLE	3. LAST (FAMILY)
JEANETTE	--	MC INTIRE

4. DATE OF BIRTH MM/DD/CCYY	5. AGE YRS.	IF UNDER 1 YEAR MONTHS / DAYS	IF UNDER 24 HOURS HOURS / MINUTES	6. SEX	7. DATE OF DEATH MM/DD/CCYY	8. HOUR
11/30/1911	86			Female	06/05/1998	1235

9. STATE OF BIRTH	10. SOCIAL SECURITY NO.	11. MILITARY SERVICE	12. MARITAL STATUS	13. EDUCATION—YEARS COMPLETED
California	113-10-5396	☐ YES ☒ NO ☐ UNK	Widowed	14

14. RACE	15. HISPANIC—SPECIFY	16. USUAL EMPLOYER
Caucasian	☐ YES _____ ☒ NO	Self Employed

17. OCCUPATION	18. KIND OF BUSINESS	19. YEARS IN OCCUPATION
Actress	Entertainment	65

USUAL RESIDENCE

20. RESIDENCE—(STREET AND NUMBER OR LOCATION)
1850 N. Whitley

21. CITY	22. COUNTY	23. ZIP CODE	24. YRS IN COUNTY	25. STATE OR FOREIGN COUNTRY
Hollywood	Los Angeles	90028	4	California

INFORMANT

26. NAME, RELATIONSHIP	27. MAILING ADDRESS (STREET AND NUMBER OR RURAL ROUTE NUMBER, CITY OR TOWN, STATE, ZIP)
Luke Wright - Grandson	940 Locust Ave., Charlottesville, Virginia 22901

SPOUSE AND PARENT INFORMATION

28. NAME OF SURVIVING SPOUSE—FIRST	29. MIDDLE	30. LAST (MAIDEN NAME)
-	-	-

31. NAME OF FATHER—FIRST	32. MIDDLE	33. LAST	34. BIRTH STATE
Edward	Davine	Nolan	CA

35. NAME OF MOTHER—FIRST	36. MIDDLE	37. LAST (MAIDEN)	38. BIRTH STATE
Ada	Louise	Bennett	CA

DISPOSITION(S)

39. DATE MM/DD/CCYY	40. PLACE OF FINAL DISPOSITION
06/06/1998	Eureka Cemetery, Eureka, Montana

FUNERAL DIRECTOR AND LOCAL REGISTRAR

41. TYPE OF DISPOSITION(S)	42. SIGNATURE OF EMBALMER	43. LICENSE NO.
CR/TR/BU	▶ Not Embalmed	-

44. NAME OF FUNERAL DIRECTOR	45. LICENSE NO.	46. SIGNATURE OF LOCAL REGISTRAR	47. DATE MM/DD/CCYY
M.T.S.	FD-1557	▶ _Mark Zimmerman_ KH	06/05/1998

PLACE OF DEATH

101. PLACE OF DEATH	102. IF HOSPITAL, SPECIFY ONE:	103. FACILITY OTHER THAN HOSPITAL:	104. COUNTY
Cedars Sinai Med. Center	☒ IP ☐ ER/OP ☐ DOA	☐ CONV. HOSP. ☐ RES. CARE ☐ OTHER	Los Angeles

105. STREET ADDRESS—(STREET AND NUMBER OR LOCATION)	106. CITY
8700 Beverly Blvd.	Los Angeles

CAUSE OF DEATH

107. DEATH WAS CAUSED BY: (ENTER ONLY ONE CAUSE PER LINE FOR A, B, C, AND D)		TIME INTERVAL BETWEEN ONSET AND DEATH	108. DEATH REPORTED TO CORONER
IMMEDIATE CAUSE (A)	Respiratory Failure	Minutes	☐ YES ☒ NO REFERRAL NUMBER
DUE TO (B)	Cerebrovascular Accident	Days	109. BIOPSY PERFORMED ☐ YES ☒ NO
DUE TO (C)	Acute Myocardial Infarction	Days	110. AUTOPSY PERFORMED ☐ YES ☒ NO
DUE TO (D)	Atherosclerotic Cardiovascular Disease	Years	111. USED IN DETERMINING CAUSE ☐ YES ☐ NO

112. OTHER SIGNIFICANT CONDITIONS CONTRIBUTING TO DEATH BUT NOT RELATED TO CAUSE GIVEN IN 107
Atrial Fibrillation

113. WAS OPERATION PERFORMED FOR ANY CONDITION IN ITEM 107 OR 112? IF YES, LIST TYPE OF OPERATION AND DATE.
Pacemaker Implant 02/24/1994

PHYSICIAN'S CERTIFICATION

114. I CERTIFY THAT TO THE BEST OF MY KNOWLEDGE DEATH OCCURRED AT THE HOUR, DATE AND PLACE STATED FROM THE CAUSES STATED.		115. SIGNATURE AND TITLE OF CERTIFIER	116. LICENSE NO.	117. DATE MM/DD/CCYY
DECEDENT ATTENDED SINCE MM/DD/CCYY	DECEDENT LAST SEEN ALIVE MM/DD/CCYY	▶ _Helen Ruth Judelson MD_	G035161	06/05/1998
02/11/1994	06/05/1998	118. TYPE ATTENDING PHYSICIAN'S NAME, MAILING ADDRESS, ZIP		
		D.Judelson MD, 414 N. Camden Dr, Beverly Hills, CA 90210		

CORONER'S USE ONLY

I CERTIFY THAT IN MY OPINION DEATH OCCURRED AT THE HOUR, DATE AND PLACE STATED FROM THE CAUSES STATED.	120. INJURY AT WORK ☐ YES ☐ NO	121. INJURY DATE MM/DD/CCYY	122. HOUR	123. PLACE OF INJURY
119. MANNER OF DEATH	124. DESCRIBE HOW INJURY OCCURRED (EVENTS WHICH RESULTED IN INJURY)			
☐ NATURAL ☐ SUICIDE ☐ HOMICIDE ☐ ACCIDENT ☐ PENDING INVESTIGATION ☐ COULD NOT BE DETERMINED				

125. LOCATION (STREET AND NUMBER OR LOCATION AND CITY, ZIP)

126. SIGNATURE OF CORONER OR DEPUTY CORONER	127. DATE MM/DD/CCYY	128. TYPED NAME, TITLE OF CORONER OR DEPUTY CORONER
▶		

STATE REGISTRAR

A	B	C	D	E	F	G	H	FAX AUTH. #	CENSUS TRACT
								061-5866	0901

STATE OF CALIFORNIA
CERTIFICATION OF VITAL RECORD

COUNTY OF LOS ANGELES • REGISTRAR-RECORDER/COUNTY CLERK

CERTIFICATE OF DEATH   38819030431
STATE FILE NUMBER   STATE OF CALIFORNIA   LOCAL REGISTRATION DISTRICT AND CERTIFICATE NUMBER

1A. NAME OF DECEDENT—First	1B. MIDDLE	1C. LAST	2A. DATE OF DEATH (MONTH, DAY, YEAR)	2B. HOUR
ALICE	E.	NUNN	July 1, 1988	1205

3. SEX	4. RACE/ETHNICITY	5. SPANISH/HISPANIC	6. DATE OF BIRTH	7. AGE	IF UNDER 1 YEAR	IF UNDER 24 HOURS
Female	Caucasian	NO ☒	October 10, 1927	60 YEARS	MONTHS DAYS	HOURS MINUTES

DECEDENT PERSONAL DATA

8. BIRTHPLACE OF DECEDENT (STATE OR FOREIGN COUNTRY)	9. NAME AND BIRTHPLACE OF FATHER	10. BIRTH NAME AND BIRTHPLACE OF MOTHER
Florida	N.G. Nunn-Georgia	Alice E. Bush-Florida

11A. CITIZEN OF WHAT COUNTRY	11B. IF DECEASED WAS EVER IN MILITARY GIVE DATES OF SERVICE	12. SOCIAL SECURITY NUMBER	13. MARITAL STATUS	14. NAME OF SURVIVING SPOUSE (IF WIFE, ENTER BIRTH NAME)
USA	19 n/a TO 19 n/a	267-26-3064	Never Married	

15. PRIMARY OCCUPATION	16. NUMBER OF YEARS THIS OCCUPATION	17. EMPLOYER (IF SELF-EMPLOYED, SO STATE)	18. KIND OF INDUSTRY OR BUSINESS
Actress	47	Self-Employed	Entertainment

USUAL RESIDENCE

19A. USUAL RESIDENCE—STREET ADDRESS (STREET AND NUMBER OR LOCATION)	19B.	19C. CITY OR TOWN
976 N. Larrabee		West Hollywood

19D. COUNTY	19E. STATE	20. NAME AND ADDRESS OF INFORMANT—RELATIONSHIP
Los Angeles	California	Martha Harris - Executrix 11135 Burbank Blvd. No. Hollywood, CA 91601

PLACE OF DEATH

21A. PLACE OF DEATH	21B. COUNTY	
Residence	Los Angeles	
21C. STREET ADDRESS (STREET AND NUMBER OR LOCATION)	21D. CITY OR TOWN	
976 No. Larrabee	West Hollywood	

CAUSE OF DEATH

22. DEATH WAS CAUSED BY: IMMEDIATE CAUSE	(ENTER ONLY ONE CAUSE PER LINE FOR A, B, AND C)		24. WAS DEATH REPORTED TO CORONER
CONDITIONS, IF ANY, WHICH GAVE RISE TO THE IMMEDIATE CAUSE, STATING THE UNDER-LYING CAUSE LAST.	(A) Cardiorespiratory arrest	min	No
	DUE TO, OR AS A CONSEQUENCE OF	APPROXIMATE INTERVAL BETWEEN ONSET AND DEATH	25. WAS BIOPSY PERFORMED? NO
	(B) Repeated cerebrovascular accident	Days	
	DUE TO, OR AS A CONSEQUENCE OF		26. WAS AUTOPSY PERFORMED? NO
	(C) arteriosclerosis - generalized	4 years	

23. OTHER SIGNIFICANT CONDITIONS—CONTRIBUTING TO DEATH BUT NOT RELATED TO CAUSE GIVEN	27. WAS OPERATION PERFORMED FOR ANY CONDITION IN ITEMS 22 OR 23? TYPE OF OPERATION	DATE
Metastatic carcinoma of the breast, Diabetes mellitus	No	

PHYSICIAN'S CERTIFICATION

28A. I CERTIFY THAT DEATH OCCURRED AT THE HOUR, DATE AND PLACE STATED FROM THE CAUSES STATED.	28B. PHYSICIAN—SIGNATURE AND DEGREE OR TITLE	28C. DATE SIGNED	28D. PHYSICIAN'S LICENSE NUMBER
I ATTENDED DECEDENT SINCE (ENTER MO. DA. YR.) 8-76	I LAST SAW DECEDENT ALIVE (ENTER MO. DA. YR.) 6-15-88	Silverman	7-1-88	C 26 207
	28E. TYPE PHYSICIAN'S NAME AND ADDRESS Alan S. Silverman, MD; 8635 W. Third St., Los Angeles, CA		

INJURY INFORMATION

29. SPECIFY ACCIDENT, SUICIDE, ETC.	30. PLACE OF INJURY	31. INJURY AT WORK	32A. DATE OF INJURY—MONTH, DAY, YEAR	32B. HOUR
33. LOCATION (STREET AND NUMBER OR LOCATION AND CITY OR TOWN)		34. DESCRIBE HOW INJURY OCCURRED (EVENTS WHICH RESULTED IN INJURY)		

CORONER'S USE ONLY

35A. I CERTIFY THAT DEATH OCCURRED AT THE HOUR, DATE AND PLACE STATED FROM THE CAUSES STATED. AS REQUIRED BY LAW I HAVE HELD AN (INQUEST-INVESTIGATION)	35B. CORONER—SIGNATURE AND DEGREE OR TITLE	35C. DATE SIGNED

36. DISPOSITION	37. DATE—MONTH, DAY, YEAR	38. NAME AND ADDRESS OF CEMETERY OR CREMATORY	39. EMBALMER'S LICENSE NUMBER AND SIGNATURE
Cremation	7/6/88	GRAND VIEW CREMATORY: 1341 Glenwood Road, Glendale	Not Embalmed

40A. NAME OF FUNERAL DIRECTOR (OR PERSON ACTING AS SUCH)	40B. LICENSE NO.	41. LOCAL REGISTRAR—SIGNATURE	42. DATE ACCEPTED BY LOCAL REGISTRAR
CALLANAN MORTUARY	F-86	Robert Batts	JUL 6 - 1988

STATE REGISTRAR	A.	B.	C.	D.	E.	F.

This is to certify that this document is a true copy of the official record filed with the Registrar-Recorder/County Clerk.

Conny B. McCormack

CONNY B. McCORMACK
Registrar-Recorder/County Clerk

This copy not valid unless prepared on engraved border displaying the Seal and Signature of the Registrar-Recorder/County Clerk.

MAY 13 2003

190940716

ANY ALTERATION OR ERASURE VOIDS THIS CERTIFICATE

CERTIFICATE OF DEATH
STATE OF CALIFORNIA
USE BLACK INK ONLY / NO ERASURES, WHITEOUTS OR ALTERATIONS
VS-11 (REV 1/03)

STATE FILE NUMBER	LOCAL REGISTRATION NUMBER

DECEDENT'S PERSONAL DATA

1. NAME OF DECEDENT --- FIRST (Given): DONALD
2. MIDDLE: DAVID
3. LAST (Family): O'CONNOR

AKA. ALSO KNOWN AS --- Include full AKA (FIRST, MIDDLE, LAST): --
4. DATE OF BIRTH mm/dd/ccyy: 08/28/1925
5. AGE Yrs.: 78
6. SEX: M

9. BIRTH STATE/FOREIGN COUNTRY: IL
10. SOCIAL SECURITY NUMBER: 554-14-0571
11. EVER IN U.S. ARMED FORCES?: X YES
12. MARITAL STATUS: MARRIED
7. DATE OF DEATH: 09/27/2003
8. HOUR: 1036

13. EDUCATION: SOME COLLEGE
14/15. WAS DECEDENT SPANISH/HISPANIC/LATINO?: X NO
16. DECEDENT'S RACE: WHITE

17. USUAL OCCUPATION: ACTOR
18. KIND OF BUSINESS OR INDUSTRY: ENTERTAINMENT
19. YEARS IN OCCUPATION: 77

USUAL RESIDENCE

20. DECEDENT'S RESIDENCE: 57 PONDEROSA RD
21. CITY: SEDONA
22. COUNTY/PROVINCE: YAVAPAI
23. ZIP CODE: 86351
24. YEARS IN COUNTY: 10
25. STATE/FOREIGN COUNTRY: AZ

INFORMANT

26. INFORMANT'S NAME, RELATIONSHIP: GLORIA VIOLET O'CONNOR, WIFE
27. INFORMANT'S MAILING ADDRESS: 744 TUOLUMNE AVE THOUSAND OAKS CA 91360

SPOUSE AND PARENT INFORMATION

28. NAME OF SURVIVING SPOUSE --- FIRST: GLORIA
29. MIDDLE: VIOLET
30. LAST (Maiden Name): NOBLE
31. NAME OF FATHER --- FIRST: JOHN
32. MIDDLE: --
33. LAST: O'CONNOR
34. BIRTH STATE: IL
35. NAME OF MOTHER --- FIRST: EFFIE
36. MIDDLE: IRENE
37. LAST (Maiden): SEARCH CRANE
38. BIRTH STATE: FL

FUNERAL DIRECTOR/LOCAL REGISTRAR

39. DISPOSITION DATE: 10/03/2003
40. PLACE OF FINAL DISPOSITION: AT SEA OFF THE COAST OF LOS ANGELES COUNTY
41. TYPE OF DISPOSITION(S): CR/SEA
42. SIGNATURE OF EMBALMER: NOT EMBALMED
43. LICENSE NUMBER: --
44. NAME OF FUNERAL ESTABLISHMENT: FOREST LAWN HOLLYWOOD HILLS
45. LICENSE NUMBER: FD 904
46. SIGNATURE OF LOCAL REGISTRAR: Thomas W Guttwaite
47. DATE: 10/02/2003

PLACE OF DEATH

101. PLACE OF DEATH: MOTION PICTURE & TV HOSPITAL
102. IF HOSPITAL, SPECIFY ONE: X IP
104. COUNTY: LOS ANGELES
105. FACILITY ADDRESS OR LOCATION WHERE FOUND: 23388 MULHOLLAND DR
106. CITY: WOODLAND HILLS

CAUSE OF DEATH

107. CAUSE OF DEATH:
IMMEDIATE CAUSE (A): CONGESTIVE HEART FAILURE — Time Interval: 1 YR
(B): ATHEROSCLEROTIC CORONARY ARTERY DISEASE — 5 YRS

108. DEATH REPORTED TO CORONER?: X NO
109. BIOPSY PERFORMED?: X NO
110. AUTOPSY PERFORMED?: X NO
111. USED IN DETERMINING CAUSE?: X NO

112. OTHER SIGNIFICANT CONDITIONS: NONE
113. WAS OPERATION PERFORMED: NO

PHYSICIAN'S CERTIFICATION

114. Decedent Attended Since (A): 08/08/2003; Last Seen Alive (B): 09/27/2003
115. SIGNATURE AND TITLE OF CERTIFIER: [signature] MD
116. LICENSE NUMBER: A39209
117. DATE: 09/29/2003
118. TYPE ATTENDING PHYSICIAN'S NAME: S HUMAYUN MD 23388 MULHOLLAND DR WOODLAND HILLS CA 91364

CORONER'S USE ONLY

119. MANNER OF DEATH / 120. INJURED AT WORK? / 121. INJURY DATE / 122. HOUR
123. PLACE OF INJURY
124. DESCRIBE HOW INJURY OCCURRED
125. LOCATION OF INJURY

INFORMATIONAL, NOT A VALID DOCUMENT TO ESTABLISH IDENTITY

126. SIGNATURE OF CORONER / 127. DATE / 128. TYPE NAME, TITLE OF CORONER

STATE REGISTRAR: A B C D E
FAX AUTH. #: 273/9866
CENSUS TRACT

CERTIFICATE OF DEATH
STATE OF CALIFORNIA
USE BLACK INK ONLY/NO ERASURES, WHITEOUTS OR ALTERATIONS
VS-11 (REV. 7/83)

STATE FILE NUMBER | LOCAL REGISTRATION NUMBER

1. NAME OF DECEDENT — FIRST (GIVEN)	2. MIDDLE	3. LAST (FAMILY)
HUGH	EDWARD	O'CONNOR

4. DATE OF BIRTH MM/DD/CCYY	5. AGE YRS.	IF UNDER 1 YEAR / IF UNDER 24 HOURS	6. SEX	7. DATE OF DEATH MM/DD/CCYY	8. HOUR
04/07/1962	32	MONTHS DAYS / HOURS MINUTES	MALE	03/28/1995	1845

9. STATE OF BIRTH	10. SOCIAL SECURITY NO.	11. MILITARY SERVICE	12. MARITAL STATUS	13. EDUCATION — YEARS COMPLETED
ITALY	559-41-2641	19 __ TO 19 __ [X] NONE	MARRIED	12

14. RACE	15. HISPANIC — SPECIFY	16. USUAL EMPLOYER
CAUCASIAN	[ ] YES [X] NO	MGM

17. OCCUPATION	18. KIND OF BUSINESS	19. YEARS IN OCCUPATION
ACTOR	ENTERTAINMENT	15

DECEDENT PERSONAL DATA

USUAL RESIDENCE

20. RESIDENCE — STREET AND NUMBER OR LOCATION
219 ADERNO WAY

21. CITY	22. COUNTY	23. ZIP CODE	24. YRS IN COUNTY	25. STATE OR FOREIGN COUNTRY
PACIFIC PALISADES	LOS ANGELES	90272	32	CALIFORNIA

INFORMANT

26. NAME, RELATIONSHIP	27. MAILING ADDRESS (STREET AND NUMBER OR RURAL ROUTE NUMBER, CITY OR TOWN, STATE, ZIP)
ANGELA O'CONNOR - WIFE	219 ADERNO WAY, PACIFIC PALISADES, CA 90272

SPOUSE AND PARENT INFORMATION

28. NAME OF SURVIVING SPOUSE — FIRST	29. MIDDLE	30. LAST (MAIDEN NAME)
ANGELA	GRACE	CLAYTON

31. NAME OF FATHER — FIRST	32. MIDDLE	33. LAST	34. BIRTH STATE
CARROLL	–	O'CONNOR	NEW YORK

35. NAME OF MOTHER — FIRST	36. MIDDLE	37. LAST MAIDEN	38. BIRTH STATE
NANCY	–	FIELDS	NEW YORK

DISPOSITION(S)

39. DATE MM/DD/CCYY	40. PLACE OF FINAL DISPOSITION
04/03/1995	RESIDENCE - ANGELA O'CONNOR, 219 ADERNO WY., PACIFIC PALISADES, CA 90272

FUNERAL DIRECTOR AND LOCAL REGISTRAR

41. TYPE OF DISPOSITION	42. SIGNATURE OF EMBALMER	43. LICENSE NO.
CR/RESIDENCE	*William Pierce*	5595

44. NAME OF FUNERAL DIRECTOR	45. LICENSE NO	46. SIGNATURE OF LOCAL REGISTRAR	47. DATE MM/DD/CCYY
PIERCE BROS. WESTWOOD VILLAGE	F-951	*Robert C. Gate*	03/31/1995

PLACE OF DEATH

101. PLACE OF DEATH	102. IF HOSPITAL, SPECIFY ONE	103. FACILITY OTHER THAN HOSPITAL	104. COUNTY
Residence	[ ] IP [ ] ER/OP [ ] DOA	[ ] CONV. HOSP [X] RES [ ] OTHER	Los Angeles

105. STREET ADDRESS — STREET AND NUMBER OR LOCATION	106. CITY
219 Aderno Way	Pacific Palisades

CAUSE OF DEATH

107. DEATH WAS CAUSED BY (ENTER ONLY ONE CAUSE PER LINE FOR A, B, C, AND D)		TIME INTERVAL BETWEEN ONSET AND DEATH	108. DEATH REPORTED TO CORONER
IMMEDIATE CAUSE	(A) Gunshot Wound To Head	Rapid	[X] YES [ ] NO
			REFERRAL NUMBER 95-02412
DUE TO	(B)		109. BIOPSY PERFORMED [ ] YES [X] NO
DUE TO	(C)		110. AUTOPSY PERFORMED [ ] YES [X] NO
DUE TO	(D)		111. USED IN DETERMINING CAUSE [ ] YES [X] NO

112. OTHER SIGNIFICANT CONDITIONS CONTRIBUTING TO DEATH BUT NOT RELATED TO CAUSE GIVEN IN 107
None

113. WAS OPERATION PERFORMED FOR ANY CONDITION IN ITEM 107 OR 112? IF YES LIST TYPE OF OPERATION AND DATE.
No

PHYSICIAN'S CERTIFICATION

114. I CERTIFY THAT TO THE BEST OF MY KNOWLEDGE DEATH OCCURRED AT THE HOUR, DATE AND PLACE STATED FROM THE CAUSES STATED. DECEDENT ATTENDED SINCE MM/DD/CCYY / DECEDENT LAST SEEN ALIVE MM/DD/CCYY	115. SIGNATURE AND TITLE OF CERTIFIER	116. LICENSE NO.	117. DATE MM/DD/CCYY
	118. TYPE ATTENDING PHYSICIAN'S NAME, MAILING ADDRESS, ZIP		

CORONER'S USE ONLY

I CERTIFY THAT IN MY OPINION DEATH OCCURRED AT THE HOUR, DATE AND PLACE STATED FROM THE CAUSES STATED. 119. MANNER OF DEATH	120. INJURY AT WORK	121. INJURY DATE MM/DD/CCYY	122. HOUR	123. PLACE OF INJURY
[ ] NATURAL [X] SUICIDE [ ] HOMICIDE [ ] ACCIDENT [ ] PENDING INVESTIGATION [ ] COULD NOT BE DETERMINED	[ ] YES [X] NO	03/28/1995	1500	Residence
	124. DESCRIBE HOW INJURY OCCURRED (EVENTS WHICH RESULTED IN INJURY) Handgun			

125. LOCATION (STREET AND NUMBER OR LOCATION AND CITY AND ZIP CODE)
219 Aderno Way, Pacific Palisades 90272

126. SIGNATURE OF CORONER OR DEPUTY CORONER	127. DATE MM/DD/CCYY	128. TYPED NAME, TITLE OF CORONER OR DEPUTY CORONER
[signature]	03/30/1995	Juana Garcia/Deputy Coroner

STATE REGISTRAR

A	B	C	D	E	F	G	H	FAX AUTH #	CENSUS TRACT

95-088883

STATE FILE NUMBER

AFFIDAVIT TO AMEND A RECORD

☐ BIRTH   ☒ DEATH   ☐ FETAL DEATH

NO ERASURES, WHITEOUTS, OR ALTERATIONS

39519013854

LOCAL REGISTRATION DISTRICT AND CERTIFICATE NUMBER

96-0001416

STATE/LOCAL REGISTRAR USE ONLY

1.	2.	3.

PART I   INFORMATION TO LOCATE RECORD—TYPE OR PRINT IN BLACK INK ONLY

NAME AS IT APPEARS ON RECORD

1. NAME—FIRST (GIVEN)	2. MIDDLE		3. LAST (FAMILY)
HUGH	EDWARD	2 OF 2	O'CONNOR

ADDITIONAL INFORMATION TO LOCATE RECORD

4. SEX	5. DATE OF EVENT—MM/DD/CCYY	6. CITY OF OCCURRENCE	7. COUNTY OF OCCURRENCE
MALE	03/28/1995	PACIFIC PALISADES	LOS ANGELES

8. FATHER'S NAME AS STATED ON ORIGINAL	9. MOTHER'S NAME AS STATED ON ORIGINAL
CARROLL O'CONNOR	NANCY FIELDS

PART II   STATEMENT OF CORRECTIONS—NO ERASURES, WHITEOUTS, OR ALTERATIONS

LIST ONE ITEM PER LINE

10. CERTIFICATE ITEM NUMBER	11. INFORMATION AS IT APPEARS ON ORIGINAL RECORD	12. INFORMATION AS IT SHOULD APPEAR
40	RESIDENCE - ANGELA O'CONNOR, 219 ADERNO WY., PACIFIC PALISADES, CA 90272	CHURCH OF SANTA SUSANNA VIA VENTI SETTEMBRE, 14 00187 ROME, ITALY
41	CR/RESIDENCE	CR/IR/BU

REASON FOR CORRECTION

13.	TO CHANGE DISPOSITION

AFFIDAVITS AND SIGNATURES

We, the undersigned, hereby certify under penalty of perjury that we have personal knowledge of the above facts and that the information given above is true and correct.

TWO PERSONS MUST SIGN THIS FORM

14. SIGNATURE OF FIRST PERSON	15. TITLE/RELATIONSHIP TO PERSON IN PART I	16. DATE SIGNED—MM/DD/CCYY
[signature]	WIFE	09/07/1995

17. AGE	18. ADDRESS (STREET, CITY, STATE, ZIP)
LEGAL	219 ADERNO WAY, PACIFIC PALISADES, CA 90272

USE BLACK INK ONLY

19. SIGNATURE OF SECOND PERSON	20. TITLE/RELATIONSHIP TO PERSON IN PART I	21. DATE SIGNED—MM/DD/CCYY
[signature]	FUNERAL DIRECTOR	09/07/1995

22. AGE	23. ADDRESS (STREET, CITY, STATE, ZIP)
LEGAL	1218 GLENDON AVE. LOS ANGELES, CA 90024

STATE/LOCAL REGISTRAR USE ONLY

24. SIGNATURE OF STATE OR LOCAL REGISTRAR	25. DATE ACCEPTED FOR REGISTRATION—MM/DD/CCYY
OFFICE OF THE STATE REGISTRAR OF VITAL STATISTICS	JAN 1 2 1996

STATE OF CALIFORNIA, DEPARTMENT OF HEALTH SERVICES, OFFICE OF STATE REGISTRAR

CERTIFICATE OF DEATH
STATE OF CALIFORNIA
USE BLACK INK ONLY/NO ERASURES, WHITEOUTS OR ALTERATIONS
VS-11 (REV 1/00)

STATE FILE NUMBER

3 2002 9039065

LOCAL REGISTRATION NUMBER

1 NAME OF DECEDENT—FIRST (GIVEN)	2 MIDDLE	3 LAST (FAMILY)
Alberta	-	Peal

4 DATE OF BIRTH MM/DD/CCYY	5 AGE YRS	IF UNDER 1 YEAR MONTHS / DAYS	IF UNDER 24 HOURS HOURS / MINUTES	6 SEX	7 DATE OF DEATH MM/DD/CCYY	8 HOUR
10/19/1920	81			Female	09/14/2002	1102

9 STATE OF BIRTH	10 SOCIAL SECURITY NO	11 MILITARY SERVICE	12 MARITAL STATUS	13 EDUCATION—YEARS COMPLETED
Ohio	262-30-3965	YES [X] NO UNK	Widow	4

14 RACE	15 HISPANIC—SPECIFY	16 USUAL EMPLOYER
Black	YES [X] NO	AFTRA SAG

17 OCCUPATION	18 KIND OF BUSINESS	19 YEARS IN OCCUPATION
Actress	Entertainment	55

DECEDENT PERSONAL DATA

USUAL RESIDENCE

20 RESIDENCE—(STREET AND NUMBER OR LOCATION)
1056 W. 84th St.

21 CITY	22 COUNTY	23 ZIP CODE	24 YRS IN COUNTY	25 STATE OR FOREIGN COUNTRY
Los Angeles	Los Angeles	90044	50	California

INFORMANT

26 NAME RELATIONSHIP	27 MAILING ADDRESS (STREET AND NUMBER OR RURAL ROUTE NUMBER, CITY OR TOWN, STATE, ZIP)
Clara Johnson - Daughter	4075 S.Figueroa St. #112 Los Angeles,CA. 90037

SPOUSE AND PARENT INFORMATION

28 NAME OF SURVIVING SPOUSE—FIRST	29 MIDDLE	30 LAST (MAIDEN NAME)
	-	

31 NAME OF FATHER—FIRST	32 MIDDLE	33 LAST	34 BIRTH STATE
Unknown	Unknown	Unknown	Unknown

35 NAME OF MOTHER—FIRST	36 MIDDLE	37 LAST (MAIDEN)	38 BIRTH STATE
Estella	-	Small	Florida

DISPOSITION(S)

39 DATE MM/DD/CCYY	40 PLACE OF FINAL DISPOSITION
09/20/2002	Inglewood Park Cemetery, Inglewood,CA.

FUNERAL DIRECTOR AND LOCAL REGISTRAR

41 TYPE OF DISPOSITION(S)	42 SIGNATURE OF EMBALMER	43 LICENSE NO
Burial	► Curtis w Pike	5147

44 NAME OF FUNERAL DIRECTOR	45 LICENSE NO	46 SIGNATURE OF LOCAL REGISTRAR	47 DATE MM/DD/CCYY
Hobbs,J.S.Williams Albert L.Cooper	FD-161	► Thomas Whitmore	09/19/2002

PLACE OF DEATH

101 PLACE OF DEATH	102 IF HOSPITAL, SPECIFY ONE	103 FACILITY OTHER THAN HOSPITAL	104 COUNTY
Centinela Hospital Medical Center	[X] IP ER/OP DOA	CONV HOSP RES CARE OTHER	Los Angeles

105 STREET ADDRESS—(STREET AND NUMBER OR LOCATION)	106 CITY
555 E.Hardy St.	Inglewood

CAUSE OF DEATH

107 DEATH WAS CAUSED BY (ENTER ONLY ONE CAUSE PER LINE FOR A, B, C, AND D)		TIME INTERVAL BETWEEN ONSET AND DEATH	108 DEATH REPORTED TO CORONER
IMMEDIATE CAUSE	(A) Cardiopulmonary Arrest	min.	YES [X] NO REFERRAL NUMBER
DUE TO	(B) Septic Shock	hrs.	109 BIOPSY PERFORMED YES [X] NO
DUE TO	(C) Fungal Sepsis	hrs.	110 AUTOPSY PERFORMED YES [X] NO
DUE TO	(D) Diabetes	yrs.	111 USED IN DETERMINING CAUSE YES NO

112 OTHER SIGNIFICANT CONDITIONS CONTRIBUTING TO DEATH BUT NOT RELATED TO CAUSE GIVEN IN 107
None

113 WAS OPERATION PERFORMED FOR ANY CONDITION IN ITEM 107 OR 112? IF YES, LIST TYPE OF OPERATION AND DATE
No

PHYSICIAN'S CERTIFICATION

114 I CERTIFY THAT TO THE BEST OF MY KNOWLEDGE DEATH OCCURRED AT THE HOUR, DATE AND PLACE STATED FROM THE CAUSES STATED		115 SIGNATURE AND TITLE OF CERTIFIER	116 LICENSE NO	117 DATE MM/DD/CCYY
DECEDENT ATTENDED SINCE MM/DD/CCYY	DECEDENT LAST SEEN ALIVE MM/DD/CCYY	►	G49354	09/17/2002
09/07/2000	09/13/2002	118 TYPE ATTENDING PHYSICIAN'S NAME, MAILING ADDRESS, ZIP Randy W. Hawkins,M.D. 644 E.Regent St. #200 Inglewood,CA 90301		

CORONER'S USE ONLY

I CERTIFY THAT IN MY OPINION DEATH OCCURRED AT THE HOUR, DATE AND PLACE STATED FROM THE CAUSES STATED

119 MANNER OF DEATH

120 INJURY AT WORK	121 INJURY DATE MM/DD/CCYY	122 HOUR	123 PLACE OF INJURY
YES NO			

124 DESCRIBE HOW INJURY OCCURRED (EVENTS WHICH RESULTED IN INJURY)

NATURAL   SUICIDE   HOMICIDE
ACCIDENT   PENDING INVESTIGATION   COULD NOT BE DETERMINED

125 LOCATION (STREET AND NUMBER OR LOCATION AND CITY, ZIP)

126 SIGNATURE OF CORONER OR DEPUTY CORONER	127 DATE MM/DD/CCYY	128 TYPED NAME, TITLE OF CORONER OR DEPUTY CORONER
►		

STATE REGISTRAR

A	B	C	D	E	F	G	H	FAX AUTH #	CENSUS TRACT

CERTIFICATE OF DEATH
STATE OF CALIFORNIA
USE BLACK INK ONLY

LOCAL REGISTRATION DISTRICT AND CERTIFICATE NUMBER
3923700I754

STATE FILE NUMBER				
1A. NAME OF DECEDENT—First (Given) BERT	1B. MIDDLE ---	1C. LAST (FAMILY) PARKS	2A. DATE OF DEATH—Mo. Day. Yr. FEBRUARY 2, 1992	2B. Hour 0135	3. SEX MALE

| 4. RACE White | 5. HISPANIC—SPECIFY ☐ YES ___ ☒ No | 6. DATE OF BIRTH—Mo. Day. Yr December 30, 1914 | 7. AGE IN YEARS 77 | IF UNDER 1 YEAR MONTHS / DAYS | IF UNDER 24 HOURS HOURS / MINUTES |

| 8. STATE OF BIRTH GA | 9. CITIZEN OF WHAT COUNTRY USA | 10A. FULL NAME OF FATHER Aaron Parks | 10B. STATE OF BIRTH Russia | 11A. FULL MAIDEN NAME OF MOTHER Hattie Spiegel | 11B. STATE OF BIRTH WI |

| 12. MILITARY SERVICE? 19 41 to 19 45 ☐ NONE | 13. SOCIAL SECURITY No. 093-1G-7904 | 14. MARITAL STATUS Married | 15. NAME OF SURVIVING SPOUSE (IF WIFE, ENTER MAIDEN NAME) Annette Liebman |

| 16A. USUAL OCCUPATION Entertainer | 16B. USUAL KIND OF BUSINESS OR INDUSTRY Entertainment | 16C. USUAL EMPLOYER Self | 16D. YEARS IN OCCUPATION 60 | 17. EDUCATION—YEARS COMPLETED 12 |

| 18A. RESIDENCE—STREET AND NUMBER OR LOCATION 21 Skyridge Road | 18B. CITY Greenwich | 18C. ZIP CODE 06831 |

| 18D. COUNTY Fairfield | 18E. NUMBER OF YEARS IN THIS COUNTY 45 | 18F. STATE OR FOREIGN COUNTRY CT | 20. NAME, RELATIONSHIP, MAILING ADDRESS AND ZIP CODE OF INFORMANT Annette Parks, wife P.O. Box 606 Rancho Santa Fe, CA 92067 |

| 19A. PLACE OF DEATH SCRIPPS MEM. HOSPITAL | 19B. IF HOSPITAL, SPECIFY ONE: IP, ER/OP, DOA IP | 19C. COUNTY SAN DIEGO | |

| 19D. STREET ADDRESS—STREET AND NUMBER OR LOCATION 9888 GENESEE AVENUE | 19E. CITY LA JOLLA | |

21. DEATH WAS CAUSED BY: (ENTER ONLY ONE CAUSE PER LINE FOR A, B, AND C)	TIME INTERVAL BETWEEN ONSET AND DEATH	22. WAS DEATH REPORTED TO CORONER? REFERRAL NUMBER ☐ YES ___ ☒ NO
IMMEDIATE CAUSE (A) Interstitial Pneumonia ▶	4 days	23. WAS BIOPSY PERFORMED? ☐ YES ☐ NO
DUE TO (B) Lung Cancer ▶	5 mos	24A. WAS AUTOPSY PERFORMED? ☐ YES ☒ NO
DUE TO (C) ▶		24B. WAS IT USED IN DETERMINING CAUSE OF DEATH ☐ YES ☐ NO

| 25. OTHER SIGNIFICANT CONDITIONS CONTRIBUTING TO DEATH BUT NOT RELATED TO CAUSE GIVEN IN 21 None | 26. WAS OPERATION PERFORMED FOR ANY CONDITION IN ITEM 21 OR 25? IF YES, LIST TYPE OF OPERATION AND DATE. No |

I CERTIFY THAT TO THE BEST OF MY KNOWLEDGE DEATH OCCURRED AT THE HOUR, DATE AND PLACE STATED FROM THE CAUSES STATED.	27B. SIGNATURE AND DEGREE OR TITLE OF CERTIFIER R. Anderson MD ▶	27C. CERTIFIER'S LICENSE NUMBER G28271	27D. DATE SIGNED 2/4/92
27A. DECEDENT ATTENDED SINCE 1/4/92 / DECEDENT LAST SEEN ALIVE 2/1/92	27E. TYPE ATTENDING PHYSICIAN'S NAME AND ADDRESS Richard Anderson, M.D. Ste. 311, 9834 Genesee Ave., La Jolla, CA 92037		

| I CERTIFY THAT IN MY OPINION DEATH OCCURRED AT THE HOUR, DATE AND PLACE STATED FROM THE CAUSES STATED. | 28A. SIGNATURE AND TITLE OF CORONER OR DEPUTY CORONER ▶ | 28B. DATE SIGNED |

| 29. MANNER OF DEATH—specify one: natural, accident, suicide, homicide, pending investigation or could not be determined | 30A. PLACE OF INJURY | 30B. INJURY AT WORK ☐ YES ☐ NO | 30C. DATE OF INJURY MONTH, DAY, YEAR | 31. HOUR |

| 32. LOCATION (STREET AND NUMBER OR LOCATION AND CITY) | 33. DESCRIBE HOW INJURY OCCURRED (EVENTS WHICH RESULTED IN INJURY) |

| 34A. DISPOSITION(S) CR/TR/RES | 34B. PLACE OF FINAL DISPOSITION—NAME AND ADDRESS Annette Parks:21 Skyridge Road Greenwich, CT 06831 | 34C. DATE MO. DAY. YEAR 2-5-1992 | 35A. SIGNATURE OF EMBALMER Not Embalmed | 35B. LICENSE NUMBER |

| 36A. NAME OF FUNERAL DIRECTOR (OR PERSON ACTING AS SUCH) Telophase Society — San Marcos | 36B. LICENSE NO. FD-1470 | 37. SIGNATURE OF LOCAL REGISTRAR Arnold G. Ramos, M.D. ▶ | 38. REGISTRATION DATE FEB 0 5 1992 |

A.	B.	C.	D.	E.	F.	CENSUS TRACT

CERTIFICATE OF DEATH
STATE OF CALIFORNIA
USE BLACK INK ONLY/NO ERASURES, WHITEOUTS OR ALTERATIONS
VS-11 (REV. 1/00)

STATE FILE NUMBER		LOCAL REGISTRATION NUMBER

DECEDENT PERSONAL DATA

1. NAME OF DECEDENT—FIRST (GIVEN)	2. MIDDLE	3. LAST (FAMILY)
DENNIS	PATRICK	HARRISON

4. DATE OF BIRTH MM/DD/CCYY	5. AGE YRS.	IF UNDER 1 YEAR MONTHS / DAYS	IF UNDER 24 HOURS HOURS / MINUTES	6. SEX	7. DATE OF DEATH MM/DD/CCYY	8. HOUR
03/14/1918	84			M	10/13/2002	1350

9. STATE OF BIRTH	10. SOCIAL SECURITY NO.	11. MILITARY SERVICE	12. MARITAL STATUS	13. EDUCATION—YEARS COMPLETED
PENNSYLVANIA	177-01-5078	YES [ ] NO [X] UNK [ ]	WIDOWED	12

14. RACE	15. HISPANIC—SPECIFY	16. USUAL EMPLOYER
CAUCASIAN	YES [ ] _____ NO [X]	SELF EMPLOYED

17. OCCUPATION	18. KIND OF BUSINESS	19. YEARS IN OCCUPATION
ACTOR/DIRECTOR	ENTERTAINMENT	1 OF 2 / 47

USUAL RESIDENCE

20. RESIDENCE—(STREET AND NUMBER OR LOCATION)
7847 TORREYSON DR.

21. CITY	22. COUNTY	23. ZIP CODE	24. YRS IN COUNTY	25. STATE OR FOREIGN COUNTRY
LOS ANGELES	LOS ANGELES	90046	45	CALIFORNIA

INFORMANT

26. NAME, RELATIONSHIP	27. MAILING ADDRESS (STREET AND NUMBER OR RURAL ROUTE NUMBER, CITY OR TOWN, STATE, ZIP)
CHRISTINE HARRISON, DAUGHTER	7321 S.E. TAYLOR PORTLAND, OR 97215

SPOUSE AND PARENT INFORMATION

28. NAME OF SURVIVING SPOUSE—FIRST	29. MIDDLE	30. LAST (MAIDEN NAME)
-	-	-

31. NAME OF FATHER—FIRST	32. MIDDLE	33. LAST	34. BIRTH STATE
WILLIAM	JOHN	HARRISON	IRELAND

35. NAME OF MOTHER—FIRST	36. MIDDLE	37. LAST (MAIDEN)	38. BIRTH STATE
MARY	K.	TYDINGS	IRELAND

DISPOSITION(S)

39. DATE MM/DD/CCYY	40. PLACE OF FINAL DISPOSITION
10/21/2002	AT SEA OFF THE COAST OF LOS ANGELES COUNTY

FUNERAL DIRECTOR AND LOCAL REGISTRAR

41. TYPE OF DISPOSITION(S)	42. SIGNATURE OF EMBALMER	43. LICENSE NO.
CR/SEA	▶ NOT EMBALMED	-

44. NAME OF FUNERAL DIRECTOR	45. LICENSE NO.	46. SIGNATURE OF LOCAL REGISTRAR	47. DATE MM/DD/CCYY
NEPTUNE SOCIETY, S.O.	FD-1359	▶ Thomas H. Hawthorne	10/18/2002

PLACE OF DEATH

101. PLACE OF DEATH	102. IF HOSPITAL, SPECIFY ONE:	103. FACILITY OTHER THAN HOSPITAL:	104. COUNTY
Own Residence	IP [ ] ER/OP [ ] DOA [ ]	CONV. HOSP. [ ] RES. CARE [ ] OTHER [ ]	Los Angeles

105. STREET ADDRESS—(STREET AND NUMBER OR LOCATION)	106. CITY
7847 Torreyson Drive	Los Angeles

CAUSE OF DEATH

107. DEATH WAS CAUSED BY: (ENTER ONLY ONE CAUSE PER LINE FOR A, B, C, AND D)	TIME INTERVAL BETWEEN ONSET AND DEATH.	
IMMEDIATE CAUSE (A) Deferred		108. DEATH REPORTED TO CORONER [X] YES [ ] NO REFERRAL NUMBER 2002-07711
DUE TO (B)		109. BIOPSY PERFORMED [ ] YES [ ] NO
DUE TO (C)		110. AUTOPSY PERFORMED [X] YES [ ] NO
DUE TO (D)		111. USED IN DETERMINING CAUSE [ ] YES [ ] NO

112. OTHER SIGNIFICANT CONDITIONS CONTRIBUTING TO DEATH BUT NOT RELATED TO CAUSE GIVEN IN 107

113. WAS OPERATION PERFORMED FOR ANY CONDITION IN ITEM 107 OR 112? IF YES, LIST TYPE OF OPERATION AND DATE.

PHYSICIAN'S CERTIFICATION

114. I CERTIFY THAT TO THE BEST OF MY KNOWLEDGE DEATH OCCURRED AT THE HOUR, DATE AND PLACE STATED FROM THE CAUSES STATED. DECEDENT ATTENDED SINCE MM/DD/CCYY / DECEDENT LAST SEEN ALIVE MM/DD/CCYY	115. SIGNATURE AND TITLE OF CERTIFIER ▶	116. LICENSE NO.	117. DATE MM/DD/CCYY
	118. TYPE ATTENDING PHYSICIAN'S NAME, MAILING ADDRESS, ZIP		

CORONER'S USE ONLY

I CERTIFY THAT IN MY OPINION DEATH OCCURRED AT THE HOUR, DATE AND PLACE STATED FROM THE CAUSES STATED.

119. MANNER OF DEATH	120. INJURY AT WORK	121. INJURY DATE MM/DD/CCYY	122. HOUR	123. PLACE OF INJURY
NATURAL [ ] SUICIDE [ ] HOMICIDE [ ] ACCIDENT [ ] PENDING INVESTIGATION [X] COULD NOT BE DETERMINED [ ]	YES [ ] NO [ ]			

124. DESCRIBE HOW INJURY OCCURRED (EVENTS WHICH RESULTED IN INJURY)

125. LOCATION (STREET AND NUMBER OR LOCATION AND CITY, ZIP)

126. SIGNATURE OF CORONER OR DEPUTY CORONER ▶ Lavette Egans	127. DATE MM/DD/CCYY 10/17/2002	128. TYPED NAME, TITLE OF CORONER OR DEPUTY CORONER Lavette Egans Deputy Coroner 09

STATE REGISTRAR

A	B	C	D	E	F	G	H	FAX AUTH. #	CENSUS TRACT
								195/6918	

AMENDMENT OF MEDICAL AND HEALTH DATA—DEATH

STATE FILE NUMBER	USE BLACK INK ONLY—NO ERASURES, WHITEOUT, OR ALTERATIONS	LOCAL REGISTRATION DISTRICT AND CERTIFICATE NUMBER
STATE/LOCAL REGISTRAR USE ONLY	1	2	3

TYPE OR PRINT IN BLACK INK ONLY

PART I — INFORMATION TO LOCATE RECORD

1. NAME—FIRST (GIVEN)	2. MIDDLE	3. LAST (FAMILY)	4. SEX
DENNIS	PATRICK	HARRISON	M

5. DATE OF EVENT—MM/DD/CCYY	6. CITY OF OCCURENCE	7. COUNTY OF OCCURRENCE	
10/13/2002	Los Angeles	Los Angeles	2OF2

PART II — INFORMATION AS IT APPEARS ON RECORD

107. DEATH WAS CAUSED BY ENTER ONLY ONE CAUSE PER LINE FOR A, B, C, AND D)

IMMEDIATE CAUSE (A) **Deferred**

(B)

(C)

DUE TO (D)

TIME INTERVAL BETWEEN ONSET AND DEATH	108. DEATH REPORTED TO CORONER
	[X] YES [ ] NO
	REFERRAL NUMBER 2002-07711
	109. BIOPSY PERFORMED [ ] YES [ ] NO
	110. AUTOPSY PERFORMED [X] YES [ ] NO
	111. USED IN DETERMINING CAUSE [ ] YES [ ] NO

112. OTHER SIGNIFICANT CONDITIONS CONTRIBUTING TO DEATH BUT NOT RELATED TO CAUSE GIVEN IN 107

113. WAS OPERATION PERFORMED FOR ANY CONDITION IN ITEM 107 or 112? IF YES, LIST TYPE OF OPERATION AND DATE.

119. MANNER OF DEATH	120. INJURY AT WORK [ ] YES [ ] NO	121. INJURY DATE—MM/DD/CCYY	122. HOUR	123. PLACE OF INJURY
[ ] NATURAL [ ] SUICIDE [ ] HOMICIDE [ ] ACCIDENT [X] PENDING INVESTIGATION [ ] COULD NOT BE DETERMINED	124. DESCRIBE HOW INJURY OCCURED (EVENTS WHICH RESULTED IN INJURY)			

125. LOCATION (STREET AND NUMBER OR LOCATION AND CITY AND ZIP CODE)

INFORMATION AS IT SHOULD APPEAR

107. DEATH WAS CAUSED BY ENTER ONLY ONE CAUSE PER LINE FOR A, B, C, AND D)

IMMEDIATE CAUSE (A) COMBINED EFFECT OF SMOKE INHALATION AND

(B) ARTERIOSCLEROTIC CARDIOVASCULAR DISEASE   RAPID

(C)

DUE TO (D)

TIME INTERVAL BETWEEN ONSET AND DEATH	108. DEATH REPORTED TO CORONER
	[X] YES [ ] NO
	REFERRAL NUMBER 2002-07711
	109. BIOPSY PERFORMED [ ] YES [X] NO
	110. AUTOPSY PERFORMED [X] YES [ ] NO
	111. USED IN DETERMINING CAUSE [X] YES [ ] NO

112. OTHER SIGNIFICANT CONDITIONS CONTRIBUTING TO DEATH BUT NOT RELATED TO CAUSE GIVEN IN 107
NONE

113. WAS OPERATION PERFORMED FOR ANY CONDITION IN ITEM 107 or 112? IF YES, LIST TYPE OF OPERATION AND DATE.
NO

119. MANNER OF DEATH	120. INJURY AT WORK [ ] YES [X] NO	121. INJURY DATE—MM/DD/CCYY 10/13/2002	122. HOUR 1317	123. PLACE OF INJURY RESIDENCE
[ ] NATURAL [ ] SUICIDE [ ] HOMICIDE [X] ACCIDENT [ ] PENDING INVESTIGATION [ ] COULD NOT BE DETERMINED	124. DESCRIBE HOW INJURY OCCURRED (EVENTS WHICH RESULTED IN INJURY) IN HOUSE FIRE			

125. LOCATION (STREET AND NUMBER OR LOCATION AND CITY AND ZIP CODE)
7847 TORREYSON DRIVE, LOS ANGELES, CALIFORNIA 90046

DECLARATION OF CERTIFYING PHYSICIAN OR CORONER

I HEREBY DECLARE UNDER PENALTY OF PERJURY THAT THE ABOVE INFORMATION IS TRUE AND CORRECT TO THE BEST OF MY KNOWLEDGE.

8. SIGNATURE OF CERTIFYING PHYSICIAN OR CORONER	9. DATE SIGNED—MM/DD/CCYY 11/27/2002	10. TYPED OR PRINTED NAME AND DEGREE/TITLE OF CERTIFIER YULAI WANG, M.D. DME
11. ADDRESS—STREET AND NUMBER 1104 NORTH MISSION ROAD	12. CITY LOS ANGELES	13. STATE CA.	14. ZIP CODE 90033

STATE/LOCAL REGISTRAR USE ONLY

15. OFFICE OF STATE REGISTRAR OR SIGNATURE OF LOCAL REGISTRAR	16. DATE ACCEPTED FOR REGISTRATION—MM/DD/CCYY 12/04/2002

STATE OF CALIFORNIA, DEPARTMENT OF HEALTH SERVICES, OFFICE OF STATE REGISTRAR

VS-24 B (1/94)

CERTIFICATE OF DEATH
STATE OF CALIFORNIA
USE BLACK INK ONLY / NO ERASURES, WHITEOUTS OR ALTERATIONS
VS-11 (REV 1/03)

STATE FILE NUMBER	LOCAL REGISTRATION NUMBER

DECEDENT'S PERSONAL DATA

1. NAME OF DECEDENT --- FIRST (Given)	2. MIDDLE	3. LAST (Family)
Gregory	--	Peck

AKA. ALSO KNOWN AS --- Include full AKA (FIRST, MIDDLE, LAST)	4. DATE OF BIRTH mm/dd/ccyy	5. AGE Yrs.	IF UNDER ONE YEAR Months / Days	IF UNDER 24 HOURS Hours / Minutes	6. SEX
	04/05/1916	87			M

9. BIRTH STATE/FOREIGN COUNTRY	10. SOCIAL SECURITY NUMBER	11. EVER IN U.S. ARMED FORCES?	12. MARITAL STATUS (at Time of Death)	7. DATE OF DEATH mm/dd/ccyy	8. HOUR (24 Hours)
California	547-16-9811	YES [ ] NO [x] UNK [ ]	Married	06/12/2003	0700

13. EDUCATION --- Highest Level/Degree (see worksheet on back)	14/15. WAS DECEDENT SPANISH/HISPANIC/LATINO? (If yes, see worksheet on back.)	16. DECEDENT'S RACE --- Up to 3 races may be listed (see worksheet on back)
Bachelor's	YES [ ] ___ NO [x]	Caucasian

17. USUAL OCCUPATION --- Type of work for most of life. DO NOT USE RETIRED	18. KIND OF BUSINESS OR INDUSTRY (e.g., grocery store, road construction, employment agency, etc.)	19. YEARS IN OCCUPATION
Actor	Entertainment	60

USUAL RESIDENCE

20. DECEDENT'S RESIDENCE (Street and number or location)
375 N. Carolwood Drive

21. CITY	22. COUNTY/PROVINCE	23. ZIP CODE	24. YEARS IN COUNTY	25. STATE/FOREIGN COUNTRY
Los Angeles	Los Angeles	90077	87	California

INFORMANT

26. INFORMANT'S NAME, RELATIONSHIP	27. INFORMANT'S MAILING ADDRESS (Street and number or rural route number, city or town, state, ZIP)
Veronique Peck - Wife	375 N. Carolwood Drive, Los Angeles, CA 90077

SPOUSE AND PARENT INFORMATION

28. NAME OF SURVIVING SPOUSE --- FIRST	29. MIDDLE	30. LAST (Maiden Name)
Veronique	-	Passani

31. NAME OF FATHER --- FIRST	32. MIDDLE	33. LAST	34. BIRTH STATE
Gregory	P.	Peck	NY

35. NAME OF MOTHER --- FIRST	36. MIDDLE	37. LAST (Maiden)	38. BIRTH STATE
Bernice	-	Ayres	MO

FUNERAL DIRECTOR/ LOCAL REGISTRAR

39. DISPOSITION DATE mm/dd/ccyy	40. PLACE OF FINAL DISPOSITION
06/16/2003	Cathedral of Our Lady of the Angels, 555 W. Temple St, Los Angeles, CA 90012

41. TYPE OF DISPOSITION(S)	42. SIGNATURE OF EMBALMER	43. LICENSE NUMBER
REL/BU	▶ Not Embalmed	

44. NAME OF FUNERAL ESTABLISHMENT	45. LICENSE NUMBER	46. SIGNATURE OF LOCAL REGISTRAR	47. DATE mm/dd/ccyy
Holy Cross Mortuary	FD-1711	▶ Thomas M Montecito	06/13/2003

PLACE OF DEATH

101. PLACE OF DEATH	102. IF HOSPITAL, SPECIFY ONE	103. IF OTHER THAN HOSPITAL, SPECIFY ONE
Residence	IP [ ] ER/OP [ ] DOA [ ]	Hospice [ ] Nursing Home/LTC [ ] Decedent's Home [x] Other [ ]

104. COUNTY	105. FACILITY ADDRESS OR LOCATION WHERE FOUND (Street and number or location)	106. CITY
Los Angeles	375 N. Carolwood Drive	Los Angeles

CAUSE OF DEATH

107. CAUSE OF DEATH		Time Interval Between Onset and Death	108. DEATH REPORTED TO CORONER?
IMMEDIATE CAUSE (A) (Final disease or condition resulting in death)	Cardiorespiratory Arrest	(AT) 10 Mins	YES [ ] NO [x] REFERRAL NUMBER
Sequentially list conditions, if any, leading to cause on Line A. Enter UNDERLYING CAUSE (disease or injury that initiated the events resulting in death) LAST (B)	Bronchopneumonia	(BT) 5 Days	109. BIOPSY PERFORMED? YES [ ] NO [x]
(C)		(CT)	110. AUTOPSY PERFORMED? YES [ ] NO [x]
(D)		(DT)	111. USED IN DETERMINING CAUSE? YES [ ] NO [ ]

112. OTHER SIGNIFICANT CONDITIONS CONTRIBUTING TO DEATH BUT NOT RESULTING IN THE UNDERLYING CAUSE GIVEN IN 107
Coronary Artery Disease

113. WAS OPERATION PERFORMED FOR ANY CONDITION IN ITEM 107 OR 112? (If yes, list type of operation and date.)	113A. IF FEMALE, PREGNANT IN LAST YEAR?
No	YES [ ] NO [ ] UNK [ ]

PHYSICIAN'S CERTIFICATION

114. I CERTIFY THAT TO THE BEST OF MY KNOWLEDGE DEATH OCCURRED AT THE HOUR, DATE, AND PLACE STATED FROM THE CAUSES STATED.	115. SIGNATURE AND TITLE OF CERTIFIER	116. LICENSE NUMBER	117. DATE mm/dd/ccyy
Decedent Attended Since / Decedent Last Seen Alive	▶ Gary Sugarman MD	G20608	06/12/2003
(A) mm/dd/ccyy 07/01/1973	(B) mm/dd/ccyy 06/11/2003	118. TYPE ATTENDING PHYSICIAN'S NAME, MAILING ADDRESS, ZIP CODE Gary Sugarman, MD 436 N. Roxbury #222, Beverly Hills, CA 90210	

CORONER'S USE ONLY

119. I CERTIFY THAT IN MY OPINION DEATH OCCURRED AT THE HOUR, DATE, AND PLACE STATED FROM THE CAUSES STATED. MANNER OF DEATH	120. INJURED AT WORK?	121. INJURY DATE mm/dd/ccyy	122. HOUR (24 Hours)
Natural [ ] Accident [ ] Homicide [ ] Suicide [ ] Pending Investigation [ ] Could not be determined [ ]	YES [ ] NO [ ] UNK [ ]		

123. PLACE OF INJURY (e.g., home, construction site, wooded area, etc.)

INFORMATIONAL, NOT A VALID DOCUMENT TO ESTABLISH IDENTITY

124. DESCRIBE HOW INJURY OCCURRED (Events which resulted in injury)

125. LOCATION OF INJURY (Street and number, or location, and city, and ZIP)

126. SIGNATURE OF CORONER / DEPUTY CORONER	127. DATE mm/dd/ccyy	128. TYPE NAME, TITLE OF CORONER / DEPUTY CORONER
▶		

STATE REGISTRAR	A	B	C	D	E	FAX AUTH. #	CENSUS TRACT

STATE OF CALIFORNIA
CERTIFICATION OF VITAL RECORD

COUNTY OF LOS ANGELES • REGISTRAR-RECORDER/COUNTY CLERK

INFORMATIONAL, NOT A
VALID DOCUMENT TO
ESTABLISH IDENTITY

CERTIFICATE OF DEATH
STATE OF CALIFORNIA—DEPARTMENT OF PUBLIC HEALTH

STATE FILE NUMBER

LOCAL REGISTRATION DISTRICT AND CERTIFICATE NUMBER **7080 21222**

DECEDENT PERSONAL DATA	1A. NAME OF DECEASED—FIRST NAME **Cole**	1B. MIDDLE NAME
	1C. LAST NAME **Porter**	2A. DATE OF DEATH **Oct 15, 1964** / 2B. HOUR **11:05 P** M

3. SEX **male**	4. COLOR OR RACE **cauc**	5. BIRTHPLACE **Indiana**	6. DATE OF BIRTH **June 9, 1891**	7. AGE (LAST BIRTHDAY) **73** YEARS	IF UNDER 1 YEAR	IF UNDER 24 HOURS

8. NAME AND BIRTHPLACE OF FATHER **Samuel F Porter - unknown**	9. MAIDEN NAME AND BIRTHPLACE OF MOTHER **Kate Cole - unknown**	10. CITIZEN OF WHAT COUNTRY **USA**	11. SOCIAL SECURITY NUMBER **527-07-6407**

12. LAST OCCUPATION **Composer**	13. NUMBER OF YEARS IN THIS OCCUPATION **50**	14. NAME OF LAST EMPLOYING COMPANY OR FIRM **self employed**	15. KIND OF INDUSTRY OR BUSINESS **entertainment**

16. IF DECEASED WAS EVER IN U.S. ARMED FORCES, GIVE WAR OR DATES OF SERVICE **none**	17. SPECIFY MARRIED, NEVER MARRIED, WIDOWED, DIVORCED **widowed**	16A. NAME OF PRESENT SPOUSE —	18B. PRESENT OR LAST OCCUPATION OF SPOUSE —

PLACE OF DEATH	19A. PLACE OF DEATH—NAME OF HOSPITAL **St. John's Hospital**	19B. STREET ADDRESS **1328 22nd St.**	☒ INSIDE CITY CORPORATE LIMITS □ OUTSIDE CITY LIMITS
	19C. CITY OR TOWN **Santa Monica**	19D. COUNTY **Los Angeles**	19E. LENGTH OF STAY IN COUNTY OF DEATH **3½ mo** / 19F. LENGTH OF STAY IN CALIFORNIA **3½ mo**

LAST USUAL RESIDENCE (WHERE DID DECEASED LIVE—IF IN INSTITUTION ENTER RESIDENCE BEFORE ADMISSION)	20A. LAST USUAL RESIDENCE—STREET ADDRESS **Waldorf Towers**	20B. IF INSIDE CITY CORPORATE LIMITS ☒ CHECK HERE	IF OUTSIDE CITY CORPORATE LIMITS CHECK ONE □ ON A FARM □ NOT ON A FARM	21A. NAME OF INFORMANT (IF OTHER THAN SPOUSE) **Elkenberry Funeral Home**
	20C. CITY OR TOWN **New York** **3300**	20D. COUNTY **New York**	20E. STATE **New York**	21B. ADDRESS OF INFORMANT **84 W. Main St. - Peru, Ind.**

PHYSICIAN'S OR CORONER'S CERTIFICATION	22A. PHYSICIAN: I HEREBY CERTIFY THAT DEATH OCCURRED AT THE HOUR, DATE AND PLACE STATED ABOVE FROM THE CAUSES STATED BELOW AND THAT I ATTENDED THE DECEASED FROM **10/15/64** AND THAT I LAST SAW THE DECEASED ALIVE ON **10/4/24/64**	22C. PHYSICIAN OR CORONER—SIGNATURE *Wm Welt*	DEGREE OR TITLE
	22B. CORONER: I HEREBY CERTIFY THAT DEATH OCCURRED AT THE HOUR, DATE AND PLACE STATED ABOVE FROM THE CAUSES STATED BELOW AND THAT I HAVE HELD AN INVESTIGATION/AUTOPSY/INQUEST ON THE REMAINS OF DECEASED AS REQUIRED BY LAW	22D. ADDRESS **135 Lasky Dr Bevly Hills**	22E. DATE SIGNED **10/16/64**

FUNERAL DIRECTOR AND LOCAL REGISTRAR	23. SPECIFY BURIAL, ENTOMBMENT OR CREMATION **burial**	24. DATE **10/17/64**	25. NAME OF CEMETERY OR CREMATORY **Mt Hope Cemetery Peru, Indiana**	26. EMBALMER—SIGNATURE *John A. Hardin* / LICENSE NUMBER **5016** IF BODY EMBALMED
	27. NAME OF FUNERAL DIRECTOR **Pierce Bros. Los Angeles**	28. DATE ACCEPTED FOR REGISTRATION BY LOCAL REGISTRAR **OCT 17 1964**	29. LOCAL REGISTRAR—SIGNATURE ▶ *K.H. Sutherland M.D.*	

CAUSE OF DEATH	30. CAUSE OF DEATH — PART I. DEATH WAS CAUSED BY: IMMEDIATE CAUSE (A) *Myocardial Infarction*	**1 hr**	**APPROXIMATE INTERVAL BETWEEN ONSET AND DEATH**
	CONDITIONS, IF ANY, WHICH GAVE RISE TO THE ABOVE CAUSE (A) STATING THE UNDERLYING CAUSE LAST — DUE TO (B) *Pyelonephritis, bilat. Bronchopneumonia*	**1 wk**	
	DUE TO (C) *Chr Emphysema, Gen Arteriosclerosis*		
	PART II: OTHER SIGNIFICANT CONDITIONS CONTRIBUTING TO DEATH BUT NOT RELATED TO THE TERMINAL DISEASE CONDITION GIVEN IN PART I (A)		

OPERATION AND AUTOPSY	31. OPERATION—CHECK ONE ☒ NO OPERATION PERFORMED □ OPERATION PERFORMED—FINDINGS USED IN DETERMINING ABOVE STATED CAUSES OF DEATH □ OPERATION PERFORMED—FINDINGS NOT USED IN DETERMINING ABOVE STATED CAUSES OF DEATH	32. DATE OF OPERATION	33. AUTOPSY—CHECK ONE □ NO AUTOPSY PERFORMED ☒ AUTOPSY PERFORMED—GROSS FINDINGS USED IN DETERMINING ABOVE STATED CAUSES OF DEATH □ AUTOPSY PERFORMED—GROSS FINDINGS NOT USED IN DETERMINING ABOVE STATED CAUSES OF DEATH

INJURY INFORMATION	34A. SPECIFY ACCIDENT, SUICIDE OR HOMICIDE	34B. DESCRIBE HOW INJURY OCCURRED
	35A. TIME OF INJURY — HOUR / MONTH / DAY / YEAR — M	
	35B. INJURY OCCURRED □ WHILE AT WORK □ NOT WHILE AT WORK	35C. PLACE OF INJURY	35D. CITY, TOWN, OR LOCATION	COUNTY	STATE

REV 11 58 FORM VS 11

Filed NOV 20 1964 RAY E. LEE, COUNTY RECORDER

This is to certify that this document is a true copy of the official record filed with the Registrar-Recorder/County Clerk.

Conny B. McCormack

CONNY B. McCORMACK
Registrar-Recorder/County Clerk

This copy not valid unless prepared on engraved border displaying the Seal and Signature of the Registrar-Recorder/County Clerk.

JAN 31 2005

019158094

MIDWEST BANK NOTE COMPANY   ANY ALTERATION OR ERASURE VOIDS THIS CERTIFICATE

CERTIFICATE OF DEATH
STATE OF CALIFORNIA

42   87-576

STATE FILE NUMBER				LOCAL REGISTRATION DISTRICT AND CERTIFICATE NUMBER

	1A. NAME OF DECEDENT—FIRST	1B. MIDDLE	1C. LAST	2A. DATE OF DEATH (MONTH, DAY, YEAR)	2B. HOUR
DECEDENT PERSONAL DATA	ROBERT	–	PRESTON	March 21, 1987	1715

3. SEX	4. RACE/ETHNICITY	5. SPANISH/HISPANIC	6. DATE OF BIRTH	7. AGE	IF UNDER 1 YEAR — MONTHS / DAYS	IF UNDER 24 HOURS — HOURS / MINUTES
Male	White	NO	June 8, 1918	68 YEARS		

8. BIRTHPLACE OF DECEDENT (STATE OR FOREIGN COUNTRY)	9. NAME AND BIRTHPLACE OF FATHER	10. BIRTH NAME AND BIRTHPLACE OF MOTHER
MA	Frank W. Meservey - MA	Ruth Rea - MA

11A. CITIZEN OF WHAT COUNTRY	11B. IF DECEASED WAS EVER IN MILITARY GIVE DATES OF SERVICE	12. SOCIAL SECURITY NUMBER	13. MARITAL STATUS	14. NAME OF SURVIVING SPOUSE (IF WIFE ENTER BIRTH NAME)
USA	1942 TO 1945	550-14-3561	Married	Catherine Feltus

15. PRIMARY OCCUPATION	16. NUMBER OF YEARS THIS OCCUPATION	17. EMPLOYER (IF SELF-EMPLOYED, SO STATE)	18. KIND OF INDUSTRY OR BUSINESS
Actor	adult life	Self Employed	Entertainment

	19A. USUAL RESIDENCE—STREET ADDRESS (STREET AND NUMBER OR LOCATION)	19B.	19C. CITY OR TOWN
USUAL RESIDENCE	1035 Fairway Road		Santa Barbara

19D. COUNTY	19E. STATE	20. NAME AND ADDRESS OF INFORMANT — RELATIONSHIP
Santa Barbara	CA	Catherine Preston, Wife 1035 Fairway Road Santa Barbara, CA

	21A. PLACE OF DEATH	21B. COUNTY	
PLACE OF DEATH	Cottage Hospital	Santa Barbara	

21C. STREET ADDRESS (STREET AND NUMBER OR LOCATION)	21D. CITY OR TOWN
Pueblo at Bath	Santa Barbara

	22. DEATH WAS CAUSED BY: (ENTER ONLY ONE CAUSE PER LINE FOR A, B, AND C) IMMEDIATE CAUSE		23. APPROXIMATE INTERVAL BETWEEN ONSET AND DEATH	24. WAS DEATH REPORTED TO CORONER?
CAUSE OF DEATH	(A) *Renal Failure*	◄ *4 weeks*		*No*
	CONDITIONS, IF ANY, WHICH GAVE RISE TO THE IMMEDIATE CAUSE, STATING THE UNDERLYING CAUSE LAST. (B) *Metastatic Carcinoma - Liver & Lung*	◄ *3 months*	25. WAS BIOPSY PERFORMED? *Yes*	
	(C) *Primary Carcinoma Tonsil / Floor of Mouth*	*14 months*	26. WAS AUTOPSY PERFORMED? *No*	

23. OTHER SIGNIFICANT CONDITIONS—CONTRIBUTING TO DEATH BUT NOT RELATED TO CAUSE GIVEN IN 22A	27. WAS OPERATION PERFORMED FOR ANY CONDITION IN ITEMS 22 OR 23? TYPE OF OPERATION	DATE
	Resection Left Floor of Mouth	*1-14-8_*

	28A. I CERTIFY THAT DEATH OCCURRED AT THE HOUR, DATE AND PLACE STATED FROM THE CAUSES STATED. I ATTENDED DECEDENT SINCE	I LAST SAW DECEDENT ALIVE	28B. PHYSICIAN—SIGNATURE AND DEGREE OR TITLE	28C. DATE SIGNED	28D. PHYSICIAN'S LICENSE NUMBER
PHYSICIAN'S CERTIFICATION	(ENTER MO. DA. YR.) *1-8-1986*	(ENTER MO. DA. YR.) *3-21-87*	*Albert Medwid M.D.*	*3/23/87*	*C18009*
			28E. TYPE PHYSICIAN'S NAME AND ADDRESS Albert Medwid MD, 2410 Fletcher, Santa Barbara, CA		

	29. SPECIFY ACCIDENT, SUICIDE, ETC.	30. PLACE OF INJURY	31. INJURY AT WORK	32A. DATE OF INJURY—MONTH, DAY, YEAR	32B. HOUR
INJURY INFORMATION					

33. LOCATION (STREET AND NUMBER OR LOCATION AND CITY OR TOWN)	34. DESCRIBE HOW INJURY OCCURRED (EVENTS WHICH RESULTED IN INJURY)

CORONER'S USE ONLY	35A. I CERTIFY THAT DEATH OCCURRED AT THE HOUR, DATE AND PLACE STATED FROM THE CAUSES STATED. AS REQUIRED BY LAW I HAVE HELD AN INQUEST-INVESTIGATION	35B. CORONER—SIGNATURE AND DEGREE OR TITLE	35C. DATE SIGNED

36. DISPOSITION	37. DATE—MONTH, DAY, YEAR	38. NAME AND ADDRESS OF CEMETERY OR CREMATORY	39. EMBALMER'S LICENSE NUMBER AND SIGNATURE
Cremation	3/24/87	Santa Barbara Cemetery, Santa Barbara, CA	Not Embalmed

40A. NAME OF FUNERAL DIRECTOR (OR PERSON ACTING AS SUCH)	40B. LICENSE NO.	41. LOCAL REGISTRAR—SIGNATURE	42. DATE ACCEPTED BY LOCAL REGISTRAR
McDermott-Crockett Mortuary	F 383	*Lawrence Hart M.D. JR*	MAR 23 1987

STATE REGISTRAR	A.	B.	C.	D.	E.

VS-11-11-85

STATE OF CALIFORNIA
CERTIFICATION OF VITAL RECORD

COUNTY OF LOS ANGELES • REGISTRAR-RECORDER/ COUNTY CLERK

CERTIFICATE OF DEATH
STATE OF CALIFORNIA
USE BLACK INK ONLY

39319046906

LOCAL REGISTRATION DISTRICT AND CERTIFICATE NUMBER

	STATE FILE NUMBER					
	1A. NAME OF DECEDENT—FIRST (GIVEN)	1B. MIDDLE	1C. LAST (FAMILY)	2A. DATE OF DEATH—MO, DAY, YR	2B. HOUR	3. SEX
DECEDENT PERSONAL DATA	Vincent	Leonard	Price	10/25/1993	1930	Male
	4. RACE	5. HISPANIC—SPECIFY	6. DATE OF BIRTH—MO, DAY, YR	7 AGE IN YEARS	IF UNDER 1 YEAR / IF UNDER 24 HOURS	
	Caucasion	☐ YES ☒ NO	05/27/1911	82		
	8. STATE OF BIRTH	9. CITIZEN OF WHAT COUNTRY	10A. FULL NAME OF FATHER	10B. STATE OF BIRTH	11A. FULL MAIDEN NAME OF MOTHER	11B. STATE OF BIRTH
	MO	USA	Vincent L. Price Sr.	ILL	Marguerite Wilcox	N.Y.
	12. MILITARY SERVICE	13. SOCIAL SECURITY NO.	14. MARITAL STATUS	15. NAME OF SURVIVING SPOUSE (IF WIFE, ENTER MAIDEN NAME)		
	19__ TO 19__ ☑ NONE	089-10-7381	Widow	None		
	16A. USUAL OCCUPATION	16B. USUAL KIND OF BUSINESS OR INDUSTRY	16C. USUAL EMPLOYER	16D. YEARS IN OCCUPATION	17. EDUCATION—YEARS COMPLETED	
	Actor	Movie/TV	20th Cen. Fox	57	20+	

	18A. RESIDENCE—STREET AND NUMBER OR LOCATION		18B. CITY	18C. ZIP CODE
USUAL RESIDENCE	9255 Swallow Drive		Los Angeles	90069
	18D. COUNTY	18E. NUMBER OF YEARS IN THIS COUNTY / 18F. STATE OR FOREIGN COUNTRY	20. NAME, RELATIONSHIP, MAILING ADDRESS AND ZIP CODE OF INFORMANT	
	Los Angeles	50 / California	Victoria Price (Daughter) 9255 Swallow Dr. Los Angeles, Ca. 90069	

	19A. PLACE OF DEATH	19B. IF HOSPITAL, SPECIFY ONE: IP, ER/OP, DOA / 19C. COUNTY		
PLACE OF DEATH	Residence	Los Angeles		
	19D. STREET ADDRESS—STREET AND NUMBER OR LOCATION / 19E. CITY	TIME INTERVAL BETWEEN ONSET AND DEATH	22. WAS DEATH REPORTED TO CORONER REFERRAL NUMBER	
	9255 Swallow Drive / Los Angeles		☐ YES ☒ NO	

	21. DEATH WAS CAUSED BY: (ENTER ONLY ONE CAUSE PER LINE FOR A, B AND C)			
CAUSE OF DEATH	IMMEDIATE CAUSE (A) Emphysema	Mos.	23. WAS BIOPSY PERFORMED ☐ YES ☑ NO	
	DUE TO (B) Carcinoma of Lung	1 Yr.	24A. WAS AUTOPSY PERFORMED ☐ YES ☒ NO	
	DUE TO (C)		24B. WAS IT USED IN DETERMINING CAUSE OF DEATH ☐ YES ☐ NO	
	25. OTHER SIGNIFICANT CONDITIONS CONTRIBUTING TO DEATH BUT NOT RELATED TO CAUSE GIVEN IN 21	26. WAS OPERATION PERFORMED FOR ANY CONDITION IN ITEM 21 OR 25. IF YES, LIST TYPE OF OPERATION AND DATE.		
	Parkinson Disease	No		

	I CERTIFY THAT TO THE BEST OF MY KNOWLEDGE DEATH OCCURRED AT THE HOUR, DATE AND PLACE STATED FROM THE CAUSES STATED.	27B. SIGNATURE AND DEGREE OR TITLE OF CERTIFIER	27C. CERTIFIER'S LICENSE NUMBER	27D. DATE SIGNED
PHYSICIAN'S CERTIFICATION			620755	10/26/93
	27A. DECEDENT ATTENDED SINCE MONTH, DAY, YEAR / DECEDENT LAST SEEN ALIVE MONTH, DAY, YEAR	27E. TYPE ATTENDING PHYSICIAN'S NAME AND ADDRESS		
	6/22/1989 / 10/25/1993	Richard Wulfsberg MD 16030 Ventura Encino, Ca.		

	I CERTIFY THAT IN MY OPINION DEATH OCCURRED AT THE HOUR, DATE AND PLACE STATED FROM THE CAUSES STATED.	28A. SIGNATURE AND TITLE OF CORONER OR DEPUTY CORONER	28B. DATE SIGNED
CORONER'S USE ONLY	29. MANNER OF DEATH—specify one: natural, accident, suicide, homicide, pending investigation or could not be determined	30A. PLACE OF INJURY	30B. INJURY AT WORK ☐ YES ☐ NO / 30C. DATE OF INJURY MONTH, DAY, YEAR / 31. HOUR
	32. LOCATION (STREET AND NUMBER OR LOCATION AND CITY)	33. DESCRIBE HOW INJURY OCCURRED (EVENTS WHICH RESULTED IN INJURY)	

	34A. DISPOSITION(S)	34B. PLACE OF FINAL DISPOSITION—NAME AND ADDRESS	34C. DATE MO, DAY, YR	35A. SIGNATURE OF EMBALMER	35B. LICENSE NO.
FUNERAL DIRECTOR AND LOCAL REGISTRAR	CR/SC	3 Miles out to Sea Santa Monica Ca.	10/29/93	Not Embalmed	None
	36A. NAME OF FUNERAL DIRECTOR (OR PERSON ACTING AS SUCH)	36B. LICENSE NO.	37. SIGNATURE OF LOCAL REGISTRAR	38. REGISTRATION DATE	
	Gold Cross Mortuary	FD 1303	Robert c. Bath IV	OCT 2 6 1993	

	A.	B.	C.	D.	E.	F.	CENSUS TRACT
STATE REGISTRAR							

VS-11 (REV. 7-92)   1629   MAKE NO ERASURES, WHITEOUTS, OR OTHER ALTERATIONS   01-9-1-2005

This is to certify that this document is a true copy of the official record filed with the Registrar-Recorder/County Clerk.

Conny B. McCormack

CONNY B. McCORMACK
Registrar-Recorder/County Clerk

NOV 0 9 1998
19-604808

This copy not valid unless prepared on engraved border displaying the Seal and Signature of the Registrar-Recorder/County Clerk.

ANY ALTERATION OR ERASURE VOIDS THIS CERTIFICATE

CERTIFICATE OF DEATH
STATE OF CALIFORNIA
USE BLACK INK ONLY/NO ERASURES, WHITEOUTS OR ALTERATIONS
VS-11 (REV. 7/93)

STATE FILE NUMBER	LOCAL REGISTRATION NUMBER

DECEDENT PERSONAL DATA

1. NAME OF DECEDENT—FIRST (GIVEN)	2. MIDDLE	3. LAST (FAMILY)
JULIET	ANNE	PROWSE

4. DATE OF BIRTH MM/DD/CCYY	5. AGE YRS.	IF UNDER 1 YEAR MONTHS / DAYS	IF UNDER 24 HOURS HOURS / MINUTES	6. SEX	7. DATE OF DEATH MM/DD/CCYY	8. HOUR
09/25/1936	59			FE	09/14/1996	0345

9. STATE OF BIRTH	10. SOCIAL SECURITY NO.	11. MILITARY SERVICE	12. MARITAL STATUS	13. EDUCATION—YEARS COMPLETED
INDIA	567-58-1520	19___ To 19___ [X] NONE	DIVORCED	12

14. RACE	15. HISPANIC—SPECIFY	16. USUAL EMPLOYER
CAUCASIAN	[ ] YES _____ [X] No	SELF EMPLOYED

17. OCCUPATION	18. KIND OF BUSINESS	19. YEARS IN OCCUPATION
DANCER	ENTERTAINMENT	53

USUAL RESIDENCE

20. RESIDENCE—STREET AND NUMBER OR LOCATION
343 S. BEVERLY GLEN BLVD

21. CITY	22. COUNTY	23. ZIP CODE	24. YRS IN COUNTY	25. STATE OR FOREIGN COUNTRY
LOS ANGELES	LOS ANGELES	90024	37	CALIFORNIA

INFORMANT

26. NAME, RELATIONSHIP	27. MAILING ADDRESS (STREET AND NUMBER OR RURAL ROUTE NUMBER, CITY OR TOWN, STATE, ZIP)
MARK MORDAH - D.P.O.A.	344 RED RIVER RD., PALM DESERT, CA 92211

SPOUSE AND PARENT INFORMATION

28. NAME OF SURVIVING SPOUSE—FIRST	29. MIDDLE	30. LAST (MAIDEN NAME)
—	—	—

31. NAME OF FATHER—FIRST	32. MIDDLE	33. LAST	34. BIRTH STATE
REGINALD	—	PROWSE	SO. AFRICA

35. NAME OF MOTHER—FIRST	36. MIDDLE	37. LAST (MAIDEN)	38. BIRTH STATE
PHYLLIS	—	DONNE	INDIA

DISPOSITION(S)

39. DATE MM/DD/CCYY	40. PLACE OF FINAL DISPOSITION
09/18/1996	RES:DR.CLIVE PROWSE, #32 BEETHOVEN ST. VANDRBIJL PK,TRAANSVAL S. AFRICA

FUNERAL DIRECTOR AND LOCAL REGISTRAR

41. TYPE OF DISPOSITION(S)	42. SIGNATURE OF EMBALMER	43. LICENSE NO.
CR/TR	▶ NOT EMBALMED	

44. NAME OF FUNERAL DIRECTOR	45. LICENSE NO.	46. SIGNATURE OF LOCAL REGISTRAR	47. DATE MM/DD/CCYY
PIERCE BROS WESTWOOD VILLAGE	FD-951	▶ Mark Sunm____	09/17/1996

PLACE OF DEATH

101. PLACE OF DEATH	102. IF HOSPITAL, SPECIFY ONE:	103. FACILITY OTHER THAN HOSPITAL:	104. COUNTY
RESIDENCE	[ ] IP [ ] ER/OP [ ] DOA	[ ] CONV. HOSP. [X] RES. [ ] OTHER	LOS ANGELES

105. STREET ADDRESS—STREET AND NUMBER OR LOCATION	106. CITY
343 S. BEVERLY GLEN BLVD	LOS ANGELES

CAUSE OF DEATH

107. DEATH WAS CAUSED BY: (ENTER ONLY ONE CAUSE PER LINE FOR A, B, C, AND D)	TIME INTERVAL BETWEEN ONSET AND DEATH	108. DEATH REPORTED TO CORONER
IMMEDIATE CAUSE (A) PANCREATIC CANCER	21 MOS	[ ] YES [X] No — REFERRAL NUMBER
DUE TO (B)		109. BIOPSY PERFORMED [ ] YES [X] No
DUE TO (C)		110. AUTOPSY PERFORMED [ ] YES [X] No
DUE TO (D)		111. USED IN DETERMINING CAUSE [ ] YES [X] No

112. OTHER SIGNIFICANT CONDITIONS CONTRIBUTING TO DEATH BUT NOT RELATED TO CAUSE GIVEN IN 107
NONE

113. WAS OPERATION PERFORMED FOR ANY CONDITION IN ITEM 107 OR 112? IF YES, LIST TYPE OF OPERATION AND DATE.
WHIPPLE PROCEDURE 12/08/1994

PHYSICIAN'S CERTIFICATION

114. I CERTIFY THAT TO THE BEST OF MY KNOWLEDGE DEATH OCCURRED AT THE HOUR, DATE AND PLACE STATED FROM THE CAUSES STATED.	115. SIGNATURE AND TITLE OF CERTIFIER	116. LICENSE NO.	117. DATE MM/DD/CCYY
	▶ Willam K. Isacoff	MG 24596	09/16/1996

DECEDENT ATTENDED SINCE MM/DD/CCYY	DECEDENT LAST SEEN ALIVE MM/DD/CCYY	118. TYPE ATTENDING PHYSICIAN'S NAME, MAILING ADDRESS, ZIP
01/24/1995	09/13/1996	WILLIAM ISACOFF MD. 100 UCLA MEDICAL PLAZA,L.A. CA 90024

CORONER'S USE ONLY

119. MANNER OF DEATH	120. INJURY AT WORK	121. INJURY DATE MM/DD/CCYY	122. HOUR	123. PLACE OF INJURY
[ ] NATURAL [ ] SUICIDE [ ] HOMICIDE [ ] ACCIDENT [ ] PENDING INVESTIGATION [ ] COULD NOT BE DETERMINED	[ ] YES [ ] No			

I CERTIFY THAT IN MY OPINION DEATH OCCURRED AT THE HOUR, DATE AND PLACE STATED FROM THE CAUSES STATED.

124. DESCRIBE HOW INJURY OCCURRED (EVENTS WHICH RESULTED IN INJURY)

125. LOCATION (STREET AND NUMBER OR LOCATION AND CITY AND ZIP CODE)

1579

126. SIGNATURE OF CORONER OR DEPUTY CORONER	127. DATE MM/DD/CCYY	128. TYPED NAME, TITLE OF CORONER OR DEPUTY CORONER
▶		

STATE REGISTRAR

A	B	C	D	E	F	G	H	FAX AUTH. #	CENSUS TRACT

CERTIFICATE OF DEATH
STATE OF CALIFORNIA

0190-053427

STATE FILE NUMBER	LOCAL REGISTRATION DISTRICT AND CERTIFICATE NU

	1A. NAME OF DECEDENT—FIRST	1B. MIDDLE	1C. LAST	2A. DATE OF DEATH (MONTH, DAY, YEAR)	2B.
DECEDENT PERSONAL DATA	GEORGE		RAFT	NOVEMBER 24, 1980	12

3. SEX	4. RACE	5. ETHNICITY	6. DATE OF BIRTH	7. AGE	IF UNDER 1 YEAR	IF UNDER 24
Male	White	Italian/German	September 26,1895	85 YEARS	MONTHS / DAYS	HOURS / M

8. BIRTHPLACE OF DECEDENT (STATE OR FOREIGN COUNTRY)	9. NAME AND BIRTHPLACE OF FATHER	10. BIRTH NAME AND BIRTHPLACE OF MOTHER
New York	Conrad Ranft, Germany	Eva (Unknown),New York

11. CITIZEN OF WHAT COUNTRY	12. SOCIAL SECURITY NUMBER	13. MARITAL STATUS	14. NAME OF SURVIVING SPOUSE (IF WIFE, ENTER BIRTH NAME)
United States	562-01-3281A	Widowed	

15. PRIMARY OCCUPATION	16. NUMBER OF YEARS THIS OCCUPATION	17. EMPLOYER (IF SELF-EMPLOYED, SO STATE)	18. KIND OF INDUSTRY OR BUSINESS
Actor	55	self employed	mot'on pictures

	19A. USUAL RESIDENCE—STREET ADDRESS (STREET AND NUMBER OR LOCATION)	19B.	19C. CITY OR TOWN
USUAL RESIDENCE	2220 Avenue of the Stars, Apt #703		Los Angeles

19D. COUNTY	19E. STATE	20. NAME AND ADDRESS OF INFORMANT—RELATIONSHIP
Los Angeles	California	Mr. James J. Collins (friend)

	21A. PLACE OF DEATH	21B. COUNTY	1310 Olive Drive
PLACE OF DEATH	Los Angeles New Hospital	Los Angeles	Los Angeles,

21C. STREET ADDRESS (STREET AND NUMBER OR LOCATION)	21D. CITY OR TOWN	California 90069
1177 So. Beverly Drive	Los Angeles	

	22. DEATH WAS CAUSED BY: (ENTER ONLY ONE CAUSE PER LINE FOR A, B, AND C)			24. WAS DEATH REPORTED TO CORONER?
CAUSE OF DEATH	IMMEDIATE CAUSE (A) CARDIO-RESPIRATORY ARREST	20 min	APPROXIMATE INTERVAL BETWEEN ONSET AND DEATH	No
	CONDITIONS, IF ANY, WHICH GAVE RISE TO THE IMMEDIATE CAUSE, STATING THE UNDERLYING CAUSE LAST. (B) ACUTE BRONCHOPNEUMONIA	4 DAYS		25. WAS AUTOPSY PERFORMED No
	(C) SEVERE PULMONARY EMPHYSEMA	20 YR.		26. WAS AUTOPSY PERFORMED No

23. OTHER CONDITIONS CONTRIBUTING BUT NOT RELATED TO THE IMMEDIATE CAUSE OF DEATH	27. WAS OPERATION PERFORMED FOR ANY CONDITION IN ITEMS 22 OR 23?	TYPE OF OPERATION	DATE
Acute Myelogenous Leukemia, Peripheral Vascular Disease			No

	28A. I CERTIFY THAT DEATH OCCURRED AT THE HOUR, DATE AND PLACE STATED FROM THE CAUSES STATED.	28B. PHYSICIAN—SIGNATURE AND DEGREE OR TITLE	28C. DATE SIGNED	28D. PHYSICIAN'S LICENSE NUMBER
PHYSICIAN'S CERTIFICATION	I ATTENDED DECEDENT SINCE / I LAST SAW DECEDENT ALIVE	Gary Sugarman, MD	11-25-80	620608
	7-1-60 / 11-24-80	28E. TYPE THE PHYSICIAN'S NAME AND ADDRESS GARY SUGARMAN 436 N. ROXBURY DR	Gary Sugarman, M.D.	

	29. SPECIFY ACCIDENT, SUICIDE, ETC.	30. PLACE OF INJURY	31. INJURY AT WORK	32A. DATE OF INJURY—MONTH, DAY, YEAR	32B. HOUR
INJURY INFORMATION					

	33. LOCATION (STREET AND NUMBER OR LOCATION AND CITY OR TOWN)	34. DESCRIBE HOW INJURY OCCURRED (EVENTS WHICH RESULTED IN INJURY)

CORONER'S USE ONLY	35A. I CERTIFY THAT DEATH OCCURRED AT THE HOUR, DATE AND PLACE FROM THE CAUSES STATED, AS REQUIRED BY LAW I HAVE HELD AN (INQUEST-INVESTIGATION)	35B. CORONER—SIGNATURE AND DEGREE OR TITLE	35C. DATE SIGN

36. DISPOSITION	37. DATE—MONTH, DAY, YEAR	38. NAME AND ADDRESS OF CEMETERY OR CREMATORY	39. EMBALMER'S LICENSE NUMBER AND SIGNATURE
Burial	Nov. 28,1980	FOREST LAWN MEMORIAL PARK 6300 Forest Lawn Drive, Los Angeles, CA	V. Jeanne Morris 70

40. NAME OF FUNERAL DIRECTOR (OR PERSON ACTING AS SUCH)	41. LOCAL REGISTRAR SIGNATURE	42. DATE ACCEPTED BY LOCAL REGISTRAR
Forest Lawn - Hollywood Hills		NOV 26 1980

STATE REGISTRAR	A.	B.	C.	D.	E.	F.

VS-11 (10-78)   01-4-1-048

CERTIFICATE OF DEATH
STATE OF CALIFORNIA
USE BLACK INK ONLY / NO ERASURES, WHITEOUTS OR ALTERATIONS
VS-11 (REV 1/04)

STATE FILE NUMBER

LOCAL REGISTRATION NUMBER

DECEDENT'S PERSONAL DATA

1. NAME OF DECEDENT --- FIRST (Given)	2. MIDDLE	3. LAST (Family)
RONALD	WILSON	REAGAN

AKA, ALSO KNOWN AS --- Include full AKA (FIRST, MIDDLE, LAST): –

4. DATE OF BIRTH mm/dd/ccyy	5. AGE Yrs.	IF UNDER ONE YEAR Months / Days	IF UNDER 24 HOURS Hours / Minutes	6. SEX
02/06/1911	93			M

9. BIRTH STATE/FOREIGN COUNTRY	10. SOCIAL SECURITY NUMBER	11. EVER IN U.S. ARMED FORCES?	12. MARITAL STATUS (at Time of Death)	7. DATE OF DEATH mm/dd/ccyy	8. HOUR (24 Hours)
ILLINOIS	480-07-7456	X YES	MARRIED	06/05/2004	1300

13. EDUCATION Highest Level/Degree	14/15. WAS DECEDENT HISPANIC/LATINO(A)/SPANISH?	16. DECEDENT'S RACE --- Up to 3 races may be listed
BACHELOR'S	YES / X NO	WHITE

17. USUAL OCCUPATION --- Type of work for most of life. DO NOT USE RETIRED	18. KIND OF BUSINESS OR INDUSTRY	19. YEARS IN OCCUPATION
PRESIDENT OF THE UNITED STATES	GOVERNMENT	8

USUAL RESIDENCE

20. DECEDENT'S RESIDENCE (Street and number or location): 668 ST. CLOUD ROAD

21. CITY	22. COUNTY/PROVINCE	23. ZIP CODE	24. YEARS IN COUNTY	25. STATE/FOREIGN COUNTRY
LOS ANGELES	LOS ANGELES	90077	59	CALIFORNIA

INFORMANT

26. INFORMANT'S NAME, RELATIONSHIP	27. INFORMANT'S MAILING ADDRESS
KAY PAIETTA-ADMINISTRATIVE ASSISTANT	10880 WILSHIRE BLVD STE 870, LOS ANGELES CA 90024

SPOUSE AND PARENT INFORMATION

28. NAME OF SURVIVING SPOUSE --- FIRST	29. MIDDLE	30. LAST (Maiden Name)
NANCY	–	DAVIS

31. NAME OF FATHER --- FIRST	32. MIDDLE	33. LAST	34. BIRTH STATE
JOHN	EDWARD	REAGAN	ILLINOIS

35. NAME OF MOTHER --- FIRST	36. MIDDLE	37. LAST (Maiden)	38. BIRTH STATE
NELLE	–	WILSON	ILLINOIS

FUNERAL DIRECTOR/LOCAL REGISTRAR

39. DISPOSITION DATE mm/dd/ccyy	40. PLACE OF FINAL DISPOSITION
06/11/2004	RONALD REAGAN PRESIDENTIAL LIBRARY, SIMI VALLEY, CALIFORNIA 93065

41. TYPE OF DISPOSITION(S)	42. SIGNATURE OF EMBALMER	43. LICENSE NUMBER
BU	Robert M. Boetticher	6153

44. NAME OF FUNERAL ESTABLISHMENT	45. LICENSE NUMBER	46. SIGNATURE OF LOCAL REGISTRAR	47. DATE mm/dd/ccyy
GATES, KINGSLEY & GATES MOELLER MURPHY	FD451	Thomas W. Gutterate	06/10/2004

PLACE OF DEATH

101. PLACE OF DEATH	102. IF HOSPITAL, SPECIFY ONE	103. IF OTHER THAN HOSPITAL, SPECIFY ONE
RESIDENCE	IP / ER/OP / DOA	Hospice / Nursing Home/LTC / X Decedent's Home / Other

104. COUNTY	105. FACILITY ADDRESS OR LOCATION WHERE FOUND	106. CITY
LOS ANGELES	668 ST. CLOUD ROAD	LOS ANGELES

CAUSE OF DEATH

107. CAUSE OF DEATH — Enter the chain of events --- diseases, injuries, or complications --- that directly caused death. DO NOT enter terminal events such as cardiac arrest, respiratory arrest, or ventricular fibrillation without showing the etiology. DO NOT ABBREVIATE.

		Time Interval Between Onset and Death
IMMEDIATE CAUSE (A) (Final disease or condition resulting in death) →	PNEUMONIA	(AT) 2 DAYS
Sequentially list conditions, if any, leading to cause on Line A. Enter UNDERLYING CAUSE (disease or injury that initiated the events resulting in death) LAST (B)		(BT)
(C)		(CT)
(D)		(DT)

108. DEATH REPORTED TO CORONER?	YES / X NO REFERRAL NUMBER
109. BIOPSY PERFORMED?	YES / X NO
110. AUTOPSY PERFORMED?	YES / X NO
111. USED IN DETERMINING CAUSE?	YES / NO

112. OTHER SIGNIFICANT CONDITIONS CONTRIBUTING TO DEATH BUT NOT RESULTING IN THE UNDERLYING CAUSE GIVEN IN 107: ALZHEIMER'S DISEASE

113. WAS OPERATION PERFORMED FOR ANY CONDITION IN ITEM 107 OR 112?	113A. IF FEMALE, PREGNANT IN LAST YEAR?
NO	YES / NO / UNK

PHYSICIAN'S CERTIFICATION

114. I CERTIFY THAT TO THE BEST OF MY KNOWLEDGE DEATH OCCURRED AT THE HOUR, DATE, AND PLACE STATED FROM THE CAUSES STATED.

Decedent Attended Since (A) mm/dd/ccyy	Decedent Last Seen Alive (B) mm/dd/ccyy	115. SIGNATURE AND TITLE OF CERTIFIER	116. LICENSE NUMBER	117. DATE mm/dd/ccyy
06/13/2001	06/05/2004	Terry Schaack MD	A43132	06/07/2004

118. TYPE ATTENDING PHYSICIAN'S NAME, MAILING ADDRESS, ZIP CODE: TERRY M. SCHAACK, MD-9675 BRIGHTON WAY, BEVERLY HILLS CA 90210

CORONER'S USE ONLY

119. I CERTIFY THAT IN MY OPINION DEATH OCCURRED AT THE HOUR, DATE, AND PLACE STATED FROM THE CAUSES STATED.

MANNER OF DEATH	Natural / Accident / Homicide / Suicide / Pending Investigation / Could not be determined	120. INJURED AT WORK? YES / NO / UNK	121. INJURY DATE mm/dd/ccyy	122. HOUR (24 Hours)

123. PLACE OF INJURY (e.g., home, construction site, wooded area, etc.)

INFORMATIONAL, NOT A VALID DOCUMENT TO ESTABLISH IDENTITY

124. DESCRIBE HOW INJURY OCCURRED (Events which resulted in injury)

125. LOCATION OF INJURY (Street and number, or location, and city, and ZIP)

126. SIGNATURE OF CORONER / DEPUTY CORONER	127. DATE mm/dd/ccyy	128. TYPE NAME, TITLE OF CORONER / DEPUTY CORONER

STATE REGISTRAR	A	B	C	D	E		FAX AUTH. #	CENSUS TRACT *090

CERTIFICATION OF VITAL RECORD

COUNTY OF LOS ANGELES • REGISTRAR-RECORDER/COUNTY CLERK

CERTIFICATE OF DEATH   38619002928
STATE OF CALIFORNIA

STATE FILE NUMBER		LOCAL REGISTRATION DISTRICT AND CERTIFICATE NUMBER

DECEDENT PERSONAL DATA

1A. NAME OF DECEDENT—FIRST	1B. MIDDLE	1C. LAST	2A. DATE OF DEATH (MONTH, DAY, YEAR)	2B. HOUR
Donna	Mullenger	Asmus	Jan. 14, 1986	0917

3. SEX	4. RACE/ETHNICITY	5. SPANISH/HISPANIC	6. DATE OF BIRTH	7. AGE	IF UNDER 1 YEAR MONTHS / DAYS	IF UNDER 24 HOURS HOURS / MINUTES
Fem.	White	NO	Jan. 27, 1921	64 YEARS		

8. BIRTHPLACE OF DECEDENT (STATE OR FOREIGN COUNTRY)	9. NAME AND BIRTHPLACE OF FATHER	10. BIRTH NAME AND BIRTHPLACE OF MOTHER
Iowa	William Mullenger, Iowa	Violet Shives, Iowa

11A. CITIZEN OF WHAT COUNTRY	11B. IF DECEASED WAS EVER IN MILITARY GIVE DATES OF SERVICE	12. SOCIAL SECURITY NUMBER	13. MARITAL STATUS	14. NAME OF SURVIVING SPOUSE (IF WIFE, ENTER BIRTH NAME)
U.S.A.	19 n/a TO 19 ___	557-24-7690	Married	Grover Asmus

15. PRIMARY OCCUPATION	16. NUMBER OF YEARS THIS OCCUPATION	17. EMPLOYER (IF SELF-EMPLOYED, SO STATE)	18. KIND OF INDUSTRY OR BUSINESS
Actress	40	Free-Lance	Motion Picture and Television

USUAL RESIDENCE

19A. USUAL RESIDENCE—STREET ADDRESS (STREET AND NUMBER OR LOCATION)	19B.	19C. CITY OR TOWN	
518 Linden Dr.		Beverly Hills	1 OF 2

19D. COUNTY	19E. STATE	20. NAME AND ADDRESS OF INFORMANT—RELATIONSHIP
Los Angeles	California	Grover Asmus - Husband 518 Linden Dr. Beverly Hills, CA 90210

PLACE OF DEATH

21A. PLACE OF DEATH	21B. COUNTY
Residence	Los Angeles

21C. STREET ADDRESS (STREET AND NUMBER OR LOCATION)	21D. CITY OR TOWN
518 Linden Dr.	Beverly Hills

CAUSE OF DEATH

22. DEATH WAS CAUSED BY: (ENTER ONLY ONE CAUSE PER LINE FOR A, B, AND C) IMMEDIATE CAUSE		24. WAS DEATH REPORTED TO CORONER?
(A) Metastatic Carcinoma of the Pancreas 3 mo.	APPROXIMATE INTERVAL BETWEEN ONSET AND DEATH	No
CONDITIONS, IF ANY, WHICH GAVE RISE TO THE IMMEDIATE CAUSE, STATING THE UNDERLYING CAUSE LAST. (B) DUE TO, OR AS A CONSEQUENCE OF		25. WAS BIOPSY PERFORMED? Yes
(C) DUE TO, OR AS A CONSEQUENCE OF		26. WAS AUTOPSY PERFORMED? No

23. OTHER SIGNIFICANT CONDITIONS—CONTRIBUTING TO DEATH BUT NOT RELATED TO CAUSE GIVEN IN 22A	27. WAS OPERATION PERFORMED FOR ANY CONDITION IN ITEMS 22 OR 23? TYPE OF OPERATION	DATE
	Laparotomy	10/30/85

PHYSICIAN'S CERTIFICATION

28A. I CERTIFY THAT DEATH OCCURRED AT THE HOUR, DATE AND PLACE STATED FROM THE CAUSES STATED. I ATTENDED DECEDENT SINCE (ENTER MO, DA, YR)	I LAST SAW DECEDENT ALIVE (ENTER MO, DA, YR)	28B. PHYSICIAN—SIGNATURE AND DEGREE OR TITLE P. Levine MD	28C. DATE SIGNED 1/15/86	28D. PHYSICIAN'S LICENSE NUMBER G035171
9/24/81	1/14/86	28E. TYPE PHYSICIAN'S NAME AND ADDRESS Phillip Levine, MD	8631 W. 3rd St. #815-W Los Angeles, CA 90048	

INJURY INFORMATION

29. SPECIFY ACCIDENT, SUICIDE, ETC.	30. PLACE OF INJURY	31. INJURY AT WORK	32A. DATE OF INJURY—MONTH, DAY, YEAR	32B. HOUR

33. LOCATION (STREET AND NUMBER OR LOCATION AND CITY OR TOWN)	34. DESCRIBE HOW INJURY OCCURRED (EVENTS WHICH RESULTED IN INJURY)

CORONER'S USE ONLY

35A. I CERTIFY THAT DEATH OCCURRED AT THE HOUR, DATE AND PLACE STATED FROM THE CAUSES STATED. AS REQUIRED BY LAW I HAVE HELD AN (INQUEST-INVESTIGATION)	35B. CORONER—SIGNATURE AND DEGREE OR TITLE	35C. DATE SIGNED

36. DISPOSITION	37. DATE—MONTH, DAY, YEAR	38. NAME AND ADDRESS OF CEMETERY OR CREMATORY	39. EMBALMER'S LICENSE NUMBER AND SIGNATURE
Burial	Jan. 17, 1986	Westwood Memorial Park, L.A.	5595 W. R. Pierce

40A. NAME OF FUNERAL DIRECTOR (OR PERSON ACTING AS SUCH)	40B. LICENSE NO.	41. LOCAL REGISTRAR—SIGNATURE	42. DATE ACCEPTED BY LOCAL REGISTRAR
Westwood Village Mortuary	951	Robert Platz L.W.	JAN 16 1986

STATE REGISTRAR

A	B	C	D	E	F
VS-11 (1-85) 1579					01-9-1-7005

This is to certify that this document is a true copy of the official record filed with the Registrar-Recorder/County Clerk.

Beatriz Valdez
BEATRIZ VALDEZ
Registrar-Recorder/County Clerk

AUG 1 0 1995

19-389409

This copy not valid unless prepared on engraved border displaying the Seal and Signature of the Registrar-Recorder/County Clerk.

ANY ALTERATION OR ERASURE VOIDS THIS CERTIFICATE

CERTIFICATE OF DEATH
STATE OF CALIFORNIA
USE BLACK INK ONLY/NO ERASURES, WHITEOUTS OR ALTERATIONS
VS-11 (REV. 7/93)

STATE FILE NUMBER | LOCAL REGISTRATION NUMBER

DECEDENT PERSONAL DATA

1. NAME OF DECEDENT—FIRST (GIVEN)	2. MIDDLE	3. LAST (FAMILY)
Thomas	N.	Rettig

4. DATE OF BIRTH MM/DD/CCYY	5. AGE YRS.	IF UNDER 1 YEAR MONTHS/DAYS	IF UNDER 24 HOURS HOURS/MINUTES	6. SEX	7. DATE OF DEATH MM/DD/CCYY	8. HOUR
12/10/1941	54			M	02/15/1996	1045

9. STATE OF BIRTH	10. SOCIAL SECURITY NO.	11. MILITARY SERVICE	12. MARITAL STATUS	13. EDUCATION—YEARS COMPLETED
NY	111-22-5489	19 __ TO 19 __ [X] NONE	Divorced	12

14. RACE	15. HISPANIC—SPECIFY	16. USUAL EMPLOYER
Caucasian	[ ] YES [X] NO	Self Employed

1 OF 2

17. OCCUPATION	18. KIND OF BUSINESS	19. YEARS IN OCCUPATION
Software Developer	Computer	15

USUAL RESIDENCE

20. RESIDENCE—STREET AND NUMBER OR LOCATION
13802 Northwest Passage # 301

21. CITY	22. COUNTY	23. ZIP CODE	24. YRS IN COUNTY	25. STATE OR FOREIGN COUNTRY
Marina Del Rey	Los Angeles	90292	42	CA

INFORMANT

26. NAME, RELATIONSHIP	27. MAILING ADDRESS (STREET AND NUMBER OR RURAL ROUTE NUMBER, CITY OR TOWN, STATE, ZIP)
Tom Rettig -Son	631 Sonoma St. Richmond, CA 94805

SPOUSE AND PARENT INFORMATION

28. NAME OF SURVIVING SPOUSE—FIRST	29. MIDDLE	30. LAST (MAIDEN NAME)
--	--	--

31. NAME OF FATHER—FIRST	32. MIDDLE	33. LAST	34. BIRTH STATE
Robert	E.	Rettig	NY

35. NAME OF MOTHER—FIRST	36. MIDDLE	37. LAST (MAIDEN)	38. BIRTH STATE
Rosemary	--	Nibali	NY

DISPOSITION(S)

39. DATE MM/DD/CCYY	40. PLACE OF FINAL DISPOSITION
02/26/1996	3 miles off Marina Del Rey, CA shoreline

FUNERAL DIRECTOR AND LOCAL REGISTRAR

41. TYPE OF DISPOSITION(S)	42. SIGNATURE OF EMBALMER	43. LICENSE NO.
CR/SEA	▶ Not Embalmed	--

44. NAME OF FUNERAL DIRECTOR	45. LICENSE NO.	46. SIGNATURE OF LOCAL REGISTRAR	47. DATE MM/DD/CCYY
Inglewood Mortuary	FD905	▶ Robert Mott	02/21/1996

PLACE OF DEATH

101. PLACE OF DEATH	102. IF HOSPITAL, SPECIFY ONE:	103. FACILITY OTHER THAN HOSPITAL:	104. COUNTY
Residence	[ ] IP [ ] ER/OP [ ] DOA	[ ] CONV. HOSP. [X] RES. [ ] OTHER	Los Angeles

105. STREET ADDRESS—STREET AND NUMBER OR LOCATION	106. CITY
13802 Northwest Passage # 301	Marina Del Rey

CAUSE OF DEATH

107. DEATH WAS CAUSED BY: (ENTER ONLY ONE CAUSE PER LINE FOR A, B, C, AND D)

			TIME INTERVAL BETWEEN ONSET AND DEATH	108. DEATH REPORTED TO CORONER
IMMEDIATE CAUSE	(A)	DEFERRED		[X] YES [ ] NO
				REFERRAL NUMBER 96-01387
DUE TO	(B)			109. BIOPSY PERFORMED [ ] YES [X] NO
DUE TO	(C)			110. AUTOPSY PERFORMED [X] YES [ ] NO
DUE TO	(D)			111. USED IN DETERMINING CAUSE [ ] YES [ ] NO

112. OTHER SIGNIFICANT CONDITIONS CONTRIBUTING TO DEATH BUT NOT RELATED TO CAUSE GIVEN IN 107

113. WAS OPERATION PERFORMED FOR ANY CONDITION IN ITEM 107 OR 112? IF YES, LIST TYPE OF OPERATION AND DATE.

PHYSICIAN'S CERTIFICATION

114. I CERTIFY THAT TO THE BEST OF MY KNOWLEDGE DEATH OCCURRED AT THE HOUR, DATE AND PLACE STATED FROM THE CAUSES STATED.	115. SIGNATURE AND TITLE OF CERTIFIER	116. LICENSE NO.	117. DATE MM/DD/CCYY
DECEDENT ATTENDED SINCE MM/DD/CCYY	DECEDENT LAST SEEN ALIVE MM/DD/CCYY	▶		
		118. TYPE ATTENDING PHYSICIAN'S NAME, MAILING ADDRESS + ZIP		

CORONER'S USE ONLY

I CERTIFY THAT IN MY OPINION DEATH OCCURRED AT THE HOUR, DATE AND PLACE STATED FROM THE CAUSES STATED.	120. INJURY AT WORK	121. INJURY DATE MM/DD/CCYY	122. HOUR	123. PLACE OF INJURY
119. MANNER OF DEATH	[ ] YES [ ] NO			
[ ] NATURAL [ ] SUICIDE [ ] HOMICIDE [ ] ACCIDENT [X] PENDING INVESTIGATION [ ] COULD NOT BE DETERMINED	124. DESCRIBE HOW INJURY OCCURRED (EVENTS WHICH RESULTED IN INJURY)			

125. LOCATION (STREET AND NUMBER OR LOCATION AND CITY AND ZIP CODE)

126. SIGNATURE OF CORONER OR DEPUTY CORONER	127. DATE MM/DD/CCYY	128. TYPED NAME, TITLE OF CORONER OR DEPUTY CORONER
▶ Mary T. Macias	02/20/1996	MARY T. MACIAS/DEPUTY CORONER

4410

STATE | A | B | C | D | E | F | G | H | FAX AUTH. # | CENSUS TRACT

STATE OF CALIFORNIA
CERTIFICATION OF VITAL RECORD

COUNTY OF LOS ANGELES
DEPARTMENT OF HEALTH SERVICES

CERTIFICATE OF DEATH
STATE OF CALIFORNIA
USE BLACK INK ONLY / NO ERASURES, WHITEOUTS OR ALTERATIONS
VS-11 (REV 1/03)

STATE FILE NUMBER		LOCAL REGISTRATION NUMBER

DECEDENT'S PERSONAL DATA

1. NAME OF DECEDENT --- FIRST (Given)	2. MIDDLE	3. LAST (Family)
JOHNATHAN	SOUTHWORTH	RITTER

AKA, ALSO KNOWN AS --- Include full AKA (FIRST, MIDDLE, LAST)	4. DATE OF BIRTH mm/dd/ccyy	5. AGE Yrs.	IF UNDER ONE YEAR Months / Days	IF UNDER 24 HOURS Hours / Minutes	6. SEX
-	09/17/1948	54			MALE

9. BIRTH STATE/FOREIGN COUNTRY	10. SOCIAL SECURITY NUMBER	11. EVER IN U.S. ARMED FORCES?	12. MARITAL STATUS (at Time of Death)	7. DATE OF DEATH mm/dd/ccyy	8. HOUR (24 Hours)
CA	548-80-3559	YES [X] NO UNK	MARRIED	09/11/2003	2248

13. EDUCATION --- Highest Level/Degree	14/15. WAS DECEDENT SPANISH/HISPANIC/LATINO? (If yes, see worksheet on back)	16. DECEDENT'S RACE --- Up to 3 races may be listed (see worksheet on back)
BACHELOR'S	YES [X] NO	WHITE

17. USUAL OCCUPATION --- Type of work for most of life. DO NOT USE RETIRED	18. KIND OF BUSINESS OR INDUSTRY (e.g., grocery store, road construction, employment agency, etc.)	19. YEARS IN OCCUPATION
ACTOR	ENTERTAINMENT	35

USUAL RESIDENCE

20. DECEDENT'S RESIDENCE (Street and number or location)
1205 BENEDICT CANYON DRIVE

21. CITY	22. COUNTY/PROVINCE	23. ZIP CODE	24. YEARS IN COUNTY	25. STATE/FOREIGN COUNTRY
BEVERLY HILLS	LOS ANGELES	90210	54	CA

INFORMANT

26. INFORMANT'S NAME, RELATIONSHIP	27. INFORMANT'S MAILING ADDRESS (Street and number or rural route number, city or town, state, ZIP)
AMY YASBECK, WIFE	1205 BENEDICT CANYON DRIVE BEVERLY HILLS CA 90210

SPOUSE AND PARENT INFORMATION

28. NAME OF SURVIVING SPOUSE --- FIRST	29. MIDDLE	30. LAST (Maiden Name)
AMY	-	YASBECK

31. NAME OF FATHER --- FIRST	32. MIDDLE	33. LAST	34. BIRTH STATE
MAURICE	WOODWARD	RITTER	TEXAS

35. NAME OF MOTHER --- FIRST	36. MIDDLE	37. LAST (Maiden)	38. BIRTH STATE
DOROTHY	FAY	SOUTHWORTH	ARIZONA

FUNERAL DIRECTOR/ LOCAL REGISTRAR

39. DISPOSITION DATE mm/dd/ccyy	40. PLACE OF FINAL DISPOSITION
09/15/2003	FOREST LAWN MEMORIAL PARK 6300 FOREST LAWN DRIVE LOS ANGELES CA 90068

41. TYPE OF DISPOSITION(S)	42. SIGNATURE OF EMBALMER	43. LICENSE NUMBER
BU	▶ Michael Stock	8755

44. NAME OF FUNERAL ESTABLISHMENT	45. LICENSE NUMBER	46. SIGNATURE OF LOCAL REGISTRAR	47. DATE mm/dd/ccyy
FOREST LAWN HOLLYWOOD HILLS	FD904	▶ Thomas L. Garthwaite wgm	09/15/2003

PLACE OF DEATH

101. PLACE OF DEATH	102. IF HOSPITAL, SPECIFY ONE	103. IF OTHER THAN HOSPITAL, SPECIFY ONE
PROVIDENCE ST JOSEPH MEDICAL CENTER	[X] IP ER/OP DOA	Hospice / Nursing Home/LTC / Decedent's Home / Other

104. COUNTY	105. FACILITY ADDRESS OR LOCATION WHERE FOUND (Street and number or location)	106. CITY
LOS ANGELES	501 S BUENA VISTA STREET	BURBANK

CAUSE OF DEATH

107. CAUSE OF DEATH		Time Interval Between Onset and Death	108. DEATH REPORTED TO CORONER?
IMMEDIATE CAUSE (A) (Final disease or condition resulting in death) →	CARDIO PULMONARY ARREST	(AT) MINS	[X] YES NO
Sequentially list conditions, if any, leading to cause on Line A. Enter UNDERLYING CAUSE (disease or injury that initiated the events resulting in death) LAST (B)	THORACIC ASCENDING AORTIC DISSECTING ANEURYSM	(BT) HOURS	REFERRAL NUMBER 2003-56867
(C)		(CT)	109. BIOPSY PERFORMED? YES [X] NO
(D)		(DT)	110. AUTOPSY PERFORMED? YES [X] NO
			111. USED IN DETERMINING CAUSE? YES [X] NO

112. OTHER SIGNIFICANT CONDITIONS CONTRIBUTING TO DEATH BUT NOT RESULTING IN THE UNDERLYING CAUSE GIVEN IN 107
HYPERLIPIDEMIA

113. WAS OPERATION PERFORMED FOR ANY CONDITION IN ITEM 107 OR 112? (If yes, list type of operation and date.)	113A. IF FEMALE, PREGNANT IN LAST YEAR?
THORACOTOMY, ANGIOGRAM 09/11/2003	YES NO UNK

PHYSICIAN'S CERTIFICATION

114. I CERTIFY THAT TO THE BEST OF MY KNOWLEDGE DEATH OCCURRED AT THE HOUR, DATE, AND PLACE STATED FROM THE CAUSES STATED.	115. SIGNATURE AND TITLE OF CERTIFIER	116. LICENSE NUMBER	117. DATE mm/dd/ccyy
Decedent Attended Since (A) 09/11/2003 / Decedent Last Seen Alive (B) 09/11/2003	▶ Richard Kroop MD	G36316	09/12/2003

118. TYPE ATTENDING PHYSICIAN'S NAME, MAILING ADDRESS, ZIP CODE
RICHARD KROOP MD 2031 W ALAMEDA AVE BURBANK CA 91505

CORONER'S USE ONLY

119. I CERTIFY THAT IN MY OPINION DEATH OCCURRED AT THE HOUR, DATE, AND PLACE STATED FROM THE CAUSES STATED.	120. INJURED AT WORK?	121. INJURY DATE mm/dd/ccyy	122. HOUR (24 Hours)
MANNER OF DEATH: Natural / Accident / Homicide / Suicide / Pending Investigation / Could not be determined	YES NO UNK		

123. PLACE OF INJURY (e.g., home, construction site, wooded area, etc.)

124. DESCRIBE HOW INJURY OCCURRED (Events which resulted in injury)

125. LOCATION OF INJURY (Street and number, or location, and city, and ZIP)

126. SIGNATURE OF CORONER / DEPUTY CORONER	127. DATE mm/dd/ccyy	128. TYPE NAME, TITLE OF CORONER / DEPUTY CORONER

STATE REGISTRAR	A	B	C	D	E	FAX AUTH. #	CENSUS TRACT

090673558

09067355558

This is a true certified copy of the record filed in the County of Los Angeles Department of Health Services if it bears the Registrar's signature in purple ink.

Thomas L. Garthwaite
Director of Health Services and Registrar

219 DATE ISSUED
NOV 1 9 2003

This copy not valid unless prepared on engraved border displaying seal and signature of Registrar.

ANY ALTERATION OR ERASURE VOIDS THIS CERTIFICATE

COUNTY OF LOS ANGELES
DEPARTMENT OF HEALTH SERVICES

STATE OF CALIFORNIA — CERTIFICATION OF VITAL RECORD

CERTIFICATE OF DEATH
STATE OF CALIFORNIA
USE BLACK INK ONLY / NO ERASURES, WHITEOUTS OR ALTERATIONS
VS-11 (REV 1/03)

STATE FILE NUMBER — LOCAL REGISTRATION NUMBER: 3 2003 19 003935

1. NAME OF DECEDENT — FIRST (Given)	ROBERT
2. MIDDLE	G.
3. LAST (Family)	ROCKWELL
AKA, ALSO KNOWN AS	-
4. DATE OF BIRTH mm/dd/ccyy	10/15/1916
5. AGE Yrs.	86
6. SEX	M
8. BIRTH STATE/FOREIGN COUNTRY	ILLINOIS
10. SOCIAL SECURITY NUMBER	332-05-8423
11. EVER IN U.S. ARMED FORCES?	X YES
12. MARITAL STATUS	MARRIED
7. DATE OF DEATH	01/25/2003
6. HOUR (24 Hours)	1935
13. EDUCATION	ASSOCIATE
14/15. WAS DECEDENT SPANISH/HISPANIC/LATINO?	X NO
16. DECEDENT'S RACE	CAUCASIAN
17. USUAL OCCUPATION	ACTOR
18. KIND OF BUSINESS OR INDUSTRY	TELEVISION
19. YEARS IN OCCUPATION	50
20. DECEDENT'S RESIDENCE	18428 COASTLINE DR.
21. CITY	MALIBU
22. COUNTY/PROVINCE	LOS ANGELES
23. ZIP CODE	90265
24. YEARS IN COUNTY	50
25. STATE/FOREIGN COUNTRY	CA
26. INFORMANT'S NAME, RELATIONSHIP	BETTY ANNE ROCKWELL - WIFE
27. INFORMANT'S MAILING ADDRESS	18428 COASTLINE DR. MALIBU, CA. 90265
28. NAME OF SURVIVING SPOUSE — FIRST	BETTY
29. MIDDLE	ANNE
30. LAST (Maiden Name)	WEISS
31. NAME OF FATHER — FIRST	HAROLD
32. MIDDLE	GRISWOLD
33. LAST	ROCKWELL
34. BIRTH STATE	IL
35. NAME OF MOTHER — FIRST	MARGARET
36. MIDDLE	BROWN
37. LAST (Maiden)	HAWKINS
38. BIRTH STATE	WI
39. DISPOSITION DATE	02/05/2003
40. PLACE OF FINAL DISPOSITION	RES: BETTY ANNE ROCKWELL 18428 COASTLINE DR. MALIBU, CA. 90265
41. TYPE OF DISPOSITION(S)	CR/RES
42. SIGNATURE OF EMBALMER	NOT EMBALMED
43. LICENSE NUMBER	-
44. NAME OF FUNERAL ESTABLISHMENT	PIERCE BROS. WESTWOOD
45. LICENSE NUMBER	FD-951
46. SIGNATURE OF LOCAL REGISTRAR	Thomas J. Garthwaite
47. DATE	02/04/2003
101. PLACE OF DEATH	OWN RESIDENCE
103. IF OTHER THAN HOSPITAL	X Decedent's Home
104. COUNTY	LOS ANGELES
105. FACILITY ADDRESS OR LOCATION WHERE FOUND	18428 COASTLINE DR.
106. CITY	MALIBU

107. CAUSE OF DEATH

	Cause	Time Interval Between Onset and Death
IMMEDIATE CAUSE (A)	CARDIOPULMONARY ARREST	1 day
(B)	METASTATIC PROSTATE CANCER	2 years
(C)		
(D)		

108. DEATH REPORTED TO CORONER? X YES — REFERRAL NUMBER 2003-50884
109. BIOPSY PERFORMED? X YES
110. AUTOPSY PERFORMED? X NO
111. USED IN DETERMINING CAUSE?

112. OTHER SIGNIFICANT CONDITIONS	NONE
113. WAS OPERATION PERFORMED	NO
114. CERTIFY death occurred — Decedent Attended Since (A)	02/12/2001
Decedent Last Seen Alive	11/26/2002
115. SIGNATURE AND TITLE OF CERTIFIER	(signature)
116. LICENSE NUMBER	G36051
117. DATE	01/27/2003
118. TYPE ATTENDING PHYSICIAN'S NAME, MAILING ADDRESS, ZIP CODE	DANIEL J. LIEBER, MD. 2001 SANTA MONICA BLVD. SANTA MONICA, CA. 90404
119. MANNER OF DEATH	
120. INJURED AT WORK?	
121. INJURY DATE	
122. HOUR	
123. PLACE OF INJURY	
124. DESCRIBE HOW INJURY OCCURRED	
125. LOCATION OF INJURY	
126. SIGNATURE OF CORONER / DEPUTY CORONER	
127. DATE	
128. TYPE NAME, TITLE OF CORONER / DEPUTY CORONER	

STATE REGISTRAR: A B C D E — FAX AUTH. # — CENSUS TRACT

090610363

This is a true certified copy of the record filed in the County of Los Angeles Department of Health Services if it bears the Registrar's signature in purple ink.

Thomas L. Garthwaite
Director of Health Services and Registrar

DATE ISSUED 234 APR 07 2003

This copy not valid unless prepared on engraved border displaying seal and signature of Registrar.

STATE OF CALIFORNIA
CERTIFICATION OF VITAL RECORD

COUNTY OF LOS ANGELES
DEPARTMENT OF HEALTH SERVICES

CERTIFICATE OF DEATH
STATE OF CALIFORNIA
USE BLACK INK ONLY/NO ERASURES, WHITEOUTS OR ALTERATIONS
VS-11 (REV. 7/97)

STATE FILE NUMBER   LOCAL REGISTRATION NUMBER

	1. NAME OF DECEDENT—FIRST (GIVEN)	2. MIDDLE	3. LAST (FAMILY)	
	ESTHER		ROLLE	

DECEDENT PERSONAL DATA

4. DATE OF BIRTH MM/DD/CCYY	5. AGE YRS.	IF UNDER 1 YEAR MONTHS / DAYS	IF UNDER 24 HOURS HOURS / MINUTES	6. SEX	7. DATE OF DEATH MM/DD/CCYY	8. HOUR
11/08/1920	78			FE	11/17/1998	2318

9. STATE OF BIRTH	10. SOCIAL SECURITY NO.	11. MILITARY SERVICE	12. MARITAL STATUS	13. EDUCATION—YEARS COMPLETED
FL	056-18-8794	YES / [X] NO / UNK	Divorced	16

14. RACE	15. HISPANIC—SPECIFY		16. USUAL EMPLOYER	
Black	YES	[X] NO	Various	

17. OCCUPATION	18. KIND OF BUSINESS	19. YEARS IN OCCUPATION
Actress	Entertainment	50

USUAL RESIDENCE

20. RESIDENCE—(STREET AND NUMBER OR LOCATION)				
4421 Don Felipe Drive				

21. CITY	22. COUNTY	23. ZIP CODE	24. YRS IN COUNTY	25. STATE OR FOREIGN COUNTRY
Los Angeles	Los Angeles	90008	27	California

INFORMANT

26. NAME, RELATIONSHIP	27. MAILING ADDRESS (STREET AND NUMBER OR RURAL ROUTE NUMBER, CITY OR TOWN, STATE, ZIP)
Isaiah Rolle-Brother	134 N.W. 15th Street Pompano Bch Fl 33060

SPOUSE AND PARENT INFORMATION

28. NAME OF SURVIVING SPOUSE—FIRST	29. MIDDLE	30. LAST (MAIDEN NAME)	
-		-	

31. NAME OF FATHER—FIRST	32. MIDDLE	33. LAST	34. BIRTH STATE
Jonathan	-	Rolle	Bahamas

35. NAME OF MOTHER—FIRST	36. MIDDLE	37. LAST (MAIDEN)	38. BIRTH STATE
Elizabeth	-	Dames	Bahamas

DISPOSITION(S)

39. DATE MM/DD/CCYY	40. PLACE OF FINAL DISPOSITION
11/25/1998	Westview Cemetery Broward County, Pompano Beach, Florida

FUNERAL DIRECTOR AND LOCAL REGISTRAR

41. TYPE OF DISPOSITION(S)	42. SIGNATURE OF EMBALMER	43. LICENSE NO.
Tr/Burial	▶ Keri McWilliams	8163

44. NAME OF FUNERAL DIRECTOR	45. LICENSE NO.	46. SIGNATURE OF LOCAL REGISTRAR	47. DATE MM/DD/CCYY
HARRISON-ROSS MORTUARY	FD 551	Mark Amano	11/24/1998

PLACE OF DEATH

101. PLACE OF DEATH	102. IF HOSPITAL, SPECIFY ONE:	103. FACILITY OTHER THAN HOSPITAL	104. COUNTY
BROTMAN MEDICAL CENTER	[X] IP / ER/OP / DOA	CONV. HOSP. / RES. CARE / OTHER	LOS ANGELES

105. STREET ADDRESS—(STREET AND NUMBER OR LOCATION)	106. CITY
3828 DELMAS TERRACE	CULVER CITY

CAUSE OF DEATH

107. DEATH WAS CAUSED BY: (ENTER ONLY ONE CAUSE PER LINE FOR A, B, C, AND D)		TIME INTERVAL BETWEEN ONSET AND DEATH	108. DEATH REPORTED TO CORONER
IMMEDIATE CAUSE (A)	ACUTE MYOCARDIAL INFARCTION	MINS	YES / [X] NO REFERRAL NUMBER
DUE TO (B)	GENERALIZED ARTERIOSCLEROSIS	YEARS	109. BIOPSY PERFORMED YES / [X] NO
DUE TO (C)	DIABETES TYPE II	YEARS	110. AUTOPSY PERFORMED YES / [X] NO
DUE TO (D)			111. USED IN DETERMINING CAUSE YES / [X] NO

112. OTHER SIGNIFICANT CONDITIONS CONTRIBUTING TO DEATH BUT NOT RELATED TO CAUSE GIVEN IN 107
CHRONIC RENAL FAILURE

113. WAS OPERATION PERFORMED FOR ANY CONDITION IN ITEM 107 OR 112? IF YES, LIST TYPE OF OPERATION AND DATE.
NO

PHYSICIAN'S CERTIFICATION

114. I CERTIFY THAT TO THE BEST OF MY KNOWLEDGE DEATH OCCURRED AT THE HOUR, DATE AND PLACE STATED FROM THE CAUSES STATED.	115. SIGNATURE AND TITLE OF CERTIFIER	116. LICENSE NO.	117. DATE MM/DD/CCYY
DECEDENT ATTENDED SINCE 08/22/1996 — DECEDENT LAST SEEN ALIVE 10/29/1998	▶ Wms E Young	G034511	11/23/1998

118. TYPE ATTENDING PHYSICIAN'S NAME, MAILING ADDRESS, ZIP
William Young M.D. 8631 W. 3rd Street #1135E L.A., CA 90048

CORONER'S USE ONLY

I CERTIFY THAT IN MY OPINION DEATH OCCURRED AT THE HOUR, DATE AND PLACE STATED FROM THE CAUSES STATED.	120. INJURY AT WORK	121. INJURY DATE MM/DD/CCYY	122. HOUR	123. PLACE OF INJURY
	YES / NO			

119. MANNER OF DEATH	124. DESCRIBE HOW INJURY OCCURRED (EVENTS WHICH RESULTED IN INJURY)
NATURAL / SUICIDE / HOMICIDE / ACCIDENT / PENDING INVESTIGATION / COULD NOT BE DETERMINED	

125. LOCATION (STREET AND NUMBER OR LOCATION AND CITY, ZIP)

12

2500

STATE REGISTRAR

126. SIGNATURE OF CORONER OR DEPUTY CORONER	127. DATE MM/DD/CCYY	128. TYPED NAME, TITLE OF CORONER OR DEPUTY CORONER
▶		

A	B	C	D	E	F	G	H	FAX AUTH. #	CENSUS TRACT
									090190793

This is a true certified copy of the record filed in the County of Los Angeles
Department of Health Services if it bears the Registrar's signature in purple ink.

DATE ISSUED   DEC 01 1998

Director of Health Service and Registrar

This copy not valid unless prepared on engraved border displaying seal and signature of Registrar.

DE LA RUE   ANY ALTERATION OR ERASURE VOIDS THIS CERTIFICATE

STATE OF CALIFORNIA
CERTIFICATION OF VITAL RECORD

COUNTY OF LOS ANGELES
DEPARTMENT OF HEALTH SERVICES

CERTIFICATE OF DEATH
STATE OF CALIFORNIA
USE BLACK INK ONLY/NO ERASURES, WHITEOUTS OR ALTERATIONS
VS-11 (REV. 1/00)

3 2000 19 002970

1. NAME OF DECEDENT—FIRST (GIVEN) FRAN	2. MIDDLE RYAN	3. LAST (FAMILY) SHAFER

4. DATE OF BIRTH 11/29/1916 | 5. AGE YRS 83 | 6. SEX F | 7. DATE OF DEATH 01/15/2000 | 8. HOUR 2126

9. STATE OF BIRTH CA | 10. SOCIAL SECURITY NO. 572-09-6495 | 11. MILITARY SERVICE X No | 12. MARITAL STATUS WIDOWED | 13. EDUCATION 15

14. RACE CAUCASIAN | 15. HISPANIC X No | 16. USUAL EMPLOYER SELF EMPLOYED

17. OCCUPATION ACTRESS | 18. KIND OF BUSINESS ENTERTAINMENT | 19. YEARS IN OCCUPATION 75

20. RESIDENCE 4204 WOODLAND AVE

21. CITY BURBANK | 22. COUNTY LOS ANGELES | 23. ZIP CODE 91505 | 24. YRS IN COUNTY 35 | 25. STATE CA

26. NAME, RELATIONSHIP CHRIS SHAFER, SON | 27. MAILING ADDRESS 10821 OSTEGO ST, NORTH HOLLYWOOD, CA. 91601

31. NAME OF FATHER JACK | 33. LAST RYAN | 34. BIRTH STATE UNK

35. NAME OF MOTHER MARY | 37. LAST (MAIDEN) BURTON | 38. BIRTH STATE UNK

39. DATE 01/26/2000 | 40. PLACE OF FINAL DISPOSITION RESIDENCE: CHRIS SHAFER, 10821 OSTEGO ST, NORTH HOLLYWOOD, CA 91601

41. TYPE OF DISPOSITION CR/RES | 42. NOT EMBALMED | 43. LICENSE NO. -

44. NAME OF FUNERAL DIRECTOR FOREST LAWN HOLLYWOOD HILLS | 45. LICENSE NO. FD 904 | 47. DATE 01/20/2000

101. PLACE OF DEATH RESIDENCE | 104. COUNTY LOS ANGELES

105. STREET ADDRESS 4204 WOODLAND AVE | 106. CITY BURBANK

107. DEATH WAS CAUSED BY:
IMMEDIATE CAUSE (A) CARDIAC ARRHYTHMIA — 5 MIN
DUE TO (B) CORONARY ARTERY DISEASE — 10 YRS

108. DEATH REPORTED TO CORONER X No
109. BIOPSY PERFORMED X No
110. AUTOPSY PERFORMED X No
111. USED IN DETERMINING CAUSE X No

112. OTHER SIGNIFICANT CONDITIONS NONE

113. WAS OPERATION PERFORMED NO

114. DECEDENT ATTENDED SINCE 01/15/1997 | DECEDENT LAST SEEN ALIVE 01/15/2000

115. SIGNATURE AND TITLE OF CERTIFIER James W Davis Jr M.D. | 116. LICENSE NO. G032480 | 117. DATE 01/18/2000

118. JAMES W DAVIS, JR, MD 200 MED CTR PLAZA #420, LA, CA 90095

119. MANNER OF DEATH (CORONER'S USE ONLY)
15
4149

FAX AUTH. # 273/13457

00323663

CERTIFICATE OF DEATH
STATE OF CALIFORNIA
USE BLACK INK ONLY/NO ERASURES, WHITEOUTS OR ALTERATIONS
VS-11 (REV. 7/93)

39419030456

STATE FILE NUMBER   LOCAL REGISTRATION NUMBER

1. NAME OF DECEDENT—FIRST (GIVEN) Richard	2. MIDDLE –	3. LAST (FAMILY) Sargent

DECEDENT PERSONAL DATA

4. DATE OF BIRTH MM/DD/CCYY 04/19/1930	5. AGE YRS. 64	IF UNDER 1 YEAR MONTHS / DAYS	IF UNDER 24 HOURS HOURS / MINUTES	6. SEX M	7. DATE OF DEATH MM/DD/CCYY 07/08/1994	8. HOUR 1300

9. STATE OF BIRTH CA	10. SOCIAL SECURITY NO. 567-46-1303	11. MILITARY SERVICE 19__ TO 19__ [X] NONE	12. MARITAL STATUS NEVER MARRIED	13. EDUCATION —YEARS COMPLETED 14

14. RACE CAUCASIAN	15. HISPANIC—SPECIFY [ ] YES ____ [X] NO	16. USUAL EMPLOYER SELF EMPLOYED

17. OCCUPATION ACTOR	18. KIND OF BUSINESS ENTERTAINMENT	19. YEARS IN OCCUPATION 40

USUAL RESIDENCE

20. RESIDENCE—STREET AND NUMBER OR LOCATION 7422 PALO VISTA DR.				
21. CITY LOS ANGELES	22. COUNTY LOS ANGELES	23. ZIP CODE 90046	24. YRS IN COUNTY 45	25. STATE OR FOREIGN COUNTRY CALIFORNIA

INFORMANT

26. NAME, RELATIONSHIP NORMAN K. McINNIS, JR., EXECUTOR	27. MAILING ADDRESS (STREET AND NUMBER OR RURAL ROUTE NUMBER, CITY OR TOWN, STATE, ZIP) 8456 W. FOUNTAIN #18 LOS ANGELES, CA. 90069

SPOUSE AND PARENT INFORMATION

28. NAME OF SURVIVING SPOUSE—FIRST –	29. MIDDLE –	30. LAST (MAIDEN NAME) –
31. NAME OF FATHER—FIRST ELMER	32. MIDDLE –	33. LAST COX	34. BIRTH STATE CA
35. NAME OF MOTHER—FIRST RUTH	36. MIDDLE –	37. LAST (MAIDEN) McNAUGHTON	38. BIRTH STATE KS

DISPOSITION(S)

39. DATE MM/DD/CCYY 07/22/1994	40. PLACE OF FINAL DISPOSITION RES: ALBERT K. WILLIAMS, 7422 PALO VISTA DR., LOS ANGELES, CA. 90046

FUNERAL DIRECTOR AND LOCAL REGISTRAR

41. TYPE OF DISPOSITION(S) CR/RES	42. SIGNATURE OF EMBALMER ▶ *Mark Hatchard*	43. LICENSE NO. 7503
44. NAME OF FUNERAL DIRECTOR FOREST LAWN HOLLYWOOD HILLS	45. LICENSE NO. F 904	46. SIGNATURE OF LOCAL REGISTRAR ▶ *Robert C. Finch Jr*	47. DATE MM/DD/CCYY 07/19/1994

PLACE OF DEATH

101. PLACE OF DEATH Cedars Sinai Med Ctr	102. IF HOSPITAL, SPECIFY ONE: [X] IP [ ] ER/OP [ ] DOA	103. FACILITY OTHER THAN HOSPITAL: [ ] CONV. HOSP. [ ] RES. [ ] OTHER	104. COUNTY Los Angeles
105. STREET ADDRESS—STREET AND NUMBER OR LOCATION 8700 Beverly Blvd			106. CITY Los Angeles

CAUSE OF DEATH

107. DEATH WAS CAUSED BY: (ENTER ONLY ONE CAUSE PER LINE FOR A, B, C, AND D)	TIME INTERVAL BETWEEN ONSET AND DEATH	108. DEATH REPORTED TO CORONER [ ] YES [X] NO REFERRAL NUMBER
IMMEDIATE CAUSE (A) METASTATIC PROSTATE CARCINOMA	55 MOS.	
DUE TO (B)		109. BIOPSY PERFORMED [ ] YES [X] NO
DUE TO (C)		110. AUTOPSY PERFORMED [ ] YES [X] NO
DUE TO (D)		111. USED IN DETERMINING CAUSE [ ] YES [ ] NO

112. OTHER SIGNIFICANT CONDITIONS CONTRIBUTING TO DEATH BUT NOT RELATED TO CAUSE GIVEN IN 107 NONE
113. WAS OPERATION PERFORMED FOR ANY CONDITION IN ITEM 107 OR 112? IF YES, LIST TYPE OF OPERATION AND DATE. NO

PHYSICIAN'S CERTIFICATION

114. I CERTIFY THAT TO THE BEST OF MY KNOWLEDGE DEATH OCCURRED AT THE HOUR, DATE AND PLACE STATED FROM THE CAUSES STATED. DECEDENT ATTENDED SINCE MM/DD/CCYY 10/29/1992	DECEDENT LAST SEEN ALIVE MM/DD/CCYY 07/05/1994	115. SIGNATURE AND TITLE OF CERTIFIER ▶ *Solomon J. Hamburg MD*	116. LICENSE NO. G53431	117. DATE MM/DD/CCYY 07/11/1994
		118. TYPE ATTENDING PHYSICIAN'S NAME, MAILING ADDRESS + ZIP SOLOMON I. HAMBURG, MD, 8635 W. THIRD ST., LOS ANGELES, CA. 90048		

CORONER'S USE ONLY

I CERTIFY THAT IN MY OPINION DEATH OCCURRED AT THE HOUR, DATE AND PLACE STATED FROM THE CAUSES STATED.	120. INJURY AT WORK [ ] YES [ ] NO	121. INJURY DATE MM/DD/CCYY	122. HOUR	123. PLACE OF INJURY
119. MANNER OF DEATH [ ] NATURAL [ ] SUICIDE [ ] HOMICIDE [ ] ACCIDENT [ ] PENDING INVESTIGATION [ ] COULD NOT BE DETERMINED	124. DESCRIBE HOW INJURY OCCURRED (EVENTS WHICH RESULTED IN INJURY)			
125. LOCATION (STREET AND NUMBER OR LOCATION AND CITY AND ZIP CODE)				

126. SIGNATURE OF CORONER OR DEPUTY CORONER ▶	127. DATE MM/DD/CCYY	128. TYPED NAME, TITLE OF CORONER OR DEPUTY CORONER

12

STATE REGISTRAR

A	B	C	D	E	F	G	H	FAX AUTH. #	CENSUS TRACT

CERTIFICATE OF DEATH
STATE OF CALIFORNIA
USE BLACK INK ONLY/NO ERASURES, WHITEOUTS OR ALTERATIONS
VS-11 (REV. 7/93)

STATE FILE NUMBER		LOCAL REGISTRATION NUMBER

DECEDENT PERSONAL DATA

1. NAME OF DECEDENT—FIRST (GIVEN)	2. MIDDLE	3. LAST (FAMILY)
ARISTOTELES	–	SAVALAS

4. DATE OF BIRTH MM/DD/CCYY	5. AGE YRS.	IF UNDER 1 YEAR — MONTHS / DAYS	IF UNDER 24 HOURS — HOURS / MINUTES	6. SEX	7. DATE OF DEATH MM/DD/CCYY	8. HOUR
01/21/1922	72			M	01/22/1994	1539

9. STATE OF BIRTH	10. SOCIAL SECURITY NO.	11. MILITARY SERVICE	12. MARITAL STATUS	13. EDUCATION — YEARS COMPLETED
NY	065-16-0946	19 UNK TO 19 UNK □ NONE	MARRIED	16

14. RACE	15. HISPANIC—SPECIFY	16. USUAL EMPLOYER
CAUCASIAN	□ YES ☒ NO	SELF EMPLOYED

17. OCCUPATION	18. KIND OF BUSINESS	19. YEARS IN OCCUPATION
ACTOR	ENTERTAINMENT	35

USUAL RESIDENCE

20. RESIDENCE—STREET AND NUMBER OR LOCATION
333 UNIVERSAL TERRACE PARKWAY

21. CITY	22. COUNTY	23. ZIP CODE	24. YRS IN COUNTY	25. STATE OR FOREIGN COUNTRY
UNIVERSAL CITY	LOS ANGELES	91607	33	CALIFORNIA

INFORMANT

26. NAME, RELATIONSHIP	27. MAILING ADDRESS (STREET AND NUMBER OR RURAL ROUTE NUMBER, CITY OR TOWN, STATE, ZIP)
JULIE SAVALAS, WIFE	333 UNIVERSAL TERRACE PARKWAY, UNIVERSAL CITY, CA. 91607

SPOUSE AND PARENT INFORMATION

28. NAME OF SURVIVING SPOUSE—FIRST	29. MIDDLE	30. LAST (MAIDEN NAME)	
JULIE	–	HOVLAND	

31. NAME OF FATHER—FIRST	32. MIDDLE	33. LAST	34. BIRTH STATE
NICHOLAS	CONSTANTINE	SAVALAS	GREECE

35. NAME OF MOTHER—FIRST	36. MIDDLE	37. LAST (MAIDEN)	38. BIRTH STATE
CHRISTINA	–	KAPSALIS	GREECE

DISPOSITION(S)

39. DATE MM/DD/CCYY	40. PLACE OF FINAL DISPOSITION
01/25/1994	FOREST LAWN MEMORIAL PARK, LOS ANGELES, CA. 90068

FUNERAL DIRECTOR AND LOCAL REGISTRAR

41. TYPE OF DISPOSITION(S)	42. SIGNATURE OF EMBALMER	43. LICENSE NO.
BURIAL	► Kim Evans	7917

44. NAME OF FUNERAL DIRECTOR	45. LICENSE NO.	46. SIGNATURE OF LOCAL REGISTRAR	47. DATE MM/DD/CCYY
FOREST LAWN HOLLYWOOD HILLS	F 904	► Robert c. Slate	01/25/1994

PLACE OF DEATH

101. PLACE OF DEATH	102. IF HOSPITAL, SPECIFY ONE:	103. FACILITY OTHER THAN HOSPITAL:	104. COUNTY
RESIDENCE	□ IP □ ER/OP □ DOA	□ CONV. HOSP. ☒ RES. □ OTHER	LOS ANGELES

105. STREET ADDRESS—STREET AND NUMBER OR LOCATION	106. CITY
333 UNIVERSAL TERRACE PARKWAY	UNIVERSAL CITY

CAUSE OF DEATH

107. DEATH WAS CAUSED BY: (ENTER ONLY ONE CAUSE PER LINE FOR A, B, C, AND D)	TIME INTERVAL BETWEEN ONSET AND DEATH	108. DEATH REPORTED TO CORONER
IMMEDIATE CAUSE (A) RENAL FAILURE	WEEKS	□ YES ☒ NO REFERRAL NUMBER
DUE TO (B) METASTATIC DISEASE	YEARS	109. BIOPSY PERFORMED ☒ YES □ NO
DUE TO (C) TRANSITIONAL CELL CANCER OF BLADDER	YEARS	110. AUTOPSY PERFORMED □ YES ☒ NO
DUE TO (D)		111. USED IN DETERMINING CAUSE □ YES □ NO

112. OTHER SIGNIFICANT CONDITIONS CONTRIBUTING TO DEATH BUT NOT RELATED TO CAUSE GIVEN IN 107
NONE

113. WAS OPERATION PERFORMED FOR ANY CONDITION IN ITEM 107 OR 112? IF YES, LIST TYPE OF OPERATION AND DATE.
NO

PHYSICIAN'S CERTIFICATION

114. I CERTIFY THAT TO THE BEST OF MY KNOWLEDGE DEATH OCCURRED AT THE HOUR, DATE AND PLACE STATED FROM THE CAUSES STATED.	115. SIGNATURE AND TITLE OF CERTIFIER	116. LICENSE NO.	117. DATE MM/DD/CCYY
DECEDENT ATTENDED SINCE MM/DD/CCYY 01/05/1994 — DECEDENT LAST SEEN ALIVE MM/DD/CCYY 01/22/1994	► Jayson Hymes M.D.	G56728	01/22/1994

118. TYPE ATTENDING PHYSICIAN'S NAME, MAILING ADDRESS + ZIP
JAYSON A. HYMES, MD, 9665 WILSHIRE BLVD., BEVERLY HILLS, CA. 90212

CORONER'S USE ONLY

I CERTIFY THAT IN MY OPINION DEATH OCCURRED AT THE HOUR, DATE AND PLACE STATED FROM THE CAUSES STATED. 119. MANNER OF DEATH	120. INJURY AT WORK	121. INJURY DATE MM/DD/CCYY	122. HOUR	123. PLACE OF INJURY
□ NATURAL □ SUICIDE □ HOMICIDE □ ACCIDENT □ PENDING INVESTIGATION □ COULD NOT BE DETERMINED	□ YES □ NO			

124. DESCRIBE HOW INJURY OCCURRED (EVENTS WHICH RESULTED IN INJURY)

125. LOCATION (STREET AND NUMBER OR LOCATION AND CITY AND ZIP CODE)

126. SIGNATURE OF CORONER OR DEPUTY CORONER	127. DATE MM/DD/CCYY	128. TYPED NAME, TITLE OF CORONER OR DEPUTY CORONER
►		

25

STATE REGISTRAR

A	B	C	D	E	F	G	H	FAX AUTH. #	CENSUS TRACT

CERTIFICATION OF VITAL RECORD

COUNTY OF LOS ANGELES • REGISTRAR-RECORDER/COUNTY CLERK

CERTIFICATE OF DEATH
STATE OF CALIFORNIA
USE BLACK INK ONLY

38919033136

| STATE FILE NUMBER | | | | | LOCAL REGISTRATION DISTRICT AND CERTIFICATE NUMBER |

DECEDENT PERSONAL DATA

1A. NAME OF DECEDENT--FIRST (GIVEN)	1B. MIDDLE	1C. LAST (FAMILY)	2A. DATE OF DEATH-- MONTH, DAY, YEAR	2B. HOUR	3. SEX
REBECCA	LUCILE	SCHAEFFER	July 18, 1989	1045	Fem.

4. RACE	5. SPANISH/HISPANIC	6. DATE OF BIRTH-- MONTH, DAY, YEAR	7 AGE IN YEARS	IF UNDER 1 YEAR MONTHS DAYS	IF UNDER 24 HOURS HOURS MINUTES
Caucasian	[ ] YES [X] NO SPECIFY	November 6, 1967	21		

8. STATE OF BIRTH	9. CITIZEN OF WHAT COUNTRY	10A. FULL NAME OF FATHER	10B. STATE OF BIRTH	11A. FULL MAIDEN NAME OF MOTHER	11B. STATE OF BIRTH
Oregon	U.S.A.	Benson Schaeffer	N.Y.	Danna Wilner	Georgia

12. MILITARY SERVICE?	13. SOCIAL SECURITY NUMBER	14. MARITAL STATUS	15. NAME OF SURVIVING SPOUSE (IF WIFE, ENTER MAIDEN NAME)
19___ TO 19___ [X] NONE	542-64-0524	Nev.Mar.	---

16A. USUAL OCCUPATION	16B. USUAL KIND OF BUSINESS OR INDUSTRY	16C. USUAL EMPLOYER	16D. YEARS IN USUAL OCCUPATION	17. NUMBER OF HIGHEST GRADE COMPLETED (1-12 OR COLLEGE 13-17+)
Actress	Entertainment	Self-Employed	5	12

USUAL RESIDENCE

18A. RESIDENCE—STREET AND NUMBER OR LOCATION	18B. CITY	18C. ZIP CODE
120 North Sweetzer Apt. #4	Los Angeles	90036

18D. COUNTY	18E. NUMBER OF YEARS IN THIS COUNTY	18F. STATE OR FOREIGN COUNTRY	20. NAME, RELATIONSHIP, MAILING ADDRESS AND ZIP CODE OF INFORMANT
Los Angeles	3	California	Benson Schaeffer (father) 3422 N.E. Pacific Street Portland, Oregon 97232

PLACE OF DEATH

19A. PLACE OF DEATH	19B. IF HOSPITAL, SPECIFY ONE: IP, ER/OP, DOA	19C. COUNTY
Cedars-Sinai Med Center	ER	Los Angeles

19D. STREET ADDRESS—STREET AND NUMBER OR LOCATION	19E. CITY	21. TIME INTERVAL BETWEEN ONSET AND DEATH	22. WAS DEATH REPORTED TO CORONER?
8700 Beverly Blvd	Los Angeles		[X] YES 89-7055 REFERRAL NUMBER [ ] NO

CAUSE OF DEATH

21. DEATH WAS CAUSED BY: (ENTER ONLY ONE CAUSE PER LINE FOR A, B, AND C)—TYPE OR PRINT		23. WAS BIOPSY PERFORMED?
IMMEDIATE CAUSE {(A)	Penetrating Gunshot Wound, Chest ▶ Mins	[ ] YES [X] NO
DUE TO {(B)	▶	24A. WAS AUTOPSY PERFORMED? [X] YES [ ] NO
DUE TO {(C)	▶	24B. IF YES, WAS IT USED IN DETERMINING CAUSE OF DEATH? [X] YES [ ] NO

25. OTHER SIGNIFICANT CONDITIONS CONTRIBUTING TO DEATH BUT NOT RELATED TO CAUSE GIVEN IN 21	26. WAS OPERATION PERFORMED FOR ANY CONDITION IN ITEM 21 OR 25? MONTH, DAY, YEAR
None	7-18-89 Thoracotomy

PHYSICIAN'S CERTIFICATION

I CERTIFY THAT DEATH OCCURRED AT THE HOUR, DATE AND PLACE STATED FROM THE CAUSES STATED.	27B. SIGNATURE AND DEGREE OR TITLE OF PHYSICIAN	27C. PHYSICIAN'S LICENSE NUMBER	27D. DATE SIGNED
27A. DECEDENT ATTENDED SINCE MONTH, DAY, YEAR / DECEDENT LAST SEEN ALIVE MONTH, DAY, YEAR	▶ 27E. TYPE ATTENDING PHYSICIAN'S NAME AND ADDRESS		

CORONER'S USE ONLY

I CERTIFY THAT DEATH OCCURRED AT THE HOUR, DATE AND PLACE STATED FROM THE CAUSES STATED.	28A. SIGNATURE OF CORONER OR DEPUTY CORONER	28B. DATE SIGNED
	▶ Deputy Coroner [signature]	7-20-89

29. MANNER OF DEATH—specify one: natural, accident, suicide, homicide, pending investigation or could not be determined	30A. PLACE OF INJURY	30B. INJURY AT WORK	30C. DATE OF INJURY MONTH, DAY, YEAR	31. HOUR
Homicide	Residence	[ ] YES [X] NO	7-18-89	1015

32. LOCATION (STREET AND NUMBER OR LOCATION AND CITY)	33. DESCRIBE HOW INJURY OCCURRED (EVENTS WHICH RESULTED IN INJURY)
120 N. Sweetzer, Los Angeles	Shot by Assailant

FUNERAL DIRECTOR AND LOCAL REGISTRAR

34A. DISPOSITION	34B. PLACE OF FINAL DISPOSITION	34C. DATE OF DISPOSITION MONTH, DAY, YEAR	35A. SIGNATURE OF EMBALMER	35B. LICENSE NUMBER
TR/BURIAL	Ahavai Sholom, 9323 S.W. 1st Ave.,Portland,Oregon	July 21, 1989	Cay Conseli	7520

36A. NAME OF FUNERAL DIRECTOR (OR PERSON ACTING AS SUCH)	36B. LICENSE NO.	37. SIGNATURE OF LOCAL REGISTRAR	38. REGISTRATION DATE
GLASBAND-WILLEN MORTUARY	F727	[signature]	JUL 21 1989

STATE REGISTRAR

A	B	C	D	E	F	CENSUS TRACT

VS-11 (REV. 1-89)   654   MAKE NO ERASURES, WHITEOUTS, OR OTHER ALTERATIONS

CERTIFICATION OF VITAL RECORD

COUNTY OF LOS ANGELES • REGISTRAR-RECORDER/COUNTY CLERK

CERTIFICATE OF DEATH
STATE OF CALIFORNIA
USE BLACK INK ONLY

39119016095

LOCAL REGISTRATION DISTRICT AND CERTIFICATE NUMBER

STATE FILE NUMBER					
1A. NAME OF DECEDENT—FIRST (Given) NATALIE	1B. MIDDLE ---	1C. LAST (FAMILY) SCHAFER	2A. DATE OF DEATH—MO, DAY, YR APRIL 10, 1991	2B. HOUR 1855	3. SEX F

| 4. RACE CAU/AMERICAN | 5. HISPANIC—SPECIFY ☐ YES ☒ NO | 6. DATE OF BIRTH—MO. DAY. YR NOVEMBER 5, 1900 | 7. AGE IN YEARS 90 | IF UNDER 1 YEAR MONTHS / DAYS | IF UNDER 24 HOURS HOURS / MINUTES |

DECEDENT PERSONAL DATA

| 8. STATE OF BIRTH NEW JERSEY | 9. CITIZEN OF WHAT COUNTRY USA | 10A. FULL NAME OF FATHER CHARLES SCHAFER | 10B. STATE OF BIRTH NEW YORK | 11A. FULL MAIDEN NAME OF MOTHER JENNIE TIM | 11B. STATE OF BIRTH NEW YORK |

| 12. MILITARY SERVICE? 19___ TO 19___ ☒ NONE | 13. SOCIAL SECURITY NO. 114-01-8100 | 14. MARITAL STATUS DIVORCED | 15. NAME OF SURVIVING SPOUSE (IF WIFE, ENTER MAIDEN NAME) |

| 16A. USUAL OCCUPATION ACTRESS | 16B. USUAL KIND OF BUSINESS OR INDUSTRY ACTING | 16C. USUAL EMPLOYER FREE LANCE | 16D. YEARS IN OCCUPATION 50 | 17. EDUCATION—YEARS COMPLETED 14 |

USUAL RESIDENCE

| 18A. RESIDENCE—STREET AND NUMBER OR LOCATION 514 NORTH RODEO DRIVE | | 18B. CITY BEVERLY HILLS | 18C. ZIP CODE 90210 |
| 18D. COUNTY LOS ANGELES | 18E. NUMBER OF YEARS IN THIS COUNTY 40 | 18F. STATE OR FOREIGN COUNTRY CALIFORNIA | 20. NAME, RELATIONSHIP, MAILING ADDRESS AND ZIP CODE OF INFORMANT NELL B. MC CORMICK-BUSINESS 263 NORTH REXFORD DR.   MANAGER BEVERLY HILLS, CA   90210 |

PLACE OF DEATH

| 19A. PLACE OF DEATH RESIDENCE | 19B. IF HOSPITAL SPECIFY ONE: IP, ER/OP, DOA | 19C. COUNTY LOS ANGELES | |
| 19D. STREET ADDRESS—STREET AND NUMBER OR LOCATION 514 NORTH RODEO DRIVE | 19E. CITY BEVERLY HILLS | TIME INTERVAL BETWEEN ONSET AND DEATH | 22. WAS DEATH REPORTED TO CORONER? REFERRAL NUMBER ☐ YES ☒ NO |

CAUSE OF DEATH

21. DEATH WAS CAUSED BY: (ENTER ONLY ONE CAUSE PER LINE FOR A, B, AND C)		
IMMEDIATE CAUSE (A) *Hepatic disease* ▶ 2 mos		23. WAS BIOPSY PERFORMED? ☐ YES ☒ NO
DUE TO (B) *Metastatic Carcinoma of breast* ▶ 1 year		24A. WAS AUTOPSY PERFORMED? ☐ YES ☒ NO
DUE TO (C) *Carcinoma of breast* ▶ 2 years		24B. WAS IT USED IN DETERMINING CAUSE OF DEATH? ☐ YES ☒ NO

| 25. OTHER SIGNIFICANT CONDITIONS CONTRIBUTING TO DEATH BUT NOT RELATED TO CAUSE GIVEN IN 21 *no* | 26. WAS OPERATION PERFORMED FOR ANY CONDITION IN ITEM 21 OR 25? IF SO TYPE OF OPERATION AND DATE. |

PHYSICIAN'S CERTIFICATION

| I CERTIFY THAT TO THE BEST OF MY KNOWLEDGE DEATH OCCURRED AT THE HOUR, DATE AND PLACE STATED FROM THE CAUSES STATED. | 27B. SIGNATURE AND DEGREE OR TITLE OF CERTIFIER *Herbert Resnick M.D.* | 27C. CERTIFIER'S LICENSE NUMBER 91507 | 27D. DATE SIGNED 4/11/91 |
| 27A. DECEDENT ATTENDED SINCE MONTH, DAY, YEAR 3/4/91 | DECEDENT LAST SEEN ALIVE MONTH, DAY, YEAR 4/4/91 | 27E. TYPE ATTENDING PHYSICIAN'S NAME AND ADDRESS HERBERT RESNICK M.D. 465 NORTH ROXBURY #711, BEVERLY | HILLS, CA |

CORONER'S USE ONLY

I CERTIFY THAT IN MY OPINION DEATH OCCURRED AT THE HOUR, DATE AND PLACE STATED FROM THE CAUSES STATED.	28A. SIGNATURE AND TITLE OF CORONER OR DEPUTY CORONER		28B. DATE SIGNED
29. MANNER OF DEATH—specify one: natural, accident, suicide, homicide, pending investigation or could not be determined.	30A. PLACE OF INJURY	30B. INJURY AT WORK ☐ YES ☐ NO	30C. DATE OF INJURY MONTH, DAY, YEAR	31. HOUR
32. LOCATION (STREET AND NUMBER OR LOCATION AND CITY)	33. DESCRIBE HOW INJURY OCCURRED (EVENTS WHICH RESULTED IN INJURY)			

FUNERAL DIRECTOR AND LOCAL REGISTRAR

| 34A. DISPOSITION(S) CR/SEA | 34B. PLACE OF FINAL DISPOSITION—NAME AND ADDRESS AT SEA:PT.FERMIN LOS ANGELES, CA | 34C. DATE MO, DAY, YEAR 4-24-91 | 35A. SIGNATURE OF EMBALMER NOT EMBALMED | 35B. LICENSE NUMBER NONE |
| 36A. NAME OF FUNERAL DIRECTOR (OR PERSON ACTING AS SUCH) NEPTUNE SOCIETY | 36B. LICENSE NO. F-1289 | 37. SIGNATURE OF LOCAL REGISTRAR *Robert C. Stutz Jr.* | 38. REGISTRATION DATE APR 18 1991 |

STATE REGISTRAR

| A. | B. | C. | D. | E. | F. | CENSUS TRACT |

VS-11 (REV. 1-90) *174.9*   MAKE NO ERASURES, WHITEOUTS, OR OTHER ALTERATIONS   01-9-1-7805

STATE OF CALIFORNIA
CERTIFICATION OF VITAL RECORD

COUNTY OF SONOMA
SANTA ROSA, CALIFORNIA

CERTIFICATE OF DEATH
STATE OF CALIFORNIA
USE BLACK INK ONLY/NO ERASURES, WHITEOUTS OR ALTERATIONS
VS-11 (REV. 1/00)

3-2000-49-000564
LOCAL REGISTRATION NUMBER

STATE FILE NUMBER

DECEDENT PERSONAL DATA

1. NAME OF DECEDENT—FIRST (GIVEN)	2. MIDDLE	3. LAST (FAMILY)
CHARLES	M.	SCHULZ

4. DATE OF BIRTH MM/DD/CCYY	5. AGE YRS.	IF UNDER 1 YEAR MONTHS/DAYS	IF UNDER 24 HOURS HOURS/MINUTES	6. SEX	7. DATE OF DEATH MM/DD/CCYY	8. HOUR
11/26/1922	77			M	02/12/2000	2218

9. STATE OF BIRTH	10. SOCIAL SECURITY NO.	11. MILITARY SERVICE	12. MARITAL STATUS	13. EDUCATION—YEARS COMPLETED
MN	468-20-4650	[X] YES [ ] NO [ ] UNK	Married	12

14. RACE	15. HISPANIC—SPECIFY	16. USUAL EMPLOYER
White	[ ] YES [X] NO	Self Employed

17. OCCUPATION	18. KIND OF BUSINESS	19. YEARS IN OCCUPATION
Artist	Media Cartoonist	65

USUAL RESIDENCE

20. RESIDENCE—STREET AND NUMBER OR LOCATION: 4900 Upper Ridge Road

21. CITY	22. COUNTY	23. ZIP CODE	24. YRS IN COUNTY	25. STATE OR FOREIGN COUNTRY
Santa Rosa	Sonoma	95404	42	CA

INFORMANT

26. NAME, RELATIONSHIP	27. MAILING ADDRESS (STREET AND NUMBER OR RURAL ROUTE NUMBER, CITY OR TOWN, STATE, ZIP)
Jean Schulz Spouse	4900 Upper Ridge Road, Santa Rosa, CA 95404

SPOUSE AND PARENT INFORMATION

28. NAME OF SURVIVING SPOUSE—FIRST	29. MIDDLE	30. LAST (MAIDEN NAME)
Jean	–	Forsyth

31. NAME OF FATHER—FIRST	32. MIDDLE	33. LAST	34. BIRTH STATE
Carl	Friedrich Augustus	Schulz	Germany

35. NAME OF MOTHER—FIRST	36. MIDDLE	37. LAST (MAIDEN)	38. BIRTH STATE
Dena	Bertina	Halvorson	WI

DISPOSITION(S)

39. DATE MM/DD/CCYY	40. PLACE OF FINAL DISPOSITION
02/16/2000	Pleasant Hills Memorial Park,1700 Pleasant Hill Rd. Sebastopol, CA 95472

FUNERAL DIRECTOR AND LOCAL REGISTRAR

41. TYPE OF DISPOSITION(S)	42. SIGNATURE OF EMBALMER	43. LICENSE NO.
BU	▶ Not Embalmed	–

44. NAME OF FUNERAL DIRECTOR	45. LICENSE NO.	46. SIGNATURE OF LOCAL REGISTRAR	47. DATE MM/DD/CCYY
PARENT-SORENSEN MORTUARY-SEB	FD 1415	▶ *Mary Maddux-Gonzales*	02/16/2000

PLACE OF DEATH

101. PLACE OF DEATH	102. IF HOSPITAL, SPECIFY ONE:	103. FACILITY OTHER THAN HOSPITAL:	104. COUNTY
Own Residence	[ ] IP [ ] ER/OP [ ] DOA	[ ] CONV. HOSP. [ ] RES. CARE [ ] OTHER	Sonoma

105. STREET ADDRESS—STREET AND NUMBER OR LOCATION	106. CITY
4900 Upper Ridge Road	Santa Rosa

CAUSE OF DEATH

107. DEATH WAS CAUSED BY: (ENTER ONLY ONE CAUSE PER LINE FOR A, B, C, AND D)

			TIME INTERVAL BETWEEN ONSET AND DEATH	108. DEATH REPORTED TO CORONER
IMMEDIATE CAUSE	(A)	Metastatic Colon Cancer	3 Mos	[X] YES [ ] NO REFERRAL NUMBER 00-0242
DUE TO	(B)			109. BIOPSY PERFORMED [X] YES [ ] NO
DUE TO	(C)			110. AUTOPSY PERFORMED [ ] YES [X] NO
DUE TO	(D)			111. USED IN DETERMINING CAUSE [ ] YES [ ] NO

112. OTHER SIGNIFICANT CONDITIONS CONTRIBUTING TO DEATH BUT NOT RELATED TO CAUSE GIVEN IN 107

113. WAS OPERATION PERFORMED FOR ANY CONDITION IN ITEM 107 OR 112? IF YES, LIST TYPE OF OPERATION AND DATE.
Omentectomy, Aorta Thrombectomy 11/17/1999

PHYSICIAN'S CERTIFICATION

114. I CERTIFY THAT TO THE BEST OF MY KNOWLEDGE DEATH OCCURRED AT THE HOUR, DATE AND PLACE STATED FROM THE CAUSES STATED.		115. SIGNATURE AND TITLE OF CERTIFIER	116. LICENSE NO.	117. DATE MM/DD/CCYY
DECEDENT ATTENDED SINCE MM/DD/CCYY	DECEDENT LAST SEEN ALIVE MM/DD/CCYY	▶ *signature*	A 050966	02/14/2000
11/12/1999	02/12/2000	118. TYPE ATTENDING PHYSICIAN'S NAME, MAILING ADDRESS, ZIP — HELEN COLLINS MD 121 Sotoyome St. Santa Rosa,CA 95405		

CORONER'S USE ONLY

119. I CERTIFY THAT IN MY OPINION DEATH OCCURRED AT THE HOUR, DATE AND PLACE STATED FROM THE CAUSES STATED.	120. INJURY AT WORK [ ] YES [ ] NO	121. INJURY DATE MM/DD/CCYY	122. HOUR	123. PLACE OF INJURY
119. MANNER OF DEATH [ ] NATURAL [ ] SUICIDE [ ] HOMICIDE [ ] ACCIDENT [ ] PENDING INVESTIGATION [ ] COULD NOT BE DETERMINED	124. DESCRIBE HOW INJURY OCCURRED (EVENTS WHICH RESULTED IN INJURY)			

125. LOCATION (STREET AND NUMBER OR LOCATION AND CITY, ZIP)

126. SIGNATURE OF CORONER OR DEPUTY CORONER	127. DATE MM/DD/CCYY	128. TYPED NAME, TITLE OF CORONER OR DEPUTY CORONER
▶		

STATE REGISTRAR

A	B	C	D	E	F	G	H	FAX AUTH. #	CENSUS TRACT
								2030	

CERTIFIED COPY OF VITAL RECORDS

STATE OF CALIFORNIA
COUNTY OF SONOMA } SS

04/06/2000
DATE ISSUED

This is true and exact reproduction of the document officially registered and placed on file in the Vital Statistics office. Sonoma County Department of Health Services.

Mary Maddux-Gonzales
LOCAL REGISTRAR
SONOMA COUNTY, CALIFORNIA

This copy not valid unless prepared on engraved border displaying seal and signature of Registrar.

STATE OF CALIFORNIA
CERTIFICATION OF VITAL RECORD

COUNTY OF LOS ANGELES • REGISTRAR-RECORDER/COUNTY CLERK

CERTIFICATE OF DEATH
STATE OF CALIFORNIA

38719010281

STATE FILE NUMBER			LOCAL REGISTRATION DISTRICT AND CERTIFICATE NUMBER
1A. NAME OF DECEDENT—FIRST: GEORGE	1B. MIDDLE: RANDOLPH	1C. LAST: SCOTT	2A. DATE OF DEATH (MONTH, DAY, YEAR): MARCH 2, 1987 — 2B. HOUR: 0600
3. SEX: MALE	4. RACE/ETHNICITY: CAUCASIAN	5. SPANISH/HISPANIC NO K	6. DATE OF BIRTH: JANUARY 23, 1898 — 7. AGE: 89 YEARS

DECEDENT PERSONAL DATA

8. BIRTHPLACE OF DECEDENT (STATE OR FOREIGN COUNTRY): VIRGINIA	9. NAME AND BIRTHPLACE OF FATHER: GEORGE GRANT SCOTT – VIRGINIA	10. BIRTH NAME AND BIRTHPLACE OF MOTHER: LUCY CRANE – VIRGINIA
11A. CITIZEN OF WHAT COUNTRY: USA	11B. IF DECEASED WAS EVER IN MILITARY GIVE DATES OF SERVICE: 19__ TO 19__	12. SOCIAL SECURITY NUMBER: 562-16-0863 — 13. MARITAL STATUS: MARRIED — 14. NAME OF SURVIVING SPOUSE (IF WIFE, ENTER BIRTH NAME): PATRICIA STILLMAN
15. PRIMARY OCCUPATION: ACTOR	16. NUMBER OF YEARS THIS OCCUPATION: ADULT LIFE — 17. EMPLOYER (IF SELF-EMPLOYED, SO STATE): SELF EMPLOYED	18. KIND OF INDUSTRY OR BUSINESS: MOTION PICTURE

USUAL RESIDENCE

19A. USUAL RESIDENCE—STREET ADDRESS (STREET AND NUMBER OR LOCATION): 156 COPLEY PLACE	19B.	19C. CITY OR TOWN: BEVERLY HILLS
19D. COUNTY: LOS ANGELES	19E. STATE: CALIFORNIA	20. NAME AND ADDRESS OF INFORMANT—RELATIONSHIP

PLACE OF DEATH

21A. PLACE OF DEATH: RESIDENCE	21B. COUNTY: LOS ANGELES	PATRICIA SCOTT – WIFE
21C. STREET ADDRESS (STREET AND NUMBER OR LOCATION): 156 COPLEY PLACE	21D. CITY OR TOWN: BEVERLY HILLS	156 COPLEY PLACE BEVERLY HILLS, CALIFORNIA 90210

CAUSE OF DEATH

22. DEATH WAS CAUSED BY: (ENTER ONLY ONE CAUSE PER LINE FOR A, B, AND C) IMMEDIATE CAUSE		
CONDITIONS, IF ANY, WHICH GAVE RISE TO THE IMMEDIATE CAUSE, STATING THE UNDERLYING CAUSE LAST.	(A) Cardiac decompensation — 12 hr	24. WAS DEATH REPORTED TO CORONER? no
	(B) arteriosclerotic coronary, cerebral disease — 15 yrs	25. WAS BIOPSY PERFORMED? no
	(C)	26. WAS AUTOPSY PERFORMED? no

APPROXIMATE INTERVAL BETWEEN ONSET AND DEATH

23. OTHER SIGNIFICANT CONDITIONS—CONTRIBUTING TO DEATH BUT NOT RELATED TO CAUSE GIVEN IN 22A: none	27. WAS OPERATION PERFORMED FOR ANY CONDITION IN ITEMS 22 OR 23? no — 27. TYPE OF OPERATION — DATE

PHYSICIAN'S CERTIFICATION

28A. I CERTIFY THAT DEATH OCCURRED AT THE HOUR, DATE AND PLACE STATED FROM THE CAUSES STATED.	28B. PHYSICIAN—SIGNATURE AND DEGREE OR TITLE: Eliot Corday M.D. — 28C. DATE SIGNED: mar 2/87 — 28D. PHYSICIAN'S LICENSE NUMBER: A 12329
I ATTENDED DECEDENT SINCE (ENTER MO. DA. YR.): 7-11-74 — I LAST SAW DECEDENT ALIVE (ENTER MO. DA. YR.): 2-20-87	28E. TYPE PHYSICIAN'S NAME AND ADDRESS: ELIOT CORDAY M.D. 8635 WEST THIRD STREET, LOS ANGELES

INJURY INFORMATION

29. SPECIFY ACCIDENT, SUICIDE, ETC.	30. PLACE OF INJURY	31. INJURY AT WORK	32A. DATE OF INJURY—MONTH, DAY, YEAR	32B. HOUR
33. LOCATION (STREET AND NUMBER OR LOCATION AND CITY OR TOWN)		34. DESCRIBE HOW INJURY OCCURRED (EVENTS WHICH RESULTED IN INJURY)		

CORONER'S USE ONLY

35A. I CERTIFY THAT DEATH OCCURRED AT THE HOUR, DATE AND PLACE STATED FROM THE CAUSES STATED, AS REQUIRED BY LAW I HAVE HELD AN (INQUEST-INVESTIGATION)	35B. CORONER—SIGNATURE AND DEGREE OR TITLE	35C. DATE SIGNED

36. DISPOSITION: BURIAL	37. DATE—MONTH, DAY, YEAR: SHIP-OUT MAR. 3, 1987	38. NAME AND ADDRESS OF CEMETERY OR CREMATORY: ELMWOOD CEMETERY, CHARLOTTE, NORTH CAROLINA	39. EMBALMER'S LICENSE NUMBER AND SIGNATURE: 5595 William R. Pierce
40A. NAME OF FUNERAL DIRECTOR (OR PERSON ACTING AS SUCH): PIERCE BROTHERS WESTWOOD VILLAGE	40B. LICENSE NO.: F 951	41. LOCAL REGISTRAR—SIGNATURE: Robert Massksh	42. DATE ACCEPTED BY LOCAL REGISTRAR: MAR 02 1987

STATE REGISTRAR	A. 4140	B.	C.	D.	E.	F. 01-97-7005

VS-11 (1-85)

This is to certify that this document is a true copy of the official record filed with the Registrar-Recorder/County Clerk.

Conny B. McCormack

CONNY B. McCORMACK
Registrar-Recorder/County Clerk

MAY 14 2002
19-254951

This copy not valid unless prepared on engraved border displaying the Seal and Signature of the Registrar-Recorder/County Clerk.

THE GREAT SEAL OF THE STATE OF CALIFORNIA • EUREKA

COUNTY OF LOS ANGELES CALIFORNIA

ANY ALTERATION OR ERASURE VOIDS THIS CERTIFICATE

STATE OF CALIFORNIA
CERTIFICATION OF VITAL RECORD

COUNTY OF LOS ANGELES • REGISTRAR-RECORDER/COUNTY CLERK

STATE OF CALIFORNIA
DEPARTMENT OF PUBLIC HEALTH
VITAL STATISTICS
STANDARD CERTIFICATE OF DEATH

1. PLACE OF DEATH: DIST. NO. 1906   LOCAL REGISTERED NO. 464

COUNTY OF Los Angeles
CITY, TOWN OR
RURAL DISTRICT OF Santa Monica   STREET AND NO. 350 - 17th Street
IF DEATH OCCURRED IN A HOSPITAL OR INSTITUTION, GIVE ITS NAME INSTEAD OF STREET AND NO.

2. FULL NAME Elzie C. Segar

RESIDENCE: NO. 350-17th   IF NON-RESIDENT, GIVE
USUAL PLACE OF ABODE   ST. CITY OR TOWN, AND STATE

3. SEX	4. COLOR OR RACE	5. SINGLE, MARRIED, WIDOWED OR DIVORCED? (WRITE THE WORD)
Male	Cauc.	Married

5A. IF MARRIED, WIDOWED OR DIVORCED, NAME OF HUSBAND OR WIFE
Myrtle A. Segar

6. DATE OF BIRTH Dec. 8 1894
MONTH DAY YEAR

7. AGE 43 YR. 10 MO. 5 DAYS. IF LESS THAN ONE DAY HRS. MIN.

OCCUPATION
8. TRADE, PROFESSION OR KIND OF WORK DONE AS SPINNER, SAWYER, BOOKKEEPER, ETC. Cartoonist
9. INDUSTRY OR BUSINESS IN WHICH WORK WAS DONE, AS SILKMILL, SAWMILL, BANK, ETC. Newspapers
10. DATE DECEASED LAST WORKED AT THIS OCCUPATION (MO. AND YR.) 1937
11. TOTAL YEARS SPENT IN THIS OCCUPATION 20

12. BIRTHPLACE (CITY OR TOWN) Chester
STATE OR COUNTRY Ill.

FATHER
13. NAME Amzie Segar
14. BIRTHPLACE (CITY OR TOWN) Chester
STATE OR COUNTRY Ill.

MOTHER
15. MAIDEN NAME Erma Crisler
16. BIRTHPLACE (CITY OR TOWN) Chester
STATE OR COUNTRY Ill.

17. LENGTH OF RESIDENCE
A. CITY, TOWN OR RURAL DISTRICT OF DEATH 12 YRS. MOS. DAYS
B. IN CALIFORNIA 15 YRS. MOS. DAYS
C. IN U.S., IF OF FOREIGN BIRTH YRS. MOS. DAYS

18. INFORMANT (SIGNATURE) Myrtle A. Segar
ADDRESS 350-17th St. Santa Monica, Cal

19. BURIAL, CREMATION OR REMOVAL? Burial WRITE THE WORD
PLACE Woodlawn Cemetery DATE 10/17/38
Santa Monica

20. EMBALMER LICENSE NO. 1484
SIGNATURE Henry G. Moeller
FUNERAL DIRECTOR MOELLER & SONS: Henry G. Moeller
ADDRESS Santa Monica, Cal.

21. FILED OCT 17 1938
DATE
By Faye M Halter
LOCAL REGISTRAR

22. DATE OF DEATH Oct. 13 1938
MONTH DAY YEAR

23. MEDICAL CERTIFICATE OF DEATH
I HEREBY CERTIFY, THAT I ATTENDED DECEASED FROM Oct. 1-1937
TO Oct 13, 1938;
THAT I LAST SAW HIM 1m ALIVE
ON Oct. 13, 1938
AND THAT DEATH OCCURRED ON THE ABOVE STATED DATE AT THE HOUR OF 9:32 P. M.

THE PRINCIPAL CAUSE OF DEATH AND RELATED CAUSES OF IMPORTANCE, IN ORDER OF ONSET, WERE AS FOLLOWS:
Portal Cirrhosis   DATE OF ONSET Oct. 1-1937
① 124k

OTHER CONTRIBUTORY CAUSES OF IMPORTANCE:

24. CORONER'S CERTIFICATE OF DEATH
I HEREBY CERTIFY, THAT I TOOK CHARGE OF THE REMAINS DESCRIBED ABOVE, HELD

AN
INQUEST, AUTOPSY OR INQUIRY THEREON, AND FROM SUCH ACTION FIND THAT SAID DECEASED CAME TO HIS DEATH ON THE DATE STATED ABOVE.

WAS THERE AN AUTOPSY? Yes.

IF OPERATION, DATE OF
CONDITION FOR WHICH PERFORMED
NAME LABORATORY TEST CONFIRMING DIAGNOSIS

25. IF DEATH WAS DUE TO EXTERNAL CAUSES (VIOLENCE) FILL IN THE FOLLOWING:
ACCIDENT, SUICIDE OR HOMICIDE?   DATE OF INJURY
INJURED   CITY OR TOWN OF
AT   COUNTY AND STATE OF
DID INJURY OCCUR IN HOME, INDUSTRY, OR PUBLIC PLACE?
MANNER OF INJURY
NATURE OF INJURY

26. IF DISEASE/INJURY RELATED TO OCCUPATION, SPECIFY No.

27. SIGNATURE Raymond Sands M.D.
PHYSICIAN, AUTOPSY SURGEON
ADDRESS Santa Monica Calif

28. WHEN REQUIRED BY LAW   CORONER
COUNTY OF

NOV 8 1938 MAMI E. BEATTY, Registrar of Vital Statistics

STATE OF CALIFORNIA
CERTIFICATION OF VITAL RECORD

COUNTY OF LOS ANGELES • REGISTRAR-RECORDER/COUNTY CLERK

STATE FILE NUMBER	**CERTIFICATE OF DEATH** STATE OF CALIFORNIA—DEPARTMENT OF PUBLIC HEALTH
LOCAL REGISTRATION DISTRICT AND CERTIFICATE NUMBER	7053 24883

DECEDENT PERSONAL DATA

1A. NAME OF DECEASED—FIRST NAME	1B MIDDLE NAME	1C. LAST NAME	2A. DATE OF DEATH	2B. HOUR
DAVID	OLIVER	SELZNICK	June 22, 1965	2:22 P.M.

3. SEX	4. COLOR OR RACE	5. BIRTHPLACE (STATE OR FOREIGN COUNTRY)	6. DATE OF BIRTH	7. AGE (LAST BIRTHDAY)
Male	Cauc.	Pennsylvania 6	May 10, 1902	63 YEARS

8. NAME AND BIRTHPLACE OF FATHER	9. MAIDEN NAME AND BIRTHPLACE OF MOTHER	10. CITIZEN OF WHAT COUNTRY	11. SOCIAL SECURITY NUMBER
Louis Selznick-Russia	Florence Sachs-Russia	U.S.A.	547-10-7379

12. LAST OCCUPATION	13. NUMBER OF YEARS IN THIS OCCUPATN.	14. NAME OF LAST EMPLOYING COMPANY OR FIRM	15. KIND OF INDUSTRY OR BUSINESS
Producer	40	Self Employed	Motion Picture

16. IF DECEASED WAS EVER IN U.S. ARMED FORCES, GIVE WAR OR DATES OF SERVICE	17. SPECIFY MARRIED NEVER MARRIED WIDOWED DIVORCED	18A. NAME OF PRESENT SPOUSE	18B. PRESENT OR LAST OCCUPATION OF SPOUSE
No	Married	Jennifer Selznick	Housewife

PLACE OF DEATH

19A. PLACE OF DEATH—NAME OF HOSPITAL	19B. STREET ADDRESS	19C. COUNTY	19D. LENGTH OF STAY IN COUNTY OF DEATH	19E. LENGTH OF STAY IN CALIFORNIA
Mt. Sinai Hospital	8720 Beverly Blvd.			
19C. CITY OR TOWN: Los Angeles		Los Angeles	40 YEARS	40 YEARS

LAST USUAL RESIDENCE (WHERE DID DECEASED LIVE—IF IN INSTITUTION ENTER RESIDENCE BEFORE ADMISSION)

20A. LAST USUAL RESIDENCE—STREET ADDRESS	20B. IF INSIDE CITY CORPORATE LIMITS		21A. NAME OF INFORMANT (IF OTHER THAN SPOUSE)
1400 Tower Grove	CHECK HERE		Barry Brannen
20C. CITY OR TOWN: Los Angeles, 6349	20D. COUNTY: Los Angeles	20E. STATE: California	21B. ADDRESS OF INFORMANT: 404 N. Roxbury Dr. Beverly Hills, Calif.

PHYSICIAN'S OR CORONER'S CERTIFICATION

22A. PHYSICIAN: I HEREBY CERTIFY THAT DEATH OCCURRED AT THE HOUR, DATE AND PLACE STATED FROM THE CAUSES STATED BELOW AND THAT I ATTENDED THE DECEASED FROM June 22, 1965 TO June 22, 1965 THAT I LAST SAW THE DECEASED ALIVE ON	22. PHYSICIAN OR CORONER—SIGNATURE Harold Miller M.D.	DEGREE OR TITLE
22B. CORONER: I HEREBY CERTIFY THAT DEATH OCCURRED AT THE HOUR, DATE AND PLACE ABOVE FROM THE CAUSES STATED BELOW AND THAT I HAVE HELD __ ON THE REMAINS OF DECEASED AS REQUIRED BY LAW	22C. ADDRESS Los Angeles 6221 Wilshire	22E. DATE SIGNED 6/23/65

FUNERAL DIRECTOR AND LOCAL REGISTRAR

23. SPECIFY BURIAL ENTOMBMENT OR CREMATION	24. DATE	25. NAME OF CEMETERY OR CREMATORY	26. EMBALMER—SIGNATURE / LICENSE NUMBER
Entombment	6/25/65	Forest Lawn Mausoleum Glendale, California	Charles W. Kessel 5049

27. NAME OF FUNERAL DIRECTOR (OR PERSON ACTING AS SUCH)	28. DATE ACCEPTED FOR REGISTRATION BY LOCAL REGISTRAR	29. LOCAL REGISTRAR—SIGNATURE
MALINOW & SILVERMAN MORTUARY	JUN 24 1965	K.H. Sutherland M.D.

CAUSE OF DEATH

30. CAUSE OF DEATH		APPROXIMATE INTERVAL BETWEEN ONSET AND DEATH
PART I. DEATH WAS CAUSED BY IMMEDIATE CAUSE (A) 5	Acute cardio respiratory failure	
CONDITIONS, IF ANY WHICH GAVE RISE TO THE ABOVE CAUSE (A) STATING THE UNDERLYING CAUSE LAST. DUE TO (B)	Acute myocardial infarction	3 hours
DUE TO (C)	arteriosclerotic cardio vasc disease	
PART II. OTHER SIGNIFICANT CONDITIONS CONTRIBUTING TO DEATH BUT NOT RELATED TO THE TERMINAL DISEASE CONDITION GIVEN IN PART I (A)	diabetes mellitus	

OPERATION AND AUTOPSY

31. OPERATION—CHECK ONE	32. DATE OF OPERATION	33. AUTOPSY—CHECK ONE
☑ OPERATION PERFORMED		☑

34A. SPECIFY ACCIDENT, SUICIDE OR HOMICIDE	34B. DESCRIBE HOW INJURY OCCURRED

INJURY INFORMATION

35A. TIME OF INJURY	HOUR	MONTH	DAY	YEAR

35B. INJURY OCCURRED	35C. PLACE OF INJURY	35D. CITY TOWN OR LOCATION	COUNTY	STATE
☐ WHILE AT WORK ☐ NOT WHILE AT WORK				

INFORMATIONAL, NOT A VALID DOCUMENT TO ESTABLISH IDENTITY

This is to certify that this document is a true copy of the official record filed with the Registrar-Recorder/County Clerk.

JAN 24 2005

Conny B. McCormack
CONNY B. McCORMACK
Registrar-Recorder/County Clerk

This copy not valid unless prepared on engraved border displaying the Seal and Signature of the Registrar-Recorder/County Clerk.

019113705

CERTIFICATION OF VITAL RECORD

COUNTY OF LOS ANGELES • REGISTRAR-RECORDER/COUNTY CLERK

CERTIFICATE OF DEATH
STATE OF CALIFORNIA—DEPARTMENT OF PUBLIC HEALTH

STATE FILE NUMBER

LOCAL REGISTRATION DISTRICT AND CERTIFICATE NUMBER: 7097-003221

DECEDENT PERSONAL DATA	1A. NAME OF DECEASED—FIRST NAME: Clara Ann	1B. MIDDLE NAME: Lou	1C. LAST NAME: McKay AKA Sheridan	2A. DATE OF DEATH—MONTH, DAY, YEAR: January 21, 1967	2B. HOUR: 3:?0P M.
	3. SEX: Female	4. COLOR OR RACE: Cauc.	5. BIRTHPLACE (STATE OR FOREIGN COUNTRY): Texas	6. DATE OF BIRTH: February 21, 1915	7. AGE (LAST BIRTHDAY): 51 YEARS
	8. NAME AND BIRTHPLACE OF FATHER: George Sheridan-Texas		9. MAIDEN NAME AND BIRTHPLACE OF MOTHER: Lula Stuart Warren-W. VA	10. CITIZEN OF WHAT COUNTRY: U.S.A.	11. SOCIAL SECURITY NUMBER: Unk.
	12. LAST OCCUPATION: Actress	13. NUMBER OF YEARS IN THIS OCCUPATION: 35	14. NAME OF LAST EMPLOYING COMPANY OR FIRM: Stage Screen T.V.	15. KIND OF INDUSTRY OR BUSINESS: Movies	
	16. IF DECEASED WAS EVER IN U.S. ARMED FORCES, GIVE WAR OR DATES OF SERVICE: NO	17. SPECIFY MARRIED, NEVER MARRIED, WIDOWED, DIVORCED: Married	18A. NAME OF PRESENT SPOUSE: Scott McKay	18B. PRESENT OR LAST OCCUPATION OF SPOUSE: Actor	

PLACE OF DEATH	19A. PLACE OF DEATH—NAME OF HOSPITAL: 1437	19B. STREET ADDRESS: 3204 Oakley Drive
	19C. CITY OR TOWN: Hollywood	19D. COUNTY: Los Angeles
		19E. LENGTH OF STAY IN COUNTY OF DEATH: 8Mo.	19F. LENGTH OF STAY IN CALIFORNIA: 8Mo.

| LAST USUAL RESIDENCE | 20A. LAST USUAL RESIDENCE—STREET ADDRESS: 3204 Oakley Drive | 20B. IF INSIDE CITY CORPORATE LIMITS: CHECK HERE | 21A. NAME OF INFORMANT: |
| | 20C. CITY OR TOWN: Hollywood | 20D. COUNTY: Los Angeles | 20E. STATE: California | 21B. ADDRESS OF INFORMANT: |

| PHYSICIAN'S OR CORONER'S CERTIFICATION | 22A. PHYSICIAN: I HEREBY CERTIFY THAT DEATH OCCURRED AT THE HOUR, DATE AND PLACE STATED ABOVE FROM THE CAUSES STATED BELOW AND THAT I ATTENDED THE DECEASED FROM APRIL 66 TO JAN 21, 67 AND THAT I LAST SAW THE DECEASED ALIVE ON JAN 20, 67 | 22C. PHYSICIAN OR CORONER—SIGNATURE: Frederick W Pobirs | DEGREE OR TITLE: M.D |
| | 22B. CORONER | 22D. ADDRESS: 240 So. La Cienega Bev. Hill | 22E. DATE SIGNED: Jan 21, 67 |

| FUNERAL DIRECTOR AND LOCAL REGISTRAR | 23. SPECIFY BURIAL, ENTOMBMENT, OR CREMATION: Cremation | 24. DATE: 1-23-67 | 25. NAME OF CEMETERY OR CREMATORY: Chapel of the Pines | 26. EMBALMER—SIGNATURE: Andrew P. Smith-5437 |
| | 27. NAME OF FUNERAL DIRECTOR: Pierce Bros. Valhalla | 28. JAN 23 1967 | 29. LOCAL REGISTRAR—SIGNATURE: |

CAUSE OF DEATH	30. CAUSE OF DEATH
	PART I. DEATH WAS CAUSED BY: IMMEDIATE CAUSE (A): Adenocarcinoma, gastric-esophageal
	CONDITIONS, IF ANY, WHICH GAVE RISE TO THE ABOVE CAUSE (A) STATING THE UNDERLYING CAUSE LAST: DUE TO (B): with massive liver metastasis —
	DUE TO (C):
	APPROXIMATE INTERVAL BETWEEN ONSET AND DEATH: 11 mos
	PART II. OTHER SIGNIFICANT CONDITIONS CONTRIBUTING TO DEATH BUT NOT RELATED TO THE TERMINAL DISEASE CONDITION GIVEN IN PART I (A):

| OPERATION AND AUTOPSY | 31. OPERATION—CHECK ONE: [X] FINDING USED IN DETERMINING ABOVE STATED CAUSES OF DEATH | 32. DATE OF OPERATION: April 25, 1966 | 33. AUTOPSY—CHECK ONE: [X] NO AUTOPSY PERFORMED |

| INJURY INFORMATION | 34A. SPECIFY ACCIDENT, SUICIDE OR HOMICIDE: | 34B. DESCRIBE HOW INJURY OCCURRED: |
| | 35A. TIME OF INJURY: | 35B. INJURY OCCURRED: | 35C. PLACE OF INJURY: | 35D. CITY, TOWN, OR LOCATION: COUNTY STATE |

This is to certify that this document is a true copy of the official record filed with the Registrar-Recorder/County Clerk.

Beatriz Valdez
BEATRIZ VALDEZ
Registrar-Recorder/County Clerk

AUG 1 0 1995
19-389294

This copy not valid unless prepared on engraved border displaying the Seal and Signature of the Registrar-Recorder/County Clerk.

American Bank Note Company — ANY ALTERATION OR ERASURE VOIDS THIS CERTIFICATE

CERTIFICATION OF VITAL RECORD

COUNTY OF LOS ANGELES • REGISTRAR-RECORDER/COUNTY CLERK

1947

DISTRICT NO. _____ REGISTRAR'S NO. **1721**

1. FULL NAME: Elizabeth Short

2. PLACE OF DEATH: (A) COUNTY: Los Angeles
   (B) CITY OR TOWN: Los Angeles
   IF OUTSIDE CITY OR TOWN LIMITS, WRITE RURAL
   (C) NAME OF HOSPITAL OR INSTITUTION: Found on Norton between Norton and Colliseum
   IF NOT IN HOSPITAL OR INSTITUTION, GIVE STREET NUMBER OR LOCATION
   (D) LENGTH OF STAY: (SPECIFY WHETHER YEARS, MONTHS OR DAYS)
   IN HOSPITAL OR INSTITUTION:
   IN THIS COMMUNITY: unknown   IN CALIFORNIA: 9 mo
   (E) IF FOREIGN BORN, HOW LONG IN THE U.S.A.: _____ YEARS

3. (E) IF VETERAN, NAME OF WAR: no
   3. (F) SOCIAL SECURITY NO.: unknown

4. SEX: female
5. COLOR OR RACE: cauc
6. (A) SINGLE, MARRIED, WIDOWED OR DIVORCED: single
6. (B) NAME OF HUSBAND OR WIFE:
6. (C) AGE OF HUSBAND OR WIFE IF ALIVE: _____ YEARS

7. BIRTHDATE OF DECEASED: July 29, 1924

8. AGE: 22 YRS   5 MOS   16 DAYS   IF LESS THAN ONE DAY OLD: HRS ___ MIN

9. BIRTHPLACE: Hyde Park, Mass.

10. USUAL OCCUPATION: Waitress

11. INDUSTRY OR BUSINESS: restaurant

FATHER
12. NAME: Cleo Alvin Short
13. BIRTHPLACE: Virginia

MOTHER
14. MAIDEN NAME: Phoebe M Sawyer
15. BIRTHPLACE: Maine

16. (A) INFORMANT: Phoebe Sawyer
    (B) ADDRESS: 115 Salem St, Medford Mass.

17. (A) removal   (B) DATE: 1-21-47
    BURIAL, CREMATION OR REMOVAL
    (C) PLACE: Sunset View Cem. Berkeley Cal

18. (A) EMBALMER'S SIGNATURE: Floyd P Dall   LICENSE NO. 1473
    (B) FUNERAL DIRECTOR: Pierce Brothers
    ADDRESS: 720 W. Washington Blvd.
    By: Stokes

19. (A) DATE FILED: JAN 27 1947   (B)
    REGISTRAR'S SIGNATURE: LaRue Robinson, DEPUTY REGISTRAR

20. DATE OF DEATH: MONTH January   DAY 14 or 15   YEAR 1947   HOUR ___ MINUTE ___

21. MEDICAL CERTIFICATE
    I HEREBY CERTIFY, THAT I ATTENDED THE DECEASED
    FROM _____ 19___
    TO _____ 19___
    THAT I LAST SAW H_____ ALIVE ON _____ 19___ AND THAT DEATH OCCURRED ON THE DATE AND HOUR STATED ABOVE.
    IMMEDIATE CAUSE OF DEATH: Hemorrhage + Shock
    DUE TO: Concussion of the brain + lacerations
    DUE TO: of the face
    OTHER CONDITIONS: (INCLUDE PREGNANCY WITHIN THREE MONTHS OF DEATH)
    MAJOR FINDINGS: OF OPERATIONS _____ DATE OF OPERATION _____
    OF AUTOPSY: As above

22. CORONER'S CERTIFICATE
    I HEREBY CERTIFY, THAT I HELD AN Autopsy AUTOPSY, INQUEST OR INVESTIGATION inquest ON THE REMAINS OF THE DECEASED AND FIND FROM SUCH ACTION THAT DECEASED CAME TO her DEATH ON THE DATE AND HOUR STATED ABOVE.

DURATION

PHYSICIAN
UNDERLINE THE CAUSE TO WHICH DEATH SHOULD BE CHARGED STATISTICALLY

23. IF DEATH WAS DUE TO EXTERNAL CAUSES, FILL IN THE FOLLOWING:
    (A) ACCIDENT, SUICIDE, OR HOMICIDE: Homicide   (B) DATE OF INJURY: 1/14 or 1/15/47
    (C) WHERE DID INJURY OCCUR: Los Angeles, Los Angeles, Calif   CITY OR TOWN   COUNTY   STATE
    (D) DID INJURY OCCUR IN OR ABOUT HOME, ON FARM, IN INDUSTRIAL PLACE, OR IN PUBLIC PLACE: Unknown   WHILE AT WORK: No   SPECIFY TYPE OF PLACE
    (E) MEANS OF INJURY: struck with unknown instrument

24. CORONER'S or PHYSICIAN'S SIGNATURE: Ben H. Brown (SPECIFY WHICH) By Edwin O. Lewis Deputy
    ADDRESS: Los Angeles, Calif   DATE: 1/25/47

STATE OF CALIFORNIA
DEPARTMENT OF PUBLIC HEALTH

CERTIFICATE OF DEATH

U.S. DEPT. OF COMMERCE
BUREAU OF THE CENSUS

This is to certify that this document is a true copy ... Registrar-Recorder/County Clerk.

Conny B. McCormack

CONNY B. McCORMACK
Registrar-Recorder/County Clerk

JAN 10 1997

19-482658

This copy not valid unless prepared on engraved border displaying the Seal and Signature of the Registrar-Recorder/County Clerk.

American Bank Note Company   ANY ALTERATION OR ERASURE VOIDS THIS CERTIFICATE

CERTIFICATION OF VITAL RECORD

COUNTY OF LOS ANGELES • REGISTRAR-RECORDER/COUNTY CLERK

CERTIFICATE OF DEATH　3 8 5 1 9 0 5 1 8 3 4
STATE OF CALIFORNIA

	STATE FILE NUMBER				LOCAL REGISTRATION DISTRICT AND CERTIFICATE NUMBER

DECEDENT PERSONAL DATA	1A. NAME OF DECEDENT—FIRST	1B. MIDDLE	1C. LAST SILVERS	2A. DATE OF DEATH (MONTH, DAY, YEAR) November 1, 1985	2B. HOUR 1412

1A. NAME OF DECEDENT—FIRST: PHIL
1C. LAST: SILVERS

3. SEX: Male | 4. RACE/ETHNICITY: Cauc. / Hebrew | 5. SPANISH/HISPANIC: NO | 6. DATE OF BIRTH: May 11, 1911 | 7. AGE: 74 YEARS

8. BIRTHPLACE OF DECEDENT (STATE OR FOREIGN COUNTRY): New York | 9. NAME AND BIRTHPLACE OF FATHER: Sol Silver / Russia | 10. BIRTH NAME AND BIRTHPLACE OF MOTHER: Sarah Handler / Russia

11A. CITIZEN OF WHAT COUNTRY: U.S.A. | 11B. IF DECEASED WAS EVER IN MILITARY GIVE DATES OF SERVICE: 19___ TO 19___ | 12. SOCIAL SECURITY NUMBER: UNKNOWN | 13. MARITAL STATUS: Divorced | 14. NAME OF SURVIVING SPOUSE (IF WIFE, ENTER BIRTH NAME)

15. PRIMARY OCCUPATION: Comedian | 16. NUMBER OF YEARS THIS OCCUPATION | 17. EMPLOYER (IF SELF-EMPLOYED, SO STATE): Self - Employed | 18. KIND OF INDUSTRY OR BUSINESS: Entertainment

USUAL RESIDENCE
19A. USUAL RESIDENCE—STREET ADDRESS (STREET AND NUMBER OR LOCATION): 2220 Ave of the Stars #1505 | 19B. | 19C. CITY OR TOWN: Century City | 1 OF 2
19D. COUNTY: Los Angeles | 19E. STATE: California | 20. NAME AND ADDRESS OF INFORMANT—RELATIONSHIP: Tracey Silvers - Daughter, 155 S. Elm Drive, Beverly Hills, California 90212

PLACE OF DEATH
21A. PLACE OF DEATH: Residence | 21B. COUNTY: Los Angeles
21C. STREET ADDRESS (STREET AND NUMBER OR LOCATION): 2220 Ave. of the Stars #1505 West Tower | 21D. CITY OR TOWN: Beverly Hills

CAUSE OF DEATH
22. DEATH WAS CAUSED BY: (ENTER ONLY ONE CAUSE PER LINE FOR A, B, AND C)
IMMEDIATE CAUSE (A): Cardiac Arrest — acute
DUE TO, OR AS A CONSEQUENCE OF (B): Coronary Arteriosclerotic Heart Disease — Chronic
DUE TO, OR AS A CONSEQUENCE OF (C):

APPROXIMATE INTERVAL BETWEEN ONSET AND DEATH
24. WAS DEATH REPORTED TO CORONER?: No
25. WAS BIOPSY PERFORMED?: No
26. WAS AUTOPSY PERFORMED?: No

23. OTHER SIGNIFICANT CONDITIONS—CONTRIBUTING TO DEATH BUT NOT RELATED TO CAUSE GIVEN IN 22A: Old Cerebrovascular accident
27. WAS OPERATION PERFORMED FOR ANY CONDITION IN ITEMS 22 OR 23? TYPE OF OPERATION: No | DATE

PHYSICIAN'S CERTIFICATION
28A. I CERTIFY THAT DEATH OCCURRED AT THE HOUR, DATE AND PLACE STATED FROM THE CAUSES STATED. I ATTENDED DECEDENT SINCE (ENTER MO. DA. YR.): 1952 | I LAST SAW DECEDENT ALIVE (ENTER MO. DA. YR.): 10-16-85
28B. PHYSICIAN—SIGNATURE AND DEGREE OR TITLE: Clarence M. Agress M.D. | 28C. DATE SIGNED: 11-2-85 | 28D. PHYSICIAN'S LICENSE NUMBER: C-6285
28E. TYPE PHYSICIAN'S NAME AND ADDRESS: Clarence M. Agress, M.D. 2080 Century Park East, Los Angeles, Ca. 90067

INJURY INFORMATION
29. SPECIFY ACCIDENT, SUICIDE, ETC. | 30. PLACE OF INJURY | 31. INJURY AT WORK | 32A. DATE OF INJURY—MONTH, DAY, YEAR | 32B. HOUR
33. LOCATION (STREET AND NUMBER OR LOCATION AND CITY OR TOWN) | 34. DESCRIBE HOW INJURY OCCURRED (EVENTS WHICH RESULTED IN INJURY)

CORONER'S USE ONLY
35A. I CERTIFY THAT DEATH OCCURRED AT THE HOUR, DATE AND PLACE STATED FROM THE CAUSES STATED. AS REQUIRED BY LAW I HAVE HELD AN (INQUEST-INVESTIGATION) | 35B. CORONER—SIGNATURE AND DEGREE OR TITLE | 35C. DATE SIGNED

DISPOSITION
36. DISPOSITION: Burial | 37. DATE—MONTH, DAY, YEAR: Nov. 3, 1985 | 38. NAME AND ADDRESS OF CEMETERY OR CREMATORY: Mt. Sinai Memorial Park, 5950 Forest Lawn #7516 Los Angeles, Ca | 39. EMBALMER'S LICENSE NUMBER AND SIGNATURE: Randy N. Pugh
40A. NAME OF FUNERAL DIRECTOR (OR PERSON ACTING AS SUCH): Groman Mortuary | cj | 40B. LICENSE NO.: 696 | 41. LOCAL REGISTRAR—SIGNATURE: Robert S. Gates | 42. DATE ACCEPTED BY LOCAL REGISTRAR: NOV __ 1985

STATE REGISTRAR | A. | B. | C. | D. | E. | F.

VS-11 (1-85)　49

This is to certify that this document is a true copy of the official record filed with the Registrar-Recorder/County Clerk.

Beatriz Valdez
BEATRIZ VALDEZ
Registrar-Recorder/County Clerk

AUG 10 1995

19-389407

This copy not valid unless prepared on engraved border displaying the Seal and Signature of the Registrar-Recorder/County Clerk.

American Bank Note Company　ANY ALTERATION OR ERASURE VOIDS THIS CERTIFICATE

CERTIFICATE OF DEATH
STATE OF CALIFORNIA
USE BLACK INK ONLY/NO ERASURES, WHITEOUTS OR ALTERATIONS
VS-11 (REV. 7/93)

39619007760

STATE FILE NUMBER		LOCAL REGISTRATION NUMBER

DECEDENT PERSONAL DATA

1. NAME OF DECEDENT—FIRST (GIVEN)	2. MIDDLE	3. LAST (FAMILY)
DONALD	CLARENCE	SIMPSON

4. DATE OF BIRTH MM/DD/CCYY	5. AGE YRS.	IF UNDER 1 YEAR MONTHS / DAYS	IF UNDER 24 HOURS HOURS / MINUTES	6. SEX	7. DATE OF DEATH MM/DD/CCYY	8. HOUR
10/29/1943	52			MALE	01/19/1996 Fnd	1707

9. STATE OF BIRTH	10. SOCIAL SECURITY NO.	11. MILITARY SERVICE	12. MARITAL STATUS	13. EDUCATION —YEARS COMPLETED
WASHINGTON	574-14-4976	19___ To 19___ NONE	NEVER MARRIED	16

1 OF 2

14. RACE	15. HISPANIC—SPECIFY	16. USUAL EMPLOYER
CAUCASIAN	YES _____ X No	SELF EMPLOYED

17. OCCUPATION	18. KIND OF BUSINESS	19. YEARS IN OCCUPATION
MOVIE PRODUCER	ENTERTAINMENT	20

USUAL RESIDENCE

20. RESIDENCE—STREET AND NUMBER OR LOCATION
685 STONE CANYON ROAD

21. CITY	22. COUNTY	23. ZIP CODE	24. YRS IN COUNTY	25. STATE OR FOREIGN COUNTRY
LOS ANGELES	LOS ANGELES	90077	20	CALIFORNIA

INFORMANT

26. NAME, RELATIONSHIP	27. MAILING ADDRESS (STREET AND NUMBER OR RURAL ROUTE NUMBER, CITY OR TOWN, STATE, ZIP)
LARY SIMPSON - BROTHER	150 SO. RODEO DRIVE, BEVERLY HILLS, CA. 90212

SPOUSE AND PARENT INFORMATION

28. NAME OF SURVIVING SPOUSE—FIRST	29. MIDDLE	30. LAST (MAIDEN NAME)
-	-	-

31. NAME OF FATHER—FIRST	32. MIDDLE	33. LAST	34. BIRTH STATE
RUSSELL	J.	SIMPSON	IA

35. NAME OF MOTHER—FIRST	36. MIDDLE	37. LAST (MAIDEN)	38. BIRTH STATE
JUNE	H.	CLARK	SD

DISPOSITION(S)

39. DATE MM/DD/CCYY	40. PLACE OF FINAL DISPOSITION
01/26/1996	RES. LARY SIMPSON, 685 STONE CANYON RD. LOS ANGELES, CA. 90077

FUNERAL DIRECTOR AND LOCAL REGISTRAR

41. TYPE OF DISPOSITION(S)	42. SIGNATURE OF EMBALMER	43. LICENSE NO.
CR/RES	▶ NOT EMBALMED	

44. NAME OF FUNERAL DIRECTOR	45. LICENSE NO.	46. SIGNATURE OF LOCAL REGISTRAR	47. DATE MM/DD/CCYY
PIERCE BROS. WESTWOOD VILLAGE	F-951	▶ Robert C. Nash	01/25/1996

PLACE OF DEATH

101. PLACE OF DEATH	102. IF HOSPITAL, SPECIFY ONE:	103. FACILITY OTHER THAN HOSPITAL:	104. COUNTY
Residence	IP / ER/OP / DOA	CONV. HOSP. / RES. / OTHER	Los Angeles

105. STREET ADDRESS—STREET AND NUMBER OR LOCATION	106. CITY
685 Stone Canyon Rd.	Los Angeles

CAUSE OF DEATH

107. DEATH WAS CAUSED BY: (ENTER ONLY ONE CAUSE PER LINE FOR A, B, C, AND D)	TIME INTERVAL BETWEEN ONSET AND DEATH	108. DEATH REPORTED TO CORONER
IMMEDIATE CAUSE (A) Deferred		X YES / NO
		REFERRAL NUMBER 96-00611
DUE TO (B)		109. BIOPSY PERFORMED YES / NO
DUE TO (C)		110. AUTOPSY PERFORMED X YES / NO
DUE TO (D)		111. USED IN DETERMINING CAUSE YES / NO

112. OTHER SIGNIFICANT CONDITIONS CONTRIBUTING TO DEATH BUT NOT RELATED TO CAUSE GIVEN IN 107

113. WAS OPERATION PERFORMED FOR ANY CONDITION IN ITEM 107 OR 112? IF YES, LIST TYPE OF OPERATION AND DATE.

PHYSICIAN'S CERTIFICATION

114. I CERTIFY THAT TO THE BEST OF MY KNOWLEDGE DEATH OCCURRED AT THE HOUR, DATE AND PLACE STATED FROM THE CAUSES STATED. DECEDENT ATTENDED SINCE MM/DD/CCYY / DECEDENT LAST SEEN ALIVE MM/DD/CCYY	115. SIGNATURE AND TITLE OF CERTIFIER ▶	116. LICENSE NO.	117. DATE MM/DD/CCYY
	118. TYPE ATTENDING PHYSICIAN'S NAME, MAILING ADDRESS + ZIP		

CORONER'S USE ONLY

I CERTIFY THAT IN MY OPINION DEATH OCCURRED AT THE HOUR, DATE AND PLACE STATED FROM THE CAUSES STATED.	120. INJURY AT WORK YES / No	121. INJURY DATE MM/DD/CCYY	122. HOUR	123. PLACE OF INJURY
119. MANNER OF DEATH	124. DESCRIBE HOW INJURY OCCURRED (EVENTS WHICH RESULTED IN INJURY)			

119. MANNER OF DEATH: NATURAL / SUICIDE / HOMICIDE / ACCIDENT / X PENDING INVESTIGATION / COULD NOT BE DETERMINED

125. LOCATION (STREET AND NUMBER OR LOCATION AND CITY AND ZIP CODE)

126. SIGNATURE OF CORONER OR DEPUTY CORONER ▶ Maria C. Arreola	127. DATE MM/DD/CCYY 01/24/1996	128. TYPED NAME, TITLE OF CORONER OR DEPUTY CORONER Deputy Coroner Maria C. Arreola

STATE REGISTRAR

A	B	C	D	E	F	G	H	FAX AUTH. #	CENSUS TRACT

AMENDMENT OF MEDICAL AND HEALTH DATA—DEATH

STATE FILE NUMBER	USE BLACK INK ONLY—NO ERASURES, WHITEOUT, OR ALTERATIONS	37619007760
		LOCAL REGISTRATION DISTRICT AND CERTIFICATE NUMBER

STATE/LOCAL REGISTRAR USE ONLY	1	2	3

TYPE OR PRINT IN BLACK INK ONLY

PART I — INFORMATION TO LOCATE RECORD

1. NAME—FIRST (GIVEN)	2. MIDDLE	3. LAST (FAMILY)	4. SEX
DONALD	CLARENCE	SIMPSON	MALE

5. DATE OF EVENT—MM/DD/CCYY	6. CITY OF OCCURENCE	7. COUNTY OF OCCURRENCE
01/19/1996 Fnd	Los Angeles	Los Angeles

2OF2

PART II — INFORMATION AS IT APPEARS ON RECORD

107. DEATH WAS CAUSED BY ENTER ONLY ONE CAUSE PER LINE FOR A, B, C, AND D)

			TIME INTERVAL BETWEEN ONSET AND DEATH
IMMEDIATE CAUSE	(A)	Deferred	
	(B)		
	(C)		
DUE TO	(D)		

108. DEATH REPORTED TO CORONER: [X] YES [ ] NO
REFERRAL NUMBER 96-00611

109. BIOPSY PERFORMED: [ ] YES [ ] NO

110. AUTOPSY PERFORMED: [X] YES [ ] NO

111. USED IN DETERMINING CAUSE: [ ] YES [ ] NO

112. OTHER SIGNIFICANT CONDITIONS CONTRIBUTING TO DEATH BUT NOT RELATED TO CAUSE GIVEN IN 107

113. WAS OPERATION PERFORMED FOR ANY CONDITION IN ITEM 107 or 112? IF YES, LIST TYPE OF OPERATION AND DATE.

119. MANNER OF DEATH	120. INJURY AT WORK	121. INJURY DATE—MM/DD/CCYY	122. HOUR	123. PLACE OF INJURY
[ ] NATURAL [ ] SUICIDE [ ] HOMICIDE	[ ] YES [ ] NO			
[ ] ACCIDENT [X] PENDING INVESTIGATION [ ] COULD NOT BE DETERMINED	124. DESCRIBE HOW INJURY OCCURED (EVENTS WHICH RESULTED IN INJURY)			

125. LOCATION (STREET AND NUMBER OR LOCATION AND CITY AND ZIP CODE)

PART III — INFORMATION AS IT SHOULD APPEAR

107. DEATH WAS CAUSED BY ENTER ONLY ONE CAUSE PER LINE FOR A, B, C, AND D)

			TIME INTERVAL BETWEEN ONSET AND DEATH
IMMEDIATE CAUSE	(A)	COMBINED EFFECTS OF MULTIPLE DRUG INTAKE	Unk
	(B)		
	(C)		
DUE TO	(D)		

108. DEATH REPORTED TO CORONER: [X] YES [ ] NO
REFERRAL NUMBER 96-00611

109. BIOPSY PERFORMED: [ ] YES [X] NO

110. AUTOPSY PERFORMED: [X] YES [ ] NO

111. USED IN DETERMINING CAUSE: [X] YES [ ] NO

112. OTHER SIGNIFICANT CONDITIONS CONTRIBUTING TO DEATH BUT NOT RELATED TO CAUSE GIVEN IN 107
Myocardial Fibrosis, Nonspecific

113. WAS OPERATION PERFORMED FOR ANY CONDITION IN ITEM 107 or 112? IF YES, LIST TYPE OF OPERATION AND DATE.
No

119. MANNER OF DEATH	120. INJURY AT WORK	121. INJURY DATE—MM/DD/CCYY	122. HOUR	123. PLACE OF INJURY
[ ] NATURAL [ ] SUICIDE [ ] HOMICIDE	[ ] YES [X] NO	Unknown	Unk	Unknown
[X] ACCIDENT [ ] PENDING INVESTIGATION [ ] COULD NOT BE DETERMINED	124. DESCRIBE HOW INJURY OCCURRED (EVENTS WHICH RESULTED IN INJURY) Drug Intake			

125. LOCATION (STREET AND NUMBER OR LOCATION AND CITY AND ZIP CODE)
Unknown

DECLARATION OF CERTIFYING PHYSICIAN OR CORONER

I HEREBY DECLARE UNDER PENALTY OF PERJURY THAT THE ABOVE INFORMATION IS TRUE AND CORRECT TO THE BEST OF MY KNOWLEDGE.

8. SIGNATURE OF CERTIFYING PHYSICIAN OR CORONER	9. DATE SIGNED—MM/DD/CCYY	10. TYPED OR PRINTED NAME AND DEGREE/TITLE OF CERTIFIER
Christopher Rogers	3-26-96	CHRISTOPHER B. ROGERS, M.D. DME

11. ADDRESS—STREET AND NUMBER	12. CITY	13. STATE	14. ZIP CODE
1104 North Mission Road	Los Angeles	CA	90033

STATE/LOCAL REGISTRAR USE ONLY

15. OFFICE OF STATE REGISTRAR OR SIGNATURE OF LOCAL REGISTRAR	16. DATE ACCEPTED FOR REGISTRATION—MM/DD/CCYY
Robert C. Gates	04/02/1996

STATE OF CALIFORNIA, DEPARTMENT OF HEALTH SERVICES, OFFICE OF STATE REGISTRAR

VS-24 B (1/94)
93 24457

CERTIFICATE OF DEATH
STATE OF CALIFORNIA
USE BLACK INK ONLY/NO ERASURES, WHITEOUTS OR ALTERATIONS
VS-11 (REV. 7/93)

STATE FILE NUMBER		LOCAL REGISTRATION NUMBER

DECEDENT PERSONAL DATA

1. NAME OF DECEDENT—FIRST (GIVEN)	2. MIDDLE	3. LAST (FAMILY)
MADGE	DORITA	SINCLAIR-COMPTON

4. DATE OF BIRTH MM/DD/CCYY	5. AGE YRS.	IF UNDER 1 YEAR MONTHS / DAYS	IF UNDER 24 HOURS HOURS / MINUTES	6. SEX	7. DATE OF DEATH MM/DD/CCYY	8. HOUR
04/28/1938	57			FEMALE	12/20/1995	0430

9. STATE OF BIRTH	10. SOCIAL SECURITY NO.	11. MILITARY SERVICE	12. MARITAL STATUS	13. EDUCATION —YEARS COMPLETED
JAMAICA	075-44-4392	19___ TO 19___ ☒ NONE	MARRIED	12

14. RACE	15. HISPANIC—SPECIFY		16. USUAL EMPLOYER
BLACK	☐ YES	☒ No	A B C PRODUCTIONS

17. OCCUPATION	18. KIND OF BUSINESS	19. YEARS IN OCCUPATION
ACTRESS	MOVIES & TELEVISION	25

USUAL RESIDENCE

20. RESIDENCE—STREET AND NUMBER OR LOCATION
14000 OLD HARBOUR LANE #301

21. CITY	22. COUNTY	23. ZIP CODE	24. YRS IN COUNTY	25. STATE OR FOREIGN COUNTRY
MARINA DEL REY	LOS ANGELES	90292	22	CALIFORNIA

INFORMANT

26. NAME, RELATIONSHIP	27. MAILING ADDRESS (STREET AND NUMBER OR RURAL ROUTE NUMBER, CITY OR TOWN, STATE, ZIP)
GARRY SINCLAIR - SON	566 TAMARAC DR., PASADENA, CA 91105

SPOUSE AND PARENT INFORMATION

28. NAME OF SURVIVING SPOUSE—FIRST	29. MIDDLE	30. LAST (MAIDEN NAME)	
DEAN	R	COMPTON	

31. NAME OF FATHER—FIRST	32. MIDDLE	33. LAST	34. BIRTH STATE
HERBERT	L	WALTERS	JAMAICA

35. NAME OF MOTHER—FIRST	36. MIDDLE	37. LAST (MAIDEN)	38. BIRTH STATE
JEMIMA	E	AUSTIN	JAMAICA

DISPOSITION(S)

39. DATE MM/DD/CCYY	40. PLACE OF FINAL DISPOSITION
12/27/1995	GARRY SINCLAIR RES 566 TAMARAC DR., PASADENA, CA

FUNERAL DIRECTOR AND LOCAL REGISTRAR

41. TYPE OF DISPOSITION(S)	42. SIGNATURE OF EMBALMER	43. LICENSE NO.
CR/RES	▶ NOT EMBALMED	—

44. NAME OF FUNERAL DIRECTOR	45. LICENSE NO.	46. SIGNATURE OF LOCAL REGISTRAR	47. DATE MM/DD/CCYY
NEPTUNE SOCIETY	F-1289	▶ *Robert C. Matt*	12/26/1995

PLACE OF DEATH

101. PLACE OF DEATH	102. IF HOSPITAL, SPECIFY ONE:	103. FACILITY OTHER THAN HOSPITAL:	104. COUNTY
GOOD SAMARITAN HOSPITAL	☒ IP ☐ ER/OP ☐ DOA	☐ CONV. HOSP. ☐ RES. ☐ OTHER	LOS ANGELES

105. STREET ADDRESS—STREET AND NUMBER OR LOCATION	106. CITY
1225 WILSHIRE BL.	LOS ANGELES

CAUSE OF DEATH

107. DEATH WAS CAUSED BY: (ENTER ONLY ONE CAUSE PER LINE FOR A, B, C, AND D)	TIME INTERVAL BETWEEN ONSET AND DEATH	108. DEATH REPORTED TO CORONER
IMMEDIATE CAUSE (A) HEPATORENAL FAILURE	1 WEEK	☐ YES ☒ NO REFERRAL NUMBER
DUE TO (B) CHRONIC LYMPHOCYTIC LEUKEMIA	6 YEARS	109. BIOPSY PERFORMED ☒ YES ☐ NO
DUE TO (C)		110. AUTOPSY PERFORMED ☐ YES ☒ NO
DUE TO (D)		111. USED IN DETERMINING CAUSE ☐ YES ☐ NO

112. OTHER SIGNIFICANT CONDITIONS CONTRIBUTING TO DEATH BUT NOT RELATED TO CAUSE GIVEN IN 107
NONE

113. WAS OPERATION PERFORMED FOR ANY CONDITION IN ITEM 107 OR 112? IF YES, LIST TYPE OF OPERATION AND DATE.
BONE MARROW 12/13/1995

PHYSICIAN'S CERTIFICATION

114. I CERTIFY THAT TO THE BEST OF MY KNOWLEDGE DEATH OCCURRED AT THE HOUR, DATE AND PLACE STATED FROM THE CAUSES STATED.	115. SIGNATURE AND TITLE OF CERTIFIER	116. LICENSE NO.	117. DATE MM/DD/CCYY
DECEDENT ATTENDED SINCE MM/DD/CCYY / DECEDENT LAST SEEN ALIVE MM/DD/CCYY	▶	C35803	12/20/1995
07/12/1989 / 12/19/1995	118. TYPE ATTENDING PHYSICIAN'S NAME, MAILING ADDRESS + ZIP L.ORR M.D., 1245 WILSHIRE BL., L.A., CA. 90017		

CORONER'S USE ONLY

119. MANNER OF DEATH — I CERTIFY THAT IN MY OPINION DEATH OCCURRED AT THE HOUR, DATE AND PLACE STATED FROM THE CAUSES STATED.	120. INJURY AT WORK	121. INJURY DATE MM/DD/CCYY	122. HOUR	123. PLACE OF INJURY
☐ NATURAL ☐ SUICIDE ☐ HOMICIDE ☐ ACCIDENT ☐ PENDING INVESTIGATION ☐ COULD NOT BE DETERMINED	☐ YES ☐ NO			

124. DESCRIBE HOW INJURY OCCURRED (EVENTS WHICH RESULTED IN INJURY)

125. LOCATION (STREET AND NUMBER OR LOCATION AND CITY AND ZIP CODE)

126. SIGNATURE OF CORONER OR DEPUTY CORONER	127. DATE MM/DD/CCYY	128. TYPED NAME, TITLE OF CORONER OR DEPUTY CORONER
▶		

STATE REGISTRAR

A	B	C	D	E	F	G	H	FAX AUTH. #	CENSUS TRACT

2041

STATE OF CALIFORNIA
CERTIFICATION OF VITAL RECORD

COUNTY OF RIVERSIDE
RIVERSIDE, CALIFORNIA

CERTIFICATE OF DEATH
STATE OF CALIFORNIA

3 1997 33007745

STATE FILE NUMBER   USE BLACK INK ONLY/NO ERASURES, WHITEOUTS OR ALTERATIONS VS-11 (REV. 11/96)   LOCAL REGISTRATION NUMBER

DECEDENT PERSONAL DATA

1. NAME OF DECEDENT—FIRST (GIVEN)	2. MIDDLE	3. LAST (FAMILY)
RICHARD	RED	SKELTON

4. DATE OF BIRTH MM/DD/CCYY	5. AGE YRS.	IF UNDER 1 YEAR MONTHS / DAYS	IF UNDER 24 HOURS HOURS / MINUTES	6. SEX	7. DATE OF DEATH MM/DD/CCYY	8. HOUR
07/18/1913	84			MALE	09/17/1997	0748

9. STATE OF BIRTH	10. SOCIAL SECURITY NO.	11. MILITARY SERVICE	12. MARITAL STATUS	13. EDUCATION—YEARS COMPLETED
IN	290-05-1445	X YES ☐ NO	MARRIED	12

14. RACE	15. HISPANIC—SPECIFY	16. USUAL EMPLOYER
CAUC.	☐ YES X NO	SELF EMPLOYED

17. OCCUPATION	18. KIND OF BUSINESS	19. YEARS IN OCCUPATION
COMEDIAN	ENTERTAINMENT	74

USUAL RESIDENCE

20. RESIDENCE—STREET AND NUMBER OR LOCATION
37801 THOMPSON ROAD

21. CITY	22. COUNTY	23. ZIP CODE	24. YRS IN COUNTY	25. STATE OR FOREIGN COUNTRY
RANCHO MIRAGE	RIVERSIDE	92270	36	CALIFORNIA

INFORMANT

26. NAME, RELATIONSHIP	27. MAILING ADDRESS (STREET AND NUMBER OR RURAL ROUTE NUMBER, CITY OR TOWN, STATE, ZIP)
LOTHIAN T. SKELTON - WIFE	37801 THOMPSON ROAD, RANCHO MIRAGE CA 92270

SPOUSE AND PARENT INFORMATION

28. NAME OF SURVIVING SPOUSE—FIRST	29. MIDDLE	30. LAST (MAIDEN NAME)
LOTHIAN	–	TOLAND

31. NAME OF FATHER—FIRST	32. MIDDLE	33. LAST	34. BIRTH STATE
JOSEPH	–	SKELTON	IN

35. NAME OF MOTHER—FIRST	36. MIDDLE	37. LAST (MAIDEN)	38. BIRTH STATE
IDA	MAE	FIELDS	IN

FUNERAL DIRECTOR AND LOCAL REGISTRAR

39. DATE MM/DD/CCYY	40. PLACE OF FINAL DISPOSITION
09/23/1997	FOREST LAWN MEM. PARK 1712 S GLENDALE AVE, GLENDALE CA 91205

41. TYPE OF DISPOSITION(S)	42. SIGNATURE OF EMBALMER	43. LICENSE NO.
BURIAL	▶ Scott Low	8257

44. NAME OF FUNERAL DIRECTOR	45. LICENSE NO.	46. SIGNATURE OF LOCAL REGISTRAR	47. DATE MM/DD/CCYY
FOREST LAWN MTY GLENDALE	FD 656	▶ Gary Feldman MD	09/22/1997

PLACE OF DEATH

101. PLACE OF DEATH	102. IF HOSPITAL SPECIFY ONE:	103. FACILITY OTHER THAN HOSPITAL	104. COUNTY
EISENHOWER MEDICAL CENTER	X IP ☐ ER/OP ☐ DOA	☐ CONV. HOSP. ☐ RES. CARE ☐ OTHER	RIVERSIDE

105. STREET ADDRESS—STREET AND NUMBER OR LOCATION	106. CITY
39000 BOB HOPE DRIVE	RANCHO MIRAGE

CAUSE OF DEATH

107. DEATH WAS CAUSED BY: (ENTER ONLY ONE CAUSE PER LINE FOR A, B, C, AND D)

			TIME INTERVAL BETWEEN ONSET AND DEATH	108. DEATH REPORTED TO CORONER
IMMEDIATE CAUSE	(A)	RESPIRATORY FAILURE	IMMED.	☐ YES X NO REFERRAL NUMBER
DUE TO	(B)	PNEUMONIA	1 MTH.	109. BIOPSY PERFORMED ☐ YES X NO
DUE TO	(C)			110. AUTOPSY PERFORMED ☐ YES X NO
DUE TO	(D)			111. USED IN DETERMINING CAUSE ☐ YES X NO

112. OTHER SIGNIFICANT CONDITIONS CONTRIBUTING TO DEATH BUT NOT RELATED TO CAUSE GIVEN IN 107
NONE

113. WAS OPERATION PERFORMED FOR ANY CONDITION IN ITEM 107 OR 112? IF YES, LIST TYPE OF OPERATION AND DATE.
NO

PHYSICIAN'S CERTIFICATION

114. I CERTIFY THAT TO THE BEST OF MY KNOWLEDGE DEATH OCCURRED AT THE HOUR, DATE AND PLACE STATED FROM THE CAUSES STATED.		115. SIGNATURE AND TITLE OF CERTIFIER	116. LICENSE NO.	117. DATE MM/DD/CCYY
DECEDENT ATTENDED SINCE MM/DD/CCYY	DECEDENT LAST SEEN ALIVE MM/DD/CCYY	▶ Andr J Silver MD	G55448	09/17/1997
08/15/1997	09/16/1997	118. TYPE ATTENDING PHYSICIAN'S NAME, MAILING ADDRESS, ZIP: ANDREW J. SILVER, MD, 72027 HIGHWAY 111, RANCHO MIRAGE, CA 92270		

CORONER'S USE ONLY

I CERTIFY THAT IN MY OPINION DEATH OCCURRED AT THE HOUR, DATE AND PLACE STATED FROM THE CAUSES STATED. 119. MANNER OF DEATH	120. INJURY AT WORK	121. INJURY DATE MM/DD/CCYY	122. HOUR	123. PLACE OF INJURY
☐ NATURAL ☐ SUICIDE ☐ HOMICIDE ☐ ACCIDENT ☐ PENDING INVESTIGATION ☐ COULD NOT BE DETERMINED	☐ YES ☐ NO			

124. DESCRIBE HOW INJURY OCCURRED (EVENTS WHICH RESULTED IN INJURY)

125. LOCATION (STREET AND NUMBER OR LOCATION AND CITY, ZIP)

126. SIGNATURE OF CORONER OR DEPUTY CORONER	127. DATE MM/DD/CCYY	128. TYPED NAME, TITLE OF CORONER OR DEPUTY CORONER
▶		

STATE REGISTRAR

A	B	C	D	E	F	G	H	FAX AUTH. #	CENSUS TRACT
								925103	

33373653

CERTIFIED COPY OF VITAL RECORDS
STATE OF CALIFORNIA, COUNTY OF RIVERSIDE

This is a true and exact reproduction of the document officially registered and placed on file in the office of the County of Riverside, County Clerk-Recorder.

DATE ISSUED   JAN 03 2003

Gary L. Orso
GARY L. ORSO
COUNTY CLERK-RECORDER
RIVERSIDE COUNTY, CALIFORNIA

This copy is not valid unless prepared on engraved border displaying date, seal and signature of the County Clerk-Recorder.

ANY ALTERATION OR ERASURE VOIDS THIS CERTIFICATE

CERTIFICATE OF DEATH
STATE OF CALIFORNIA
USE BLACK INK ONLY/NO ERASURES, WHITEOUTS OR ALTERATIONS
VS-11 (REV. 7/93)

39419005212

STATE FILE NUMBER		LOCAL REGISTRATION NUMBER

DECEDENT PERSONAL DATA

1. NAME OF DECEDENT—FIRST (GIVEN)	2. MIDDLE	3. LAST (FAMILY)
HAROLD	JOHN	SMITH

4. DATE OF BIRTH MM/DD/CCYY	5. AGE YRS.	IF UNDER 1 YEAR MONTHS / DAYS	IF UNDER 24 HOURS HOURS / MINUTES	6. SEX	7. DATE OF DEATH MM/DD/CCYY	8. HOUR
08/24/1916	77			MALE	01/28/1994 FOUND	1630

9. STATE OF BIRTH	10. SOCIAL SECURITY NO.	11. MILITARY SERVICE	12. MARITAL STATUS	13. EDUCATION — YEARS COMPLETED
MI	069-07-9438	1945 to 1947 ☐ NONE	WIDOW	12

14. RACE	15. HISPANIC—SPECIFY	16. USUAL EMPLOYER
CAUCASIAN	☐ YES _____ ☒ NO	SELF

17. OCCUPATION	18. KIND OF BUSINESS	19. YEARS IN OCCUPATION
ACTOR	ENTERTAINMENT	71

USUAL RESIDENCE

20. RESIDENCE—STREET AND NUMBER OR LOCATION
242 N ENTRADA DR

21. CITY	22. COUNTY	23. ZIP CODE	24. YRS IN COUNTY	25. STATE OR FOREIGN COUNTRY
PACIFIC PALISADES	LOS ANGELES	90402	46	CALIFORNIA

INFORMANT

26. NAME, RELATIONSHIP	27. MAILING ADDRESS (STREET AND NUMBER OR RURAL ROUTE NUMBER, CITY OR TOWN, STATE, ZIP)
TERRY J SMITH- SON	330 S MYERS ST BURBANK CA, 91506

SPOUSE AND PARENT INFORMATION

28. NAME OF SURVIVING SPOUSE—FIRST	29. MIDDLE	30. LAST (MAIDEN NAME)
-	-	-

31. NAME OF FATHER—FIRST	32. MIDDLE	33. LAST	34. BIRTH STATE
JAY	-	SMITH	-

35. NAME OF MOTHER—FIRST	36. MIDDLE	37. LAST (MAIDEN)	38. BIRTH STATE
EMMA	-	LePLEUFF	-

DISPOSITION(S)

39. DATE MM/DD/CCYY	40. PLACE OF FINAL DISPOSITION
02/02/1994	WOODLAWN CEMETERY 1847 14TH ST SANTA MONICA CA, 90404

FUNERAL DIRECTOR AND LOCAL REGISTRAR

41. TYPE OF DISPOSITION(S)	42. SIGNATURE OF EMBALMER	43. LICENSE NO.
BURIAL	Richard N. White	4485

44. NAME OF FUNERAL DIRECTOR	45. LICENSE NO.	46. SIGNATURE OF LOCAL REGISTRAR	47. DATE MM/DD/CCYY
PIERCE BROS MOELLER MURPHY	FD-695	Robert C. Mitz	02/01/1994

PLACE OF DEATH

101. PLACE OF DEATH	102. IF HOSPITAL, SPECIFY ONE:	103. FACILITY OTHER THAN HOSPITAL	104. COUNTY
RESIDENCE	☐ IP ☐ ER/OP ☐ DOA	☐ CONV. HOSP. ☒ RES. ☐ OTHER	LOS ANGELES

105. STREET ADDRESS—STREET AND NUMBER OR LOCATION	106. CITY
242 N ENTRADA	PACIFIC PALISADES

CAUSE OF DEATH

107. DEATH WAS CAUSED BY: (ENTER ONLY ONE CAUSE PER LINE FOR A, B, C, AND D)	TIME INTERVAL BETWEEN ONSET AND DEATH	108. DEATH REPORTED TO CORONER
IMMEDIATE CAUSE (A) Arteriosclerotic Cardiovascular Disease	YEARS	☒ YES ☐ NO REFERRAL NUMBER 94-01028
DUE TO (B)		109. BIOPSY PERFORMED ☐ YES ☒ NO
DUE TO (C)		110. AUTOPSY PERFORMED ☐ YES ☒ NO
DUE TO (D)		111. USED IN DETERMINING CAUSE ☐ YES ☒ NO

112. OTHER SIGNIFICANT CONDITIONS CONTRIBUTING TO DEATH BUT NOT RELATED TO CAUSE GIVEN IN 107
NONE

113. WAS OPERATION PERFORMED FOR ANY CONDITION IN ITEM 107 OR 112? IF YES, LIST TYPE OF OPERATION AND DATE.
NO

PHYSICIAN'S CERTIFICATION

114. I CERTIFY THAT TO THE BEST OF MY KNOWLEDGE DEATH OCCURRED AT THE HOUR, DATE AND PLACE STATED FROM THE CAUSES STATED. DECEDENT ATTENDED SINCE MM/DD/CCYY / DECEDENT LAST SEEN ALIVE MM/DD/CCYY	115. SIGNATURE AND TITLE OF CERTIFIER	116. LICENSE NO.	117. DATE MM/DD/CCYY
	▶		
	118. TYPE ATTENDING PHYSICIAN'S NAME, MAILING ADDRESS · ZIP		

CORONER'S USE ONLY

I CERTIFY THAT IN MY OPINION DEATH OCCURRED AT THE HOUR, DATE AND PLACE STATED FROM THE CAUSES STATED. 119. MANNER OF DEATH	120. INJURY AT WORK ☐ YES ☐ NO	121. INJURY DATE MM/DD/CCYY	122. HOUR	123. PLACE OF INJURY
☒ NATURAL ☐ SUICIDE ☐ HOMICIDE ☐ ACCIDENT ☐ PENDING INVESTIGATION ☐ COULD NOT BE DETERMINED	124. DESCRIBE HOW INJURY OCCURRED (EVENTS WHICH RESULTED IN INJURY)			

125. LOCATION (STREET AND NUMBER OR LOCATION AND CITY AND ZIP CODE)
242 N ENTRADA DR PACIFIC PALISADES CA, 90402

126. SIGNATURE OF CORONER OR DEPUTY CORONER	127. DATE MM/DD/CCYY	128. TYPED NAME, TITLE OF CORONER OR DEPUTY CORONER
▶ Philip D.	01/29/1994	PHILIP DITURI. DEPUTY CORNER

STATE REGISTRAR

A	B	C	D	E	F	G	H	FAX AUTH. #	CENSUS TRACT
4292									

STATE OF CALIFORNIA
CERTIFICATION OF VITAL RECORD

COUNTY OF LOS ANGELES
DEPARTMENT OF HEALTH SERVICES

CERTIFICATE OF DEATH
STATE OF CALIFORNIA
USE BLACK INK ONLY / NO ERASURES, WHITEOUTS OR ALTERATIONS
VS-11 (REV 1/03)

STATE FILE NUMBER		LOCAL REGISTRATION NUMBER

1. NAME OF DECEDENT --- FIRST (Given)	2. MIDDLE	3. LAST (Family)
ROBERT	LANGFORD	STACK

AKA, ALSO KNOWN AS --- Include full AKA (FIRST, MIDDLE, LAST)	4. DATE OF BIRTH mm/dd/ccyy	5. AGE Yrs.	IF UNDER ONE YEAR Months / Days	IF UNDER 24 HOURS Hours / Minutes	6. SEX
	01/13/1919	84			M

9. BIRTH STATE/FOREIGN COUNTRY	10. SOCIAL SECURITY NUMBER	11. EVER IN U.S. ARMED FORCES?	12. MARITAL STATUS (at Time of Death)	7. DATE OF DEATH mm/dd/ccyy	8. HOUR (24 Hours)
CA	548-28-3552	X YES ☐ NO ☐ UNK	MARRIED	05/14/2003	1725

13. EDUCATION --- Highest Level/Degree (see worksheet on back)	14/15. WAS DECEDENT SPANISH/HISPANIC/LATINO? (If yes, see worksheet on back)	16. DECEDENT'S RACE --- Up to 3 races may be listed (see worksheet on back)
SOME COLLEGE	☐ YES X NO	CAUCASIAN

17. USUAL OCCUPATION --- Type of work for most of life. DO NOT USE RETIRED	18. KIND OF BUSINESS OR INDUSTRY (e.g., grocery store, road construction, employment agency, etc.)	19. YEARS IN OCCUPATION
ACTOR	ENTERTAINMENT	63

20. DECEDENT'S RESIDENCE (Street and number or location)
321 SAINT PIERRE RD.

21. CITY	22. COUNTY/PROVINCE	23. ZIP CODE	24. YEARS IN COUNTY	25. STATE/FOREIGN COUNTRY
LOS ANGELES	LOS ANGELES	90077	84	CA

26. INFORMANT'S NAME, RELATIONSHIP	27. INFORMANT'S MAILING ADDRESS (Street and number or rural route number, city or town, state, ZIP)
ROSEMARIE STACK - WIFE	321 SAINT PIERRE RD. LOS ANGELES, CA 90077

28. NAME OF SURVIVING SPOUSE --- FIRST	29. MIDDLE	30. LAST (Maiden Name)
ROSEMARIE	-	BOWE

31. NAME OF FATHER --- FIRST	32. MIDDLE	33. LAST	34. BIRTH STATE
JAMES	LANGFORD	STACK	UNK

35. NAME OF MOTHER --- FIRST	36. MIDDLE	37. LAST (Maiden)	38. BIRTH STATE
ELIZABETH	-	WOOD	CA

39. DISPOSITION DATE mm/dd/ccyy	40. PLACE OF FINAL DISPOSITION
05/22/2003	WESTWOOD VILLAGE MEMORIAL PARK 1218 GLENDON AVE. LOS ANGELES, CA 90024

41. TYPE OF DISPOSITION(S)	42. SIGNATURE OF EMBALMER	43. LICENSE NUMBER
CR/BU	▶ NOT EMBALMED	

44. NAME OF FUNERAL ESTABLISHMENT	45. LICENSE NUMBER	46. SIGNATURE OF LOCAL REGISTRAR	47. DATE mm/dd/ccyy
PIERCE BROS. WESTWOOD	FD-951	▶ *Thomas L Gawhannie*	05/21/2003

101. PLACE OF DEATH	102. IF HOSPITAL, SPECIFY ONE	103. IF OTHER THAN HOSPITAL, SPECIFY ONE
RESIDENCE	☐ IP ☐ ER/OP ☐ DOA	☐ Hospice ☐ Nursing Home/LTC X Decedent's Home ☐ Other

104. COUNTY	105. FACILITY ADDRESS OR LOCATION WHERE FOUND (Street and number or location)	106. CITY
LOS ANGELES	321 SAINT PIERRE RD.	LOS ANGELES

107. CAUSE OF DEATH	Enter the chain of events --- diseases, injuries, or complications --- that directly caused death. DO NOT enter terminal events such as cardiac arrest, respiratory arrest, or ventricular fibrillation without showing the etiology. DO NOT ABBREVIATE.	Time Interval Between Onset and Death	108. DEATH REPORTED TO CORONER?
IMMEDIATE CAUSE (A) (Final disease or condition resulting in death) →	MYOCARDIAL INFARCTION	(A) 10mins.	☐ YES X NO REFERRAL NUMBER
Sequentially list conditions, if any, leading to cause on Line A. Enter UNDERLYING CAUSE (disease or injury that initiated the events resulting in death) LAST (B)	CORONARY ARTERY DISEASE	(B) 5years	109. BIOPSY PERFORMED? ☐ YES X NO
(C)		(C)	110. AUTOPSY PERFORMED? ☐ YES X NO
(D)		(D)	111. USED IN DETERMINING CAUSE? ☐ YES ☐ NO

112. OTHER SIGNIFICANT CONDITIONS CONTRIBUTING TO DEATH BUT NOT RESULTING IN THE UNDERLYING CAUSE GIVEN IN 107
CANCER OF PROSTATE

113. WAS OPERATION PERFORMED FOR ANY CONDITION IN ITEM 107 OR 112? (If yes, list type of operation and date.)	113A. IF FEMALE, PREGNANT IN LAST YEAR?
NO	☐ YES ☐ NO ☐ UNK

114. I CERTIFY THAT TO THE BEST OF MY KNOWLEDGE DEATH OCCURRED AT THE HOUR, DATE, AND PLACE STATED FROM THE CAUSES STATED.	115. SIGNATURE AND TITLE OF CERTIFIER	116. LICENSE NUMBER	117. DATE mm/dd/ccyy
Decedent Attended Since / Decedent Last Seen Alive	▶ *Richard N Gold M D*	G25587	05/20/2003
(A) mm/dd/ccyy 02/21/1997	(B) mm/dd/ccyy 04/30/2003	118. TYPE ATTENDING PHYSICIANS' NAME, MAILING ADDRESS, ZIP CODE: RICHARD N.GOLD,MD. 8631 W.3RD ST. LOS ANGELES, CA. 90048	

119. I CERTIFY THAT IN MY OPINION DEATH OCCURRED AT THE HOUR, DATE, AND PLACE STATED FROM THE CAUSES STATED.		
MANNER OF DEATH ☐ Natural ☐ Accident ☐ Homicide ☐ Suicide ☐ Pending Investigation ☐ Could not be determined	120. INJURED AT WORK? ☐ YES ☐ NO ☐ UNK	121. INJURY DATE mm/dd/ccyy 122. HOUR (24 Hours)

123. PLACE OF INJURY (e.g., home, construction site, wooded area, etc.)

124. DESCRIBE HOW INJURY OCCURRED (Events which resulted in injury)

125. LOCATION OF INJURY (Street and number, or location, and city, and ZIP)

126. SIGNATURE OF CORONER / DEPUTY CORONER	127. DATE mm/dd/ccyy	128. TYPE NAME, TITLE OF CORONER / DEPUTY CORONER
▶		

STATE REGISTRAR	A	B	C	D	E		FAX AUTH. #	CENSUS TRACT

090627733

This is a true certified copy of the record filed in the County of Los Angeles Department of Health Services if it bears the Registrar's signature in purple ink.

Thomas L Gawhannie   ISSUED   234   JUN 16 2003

Director of Health Services and Registrar

This copy not valid unless prepared on engraved border displaying seal and signature of Registrar.

ANY ALTERATION OR ERASURE VOIDS THIS CERTIFICATE

CERTIFICATE OF DEATH
STATE OF CALIFORNIA
USE BLACK INK ONLY / NO ERASURES, WHITEOUTS OR ALTERATIONS
VS-11 (REV 1/03)

STATE FILE NUMBER	LOCAL REGISTRATION NUMBER

DECEDENT'S PERSONAL DATA

1. NAME OF DECEDENT --- FIRST (Given): FLORENCE
2. MIDDLE: L.
3. LAST (Family): NEWMAN

AKA: --
4. DATE OF BIRTH: 07/01/1924
5. AGE Yrs.: 79
6. SEX: F

9. BIRTH STATE/FOREIGN COUNTRY: ILLINOIS
10. SOCIAL SECURITY NUMBER: 336-14-0662
11. EVER IN U.S. ARMED FORCES?: NO [X]
12. MARITAL STATUS: MARRIED
7. DATE OF DEATH: 10/03/2003
8. HOUR: 1435

13. EDUCATION: BACHELOR'S
14/15. SPANISH/HISPANIC/LATINO?: NO [X]
16. RACE: WHITE

17. USUAL OCCUPATION: ACTOR
18. KIND OF BUSINESS OR INDUSTRY: ENTERTAINMENT
19. YEARS IN OCCUPATION: 57

USUAL RESIDENCE

20. DECEDENT'S RESIDENCE: 68-09 BOOTH STREET
21. CITY: FOREST HILLS
22. COUNTY/PROVINCE: QUEENS
23. ZIP CODE: 11375
24. YEARS IN COUNTY: 56
25. STATE/FOREIGN COUNTRY: NEW YORK

INFORMANT

26. INFORMANT'S NAME, RELATIONSHIP: MARTIN M. NEWMAN - HUSBAND
27. INFORMANT'S MAILING ADDRESS: 10630 WILKINS AVENUE #303, LOS ANGELES, CA 90024

SPOUSE AND PARENT INFORMATION

28. NAME OF SURVIVING SPOUSE --- FIRST: MARTIN
29. MIDDLE: M.
30. LAST (Maiden Name): NEWMAN

31. NAME OF FATHER: JACK
32. MIDDLE: --
33. LAST: SCHWARTZ
34. BIRTH STATE: NEW YORK

35. NAME OF MOTHER: HANNA
36. MIDDLE: --
37. LAST (Maiden): WEIL
38. BIRTH STATE: ILLINOIS

FUNERAL DIRECTOR / LOCAL REGISTRAR

39. DISPOSITION DATE: 10/07/2003
40. PLACE OF FINAL DISPOSITION: MOUNT SINAI MEMORIAL PARK 5950 FOREST LAWN DRIVE, L.A., CA 90068

41. TYPE OF DISPOSITION(S): BURIAL
42. SIGNATURE OF EMBALMER: NOT EMBALMED
43. LICENSE NUMBER: --

44. NAME OF FUNERAL ESTABLISHMENT: MOUNT SINAI MORTUARY
45. LICENSE NUMBER: FD-1010
46. SIGNATURE OF LOCAL REGISTRAR: Thomas W Guttuvire
47. DATE: 10/07/2003

PLACE OF DEATH

101. PLACE OF DEATH: CEDARS-SINAI MEDICAL CENTER
102. IF HOSPITAL, SPECIFY ONE: IP [X]
104. COUNTY: LOS ANGELES
105. FACILITY ADDRESS: 8700 BEVERLY BLVD
106. CITY: LOS ANGELES

CAUSE OF DEATH

107. CAUSE OF DEATH:
IMMEDIATE CAUSE (A): CEREBROVASCULAR ACCIDENT — HOURS
108. DEATH REPORTED TO CORONER?: NO [X]
109. BIOPSY PERFORMED?: NO [X]
110. AUTOPSY PERFORMED?: NO [X]
111. USED IN DETERMINING CAUSE?:

112. OTHER SIGNIFICANT CONDITIONS: ATRIAL FIBRILLATION

113. WAS OPERATION PERFORMED: NO
113A. IF FEMALE, PREGNANT IN LAST YEAR?: NO [X]

PHYSICIAN'S CERTIFICATION

114. I CERTIFY... DECEDENT ATTENDED SINCE: --/--/1997 DECEDENT LAST SEEN ALIVE: 10/03/2003
115. SIGNATURE AND TITLE OF CERTIFIER: [signature]
116. LICENSE NUMBER: G46165
117. DATE: 10/06/2003
118. ATTENDING PHYSICIAN'S NAME: MARK G BAMBERGER M.D. 8920 WILSHIRE BLVD #635, BEVERLY HILLS, CA 90211

CORONER'S USE ONLY

119. I CERTIFY...
120. INJURED AT WORK?:
121. INJURY DATE:
122. HOUR:

INFORMATIONAL, NOT A VALID DOCUMENT TO ESTABLISH IDENTITY

FAX AUTH. #: 344/2052

CERTIFICATE OF DEATH

STATE OF CALIFORNIA
USE BLACK INK ONLY/NO ERASURES, WHITEOUTS OR ALTERATIONS
VS-11 (REV. 1/00)

STATE FILE NUMBER

3 2002 19 029765

LOCAL REGISTRATION NUMBER

DECEDENT PERSONAL DATA

1. NAME OF DECEDENT—FIRST (GIVEN)	2. MIDDLE	3. LAST (FAMILY)
RODNEY	STEPHAN	STEIGER

4. DATE OF BIRTH MM/DD/CCYY	5. AGE YRS.	IF UNDER 1 YEAR MONTHS / DAYS	IF UNDER 24 HOURS HOURS / MINUTES	6. SEX	7. DATE OF DEATH MM/DD/CCYY	8. HOUR
04/14/1925	77			MALE	07/09/2002	0853

9. STATE OF BIRTH	10. SOCIAL SECURITY NO.	11. MILITARY SERVICE	12. MARITAL STATUS	13. EDUCATION—YEARS COMPLETED
NY	145-22-6295	[X] YES [ ] No [ ] UNK	MARRIED	10

14. RACE	15. HISPANIC—SPECIFY		16. USUAL EMPLOYER
CAUC.	[ ] Yes	[X] No	FALCONHURST INC.

17. OCCUPATION	18. KIND OF BUSINESS	19. YEARS IN OCCUPATION
ACTOR	ENTERTAINMENT	50

USUAL RESIDENCE

20. RESIDENCE—(STREET AND NUMBER OR LOCATION)
6324 ZUMIREZ DR.

21. CITY	22. COUNTY	23. ZIP CODE	24. YRS IN COUNTY	25. STATE OR FOREIGN COUNTRY
MALIBU	LOS ANGELES	90265	30	CA

INFORMANT

26. NAME, RELATIONSHIP	27. MAILING ADDRESS (STREET AND NUMBER OR RURAL ROUTE NUMBER, CITY OR TOWN, STATE, ZIP)
JOAN STEIGER - WIFE	6324 ZUMIREZ DR., MALIBU, CA. 90265

SPOUSE AND PARENT INFORMATION

28. NAME OF SURVIVING SPOUSE—FIRST	29. MIDDLE	30. LAST (MAIDEN NAME)	
JOAN	B.	BENEDICT	

31. NAME OF FATHER—FIRST	32. MIDDLE	33. LAST	34. BIRTH STATE
FREDERICK	–	STEIGER	NY

35. NAME OF MOTHER—FIRST	36. MIDDLE	37. LAST (MAIDEN)	38. BIRTH STATE
AUGUSTA	AMELIA	DRIVER	NY

DISPOSITION(S)

39. DATE MM/DD/CCYY	40. PLACE OF FINAL DISPOSITION
07/11/2002	FOREST LAWN MEM. PARK 6300 FOREST LAWN DR. LOS ANGELES, CA. 90068

FUNERAL DIRECTOR AND LOCAL REGISTRAR

41. TYPE OF DISPOSITION(S)	42. SIGNATURE OF EMBALMER	43. LICENSE NO.
CR/BU	▶ NOT EMBALMED	–

44. NAME OF FUNERAL DIRECTOR	45. LICENSE NO.	46. SIGNATURE OF LOCAL REGISTRAR	47. DATE MM/DD/CCYY
FOREST LAWN HOLLYWOOD HILLS	FD 904	▶ Thomas G Whitworth	07/11/2002

PLACE OF DEATH

101. PLACE OF DEATH	102. IF HOSPITAL, SPECIFY ONE:	103. FACILITY OTHER THAN HOSPITAL:	104. COUNTY
ST JOHN HEALTH CENTER	[X] IP [ ] ER/OP [ ] DOA	[ ] CONV. HOSP. [ ] RES. CARE [ ] OTHER	LOS ANGELES

105. STREET ADDRESS—(STREET AND NUMBER OR LOCATION)	106. CITY
1328 22ND ST	SANTA MONICA

CAUSE OF DEATH

107. DEATH WAS CAUSED BY: (ENTER ONLY ONE CAUSE PER LINE FOR A, B, C, AND D)	TIME INTERVAL BETWEEN ONSET AND DEATH	108. DEATH REPORTED TO CORONER
IMMEDIATE CAUSE (A) RESPIRATORY FAILURE	13 DAYS	[ ] YES [X] No REFERRAL NUMBER
DUE TO (B) SEPSIS	2 WKS	109. BIOPSY PERFORMED [ ] YES [X] No
DUE TO (C) RENAL FAILURE	2 WKS	110. AUTOPSY PERFORMED [ ] YES [X] No
DUE TO (D) PANCREATIC CANCER	3 WKS	111. USED IN DETERMINING CAUSE [ ] YES [X] No

112. OTHER SIGNIFICANT CONDITIONS CONTRIBUTING TO DEATH BUT NOT RELATED TO CAUSE GIVEN IN 107
CORONARY ARTERY DISEASE

113. WAS OPERATION PERFORMED FOR ANY CONDITION IN ITEM 107 OR 112? IF YES, LIST TYPE OF OPERATION AND DATE.
RESECTION OF PANCREAS 06/17/2002

PHYSICIAN'S CERTIFICATION

114. I CERTIFY THAT TO THE BEST OF MY KNOWLEDGE DEATH OCCURRED AT THE HOUR, DATE AND PLACE STATED FROM THE CAUSES STATED.	115. SIGNATURE AND TITLE OF CERTIFIER	116. LICENSE NO.	117. DATE MM/DD/CCYY
DECEDENT ATTENDED SINCE MM/DD/CCYY: 06/11/2002 — DECEDENT LAST SEEN ALIVE MM/DD/CCYY: 07/09/2002	▶ Bilchik M.D.	A69766	07/10/2002
	118. TYPE ATTENDING PHYSICIAN'S NAME, MAILING ADDRESS, ZIP: ANTON J BILCHIK, MD 2200 SANTA MONICA BLVD, SANTA MONICA, CA		90404

CORONER'S USE ONLY

I CERTIFY THAT IN MY OPINION DEATH OCCURRED AT THE HOUR, DATE AND PLACE STATED FROM THE CAUSES STATED.	120. INJURY AT WORK	121. INJURY DATE MM/DD/CCYY	122. HOUR	123. PLACE OF INJURY
119. MANNER OF DEATH	[ ] YES [ ] No			

119. MANNER OF DEATH	124. DESCRIBE HOW INJURY OCCURRED (EVENTS WHICH RESULTED IN INJURY)
[ ] NATURAL [ ] SUICIDE [ ] HOMICIDE [ ] ACCIDENT [ ] PENDING INVESTIGATION [ ] COULD NOT BE DETERMINED	

INFORMATIONAL, NOT A VALID DOCUMENT TO ESTABLISH IDENTITY

125. LOCATION (STREET AND NUMBER OR LOCATION AND CITY, ZIP)

126. SIGNATURE OF CORONER OR DEPUTY CORONER	127. DATE MM/DD/CCYY	128. TYPED NAME, TITLE OF CORONER OR DEPUTY CORONER
▶		

STATE REGISTRAR

A	B	C	D	E	F	G	H	FAX AUTH. #	CENSUS TRACT

CERTIFICATION OF VITAL RECORD

COUNTY OF LOS ANGELES • REGISTRAR-RECORDER/COUNTY CLERK

CERTIFICATE OF DEATH
STATE OF CALIFORNIA—DEPARTMENT OF PUBLIC HEALTH

7097-023490

STATE FILE NUMBER	LOCAL REGISTRATION DISTRICT AND CERTIFICATE NUMBER

DECEDENT PERSONAL DATA

1A. NAME OF DECEASED—FIRST NAME	1B. MIDDLE NAME	1C. LAST NAME	2A. DATE OF DEATH—MONTH DAY YEAR	2B. HOUR
Inger	Stensland	Jones aka Stevens	4-30-70	PRIOR T. 1030 A

3 SEX	4 COLOR OR RACE	5. BIRTHPLACE (STATE OR FOREIGN COUNTRY)	6. DATE OF BIRTH	7. AGE LAST BIRTHDAY	IF UNDER 1 YEAR	IF UNDER 24 HOURS
Female	Caucasian	Sweden	October 18, 1934	35 YEARS		

8 NAME AND BIRTHPLACE OF FATHER	9. MAIDEN NAME AND BIRTHPLACE OF MOTHER
Per Gustaf Stensland, Sweden	Lisbeth Potthoff, Sweden.

AMENDED 1 OF 2

10 CITIZEN OF WHAT COUNTRY	11 SOCIAL SECURITY NUMBER	12. MARRIED, NEVER MARRIED, WIDOWED DIVORCED (SPECIFY)	13. NAME OF SURVIVING SPOUSE (IF WIFE ENTER MAIDEN NAME)
USA	511 20 0818	Married	Isaac L. Jones

14 LAST OCCUPATION	15. NUMBER OF YEARS IN THIS OCCUPATION	16. NAME OF LAST EMPLOYING COMPANY OR FIRM (IF SELF EMPLOYED SO STATE)	17. KIND OF INDUSTRY OR BUSINESS
Actress	17 yrs	Free Lance Actress	Motion Picture

PLACE OF DEATH

18A. PLACE OF DEATH—NAME OF HOSPITAL OR OTHER IN PATIENT FACILITY	18A. STREET ADDRESS—(STREET AND NUMBER, OR LOCATION)	18C. INSIDE CITY CORPORATE LIMITS SPECIFY YES OR NO
	8000 Woodrow Wilson Drive	Yes

18D. CITY OR TOWN	18E. COUNTY	18F. LENGTH OF STAY IN COUNTY OF DEATH	18G. LENGTH OF STAY IN CALIFORNIA
Los Angeles	Los Angeles	11 YEARS	11 YEARS

USUAL RESIDENCE (IF DEATH OCCURRED IN INSTITUTION, ENTER RESIDENCE BEFORE ADMISSION)

19A. USUAL RESIDENCE—STREET ADDRESS (STREET AND NUMBER OR LOCATION)	19B. INSIDE CITY CORPORATE LIMITS (SPECIFY YES OR NO)	20 NAME AND MAILING ADDRESS OF INFORMANT
8000 Woodrow Wilson Drive	Yes	Mr. Isaac L. Jones

19C. CITY OR TOWN	19D. COUNTY	19E. STATE	
Los Angeles	Los Angeles	California	Malibu, California

PHYSICIAN'S OR CORONER'S CERTIFICATION

21A. CORONER: I HEREBY CERTIFY THAT DEATH OCCURRED AT THE HOUR DATE AND PLACE STATED ABOVE FROM THE CAUSES STATED BELOW AND THAT I HAVE HELD ON THE REMAINS OF DECEASED AS REQUIRED BY LAW	21B. PHYSICIAN: I HEREBY CERTIFY THAT DEATH OCCURRED AT THE HOUR DATE AND PLACE STATED ABOVE FROM THE CAUSES STATED BELOW AND THAT I ATTENDED THE DECEASED FROM / TO	21C. PHYSICIAN OR CORONER—SIGNATURE AND TITLE	21D DATE SIGNED
Investigation		Harold Wise	5-5-70
	21E ADDRESS	HALL OF JUSTICE LOS ANGELES CA.	

FUNERAL DIRECTOR AND LOCAL REGISTRAR

22A. SPECIFY BURIAL ENTOMBMENT OR CREMATION	22B. DATE	23. NAME OF CEMETERY OR CREMATORY	24. EMBALMER—SIGNATURE (IF BODY EMBALMED) LICENSE NUMBER
Cremation	5/5/70	Burial At Sea Inglewood Cemetery	Walter R Rainey 5373

25 NAME OF FUNERAL DIRECTOR (OR PERSON ACTING AS SUCH)	26. IF NOT CERTIFIED BY CORONER WAS THIS DEATH REPORTED TO CORONER? SPECIFY YES OR NO	28 LOCAL REGISTRAR—SIGNATURE	28 DATE
Angelus Funeral Home	Yes	Dickerson MD	MAY 5 1970

CAUSE OF DEATH / MEDICAL AND HEALTH DATA

29 PART I. DEATH WAS CAUSED BY:	ENTER ONLY ONE CAUSE PER LINE FOR A, B, AND C	APPROXIMATE INTERVAL BETWEEN ONSET AND DEATH
IMMEDIATE CAUSE (A)	Deferred	
CONDITIONS, IF ANY, WHICH GAVE RISE TO THE IMMEDIATE CAUSE (A), STATING THE UNDERLYING CAUSE LAST. DUE TO, OR AS A CONSEQUENCE OF (B)		
DUE TO, OR AS A CONSEQUENCE OF (C)		

30. PART II. OTHER SIGNIFICANT CONDITIONS— CONTRIBUTING TO DEATH BUT NOT RELATED TO THE IMMEDIATE CAUSE GIVEN IN PART I	31. WAS OPERATION OR BIOPSY PERFORMED FOR ANY CONDITION IN ITEMS 29 OR 30? SPECIFY OPERATION AND/OR BIOPSY	32A. AUTOPSY	32B
		Yes	

INJURY INFORMATION

33 SPECIFY ACCIDENT, SUICIDE OR HOMICIDE	34. PLACE OF INJURY (SPECIFY HOME, FARM, FACTORY, OFFICE BUILDING, ETC.)	35. INJURY AT WORK (SPECIFY YES OR NO)	36A. DATE OF INJURY—MONTH DAY YEAR	36B HOUR
				M

37A. PLACE OF INJURY (STREET AND NUMBER OR LOCATION AND CITY OR TOWN)	37B. DISTANCE FROM PLACE OF INJURY TO USUAL RESIDENCE ITEM 19 MILES	38. WERE LABORATORY TESTS DONE FOR DRUGS OR TOXIC CHEMICALS (SPECIFY YES OR NO.)	39 WERE LABORATORY TESTS DONE FOR ALCOHOL (SPECIFY YES OR NO.)

40. DESCRIBE HOW INJURY OCCURRED (ENTER SEQUENCE OF EVENTS WHICH RESULTED IN INJURY, NATURE OF INJURY SHOULD BE ENTERED IN ITEM 29)

STATE REGISTRAR

A.	B.	C.	D.	E.	F.
					1941

REV 1-1-68 Form VS-11

This is to certify that this document is a true copy of the official record filed with the Registrar-Recorder/County Clerk.

Beatriz Valdez

BEATRIZ VALDEZ
Registrar-Recorder/County Clerk

AUG 10 1995

19-388001

This copy not valid unless prepared on engraved border displaying the Seal and Signature of the Registrar-Recorder/County Clerk.

American Bank Note Company | ANY ALTERATION OR ERASURE VOIDS THIS CERTIFICATE

CERTIFICATION OF VITAL RECORD

COUNTY OF LOS ANGELES • REGISTRAR-RECORDER/COUNTY CLERK

704888

AMENDMENT OF MEDICAL AND HEALTH SECTION DATA—DEATH 709⁻ 023490

STATE CERTIFICATE NUMBER	(INSTRUCTIONS ON REVERSE)		LOCAL REGISTRATION DISTRICT AND CERTIFICATE NUMBER

IDENTIFICATION OF THE RECORD

1A. FIRST NAME INGER	1B. MIDDLE NAME STENSLAND	1C. LAST NAME JONES aka: STEVENS

2 of 2

2. PLACE OF OCCURRENCE—CITY OR COUNTY LOS ANGELES	3. DATE OF EVENT 4-30-70	4. DATE ORIGINAL FILED 5-5-70

INFORMATION AS REPORTED ON THE ORIGINALLY REGISTERED CERTIFICATE

ORIGINALLY REPORTED INFORMATION

29. PART I. DEATH WAS CAUSED BY: ENTER ONLY ONE CAUSE PER LINE FOR A. B. AND C
IMMEDIATE CAUSE (A) DEFERRED
CONDITIONS. IF ANY. WHICH GAVE RISE TO THE IMMEDIATE CAUSE (A). STATING THE UNDERLYING CAUSE LAST.
DUE TO. OR AS A CONSEQUENCE OF (B)
DUE TO. OR AS A CONSEQUENCE OF (C)

APPROXIMATE INTERVAL BETWEEN ONSET AND DEATH

30. PART II. OTHER SIGNIFICANT CONDITIONS
31. WAS OPERATION OR BIOPSY PERFORMED
32A. AUTOPSY YES
32B. IF YES WERE FINDINGS CONSIDERED IN DETERMINING CAUSE OF DEATH

33. SPECIFY ACCIDENT. SUICIDE OR HOMICIDE | 34. PLACE OF INJURY | 35. INJURY AT WORK | 36A. DATE OF INJURY | 36B. HOUR M.

37A. PLACE OF INJURY | 37B. DISTANCE FROM PLACE OF INJURY TO USUAL RESIDENCE | 38. WERE LABORATORY TESTS DONE FOR DRUGS | 39. WERE LABORATORY TESTS DONE FOR ALCOHOL
MILES

40. DESCRIBE HOW INJURY OCCURRED

INFORMATION AS IT SHOULD BE STATED ON THE ORIGINALLY REGISTERED CERTIFICATE

INFORMATION AS IT SHOULD BE STATED ON THE ORIGINALLY REGISTERED CERTIFICATE

29. PART I. DEATH WAS CAUSED BY: ENTER ONLY ONE CAUSE PER LINE FOR A. B. AND C
IMMEDIATE CAUSE (A) ACUTE BARBITURATE INTOXICATION.
CONDITIONS. IF ANY. WHICH GAVE RISE TO THE IMMEDIATE CAUSE (A). STATING THE UNDERLYING CAUSE LAST.
DUE TO. OR AS A CONSEQUENCE OF (B) INGESTION OF OVERDOSE.
DUE TO. OR AS A CONSEQUENCE OF (C)

APPROXIMATE INTERVAL BETWEEN ONSET AND DEATH

30. PART II. OTHER SIGNIFICANT CONDITIONS
31. WAS OPERATION OR BIOPSY PERFORMED NO
32A. AUTOPSY YES
32B. IF YES WERE FINDINGS CONSIDERED IN DETERMINING CAUSE OF DEATH YES

33. SPECIFY ACCIDENT. SUICIDE OR HOMICIDE SUICIDE | 34. PLACE OF INJURY HOME | 35. INJURY AT WORK NO | 36A. DATE OF INJURY 4-30-70 | 36B. HOUR PRIOR TO; 1030 M.

37A. PLACE OF INJURY 8000 WOODROW WILSON DRIVE LOS ANGELES | 37B. DISTANCE 0 MILES | 38. WERE LABORATORY TESTS DONE FOR DRUGS YES | 39. WERE LABORATORY TESTS DONE FOR ALCOHOL YES

40. DESCRIBE HOW INJURY OCCURRED
AS ABOVE

DECLARATION OF CERTIFYING PHYSICIAN OR CORONER

5. I. THE CERTIFYING PHYSICIAN OR CORONER HAVING PERSONAL KNOWLEDGE OF SUPPLEMENTAL INFORMATION WHICH MODIFIES THE INFORMATION ORIGINALLY REPORTED. DECLARE UNDER PENALTY OF PERJURY THAT THE ABOVE INFORMATION IS TRUE AND CORRECT TO THE BEST OF MY KNOWLEDGE.

6A. SIGNATURE OF PHYSICIAN OR CORONER	6B. DATE SIGNED JUN 9 1970
7A. NAME OF PHYSICIAN OR CORONER (PRINT OR TYPE) THOMAS T. NOGUCHI, M.D., CORONER	7B. DEGREE OR TITLE
7C. ADDRESS DEPUTY	

HALL OF JUSTICE LOS ANGELES, CALIFORNIA

REGISTRAR'S OFFICE

8A. OFFICE OF STATE OR LOCAL REGISTRAR
STATE OF CALIFORNIA. DEPARTMENT OF PUBLIC HEALTH. BUREAU OF VITAL STATISTICS

8B. DATE ACCEPTED JUN 1 0 1970
(REV. 1-1-69) FORM VS-24B

This is to certify that this document is a true copy of the official record filed with the Registrar-Recorder/County Clerk.

Beatriz Valdez
BEATRIZ VALDEZ
Registrar-Recorder/County Clerk

AUG 1 0 1995
19-388008

This copy not valid unless prepared on engraved border displaying the Seal and Signature of the Registrar-Recorder/County Clerk.

ANY ALTERATION OR ERASURE VOIDS THIS CERTIFICATE

STATE OF CALIFORNIA
CERTIFICATION OF VITAL RECORD

COUNTY OF LOS ANGELES • REGISTRAR-RECORDER/COUNTY CLERK

CERTIFICATE OF DEATH
STATE OF CALIFORNIA
USE BLACK INK ONLY

38919042278

STATE FILE NUMBER				LOCAL REGISTRATION DISTRICT AND CERTIFICATE NUMBER		

DECEDENT PERSONAL DATA

1A. NAME OF DECEDENT—FIRST (GIVEN)	1B. MIDDLE	1C. LAST (FAMILY)	2A. DATE OF DEATH—MO. DAY. YR	2B. HOUR	3. SEX
JAY	CLEVE	FIX-STEWART	Sept. 17, 1989	1613	M

4. RACE	5. SPANISH/HISPANIC—SPECIFY	6. DATE OF BIRTH—MO. DAY. YR	7. AGE IN YEARS	IF UNDER 1 YEAR MONTHS / DAYS	IF UNDER 24 HOURS HOURS / MINUTES
WHITE	YES [ ] [X] NO	SEPTEMBER 6,1918	71		

8. STATE OF BIRTH	9. CITIZEN OF WHAT COUNTRY	10A. FULL NAME OF FATHER	10B. STATE OF BIRTH	11A. FULL MAIDEN NAME OF MOTHER	11B. STATE OF BIRTH
IN	U.S.A.	JULIAN FIX	IN	RESSIE JENKINS	IN

12. MILITARY SERVICE?	13. SOCIAL SECURITY NO.	14. MARITAL STATUS	15. NAME OF SURVIVING SPOUSE (IF WIFE, ENTER MAIDEN NAME)
19 41 TO 19 41 [ ] NONE	315-07-7446	MARRIED	PHYLLIS KISER

16A. USUAL OCCUPATION	16B. USUAL KIND OF BUSINESS OR INDUSTRY	16C. USUAL EMPLOYER	16D. YEARS IN OCCUPATION	17. EDUCATION—YEARS COMPLETED
ANNOUNCER	ENTERTAINMENT	A.F.T.R.A.	50	16

USUAL RESIDENCE

18A. RESIDENCE—STREET AND NUMBER OR LOCATION	18B. CITY	18C. ZIP CODE
1979 GRACE AVENUE TOWN HOUSE A-2	LOS ANGELES	90068

18D. COUNTY	18E. NUMBER OF YEARS IN THIS COUNTY	18F. STATE OR FOREIGN COUNTRY	20. NAME, RELATIONSHIP, MAILING ADDRESS AND ZIP CODE OF INFORMANT
LOS ANGELES	46	CALIFORNIA	MRS. PHYLLIS FIX, WIFE

PLACE OF DEATH

19A. PLACE OF DEATH	19B. IF HOSPITAL, SPECIFY ONE: IP, ER/OP, DOA	19C. COUNTY	1979 GRACE AVENUE TOWN HOUSE A-2 LOS ANGELES, CA. 90068
Residence - Outside Garage		Los Angeles	

19D. STREET ADDRESS—STREET AND NUMBER OR LOCATION	19E. CITY	TIME INTERVAL BETWEEN ONSET AND DEATH	22. WAS DEATH REPORTED TO CORONER? REFERRAL NUMBER
1917 Grace Avenue	Los Angeles		[X] YES 89-9020 [ ] NO

CAUSE OF DEATH

21. DEATH WAS CAUSED BY: (ENTER ONLY ONE CAUSE PER LINE FOR A, B AND C)		23. WAS BIOPSY PERFORMED?
IMMEDIATE CAUSE (A)	GUNSHOT WOUND TO HEAD ▶	[ ] YES [X] NO
DUE TO (B)	▶	24A. WAS AUTOPSY PERFORMED? [ ] YES [X] NO
DUE TO (C)	▶	24B. WAS IT USED IN DETERMINING CAUSE OF DEATH? [ ] YES [ ] NO

25. OTHER SIGNIFICANT CONDITIONS CONTRIBUTING TO DEATH BUT NOT RELATED TO CAUSE GIVEN IN 21	26. WAS OPERATION PERFORMED FOR ANY CONDITION IN ITEM 21 OR 25? IF YES, LIST TYPE OF OPERATION AND DATE.
None	No

PHYSICIAN'S CERTIFICATION

I CERTIFY THAT TO THE BEST OF MY KNOWLEDGE DEATH OCCURRED AT THE HOUR, DATE AND PLACE STATED FROM THE CAUSES STATED.	27B. SIGNATURE AND DEGREE OR TITLE OF PHYSICIAN	27C. PHYSICIAN'S LICENSE NUMBER	27D. DATE SIGNED
27A. DECEDENT ATTENDED SINCE MONTH, DAY, YEAR / DECEDENT LAST SEEN ALIVE MONTH, DAY, YEAR	27E. TYPE ATTENDING PHYSICIAN'S NAME AND ADDRESS		

CORONER'S USE ONLY

I CERTIFY THAT IN MY OPINION DEATH OCCURRED AT THE HOUR, DATE AND PLACE STATED FROM THE CAUSES STATED.	28A. SIGNATURE AND TITLE OF CORONER OR DEPUTY CORONER ▶ Deputy Coroner	28B. DATE SIGNED 9-21-89
29. MANNER OF DEATH—specify one; natural, accident, suicide, homicide, pending investigation or could not be determined Suicide	30A. PLACE OF INJURY Garage	30B. INJURY AT WORK [ ] YES [X] NO	30C. DATE OF INJURY MONTH, DAY, YEAR 9-17-89	31. HOUR 1600

32. LOCATION (STREET AND NUMBER OR LOCATION AND CITY)	33. DESCRIBE HOW INJURY OCCURRED (EVENTS WHICH RESULTED IN INJURY)
1917 Grace - Los Angeles	Self-Inflicted Gunshot Wound

FUNERAL DIRECTOR AND LOCAL REGISTRAR

34A. DISPOSITION(S)	34B. PLACE OF FINAL DISPOSITION—NAME AND ADDRESS	34C. DATE MO. DAY. YEAR	35A. SIGNATURE OF EMBALMER	35B. LICENSE NUMBER
CR/BU	Forest Lawn memorial Park Los Angeles, CA 90068	Sept 25, 1989	Elizabeth Derridh	7435

36A. NAME OF FUNERAL DIRECTOR (OR PERSON ACTING AS SUCH)	36B. LICENSE NO.	37. SIGNATURE OF LOCAL REGISTRAR	38. REGISTRATION DATE
FOREST LAWN HOLLYWOOD HILLS MTY.	F 904	▶ Robert Mate Jr	SEP 2 2 1989

STATE REGISTRAR

A.	B.	C.	D.	E.	F.	CENSUS TRACT

This is to certify that this document is a true copy of the official record filed with the Registrar-Recorder/County Clerk.

Conny B. McCormack

CONNY B. McCORMACK
Registrar-Recorder/County Clerk

DEC 07 2000

19-149009

This copy not valid unless prepared on engraved border displaying the Seal and Signature of the Registrar-Recorder/County Clerk.

MIDWEST BANK NOTE COMPANY • ANY ALTERATION OR ERASURE VOIDS THIS CERTIFICATE

CERTIFICATION OF VITAL RECORD

STATE OF CALIFORNIA
DEPARTMENT OF HEALTH SERVICES

3 051996 061105   CERTIFICATE OF DEATH   3 1996 38 001394

STATE OF CALIFORNIA
USE BLACK INK ONLY/NO ERASURES, WHITEOUTS OR ALTERATIONS
VS-11 (REV. 7/93)

STATE FILE NUMBER		LOCAL REGISTRATION NUMBER

DECEDENT PERSONAL DATA

1. NAME OF DECEDENT—FIRST (GIVEN)	2. MIDDLE	3. LAST (FAMILY)
LYLE	—	TALBOT

4. DATE OF BIRTH MM/DD/CCYY	5. AGE YRS.	IF UNDER 1 YEAR / IF UNDER 24 HOURS	6. SEX	7. DATE OF DEATH MM/DD/CCYY	8. HOUR
02/08/1902	94	MONTHS DAYS / HOURS MINUTES	M	03/03/1996	0715

9. STATE OF BIRTH	10. SOCIAL SECURITY NO.	11. MILITARY SERVICE	12. MARITAL STATUS	13. EDUCATION — YEARS COMPLETED
PA	569-18-8431	19___ TO 19___ NONE	WIDOWER	11

14. RACE	15. HISPANIC—SPECIFY		16. USUAL EMPLOYER
WHITE	YES	X NO	VARIOUS

17. OCCUPATION	18. KIND OF BUSINESS	19. YEARS IN OCCUPATION
ACTOR	ACTING	78

USUAL RESIDENCE

20. RESIDENCE—STREET AND NUMBER OR LOCATION
601 VAN NESS, #451

21. CITY	22. COUNTY	23. ZIP CODE	24. YRS IN COUNTY	25. STATE OR FOREIGN COUNTRY
SAN FRANCISCO	SAN FRANCISCO	94102	7	CA

INFORMANT

26. NAME, RELATIONSHIP	27. MAILING ADDRESS (STREET AND NUMBER OR RURAL ROUTE NUMBER, CITY OR TOWN, STATE, ZIP)
STEVEN TALBOT, SON	149 FAIRMOUNT STREET, SAN FRANCISCO, CA 94131

SPOUSE AND PARENT INFORMATION

28. NAME OF SURVIVING SPOUSE—FIRST	29. MIDDLE	30. LAST (MAIDEN NAME)
—	—	—

31. NAME OF FATHER—FIRST	32. MIDDLE	33. LAST	34. BIRTH STATE
EDWARD	—	HENDERSON	NB

35. NAME OF MOTHER—FIRST	36. MIDDLE	37. LAST (MAIDEN)	38. BIRTH STATE
FLORENCE	—	HOLLYWOOD	NB

DISPOSITION(S)

39. DATE MM/DD/CCYY	40. PLACE OF FINAL DISPOSITION
03/06/1996	SCATTERED AT SEA, OFF THE MARIN COUNTY COAST

FUNERAL DIRECTOR AND LOCAL REGISTRAR

41. TYPE OF DISPOSITION(S)	42. SIGNATURE OF EMBALMER	43. LICENSE NO.
CR/SEA	▶ NOT EMBALMED	

44. NAME OF FUNERAL DIRECTOR	45. LICENSE NO.	46. SIGNATURE OF LOCAL REGISTRAR	47. DATE MM/DD/CCYY
NEPTUNE SOCIETY OF NO. CA	FD1306	▶	03/06/1996

PLACE OF DEATH

101. PLACE OF DEATH	102. IF HOSPITAL, SPECIFY ONE:					103. COUNTY
RESIDENCE	IP	ER/OP	DOA	CONV. HOSP.	RES. OTHER	SAN FRANCISCO

105. STREET ADDRESS—STREET AND NUMBER OR LOCATION	106. CITY
601 VAN NESS, #451	SAN FRANCISCO

CAUSE OF DEATH

107. DEATH WAS CAUSED BY: (ENTER ONLY ONE CAUSE PER LINE FOR A, B, C, AND D)	TIME INTERVAL BETWEEN ONSET AND DEATH	108. DEATH REPORTED TO CORONER
IMMEDIATE CAUSE (A) CONGESTIVE HEART FAILURE	7 YRS.	X YES NO REFERRAL NUMBER NC-0545
DUE TO (B) CORONARY ATHEROSCLEROSIS	20 YRS.	109. BIOPSY PERFORMED YES X NO
DUE TO (C)		110. AUTOPSY PERFORMED YES X NO
DUE TO (D)		111. USED IN DETERMINING CAUSE YES NO

112. OTHER SIGNIFICANT CONDITIONS CONTRIBUTING TO DEATH BUT NOT RELATED TO CAUSE GIVEN IN 107
—

113. WAS OPERATION PERFORMED FOR ANY CONDITION IN ITEM 107 OR 112? IF YES, LIST TYPE OF OPERATION AND DATE.

PHYSICIAN'S CERTIFICATION

114. I CERTIFY THAT TO THE BEST OF MY KNOWLEDGE DEATH OCCURRED AT THE HOUR, DATE AND PLACE STATED FROM THE CAUSES STATED.	115. SIGNATURE AND TITLE OF CERTIFIER	116. LICENSE NO.	117. DATE MM/DD/CCYY
DECEDENT ATTENDED SINCE MM/DD/CCYY: 03/28/1989 — DECEDENT LAST SEEN ALIVE MM/DD/CCYY: 01/10/1996	▶	022240	3/4/96

118. TYPE ATTENDING PHYSICIAN'S NAME, MAILING ADDRESS + ZIP
EDWARD KERSH, M.D., 3838 CALIFORNIA ST., SAN FRANCISCO, CA 94118

CORONER'S USE ONLY

I CERTIFY THAT IN MY OPINION DEATH OCCURRED AT THE HOUR, DATE AND PLACE STATED FROM THE CAUSES STATED.	120. INJURY AT WORK YES NO	121. INJURY DATE MM/DD/CCYY	122. HOUR	123. PLACE OF INJURY
119. MANNER OF DEATH: NATURAL / SUICIDE / HOMICIDE / ACCIDENT / PENDING INVESTIGATION / COULD NOT BE DETERMINED	124. DESCRIBE HOW INJURY OCCURRED (EVENTS WHICH RESULTED IN INJURY)			

125. LOCATION (STREET AND NUMBER OR LOCATION AND CITY AND ZIP CODE)

126. SIGNATURE OF CORONER OR DEPUTY CORONER	127. DATE MM/DD/CCYY	128. TYPED NAME, TITLE OF CORONER OR DEPUTY CORONER
▶		

STATE REGISTRAR

A	B	C	D	E	F	G	H	FAX AUTH. #	CENSUS TRACT
8	X	2							

183375

This is to certify that this document is a true copy of the official record filed with the Office of Vital Records and Statistics.

S. Kimberly Belshe, Director and State Registrar of Vital Records and Statistics
by:

GEORGE B. (PETER) ABBOTT, JR., M.D., M.P.H., CHIEF
OFFICE OF VITAL RECORDS AND STATISTICS

DATE ISSUED
OCT 23 1996

This copy not valid unless prepared on engraved border displaying seal and signature of Registrar.

ANY ALTERATION OR ERASURE VOIDS THIS CERTIFICATE

CERTIFICATION OF VITAL RECORD

COUNTY OF LOS ANGELES • REGISTRAR-RECORDER/COUNTY CLERK

CERTIFICATE OF DEATH
STATE OF CALIFORNIA—DEPARTMENT OF PUBLIC HEALTH

7097-048200
LOCAL REGISTRATION DISTRICT AND CERTIFICATE NUMBER
STATE FILE NUMBER

1A. NAME OF DECEASED—FIRST NAME: Constance	1B. MIDDLE NAME: Talmadge	1C. LAST NAME: Giblin
2A. DATE OF DEATH—MONTH, DAY, YEAR: Nov 23, 1973	2B. HOUR: 8:25P M	

DECEDENT PERSONAL DATA

3. SEX: Female	4. COLOR OR RACE: Cauc	5. BIRTHPLACE (STATE OR FOREIGN COUNTRY): New York	6. DATE OF BIRTH: April 19, 1903	7. AGE—LAST BIRTHDAY: 70 YEARS	IF UNDER 1 YEAR	IF UNDER 24 HOURS

8. NAME AND BIRTHPLACE OF FATHER: Fred Talmadge-Unknown
9. MAIDEN NAME AND BIRTHPLACE OF MOTHER: Margaret Jose-Spain

10. CITIZEN OF WHAT COUNTRY: U.S.A.	11. SOCIAL SECURITY NUMBER: 111-36-2117	12. MARRIED-NEVER MARRIED, WIDOWED, DIVORCED (SPECIFY): Widowed	13. NAME OF SURVIVING SPOUSE (IF WIFE ENTER MAIDEN NAME):

14. LAST OCCUPATION: Actress	15. NUMBER OF YEARS IN THIS OCCUPATION: 10	16. NAME OF LAST EMPLOYING COMPANY OR FIRM (IF SELF EMPLOYED, SO STATE): Free Lance	17. KIND OF INDUSTRY OR BUSINESS: Motion Pictures

PLACE OF DEATH

18A. PLACE OF DEATH—NAME OF HOSPITAL OR OTHER IN-PATIENT FACILITY: California Hospital	18B. STREET ADDRESS—(STREET AND NUMBER, OR LOCATION): 1414 S Hope St	18C. INSIDE CITY CORPORATE LIMITS (SPECIFY YES OR NO): YES
18D. CITY OR TOWN: Los Angeles	18E. COUNTY: Los Angeles	18F. LENGTH OF STAY IN COUNTY OF DEATH: 3 YEARS	18G. LENGTH OF STAY IN CALIFORNIA: 3 YEARS

USUAL RESIDENCE (IF DEATH OCCURRED IN INSTITUTION, ENTER RESIDENCE BEFORE ADMISSION)

19A. USUAL RESIDENCE—STREET ADDRESS (STREET AND NUMBER OR LOCATION): 9200 Wilshire Blvd	19B. INSIDE CITY CORPORATE LIMITS (SPECIFY YES OR NO): Yes	20. NAME AND MAILING ADDRESS OF INFORMANT: John C Goff, 3600 Wilshire Blvd
19C. CITY OR TOWN: Beverly Hills	19D. COUNTY: Los Angeles	19E. STATE: California	Los Angeles, Calif

PHYSICIAN'S OR CORONER'S CERTIFICATION

21A. CORONER	21B. PHYSICIAN	21C. PHYSICIAN OR CORONER—SIGNATURE AND DEGREE OR TITLE: Phillip E Lue MD	21D. DATE SIGNED: Nov 26. 1973
8/18/70	11/23/73	11/23/73	21E. ADDRESS: 1401 S Hope St L.A.	21F. PHYSICIAN'S LICENSE NUMBER: A08681

FUNERAL DIRECTOR AND LOCAL REGISTRAR

22A. SPECIFY BURIAL, ENTOMBMENT OR CREMATION: Entombment	22B. DATE: 11-29-73	23. NAME OF CEMETERY OR CREMATORY: Hollywood Mausoleum	24. EMBALMER—SIGNATURE (IF BODY EMBALMED) LICENSE NUMBER: 5063
25. NAME OF FUNERAL DIRECTOR (OR PERSON ACTING AS SUCH): Pierce Bros-Hollywood	26. IF NOT CERTIFIED BY CORONER WAS THIS DEATH REPORTED TO CORONER? (SPECIFY YES OR NO): no	27. LOCAL REGISTRAR—SIGNATURE	28. DATE ACCEPTED FOR REGISTRATION BY LOCAL REGISTRAR: NOV 20 1973

MEDICAL AND HEALTH DATA

CAUSE OF DEATH

29. PART I. DEATH WAS CAUSED BY: ENTER ONLY ONE CAUSE PER LINE FOR A, B, AND C

IMMEDIATE CAUSE (A) Pneumonia, Bronchia Terminal — 1 wk

CONDITIONS, IF ANY, WHICH GAVE RISE TO THE IMMEDIATE CAUSE (A) STATING THE UNDERLYING CAUSE LAST
DUE TO, OR AS A CONSEQUENCE OF (B) Hepatitis Chronic Aggressive, Idiopathic — Unk

DUE TO, OR AS A CONSEQUENCE OF (C)

APPROXIMATE INTERVAL BETWEEN ONSET AND DEATH

30. PART II. OTHER SIGNIFICANT CONDITIONS—CONTRIBUTING TO DEATH BUT NOT RELATED TO THE IMMEDIATE CAUSE GIVEN IN PART I	31. WAS OPERATION OR BIOPSY PERFORMED FOR ANY CONDITION IN ITEMS 29 OR 30? SPECIFY OPERATION AND/OR BIOPSY: no	32A. AUTOPSY (SPECIFY YES OR NO): no	32B. IF YES, WERE FINDINGS CONSIDERED IN DETERMINING CAUSE OF DEATH? SPECIFY YES OR NO

INJURY INFORMATION

33. SPECIFY ACCIDENT, SUICIDE OR HOMICIDE	34. PLACE OF INJURY (SPECIFY HOME, FARM, FACTORY, OFFICE BUILDING, ETC.)	35. INJURY AT WORK (SPECIFY YES OR NO)	36A. DATE OF INJURY—MONTH DAY YEAR	36B. HOUR M

37A. PLACE OF INJURY (STREET AND NUMBER OR LOCATION AND CITY OR TOWN)	37B. DISTANCE FROM PLACE OF USUAL RESIDENCE IS MILES	38. WERE LABORATORY TESTS DONE FOR DRUGS OR TOXIC CHEMICALS (SPECIFY YES OR NO)	39. WERE LABORATORY TESTS DONE FOR ALCOHOL (SPECIFY YES OR NO)

40. DESCRIBE HOW INJURY OCCURRED (ENTER SEQUENCE OF EVENTS WHICH RESULTED IN INJURY, NATURE OF INJURY SHOULD BE ENTERED IN ITEM 29)

STATE REGISTRAR	A.	B.	C.	D.	E.	F.

REV 1-1-66 Form VS-11

This is to certify that this document is a true copy of the official record filed with the Registrar-Recorder/County Clerk.

Conny B. McCormack
CONNY B. McCORMACK
Registrar-Recorder/County Clerk

OCT 1 1996
19-384184

This copy not valid unless prepared on engraved border displaying the Seal and Signature of the Registrar-Recorder/County Clerk.

BANKNOTE CORPORATION OF AMERICA
ANY ALTERATION OR ERASURE VOIDS THIS CERTIFICATE

CERTIFICATION OF VITAL RECORD

COUNTY OF LOS ANGELES • REGISTRAR-RECORDER/COUNTY CLERK

CERTIFICATE OF DEATH

STATE OF CALIFORNIA—DEPARTMENT OF PUBLIC HEALTH

7097-026379

LOCAL REGISTRATION DISTRICT AND CERTIFICATE NUMBER

1A. NAME OF DECEASED—FIRST NAME: Natalie	1B. MIDDLE NAME: M	1C. LAST NAME: Talmadge	2A. DATE OF DEATH—MONTH, DAY, YEAR: June 19, 1969	2B. HOUR: 11:58P M

DECEDENT PERSONAL DATA

3. SEX: female	4. COLOR OR RACE: cauc	5. BIRTHPLACE (STATE OR FOREIGN COUNTRY): New York	6. DATE OF BIRTH: April 29 1900	7. AGE (LAST BIRTHDAY): 69 YEARS	IF UNDER 1 YEAR	IF UNDER 24 HOURS

8. NAME AND BIRTHPLACE OF FATHER: Frederick T Talmadge- Conn	9. MAIDEN NAME AND BIRTHPLACE OF MOTHER: Margaret L Jose- Spain

10. CITIZEN OF WHAT COUNTRY: U.S.A.	11. SOCIAL SECURITY NUMBER: none	12. MARRIED, NEVER MARRIED, WIDOWED, DIVORCED (SPECIFY): divorced	13. NAME OF SURVIVING SPOUSE (IF WIFE, ENTER MAIDEN NAME):

14. LAST OCCUPATION: housewife	15. NUMBER OF YEARS IN THIS OCCUPATION: 30	16. NAME OF LAST EMPLOYING COMPANY OR FIRM (IF SELF EMPLOYED, SO STATE): own home	17. KIND OF INDUSTRY OR BUSINESS: own home

PLACE OF DEATH

18A. PLACE OF DEATH—NAME OF HOSPITAL OR OTHER IN-PATIENT FACILITY: Santa Monica Hospital	18B. STREET ADDRESS—(STREET AND NUMBER, OR LOCATION): 1250 16th. Street	18C. INSIDE CITY CORPORATE LIMITS (SPECIFY YES OR NO): yes

18D. CITY OR TOWN: Santa Monica	18E. COUNTY: Los Angeles	18F. LENGTH OF STAY IN COUNTY OF DEATH: 50 YEARS	18G. LENGTH OF STAY IN CALIFORNIA: 50 YEARS

USUAL RESIDENCE (IF DEATH OCCURRED IN INSTITUTION, ENTER RESIDENCE BEFORE ADMISSION)

19A. USUAL RESIDENCE—STREET ADDRESS (STREET AND NUMBER OR LOCATION): 9641 Sunset Blvd.	19B. INSIDE CITY CORPORATE LIMITS (SPECIFY YES OR NO): yes	20. NAME AND MAILING ADDRESS OF INFORMANT: Constance Talmadge Giblin

19C. CITY OR TOWN: Beverly Hills	19D. COUNTY: Los Angeles	19E. STATE: Calif	same

PHYSICIAN'S OR CORONER'S CERTIFICATION

21A. CORONER: I HEREBY CERTIFY THAT DEATH OCCURRED AT THE HOUR, DATE AND PLACE STATED ABOVE FROM THE CAUSES STATED BELOW AND THAT I HAVE HELD ON THE REMAINS OF DECEASED AS REQUIRED BY LAW	21B. PHYSICIAN: I HEREBY CERTIFY THAT DEATH OCCURRED AT THE HOUR, DATE, AND PLACE STATED ABOVE FROM THE CAUSES STATED BELOW AND THAT I ATTENDED THE DECEASED	21C. PHYSICIAN OR CORONER—SIGNATURE AND DEGREE OR TITLE: Robert M. Kahn MD	21D. DATE SIGNED: 6/21/69
(INVESTIGATION OR INQUEST) FROM 1/20/69 TO 6/19/69 ... 6/19/69		21E. ADDRESS: 984 Monument St. Pacific Palisades	21F. PHYSICIAN'S CALIFORNIA LICENSE NUMBER: 18582

FUNERAL DIRECTOR AND LOCAL REGISTRAR

22A. SPECIFY BURIAL, ENTOMBMENT OR CREMATION: entombment	22B. DATE: 6-23-69	23. NAME OF CEMETERY OR CREMATORY: Hollywood Mausoleum	24. EMBALMER—SIGNATURE (IF BODY EMBALMED): Henry Petracchi LICENSE NUMBER: 4281
25. NAME OF FUNERAL DIRECTOR (OR PERSON ACTING AS SUCH): Pierce Bros Hollywood	26. IF NOT CERTIFIED BY CORONER, WAS THIS DEATH REFERRED TO CORONER? (SPECIFY YES OR NO): no	27. LOCAL REGISTRAR—SIGNATURE: [signature]	28. DATE ACCEPTED FOR REGISTRATION BY LOCAL REGISTRAR: JUN 22 1969

CAUSE OF DEATH

29. PART I. DEATH WAS CAUSED BY:	ENTER ONLY ONE CAUSE PER LINE FOR A, B. AND C		APPROXIMATE INTERVAL BETWEEN ONSET AND DEATH
	IMMEDIATE CAUSE (A)	Massive acute Pulmonary Edema -	Hours
CONDITIONS, IF ANY, WHICH GAVE RISE TO THE IMMEDIATE CAUSE (A), STATING THE UNDERLYING CAUSE LAST.	DUE TO, OR AS A CONSEQUENCE OF (B)	Arteriosclerotic Cardiovascular Disease	Years
	DUE TO, OR AS A CONSEQUENCE OF (C)		

30. PART II. OTHER SIGNIFICANT CONDITIONS—CONTRIBUTING TO DEATH BUT NOT RELATED TO THE IMMEDIATE CAUSE GIVEN IN PART I: Previous Cerebral Vascular Accident Arthritis	31. WAS OPERATION OR BIOPSY PERFORMED FOR ANY CONDITION IN ITEMS 29 OR 30? (SPECIFY): no	32A. AUTOPSY (SPECIFY YES OR NO): no	32B. IF YES WERE FINDINGS CONSIDERED IN DETERMINING CAUSE OF DEATH? (SPECIFY YES OR NO):

INJURY INFORMATION

33. SPECIFY ACCIDENT, SUICIDE OR HOMICIDE	34. PLACE OF INJURY (SPECIFY HOME, FARM, FACTORY, OFFICE BUILDING, ETC.)	35. INJURY AT WORK (SPECIFY YES OR NO)	36A. DATE OF INJURY—MONTH DAY YEAR	36B. HOUR

37A. PLACE OF INJURY (STREET AND NUMBER OR LOCATION AND CITY OR TOWN)	37B. DISTANCE FROM PLACE OF INJURY TO USUAL RESIDENCE ITEM 19: MILES	38. WERE LABORATORY TESTS DONE FOR DRUGS OR TOXIC CHEMICALS (SPECIFY YES OR NO)	39. WERE LABORATORY TESTS DONE FOR ALCOHOL (SPECIFY YES OR NO)

40. DESCRIBE HOW INJURY OCCURRED (ENTER SEQUENCE OF EVENTS WHICH RESULTED IN INJURY. NATURE OF INJURY SHOULD BE ENTERED IN ITEM 29)					

STATE REGISTRAR

A.	B.	C.	D.	E.	F. 7006

REV. 1-1-68 FORM VS-11

Filed 7-3-59   RAY E. LEE, COUNTY RECORDER

CERTIFICATE OF DEATH

STATE OF CALIFORNIA—DEPARTMENT OF PUBLIC HEALTH

LOCAL REGISTRATION DISTRICT AND CERTIFICATE NUMBER 7007-025209

1A. NAME OF DECEASED—FIRST NAME	1B. MIDDLE NAME	1C. LAST NAME	2A. DATE OF DEATH—MONTH, DAY, YEAR	2B. HOUR
WILLIAM	WHITNEY	TALMAN JR.	August 30, 1968	8:30 A

3. SEX	4. COLOR OR RACE	5. BIRTHPLACE (STATE OR FOREIGN COUNTRY)	6. DATE OF BIRTH	7. AGE (LAST BIRTHDAY)	IF UNDER 1 YEAR	IF UNDER 24 HOURS
Male	Caucasian	Michigan	February 4, 1915	53 YEARS		

8. NAME AND BIRTHPLACE OF FATHER	9. MAIDEN NAME AND BIRTHPLACE OF MOTHER
William Whitney Talman - Michigan	Ada Barber- New Jersey

10. CITIZEN OF WHAT COUNTRY	11. SOCIAL SECURITY NUMBER	12. MARRIED, NEVER MARRIED, WIDOWED, DIVORCED (SPECIFY)	13. NAME OF SURVIVING SPOUSE (IF WIFE, ENTER MAIDEN NAME)
U.S.A.	372-05-0619	Married	Margaret Larkin

14. LAST OCCUPATION	15. NUMBER OF YEARS IN THIS OCCUPATION	16. NAME OF LAST EMPLOYING COMPANY OR FIRM (IF SELF EMPLOYED, SO STATE)	17. KIND OF INDUSTRY OR BUSINESS
Actor	30	Self Employed	Stage, Motion Pictures, Televi

18A. PLACE OF DEATH—NAME OF HOSPITAL OR OTHER IN-PATIENT FACILITY	18B. STREET ADDRESS—(STREET AND NUMBER, OR LOCATION)	18C. INSIDE CITY CORPORATE LIMITS (SPECIFY YES OR NO)
West Valley Community Hospital	5333 Balboa Boulevard	

18D. CITY OR TOWN	18E. COUNTY	18F. LENGTH OF STAY IN COUNTY OF DEATH	18G. LENGTH OF STAY IN CALIFORNIA
(Encino) Los Angeles	Los Angeles	18 YEARS	18 YE

19A. USUAL RESIDENCE—STREET ADDRESS (STREET AND NUMBER OR LOCATION)	19B. INSIDE CITY CORPORATE LIMITS (SPECIFY YES OR NO)	20. NAME AND MAILING ADDRESS OF INFORMANT
16836 Marmaduke Place	Yes	Mrs. Margaret L. Talman—Wife
19C. CITY OR TOWN	19D. COUNTY	19E. STATE	16836 Marmaduke Place
Encino	Los Angeles	California	Encino, California

21A. CORONER: I HEREBY CERTIFY THAT DEATH OCCURRED AT THE HOUR, DATE AND PLACE STATED ABOVE FROM THE CAUSES STATED BELOW AND THAT I HAVE HELD ON THE REMAINS OF DECEASED AS REQUIRED BY LAW	21B. PHYSICIAN: I HEREBY CERTIFY THAT DEATH OCCURRED AT THE HOUR, DATE, AND PLACE STATED ABOVE, AND FROM THE CAUSES STATED BELOW AND THAT I ATTENDED THE DECEASED	21C. PHYSICIAN OR CORONER SIGNATURE AND DEGREE OR TITLE	21D. DATE SIGNED
(INVESTIGATION OR INQUEST)	FROM 4/26/68 TO 8/30/68 AND (LAST SAW THE DECEASED ALIVE MONTH, DAY, YEAR) 8/29/68	J. Rosenbaum, M.D.	8/31/68
		21E. ADDRESS 2320 Wilshire Blvd Los Angeles, Cal.	21F. PHYSICIAN'S CALIFORNIA LICENSE NUMBER C27209

22A. SPECIFY BURIAL, ENTOMBMENT OR CREMATION	22B. DATE	23. NAME OF CEMETERY OR CREMATORY	24. EMBALMER—SIGNATURE (IF BODY EMBALMED) LICENSE NUMBER
Burial	Sept. 3, 1968	FOREST LAWN MEMORIAL PARK	Everett S. Biglee 5635

25. NAME OF FUNERAL DIRECTOR (OR PERSON ACTING AS SUCH)	26. IF NOT CERTIFIED BY CORONER, WAS THIS DEATH REPORTED TO CORONER? (SPECIFY YES OR NO)	27. LOCAL REGISTRAR—SIGNATURE	28. DATE ACCEPTED FOR REGISTRATION BY LOCAL REGISTRAR
Forest Lawn Hollywood Hills Mortuary	No	Salisbacher MD RH	SEP 3 1968

29. PART I. DEATH WAS CAUSED BY:		ENTER ONLY ONE CAUSE PER LINE FOR A, B, AND C		APPROX INTERVAL BETWEEN ONSET AND DEATH
	IMMEDIATE CAUSE (A)	Bronchogenic Carcinoma		10 mo.
CONDITIONS, IF ANY, WHICH GAVE RISE TO THE IMMEDIATE CAUSE (A), STATING THE UNDERLYING CAUSE LAST.	DUE TO, OR AS A CONSEQUENCE OF (B)			
	DUE TO, OR AS A CONSEQUENCE OF (C)			

30. PART II. OTHER SIGNIFICANT CONDITIONS—CONTRIBUTING TO DEATH BUT NOT RELATED TO THE IMMEDIATE CAUSE GIVEN IN PART I	31. WAS OPERATION OR BIOPSY PERFORMED FOR ANY CONDITION IN ITEMS 29 OR 30? (SPECIFY OPERATION AND/OR BIOPSY)	32A. AUTOPSY (SPECIFY YES OR NO)	32B. IF YES, WERE FINDINGS CONSIDERED IN DETERMINING CAUSE OF DEATH? (SPECIFY YES OR NO)
None	Yes, Thoracotomy and biopsy	Yes	Yes

33. SPECIFY ACCIDENT, SUICIDE OR HOMICIDE	34. PLACE OF INJURY (SPECIFY HOME, FARM, FACTORY, OFFICE BUILDING, ETC.)	35. INJURY AT WORK (SPECIFY YES OR NO)	36A. DATE OF INJURY—MONTH, DAY, YEAR	36B. HOUR

37A. PLACE OF INJURY (STREET AND NUMBER OR LOCATION AND CITY OR TOWN)	37B. DISTANCE FROM PLACE OF INJURY TO USUAL RESIDENCE, ITEM 19 MILES	38. WERE LABORATORY TESTS DONE FOR DRUGS OR TOXIC CHEMICALS (SPECIFY YES OR NO)	39. WERE LABORATORY TESTS DONE FOR ALCOHOL (SPECIFY YES OR NO)

40. DESCRIBE HOW INJURY OCCURRED (ENTER SEQUENCE OF EVENTS WHICH RESULTED IN INJURY, NATURE OF INJURY SHOULD BE ENTERED IN ITEM 29)

A.	B.	C.	D.	E.	F.
					1397

REV. 1-1-66 Form VS-11

STATE OF CALIFORNIA
CERTIFICATION OF VITAL RECORD

COUNTY OF LOS ANGELES • REGISTRAR-RECORDER/COUNTY CLERK

CERTIFICATE OF DEATH
STATE OF CALIFORNIA
USE BLACK INK ONLY

STATE FILE NUMBER

39019023308

LOCAL REGISTRATION DISTRICT AND CERTIFICATE NUMBER

1A. NAME OF DECEDENT—FIRST (GIVEN)	1B. MIDDLE	1C. LAST (FAMILY)	2A. DATE OF DEATH—MO. DAY, YR	2B. HOUR	3. SEX
VICTOR	--	TAYBACK	MAY 25, 1990	0156	M

4. RACE	5. HISPANIC—SPECIFY	6. DATE OF BIRTH—MO. DAY. YR	7. AGE IN YEARS	IF UNDER 1 YEAR MONTHS / DAYS	IF UNDER 24 HOURS HOURS / MINUTES
WHITE	YES / X NO	JANUARY 6, 1930	60		

DECEDENT PERSONAL DATA

8. STATE OF BIRTH	9. CITIZEN OF WHAT COUNTRY	10A. FULL NAME OF FATHER	10B. STATE OF BIRTH	11A. FULL MAIDEN NAME OF MOTHER	11B. STATE OF BIRTH
NY	USA	JAMES TABBACK	SYRIA	HELEN ASFOUR	SYRIA

12. MILITARY SERVICE?	13. SOCIAL SECURITY NO.	14. MARITAL STATUS	15. NAME OF SURVIVING SPOUSE (IF WIFE, ENTER MAIDEN NAME)
UNK To UNK ☐ NONE	071-22-1775	MARRIED	SHEILA BARNARD

16A. USUAL OCCUPATION	16B. USUAL KIND OF BUSINESS OR INDUSTRY	16C. USUAL EMPLOYER	16D. YEARS IN OCCUPATION	17. EDUCATION—YEARS COMPLETED
ACTOR	ENTERTAINMENT	SELF EMPLOYED	33	14

USUAL RESIDENCE

18A. RESIDENCE—STREET AND NUMBER OR LOCATION	18B. CITY	18C. ZIP CODE
300 CUMBERLAND ROAD	GLENDALE	91202

18D. COUNTY	18E. NUMBER OF YEARS IN THIS COUNTY	18F. STATE OR FOREIGN COUNTRY	20. NAME, RELATIONSHIP, MAILING ADDRESS AND ZIP CODE OF INFORMANT
LOS ANGELES	45	CALIFORNIA	SHEILA TAYBACK-WIFE 300 CUMBERLAND ROAD GLENDALE, CA. 91202

PLACE OF DEATH

19A. PLACE OF DEATH	19B. IF HOSPITAL, SPECIFY ONE: IP. ER/OP. DOA	19C. COUNTY
GLENDALE ADV. MEDICAL CTR.	ER	LOS ANGELES

19D. STREET ADDRESS—STREET AND NUMBER OR LOCATION	19E. CITY	TIME INTERVAL BETWEEN ONSET AND DEATH	22. WAS DEATH REPORTED TO CORONER? REFERRAL NUMBER
1509 WILSON TERRACE	GLENDALE		X YES 90-5176 ☐ NO

CAUSE OF DEATH

21. DEATH WAS CAUSED BY: (ENTER ONLY ONE CAUSE PER LINE FOR A, B, AND C)		23. WAS BIOPSY PERFORMED?
IMMEDIATE CAUSE (A)	Arteriosclerotic Cardiovascular Disease ▶ unk	☐ YES X NO
DUE TO (B)	▶	24A. WAS AUTOPSY PERFORMED? ☐ YES X NO
DUE TO (C)	▶	24B. WAS IT USED IN DETERMINING CAUSE OF DEATH? ☐ YES X NO

25. OTHER SIGNIFICANT CONDITIONS CONTRIBUTING TO DEATH BUT NOT RELATED TO CAUSE GIVEN IN 21	26. WAS OPERATION PERFORMED FOR ANY CONDITION IN ITEM 21 OR 25? IF YES, LIST TYPE OF OPERATION AND DATE.
Diabetes Mellitus	No

PHYSICIAN'S CERTIFICATION

I CERTIFY THAT TO THE BEST OF MY KNOWLEDGE DEATH OCCURRED AT THE HOUR, DATE AND PLACE STATED FROM THE CAUSES STATED.	27B. SIGNATURE AND DEGREE OR TITLE OF CERTIFIER	27C. CERTIFIER'S LICENSE NUMBER	27D. DATE SIGNED
27A. DECEDENT ATTENDED SINCE / DECEDENT LAST SEEN ALIVE — MONTH, DAY, YEAR / MONTH, DAY, YEAR	▶		
	27E. TYPE ATTENDING PHYSICIAN'S NAME AND ADDRESS		

CORONER'S USE ONLY

I CERTIFY THAT IN MY OPINION DEATH OCCURRED AT THE HOUR, DATE AND PLACE STATED FROM THE CAUSES STATED.	28A. SIGNATURE AND TITLE OF CORONER OR DEPUTY CORONER	28B. DATE SIGNED
▶	Palmer Deputy Coroner	5-29-1990

29. MANNER OF DEATH—specify one: natural, accident, suicide, homicide; pending investigation or could not be determined	30A. PLACE OF INJURY	30B. INJURY AT WORK? ☐ YES ☐ NO	30C. DATE OF INJURY MONTH, DAY, YEAR	31. HOUR

32. LOCATION (STREET AND NUMBER OR LOCATION AND CITY)	33. DESCRIBE HOW INJURY OCCURRED (EVENTS WHICH RESULTED IN INJURY)

FUNERAL DIRECTOR AND LOCAL REGISTRAR

34A. DISPOSITION(S)	34B. PLACE OF FINAL DISPOSITION	34C. DATE MO. DAY. YEAR	35A. SIGNATURE OF EMBALMER	35B. LICENSE NUMBER
BURIAL	FOREST LAWN MEMORIAL PARK LOS ANGELES, CA. 90068	MAY 30, 1990	David Sission	7653

36A. NAME OF FUNERAL DIRECTOR (OR PERSON ACTING AS SUCH)	36B. LICENSE NO.	37. SIGNATURE OF LOCAL REGISTRAR	38. REGISTRATION DATE
FOREST LAWN HOLLYWOOD HILLS MTY.	F 904	▶ Robert Nate	MAY 30 1990

STATE REGISTRAR

A.	B.	C.	D.	E.	F.	CENSUS TRACT

VS-11 (REV. 1-90)   MAKE NO ERASURES, WHITEOUTS, OR OTHER ALTERATIONS   01-9-3-0375

This is to certify that this document is a true copy of the official record filed with the Registrar-Recorder/County Clerk.

Conny B. McCormack

CONNY B. McCORMACK
Registrar-Recorder/County Clerk

This copy not valid unless prepared on engraved border displaying the Seal and Signature of the Registrar-Recorder/County Clerk.

OCT 0 4 2001

19-673793

ANY ALTERATION OR ERASURE VOIDS THIS CERTIFICATE

CERTIFICATE OF DEATH
STATE OF CALIFORNIA
USE BLACK INK ONLY/NO ERASURES, WHITEOUTS OR ALTERATIONS
VS-11 (REV. 7/93)

39519011027

STATE FILE NUMBER   LOCAL REGISTRATION NUMBER

1. NAME OF DECEDENT—FIRST (GIVEN)	2. MIDDLE	3. LAST (FAMILY)
IRENE	TEDROW	KENT

DECEDENT PERSONAL DATA						
4. DATE OF BIRTH MM/DD/CCYY	5. AGE YRS.	IF UNDER 1 YEAR MONTHS / DAYS	IF UNDER 24 HOURS HOURS / MINUTES	6. SEX	7. DATE OF DEATH MM/DD/CCYY	8. HOUR
08/03/1907	87			F	03/10/1995	0500

9. STATE OF BIRTH	10. SOCIAL SECURITY NO.	11. MILITARY SERVICE	12. MARITAL STATUS	13. EDUCATION—YEARS COMPLETED
COLORADO	093-09-6130	19___ TO 19___ [X] NONE	WIDOW	16

14. RACE	15. HISPANIC—SPECIFY	16. USUAL EMPLOYER
CAUCASIAN	[ ] YES _____ [X] NO	SELF EMPLOYED

17. OCCUPATION	18. KIND OF BUSINESS	19. YEARS IN OCCUPATION
ACTRESS	THEATRE/FILM/TELEVISION	50

USUAL RESIDENCE

20. RESIDENCE—STREET AND NUMBER OR LOCATION
5763 CORTEEN PLACE

21. CITY	22. COUNTY	23. ZIP CODE	24. YRS. IN COUNTY	25. STATE OR FOREIGN COUNTRY
NORTH HOLLYWOOD	LOS ANGELES	91607	56	CA

INFORMANT

26. NAME, RELATIONSHIP	27. MAILING ADDRESS (STREET AND NUMBER OR RURAL ROUTE NUMBER, CITY OR TOWN, STATE, ZIP)
ENID KENT (DAUGHTER)	591 N. PLYMOUTH LOS ANGELES, CA 90004

SPOUSE AND PARENT INFORMATION

28. NAME OF SURVIVING SPOUSE—FIRST	29. MIDDLE	30. LAST (MAIDEN NAME)
-	-	-

31. NAME OF FATHER—FIRST	32. MIDDLE	33. LAST	34. BIRTH STATE
HARRY	BEECHER	TEDROW	COLORADO

35. NAME OF MOTHER—FIRST	36. MIDDLE	37. LAST (MAIDEN)	38. BIRTH STATE
CAMILLA	EUDORA	ROBERTS	COLORADO

DISPOSITION(S)

39. DATE MM/DD/CCYY	40. PLACE OF FINAL DISPOSITION
03/17/1995	WESTWOOD MEMORIAL PARK, 1218 GLENDON AVE. LOS ANGELES, CA 90024

FUNERAL DIRECTOR AND LOCAL REGISTRAR

41. TYPE OF DISPOSITION(S)	42. SIGNATURE OF EMBALMER	43. LICENSE NO.
CR/BU	▶ NOT EMBALMED	-

44. NAME OF FUNERAL DIRECTOR	45. LICENSE NO.	46. SIGNATURE OF LOCAL REGISTRAR	47. DATE MM/DD/CCYY
PIERCE BROS. WESTWOOD VILLAGE	F-951	▶ Robert C. Gate	03/16/1995

PLACE OF DEATH

101. PLACE OF DEATH	102. IF HOSPITAL, SPECIFY ONE:	103. FACILITY OTHER THAN HOSPITAL:	104. COUNTY
RESIDENCE	[ ] P [ ] ER/OP [ ] DOA	[ ] CONV. HOSP. [X] RES [ ] OTHER	LOS ANGELES

105. STREET ADDRESS—STREET AND NUMBER OR LOCATION	106. CITY
5763 CORTEEN PLACE	NORTH HOLLYWOOD

CAUSE OF DEATH

107. DEATH WAS CAUSED BY: (ENTER ONLY ONE CAUSE PER LINE FOR A, B, C, AND D)		TIME INTERVAL BETWEEN ONSET AND DEATH	
IMMEDIATE CAUSE (A)	CARDIOPULMONARY ARREST	½ HOUR	108. DEATH REPORTED TO CORONER [ ] YES [X] NO REFERRAL NUMBER
DUE TO (B)	ATHEROSCLEROTIC HEART DISEASE	10 YRS.	109. BIOPSY PERFORMED [ ] YES [X] NO
DUE TO (C)			110. AUTOPSY PERFORMED [ ] YES [X] NO
DUE TO (D)			111. USED IN DETERMINING CAUSE [ ] YES [ ] NO

112. OTHER SIGNIFICANT CONDITIONS CONTRIBUTING TO DEATH BUT NOT RELATED TO CAUSE GIVEN IN 107
ATRIAL FIBRILLATION, CEREBROVASCULAR ACCIDENT

113. WAS OPERATION PERFORMED FOR ANY CONDITION IN ITEM 107 OR 112? IF YES, LIST TYPE OF OPERATION AND DATE
NO

PHYSICIAN'S CERTIFICATION

114. I CERTIFY THAT TO THE BEST OF MY KNOWLEDGE DEATH OCCURRED AT THE HOUR, DATE AND PLACE STATED FROM THE CAUSES STATED.	115. SIGNATURE AND TITLE OF CERTIFIER	116. LICENSE NO.	117. DATE MM/DD/CCYY
DECEDENT ATTENDED SINCE 06/01/1992 — DECEDENT LAST SEEN ALIVE 03/05/1995	Darius Gharib M.D.	A 42217	03/10/1995
	118. TYPE ATTENDING PHYSICIAN'S NAME, MAILING ADDRESS - ZIP DARIUS GHARIB, M.D. 16500 VENTURA BL. #205 ENCINO, CA 91436		

CORONER'S USE ONLY

119. I CERTIFY THAT IN MY OPINION DEATH OCCURRED AT THE HOUR, DATE AND PLACE STATED FROM THE CAUSES STATED.	120. INJURY AT WORK	121. INJURY DATE MM/DD/CCYY	122. HOUR	123. PLACE OF INJURY
MANNER OF DEATH: [ ] NATURAL [ ] SUICIDE [ ] HOMICIDE [ ] ACCIDENT [ ] PENDING INVESTIGATION [ ] COULD NOT BE DETERMINED	[ ] YES [ ] NO			
	124. DESCRIBE HOW INJURY OCCURRED (EVENTS WHICH RESULTED IN INJURY)			

125. LOCATION (STREET AND NUMBER OR LOCATION AND CITY AND ZIP CODE)

126. SIGNATURE OF CORONER OR DEPUTY CORONER	127. DATE MM/DD/CCYY	128. TYPED NAME, TITLE OF CORONER OR DEPUTY CORONER
▶		

STATE REGISTRAR

A	B	C	D	E	F	G	H	FAX AUTH. #	CENSUS TRACT

CERTIFICATE OF DEATH
STATE OF CALIFORNIA
USE BLACK INK ONLY / NO ERASURES, WHITEOUTS OR ALTERATIONS
VS-11 (REV 1/03)

STATE FILE NUMBER		LOCAL REGISTRATION NUMBER

DECEDENT'S PERSONAL DATA

1. NAME OF DECEDENT --- FIRST (Given)	2. MIDDLE	3. LAST (Family)
CHERLYNNE	T.	THIGPEN

AKA. ALSO KNOWN AS --- include full AKA (FIRST, MIDDLE, LAST)	4. DATE OF BIRTH mm/dd/ccyy	5. AGE Yrs.	IF UNDER ONE YEAR Months / Days	IF UNDER 24 HOURS Hours / Minutes	6. SEX
LYNNE-THIGPEN	12/22/1948	54			F

9. BIRTH STATE/FOREIGN COUNTRY	10. SOCIAL SECURITY NUMBER	11. EVER IN U.S. ARMED FORCES?	12. MARITAL STATUS (at Time of Death)	7. DATE OF DEATH mm/dd/ccyy	8. HOUR (24 Hours)
IL	345-42-3412	☐ YES ☒ NO ☐ UNK	NEVER MARRIED	03/13/2003	0013

13. EDUCATION --- Highest Level/Degree (see worksheet on back)	14/15. WAS DECEDENT SPANISH/HISPANIC/LATINO? (If yes, see worksheet on back.)	16. DECEDENT'S RACE --- Up to 3 races may be listed (see worksheet on back)
BACHELOR'S	☐ YES ____ ☒ NO	AFRICAN AMERICAN

17. USUAL OCCUPATION --- Type of work for most of life. DO NOT USE RETIRED	18. KIND OF BUSINESS OR INDUSTRY (e.g., grocery store, road construction, employment agency, etc.)	19. YEARS IN OCCUPATION
ACTRESS	ENTERTAINMENT 1OF2	31

USUAL RESIDENCE

20. DECEDENT'S RESIDENCE (Street and number or location)				
4225 ALLA RD. UNIT #9				

21. CITY	22. COUNTY/PROVINCE	23. ZIP CODE	24. YEARS IN COUNTY	25. STATE/FOREIGN COUNTRY
MARINA DEL REY	LOS ANGELES	90292	2	CALIFORNIA

INFORMANT

26. INFORMANT'S NAME, RELATIONSHIP	27. INFORMANT'S MAILING ADDRESS (Street and number or rural route number, city or town, state, ZIP)
LARRY ARONSON - FRIEND	4225 ALLA RD., UNIT #9, MARINA DEL REY, CA 90292

SPOUSE AND PARENT INFORMATION

28. NAME OF SURVIVING SPOUSE --- FIRST	29. MIDDLE	30. LAST (Maiden Name)
-	-	-

31. NAME OF FATHER --- FIRST	32. MIDDLE	33. LAST	34. BIRTH STATE
GEORGE	-	THIGPEN	UNK

35. NAME OF MOTHER --- FIRST	36. MIDDLE	37. LAST (Maiden)	38. BIRTH STATE
CELIA	-	MARTIN	UNK

FUNERAL DIRECTOR/ LOCAL REGISTRAR

39. DISPOSITION DATE mm/dd/ccyy	40. PLACE OF FINAL DISPOSITION
03/17/2003	ELMHERST CEMETERY JOLIET, IL 60451

41. TYPE OF DISPOSITION(S)	42. SIGNATURE OF EMBALMER	43. LICENSE NUMBER
TR/BU	*Ellen Lade*	8251

44. NAME OF FUNERAL ESTABLISHMENT	45. LICENSE NUMBER	46. SIGNATURE OF LOCAL REGISTRAR	47. DATE mm/dd/ccyy
GATES KINGSLEY & GATES SMITH-SALSBURY	FD-1016	*Thomas W. Whitewate*	03/17/2003

PLACE OF DEATH

101. PLACE OF DEATH	102. IF HOSPITAL, SPECIFY ONE	103. IF OTHER THAN HOSPITAL, SPECIFY ONE
DANIEL FREEMAN MARINA HOSPITAL	☐ IP ☒ ER/OP ☐ DOA	☐ Hospice ☐ Nursing Home/LTC ☐ Decedent's Home ☐ Other

104. COUNTY	105. FACILITY ADDRESS OR LOCATION WHERE FOUND (Street and number or location)	106. CITY
LOS ANGELES	4650 LINCOLN BLVD.	MARINA DEL REY

CAUSE OF DEATH

107. CAUSE OF DEATH — Enter the chain of events --- diseases, injuries, or complications --- that directly caused death. DO NOT enter terminal events such as cardiac arrest, respiratory arrest, or ventricular fibrillation without showing the etiology. DO NOT ABBREVIATE.

		Time Interval Between Onset and Death	108. DEATH REPORTED TO CORONER?
IMMEDIATE CAUSE (A) (Final disease or condition resulting in death)	DEFERRED	(AT)	☒ YES ☐ NO REFERRAL NUMBER 2003-02046
Sequentially, list conditions, if any, leading to cause on Line A. Enter (B)		(BT)	109. BIOPSY PERFORMED? ☐ YES ☐ NO
UNDERLYING CAUSE (disease or injury that (C)		(CT)	110. AUTOPSY PERFORMED? ☒ YES ☐ NO
initiated the events resulting in death) LAST (D)		(DT)	111. USED IN DETERMINING CAUSE? ☐ YES ☐ NO

112. OTHER SIGNIFICANT CONDITIONS CONTRIBUTING TO DEATH BUT NOT RESULTING IN THE UNDERLYING CAUSE GIVEN IN 107

113. WAS OPERATION PERFORMED FOR ANY CONDITION IN ITEM 107 OR 112? (If yes, list type of operation and date.)	113A. IF FEMALE, PREGNANT IN LAST YEAR?
	☐ YES ☐ NO ☒ UNK

PHYSICIAN'S CERTIFICATION

114. I CERTIFY THAT TO THE BEST OF MY KNOWLEDGE DEATH OCCURRED AT THE HOUR, DATE, AND PLACE STATED FROM THE CAUSES STATED.	115. SIGNATURE AND TITLE OF CERTIFIER	116. LICENSE NUMBER	117. DATE mm/dd/ccyy
Decedent Attended Since (A) mm/dd/ccyy / Decedent Last Seen Alive (B) mm/dd/ccyy			
	118. TYPE ATTENDING PHYSICIAN'S NAME, MAILING ADDRESS, ZIP CODE		

CORONER'S USE ONLY

119. I CERTIFY THAT IN MY OPINION DEATH OCCURRED AT THE HOUR, DATE, AND PLACE STATED FROM THE CAUSES STATED.		120. INJURED AT WORK?	121. INJURY DATE mm/dd/ccyy	122. HOUR (24 Hours)
MANNER OF DEATH ☐ Natural ☐ Accident ☐ Homicide ☐ Suicide ☒ Pending Investigation ☐ Could not be determined		☐ YES ☐ NO ☐ UNK		

123. PLACE OF INJURY (e.g., home, construction site, wooded area, etc.)

124. DESCRIBE HOW INJURY OCCURRED (Events which resulted in injury)

INFORMATIONAL, NOT A VALID DOCUMENT TO ESTABLISH IDENTITY

125. LOCATION OF INJURY (Street and number, or location, and city, and ZIP)

126. SIGNATURE OF CORONER / DEPUTY CORONER	127. DATE mm/dd/ccyy	128. TYPE NAME, TITLE OF CORONER / DEPUTY CORONER	090
Mary T. Macias	03/15/2003	MARY T. MACIAS DEPUTY CORONER	

STATE REGISTRAR	A	B	C	D	E		FAX AUTH. #	CENSUS TRACT

STATE OF CALIFORNIA
CERTIFICATION OF VITAL RECORD

COUNTY OF LOS ANGELES
DEPARTMENT OF HEALTH SERVICES

AMENDMENT OF MEDICAL AND HEALTH DATA—DEATH

STATE FILE NUMBER	USE BLACK INK ONLY—NO ERASURES, WHITEOUT, OR ALTERATIONS	LOCAL REGISTRATION DISTRICT AND CERTIFICATE NUMBER
STATE/LOCAL REGISTRAR USE ONLY 1	2	3

TYPE OR PRINT IN BLACK INK ONLY

PART I — INFORMATION TO LOCATE RECORD

1. NAME—FIRST (GIVEN)	2. MIDDLE	3. LAST (FAMILY)	4. SEX
CHERLYNNE	T.	THIGPEN	F

5. DATE OF EVENT—MM/DD/CCYY	6. CITY OF OCCURENCE	7. COUNTY OF OCCURRENCE	
03/13/2003	MARINA DEL REY	LOS ANGELES	2 OF 2

PART II — INFORMATION AS IT APPEARS ON RECORD

107. DEATH WAS CAUSED BY ENTER ONLY ONE CAUSE PER LINE FOR A, B, C, AND D)

IMMEDIATE CAUSE
(A) DEFERRED
(B)
(C)
DUE TO (D)

TIME INTERVAL BETWEEN ONSET AND DEATH

108. DEATH REPORTED TO CORONER [X] YES [ ] NO
REFERRAL NUMBER 2003-02046

109. BIOPSY PERFORMED [ ] YES [ ] NO

110. AUTOPSY PERFORMED [X] YES [ ] NO

111. USED IN DETERMINING CAUSE [ ] YES [ ] NO

112. OTHER SIGNIFICANT CONDITIONS CONTRIBUTING TO DEATH BUT NOT RELATED TO CAUSE GIVEN IN 107

113. WAS OPERATION PERFORMED FOR ANY CONDITION IN ITEM 107 or 112? IF YES, LIST TYPE OF OPERATION AND DATE.

119. MANNER OF DEATH
[ ] NATURAL [ ] SUICIDE [ ] HOMICIDE
[ ] ACCIDENT [X] PENDING INVESTIGATION [ ] COULD NOT BE DETERMINED

120. INJURY AT WORK [ ] YES [ ] NO
121. INJURY DATE—MM/DD/CCYY
122. HOUR
123. PLACE OF INJURY
124. DESCRIBE HOW INJURY OCCURED (EVENTS WHICH RESULTED IN INJURY)

125. LOCATION (STREET AND NUMBER OR LOCATION AND CITY AND ZIP CODE)

PART III — INFORMATION AS IT SHOULD APPEAR

107. DEATH WAS CAUSED BY ENTER ONLY ONE CAUSE PER LINE FOR A, B, C, AND D)

IMMEDIATE CAUSE
(A) ACUTE CARDIAC DYSFUNCTION — MINS
(B) NON-TRAUMATIC SYMETRIC & SPONTANEOUS INTRAVENTRICULAR HEMORRHAGES IN THE BRAIN — UNK
(C)
DUE TO (D)

108. DEATH REPORTED TO CORONER [X] YES [ ] NO
REFERRAL NUMBER 2003-02046

109. BIOPSY PERFORMED [ ] YES [X] NO

110. AUTOPSY PERFORMED [X] YES [ ] NO

111. USED IN DETERMINING CAUSE [X] YES [ ] NO

112. OTHER SIGNIFICANT CONDITIONS CONTRIBUTING TO DEATH BUT NOT RELATED TO CAUSE GIVEN IN 107
CARDIOMEGALY

113. WAS OPERATION PERFORMED FOR ANY CONDITION IN ITEM 107 or 112? IF YES, LIST TYPE OF OPERATION AND DATE.
NO

119. MANNER OF DEATH
[X] NATURAL [ ] SUICIDE [ ] HOMICIDE
[ ] ACCIDENT [ ] PENDING INVESTIGATION [ ] COULD NOT BE DETERMINED

120. INJURY AT WORK [ ] YES [ ] NO
121. INJURY DATE—MM/DD/CCYY
122. HOUR
123. PLACE OF INJURY
124. DESCRIBE HOW INJURY OCCURRED (EVENTS WHICH RESULTED IN INJURY)

125. LOCATION (STREET AND NUMBER OR LOCATION AND CITY AND ZIP CODE)

DECLARATION OF CERTIFYING PHYSICIAN OR CORONER

I HEREBY DECLARE UNDER PENALTY OF PERJURY THAT THE ABOVE INFORMATION IS TRUE AND CORRECT TO THE BEST OF MY KNOWLEDGE.

8. SIGNATURE OF CERTIFYING PHYSICIAN OR CORONER	9. DATE SIGNED—MM/DD/CCYY	10. TYPED OR PRINTED NAME AND DEGREE/TITLE OF CERTIFIER
[signature]	05/29/2003	PEDRO M. ORTIZ-COLOM, M.D. DME

11. ADDRESS—STREET AND NUMBER	12. CITY	13. STATE	14. ZIP CODE
1104 N. MISSION ROAD	LOS ANGELES	CA	90033

STATE/LOCAL REGISTRAR USE ONLY

15. OFFICE OF STATE REGISTRAR OR SIGNATURE OF LOCAL REGISTRAR	16. DATE ACCEPTED FOR REGISTRATION—MM/DD/CCYY	
Thomas G. [signature]	06/05/2003	090625872

STATE OF CALIFORNIA, DEPARTMENT OF HEALTH SERVICES, OFFICE OF STATE REGISTRAR   VS-24 B (1/94)

This is a true certified copy of the record filed in the County of Los Angeles Department of Health Services if it bears the Registrar's signature in purple ink.

DATE ISSUED JUN 05 2003

Thomas L. [signature]
Director of Health Services and Registrar

This copy not valid unless prepared on engraved border displaying seal and signature of Registrar.

CERTIFICATE OF DEATH
STATE OF CALIFORNIA
USE BLACK INK ONLY/NO ERASURES, WHITEOUTS OR ALTERATIONS
VS-11 (REV. 1/00)

STATE FILE NUMBER | LOCAL REGISTRATION NUMBER

DECEDENT PERSONAL DATA

1. NAME OF DECEDENT—FIRST (GIVEN): Lawrence
2. MIDDLE: James
3. LAST (FAMILY): Tierney
4. DATE OF BIRTH MM/DD/CCYY: 03/15/1919
5. AGE YRS.: 82
IF UNDER 1 YEAR — MONTHS / DAYS | IF UNDER 24 HOURS — HOURS / MINUTES
6. SEX: M
7. DATE OF DEATH MM/DD/CCYY: 02/26/2002
8. HOUR: 0315
9. STATE OF BIRTH: NY
10. SOCIAL SECURITY NO.: 055-01-9213
11. MILITARY SERVICE: [ ] YES [X] NO [ ] UNK
12. MARITAL STATUS: Never Married
13. EDUCATION—YEARS COMPLETED: 14
14. RACE: White
15. HISPANIC—SPECIFY: [ ] YES ____ [X] NO
16. USUAL EMPLOYER: Self Employed
17. OCCUPATION: Actor
18. KIND OF BUSINESS: Entertainment
19. YEARS IN OCCUPATION: 58

USUAL RESIDENCE

20. RESIDENCE—(STREET AND NUMBER OR LOCATION): 1526 N. Fairfax Ave.
21. CITY: Los Angeles
22. COUNTY: Los Angeles
23. ZIP CODE: 90046
24. YRS IN COUNTY: 31
25. STATE OR FOREIGN COUNTRY: CA

INFORMANT

26. NAME, RELATIONSHIP: Michael Tierney, D.P.O.A.
27. MAILING ADDRESS (STREET AND NUMBER OR RURAL ROUTE NUMBER, CITY OR TOWN, STATE, ZIP): 1526 N. Fairfax Ave., Los Angeles, CA 90046

SPOUSE AND PARENT INFORMATION

28. NAME OF SURVIVING SPOUSE—FIRST: –
29. MIDDLE: –
30. LAST (MAIDEN NAME): –
31. NAME OF FATHER—FIRST: Lawrence
32. MIDDLE: Hugh
33. LAST: Tierney
34. BIRTH STATE: NY
35. NAME OF MOTHER—FIRST: Marion
36. MIDDLE: Alice
37. LAST (MAIDEN): Crowley
38. BIRTH STATE: NY

DISPOSITION(S)

39. DATE MM/DD/CCYY: 03/07/2002
40. PLACE OF FINAL DISPOSITION: Residence: Michael Tierney 1526 Fairfax Ave., Los Angeles, CA 90046

FUNERAL DIRECTOR AND LOCAL REGISTRAR

41. TYPE OF DISPOSITION(S): CR/RES
42. SIGNATURE OF EMBALMER: ► Not Embalmed
43. LICENSE NO.: –
44. NAME OF FUNERAL DIRECTOR: Abbott & Hast Mortuary, Inc.
45. LICENSE NO.: FD 1399
46. SIGNATURE OF LOCAL REGISTRAR: ► Fred Leaf
47. DATE MM/DD/CCYY: 03/05/2002

PLACE OF DEATH

101. PLACE OF DEATH: Sharon Care Center
102. IF HOSPITAL, SPECIFY ONE: [ ] IP [ ] ER/OP [ ] DOA
103. FACILITY OTHER THAN HOSPITAL: [X] CONV. HOSP. [ ] RES. CARE [ ] OTHER
104. COUNTY: Los Angeles
105. STREET ADDRESS—(STREET AND NUMBER OR LOCATION): 8167 W. 3rd St.
106. CITY: Los Angeles

CAUSE OF DEATH

107. DEATH WAS CAUSED BY: (ENTER ONLY ONE CAUSE PER LINE FOR A, B, C, AND D)

		TIME INTERVAL BETWEEN ONSET AND DEATH
IMMEDIATE CAUSE (A)	Cardiac Arrest	5 Min
DUE TO (B)	Congestive Heart Failure	1 Yr
DUE TO (C)	Hypertension	10 Yrs
DUE TO (D)		

108. DEATH REPORTED TO CORONER: [X] YES [ ] NO — REFERRAL NUMBER: 2002-51859
109. BIOPSY PERFORMED: [ ] YES [X] NO
110. AUTOPSY PERFORMED: [ ] YES [X] NO
111. USED IN DETERMINING CAUSE: [ ] YES [ ] NO

112. OTHER SIGNIFICANT CONDITIONS CONTRIBUTING TO DEATH BUT NOT RELATED TO CAUSE GIVEN IN 107: Cerebroascular Accident

113. WAS OPERATION PERFORMED FOR ANY CONDITION IN ITEM 107 OR 112? IF YES, LIST TYPE OF OPERATION AND DATE.: No

I 119

PHYSICIAN'S CERTIFICATION

114. I CERTIFY THAT TO THE BEST OF MY KNOWLEDGE DEATH OCCURRED AT THE HOUR, DATE AND PLACE STATED FROM THE CAUSES STATED.
DECEDENT ATTENDED SINCE MM/DD/CCYY: 01/15/2000
DECEDENT LAST SEEN ALIVE MM/DD/CCYY: 02/01/2002
115. SIGNATURE AND TITLE OF CERTIFIER: ► Ryendrc Prasd
116. LICENSE NO.: A68598
117. DATE MM/DD/CCYY: 02/28/2002
118. TYPE ATTENDING PHYSICIAN'S NAME, MAILING ADDRESS, ZIP: Raj Prassad, MD, 2080 E. Century Park, Los Angeles, CA 90067

CORONER'S USE ONLY

4

119. I CERTIFY THAT IN MY OPINION DEATH OCCURRED AT THE HOUR, DATE AND PLACE STATED FROM THE CAUSES STATED.
MANNER OF DEATH: [ ] NATURAL [ ] SUICIDE [ ] HOMICIDE [ ] ACCIDENT [ ] PENDING INVESTIGATION [ ] COULD NOT BE DETERMINED
120. INJURY AT WORK: [ ] YES [ ] NO
121. INJURY DATE MM/DD/CCYY:
122. HOUR:
123. PLACE OF INJURY:
124. DESCRIBE HOW INJURY OCCURRED (EVENTS WHICH RESULTED IN INJURY):
125. LOCATION (STREET AND NUMBER OR LOCATION AND CITY, ZIP):
126. SIGNATURE OF CORONER OR DEPUTY CORONER: ►
127. DATE MM/DD/CCYY:
128. TYPED NAME, TITLE OF CORONER OR DEPUTY CORONER:

STATE REGISTRAR

A | B | C | D | E | F | G | H | FAX AUTH. #: 092-1603 | CENSUS TRACT

STATE OF CALIFORNIA
CERTIFICATION OF VITAL RECORD

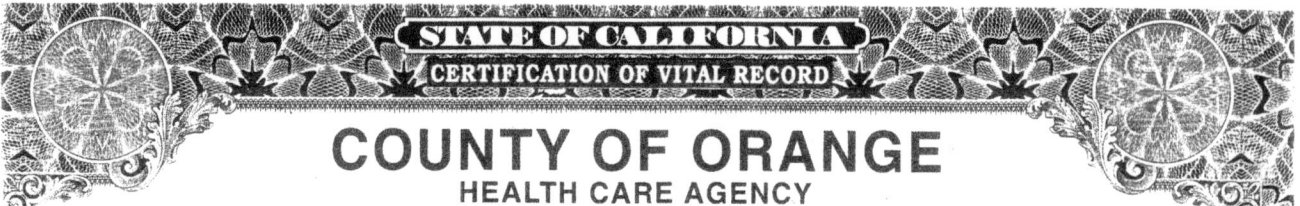

COUNTY OF ORANGE
HEALTH CARE AGENCY
1200 N. MAIN STREET, SUITE 100-A
SANTA ANA, CA 92701

CERTIFICATE OF DEATH   3 200030 004927

STATE OF CALIFORNIA
USE BLACK INK ONLY/NO ERASURES, WHITEOUTS OR ALTERATIONS
VS-11 (REV. 1/00)

STATE FILE NUMBER   LOCAL REGISTRATION NUMBER

DECEDENT PERSONAL DATA

1. NAME OF DECEDENT—FIRST (GIVEN)	2. MIDDLE	3. LAST (FAMILY)
CLAIRE	TREVOR	BREN

4. DATE OF BIRTH MM/DD/CCYY	5. AGE YRS	IF UNDER 1 YEAR MONTHS DAYS	IF UNDER 24 HOURS HOURS MINUTES	6. SEX	7. DATE OF DEATH MM/DD/CCYY	8. HOUR
03/08/1910	90			F	04/08/2000	0715

9. STATE OF BIRTH	10. SOCIAL SECURITY NO.	11. MILITARY SERVICE	12. MARITAL STATUS	13. EDUCATION—YEARS COMPLETED
NEW YORK	568-01-7925	☐ YES ☒ NO ☐ UNK	WIDOWED	14

14. RACE	15. HISPANIC—SPECIFY	16. USUAL EMPLOYER
CAUCASIAN	☐ YES ☒ NO	SELF EMPLOYED

17. OCCUPATION	18. KIND OF BUSINESS	19. YEARS IN OCCUPATION
ACTRESS	ENTERTAINMENT	60

USUAL RESIDENCE

20. RESIDENCE—STREET AND NUMBER OR LOCATION:
22 RUE VILLARS

21. CITY	22. COUNTY	23. ZIP CODE	24. YRS IN COUNTY	25. STATE OR FOREIGN COUNTRY
NEWPORT BEACH	ORANGE	92660	40	CA

INFORMANT

26. NAME, RELATIONSHIP	27. MAILING ADDRESS (STREET AND NUMBER OR RURAL ROUTE NUMBER, CITY OR TOWN, STATE, ZIP)
M.A.POPE – BUSINESS MANAGER	P.O. BOX 3090 NEWPORT BEACH, CA 92658

SPOUSE AND PARENT INFORMATION

28. NAME OF SURVIVING SPOUSE—FIRST	29. MIDDLE	30. LAST (MAIDEN NAME)
–	–	–

31. NAME OF FATHER—FIRST	32. MIDDLE	33. LAST	34. BIRTH STATE
NOEL	B.	WEMLINGER	FRANCE

35. NAME OF MOTHER—FIRST	36. MIDDLE	37. LAST (MAIDEN)	38. BIRTH STATE
BENJAMINA	–	MORRISON	IRELAND

DISPOSITION(S)

39. DATE MM/DD/CCYY	40. PLACE OF FINAL DISPOSITION
04/12/2000	AT SEA OFF THE COAST OF ORANGE COUNTY, CA

FUNERAL DIRECTOR AND LOCAL REGISTRAR

41. TYPE OF DISPOSITION(S)	42. SIGNATURE OF EMBALMER	43. LICENSE NO.
CR/SEA	▶ NOT EMBALMED	–

44. NAME OF FUNERAL DIRECTOR	45. LICENSE NO.	46. SIGNATURE OF LOCAL REGISTRAR	47. DATE MM/DD/CCYY
PACIFIC VIEW MORTUARY	FD 1176	Mark B _____	04/11/2000

PLACE OF DEATH

101. PLACE OF DEATH	102. IF HOSPITAL, SPECIFY ONE:	103. FACILITY OTHER THAN HOSPITAL:	104. COUNTY
HOAG MEMORIAL HOSPITAL PRESBYTERIAN	☒ IP ☐ ER/OP ☐ DOA	☐ CONV. HOSP. ☐ RES. CARE ☐ OTHER	ORANGE

105. STREET ADDRESS (STREET AND NUMBER OR LOCATION)	106. CITY
ONE HOAG DRIVE	NEWPORT BEACH

CAUSE OF DEATH

107. DEATH WAS CAUSED BY: (ENTER ONLY ONE CAUSE PER LINE FOR A, B, C, AND D)	TIME INTERVAL BETWEEN ONSET AND DEATH	
IMMEDIATE CAUSE (A) CARDIOPULMONARY COLLAPSE	IMMED	108. DEATH REPORTED TO CORONER ☐ YES ☒ NO REFERRAL NUMBER
DUE TO (B) ACUTE RESPIRATORY FAILURE	1 MONTH	109. BIOPSY PERFORMED ☐ YES ☒ NO
DUE TO (C) PNEUMONIA	1 MONTH	110. AUTOPSY PERFORMED ☐ YES ☒ NO
DUE TO (D) CHRONIC OBSTRUCTIVE PULMONARY DISEASE	YEARS	111. USED IN DETERMINING CAUSE ☐ YES ☐ NO

112. OTHER SIGNIFICANT CONDITIONS CONTRIBUTING TO DEATH BUT NOT RELATED TO CAUSE GIVEN IN 107
DIVERTICULITIS, SUPRAVENTRICULAR TACHYCARDIA

113. WAS OPERATION PERFORMED FOR ANY CONDITION IN ITEM 107 OR 112? IF YES, LIST TYPE OF OPERATION AND DATE.
NO

J44.9

PHYSICIAN'S CERTIFICATION

114. I CERTIFY THAT TO THE BEST OF MY KNOWLEDGE DEATH OCCURRED AT THE HOUR, DATE AND PLACE STATED FROM THE CAUSES STATED.	115. SIGNATURE AND TITLE OF CERTIFIER	116. LICENSE NO	117. DATE MM/DD/CCYY
DECEDENT ATTENDED SINCE MM/DD/CCYY 06/14/1999 DECEDENT LAST SEEN ALIVE MM/DD/CCYY 04/07/2000	▶ _____ M.D.	G29857	04/10/2000

118. TYPE ATTENDING PHYSICIAN'S NAME, MAILING ADDRESS, ZIP
DENNIS R.NOVAK, MD   320 SUPERIOR AVENUE #200 NEWPORT BEACH, CA 92663

CORONER'S USE ONLY

I CERTIFY THAT IN MY OPINION DEATH OCCURRED AT THE HOUR, DATE AND PLACE STATED FROM THE CAUSES STATED.	120. INJURY AT WORK ☐ YES ☐ NO	121. INJURY DATE MM/DD/CCYY	122. HOUR	123. PLACE OF INJURY

119. MANNER OF DEATH	124. DESCRIBE HOW INJURY OCCURRED (EVENTS WHICH RESULTED IN INJURY)
☐ NATURAL ☐ SUICIDE ☐ HOMICIDE ☐ ACCIDENT ☐ PENDING INVESTIGATION ☐ COULD NOT BE DETERMINED	

125. LOCATION (STREET AND NUMBER OR LOCATION AND CITY, ZIP)

126. SIGNATURE OF CORONER OR DEPUTY CORONER	127. DATE MM/DD/CCYY	128. TYPED NAME, TITLE OF CORONER OR DEPUTY CORONER
▶		

F22306

CERTIFIED COPY OF VITAL RECORDS

STATE OF CALIFORNIA COUNTY OF ORANGE } SS	DATE ISSUED	FAX AUTH. # 9148	CENSUS TRACT

REGISTRAR

This is a true and exact reproduction of the document o____ registered and placed on file in the office of the VITAL RECORDS SECTION, ORANGE COUNTY HEALTH CARE AGENCY.

APR 20 2000

MARK B. HORTON, M.D.
HEALTH OFFICER
ORANGE COUNTY, CALIFORNIA

This copy not valid unless prepared on engraved border displaying seal and signature of Registrar.

ANY ALTERATION OR ERASURE VOIDS THIS CERTIFICATE

STATE OF CALIFORNIA
CERTIFICATION OF VITAL RECORD

COUNTY OF LOS ANGELES • REGISTRAR-RECORDER/COUNTY CLERK

CERTIFICATE OF DEATH
STATE OF CALIFORNIA
USE BLACK INK ONLY-NO ERASURES, WHITEOUTS OR ALTERATIONS
VS 11 (REV 7-97)

3 199019 006106

STATE FILE NUMBER		LOCAL REGISTRATION NUMBER

1. NAME OF DECEDENT—FIRST (GIVEN)	2. MIDDLE	3. LAST (FAMILY)
ROBERT	WILLIAM	TROUP JR

4. DATE OF BIRTH MM DD CCYY	5. AGE YRS	6. SEX	7. DATE OF DEATH MM DD CCYY	8. HOUR
10/18/1918	80	M	02/07/1999	1925

DECEDENT PERSONAL DATA

9. STATE OF BIRTH	10. SOCIAL SECURITY NO	11. MILITARY SERVICE	12. MARITAL STATUS	13. EDUCATION—YEARS COMPLETED
PA	198-14-7654	X YES	MARRIED	16

14. RACE	15. HISPANIC SPECIFY	16. USUAL EMPLOYER
CAUCASIAN	X No	SELF EMPLOYED

17. OCCUPATION	18. KIND OF BUSINESS	19. YEARS IN OCCUPATION
SONG WRITER/ACTOR	ENTERTAINMENT	60

USUAL RESIDENCE

20. RESIDENCE—STREET AND NUMBER OR LOCATION
16074 ROYAL OAK RD

21. CITY	22. COUNTY	23. ZIP CODE	24. YRS IN COUNTY	25. STATE OR FOREIGN COUNTRY
ENCINO	LOS ANGELES	91436	52	CA

INFORMANT

26. NAME RELATIONSHIP	27. MAILING ADDRESS (STREET AND NUMBER OR RURAL ROUTE NUMBER, CITY OR TOWN, STATE, ZIP)
CYNNIE TROUP - DAUGHTER	25238 MALIBU RD MALIBU CA 90265

SPOUSE AND PARENT INFORMATION

28. NAME OF SURVIVING SPOUSE—FIRST	29. MIDDLE	30. LAST (MAIDEN) NAME
JULIE	–	PECK

31. NAME OF FATHER—FIRST	32. MIDDLE	33. LAST	34. BIRTH STATE
ROBERT	WILLIAM	TROUP SR	PA

35. NAME OF MOTHER—FIRST	36. MIDDLE	37. LAST (MAIDEN)	38. BIRTH STATE
KATHERINE	–	REESE	PA

DISPOSITION(S)

39. DATE MM/DD/CCYY	40. PLACE OF FINAL DISPOSITION
02/16/1999	RESIDENCE:JULIE TROUP - 16074 ROYAL OAK RD ENCINO CA 91436

FUNERAL DIRECTOR AND LOCAL REGISTRAR

41. TYPE OF DISPOSITION-S	42. SIGNATURE OF EMBALMER	43. LICENSE NO
CR/RES	► NOT EMBALMED	

44. NAME OF FUNERAL DIRECTOR	45. LICENSE NO	46. SIGNATURE OF LOCAL REGISTRAR	47. DATE MM/DD/CCYY
FOREST LAWN HOLLYWOOD HILLS	FD 904		02/12/1999

PLACE OF DEATH

101. PLACE OF DEATH	102. IF HOSPITAL, SPECIFY ONE	103. FACILITY OTHER THAN HOSPITAL	104. COUNTY
SHERMAN OAKS HOSPITAL	X IP □ ER/OP □ DOA	□ CONV. HOSP. □ RES. CARE □ OTHER	LOS ANGELES

105. STREET ADDRESS—STREET AND NUMBER OR LOCATION	106. CITY
4929 VAN NUYS BLVD	SHERMAN OAKS

CAUSE OF DEATH

107. DEATH WAS CAUSED BY: (ENTER ONLY ONE CAUSE PER LINE FOR A, B, C, AND D)		TIME INTERVAL BETWEEN ONSET AND DEATH	108. DEATH REPORTED TO CORONER
IMMEDIATE CAUSE (A) CARDIOPULMONARY ARREST		5 MIN	□ YES X NO
DUE TO (B) PULMONARY EDEMA		2 DAYS	109. BIOPSY PERFORMED □ YES X NO
DUE TO (C) MYOCARDIAL INFARCTION		4 DAYS	110. AUTOPSY PERFORMED □ YES X NO
DUE TO (D) PNEUMONIA		5 DAYS	111. USED IN DETERMINING CAUSE □ YES X NO

112. OTHER SIGNIFICANT CONDITIONS CONTRIBUTING TO DEATH BUT NOT RELATED TO CAUSE GIVEN IN 107
NONE

113. WAS OPERATION PERFORMED FOR ANY CONDITION IN ITEM 107 OR 112? IF YES, LIST TYPE OF OPERATION AND DATE.
NO

PHYSICIAN'S CERTIFICATION

114. I CERTIFY THAT TO THE BEST OF MY KNOWLEDGE DEATH OCCURRED AT THE HOUR, DATE AND PLACE STATED FROM THE CAUSES STATED.	115. SIGNATURE AND TITLE OF CERTIFIER	116. LICENSE NO	117. DATE MM/DD/CCYY
DECEDENT ATTENDED SINCE 02/02/1999	DECEDENT LAST SEEN ALIVE 02/07/1999	► N B Peleg MD	G53260	02/11/1999
		118. TYPE ATTENDING PHYSICIAN'S NAME, MAILING ADDRESS, ZIP N B PELEG, MD 12626 RIVERSIDE DR #404 NO HOLLYWOOD CA 91607		

CORONER'S USE ONLY

119. I CERTIFY THAT IN MY OPINION DEATH OCCURRED AT THE HOUR, DATE AND PLACE STATED FROM THE CAUSES STATED.	120. INJURY AT WORK □ YES □ NO	121. INJURY DATE MM DD CCYY	122. HOUR	123. PLACE OF INJURY
119. MANNER OF DEATH □ NATURAL □ SUICIDE □ HOMICIDE □ ACCIDENT □ PENDING INVESTIGATION □ COULD NOT BE DETERMINED	124. DESCRIBE HOW INJURY OCCURRED (EVENTS WHICH RESULTED IN INJURY)			

125. LOCATION (STREET AND NUMBER OR LOCATION AND CITY, ZIP)

126. SIGNATURE OF CORONER OR DEPUTY CORONER	127. DATE MM/DD/CCYY	128. TYPED NAME, TITLE OF CORONER OR DEPUTY CORONER
►		

STATE REGISTRAR

A	B	C	D	E	F	G	H	FAX AUTH #	CENSUS TRACT
								273/10365	

This is to certify that this document is a true copy of the official record filed with the Registrar-Recorder/County Clerk.

Conny B. McCormack

CONNY B. McCORMACK
Registrar-Recorder/County Clerk

This copy not valid unless prepared on engraved border displaying the Seal and Signature of the Registrar-Recorder/County Clerk.

APR 29 2002

19-217770

ANY ALTERATION OR ERASURE VOIDS THIS CERTIFICATE

STATE OF CALIFORNIA
CERTIFICATION OF VITAL RECORD

COUNTY OF LOS ANGELES • REGISTRAR-RECORDER/COUNTY CLERK

FILED AUG 13 1940 MAME B. BEATTY, Registrar of Vital Statistics   DISTRICT NO. 1906   REGISTRAR'S NO. 372   7620

1. FULL NAME TURPIN...Bernard

2. PLACE OF DEATH: (A) COUNTY Los Angeles
(B) CITY OR TOWN Santa Monica   2-06
IF OUTSIDE CITY OR TOWN LIMITS, WRITE RURAL
(C) NAME OF HOSPITAL OR INSTITUTION
Santa Monica Hospital   (1-1)
IF NOT IN HOSPITAL OR INSTITUTION, GIVE STREET NUMBER OR LOCATION
(D) LENGTH OF STAY: (SPECIFY WHETHER YEARS, MONTHS OR DAYS)
IN HOSPITAL OR INSTITUTION 10 hours
IN THIS COMMUNITY 10 hrs.   IN CALIFORNIA 33 yrs.
(E) IF FOREIGN BORN, HOW LONG IN THE U.S.A. _____ YEARS

3. USUAL RESIDENCE OF DECEASED:
(A) STATE California
(B) COUNTY Los Angeles
(C) CITY OR TOWN Beverly Hills   2-16
IF OUTSIDE CITY OR TOWN LIMITS, WRITE RURAL
(D) STREET No. 603 North Canon Dr.

20. DATE OF DEATH: MONTH July   DAY 1
YEAR 1940   HOUR 1   MINUTE 50 AM

3. (A) IF VETERAN, NAME OF WAR None
3. (B) SOCIAL SECURITY NO. 548-26-2770

4. SEX Male
5. COLOR OR RACE White
G. (A) SINGLE, MARRIED, WIDOWED OR DIVORCED Married

6. (B) NAME OF HUSBAND OR WIFE Babette Turpin
G. (C) AGE OF HUSBAND OR WIFE IF ALIVE 55 YEARS

21. MEDICAL CERTIFICATE
I HEREBY CERTIFY, THAT I ATTENDED THE DECEASED
FROM June - 28 - 19 40
TO July 1, 19 40
THAT I LAST SAW HIM ALIVE ON June - 30 - 19 40
AND THAT DEATH OCCURRED ON THE DATE AND HOUR STATED ABOVE.

22. CORONER'S CERTIFICATE
I HEREBY CERTIFY, THAT I HELD AN
AUTOPSY, INQUEST OR INVESTIGATION ON THE REMAINS OF THE DECEASED AND FIND FROM SUCH ACTION THAT DECEASED CAME TO _____ DEATH ON THE DATE AND HOUR STATED ABOVE.

7. BIRTHDATE OF DECEASED September 19, 1869
MONTH   DAY   YEAR

8. AGE 70 YRS 9 MOS 12 DAYS   IF LESS THAN ONE DAY OLD HRS MIN

9. BIRTHPLACE New Orleans, Louisiana

10. USUAL OCCUPATION Actor

11. INDUSTRY OR BUSINESS Motion Picture

FATHER
12. NAME Ernest Turpin
13. BIRTHPLACE New Orleans, Louisiana

MOTHER
14. MAIDEN NAME Sarah Buckley
15. BIRTHPLACE New Orleans, Louisiana

16. (A) INFORMANT Mrs Babette Turpin
(B) ADDRESS 603 North Canon Dr.

17. (A) Entombment   (B) DATE July 3, 1940
BURIAL, CREMATION OR REMOVAL
(C) PLACE Forest Lawn Cemetery

18. (A) EMBALMER'S SIGNATURE Charles L Mercer   LICENSE No. 2210
CUNNINGHAM & O'CONNOR
(B) FUNERAL DIRECTOR
ADDRESS 1031 South Grand Ave. Los Angeles
BY J. W. Cannon, Jr

19. (A) JUL 2 1940   (B) By Margery E.Nolan
DATE FILED   REGISTRAR'S SIGNATURE

DURATION

IMMEDIATE CAUSE OF DEATH
Acute heart failure
DUE TO Coronary Sclerosis   94a   2 y.
DUE TO Arteriosclerosis   83a   10 y.

OTHER CONDITIONS Hemiplegia   (4)   10 days
(INCLUDE PREGNANCY WITHIN THREE MONTHS OF DEATH)

MAJOR FINDINGS: OF OPERATIONS _____
DATE OF OPERATION _____
OF AUTOPSY None

PHYSICIAN
UNDERLINE THE CAUSE TO WHICH DEATH SHOULD BE CHARGED STATISTICALLY

23. IF DEATH WAS DUE TO EXTERNAL CAUSES, FILL IN THE FOLLOWING:
(A) ACCIDENT, SUICIDE, OR HOMICIDE? _____   (B) DATE OF INJURY _____
(C) WHERE DID INJURY OCCUR? _____ CITY OR TOWN COUNTY STATE
(D) DID INJURY OCCUR IN OR ABOUT HOME, ON FARM, IN INDUSTRIAL PLACE, OR IN PUBLIC PLACE? _____ SPECIFY TYPE OF PLACE _____ WHILE AT WORK? _____
(E) MEANS OF INJURY _____

J L POMEROY M D
24. CORONER'S PHYSICIAN'S SIGNATURE Rudolph Marx, M.D.
(SPECIFY WHICH) 1930 Wilshire Blvd
ADDRESS Los Angeles   DATE July-2-40

STATE OF CALIFORNIA
DEPARTMENT OF PUBLIC HEALTH

CERTIFICATE OF DEATH   (over)

U. S. DEPT. OF COMMERCE
BUREAU OF THE CENSUS

This is to certify that this document is a true copy of the official record filed with the Registrar-Recorder/County Clerk.

Conny B. McCormack

CONNY B. McCORMACK
Registrar-Recorder/County Clerk

NOV 2 8 2000
19-118076

This copy not valid unless prepared on engraved border displaying the Seal and Signature of the Registrar-Recorder/County Clerk.

MIDWEST BANK NOTE COMPANY   ANY ALTERATION OR ERASURE VOIDS THIS CERTIFICATE

STATE OF CALIFORNIA
CERTIFICATION OF VITAL RECORD

COUNTY OF LOS ANGELES • REGISTRAR-RECORDER/COUNTY CLERK

CERTIFICATE OF DEATH
STATE OF CALIFORNIA
USE BLACK INK ONLY

3931 9037905

			LOCAL REGISTRATION DISTRICT AND CERTIFICATE NUMBER
STATE FILE NUMBER			

DECEDENT PERSONAL DATA

1A. NAME OF DECEDENT—FIRST (GIVEN)	1B. MIDDLE	1C. LAST (FAMILY)	2A. DATE OF DEATH—MO, DAY, YR	2B. HOUR	3. SEX
HERVE	JEAN PIERRE	VILLECHAIZE	09/04/1993	0340	MALE

4. RACE	5. HISPANIC—SPECIFY	6. DATE OF BIRTH—MO, DAY, YR	7. AGE IN YEARS	IF UNDER 1 YEAR MONTHS/DAYS	IF UNDER 24 HOURS HOURS/MINUTES
CAUCASIAN	YES [ ] NO [X]	04/23/1943	50		

8. STATE OF BIRTH	9. CITIZEN OF WHAT COUNTRY	10A. FULL NAME OF FATHER	10B. STATE OF BIRTH	11A. FULL MAIDEN NAME OF MOTHER	11B. STATE OF BIRTH
FRANCE	FRANCE	ANDRE VILLECHAIZE	FRANCE	EVELINE RECCHIONI	ENGLAND

12. MILITARY SERVICE	13. SOCIAL SECURITY NO.	14. MARITAL STATUS	15. NAME OF SURVIVING SPOUSE (IF WIFE, ENTER MAIDEN NAME)
19___ TO 19___ [X] NONE	097-44-4252	DIVORCED	--

16A. USUAL OCCUPATION	16B. USUAL KIND OF BUSINESS OR INDUSTRY	16C. USUAL EMPLOYER	16D. YEARS IN OCCUPATION	17. EDUCATION—YEARS COMPLETED
ACTOR	ENTERTAINMENT	SELF	30	6

USUAL RESIDENCE

18A. RESIDENCE—STREET AND NUMBER OR LOCATION	18B. CITY	18C. ZIP CODE
11537 W KILLION ST.	NORTH HOLLYWOOD	91601

18D. COUNTY	18E. NUMBER OF YEARS IN THIS COUNTY	18F. STATE OR FOREIGN COUNTRY	20. NAME, RELATIONSHIP, MAILING ADDRESS AND ZIP CODE OF INFORMANT
LOS ANGELES	19	CALIFORNIA	KATHY SELF - FRIEND

PLACE OF DEATH

19A. PLACE OF DEATH	19B. IF HOSPITAL, SPECIFY ONE: ER/OP, OP, DOA	19C. COUNTY	126½ W. WALNUT AVENUE EL SEGUNDO, CA 90245
MEDICAL CENTER OF NO. HOLLYWOOD	ER/OP	LOS ANGELES	

19D. STREET ADDRESS—STREET AND NUMBER OR LOCATION	19E. CITY		
12629 RIVERSIDE DRIVE	NORTH HOLLYWOOD	TIME INTERVAL BETWEEN ONSET AND DEATH	22. WAS DEATH REPORTED TO CORONER REFERRAL NUMBER [X] YES 93-08264 [ ] NO

CAUSE OF DEATH

21. DEATH WAS CAUSED BY: (ENTER ONLY ONE CAUSE PER LINE FOR A, B, AND C)			
IMMEDIATE CAUSE (A) GUNSHOT WOUND OF CHEST	▶	RAPID	23. WAS BIOPSY PERFORMED [ ] YES [X] NO
DUE TO (B)	▶		24A. WAS AUTOPSY PERFORMED [ ] YES [X] NO
DUE TO (C)	▶		24B. WAS IT USED IN DETERMINING CAUSE OF DEATH [ ] YES [X] NO

25. OTHER SIGNIFICANT CONDITIONS CONTRIBUTING TO DEATH BUT NOT RELATED TO CAUSE GIVEN IN 21	26. WAS OPERATION PERFORMED FOR ANY CONDITION IN ITEM 21 OR 25. IF YES, LIST TYPE OF OPERATION AND DATE.
NONE	NO

PHYSICIAN'S CERTIFICATION

	27B. SIGNATURE AND DEGREE OR TITLE OF CERTIFIER	27C. CERTIFIER'S LICENSE NUMBER	27D. DATE SIGNED
CERTIFY THAT TO THE BEST OF MY KNOWLEDGE DEATH OCCURRED AT THE HOUR, DATE AND PLACE STATED FROM THE CAUSES STATED.	▶		
27A. DECEDENT ATTENDED SINCE MONTH, DAY, YEAR	DECEDENT LAST SEEN ALIVE MONTH, DAY, YEAR	27E. TYPE ATTENDING PHYSICIAN'S NAME AND ADDRESS	

CORONER'S USE ONLY

I CERTIFY THAT IN MY OPINION DEATH OCCURRED AT THE HOUR, DATE AND PLACE STATED FROM THE CAUSES STATED.	28A. SIGNATURE AND TITLE OF CORONER OR DEPUTY CORONER	28B. DATE SIGNED
	▶ DEPUTY CORONER	09-07-93

29. MANNER OF DEATH	30A. PLACE OF INJURY	30B. INJURY AT WORK	30C. DATE OF INJURY MONTH, DAY, YEAR	31. HOUR
SUICIDE	RESIDENCE/BACKYARD	YES [ ] NO [X]	09-04-93	0300

32. LOCATION (STREET AND NUMBER OR LOCATION AND CITY)	33. DESCRIBE HOW INJURY OCCURRED (EVENTS WHICH RESULTED IN INJURY)
11537 W. KILLION STREET, NO. HOLLYWOOD	SELF-INFLICTED GUNSHOT WOUND

FUNERAL DIRECTOR AND LOCAL REGISTRAR

34A. DISPOSITION(S)	34B. PLACE OF FINAL DISPOSITION—NAME AND ADDRESS	34C. DATE MO, DAY, YR.	35A. SIGNATURE OF EMBALMER	35B. LICENSE NO
CR/SEA	BURIAL AT SEA: OFF POINT FERMIN LOS ANGELES, CALIFORNIA	09/14/1993	NOT EMBALMED	--

36A. NAME OF FUNERAL DIRECTOR (OR PERSON ACTING AS SUCH)	36B. LICENSE NO	37. SIGNATURE OF LOCAL REGISTRAR	38. REGISTRATION DATE
THE NEPTUNE SOCIETY	F-1289	▶ Robert E. Blate	SEP 10 1993

STATE REGISTRAR

A	B	C	D	E	F	CENSUS TRACT

VS-11 (REV. 7-92)   MAKE NO ERASURES, WHITEOUTS, OR OTHER ALTERATIONS

This is to certify that this document is a true copy of the official record filed with the Registrar-Recorder/County Clerk.

Conny B. McCormack
CONNY B. McCORMACK
Registrar-Recorder/County Clerk

This copy not valid unless prepared on engraved border displaying the Seal and Signature of the Registrar-Recorder/County Clerk.

APR 10 2000
19-557836

MIDWEST BANK NOTE COMPANY   ANY ALTERATION OR ERASURE VOIDS THIS CERTIFICATE

CERTIFICATION OF VITAL RECORD

COUNTY OF LOS ANGELES • REGISTRAR-RECORDER/COUNTY CLERK

CERTIFICATE OF DEATH
STATE OF CALIFORNIA
USE BLACK INK ONLY

39219014510

LOCAL REGISTRATION DISTRICT AND CERTIFICATE NUMBER

STATE FILE NUMBER					
1A. NAME OF DECEDENT—FIRST (GIVEN)	1B. MIDDLE	1C. LAST (FAMILY)	2A. DATE OF DEATH—MO, DAY, YR	2B. HOUR	3. SEX
NANCY	WALKER	CRAIG	MARCH 25, 1992	1530	F

DECEDENT PERSONAL DATA

4. RACE	5. HISPANIC—SPECIFY	6. DATE OF BIRTH—MO, DAY, YR	7. AGE IN YEARS	IF UNDER 1 YEAR MONTHS DAYS	IF UNDER 24 HOURS HOURS MINUTES
CAU/AMERICAN	☐ YES ☒ NO	MAY 10, 1922	69		

8. STATE OF BIRTH	9. CITIZEN OF WHAT COUNTRY	10A. FULL NAME OF FATHER	10B. STATE OF BIRTH	11A. FULL MAIDEN NAME OF MOTHER	11B. STATE OF BIRTH
PA	USA	DEWEY BARTO	PA	ANNA MYRTLE LAWLER	PA

12. MILITARY SERVICE? 19___ TO 19___ ☒ NONE	13. SOCIAL SECURITY NO. 119-05-4039	14. MARITAL STATUS MARRIED	15. NAME OF SURVIVING SPOUSE (IF WIFE, ENTER MAIDEN NAME) DAVID CRAIG	

16A. USUAL OCCUPATION	16B. USUAL KIND OF BUSINESS OR INDUSTRY	16C. USUAL EMPLOYER	16D. YEARS IN OCCUPATION	17. EDUCATION—YEARS COMPLETED
ACTRESS	T.V. & MOVIES	SELF-EMPLOYED	56	12

USUAL RESIDENCE

18A. RESIDENCE—STREET AND NUMBER OR LOCATION 3702 EUREKA DRIVE		18B. CITY STUDIO CITY	18C. ZIP CODE 91604

18D. COUNTY LOS ANGELES	18E. NUMBER OF YEARS IN THIS COUNTY 22	18F. STATE OR FOREIGN COUNTRY CALIFORNIA	20. NAME, RELATIONSHIP, MAILING ADDRESS AND ZIP CODE OF INFORMANT DAVID CRAIG - HUSBAND 3702 EUREKA DRIVE STUDIO CITY, CA 91604

PLACE OF DEATH

19A. PLACE OF DEATH RESIDENCE	19B. IF HOSPITAL, SPECIFY ONE: IP, ER/OP, DOA	19C. COUNTY LOS ANGELES

19D. STREET ADDRESS—STREET AND NUMBER OR LOCATION 3702 EUREKA DRIVE	19E. CITY STUDIO CITY

CAUSE OF DEATH

21. DEATH WAS CAUSED BY: (ENTER ONLY ONE CAUSE PER LINE FOR A, B, AND C)		TIME INTERVAL BETWEEN ONSET AND DEATH
IMMEDIATE CAUSE (A) Adenocarcinoma both lungs ▶		10 years
DUE TO (B) ▶		
DUE TO (C) ▶		

22. WAS DEATH REPORTED TO CORONER? REFERRAL NUMBER ☐ YES ☒ NO
23. WAS BIOPSY PERFORMED? ☒ YES ☐ NO
24A. WAS AUTOPSY PERFORMED? ☐ YES ☒ NO
24B. WAS IT USED IN DETERMINING CAUSE OF DEATH? ☐ YES ☒ NO

25. OTHER SIGNIFICANT CONDITIONS CONTRIBUTING TO DEATH BUT NOT RELATED TO CAUSE GIVEN IN 21 Pulmonary emboli	26. WAS OPERATION PERFORMED FOR ANY CONDITION IN ITEM 21 OR 25? IF YES, LIST TYPE OF OPERATION AND DATE. Right upper lobectomy 1/5/92

PHYSICIAN'S CERTIFICATION

I CERTIFY THAT TO THE BEST OF MY KNOWLEDGE DEATH OCCURRED AT THE HOUR, DATE AND PLACE STATED FROM THE CAUSES STATED.		27B. MEDICAL AND DEGREE OR TITLE OF CERTIFIER ▶ Avrum Bluming M.D.	27C. CERTIFIER'S LICENSE NUMBER G15859	27D. DATE SIGNED 3/26/92

27A. DECEDENT ATTENDED SINCE MONTH, DAY, YEAR 4-6-82	DECEDENT LAST SEEN ALIVE MONTH, DAY, YEAR 3-23-92	27E. TYPE ATTENDING PHYSICIAN'S NAME AND ADDRESS AVRUM BLUMING M.D. 16311 VENTURA BLVD. #780, ENCINO, CA

CORONER'S USE ONLY

I CERTIFY THAT IN MY OPINION DEATH OCCURRED AT THE HOUR, DATE AND PLACE STATED FROM THE CAUSES STATED.	28A. SIGNATURE AND TITLE OF CORONER OR DEPUTY CORONER	28B. DATE SIGNED

29. MANNER OF DEATH—specify one: natural, accident, suicide, homicide, pending investigation or could not be determined	30A. PLACE OF INJURY	30B. INJURY AT WORK ☐ YES ☐ NO	30C. DATE OF INJURY MONTH, DAY, YEAR	31. HOUR

32. LOCATION (STREET AND NUMBER OR LOCATION AND CITY)	33. DESCRIBE HOW INJURY OCCURRED (EVENTS WHICH RESULTED IN INJURY)

FUNERAL DIRECTOR AND LOCAL REGISTRAR

34A. DISPOSITION(S) CR/RES.	34B. PLACE OF DISPOSITION, NAME AND ADDRESS 3702 EUREKA DRIVE STUDIO CITY, CALIFORNIA 91604	34C. DATE MO, DAY, YEAR 3-30-92	35A. SIGNATURE OF EMBALMER NOT EMBALMED	35B. LICENSE NUMBER NONE

36A. NAME OF FUNERAL DIRECTOR (OR PERSON ACTING AS SUCH) NEPTUNE SOCIETY	36B. LICENSE NO. F-1289	37. SIGNATURE OF LOCAL REGISTRAR ▶ Robert C. Gates	38. REGISTRATION DATE MAR 27 1992

STATE REGISTRAR

A.	B.	C.	D.	E.	F.	CENSUS TRACT

VS-11 (REV. 3-91) 1629   MAKE NO ERASURES, WHITEOUTS, OR OTHER ALTERATIONS   01-9-1-7005

This is to certify that this document is a true copy of the official record filed with the Registrar-Recorder/County Clerk.

Conny B. McCormack

CONNY B. McCORMACK
Registrar-Recorder/County Clerk

SEP 24 1996
19-379334

This copy not valid unless prepared on engraved border displaying the Seal and Signature of the Registrar-Recorder/County Clerk.

ANY ALTERATION OR ERASURE VOIDS THIS CERTIFICATE

CERTIFICATE OF DEATH
STATE OF CALIFORNIA
USE BLACK INK ONLY/NO ERASURES, WHITEOUTS OR ALTERATIONS
VS-11 (REV 1 00)

STATE FILE NUMBER | 3 200119 000141 | LOCAL REGISTRATION NUMBER

1. NAME OF DECEDENT—FIRST (GIVEN)	2. MIDDLE	3. LAST (FAMILY)
HERMAN	RAY	WALSTON

4. DATE OF BIRTH MM/DD/CCYY	5. AGE YRS	6. SEX	7. DATE OF DEATH MM/DD/CCYY	8. HOUR
11/02/1914	86	M	01/01/2001	1735

9. STATE OF BIRTH	10. SOCIAL SECURITY NO	11. MILITARY SERVICE	12. MARITAL STATUS	13. EDUCATION—YEARS COMPLETED
MISSISSIPPI	433-09-3688	NO	MARRIED	12

14. RACE	15. HISPANIC—SPECIFY	16. USUAL EMPLOYER
CAUCASIAN	NO	SELF EMPLOYED

17. OCCUPATION	18. KIND OF BUSINESS	19. YEARS IN OCCUPATION
ACTOR	ENTERTAINMENT	43

20. RESIDENCE: 423 SOUTH REXFORD DRIVE #106

21. CITY	22. COUNTY	23. ZIP CODE	24. YRS IN COUNTY	25. STATE
BEVERLY HILLS	LOS ANGELES	90212	39	CALIFORNIA

26. RUTH WALSTON, WIFE — 27. 423 SOUTH REXFORD DRIVE #106, BEVERLY HILLS, CA 9021

28. RUTH / 30. CALVERT
31. HARRY / 33. WALSTON / 34. TEXAS
35. MITTIE / 37. KIMBRELL / 38. ALABAMA

39. 01/11/2001 — 40. RES: RUTH WALSTON, 423 SOUTH REXFORD DRIVE #106, BEVERLY HILLS, CA 90212

41. CR/RES — 42. NOT EMBALMED
44. NEPTUNE SOCIETY BURBANK — 45. FD-1359 — 47. 01/11/2001

101. RESIDENCE — 104. LOS ANGELES
105. 423 SOUTH REXFORD DRIVE #106 — 106. BEVERLY HILLS

107. (A) CARDIORESPIRATORY ARREST — 30 MINS
(B) SYSTEMIC LUPUS ERYTHEMATOSUS — 10 YRS
112. NONE
113. NO

114. 02/02/1985 / 01/01/2001 — 115. Paul Rudnick MD — 116. G5502 — 117. 01/09/2001
118. P. RUDNICK, M.D. 8920 WILSHIRE BLVD, #635, BEVERLY HILLS, CA 90210

273/13679

STATE OF CALIFORNIA
CERTIFICATION OF VITAL RECORD

COUNTY OF LOS ANGELES
DEPARTMENT OF HEALTH SERVICES

CERTIFICATE OF DEATH
STATE OF CALIFORNIA
USE BLACK INK ONLY/NO ERASURES, WHITEOUTS OR ALTERATIONS
VS-11 (REV. 1/00)

3 2002 19 024698

STATE FILE NUMBER · LOCAL REGISTRATION NUMBER

DECEDENT PERSONAL DATA

1. NAME OF DECEDENT—FIRST (GIVEN)	2. MIDDLE	3. LAST (FAMILY)
Lew	R.	Wasserman

4. DATE OF BIRTH MM/DD/CCYY	5. AGE YRS.	IF UNDER 1 YEAR MONTHS DAYS	IF UNDER 24 HOURS HOURS MINUTES	6. SEX	7. DATE OF DEATH MM/DD/CCYY	8. HOUR
03/15/1913	89			M	06/03/2002	1115

9. STATE OF BIRTH	10. SOCIAL SECURITY NO.	11. MILITARY SERVICE	12. MARITAL STATUS	13. EDUCATION—YEARS COMPLETED
OH	283-10-0875	Yes X No UNK	Married	12

14. RACE	15. HISPANIC—SPECIFY	16. USUAL EMPLOYER
White	Yes X No	MCA

17. OCCUPATION	18. KIND OF BUSINESS	19. YEARS IN OCCUPATION
Chairman	Entertainment	67

USUAL RESIDENCE

20. RESIDENCE—(STREET AND NUMBER OR LOCATION)
911 North Foothill Road

21. CITY	22. COUNTY	23. ZIP CODE	24. YRS IN COUNTY	25. STATE OR FOREIGN COUNTRY
Beverly Hills	Los Angeles	90210	65	CA

INFORMANT

26. NAME, RELATIONSHIP	27. MAILING ADDRESS (STREET AND NUMBER OR RURAL ROUTE NUMBER, CITY OR TOWN, STATE, ZIP)
Lynne Wasserman, Daughter	514 Doheny Road, Beverly Hills, CA 90210

SPOUSE AND PARENT INFORMATION

28. NAME OF SURVIVING SPOUSE—FIRST	29. MIDDLE	30. LAST (MAIDEN NAME)
Edith	–	Beckerman

31. NAME OF FATHER—FIRST	32. MIDDLE	33. LAST	34. BIRTH STATE
Isaac	–	Wasserman	Russia

35. NAME OF MOTHER—FIRST	36. MIDDLE	37. LAST (MAIDEN)	38. BIRTH STATE
Minnie	–	Shenker	Russia

DISPOSITION(S)

39. DATE MM/DD/CCYY	40. PLACE OF FINAL DISPOSITION
06/03/2002	Hillside Memorial Park 6001 Centinela Av. Los Angeles, CA 90045

FUNERAL DIRECTOR AND LOCAL REGISTRAR

41. TYPE OF DISPOSITION(S)	42. SIGNATURE OF EMBALMER	43. LICENSE NO.
BU	▶ Not Embalmed	–

44. NAME OF FUNERAL DIRECTOR	45. LICENSE NO.	46. SIGNATURE OF LOCAL REGISTRAR	47. DATE MM/DD/CCYY
Hillside Mortuary	FD1358	▶ Thomas L. Garthwaite	06/03/2002

PLACE OF DEATH

101. PLACE OF DEATH	102. IF HOSPITAL, SPECIFY ONE:	103. FACILITY OTHER THAN HOSPITAL:	104. COUNTY
Residence	IP ER/OP DOA	CONV. HOSP. RES. CARE OTHER	Los Angeles

105. STREET ADDRESS—(STREET AND NUMBER OR LOCATION):	106. CITY
911 North Foothill Road	Beverly Hills

CAUSE OF DEATH

107. DEATH WAS CAUSED BY: (ENTER ONLY ONE CAUSE PER LINE FOR A, B, C, AND D)	TIME INTERVAL BETWEEN ONSET AND DEATH	108. DEATH REPORTED TO CORONER
IMMEDIATE CAUSE (A) Cardiorespiratory Arrest	10 Mins.	Yes X No / REFERRAL NUMBER
DUE TO (B) Cerebrovascular Accident	10 Days	109. BIOPSY PERFORMED Yes X No
DUE TO (C) Essential Hypertension	5 Years	110. AUTOPSY PERFORMED Yes X No
DUE TO (D)		111. USED IN DETERMINING CAUSE Yes No

112. OTHER SIGNIFICANT CONDITIONS CONTRIBUTING TO DEATH BUT NOT RELATED TO CAUSE GIVEN IN 107
Idiopathic Subaortic Stenosis

113. WAS OPERATION PERFORMED FOR ANY CONDITION IN ITEM 107 OR 112? IF YES, LIST TYPE OF OPERATION AND DATE.
No

PHYSICIAN'S CERTIFICATION

114. I CERTIFY THAT TO THE BEST OF MY KNOWLEDGE DEATH OCCURRED AT THE HOUR, DATE AND PLACE STATED FROM THE CAUSES STATED.	115. SIGNATURE AND TITLE OF CERTIFIER	116. LICENSE NO.	117. DATE MM/DD/CCYY
DECEDENT ATTENDED SINCE MM/DD/CCYY 07/01/1962 — DECEDENT LAST SEEN ALIVE MM/DD/CCYY 06/03/2002	▶ S. R. Kennamer MD	G1805	06/03/2002

118. TYPE ATTENDING PHYSICIAN'S NAME, MAILING ADDRESS, ZIP
S. Rex Kennamer, MD 436 N. Roxbury Dr. Beverly Hills, CA 90210

CORONER'S USE ONLY

I CERTIFY THAT IN MY OPINION DEATH OCCURRED AT THE HOUR, DATE AND PLACE STATED FROM THE CAUSES STATED.	120. INJURY AT WORK	121. INJURY DATE MM/DD/CCYY	122. HOUR	123. PLACE OF INJURY
119. MANNER OF DEATH	Yes No			

119. MANNER OF DEATH	124. DESCRIBE HOW INJURY OCCURRED (EVENTS WHICH RESULTED IN INJURY)
NATURAL SUICIDE HOMICIDE ACCIDENT PENDING INVESTIGATION COULD NOT BE DETERMINED	

125. LOCATION (STREET AND NUMBER OR LOCATION AND CITY, ZIP)

126. SIGNATURE OF CORONER OR DEPUTY CORONER	127. DATE MM/DD/CCYY	128. TYPED NAME, TITLE OF CORONER OR DEPUTY CORONER
▶		090557527

STATE REGISTRAR

A	B	C	D	E	F	G	H	FAX AUTH. #	CENSUS TRACT

This is a true certified copy of the record filed in the County of Los Angeles Department of Health Services if it bears the Registrar's signature in purple ink.

Thomas L. Garthwaite
Director of Health Services and Registrar

DATE ISSUED
234
SEP 04 2002

This copy not valid unless prepared on engraved border displaying seal and signature of Registrar.

ANY ALTERATION OR ERASURE VOIDS THIS CERTIFICATE

STATE OF CALIFORNIA
CERTIFICATION OF VITAL RECORD

COUNTY OF LOS ANGELES • REGISTRAR-RECORDER/COUNTY CLERK

CERTIFICATE OF DEATH
STATE OF CALIFORNIA

0190-058650

STATE FILE NUMBER				LOCAL REGISTRATION DISTRICT AND CERTIFICATE NUMBER	

1A. NAME OF DECEDENT—FIRST	1B. MIDDLE	1C. LAST	2A. DATE OF DEATH (MONTH, DAY, YEAR)	2B. HOUR
Dennis	Carl	Wilson	December 28, 1983	1748

3. SEX	4. RACE/ETHNICITY	5. SPANISH/HISPANIC	6. DATE OF BIRTH	7. AGE	IF UNDER 1 YEAR	IF UNDER 24 HOURS
male	white	NO	December 4, 1944	39 YEARS	MONTHS / DAYS	HOURS / MINUTES

DECEDENT PERSONAL DATA

8. BIRTHPLACE OF DECEDENT (STATE OR FOREIGN COUNTRY)	9. NAME AND BIRTHPLACE OF FATHER		10. BIRTH NAME AND BIRTHPLACE OF MOTHER
California	Murry G. Wilson	Kansas	Audree Nora Korthoff Minnesota

11. CITIZEN OF WHAT COUNTRY	12. SOCIAL SECURITY NUMBER	13. MARITAL STATUS	14. NAME OF SURVIVING SPOUSE (IF WIFE, ENTER BIRTH NAME)
U.S.A.	562-60-0767	married	Shawn Love

15. PRIMARY OCCUPATION	16. NUMBER OF YEARS THIS OCCUPATION	17. EMPLOYER (IF SELF-EMPLOYED, SO STATE)	18. KIND OF INDUSTRY OR BUSINESS
musician	22	self employed	entertainment

USUAL RESIDENCE

19A. USUAL RESIDENCE—STREET ADDRESS (STREET AND NUMBER OR LOCATION)	19B.	19C. CITY OR TOWN
9744 Wilshire		Beverly Hills

19D. COUNTY	19E. STATE	20. NAME AND ADDRESS OF INFORMANT—RELATIONSHIP
Los Angeles	California	Shawn Love Wilson (wife) 9744 Wilshire Beverly Hills, California

AMENDED
1 OF 2

PLACE OF DEATH

21A. PLACE OF DEATH	21B. COUNTY
Ocean, off pier	Los Angeles

21C. STREET ADDRESS (STREET AND NUMBER OR LOCATION)	21D. CITY OR TOWN
13929 Marquesas Way; Basin C-1100	Marina del Rey

CAUSE OF DEATH

22. DEATH WAS CAUSED BY: IMMEDIATE CAUSE (ENTER ONLY ONE CAUSE PER LINE FOR A, B, AND C)		24. WAS DEATH REPORTED TO CORONER?
(A) DROWNING	APPROXIMATE INTERVAL BETWEEN ONSET AND DEATH	83-16219
CONDITIONS, IF ANY, WHICH GAVE RISE TO THE IMMEDIATE CAUSE, STATING THE UNDERLYING CAUSE LAST. DUE TO, OR AS A CONSEQUENCE OF (B)		25. WAS BIOPSY PERFORMED? NO
DUE TO, OR AS A CONSEQUENCE OF (C)		26. WAS AUTOPSY PERFORMED? YES

23. OTHER CONDITIONS CONTRIBUTING BUT NOT RELATED TO THE IMMEDIATE CAUSE OF DEATH	27. WAS OPERATION PERFORMED FOR ANY CONDITION IN ITEMS 22 OR 23? TYPE OF OPERATION	DATE
		NO

PHYSICIAN'S CERTIFICATION

28A. I CERTIFY THAT DEATH OCCURRED AT THE HOUR, DATE AND PLACE STATED FROM THE CAUSES STATED. I ATTENDED DECEDENT SINCE / I LAST SAW DECEDENT ALIVE (ENTER MO. DA. YR.)	28B. PHYSICIAN—SIGNATURE AND DEGREE OR TITLE	28C. DATE SIGNED	28D. PHYSICIAN'S LICENSE NUMBER
	28E. TYPE PHYSICIAN'S NAME AND ADDRESS		

INJURY INFORMATION

29. SPECIFY ACCIDENT, SUICIDE, ETC.	30. PLACE OF INJURY	31. INJURY AT WORK	32A. DATE OF INJURY—MONTH DAY YEAR	32B. HOUR
Accident	Ocean Pier	No	Dec. 28, 1983	1745

33. LOCATION (STREET AND NUMBER OR LOCATION AND CITY OR TOWN)	34. DESCRIBE HOW INJURY OCCURRED (EVENTS WHICH RESULTED IN INJURY)
13929 Marquesas Way, Marina del Rey	Swimming

CORONER'S USE ONLY

2D

35A. I CERTIFY THAT DEATH OCCURRED AT THE HOUR, DATE AND PLACE STATED FROM THE CAUSES STATED. AS REQUIRED BY LAW I HAVE HELD AN INVESTIGATION	35B. CORONER—SIGNATURE AND DEGREE OR TITLE	35C. DATE SIGNED
	Deputy Coroner	12-30-83

36. DISPOSITION	37. DATE—MONTH DAY YEAR	38. NAME AND ADDRESS OF CEMETERY OR CREMATORY	39. EMBALMER'S LICENSE NUMBER AND SIGNATURE
entombment	January 3, 1983	Inglewood Cemetery 720 E. Florence Avenue Inglewood, California	not embalmed

40A. NAME OF FUNERAL DIRECTOR (OR PERSON ACTING AS SUCH)	40B. LICENSE NO.	41. LOCAL REGISTRAR—SIGNATURE	42. DATE ACCEPTED BY LOCAL REGISTRAR
Inglewood Cemetery Mortuary	1101	mp	4 1984

STATE REGISTRAR	A.	B.	C.	D.	E.	F.

This is to certify that this document is a true copy of the official record filed with the Registrar-Recorder/County Clerk.

Conny B. McCormack
CONNY B. McCORMACK
Registrar-Recorder/County Clerk

This copy not valid unless prepared on engraved border displaying the Seal and Signature of the Registrar-Recorder/County Clerk.

MAY 1 3 2003

190940718

MIDWEST BANK NOTE COMPANY   ANY ALTERATION OR ERASURE VOIDS THIS CERTIFICATE

CERTIFICATE OF DEATH
STATE OF CALIFORNIA
USE BLACK INK ONLY/NO ERASURES, WHITEOUTS OR ALTERATIONS
VS-11 (REV. 7/97)

STATE FILE NUMBER		LOCAL REGISTRATION NUMBER

DECEDENT PERSONAL DATA

1. NAME OF DECEDENT—FIRST (GIVEN)	2. MIDDLE	3. LAST (FAMILY)
Clerow	Flip	Wilson

4. DATE OF BIRTH MM/DD/CCYY	5. AGE YRS.	IF UNDER 1 YEAR MONTHS / DAYS	IF UNDER 24 HOURS HOURS / MINUTES	6. SEX	7. DATE OF DEATH MM/DD/CCYY	8. HOUR
12/08/1933	64			M	11/25/1998	1822

9. STATE OF BIRTH	10. SOCIAL SECURITY NO.	11. MILITARY SERVICE	12. MARITAL STATUS	13. EDUCATION—YEARS COMPLETED
New Jersey	149-24-0227	X YES ☐ NO ☐ UNK	Divorced	8

14. RACE	15. HISPANIC—SPECIFY		16. USUAL EMPLOYER
Black	☐ YES	X NO	Self

17. OCCUPATION	18. KIND OF BUSINESS	19. YEARS IN OCCUPATION
Entertainer	Television Entertainment	40

USUAL RESIDENCE

20. RESIDENCE—(STREET AND NUMBER OR LOCATION)
21970 Pacific Coast Highway

21. CITY	22. COUNTY	23. ZIP CODE	24. YRS IN COUNTY	25. STATE OR FOREIGN COUNTRY
Malibu	Los Angeles	90265	30	California

INFORMANT

26. NAME, RELATIONSHIP	27. MAILING ADDRESS (STREET AND NUMBER OR RURAL ROUTE NUMBER, CITY OR TOWN, STATE, ZIP)
Martell Michelle Zacharias-Daughter	250 Trevethan, Santa Cruz, California 95062

SPOUSE AND PARENT INFORMATION

28. NAME OF SURVIVING SPOUSE—FIRST	29. MIDDLE	30. LAST (MAIDEN NAME)
-	-	-

31. NAME OF FATHER—FIRST	32. MIDDLE	33. LAST	34. BIRTH STATE
Clerow	-	Wilson	New Jerse

35. NAME OF MOTHER—FIRST	36. MIDDLE	37. LAST (MAIDEN)	38. BIRTH STATE
Cornelia	Elizabeth	Bullock	USA-UNK

DISPOSITION(S)

39. DATE MM/DD/CCYY	40. PLACE OF FINAL DISPOSITION
12/09/1998	Residence, Martell M. Zacharias- DTR 250 Trevethan, Santa Cruz, CA 95062

FUNERAL DIRECTOR AND LOCAL REGISTRAR

41. TYPE OF DISPOSITION(S)	42. SIGNATURE OF EMBALMER	43. LICENSE NO.
CR/RES	▶ Not Embalmed	-

44. NAME OF FUNERAL DIRECTOR	45. LICENSE NO.	46. SIGNATURE OF LOCAL REGISTRAR	47. DATE MM/DD/CCYY
Pierce Bros. Westwood Village	FD 951	▶	12/08/1998 SN

PLACE OF DEATH

101. PLACE OF DEATH	102. IF HOSPITAL, SPECIFY ONE:	103. FACILITY OTHER THAN HOSPITAL:	104. COUNTY
Residence	☐ IP ☐ ER/OP ☐ DOA	☐ CONV. HOSP. ☐ RES. CARE ☐ OTHER	Los Angeles

105. STREET ADDRESS—(STREET AND NUMBER OR LOCATION)	106. CITY
21970 Pacific Coast Highway	Malibu

CAUSE OF DEATH

107. DEATH WAS CAUSED BY: (ENTER ONLY ONE CAUSE PER LINE FOR A, B, C, AND D)	TIME INTERVAL BETWEEN ONSET AND DEATH	108. DEATH REPORTED TO CORONER
IMMEDIATE CAUSE (A) Cariopulmonary Arrest	1 Day	☐ YES X NO REFERRAL NUMBER
DUE TO (B) Metastatic Biliary Cancer	4 Mos.	109. BIOPSY PERFORMED ☐ YES X NO
DUE TO (C)		110. AUTOPSY PERFORMED ☐ YES X NO
DUE TO (D)		111. USED IN DETERMINING CAUSE ☐ YES ☐ NO

112. OTHER SIGNIFICANT CONDITIONS CONTRIBUTING TO DEATH BUT NOT RELATED TO CAUSE GIVEN IN 107
None

113. WAS OPERATION PERFORMED FOR ANY CONDITION IN ITEM 107 OR 112? IF YES, LIST TYPE OF OPERATION AND DATE.
No

PHYSICIAN'S CERTIFICATION

114. I CERTIFY THAT TO THE BEST OF MY KNOWLEDGE DEATH OCCURRED AT THE HOUR, DATE AND PLACE STATED FROM THE CAUSES STATED.		115. SIGNATURE AND TITLE OF CERTIFIER	116. LICENSE NO.	117. DATE MM/DD/CCYY
DECEDENT ATTENDED SINCE MM/DD/CCYY 09/16/1998	DECEDENT LAST SEEN ALIVE MM/DD/CCYY 11/12/1998	▶ Daniel Lieber	G 03605	12/04/1998

118. TYPE ATTENDING PHYSICIAN'S NAME, MAILING ADDRESS, ZIP
Daniel Lieber, MD, 100 UCLA Medical Plaza, Ste 550, Los Angeles CA 90024

CORONER'S USE ONLY

I CERTIFY THAT IN MY OPINION DEATH OCCURRED AT THE HOUR, DATE AND PLACE STATED FROM THE CAUSES STATED. 119. MANNER OF DEATH	120. INJURY AT WORK ☐ YES ☐ NO	121. INJURY DATE MM/DD/CCYY	122. HOUR	123. PLACE OF INJURY
☐ NATURAL ☐ SUICIDE ☐ HOMICIDE ☐ ACCIDENT ☐ PENDING INVESTIGATION ☐ COULD NOT BE DETERMINED	124. DESCRIBE HOW INJURY OCCURRED (EVENTS WHICH RESULTED IN INJURY)			

125. LOCATION (STREET AND NUMBER OR LOCATION AND CITY, ZIP)

126. SIGNATURE OF CORONER OR DEPUTY CORONER	127. DATE MM/DD/CCYY	128. TYPED NAME, TITLE OF CORONER OR DEPUTY CORONER
▶		

STATE REGISTRAR

A	B	C	D	E	F	G	H	FAX AUTH. #	CENSUS TRACT
								849-5773	09

STATE OF CALIFORNIA
CERTIFICATION OF VITAL RECORD

COUNTY OF LOS ANGELES
DEPARTMENT OF HEALTH SERVICES

CERTIFICATE OF DEATH
STATE OF CALIFORNIA
USE BLACK INK ONLY/NO ERASURES, WHITEOUTS OR ALTERATIONS
VS-11 (REV. 1/00)

STATE FILE NUMBER | LOCAL REGISTRATION NUMBER

DECEDENT PERSONAL DATA

1. NAME OF DECEDENT—FIRST (GIVEN)	2. MIDDLE	3. LAST (FAMILY)
Emily	Marie	Bertelsen - Hupp

4. DATE OF BIRTH MM/DD/CCYY	5. AGE YRS.	IF UNDER 1 YEAR MONTHS DAYS	IF UNDER 24 HOURS HOURS MINUTES	6. SEX	7. DATE OF DEATH MM/DD/CCYY	8. HOUR
12/11/1919	80			F	12/10/2000	1345

9. STATE OF BIRTH	10. SOCIAL SECURITY NO.	11. MILITARY SERVICE	12. MARITAL STATUS	13. EDUCATION—YEARS COMPLETED
UT	529-16-8798	YES [X] NO UNK	Married	14

14. RACE	15. HISPANIC—SPECIFY	16. USUAL EMPLOYER
White	YES [X] NO	Self Employed

17. OCCUPATION	18. KIND OF BUSINESS	19. YEARS IN OCCUPATION
Actress	Movie Industry	45

USUAL RESIDENCE

20. RESIDENCE—(STREET AND NUMBER OR LOCATION)
9501 Cherokee Lane

21. CITY	22. COUNTY	23. ZIP CODE	24. YRS IN COUNTY	25. STATE OR FOREIGN COUNTRY
Beverly Hills	Los Angeles	90210	60	CA

INFORMANT

26. NAME, RELATIONSHIP		27. MAILING ADDRESS (STREET AND NUMBER OR RURAL ROUTE NUMBER, CITY OR TOWN, STATE, ZIP)
Richard Hupp	Son	23801 Haynes St. West Hills, CA 91307

SPOUSE AND PARENT INFORMATION

28. NAME OF SURVIVING SPOUSE—FIRST	29. MIDDLE	30. LAST (MAIDEN NAME)
Jack	Rodney	Hupp

31. NAME OF FATHER—FIRST	32. MIDDLE	33. LAST	34. BIRTH STATE
Lane	Joseph	Bertelsen	UT

35. NAME OF MOTHER—FIRST	36. MIDDLE	37. LAST (MAIDEN)	38. BIRTH STATE
Etta	Marie	Long	UT

DISPOSITION(S)

39. DATE MM/DD/CCYY	40. PLACE OF FINAL DISPOSITION
12/14/2000	RES: Jack Hupp. 9501 Cherokee Lane, Beverly Hills, CA 91307

FUNERAL DIRECTOR AND LOCAL REGISTRAR

41. TYPE OF DISPOSITION(S)	42. SIGNATURE OF EMBALMER	43. LICENSE NO.
CR/RES	Not Embalmed	-

44. NAME OF FUNERAL DIRECTOR	45. LICENSE NO.	46. SIGNATURE OF LOCAL REGISTRAR	47. DATE MM/DD/CCYY
Crawford Mortuary	FD1228	Mark Simmon	12/14/2000

PLACE OF DEATH

101. PLACE OF DEATH	102. IF HOSPITAL, SPECIFY ONE:	103. FACILITY OTHER THAN HOSPITAL	104. COUNTY
Residence	IP ER/OP DOA	CONV. HOSP. RES. CARE OTHER	Los Angeles

105. STREET ADDRESS—(STREET AND NUMBER OR LOCATION)	106. CITY
9501 Cherokee Lane.	Beverly Hills

CAUSE OF DEATH

107. DEATH WAS CAUSED BY: (ENTER ONLY ONE CAUSE PER LINE FOR A, B, C, AND D)

			TIME INTERVAL BETWEEN ONSET AND DEATH	108. DEATH REPORTED TO CORONER
IMMEDIATE CAUSE	(A)	Cardiopulmonary Arrest	mins	[X] YES [X] NO REFERRAL NUMBER 2000-58905
DUE TO	(B)	Arteriosclerotic Vascular Disease	yrs	109. BIOPSY PERFORMED YES [X] NO
DUE TO	(C)			110. AUTOPSY PERFORMED YES [X] NO
DUE TO	(D)			111. USED IN DETERMINING CAUSE YES [X] NO

112. OTHER SIGNIFICANT CONDITIONS CONTRIBUTING TO DEATH BUT NOT RELATED TO CAUSE GIVEN IN 107
Chronic Obstructive Pulmonary Disease

113. WAS OPERATION PERFORMED FOR ANY CONDITION IN ITEM 107 OR 112? IF YES, LIST TYPE OF OPERATION AND DATE.
No

PHYSICIAN'S CERTIFICATION

114. I CERTIFY THAT TO THE BEST OF MY KNOWLEDGE DEATH OCCURRED AT THE HOUR, DATE AND PLACE STATED FROM THE CAUSES STATED. DECEDENT ATTENDED SINCE MM/DD/CCYY	DECEDENT LAST SEEN ALIVE MM/DD/CCYY	115. SIGNATURE AND TITLE OF CERTIFIER	116. LICENSE NO.	117. DATE MM/DD/CCYY
03/18/1991	11/17/2000	John Corday M.D.	G 31116	12/13/2000

118. TYPE ATTENDING PHYSICIAN'S NAME, MAILING ADDRESS, ZIP
Stephen R. Corday, MD. 8635 W. 3rd. St. Los Angeles, CA 90048

CORONER'S USE ONLY

I CERTIFY THAT IN MY OPINION DEATH OCCURRED AT THE HOUR, DATE AND PLACE STATED FROM THE CAUSES STATED.	120. INJURY AT WORK	121. INJURY DATE MM/DD/CCYY	122. HOUR	123. PLACE OF INJURY
119. MANNER OF DEATH	YES NO			

119. MANNER OF DEATH: NATURAL, SUICIDE, HOMICIDE, ACCIDENT, PENDING INVESTIGATION, COULD NOT BE DETERMINED

124. DESCRIBE HOW INJURY OCCURRED (EVENTS WHICH RESULTED IN INJURY)

125. LOCATION (STREET AND NUMBER OR LOCATION AND CITY, ZIP)

126. SIGNATURE OF CORONER OR DEPUTY CORONER	127. DATE MM/DD/CCYY	128. TYPED NAME, TITLE OF CORONER OR DEPUTY CORONER

090392115

STATE REGISTRAR

A	B	C	D	E	F	G	H	FAX AUTH. #	CENSUS TRACT
								197/43	

This is a true certified copy of the record filed in the County of Los Angeles Department of Health Services if it bears the Registrar's signature in purple ink.

DATE ISSUED OCT 27 2000

Director of Health Services and Registrar

This copy not valid unless prepared on engraved border displaying seal and signature of Registrar.

ANY ALTERATION OR ERASURE VOIDS THIS CERTIFICATE

BIOGRAPHICAL
NOTES

Claude Akins (Professional Name); Claude A. Akins (Name on Death Certificate); Marion is often listed as his birth middle name, but his wife of over 40 years didn't use it on the Death Certificate; **p. 4**—This prolific actor appeared in 100 films and more than 180 television programs. *The Night Stalker* and *Battle for the Planet of the Apes* were two of his movies.

Jack Albertson (Professional Name, Birth Name and Name on the Death Certificate); **p. 5**—Albertson is one of the few to garner the Triple Crown for actors: an Oscar and Tony for *The Subject Was Roses*, and an Emmy for *Chico and the Man*. His look has been described as "nondescript."

Morey Amsterdam (Professional Name, Birth Name and Name on the Death Certificate); the Human Joke Machine (Nickname); **p. 6**—His career started when he was 14 in Vaudeville. His comedic wit kept him busy in radio in the 1930s and 1940s. He is best remembered for his character Buddy Sorrell on *The Dick Van Dyke Show*. His movie credits were for small roles.

Royce Applegate (Professional Name); Roy Applegate (another name used in some credits); Royce Dwayne Applegate (Birth Name and Name on the Death Certificate); **pp. 7–8**—Applegate's movie and television series kept him active for 30 years. *Seabiscuit* and *Gods and Generals* were his last two movies. He died in a fire at his home.

Jim Backus (Professional Name); James Gilmore Backus (Birth Name and Name on the Death Certificate); **p. 9**—Radio, Broadway, movie, television and cartoons Backus did it all. Perhaps his most memorable movie role was in *Rebel Without a Cause*. Thurston Howell III on *Gilligan's Island* and the cartoon character Mr. Magoo are small-screen favorites.

Red Barry (Professional Name); Donald Barry DeAcosta (Birth Name); Donald Michael Barry (Name on the Death Certificate); **p. 10**—The weekly movie serial *Adventures of Red Ryder* was the high point in his career. He continued to appear in western movies, but in smaller and smaller parts. He took his own life at home.

Billy Barty (Professional Name); William John Bertanzetti (may be his birth name, but his Death Certificate lists his father's surname as Barty); William John Barty (Name listed on the Death Certificate); **p. 11**—Film credits include *Wedded Blisters*, *Nothing Sacred* (where he bit Frederic March on the leg), and *W. C. Fields and Me*. He also made appearances on television in *Mr. Lucky*, *Get Smart*, *Peter Gunn*, and many others.

Ralph Bellamy (Professional Name); Ralph Rexford Bellamy (Birth Name and Name on the Death Certificate); **p. 12**—*The Awful Truth* in 1937 earned him an Oscar nomination. He often played "the other man" in strong supporting roles. *Sunrise at Campobello*, in which he portrayed President Franklin Delano Roosevelt, was a reprise of a role he had played on Broadway.

William Bendix (Professional Name, Birth Name and Name on the Death Certificate); **p. 13**—Bendix was often cast in supporting roles. He was nominated for an Academy Award for *Wake Island*. *The Glass Key* and *Lifeboat* were two of his films. He brought the character Chester A. Riley from radio to the small screen in *The Life of Riley*. "What a revoltin' development this is!" was his signature exclamation.

Paul Bern (Professional Name, Birth Name and Name on the Death Certificate); **p. 14**—Bern's career in motion pictures was as a writer, producer and director. Perhaps his biggest claim to fame was being the husband of Jean Harlow. His death was ruled a suicide by the coroner's office, but as with other Hollywood suicides, the suspicion of murder surrounded it.

Ted Bessell (Professional Name); Howard Weston Bessell, Jr. (Birth Name and Name listed on the Death Certificate); **p. 15**—Bessell started his career in soap operas. His role as Don Hollinger on *That Girl* was his big break. After several short-lived television comedies, he turned to direction and production.

Carl Betz (Professional Name); Carl Lawrence Betz (Birth Name and Name on the Death Certificate); **p. 16**—He started in radio, then went on to work on Broadway and in movies. He finally found his home on the small screen. He was on the *Donna Reed Show* for eight years. *Judd for the Defense* was his second series.

Madge Blake (Professional Name); Madge C. Blake (Name on Death Certificate); **p. 17**—Blake began her career in motion pictures in *Adam's Rib* in an uncredited role. Her well-known characters on television were Flora MacMichaels on the *Real McCoys*, Margaret Mondello on *Leave It to Beaver*, and Aunt Harriet Cooper on *Batman*.

Mel Blanc (Professional Name); Melvin Jerome Blank (Birth Name); Melvin Jerome Blanc (Name on the Death Certificate); **p. 18**—A voice specialist for 63 years, he had worked for Warner Bros. and Looney Tunes/Merrie Melodies. He was the voice of Bugs Bunny, Tweety, Speedy Gonzales, Porky Pig, and Daffy Duck, just to name a few. He credited being a member of the young men's Masonic organization DeMolay as the foundation for his success in life.

Dan Blocker (Professional Name); Dan Davis Blocker (Birth Name and Name on the Death Certificate); **p. 19**—Blocker got his start in the mid 1950s. His character on the television series *Bonanza* (rerun title *Ponderosa*) was Eric "Hoss" Cartwright. This series ran from 1959 to 1972.

Humphrey Bogart (Professional Name); Humphrey De Forest Bogart (Birth Name and Name on the Death Certificate); **p. 20**—He was a stage actor until his movie debut in *Broadway's Like That* in 1930. Two of the films that made him a star were *High Sierra* and *The Maltese Falcon*. "Boggy" received his Academy Award for *The African Queen*, *Casablanca* and *The Caine Mutiny*. Both earned him Oscar nominations. Many consider him the most popular male star of Hollywood's Golden Age.

Margaret Booth (Professional Name); Margaret Elizabeth Booth (Birth Name and Name on the Death Certificate); **p. 21**—Miss Booth started at Louis B. Mayer studio in 1921 as an assistant film editor. *Why Men Leave Home* was her first coeditor credit. Her final film was *Murder by Death* in 1976. She received an honorary Oscar in 1977 for the accumulation of work in her field. She died at age 104.

William Boyd (Professional Name); William Lawrence Boyd (Birth Name and Name on the Death Certificate); **p. 22**—He started his acting career in 1920. After his appearance in *The Volga Boatman* he became a matinee idol. In 1935, he was offered the lead in *Hopalong Cassidy*. He made a total of 54 "Hoppies" for the original producer and another 12 for his own production company. He was one of the few actors who purchased all the rights to his pictures. His marketing and licensing skills made him a multimillionaire.

William Boyett (Professional Name); Harry William Boyett (Birth Name and Name on the Death Certificate); **p. 23**—Boyett was a veteran stage, screen and television character. He was one of the last surviving members of the Jack Webb stock company. Boyett was seen in *Dragnet* during the 1950s and 1960s. Webb cast him as "Mac" MacDonald on *Adam-12* from 1968 to 1975

Marlon Brando (Professional Name and Name on the Death Certificate); Marlon Brando, Jr. (Birth Name); **p. 24**—The "greatest actor of all time" is a title that many consider well deserved. Whether it was *A Streetcar Named Desire*, *The Godfather*, or *Last Tango in Paris*, he brought "truth," a sense of reality to his roles.

Lloyd Bridges (Professional Name); Lloyd Vernet Bridges, Jr. (Birth Name and Name on the Death Certificate); **p. 25**—A contract player for Columbia, Bridges made B westerns, serials, and comedy shorts. *Sea Hunt* in 1958 made him a small screen star. The films *Airplane* and *Hot Shots* garnered him a new generation of fans.

Charles Bronson (Professional Name); Charles Dennis Buchinsky (Birth Name); Charles Dennis Bronson (Name on the Death Certificate); **p. 26**—*The Magnificent Seven*, *The Great Escape*, and *The Dirty Dozen* were three of his movies from the 1960s. The five *Death Wish* films had audiences flocking to see him.

Foster Brooks (Professional Name); Foster M. Brooks (Name on Death Certificate); **p. 27**—Brooks was the opening act for Perry Como at the new Hilton Hotel in Las Vegas. His guest appearance on *The Tonight Show Starring Johnny Carson* in 1962 was his national debut.

Though he gained fame portraying "The Loveable Lush," he was a teetotaler.

Rory Calhoun (Professional Name and Name on the Death Certificate); **p. 28**—Large-screen credits include *River of No Return*, *How to Marry a Millionaire* and *With a Song in My Heart*. On the small screen he starred in *The Texan*. He also appeared for five years on *Capitol*, a daytime drama.

Macdonald Carey (Professional Name); Edward Macdonald Carey (Name on the Death Certificate); **p. 29**—Carey made his film debut in *Dr. Broadway*. He had roles in a number of westerns, including *Comanche Territory*, *Copper Canyon* and *The Great Missouri Raid*. Tom Horton was his character on the daytime drama *Days of Our Lives* for more than 25 years. It was his rich, comforting voice that was heard at the beginning of each program: "...so are the days of our lives."

Johnny Carson (Professional Name); John William Carson (Birth Name and Name on the Death Certificate); The King of Late Night (Nickname); **p. 30**—For 30 years he was the host of *The Tonight Show Starring Johnny Carson*. In 1958, during his hosting of the daytime television program, *Who Do You Trust*, Ed McMahon became his longtime sidekick. Carson is not credited with any appearances on the silver screen.

Nell Carter (Professional Name); Nell Ruth Hardy (Birth Name); Nell Ruth Carter (Name on the Death Certificate); **p. 31**—This certificate includes a medical amendment that is not shown. The cause of death is probable atherosclerotic heart disease. Carter received both a Tony and an Emmy for her role in *Ain't Misbehavin'* and two Emmy nominations for her role on the television sitcom *Gimme a Break!*

Ray Charles (Professional Name); Ray Charles Robinson (Birth Name and Name on the Death Certificate); **p. 32**—Music was his entree to motion pictures and television. He played R & B, gospel, and country and western, all with raw, soulful delivery. *Ballad in Blue* and *The Blues Brothers* were two of his films.

Lana Clarkson (Professional Name); Lana Jean Clarkson (Birth Name and Name on the Death Certificate); **pp. 33–34**—*Fast Times at Ridgemont High* and *Barbarian Queen II: The Empress Strikes Back* were two of her early films. She was found shot to death at the home of Phil Spector in Alhambra, California.

Rosemary Clooney (Professional Name, Birth Name and Name on the Death Certificate); **p. 35**—She sang from an early age. At 13 she made her radio singing debut. With reluctance she recorded "Come On 'a' My House" in 1951. It became a huge success, selling over a million copies. "Hey There," "Tenderly," "This Ole House" and "Half As Much" were other top hits.

James Coburn (Professional Name); James Harrison Coburn III (Birth Name and Name on the Death Certificate); **p. 36**—*The Great Escape*, *Our Man Flint* and *The Magnificent Seven* were three of his early movies. He received an Oscar for his role in the 1977 film *Affliction*.

Imogene Coca (Professional Name); Imogene Coca Donovan (Name on the Death Certificate); **p. 37**—By age 13 Miss Coca was a seasoned Vaudeville trouper. Her biggest hit was perhaps *Your Show of Shows*, a television variety and comedy show. She was also well received as Aunt Edna in *National Lampoon's Vacation*.

Iron Eyes Cody (Professional Name); Oscar Iron Eyes Cody (Name on the Death Certificate); **p. 38**—He was considered the first American Indian to be cast as an American Indian. (There is a real question as to whether he was an American Indian or not.) He began regular work in motion pictures in the early 1930s. The "Keep America Beautiful" advertisement that portrayed an American Indian who sheds a tear for a blighted America was a perfect role for him.

Nat "King" Cole (Professional Name); Nathaniel Adams Coles (Birth Name); Nathaniel Adams Cole (Name on the Death Certificate); **p. 39**—Cole earned 28 Gold Records. He recorded such hits as "Unforgettable," "Ramblin Rose" and "Too Young." He cancelled his one-season television show, *The Nat King Cole Show*, when, by the end of the year, no national sponsors could be found.

Ray Collins (Professional Name); Ray Bidwell Collins (Name on the Death Certificate); **p. 40**—Collins started working in stock companies as a child. He was a charter member of Orson Welles' Mercury Theater group. Welles cast him in *Citizen Kane*, *The Magnificent Ambersons* and *Touch of Evil*. For seven years he portrayed Lt. Tragg on *Perry Mason* on the small screen.

Ray Combs (Professional Name); Raymond Neil Combs, Jr. (Birth Name and Name on the Death Certificate); **pp. 41–42**—Combs was the host of the TV series *Family Feud* from 1988 to 1994. His other game show, *Family Challenge*, was on cable television. He took his life by hanging himself while in the hospital.

Jackie Coogan (Professional Name and "also known as" on the Death Certificate); John Leslie Coogan, Jr.

(Birth Name and Name on the Death Certificate); **p. 43**—His career blossomed from 1919 until 1931. His two series on the small screen were *McKeever & the Colonel* and *The Addams Family*.

Ellen Corby (Professional Name and Name on the Death Certificate); Ellen Hansen (Birth Name); **p. 44**—A small part in *It's a Wonderful Life* was her first film role. She garnered a Best Supporting Actress nomination for her portrayal of Aunt Trina in *I Remember Mama* in 1948. The small screen brought her the greatest recognition as Esther "Grandma" Walton from 1972 to 1979. She received three consecutive Emmy awards: 1973, 1974, and 1975.

Joseph Cotten (Professional Name); Joseph C. Cotten (Name on the Death Certificate); **p. 45**—He had been a friend of Orson Welles since the mid–1930s. His distinctive voice served him well in radio with Welles' Mercury Players. *Citizen Kane*, *Shadow of a Doubt* and *The Third Man* were a few of his films.

Wally Cox (Professional Name); Wallace Maynard Cox (Birth Name and Name on the Death Certificate); **p. 46**—The initial Death Certificate lists "deferred" on the cause-of-death line. The medical amendment, which is not shown, lists the cause of death as acute cardiac insufficiency; coronary sclerosis, severe; and atherosclerotic heart disease. Cox was a lifelong friend of Marlon Brando, and his cremains were supposedly dispersed along with Brando's in Death Valley. *Mr. Peepers* and the voice of *Underdog* were his television roles. He was the upper-left square on *Hollywood Squares* from 1966 to 1973.

Richard Crenna (Professional Name); Richard Donald Crenna (Birth Name and Name on the Death Certificate); **p. 47**—Best known for his work on the small screen. His series include *Our Miss Brooks*, *The Real McCoys*, and *Slattery's People*. On the big screen he portrayed Sylvester Stallone's commanding office in *First Blood* and the *Rambo* sequels that followed.

Hume Cronyn (Professional Name and Name on the Death Certificate); **p. 48**—Cronyn was multi talented. He could write as well as perform. Two of his films with his wife, Jessica Tandy, were *Cocoon* and *Batteries Not Included*. He received an Emmy for his role in *Broadway Bound*.

Robert Cummings (Professional Name); Robert O. Cummings (Name on the Death Certificate); **p. 49**—He made light comedies in the 1930s and 1940s. In the 1950s he switched to television. His two series were *The Bob Cummings Show* and *My Living Doll*.

Rodney Dangerfield (Professional Name and Name on the Death Certificate); **p. 50**—An affidavit of correction, which is not shown, changes the embalmer from Randy M. Ziegler to Stephen R Cosgrove. Dangerfield started his career as a stand-up comedian. He had the unique honor of having made Ed Sullivan laugh when he appeared on Ed's *Toast of the Town* television series. His "I get no respect!" brought him in touch with the average guy. His movies included *Caddyshack*, *Easy Money*, and *Back to School*.

Selma Diamond (Professional Name and Name on the Death Certificate); **p. 51**—Nominated for an Emmy in 1956 as a writer on *Caesar's Hour* and again in 1985 as Outstanding Supporting Actress for her role as Selma Hacker on *Night Court*. In 1971 she made five appearances on *The Tonight Show Starring Johnny Carson* within eight months.

Troy Donahue (Professional Name); Merle Johnson Jr. (Birth Name); Merle Johnson (Name on the Death Certificate); **pp. 52–53**—There is also an affidavit to amend the record showing the addition of Troy Donahue as an "also known as" name. His look was the epitome of a surfer boy and teenage heartthrob. *A Summer Place* and *Susan Slade* were two of his early films. The television series *Surfside 6* showcased his blond good looks.

David Doyle (Professional Name); David Fitzgerald Doyle (Birth Name and Name on the Death Certificate); **p. 54**—An affidavit to amend a record, not shown here, changes some spellings on his last residence street name. *Will Success Spoil Rock Hunter?* was his first Broadway break in 1956. His move to Hollywood brought an assortment of character roles. On the small screen, his portrayal of Bosley on *Charlie's Angels* is perhaps his most remembered.

Marie Dressler (Professional Name and Name on the Death Certificate); **p. 55**—A stage actress in the 19th century, she moved into silent films. *Anna Christie* was her first film with sound. She received an Academy Award for her character in *Min and Bill*.

Irene Dunne (Professional Name); Irene Marie Dunn (Birth Name); Irene Dunne Griffin (Name on the Death Certificate); First Lady of Hollywood (Nickname); **p. 56**—She received five Academy Award nominations. The first was for her role in *Cimmarron*. *I Remember Mama* was the film many thought should have earned her the Oscar. *It Grows on Trees* was her last major movie.

Buddy Ebsen (Professional Name); Christian L. Ebsen, Jr. (Name on the Death Certificate); **p. 57**—Ebsen turned down Louis B. Mayer's offer to be a contract player. This caused him to be blacklisted in Hollywood. His role on the small screen in *Davy Crockett* opened the door to *The Beverly Hillbillies* and finally *Barnaby Jones*. He attributed his success to DeMolay, a young men's Masonic organization. He was inducted into the DeMolay Hall of Fame in 1996.

Hope Emerson (Professional Name, Birth Name and Name on the Death Certificate); **p. 58**—Miss Emerson worked consistently from her first movie in 1948, *Kobb's Corner*, through *The Dennis O'Keefe Show* in 1959. In the Craig Stevens' series *Peter Gun* she portrayed his confidante, "Mother," during the 1958 season. She was also the voice of Elsie the Cow in the Borden commercials.

Norman Fell (Professional Name); Norman Noah Fell (Birth Name and Name on the Death Certificate); **p. 59**—Fell had that every-man look that allowed him to be in movies and television without typecasting. He was in four television series, but his best-remembered role was Mr. Roper on *Three's Company* for which he received a Golden Globe for Best Supporting Actor.

Verna Felton (Professional Name); Verna Felton Millar (Name on the Death Certificate); **p. 60**—She was a popular actress on radio and television. Felton was the voice of a number of Disney characters: Fairy Godmother in *Cinderella*, Queen of Hearts in *Alice in Woderland*, Winnifred in *Junglebook*, Flora in *Sleeping Beauty*, and the gossipy elephant in *Dumbo*. She made several appearances on *I Love Lucy*, including that of Mrs. Porter in *Lucy Takes a Maid*.

Ella Fitzgerald (Professional Name); Ella Jane Fitzgerald (Birth Name and Name on the Death Certificate); **p. 61**—She had more than 200 albums to her credit, with 13 Grammy awards. Fitzgerald won Best Female Vocalist awards three consecutive years.

F. Scott Fitzgerald (Professional Name and Name on the Death Certificate); **p. 62**—*This Side of Paradise*, *The Great Gatsby*, and *Tender Is the Night* were but three of his novels. He was a prolific writer of both novels and short stories. There should be an affidavit of correction to change the burial location to Saint Mary's Cemetery, Rockville, Montgomery County, Maryland, but no affidavit was filed.

Susan Fleming (Professional Name and Birth Name); Susan Alva Fleming-Marx (Name on the Death Certificate); **p. 63**—While her career was short-lived, Miss Fleming appeared in over 20 movies. *God's Country* was her final film, made in 1937. She was married to Harpo Marx. In her later years, she was a politician and activist in Palm Springs, California.

Redd Foxx (Professional Name and Name on the Death Certificate); **p. 64**—There are two amendments that are not shown. One is a medical amendment that changes the time of death to military time. An affidavit to amend a record changes the date of burial from 10/12/1991 to 10/15/1991. Foxx was a "blue" comedian (meaning that he was considered too raunchy and sexual for some audiences). His first television series was *Sanford and Son* from 1972 to 1977. He was a champion for African American writers and producers. His film credits include *Harlem Nights* on the big screen and *Ghost of a Chance* on the small screen.

James Franciscus (Professional Name); James Grove Franciscus (Birth Name); James G. Franciscus (Name on the Death Certificate); **p. 65**—His television series include *Naked City*, *The Investigators*, *Mr. Novak* and *Longstreet*. When he became disenchanted with the roles offered to him, he formed his own production company, Omnibus Productions.

John Frankenheimer (Professional Name); John Michael Frankenheimer (Name on the Death Certificate); **p. 66**—Frankenheimer much preferred to direct live television rather than films. He is known for his innovative camera angles. *Birdman of Alcatraz*, *The Manchurian Candidate*, and *Seven Days in May* were three of his movies. *Studio One* and *Playhouse 90* were two of the 140 live television dramas that he directed.

Allen Funt (Professional Name); Allen Albert Funt (Name on the Death Certificate); **p. 67**—He developed the *Candid Camera* series that used a hidden camera to create comedy programming.

Eva Gabor (Professional Name and Name on the Death Certificate); **p. 68**—She made many appearances on television before her series, *Green Acres*. She was also a regular on *Match Game* from 1974 to 1976.

Magda Gabor (Professional Name and Name on the Death Certificate); **p. 69**—In career activity, the least prolific of the three Gabor sisters. She was on the premier program for *The Colgate Comedy Hour*. Her sole movie credit was *Mai la'nyok* in 1937.

Christopher George (Professional Name); Christopher John George (Birth Name and Name on the Death Certificate); **p. 70**—His swarthy good looks attest to his Greek extraction. His TV series was *Rat Patrol* from 1966 to 1968. His films include *El Dorado*, *Project X*, *The Train Robbers*, and *Midway*.

Trevor Goddard (Professional Name); Trevor John Goddard (Birth Name and Name on the Death Certificate); **pp. 71–72**—He appeared in several segments of *Silk Stalkings*, as well as a number of other series. He was a regular on *Jag* from 1998 to 2001. His films include *Pirates of the Caribbean: The Curse of the Black Pearl*, *Hollywood Vampyr*, and *Legion*.

Alexander Godunov (Professional Name); Alexander Boris Godunov (Name on the Death Certificate); **p. 73**—Not shown is an affidavit to amend a record that divides his cremains. One-half went to the residence of Alle Khanlashzici in Beverly Hills, Ca. Godunov attended the Riga State Ballet School beginning at age nine. He danced with both the Moscow Classical Ballet and the Bolshoi. His film credits include *Witness* and *Die Hard*.

Stewart Granger (Professional Name); James Stewart Granger (Name on the Death Certificate); **p. 74**—He started his film career in the United Kingdom. Stardom brought him to Hollywood. His films include *Beau Brummel* and *The Prisoner of Zenda*. *The Circle* was his Broadway debut.

Teresa Graves (Professional Name and Name on the Death Certificate); **pp. 75–76**—Movies included *That Man Bolt*, *Black Eye*, and *Vampira*. On the small screen she was regularly seen on *Rowan and Martin's Laugh-In* and *Get Christie Love*. She died following a fire at her home.

Lorne Greene (Professional Name); Lorne Hyman Greene (Birth Name and Name on the Death Certificate); **p. 77**—Began his professional career on Canadian radio. His distinctive, authoritative voice soon brought him to prominence. His small-screen successes came in *Bonanza* and *Battlestar Galactica*.

Anne Gwynne (Professional Name); Marguerite Gwynne Trice (Birth Name); Marguerite Gilford (Name on the Death Certificate); **p. 78**—The strikingly beautiful young woman spent the bulk of her career making B pictures with western, space, and horror themes. *The Black Cat*, *Men of Texas*, and *Dick Tracy Meets Gruesome* were three of her films. She was also one of the top five pin-up girls during World War II.

Buddy Hackett (Professional Name and Name on the Death Certificate); **p. 79**—By his own admission he was a "saloon comic." He enjoyed the repartee offered by a live audience as opposed to movies or television. His films include *The Music Man*, the *Herbie* series of films, and *Fireman Save My Child*.

Joan Hackett (Professional Name and Name on the Death Certificate); **p. 80**—One of her biggest claims to fame was simply that she was great to work with. She was also known for her perfection in her roles. *Harnessing the Sun*, *Dead of Night*, and *Will Penny* were a few of her films.

Jack Haley (Professional Name); John Joseph Haley (Birth Name and Name on the Death Certificate, along with an addition of an "also known as," adding Jack Haley); **p. 81**—Best remembered as the Tin Man in *The Wizard of Oz*. He reprised two of his Broadway productions when they came to the big screen. Those were *Follow Thru* and *Higher and Higher*.

Gabby Hayes (Professional Name); George Francis Hayes (Birth Name and Name on the Death Certificate); **p. 82**—His niche in the movie industry was as a sidekick. He made the Hopalong Cassidy films between 1936 and 1939. In the 1940s he played western sidekicks to John Wayne, Roy Rogers, and Randolph Scott. In real life, he was the antithesis of the characters he portrayed.

Susan Hayward (Professional Name); Edythe Marrener Chalkley (Name on the Death Certificate); **p. 83**—The nationwide search for the lead in *Gone with the Wind* brought Hayward to Hollywood, although she was not cast in the film. She received four Academy Award nominations before finally receiving one for *I Want to Live*. *My Foolish Heart*, *I'll Cry Tomorrow*, and *Farmer's Daughter* were the others for which she was nominated.

Eileen Heckart (Professional Name); Anna Eileen Heckart (Birth Name); Eileen Yankee (Name on the Death Certificate); **p. 84**—Her first love was the theater. Her films include *Miracle in the Rain*, *The Bad Seed*, and *Bus Stop*. She received an Academy Award for her role in *Butterflies Are Free*. In the television miniseries *Backstairs at the White House*, she portrayed Eleanor Roosevelt.

Paul Henreid (Professional Name and Name on the Death Certificate); **p. 85**—He began his film career in Vienna. *Casablanca* and *Now Voyager* were two of his motion picture appearances. On the small screen, he directed over 80 episodes for *Alfred Hitchcock Presents*.

Katharine Hepburn (Professional Name); Katharine Houghton Hepburn (Birth Name); Katharine H. Hepburn (Name on the Death Certificate); First Lady of Cinema (Nickname); **p. 86**—Her excellence in films garnered her 12 Academy Award nominations, of her four Oscars, *Morning Glory* was her first Academy Award and *On Golden Pond* was her last.

Bob Hope (Professional Name); Leslie Towns Hope (Birth Name and Name on the Death Certificate); **pp. 87–88**—Also shown is an affidavit to amend the record, but the affidavit is in error. It should correct only the spelling of Hope's middle name to Townes, but it also incorrectly changes his first name to Lester. Hope's *Road to ...* films co-starred Dorothy Lamour and Bing Crosby. He received five honorary Oscars for entertaining United States troops all over the world.

Jill Ireland (Professional Name); Jill Ireland Bronson (Name on the Death Certificate); **p. 89**—Her films included *Death Wish II*, *The Mechanic*, and *The Karate Killers*. She appeared in a number of television series, including five episodes of *The Man from U.N.C.L.E.*

Graham Jarvis (Professional Name); Graham Powley Jarvis (Name on the Death Certificate); **p. 90**—A character actor, Jarvis made appearances on any number of series. He made 17 episodes of *7th Heaven*. Probably he is best known for his role on *Mary Hartman, Mary Hartman*.

Carolyn Jones (Professional Name); Carolyn Sue Jones (Name on the Death Certificate); **p. 91**—She received an Academy Award nomination for her role in *The Bachelor Party*, but she is probably best remembered as Morticia, the matriarch on *The Addams Family*.

Danny Kaye (Professional Name and Name on the Death Certificate); **p. 92**—Coming up through his work in the Catskills, he honed his comic skills in the borscht belt. His strength was reciting tongue twisters in song and monologue. *The Secret Life of Walter Mitty*, *Hans Christian Andersen*, *The Court Jester*, and *Knock on Wood* were four of his films.

Gene Kelly (Professional Name); Eugene Curran Kelly (Birth Name and Name on the Death Certificate); **p. 93**—Dancer and actor Kelly had a strong, masculine, athletic dance style. *An American in Paris*, *For Me and My Gal*, *Words and Music*, and *Singin' in the Rain* were some of his pictures.

Mabel King (Professional Name); Mabel W. King (Name on the Death Certificate); **p. 94**—She was in *The Wiz I & II* and *Scrooged*. She was also on the TV series *What's Happening* and made three appearances on *Fantasy Island*.

Ernie Kovacs (Professional Name); Ernest E. Kovacs (Name on the Death Certificate); **p. 95**—Cinema did not serve Kovacs as well as the small screen. His series on television was a combination of his off-beat humor and pioneering special effects. He made three small-screen series titled with variations on his name.

Walter Lantz (Professional Name, Birth Name and Name on the Death Certificate); **p. 96**—Lantz was a successful, prolific, and durable animator. He introduced such cartoon characters as Oswald the Lucky Rabbit, Andy Panda, Chilly Willy, and his star, Woody Woodpecker. He received an honorary Oscar in 1979.

Wesley Lau (Professional Name); Wesley Albert Lau (Name on the Death Certificate); **p. 97**—As Lt. Anderson, he played on *Perry Mason* from 1961–1965. He also was on several episodes of *Mission Impossible* and *The Virginian*.

Peggy Lee (Professional Name and Name on the Death Certificate); Norma Deloris Egstrom (Birth Name); **p. 98**—An exceptional singer and talented songwriter, Miss Lee co-wrote 22 songs for her autobiographical Broadway musical *Peg*. Lee recorded countless classics, including "Fever," "Lover," "Golden Earrings," and "Is That All There Is?"

Janet Leigh (Professional Name); Janet Leigh Brandt (Name on the Death Certificate); **p. 99**—Movies included *Little Women*, *Angels in the Outfield*, *Scaramouche*, *Houdini*, and the *Black Shield of Falworth*. Her 45 seconds in *Psycho* are still what most people remember of her career.

Jack Lemmon (Professional Name); John Uhler Lemmon III (Birth Name and Name on the Death Certificate); **p. 100**—While he made what he did look easy, he left a 40-year career of quality work. *Mister Roberts*, *Some Like It Hot*, *The Apartment*, and *Days of Wine and Roses* are just a few of his many films.

Cleavon Little (Professional Name); Cleavon Jake Little (Birth Name and Name on the Death Certificate); **p. 101**—The western spoof *Blazing Saddles* was the apex of his career. His training came from Juilliard and the American Academy of Dramatic Art. He also did two television sitcoms, *Temperature's Rising* and *Bagdad Café*.

Julie London (Professional Name); Julie Peck (Birth Name); Julie London Troup (Name on the Death Certificate); **p. 102**—London was a singer who acted. She had over 40 albums released. The small screen series *Emergency* gave her an opportunity to work with her husband, Bobby Troup, and her ex-husband, Jack Webb.

Richard Long (Professional Name); Richard Mc-Cord Long (Birth Name and Name on the Death Certificate); **p. 103**—*Tomorrow Is Forever* was his first film. He also was in the *Ma and Pa Kettle* film series. The small screen showcased him in *The Big Valley* and *Nanny and the Professor*.

Rita Lynn (Professional Name and Name on the Death Certificate); **p. 104**—While she made a few movies, her work on the small screen was where she shone. She appeared on *Perry Mason* five times and *The Detectives Starring Robert Taylor* four times.

Meredith MacRae (Professional Name and Birth Name); Meredith Macrae Neal (Name on the Death Certificate); **pp. 105–106**—Also shown is an affidavit to amend a record, changing a misspelling, Macrea to Macrae. Her biggest series was *Petticoat Junction* from 1966 to 1970. Her first television series was *My Three Sons*, 1963–65.

Nancy Marchand (Professional Name); Nancy M. Sparer AKA Nancy Marchand (Name on the Death Certificate); **p. 107**—A stage actress by training, on the small screen she garnered four Emmys for her role as Mrs. Pynchon on *Lou Grant*. Her last role was on *The Sopranos*, for which she received a Golden Globe.

Helen Martin (Professional Name); Helen Dorothy Martin (Name on the Death Certificate); **p. 108**—Her role in *Native Son* made her one of the first African Americans to appear on Broadway. *That's My Mama*, *Benson*, *Good Times*, and *Full House* were her television series. Perhaps best remembered in *227*, as Pearl Shay. She had just finished filming *Something to Sing About* shortly before her death.

Mary Martin (Professional Name); Mary Virginia Martin (Birth Name); Mary Virginia Martin Halliday (Name on the Death Certificate); **p. 109**—She never had the success on the big screen that she did on Broadway, where she starred in *South Pacific*, *Peter Pan*, *The Sound of Music*, and *I Do, I Do*.

Chico Marx (Professional Name); Leo Chico Marx (Name on the Death Certificate); **p. 110**—One of the three "famous" Marx Brothers, as well as their business manager. Some of the brothers' films are *The Coconuts*, *Animal Crackers*, and *Monkey Business*.

Groucho Marx (Professional Name); Julius Henry Marx (Birth Name); Julius H. Marx (Name on the Death Certificate); **p. 111**—The best known of the Marx Brothers because of his long running program, *You Bet Your Life*. This was first on radio, then moved to television. With his brothers, he made comic films, including *A Day at the Races* and *A Night at the Opera*.

Harpo Marx (Professional Name); Arthur Harpo Marx (Name on the Death Certificate); **p. 112**—A member of the Marx Brothers comedy team, he played a mute on stage and was a self-taught harpist. In his routines, he would use pantomime and frequently a bike horn to communicate. On an *I Love Lucy* episode, he recreated the mirror scene from *Duck Soup*.

Zeppo Marx (Professional Name); Herbert Marx (Birth Name); Herbert AKA Zeppo Z. Marx (Name on the Death Certificate); **p. 113**—He made only five of the films with the Marx Brothers before leaving to start a talent management company. He is known for his keen sense of humor, but normally played the straight man to his brothers. *Horse Feathers* was the movie that showcased his fine tenor voice.

Doug McClure (Professional Name); Douglas Osborne McClure (Birth Name and Name on the Death Certificate); **p. 114**—This seemingly ageless, blond, leading man made more than 500 film and television appearances. Often times he is best remembered for his roles in *The Virginian* and *The Man from Shiloh* on the small screen and *Backtrack* on the big screen.

Burgess Meredith (Professional Named); Oliver Burgess Meredith (Birth Name and Name on the Death Certificate); **p. 115**—Meredith was multitalented; best known as an actor, he wrote and produced *Diary of a Chambermaid*. *The Story of G.I. Joe*, *Mine Own Executioner*, and *On Our Merry Way* were among the films where he did memorable performances. His career was sidetracked by the McCarthy hearings when he was branded an unfriendly witness. He played the Penguin on the television series *Batman*.

Ann Miller (Professional Name and Name on the Death Certificate); **p. 116**—*On the Town* and *Kiss Me Kate* were two of her films, which showcased her dancing skills. She was on Broadway in *Sugar Babies* for nine years.

Carmen Miranda (Professional Name); Maria do Carmo Miranda Da Cunha (Birth Name); Maria do Carmo Miranda Da Cunha Sebastian AKA Carmen Miranda (Name on the Death Certificate); **p. 117**—Born in Portugal, but became a star in Brazil. Her first film was *Down Argentine Way*. Her trademarks were her fruit adorned hat and broad smile. Following her death, she was returned to her adopted home of Brazil for burial.

Montie Montana (Professional Name); Owen Harlan Mickel (Name on the Death Certificate); **p. 118**—Not shown is an affidavit to amend a record that adds the name Montie Montana to the certificate. While he made a number of western movies, he is probably best remembered for riding a pinto horse in the Tournament of Roses parade for more than 60 years. The Secret Service was not amused when he roped President Eisenhower during the inaugural parade in 1953.

Edward Mulhare (Professional Name and Name on the Death Certificate); **p. 119**—Rex Harrison should have been his best friend. Two excellent opportunities came to him through Mr. Harrison. On Broadway, Mulhare succeeded Harrison in *My Fair Lady* when the latter joined the London company. Harrison also starred in *The Ghost and Mrs. Muir* on the silver screen; two decades later, Mulhare took this role to the small screen.

George Nader (Professional Name); George Garfield Nader, Jr. (Birth Name and Name on the Death Certificate); **p. 120**—His athletic build and good looks weren't enough to catapult him over the rest of the men in Universal's stable. His career in the states was probably sabotaged by Universal in order to save the career of Rock Hudson, who was more bankable. *Away All Boats* was probably his best movie role in the U.S. In West Germany, he made a string of films portraying Jerry Cotton.

Alan Napier (Professional Name and Name on the Death Certificate); **p. 121**—Napier had a long and varied career. From his first film, *Caste*, in 1930, he played a variety of characters. He was reluctant to play the butler on the *Batman* television series until he learned how much they would pay him. Friends told him this role could make him the most famous butler in history.

Jeannette Nolan (Professional Name and Birth Name); Jeannette McIntire (Name on the Death Certificate); **p. 122**—In 1948 she appeared with Orson Welles in *Macbeth*. This was her film debut and considered by many to be her best rule. She made over 300 television appearances including *Perry Mason*, *I Spy*, and *MacGyver*

and was a regular on *The Virginian* and *The Richard Boone Show*.

Alice Nunn (Professional Name); Alice E. Nunn (Name on the Death Certificate); **p. 123**—Her first roles were on *Camp Runamuck* and *Petticoat Junction* on the small screen. Big-screen credits include *Pee-Wee's Big Adventure*, *Mommie Dearest*, *Who's That Girl* and *Three O'Clock High*.

Donald O'Connor (Professional Name); Donald David O'Connor (Name on the Death Certificate); **p. 124**—He was considered an entertainer for 77 of his 78 years. To use his own words, "I was born and raised to entertain other people." His span of roles ran from *Singin' in the Rain* to the six *Francis the Talking Mule* films.

Hugh O'Connor (Professional Name); Hugh Edward O'Connor (Name on the Death Certificate); **pp. 125–126**—Also shown is an affidavit to amend a record, which changed the location of his cremated remains from his wife's residence to the Church of St. Susanna in Rome, Italy. Son of Carroll and Nancy O'Connor, he appeared in his father's television series, *In the Heat of the Night*. His big-screen film was *Words Upon the Window Pane*.

LaWanda Page (Professional Name); Alberta Peal (Named on the Death Certificate); **p. 127**—Not shown is an affidavit to amend a record that adds the name LaWanda Page to the certificate. Page began her career in black theaters and nightclubs as a standup comedienne. Redd Foxx gave her her biggest break when he cast her as his sister-in-law on *Sanford and Son*.

Bert Parks (Professional Name and Name on the Death Certificate); **p. 128**—Host of the Miss America Pageant from 1954 to 1979. In most of his television appearances he played himself. Even in his large-screen appearances, his role was that of host or emcee. *Circus*, *Hold That Note*, and *Double or Nothing* are three of his films.

Dennis Patrick (Professional Name); Dennis Patrick Harrison (Birth Name and Name on the Death Certificate); **pp. 129–130**—He was the first vampire on television in an episode of *Stage 13*. He is credited with over 1800 guest roles on the small screen. *Gift of Tears*, for which he won an Emmy, and *Masthead* for the large screen were two of his directing projects.

Gregory Peck (Professional Name and Name on the Death Certificate); **p. 131**—*Captain Horatio Hornblower R.N.*, *Moby Dick*, and *Roman Holiday* were films he did because they interested him. It was in *To Kill a Mockingbird* that he garnered his Academy Award for Best Actor.

Cole Porter (Professional Name and Name on the Death Certificate); **p. 132**—A prolific songwriter who became a recluse after the amputation of his right leg. "You Do Something to Me," "My Heart Belongs to Daddy," and "From This Moment On" are just three of the many standards he gave to the American songbook.

Robert Preston (Professional Name and Name on the Death Certificate); Robert Preston Meservey (Birth Name); **p. 133**—He will forever be the Music Man, the role he took from Broadway to the silver screen. Other films to his credit include *The Dark at the Top of the Stairs*, *All the Way Home*, and *Victor/Victoria*.

Vincent Price (Professional Name); Vincent Leonard Price, Jr. (Birth Name); Vincent Leonard Price (Name on the Death Certificate); **p. 134**—Known for his roles in horror films, he made six adaptations from Poe's works. *The Pit and the Pendulum*, *The Raven*, *The Masque of the Red Death*, and *Tomb of Ligeia* were four of them.

Juliet Prowse (Professional Name); Juliet Anne Prowse (Birth Name and Name on the Death Certificate); **p. 135**—Probably the only entertainer made famous by Soviet Premier Khrushchev. He was invited to watch rehearsal for *Can-Can*. The next day, he denounced the dance as immoral. Prowse's photograph was the one that accompanied the story. She did better on the stage and the nightclub circuit than in her few films.

George Raft (Professional Name and Name on the Death Certificate); **p. 136**—Some have said there was only one thing holding him back from being a star: he couldn't act. That small problem didn't stop him from making scores of films. *The Glass Key*, *Souls at Sea*, *You and Me*, *Night After Night*, and *Sextette* were but a few.

Ronald Reagan (Professional Name); Ronald Wilson Reagan (Birth Name and Name on the Death Certificate); The Great Communicator (Nicknames); **p. 137**—Before entering politics, culminating with his election as the 40th president of the United States, he had a successful entertainment career. Some of his films include *Kings Row*, *Desperate Journey*, and *This Is the Army*. He was also the host of *Death Valley Days* on the small screen.

Donna Reed (Professional Name); Donna Mullenger Asmus (Name on the Death Certificate); **p. 138**—There is an affidavit to amend a record, not shown, which changes the maiden name of her mother from Violet Shives to Hazel Shives. As a contract player for MGM she didn't seem to be put to good use, but *It's a Wonderful Life* and *From Here to Eternity* were two of her best films. She starred on *The Donna Reed Show* on the small screen from 1958 to 1966.

Tommy Rettig (Professional Name); Thomas N. Rettig (Birth Name and Name on Death Certificate); **p. 139**—A medical amendment, which is not shown, lists the cause of death as Dissecting Aortic Aneurysm and Hypertensive Cardiovascular Disease. Rettig was already a seasoned actor when he was selected from 500 young boys for the role of Jeff Miller on *Lassie*. *Annie Get Your Gun* was his stage debut in a touring company which included Mary Martin. Since audiences are not usually receptive to child actors who grow up, his career was over by age 15. *The 5,000 Fingers of Dr. T.* was his most memorable film.

John Ritter (Professional Name); Jonathan Southworth Ritter (Birth Name and Name on the Death Certificate); **p. 140**—*Three's Company* is his most popular television sitcom. He also starred in *Hooperman* and *8 Simple Rules for Dating My Teenage Daughter*. He was working on the set of the latter at the time he was stricken with his dissecting aneurysm.

Robert Rockwell (Professional Name); Robert G. Rockwell (Birth Name and Name on the Death Certificate); **p. 141**—He brought the role of Mr. Boynton on *Our Miss Brooks* from radio to television. His identification with the role was so strong that many opportunities were denied to him. On *The Loretta Young Show*, he played Young's husband in several episodes. He did more than 200 voiceovers and commercials.

Esther Rolle (Professional Name and Name on the Death Certificate); **p. 142**—*I Know Why the Caged Bird Sings*, *Driving Miss Daisy*, and *Summer of My German Soldier* were three of her films. *Maude* and *Good Times* were her sitcoms.

Fran Ryan (Professional Name); Fran Ryan Shafer (Name on the Death Certificate); **p. 143**—A lookalike for Marjorie Main, she also often played a hard, gruff woman. Her films included *Take This Job and Shove It*, *The Apple Dumpling Gang*, and *Pale Rider*. Her television credits included *The Doris Day Show*, *Green Acres*, and *Gunsmoke*.

Dick Sargent (Professional Name); Richard Cox (Birth Name); Richard Sargent (Name on the Death

Certificate); **p. 144**—He did supporting work in such films as *Operation Petticoat, That Touch of Mink, The Ghost and Mr. Chicken* and *The Private Navy of Sgt. O'Farrell.* On the small screen, he played the second Darren Stephens on *Bewitched.*

Telly Savalas (Professional Name); Aristoteles Savalas (Birth Name and Name on the Death Certificate); **p. 145**—An affidavit to amend a record (not shown) adds the name of Telly Aristotelis Savalas to the certificate. Fortunately for him, the television movie *The Marcus-Nelson Murders* was expanded into a series, *Kojak.* Other films included *The Dirty Dozen, Kelly's Heroes,* and *Birdman of Alcatraz,* for which he received an Oscar nomination for Best Supporting Actor.

Rebecca Schaeffer (Professional Name); Birth Name and Name on the Death Certificate); **p. 146**—She was only getting her start when she was murdered by an obsessed fan. *My Sister Sam* was her first evening television series. Her last film, released after her death, was aptly named *Loss of Innocence.*

Natalie Schafer (Professional Name, Birth Name and Name on the Death Certificate); **p. 147**—Society matrons or fashionable ladies were her niche market. *The Body Disappears* in 1941 was her first film. *Gilligan's Island* was her vehicle for success on the small screen

Charles Schulz (Professional Name); Charles Monroe Schulz (Birth Name); Charles M. Schulz (Name on the Death Certificate); **p. 148**—Creator of the comic strip *Peanuts.* The first paper to carry *Peanuts* was the *St. Paul Pioneer Press.* At the height of the strip's popularity there were 355 million readers enjoying the antics of his characters.

Randolph Scott (Professional Name); George Randolph Scott (Birth Name and Name on the Death Certificate); **p. 149**—The western genre was made for him. With his blond hair, blue eyes, and easy-going charm he was the epitome of the western star. His production company, Ranown, produced such films as *Man in the Saddle, The Tall T. Shootout at Medicine Bend, Ride Lonesome,* and, his final film, *Ride the High Country.*

E. C. Segar (Professional Name); Elzie C. Segar (Name on the Death Certificate); **p. 150**—Newspaper cartoonist who created Popeye the Sailor Man.

David O. Selznick (Professional Name); David Selznick (Birth Name); David Oliver Selznick (Name on the Death Certificate); **p. 151**—One of the most famous

producers of Hollywood in its Golden Age. *Gone with the Wind* was produced by his production company, Selznick International.

Ann Sheridan (Professional Name); Clara Lou Sheridan (Birth Name); Clara Lou McKay AKA Ann Sheridan (Name on the Death Certificate); **p. 152**—An affidavit to change a record (not shown) changes the interment location from Chapel of the Pines to Hollywood Forever. Sheridan was one of the few women in films who was permitted to grow from a beautiful teenager into a mature leading star. *Torrid Zone, They Drive by Night,* and *I Was a Male War Bride* are only a sampling of her films. *Pistols 'n' Petticoats* was her TV series.

Elizabeth Short (Professional Name and Name on the Death Certificate); The Black Dahlia (Nickname); **p. 153**—While she wanted to be in pictures, her desire did not translate into success. Her body was found carefully dismembered in a vacant lot in Hollywood.

Phil Silvers (Professional Name and Name on the Death Certificate); **p. 154**—An amendment to correct the record, which is not shown, adds his Social Security number to the record. He celebrated a long run of fine Broadway plays. *Top Banana* and *A Funny Thing Happened on the Way to the Forum* garnered him Tony awards. On the small screen, *You'll Never Get Rich* AKA *The Phil Silvers Show* made him a star.

Don Simpson (Professional Name); Donald Clarence Simpson (Name on the Death Certificate); **pp. 155–156**—An extravagant movie producer, he produced such films as *Flashdance, The Rock, Top Gun,* and *Days of Thunder.* His death brought into the limelight the abuse of prescription drugs in the motion picture industry.

Madge Sinclair (Professional Name); Madge Dorita Sinclair-Compton (Name on the Death Certificate); **p. 157**—Her first film was *Conrack.* Nominated for an Emmy for her performance in *Roots. Trapper John* was her other television series.

Red Skelton (Professional Name); Richard Red Skelton (Name on the Death Certificate); **p. 158**—Hosted the *Red Skelton Show on Radio* from 1941 to 1953. He then brought it to television from 1951 to 1971. Clem Kadiddlehopper, George Appleby and Gertrude and Heathcliffe were but a few of the characters he created.

Hal Smith (Professional Name); Harold John Smith (Birth Name and Name on the Death Certificate);

p. 159—A prolific cartoon voiceperson, he did most of his work for Hanna-Barbera. At Walt Disney, he and Jack Bailey were the voice of Goofy after 1967. His role as Otis, the town drunk, on *The Andy Griffith Show*, was a favorite with viewers.

Robert Stack (Professional Name); Robert Langford Stack (Name on the Death Certificate); **p. 160**—In 1952 he starred in the first 3-D movie, *Bwana Devil*. He received an Academy Award nomination for *Written on the Wind*. His television series were *The Untouchables*, *Most Wanted* and *The Name of the Game*.

Florence Stanley (Professional Name); Florence L. Newman (Name on the Death Certificate); **p. 161**—Broadway plays include *The Prisoner of Second Avenue*, *Fiddler on the Roof*, and *The Secret Affairs of Mildred Wild*. On television, she was on *Barney Miller* and *Nurses* and a guest star on any number of others.

Rod Steiger (Professional Name); Rodney Stephan Steiger (Name on the Death Certificate); **p. 162**—*On the Waterfront* was his first Academy Award nomination. *In the Heat of the Night* was his vehicle to receive the award. He was also nominated for his work in *The Pawnbroker*.

Inger Stevens (Professional Name); Inger Stensland Jones AKA Stevens (Name on the Death Certificate); **pp. 163–164**—*Man on Fire* was her first film. *Cry Terror*, *The Buccaneer*, *The World, the Flesh, and the Devil*, and *The New Interns* were just a few of her movies. She took her own life at age 35.

Jay Stewart (Professional Name); Jay Stewart Fix (Birth Name); Jay Cleve Fix-Stewart (Name on the Death Certificate); **p. 165**—His voice was his profession. He was the announcer on *The Mike Douglas Show*, *Blackout*, *Jeopardy*, and *Scrabble*, among others.

Lyle Talbot (Professional Name and Name on the Death Certificate); **p. 166**—He started as a contract player for Warner Bros. *The Thirteen Guests*, *Three Legionnaires*, *They Raid by Night*, and *Sunrise at Campobello* were some of his films. He did a serial for Columbia called *Chick Carter, Detective*.

Constance Talmadge (Professional Name); Constance Talmadge Giblin (Name on the Death Certificate); **p. 167**—A very prolific actress in the silent era. Between 1914 and 1927, she was in more than 80 films. *Venus*, *Breakfast at Sunrise*, and *The Duchess of Buffalo* were her last three movies.

Natalie Talmadge (Professional Name); Natalie M. Talmadge (Name on the Death Certificate); **p. 168**—Another silent era actress. She made only a few films in her seven-year career. After her marriage to Buster Keaton, she made only one additional movie, *Our Hospitality*. *Yes or No*, *The Love Expert*, and *A County Hero* are others she made.

William Talman (Professional Name); Willam Whitney Talman, Jr. (Birth Name and Name on the Death Certificate); **p. 169**—He received an Academy Award nomination for *The Hitch-Hiker*. *I've Lived Before* and *Joe Dakota* were films he co-wrote. His biggest success probably came from his role as the district attorney, Hamilton Burger, on *Perry Mason*. He was replaced on *Perry Mason* for a few months, but the fans insisted that he should be returned.

Jessica Tandy (Professional Name); Jessica Tandy Cronyn (Name on the Death Certificate); **p. 170**—She was one of only a handful of performers to earn the Triple Crown for actors, with her Oscar for *Driving Miss Daisy*; her Tonys for *A Streetcar Named Desire*, *The Gin Game*, and *Foxfire*; and her Emmy for the television version of *Foxfire*.

Vic Tayback (Professional Name); Victor Tayback (Name on the Death Certificate); **p. 171**—His television series was *Alice*. He also made a number of appearances on *The Love Boat*. *Horseplayer* and *Beverly Hills Bodysnatcher* were his last two films.

Irene Tedrow (Professional Name); Irene Tedrow Kent (Name on the Death Certificate); **p. 172**—A hardworking actress, she appeared in more than 60 films and on the small screen in more than 100 episodic programs. She was seen on *Dragnet* five times over three seasons. *Empire of the Ants* was one of her last big-screen appearances.

Lynne Thigpen (Professional Name); Cherylynne T. Thigpen (Name on the Death Certificate); **pp. 173–174**—Also shown is a medical amendment adding the cause of death (acute cardiac dysfunction and brain hemorrhaging). She was still at work on her series, *The District*, at the time of her death. She also had recurring roles on *The Cosby Show*, *Gimme a Break*, and *Thirtysomething*.

Lawrence Tierney (Professional Name); Lawrence James Tierney (Name on the Death Certificate); **p. 175**—The title character in *Dillinger*, made him a star. RKO capitalized on his success with such films as *San Quentin*, *Step by Step*, *The Devil Thumbs a Ride*, *Bodyguard*, and *Born to Kill*.

Claire Trevor (Professional Name); Claire Trevor Bren (Name on the Death Certificate); **p. 176**—She earned Oscar nominations for *Dead End* and *The High and the Mighty*. She received the award for Best Supporting Actress for *Key Largo*. Her talent made her acting seem effortless. Her moniker was the "Queen of the B's."

Bobby Troup (Professional Name); Robert William Troup, Jr. (Birth Name and Name on the Death Certificate); **p. 177**—On the small screen he played a doctor on *Emergency* with his wife, Julie London, playing a nurse. He worked on several segments of *Dragnet*, *Perry Mason* and *Adam 12*. "Route 66" was one of the songs he composed.

Ben Turpin (Professional Name); Bernard Turpin (Name on the Death Certificate); **p. 178**—Between 1907 and 1940, he appeared in over 200 films. His trademark was his crossed eyes. A running gag was that whenever his character was stubborn or obtuse, another character would threaten to smack him hard enough to uncross his eyes. *Cracked Nuts*, *Law of the Wild*, *Lighthouse Love*, and *The College Hero* were a few of his movies.

Herve Villechaize (Professional Name); Herve Jean Pierre Villechaize (Birth Name and Name on the Death Certificate); **p. 179**—He made eight films over eight years before making *The Man with the Golden Gun*. *Fantasy Island* was his inspiration. That television series lasted from 1978 to 1983.

Nancy Walker (Professional Name); Nancy Walker Craig (Name on the Death Certificate); **p. 180**—She was fortunate enough to go from one small screen series to another: from *Family Affair* to *McMillan and Wife*, to *Mary Tyler Moore* and finally to *Rhoda*. Perhaps best remembered for commercials for Bounty paper towels, where she played Rosie.

Ray Walston (Professional Name); Herman Ray Walston (Name on the Death Certificate); **p. 181**—Gar-

nered a Tony for the Broadway production of *Damn Yankees*. He earned two Emmys for *Picket Fences*. *My Favorite Martian* was another of his small-screen successes. *South Pacific*, *Paint Your Wagon*, and *The Apartment* were a few of his films.

Lew Wasserman (Professional Name); Lew R. Wasserman (Name on the Death Certificate); **p. 182**—Chairman and chief executive officer of MCA, the parent company of Universal Studios. The company was first sold to Matsushita in 1990 and then to Seagram's in 1995. Wasserman retained his board membership until 1998.

Dennis Wilson (Professional Name); Dennis Carl Wilson (Birth Name and Name on the Death Certificate); **p. 183**—An amendment, which is not shown, changes the location of his cremains from Inglewood Park Cemetery to dispersal at sea. He was the drummer for the Beach Boys. He also happened to be the only one who could surf. His drumming work was considered stellar, and his work as a singer and songwriter was equally great. "Forever" and "Pacific Ocean Blue" were two songs that showcased his talent.

Flip Wilson (Professional Name); Clerow Flip Wilson (Name on the Death Certificate); **p. 184**—A comedian who made a number of appearances on *Rowan & Martin's Laugh-In*. He also had his own program on the small screen, *The Flip Wilson Show*, from 1970 to 1974. He only appeared in a few films. *Skatetown, U.S.A.* and *Uptown Saturday Night* were two of them.

Marie Windsor (Professional Name); Emily Marie Bertelsen (Birth Name); Emily Marie Bertelsen-Hupp (Name on the Death Certificate); **p. 185**—She was one of the "bad girls" in films. *Hellfire*, *The Killing*, *The Narrow Margin*, and *The Little Shop of Horrors* were four of her movies.